HOUSEHOLD

HINTS & TIPS

Elsie Agnes Allen

HINKLER
BOOKS

Household Hints & Tips
First Published in 2003 by Hinkler Books Pty Ltd
17–23 Redwood Drive
Dingley VIC 3172 Australia
www.hinklerbooks.com

ISBN 1 8651 5942 5

Cover Designer: Sam Grimmer
Editor: Sally Steward
Typesetting: Midland Typesetters, Maryborough, Vic, Australia
Printed and bound in Australia by Griffin Press

CONTENTS

Introduction

HOME is called 'home' because it is where we all feel safe and comfortable. It is the place we go after we have done our work for the day, or completed our playing, leisure or recreation. Whether it is a mobile home in the great outback or a palace in the mountains, it's our place. A place of refuge, where we can do as we like and say what we wish. It's where we belong.

Importantly, most of us enjoy doing things that make our home unique. Some of us fill the back yard with a vegetable plot that will feed the hungry masses. Others construct an entertaining area where food and conversation flourish. Then there are the 'sheddies', who rule their own separate kingdom, surrounded by neatly arranged tools and intriguing bits of metal. No two homes are exactly the same. And that is where this book comes in. *Household Hints & Tips* is designed to help the home-maker turn his or her home into something special, with thousands of hints and tips right across the board.

An enjoyable, happy place – a centre of good ideas, relaxation and hospitality.
Home.

ELSIE AGNES ALLEN

1
Cleaning

Cleaning – it can occupy your time, sap your energy, get into your mind, and drag down your bank balance. We all love a clean, fresh smelling environment, and some of us get an intense satisfaction out of converting disorder and chaos into a clean house. There are certain secrets that have always been secret women's business, which have been passed from mother to daughter and sometimes to the next-door neighbour. Now it's all out in the open and the men are getting a chance to read about cleaning secrets also. This chapter will tell of ways and means of taking the sting and the cost out of cleaning.

Did you know that you could make up your own cleaning liquids? They save money, and work just as well as the over-the-counter products. Did you know that there are two ways to get a cleaning job done – the hard, sweaty way and the easy, sweaty way. Or you can hire a cleaning lady. She will know all these tips. Her mother told her!

Cleaners and cleaning tools
All-purpose cleaner
1 cup ammonia
½ cup white vinegar
½ cup baking soda
4 litres warm water

Store in containers and use as needed.

Brooms
Brooms and brushes will keep longer if washed occasionally in two litres of water to which four tablespoons of ammonia have been added. Soak for thirty minutes, rinse and dry.

Honey soap
Cut thinly 125 grams of yellow soap into a double saucepan. Stir occasionally until it is melted. Add one tablespoon of palm oil, one tablespoon of honey, and a few drops of oil of cinnamon. Let it all boil together another six or eight minutes, then pour out and let it stand. Cut up and it is ready to use.

Keeping dustcloths clean
Keep dustcloths fresh and clean with this mix:

1 jar hot sudsy water
2 teaspoons turpentine

Stuff cleaning cloths into jar and allow to soak. Hang on line to dry.

Other ways to keep dustcloths clean:

- Add olive oil to your dust rag.
- Baby oil can be added to your dust rag.
- Vaseline can be applied onto a soft cloth.

Furniture polish

Here are three great polishes:

- Furniture polish one

½ cup vinegar
1 cup linseed oil
½ cup methylated spirits

Mix, shake bottle well before using.

- Furniture polish two

1 tablespoon vinegar
2 tablespoons olive oil
4 cups water

Combine and store in a spray container.

- Furniture polish three

1 cup flaxseed oil
1 cup white vinegar
1 cup turpentine

Combine in a container and shake before use.

Linseed oil

Linseed oil:

- Protects wooden fences and gates.
- Makes brick fireplaces look fresh and new.
- Prevents veneered furniture from cracking.
- Polishes and protects outdoor furniture.

Window cleaners

- Window cleaner one

1 cup ammonia
10 litres warm water
Spray on windows; Wipe off with paper towel or screwed-up newspaper.

- Window cleaner two

1 part vinegar
3 parts water
1 drop blue food colouring

- Window cleaner three

½ cup ammonia
1 tablespoon vinegar
2 tablespoons cornflour
1 bucket warm water

- Window cleaner four

2 tablespoons vinegar
3 drops dishwashing liquid
blue food colouring

- Window cleaner five

1 bottle rubbing alcohol
2 teaspoons ammonia

Spray on window and wipe with paper towel. Cuts dirt and will not streak.

- Window cleaner Six

4 litres warm water
½ cup cornflour

Apply and wipe with paper towel.

Miracle window cleaner
Use equal parts of kerosene, cloudy ammonia, methylated spirits bottle and water. If kerosene does not mix well, shake it before using. This mixture is particularly good for seaside areas as it ploughs through the salt. After washing windows down with the mixture, polish with a soft dry cloth.

General tips
Ants
Goodbye ants! Sprinkle sugar or talcum powder where the ants are and then follow the ant trail back to the nest. Once found, pour kerosene into the nest.
   Cucumber peels deter ants.
   Sprinkle salt and pepper across the ants' path to deter them.
   Sprinkle crushed cloves near nest. They hate it!

Ant deterrent
Mix a paste made with:

2 cups sugar
1 cup hot water
2 tablespoons Borax
2 tablespoons boracic acid

Boil together for three minutes. Spread across the trail near the nest.

A quick tidy up
A quick tidy up when guests are coming unexpectedly:

- Shut doors to rooms that are not likely to be used.
- Tidy away toys and clutter.
- Give the carpet a quick clean with a carpet sweeper.
- Fluff up pillows and cushions.
- Freshen up flower arrangements or put in a new one.
- Wipe surfaces in the bathroom and put out guest towels.
- Keep the lighting low so that corners can't be peered into!

Candlesticks
Silver candlesticks that have wax dripped on them can be cleaned by placing the candlesticks in the freezer until the wax freezes, making it peel off easily.

Clothing

Use hairspray to remove pen or ink marks from clothing (or carpet). Just spray on, leave for a few seconds, and wipe with a damp cloth.

Dustpan

Wax the surface of your dustpan and watch the dirt slide off easily.

Flies

To keep the room free from flies:

- Place a few drops of eucalyptus in a bowl of hot water.
- Bruise some mint between your fingers, place in a bowl.

Flowers

To extend the life of fresh flowers and/or hold the petals and arrangements together, use hairspray.

Hard water

If water is hard and not good to clean with, add a little Borax to soften.

Laminated surfaces

To clean laminated surfaces use a cloth sprinkled with methylated spirits.

Odours

To remove a bad odour

Sprinkle cinnamon on aluminium foil and place it in a hot oven, leaving the door open. As the cinnamon heats, its scent will permeate the house.

Leave slices of fresh apple in an area with strong odours. After two to three days, the apple slices will be brown and dry and the stale air will be replaced with the scent of fresh apple.

Boil water with a little ammonia. Or put a spoonful of coffee in a container and heat in the oven to deodorise your kitchen.

Sweeten the smell of your disposal by feeding it the rind of a lemon, orange or grapefruit.

Strong odours on your hands (such as onions or fish) can be removed by lightly wetting your hands and then sprinkling with baking soda. Rub the soda all over the hands, then rinse the soda and the odour away.

Paintbrush duster

A paintbrush can be an effective way to dust those hard to reach places.

Photographs

Remove fingerprints from photos with hairspray and buff with a soft cloth.

Piano

To whiten piano keys, wash with rubbing alcohol.

Rubbish

To clean a rubbish tin, reverse it over a sprinkler and turn the hose up full. Leave it to dry.

Quick tips

- Put your liquid cleaner into a spray bottle to save on the amount of liquid that you use.
- Use an old toothbrush to clean places that are hard to get at.
- When your sponge mop begins to shred, simply place an old sock over it to make it last longer.
- Use old T-shirts cut up for polishing/cleaning rags. Simply discard after job is done.
- Cut the best parts from old tea towels and dusters and use them for cleaning.
- Place an old sock over your hand to dust surfaces and blinds.
- Remove mildew from leather surfaces, such as a suitcase, by wiping them with a cloth moistened in equal parts of water and rubbing alcohol.
- Clean the telephone with rubbing alcohol.
- To clean a soft pencil eraser, rub it against a harder ink eraser.

Staying fresh

There's nothing like the house smelling fresh.

- Make a nice aroma for the house by simmering cinnamon and cloves on the stove.
- A teaspoon of vanilla in a small pot of water and brought to the boil will take the odours out of the kitchen.
- A cotton ball with wintergreen oil on it, located in a discrete spot in any room, will keep it smelling fresh for weeks on end.
- A container of vinegar left in a room will keep it smelling fresh, even when the house is closed up for a while.
- Put some vanilla extract on a cloth and wipe it on the lights throughout the house – when the lights go on a fresh aroma is released throughout the house.
- To remove smoke from a room, dip a towel in equal parts water and vinegar, wring it out, stand in the centre of the room, and whirl the towel gently above your head.
- To stop butts burning in an ashtray and adding to the smell, line the bottom of the ashtray with two centimetres of baking soda.
- To make tap water heavily laced with chlorine more drinkable, fill a jug and let it stand overnight.
- Paint odour from a newly painted room can be eliminated by placing a large plate of salt in the room.
- Vinegar is an excellent deodoriser and sanitiser for toilet bowls, drains, sinks, etc.

Stickers

Remove price-tag glue by rubbing with paper towel and a dab of peanut butter.
Use a paper towel dabbed with vegetable oil.

Tar

Tar can be removed from the paws of your pets with eucalyptus oil. Apply the eucalyptus oil, then sponge with warm, soapy water and repeat half hourly until tar is removed.

Vomit in a car

If vomit is not removed, then the smell will very likely outlast the life of the car.

- Remove the vomit by placing a plastic bag over your hand and removing the lumps.
- Sponge the soiled area with Eucalyptus Woollen Wash.
- Any surfaces of the car that have been soiled should be cleaned.

- Pay particular attention to seams and upholstery.
- Clean up under the seats where the vomit may have been sprayed.
- Use an old toothbrush, or a soft nail-brush, to scrub seams.
- Mats can be lifted then scrubbed.
- The floor under the mats should be washed and allowed to dry.
- Replace dry mats.
- Smother the floor with Borax powder and allow to sit for several days.
- Vacuum off.

Homewares
Aluminium
Polish aluminium by rubbing with a cloth soaked in ammonia.

Brass
There are several ways to clean brass:

- Make paste with ½ cup of salt and ½ cup vinegar.
- Dip lemon peel in salt and rub.
- Rub, using soft cloth with some tomato sauce.
- Wash in water in which potatoes have been boiled.

Burnt pots
If food burns the bottom of the pan, cover it with vinegar and add one tablespoon of salt. Soak it overnight and scrub. Or try one of the following:

- Clean by putting out in the sun for a few days. The burnt part will simply peel off.
- Fill with water and add laundry powder, allow to soak.
- Fill with warm water, add bicarbonate of soda, bring to boil and let cool.
- Fill with water and add ammonia. Allow to stand.

Chandelier
Take crystals from your chandelier, place the crystals in a pillowcase, secure and place on a rack in the dishwasher. Set on glass cycle and they will come out sparkling.

China
When storing fine china, place a paper plate between each plate to prevent damage to the surface.

Casserole dishes
Season the outside of unglazed casserole dishes before use with a cut onion or garlic cloves. This strengthens them.

Mending broken china
Keep all broken pieces in a plastic bag. Use epoxy resin for repairs as this allows you to expose the piece to low heat afterwards. Before you spread glue on broken china, wipe the edges with a piece of non-fluffy material. When gluing small pieces of china use Blu-Tack or clothes pegs to hold the pieces together as it sets.

To replace a handle on a mug

Place the mug in a box of sand, handle side up, to keep it in place. Apply adhesive to the broken edges of the handle and the mug. Fix the handle in position. Wipe away any surplus glue. Leave the mug in the sand until it is dry.

Vases

If a vase is too deep for the flowers you wish to put in it, simply place crushed newspaper in the bottom.

To clean a vase with a difficult shape, pour a handful of sand into it, add vinegar and hot water and allow to stand overnight. Rinse.

Cleaning chrome

Rub with a piece of smooth, damp aluminium foil. The foil turns black but will make the chrome shine. Clean with left-over soda water.

Copper

There are many ways to clean copper:

- Use Worcestershire sauce. Rinse and rub.
- Dip soft cloth in vinegar and then in salt and scour. Rinse and buff.
- Make mixture of one tablespoon each of flour, salt and vinegar.
- Make mixture of one part salt and five parts vinegar.
- Apply toothpaste and a damp cloth.

Crystal vases

Crystal vases, particularly those that are narrow at the bottom, can be washed with warm soapy water with a little cloudy ammonia and a few broken eggshells. Shake vigorously and rinse thoroughly with warm water. This method also works for bottles or any item that has a narrow bottom.

Glass

Do not expose glassware to high temperatures as it may break.

Gilt and hand-painted decorations on glassware will come off if the glassware is soaked for too long.

Always store wine glasses upright. If you store them upside down they will develop a musty smell and the rims may become damaged

To remove smells from glass jars, wash and soak in a solution of one teaspoon dry mustard and four litres warm water overnight. Rinse well.

Make glass shine by putting cut lemons in the rinsing water after washing your glassware. Lemon cuts the grease and the acid released makes them shine and sparkle.

Chipped rims may be rubbed with a piece of extra fine sandpaper until smooth.

Remove scratches from glass by rubbing gently with Brasso.

Cleaning glassware

- Clean narrow-necked vases by using a solution of vinegar and water. Add dry rice and shake.
- Scratches on glassware will disappear if polished with toothpaste.
- Smooth a small nick in the rim of a glass object by rubbing it gently with an emery board.

- Clean vases with a solution of one teaspoon salt and one cup vinegar. Soak overnight.
- Use toilet bowl cleaner to remove mineral deposits in glass containers.

Keeping wine and beer glasses sparkling and good to drink out of is simple if you know the secret. A dishwasher does the best job. If, however you do not have a dishwasher and if your glasses look smeary after washing, or if beer goes flat in them, you must change your washing method. Use hot water and Morning Fresh detergent. When the glasses have been thoroughly washed make sure they are well rinsed with hot water and drain on paper towel. Do not use a tea towel.

Eyeglasses
If the screws of your spectacles come out easily, dab the ends of the screws with clear nail varnish. Clean.
Wash spectacles regularly in dishwashing liquid solution.
To prevent spectacles from clouding over, rub with neat dishwashing liquid.
Polish with perfume.

Mirrors
Polish your mirror to a sparkling shine by adding a few drops of methylated spirits to a damp cloth. Be careful to avoid leakage behind the frame. Buff with a soft cloth.

Pottery vases
Pottery vases should be sealed on the inside with beeswax before using them. This makes them waterproof. Simply melt the wax and coat the inside of the vase using a small brush.

Silver
- To prevent silver from tarnishing when storing, wrap it with a small piece of camphor.
- Rub silver items with a damp cloth and small amount of toothpaste. Rinse and polish.
- Gently rub with fireplace ashes.
- Use the water from your boiled potatoes to soak the silverware in overnight. Buff.

Teapots
Aluminium
Gently scrub the inside with steel wool, salt and vinegar.

Enamel
Soak overnight with salt and water or with water and ammonia.

Silver or pottery
To remove tea stains from the inside of a silver or pottery teapot, half fill the pot with water, add two or three denture-cleaning tablets and leave overnight.

Teflon pots
Never use harsh abrasive on Teflon-coated cooking utensils. If the Teflon discolours, mix:

2 tablespoons of Borax powder
¼ cup White King
1 cup water

Bring this solution to the boil in the stained pan for five minutes. Wash, rinse and dry. Wipe with oil before using.

Windows
Never wash windows when the sun is shining on them. They will dry too quickly and streak.

Window-sills are made easy to clean by coating them in wax, which protects the paint and allows dirt to be wiped off quickly.

Aluminium windows
To clean aluminium window frames, make a paste with powdered whiting (available at hardware stores) and methylated spirits. Put some of the paste onto a cloth and polish frames. Buff up with a soft, clean cloth.

If the frames are really bad with caked-on dirt, brush, wash with very hot water and Eucalyptus Wool Mix or similar product, before applying the whiting paste.

Home-made window cleaner
Mix equal parts of kerosene, cloudy ammonia, methylated spirits and water. Shake well to mix together. Spray onto windows. Wipe with screwed-up newspaper.

Painting windows
When painting windows, extend the paint onto the glass. It creates a little more clean-up work, but does a better job of sealing out moisture. After the paint has dried, use a razor-blade scraper to scrape off excess paint.

Shoe polish on walls
Shoe polish can usually be removed by putting a little methylated spirits, or kerosene, on a cloth, then dabbing the stain. Remove residual stains with warm water and a little Eucalyptus Wool Mix.

Window cleaner for seaside homes
Mix together:

4 dessertspoons of cornflour
½ cup of cloudy ammonia
½ cup brown vinegar

Shake well before using. Apply with a slightly dampened sponge. Polish with scrunched-up newspaper.

Furniture and furnishings
Bedding
Sleeping bags
Turn inside out and clean with a vacuum cleaner before storing away. Use the small nozzle to get into the corners. Hang out to air on the clothes line and place a cotton bud with a few drops of lavender oil in it before rolling it up.

Squeaky bed
Silence squeaky bed springs with a coat of spray wax.

Wooden slats
To prevent them from moving easily and falling out, slip large rubber bands over the ends of slats.

Blinds
Heavily soiled blinds can be washed in the bath. Half fill the bath with water. Add one cup of liquid detergent and ½ cup of vinegar. Swish the blinds in the tub. Rinse under the shower. Dry over a curtain rod.

Rub fabric softener sheets over Venetian blinds.

Cleaning holland blinds
Watermarks on holland blinds, particularly those over kitchen sinks, often are almost impossible to remove. A good idea is to try to invert the blind, putting the top to the bottom.

Cleaning Venetian blinds
- Take the blinds down.
- Hang on clothes line.
- Wipe with soapy water.
- Spray gently with hose.
- Brush the tapes to get rid of the dust.
- If the tapes are white, rub with white shoe cleaner.

Venetian blinds are easily cleaned by pulling a pair of old socks over the hands and rubbing the slats with both hands. Dampen the socks with a mixture of ammonia and methylated spirits.

Rub fabric softener over Venetian blinds.

Cleaning vertical blinds
A weak solution of bleach will remove the marks from vertical blinds. Use about one part bleach to three parts warm water. Because the vertical blinds are a woven fabric, it is a good idea to use a soft brush, or an old toothbrush, so the solution gets into the weave.

Curtains
Synthetic curtains can be very difficult to iron if creases are allowed to form during washing. Avoid this by washing the curtains in the bath in almost cold water. Add detergent and wash the curtains through the water. After rinsing, drip dry and rehang before they are quite dry.

Decking and fencing
Decking and fences can be preserved and made to look good by applying linseed oil.

Electronic equipment
Proper care of your electronic equipment can prevent a lot of frustration caused by poor performance, and save you much money on unnecessary repairs.

- Clean computer monitors regularly with window cleaner or methylated spirits, and buff with a paper towel.
- To prevent dust build-up on your computer monitor, occasionally spray an anti-static solution.
- Dust between keyboard keys on your computer with a cotton bud.
- Clean the tops of the keyboard keys with methylated spirits on a cotton bud.
- Clean marks off the computer case with methylated spirits on a cotton ball.
- Regularly dust portable radios, stereos, walkmans, portable CD players.
- Keep compact discs in their cases or plastic sleeves to prevent damage, or scratching and dust ruining their performance.
- Compact discs that are not playing properly can often be fixed by gently cleaning with toothpaste to get rid of dust and scratches.
- Store video tapes and audio tapes in their plastic cases. Never leave them in areas exposed to heat, such as the rear shelf of the car.
- Marks on portable radios, stereos, walkmans, and portable CD players can be removed with methylated spirits on a ball of cotton wool.
- The case of a fax/copier/scanner can be cleaned with methylated spirits and a cotton ball.
- Dust answering machines regularly, inside and out, and replace worn-out tapes.

Fireplaces
Enhance and preserve the appearance of your fireplace by giving it an annual coating of linseed oil.

Furniture stains
Tea makes a nice, inexpensive, yet permanent stain for unstained furniture.

General furniture tips
- Use a car wash glove to polish furniture. The polish will impregnate it and will be able to be used over and over again.
- Keep an elastic band around your bottle of furniture polish to attach your cloth.
- Remove scratches by rubbing a peanut over the scratch.
- To remove white patches caused by putting a hot article on the wood, apply a thin paste of salad oil and salt. Allow to stand for two hours. Wipe and polish.
- Mix cigarette ash with a little Vaseline and rub on the spot.
- To prevent pottery items from scratching furniture, put self-sticking bunion pads on the bottom.
- To prevent chairs scratching wooden floors stick self-adhesive bunion pads to the bottom, or wax chair bottoms.

Glass-topped tables
For a lint-free cleaner, clean with:

1 tablespoon of fabric softener
2 litres of water
2 cups methylated spirits

Apply with a soft cloth and polish with a chamois or a soft, dry cloth.

Heat marks
Heat marks on furniture can be removed by rubbing well with Brasso and then polishing with a soft dry cloth.

Make a paste of cigarette ash and water and rub this over the mark. Always rub with the grain of the wood.

Lampshades

Clean lampshades regularly. Otherwise they become impossible to clean. Unplug lamps at the main before cleaning them. Use the upholstery tool on your vacuum to clean a fabric shade. Do not wet as it may shrink.

Gently dust paper shades with a dry cloth.

Straw shades need to be vacuumed regularly as they are dust traps.

Silk shades need professional cleaning.

Plastic and glass shades can be washed with soap and water then dried.

Clean ruffled or pleated lampshades with a baby's hairbrush. The bristles are soft and will not shag or harm the shade.

Parchment shades should be gently dusted and the marks removed with an India rubber.

Polishing tip

When polishing furniture, put the polish on a cloth inside an old nylon stocking. The polish comes through but the nylon prevents lint or fluff being left on the furniture.

Scratches on furniture

On varnished furniture, scratches may be removed by placing a coarse cloth well soaked in linseed oil on the scratches. Leave for a short time, rub a little, then remove the excess, and polish. Deeper scratches can often be covered by applying a little shoe polish the same colour as the furniture.

Sheep skins

Some sheep skins, particularly those used for invalids or babies, can be readily washed. Usually the washing instructions are marked. If not, rub brown vinegar into the back to save it from hardening. Then scrub the surface with a wool mix in a rough cloth. Do this in sections so as not to get the skins too damp and as you go rub each section with a dry cloth.

Silverfish in cupboards

These pests are nearly impossible to eradicate except by professional treatment, but you can defer them by putting Epsom salts, Borax powder or alum in the back of your cupboards. Some people buy strongly smelling soaps and put them in the back of cupboards as a deterrent.

Soft furnishings

Regular cleaning makes soft furnishings last longer. Do not let them get so dirty that they are impossible to clean. A few blocks of camphor down the back of your sofa will help to keep the moths away and will keep it smelling fresh.

Sticking drawers

If wooden drawers stick, lubricate the slides of the drawers with a bar of soap. Try using a candle instead. Or sprinkle a rag with a little cornstarch and wipe the runners.

Suede and velvet

For suede or velvet furniture, do not use a water cleaner. Only a powder cleaner is suitable for these types of fabric.

Tapestry

Clean tapestry furniture covers by rubbing in warm bran and brushing or vacuuming surplus away.

To revive faded tapestry coverings and furniture, rub with dampened salt, leave for thirty minutes and vacuum off.

To clean a tapestry wall hanging

Make up a mixture of:

2 tablespoons Borax powder
2 cups salt
2 tablespoons dry cleaning fluid or Shellite

Sprinkle the tapestry with the mixture. Leave for about an hour. Beat the tapestry from the back to remove all the powder.

Upholstery

Never spot or clean upholstery without first testing the fabric in a part that will not show if it marks.

Urine stains

If the stains are on a mattress, they are often very difficult to remove as the smell soaks through the padding.

- Cover the stain thickly with a mixture of Borax powder and talcum powder.
- Cover the whole area with a towel and leave for a couple of days if possible.
- Sponge with cloudy ammonia or white vinegar.
- If you are unsuccessful in removing the stain, use a mattress cover.
- If the stains are on your curtains, sponge quickly with a cloth and cloudy ammonia.
- If the stain remains, curtains should be professionally cleaned.

If you have pets which live inside be careful when you choose an underlay for your carpet. You will be wise to choose one which will not stain too badly if something is spilt on it. Remember, anything you spill on the carpet will possibly go through to the underlay, and you don't want a stain from the underlay coming up to the surface of the carpet.

Veneer furniture

To prevent veneer furniture from cracking in the sunlight, apply slightly warm linseed oil on a cloth.

Vinyl

To remove marks from vinyl simply rub with toothpaste.

Furniture covered with vinyl sometimes absorbs colour from clothing. The vinyl stretches when it is sat upon and body heat opens pores. The vinyl traps the stain. Apply hot towels to open the vinyl and to expose the stain for treatment. It is always best to first try hot, soapy water before chemical cleaners. Use pure soap, not detergent.

Cleaning vinyl furniture

To clean vinyl furniture mix up this eucalyptus wash:

4 cups Lux flakes
1 cup methylated spirits
50 ml eucalyptus

Use about two tablespoons to half a bucket of water. Scrub with a soft brush. When the furniture is thoroughly dry, apply a good vinyl polish. Buff with a clean, dry towel.

Ingrained dirt
If vinyl has ingrained dirt it will need to have hot towels applied prior to cleaning. Leave for fifteen minutes. This will loosen dirt, ready for cleaning.

Pen marks on vinyl
Both vinyl and leather need to be heated with hot water before attempting to remove ball-point pen marks. Wring out a cloth in very hot water and let the cloth sit on the mark for a couple of minutes. Remove the cloth and immediately, while the vinyl is hot rub with toothpaste or shampoo or a commercial vinyl-cleaning product, on a soft cloth. If the marks change colour, rub immediately with methylated spirits. Sponge over with warm water and a little shampoo.

Hairspray may take ballpoint ink off vinyl.

Repairing tears in vinyl
Kits and 'repair a patch' kits are available at motor accessories shops. Repairs to vinyl can be made less noticeable by using a matching colour felt tip pen to colour in. It is always best to use a lighter colour and to do three coats. Spray with any good vinyl polish.

Walnut furniture
If the furniture is genuine walnut, a scratch or stain can be removed by cutting a whole walnut in half and rubbing the mark vigorously with the nut. The juice will remove the stain. Watermarks on walnut furniture can be removed with Brasso.

Watermarks
Remove watermarks from wooden furniture by rubbing with camphorated oil.

Remove rings made by wet glasses by dampening with cigarette ash.

Wicker furniture
If your wicker furniture is a little wobbly, wash it outdoors with hot soapy water.

Rinse and let it air dry. The wood and canes will shrink and tighten. Saggy seats also will tighten if treated with hot water. Vinegar can be added to the water for a freshening effect.

Woodwork
Clean with cold tea. It will sparkle.

Leather
Keep out of the direct light of the sun. Check that the leather is washable by pouring a few drops of water to an area of the couch that is out of sight. If it forms droplets, it is OK to wash. If, however, it is absorbed into the leather then it must not be washed, but must be kept dusted and simply wiped with a slightly damp cloth.

Home-made leather polish
Here's an easy, leather polish to make that brings up a beautiful shine. Take 300 ml linseed oil. Bring to the boil. Cool. Add 300 ml vinegar. Apply with a soft cloth. Buff.

Waterproof leather
Wipe clean with soapy water. Rub well with a soft cloth, which has been dipped in beaten egg white. Buff with soft cloth.

Floors
Broken glass
To sweep up broken glass, dampen the broom head and the tiny pieces of glass will stick to it.

Carpet
Before shampooing carpet, test a trial patch with the shampoo of your choice. If possible, remove all the furniture from the room then vacuum the carpet. Apply shampoo, do a small area at a time, and dry as you go so that the carpet remains as dry as possible. If a mechanical shampooer is being used, do all the room at one time. Leave until the room is completely dry before moving furniture back into it.

- Use kerosene to get rid of a greasy stain but dab, don't rub.
- Sprinkle carpet with salt before vacuuming to destroy moth larvae and brighten colour.
- To remove mud from carpet, sprinkle with cornflour. Allow to sit, then vacuum.
- To remove dirt from carpet, mix one teacup of ammonia and one cup of turpentine in a bucket of hot water. Dip the cloth in bucket, wring and rub.

Lift indents
After you have moved furniture around the room, get rid of any carpet indents by putting a damp cloth on each indentation and place an iron, on low setting, on the cloth. Hold it for just long enough to heat. The fibres will be lifted again, and you can brush them into their original position.

Moths
Sprinkle the carpet with salt before vacuuming to destroy moth larvae and brighten colour.

Mud
To remove mud from carpet, sprinkle with cornflour. Allow to sit, and vacuum.

Pet odour
To get rid of a pet odour from a carpet, spray the area with some white vinegar. An inexpensive way of deodorising carpet is to sprinkle baking soda on it, wait fifteen minutes, then vacuum.

Static shock
Static shock can be reduced or eliminated from carpet by mixing up one part liquid fabric softener and five parts water in a spray bottle, and misting the carpet lightly.

Stains
- Rub stale bread over marks on the carpet to remove stains.
- Use shaving foam. Rinse with soda water.
- Sprinkle with salt and sponge.

General stains
Dampen the stain. Cover it with Kemdex dental powder. Leave for about twenty minutes. Remove excess powder, then sponge with warm water and a little Napisan. Work from the outside edge towards the centre and mop up residual moisture with a thick towel.

Grease stains
To remove grease stains:

- Sprinkle with cornflour, leave overnight and vacuum.
- Sprinkle with baking soda, shampoo and vacuum.

Pet stains
To remove pet stains from carpet, blot the spill with a paper towel and saturate it with soda water. Let it sit for five minutes or so, and then blot again with paper towel.

Wine stains
To remove red wine:

- Soak up spill with paper towel, soak in soda water and place absorbent towel with weight on it overnight.
- Soak immediately with soda water. Continue to apply and mop until stain disappears.

Egg on the floor
If an egg breaks on the floor, sprinkle the egg with salt, allow to stand for a short time. Wipe it off with a paper towel. It comes off cleanly, leaving no mess.

Lino
To remove black shoe marks on lino, use Brasso.

Seagrass matting
If there is an unpleasant odour, you may have to clean underneath as well as lifting and scrubbing the matting. To clean the matting, put two cups of salt into a bucket of hot water. Stir to dissolve some of the salt. Scrub the matting. Dry thoroughly. Replace. Cut up some unskinned onions and place on plates around the room. Close doors and windows, and leave for forty-eight hours. Remove the onions and air the room.

Shoe polish on floors
If shoe polish has rubbed off on to the covering of your chairs, or on the carpet, check if it is coloured or black. Black will need turpentine to remove it, but cleaning fluid is best for coloured stains.

Slate floors
In the 70s, slate was being used in many modern homes. If you want your slate floors to look fresh, use equal parts of linseed oil and turpentine. It prevents smudges and makes it sparkle.

Tiled floors

Non-slip
To maintain a non-slip surface on your tiled floors, wash with a mixture of equal parts kerosene and vinegar.

Removing stains
Stains on tiled floors can be removed by rubbing the area with a slice of lemon dipped in salt. Leave for one hour then rinse.

Vacuuming

Aroma
To fill the air with a nice fresh aroma, add a cotton ball saturated with your favourite scent to the vacuum cleaner bag.

Empty it
Make sure your vacuum cleaner is emptied regularly.

Hairpins
Pick up any hairpins or other objects that are lying about the carpet as they could damage the motor.

Plastic bag
Tuck a plastic bag into your apron when vacuuming. It is handy to collect little bits of stuff that are lying on the floor.

Servicing
Regular servicing is a good idea if the vacuum cleaner is to last a lifetime.

Tubes
Use empty wrapping paper tubes as an extension to your vacuum cleaner attachment to reach out-of-the-way places. You can even flatten the end of the tube to squeeze into tight crevices.

Vacuum bags
Re-use your vacuum bags by carefully slitting open the bottom with a razor blade, emptying the bag and resealing it with tape.

Vinyl floors
Floor with built-up polish can be treated by rubbing with steel wool dipped in kerosene. Then wash with hot water and detergent.

Washing
Wash your floor in a solution of four litres warm water, two tablespoons furniture polish, and ½ cup vinegar. No need to wax.

Wax

When cleaning floors that have been waxed, use cold water to which ½ a cup of vinegar has been added. The cold water won't remove the wax and the vinegar will remove the dirt.

Removing wax

To remove floor wax, use a mixture of hot water to which one cup ammonia has been added.

Before waxing

Before waxing the floor, wet cloth thoroughly with cold water and wring out. It won't absorb so much wax.

Clean up surfaces covered in mildew with a rag soaked in lemon juice and salt.

Walls and wallpaper
Crayon marks

Crayon marks can be removed from a wall with a cloth dampened with turpentine. Or try rubbing the marks with toothpaste, leave them for a few minutes and then wash off.

Crayon marks can be removed from wallpaper by rubbing over with dry soap-filled steel wool pads.

Try rubbing with dry steel wool, then sponge with eucalyptus.

Washable wallpaper can be cleaned with warm water and a little cloudy ammonia.

Grease stains

Make a paste of Borax powder with very little water. Paste over the stain. Allow to dry. Brush off with a soft cloth.

Bread will also clean greasy wallpaper. Remove all the dust from the wallpaper. Hold the bread in the hand and wipe lightly over.

To remove grease spots from a wall, make up a paste of water and cornstarch. Let it remain on the spot until it is dry, then brush it off.

Make a paste about the consistency of cream with starch and white vinegar. Spread the paste over the line of the stain. When it dries, brush it off.

Vinyl wallpaper can be cleaned with white vinegar on a cloth wrung out in warm water.

Paste a matching piece over the stain using a ragged tear which makes it less noticeable.

Smoke stains

Wash painted walls or ceilings that have been stained by smoke or gas heaters with:

A bucket of hot soapy water
8 tablespoons of Borax powder
½ cup cloudy ammonia

Wallpaper

Washable wallpaper can be cleaned with warm water and a little cloudy ammonia.

Grease stains can be removed from non-washable wallpaper by making a paste of talcum powder with very little water and allowing to dry on the stain. Then brush off with a soft cloth.

A slice of stale bread, at least two days old, will also clean wallpaper. Remove all the dust from the wallpaper first. Then hold the bread and wipe lightly over, changing the bread as its surface becomes dirty.

Vinyl wallpaper can be cleaned with white vinegar on a warm cloth.

To wash walls, mix two litres of water and add two tablespoons of baking powder, thirty ml of vinegar and thirty ml of ammonia.

When washing walls, always start at the bottom and go upwards, to prevent streaks.

Ballpoint ink will come off walls by rubbing on toothpaste and then wiping it off with a damp cloth.

Toothpaste and a soft damp cloth will remove black marks from walls.

An art gum eraser is good for cleaning marks off non-washable wallpaper.

Window-sills are made easy to clean by coating them in wax, which protects the paint and allows dirt to be wiped off quickly.

Kitchen hints
Bench tops
To clean, sprinkle with baking soda and spray with water. Allow to stand for one hour and wipe clean.

Make a mixture of one part ammonia to four parts water and wipe.

Wipe with a sponge which has been dipped in vinegar.

Can opener
To remove the grease from the operating mechanism of your can opener, run a piece of paper towel through it.

Casserole
To remove any food stuck to a casserole dish, fill it with boiling water and add two tablespoons of salt or baking soda.

Corningware
When cleaning Corning type dishes, use baking soda.

Cupboards
Cover the inside surfaces of your cupboards with plastic wrap. You then only need to gather the wrap and bin it when you clean. Replace with clean wrap.

Out, moths!
Crumbled bay leaves in the bottom of your cupboard will discourage insects and moths.

Moth repellent
120 ml rosemary oil
1 cup mint leaves
1 tablespoon thyme
1 tablespoon cloves
1 tablespoon oris root

Mix together and let stand before placing in small muslin bags and placing in your drawers.

Detergent
Add a few drops of water to a seemingly empty bottle of liquid dish wash detergent. It will mix with the remaining dregs, and you will get a few more washes out of it.

Adding a few drops of vinegar to your dishwashing water, cuts through the grease and makes your detergent go further.

Dishwasher

An equal amount of baking soda and dishwashing liquid/powder in your dishwasher will not only make your dishes and cutlery cleaner, but keep the machine clean, too.

If you are machine-washing dishes, make sure that the detergent you use is suitable not only for the machine but for the dishes that you wash.

Do not wash good china that has gold leaf on it in a dishwashing machine.

Discolouration

To get rid of dishwasher discolouration due to iron deposits, run the washer through a cycle using one quarter of a cup of Oxalic Acid Crystals, then run a second cycle using just water.

Disinfect

Run powdered laundry bleach through the cycle in an empty dishwasher to clean and disinfect it.

Glassware

To remove scum from glassware, add half a cup of bleach to the wash cycle of the dishwasher and half a cup of vinegar to the rinse cycle.

Lime

To remove lime build-up in your dishwasher, put three quarters of a cup of laundry bleach into it, and run it through the wash cycle. After it drains, add two cups of vinegar and run the rinse cycle. Do not run the drying cycle. Instead, reset it for the full cycle and run that with the usual detergent.

Save power

To save power when using a dishwashing machine, open the door at the end of the wash cycle and allow the dishes to air dry.

Use half

Fill only half the container in your dishwasher with dishwashing liquid/ powder. It does the same job, saves on product, and ensures that your glasses will not get water-marked or scarred.

Enamelware

A paste of salt and vinegar helps brighten discoloured enamelware.

Fresh dishcloth

A tablespoon of bleach in dishwashing water not only kills germs but also keeps the dishcloth clean and smelling fresh.

Grease marks

To clean pots, burner rings and other kitchen utensils stained with grease marks, soak them in ammonia overnight.

Hot water

Always use hot water for washing dishes, to remove all grease.

Kettle

To prevent hard water from scaling the inside of your kettle, put a marble inside.

Kitchen rusts

Knife rust

Remove rust from a knife blade by plunging it into an onion and leaving it in there for about an hour. Work the blade backwards and forwards every now and then, and finally wash in soap and water.

Pan rust

To remove rust from a baking pan, scour the pan with a raw potato dipped in cleaning powder.

Save pads

Cut steel wool pads into four pieces and use them one at a time. This saves wastage through rusting.

Stop steel wool rusting

To keep a steel wool pad from rusting, put two teaspoons of baking soda in the dish in which it is kept.

Store steel wool soap pads in the freezer or refrigerator to stop them from rusting.

Kitchen shelves

Cover kitchen shelves with wipeable, plastic, self-adhesive material. Wooden shelves, which become stained, should be washed thoroughly with hot soapy water. Then wipe down with a solution of one part White King to four parts water. Don't return things to the shelves until they are perfectly dry.

Kitchen sink

For a sparkling sink:

- Soak paper towel in ammonia and lay it across the bottom of the sink. Leave overnight.
- Clean your sink with baking soda.
- Use soda water from a bottle.
- Dampen a cloth with vinegar and wipe.

Keep a rubber plunger (from hardware stores or supermarkets) in the cupboard under the sink in case of a blockage.

To make your sink sparkle like new, clean with a damp cloth and fine powdered Bon Ami, Ajax or Jif. Wipe off and then wipe over with methylated spirits.

Rust stains

- Use cream of tartar and hydrogen peroxide to clean the rust marks off the sink.
- Dampen a cloth with vinegar and clean.
- Vinegar will remove the alkali corrosion around the taps.
- Coat kitchen taps with glycerine to prevent them marking with water spots.

Kitchen stains

Coffee stains

To remove tea and coffee stains from china and porcelain, use a paste of baking soda and water.

Stained coffee pot

To clean a stained coffee pot, soak it overnight in water containing a denture-cleaning tablet.

Tea stains

Tea stains can be removed from cups and teapots with a few drops of bleach in lukewarm water.

Oven cleaning

Before you begin

Before you begin to clean your oven, rub lanolin onto your hands and under your fingernails. Your hands will wash clean.

Pull all the removable parts from the oven and stove and put into a large black garbage bag. Pour in a couple of cups of ammonia. Seal the bag and allow to stand for a few hours. Rinse the items clean.

Cleaning

To clean the oven racks, fill the bathtub with hot water, add ½ cup dishwashing detergent and allow to soak. Wipe clean.

Place racks in a black plastic bag with an open container of ammonia. Leave in the sun for the day. Rinse.

To clean the grill or roasting pan, sprinkle dry laundry detergent over the bottom. Cover with dampened paper towel and allow to sit.

Overnight

Sprinkle baking soda onto the bottom of your oven before you go to bed at night. Wipe clean in the morning.

Place a saucer of ammonia in the oven before you go to bed to soften the grease. Wipe clean in the morning.

Oven fire!!!

To douse a small fire in the oven, pour baking soda onto it.

Plastic in the toaster

Remove plastic that has melted onto your toaster with nail polish remover.

Refrigerator

To eliminate food odours from the refrigerator, place a glass of water inside with a few drops of vanilla essence in it.

Baking powder placed in the refrigerator will keep it fresh and eliminate odours.

A teaspoon of lemon extract added to your cleaning water will help eliminate bad odours from your refrigerator.

To deodorise the refrigerator, cut a raw potato in half and place it inside with the cut side up.

Two charcoal briquettes work well as a refrigerator deodoriser.

If the plastic storage containers from your refrigerator have an unsavoury smell, fill them with water, add a few drops of vanilla extract and let them stand overnight.

To remove damp, musty smells from cupboards or odours in the refrigerator, place a container of used coffee grounds inside.

Rubber gloves
Wear rubber gloves if you find the heat of the dishwashing water hard to cope with.

Thermos
To remove stains from a thermos, pour in one tablespoon of raw rice and a cup of warm water, shake well, and rinse.

If a thermos smells stale and musty, put in a tablespoon of bicarbonate of soda, fill with water and leave overnight.

Leave a piece of charcoal in the thermos when it is not in use. To prevent smells the lid should never be kept on a thermos when it is not being used.

Tinfoil
Clean your pans with a small ball of tinfoil.

Toothbrush
A toothbrush is very handy in the kitchen for cleaning beaters, graters, and other finicky implements.

Wooden cutting boards
Every six months, paint the cutting board with vegetable oil and allow to stand overnight.

Remove odours from your cutting board by sprinkling with baking soda.

Sprinkle with salt and rub with the cut side of a lemon.

Laundry hints
Bath towels
To soften towels and make them more absorbent, soak them overnight in a solution of water and Borax powder. Use one tablespoon of Borax to one litre of water.

Black clothing
Black clothing tends to look brown after several washings. To restore the black colour, add coffee or strong tea to the rinse water.

Care of your washing machine
To keep a washing machine clear of lint and soap build-up, put a packet of Epsom Salts in the detergent container and run the machine through a clear cycle. Do this regularly and the washing machine will remain clean.

Chewing gum
Remove chewing gum by:

- Gently rubbing with eucalyptus oil.
- Applying petroleum jelly and easing off.
- Putting garment in the freezer for thirty minutes and then peeling off.

Dye

To keep fabrics from bleeding, add two to three teaspoons of salt to the wash and rinse cycles.

Heavy garments

Heavy garments, which take longer to dry, can be rolled in a towel after washing, then put in the washing machine to spin dry on a slow cycle.

Mildew

Mildew spots can be removed from white fabrics by rubbing a lemon juice and salt mixture into the spots. Then let the garment dry in the sun before washing.

Paint

Paint can be removed from washable clothes with a mixture of equal parts of ammonia and turpentine. Rub the spots with the mixture then wash in soap suds.

Hot vinegar will remove paint from cotton clothes.

Save tags

When you get new clothes, save the tags with the washing instructions on them. Keep them together in the laundry for quick reference.

Scorch marks

Scorch marks can be removed from clothes by dampening them and exposing them to the sun. Remember: always use distilled water in your iron. Tap water will corrode it.

Scraps of soap

Save scraps of soap from the bathroom. Place them in an old stocking, tie the end and use them in the washing machine.

Collect the bits, cover them with boiling water and a little Borax powder. Boil a few minutes, stir well and cut into blocks when cool.

Make a small, drawstring bag with foam material. Fill the bag with the pieces of soap and hang from a tap in the bath or shower. Children love it.

Stains

Beetroot stains

Remove beetroot stains by placing a saucer of cold water under the stain and a slice of bread on top. The damp bread will absorb the stain. Wash in the usual way.

Chocolate stains

Never use hot water to remove chocolate. It sets the stain. Simply wash in cold sudsy water.

Felt-tipped pens

To remove felt-tipped pen colour from clothing, gently dab with essence of lemon.

Grass stains

Grass stains can be removed by sprinkling sugar on the dampened stain. Roll up and leave for an hour. Wash as usual.

Grease stains

To remove any stain that contains oil or grease, sprinkle with talcum powder, leave for thirty minutes, then brush off.

Perspiration stains

Perspiration stains can be removed by:

- Soaking the clothing in salt water prior to placing in the washing machine.
- Dissolving an aspirin in the water and soaking, allowing to dry, and then washing as usual.
- Applying baking soda paste to the affected area.

Rain stains on felt

To remove rain stains from a felt hat, rub gently with a piece of sandpaper to bring up the pile, then hold over a steaming kettle for a few minutes.

Sea water stains

For sea water stains on fabric, sponge with warm water to dissolve the salt. If the stain persists, spot with methylated spirits, then launder or dry clean. For sea water stains on shoes, try two teaspoons of methylated spirits to one dessertspoon of milk. Rub on, leave to dry, then repolish.

Seaweed stains

Spot with methylated spirits, then wash thoroughly.

Wine stains

Remove wine or fruit stains from table linen by rubbing the stain while still wet, with common salt.

Soda water poured on red wine stains immediately after spillage will remove the stain.

Tea towels

For tea towels that have become discoloured, soak them in boiling water with a tablespoon of Borax to every litre of water, then boil in a pot on the cook top.

Vomit

Vomit on clothing can usually be removed by sponging or washing in a solution of water and Borax powder.

Wash the garment in a wool mix as this will remove any odour.

If there is a lingering smell of vomit in the bathroom or in a car, put a few drops of Nil Odour onto a pad of cottonwool and leave it in the area.

Washing toys

Hang a child's washable toy to dry by placing it in a string bag or an old stocking and hanging that on the line.

Woollens
Drying woollens

Carefully roll the garment into a sausage shape so that it receives the same pressure all over. Spread it on two or three thicknesses of bath towel. Keep it away from direct sunlight as the sun can discolour the wool.

Wonder wool washer

Although you can use commercial products, some of which are excellent, you can make up your own wonder mix. With its use, washing woollens is not a problem. Mix together well and bottle.

2 cups Lux Flakes or similar product
200 ml eucalyptus
200 ml methylated spirits
100 ml glycerine

Use a tablespoonful for each garment. This mixture does not need to be rinsed out. Carefully knead it through the garment, squeeze it out, and lay your garment out to dry. This no-rinse method saves a lot of effort, and works better than conventional washing. Never use hot water, but use water that is warm.

Clothes and accessories
General washing tips
Beaded bags

Rub Borax powder into the handbag and leave for at least an hour, then brush and shake out.

Canvas bags

Canvas bags may be washed and scrubbed with warm soapy water. To avoid mildew forming, make sure the bag is dry before storing.

Fabric bags

For fabric handbags, use a powdered carpet cleaner.

Leather bags

Leather handbags can be cleaned with a soft cloth dipped in warm water to which a little cloudy ammonia has been added. When thoroughly dry, polish with a good cream, and spray with Tuxan Silicone Water Repellent.

Never use a coloured polish on handbags as it may come off on your clothes.

Patent leather

Polish patent leather with Vaseline and thoroughly rub off with a good soft cloth.

Ugg boots

Wash ugg boots with a wool mix using about a capful to a bowl of warm water. Rub briskly with a rough towel to dry the surface. Or simply put the ugg boots into the washing machine for cleaning.

Vinyl

Add a little cloudy ammonia to warm soapy water to clean vinyl. Polish with a cream furniture polish.

Wedding gown

Have the wedding gown cleaned by a professional cleaner. Do not store a wedding gown in plastic. Pack it in pale blue tissue paper. If possible, take it out and hang it in the air every two or three months. To keep any moths away, sprinkle Epsom Salts with the wedding gown, but be careful not to let them touch it.

Wedding veil

Before packing away, make sure a wedding veil is clean. Pack in plenty of pale blue tissue paper in a cardboard box. Sprinkle the bottom of the box with some Epsom Salts, but be careful not to touch the veil. If a veil needs stiffening use gum water.

Iron the veil under greaseproof paper.

Hems

Skirts will go up and down with fashion trends. If you are letting the hem down, to remove the line, just rub it with white vinegar. Then wring out a cloth in cloudy ammonia and a little water, and press the cloth along the line on both sides.

Jewellery
Diamond

Dip diamond jewellery in full strength vinegar, rinse and polish with a soft cloth.

Gold

To polish gold jewellery, soak in a solution of ½ ammonia, ½ water and two drops of liquid soap. Soak for a few minutes, and brush with an old, soft toothbrush. Rinse well and buff. Do not use this solution for pearls.

Costume

Clean costume jewellery by brushing it with baking soda.

Satin

Stains on satin should always be removed with dry-cleaning fluid. Water applied to satin alters the texture. Satin garments should be entrusted only to a commercial cleaner who not only cleans, but also redresses fabric.

Ironing
Dry iron

If you use a dry iron instead of a steam iron, place heavy-duty aluminium foil over the ironing board and cover it with the board's slipcover. The foil will reflect heat back to the garment being ironed, making your work easier.

Scorch marks

If you do end up doing the ironing and you get involved in *The Jerry Springer Show* so much that you scorch something, do not panic. First, make sure the mark is only a scorch and not a burn.

- A scorch can be removed by rubbing with dry steel wool to remove surface brown. If a pale-coloured material, sponge with a weak bleach about one part in four.
- On a silky synthetic, make a paste of glycerine and Borax powder and leave it to dry before brushing off. This can be used if you are worried about the colour of the material.
- Some scorch marks can be removed with a fifty-fifty solution of peroxide and water. Don't leave it soaking, do it quickly, then wash the garment thoroughly. With this

method it is always necessary to test the fabric on a seam, which will not show.
- Remember, if in doubt, don't.

Ten top ironing tips

Not everybody likes to iron, in fact most people find it tedious. However, it is usually a job that has to be done so here are the ten top ironing tips to make it simpler and more pleasant:

- Never iron anything that doesn't need to be ironed. Towels and sheets don't need ironing, simply roll tightly and put away.
- Use the clothes dryer to do as much ironing as you can. Remove the clothes as soon as the cycle finishes and as you take the clothes out, give them a good firm shake and fold them.
- When you hang clothes out to dry, take a little extra time to hang them on the line in a fashion that minimises the creasing. Fold as you put the dry clothes into the basket.
- Underclothes do not need ironing.
- Handkerchiefs do not need ironing.
- Buy clothes that don't need ironing.
- Do your ironing while you are watching your favourite television show.
- Ironing can be therapeutic; listen to music and just let your mind wander.
- Let each person who is over twelve in the household do their own ironing.
- Get an ironing lady . . .

Bathroom hints

Nobody likes cleaning the bathroom. It is a thankless, back-breaking task. However, there are some things that you should know that will make it easier.

Basin

Wipe the basin out after every use. This won't give the mould an opportunity to grow.
Save old toothbrushes and use them to clean hard-to-get-at places around the taps.
Shine chrome taps with a cloth dampened with vinegar. Buff with a dry cloth.
A sponge makes a great soap dish.

Bath

Scrub the bath, wipe the tiles and clean the shower at least once a week. Spray on cloudy ammonia. Leave for a few minutes. Go back and the dirt will rinse off. Don't let it get out of hand as that is when the mould grows and the task becomes a big one.
A mixture of salt and turpentine will remove yellow stains.
Soak your whites in Napisan in the bathtub. Stains will come out of your clothes and the bath at the same time.
Use a cloth soaked in undiluted ammonia.
Rust stains can be removed from the bath by rubbing with a cloth dipped in vinegar.
Treat stubborn bathtub stains with a mixture of cream of tartar and hydrogen peroxide.
A paste of Borax powder and lemon juice can be used to rub away rust stains from the tub.
To polish old bathtubs, use a car polish.
Use recycled orange or onion bags as scourers when cleaning your bath.

Brushes

To clean combs and brushes, place them in a little hot water and sprinkle them with bicarbonate of soda. Leave a few minutes and rinse.

Medicine cabinet

Clean out your medicine cabinet and throw out any expired medications on the last day of December each year. This will free up space and prevent you from taking out-of-date drugs.

Mirror

Prevent the bathroom mirror from misting up by wiping it with a damp cloth sprinkled with glycerine.

Shower curtains

To clean the shower curtain, wash with towels in a vinegar/water solution in the washing machine. Hang while still wet.

Mildew on rubber bathroom mats or shower curtains can be removed by soaking in the bath in a solution of water and bleach for a few hours. Hang out to dry.

Wash plastic shower curtains in the washing machine with terrycloth towels. Add a few drops of mineral oil to the rinse. This will clean the curtain and keep it soft and flexible.

The hemline of a shower curtain builds up an accumulation of soap. This can be removed with a paste made of salt and lemon. Rub firmly and then wash in lukewarm water.

After cleaning the shower doors wipe the inside down with lemon oil (furniture polish). They will stay clean much longer.

Showerhead

To remove the mineral deposits that often block the shower rose, remove the rose and boil it in white vinegar for fifteen minutes. Allow to cool and rinse.

Use a sponge mop to make quick work of cleaning a shower wall.

The naked scrubber

The best time to scrub the bath or clean the shower is when you are about to have a shower yourself. Arm yourself with the cleaning items. Get in and do the job naked. That way you won't spill bleach on your clothes.

Tiles

An easy way to whiten grout between shower tiles:

- Open the bathroom windows.
- Put a mixture of half bleach/half water in a spray bottle, and spray all over the grout.
- Return in fifteen minutes to check progress.
- Re-apply one or two more times if necessary.

A mixture of brown vinegar and kerosene will keep tiles looking very clean and shiny. For cleaning grouting use Epsom Salts.

Dip steel wool in vinegar and scrub tiles in the shower recess.

Toilet

Give the toilet bowl a good clean with the brush every day. Spray with vinegar to disinfect.

Place a denture cleaning tablet in the toilet bowl to clean.

Pour left-over cola drinks into toilet bowl, allow to stand and flush.

Toys

Use a plastic colander to hold your children's bathtub toys. You can use it like a scoop to collect small toys such as rubber ducks, plastic boats and action figures. Just leave it to drain right inside the tub.

Use that soap!

Put small soap slivers in a cotton sock. The soap-filled sock can replace a sudsy wash-cloth.

Walls

Scrub the shower walls with a mixture of baking soda and liquid dishwashing detergent.

Fill the bath with hot water, shut the door and let the room steam for ten minutes. This will loosen the dirt. Simply wipe the walls.

Wipe glass shower doors with a sponge soaked in vinegar.

Fill a spray bottle with vinegar and spray glass surfaces.

Wipe glycerine on windows and mirrors to prevent them from steaming up.

Amazing vinegar
Cooking with vinegar
Cheese

To keep cheese fresh for several weeks, place in an airtight container with a paper towel that has been dampened with vinegar at the bottom. Use a knife dipped in vinegar to prevent mould forming when you cut slices of cheese.

Hard-boiled eggs

For a hard-boiled egg, add a splash of vinegar. If one cracks, it will not boil out of the shell.

Make buttermilk

If you have a recipe that calls for sour milk (or buttermilk), add a bit of vinegar to fresh milk. This doesn't taste like vinegar. The vinegar separates the cheese from the whey.

Marinade

Utilise all of those bits and pieces of tomato sauce or chutney by adding some vinegar, oil, onion, garlic and spices to the bottle and shaking. Use as a marinade for meat.

Poaching eggs

It helps the eggs to keep their shape if you add a teaspoon of vinegar to the water, then swirl the water around with a wooden spoon.

Tenderise meat

To tenderise the toughest roast, pour one to two tablespoons of vinegar over a roast before cooking, then add salt, pepper or other condiments.

Salad dressing

Make a salad dressing by adding one part vinegar to three parts olive oil. Add a teaspoon of sugar and spices of your choice.

Stews

For stews and casseroles, add a tablespoon of vinegar to the juices when boiling ribs or meat for stews, and even the toughest meat will be so tender you can cut with a fork or it will fall off the bone.

Vinegar kills bacteria

Wash any flesh foods with vinegar before cooking to reduce the bacteria, especially chicken. Rinse fresh fruit and vegetables in vinegar. It can kill bacteria.

Cleaning with vinegar

Calcium build-up

Soak the bathroom showerhead in vinegar overnight, then rinse in hot water, to remove mineral deposits and keep it flowing freely. Vinegar is great for removing calcium deposit build-up. Heat vinegar to boiling point. Then pour over your fixtures that have deposits of lime. This will release or remove the deposit.

Chewing gum

To dissolve chewing gum, saturate the area with vinegar. If the vinegar is heated, it will work faster.

Septic tank

If you have a septic tank, use vinegar instead of harsh chemicals to clean the toilet bowl. Let it set overnight. It will help keep germs down.

Unblock drains

Pour white vinegar down the kitchen and bathroom sinks and shower drain to unclog them. It works like a wonder and has no toxins.

Vinegar and do-it-yourself

Clean paint brushes

Use boiling vinegar (no water) to clean hardened acrylic paints from paintbrushes.

De-rust nails and screws

Remove rust on screws and from nails with vinegar. Put the metal object in a container and cover with vinegar, seal the container and shake, let stand overnight or twenty-four hours.

Prepare paint surface

Wiping down clean metal surfaces with a vinegar solution (one part vinegar to five parts water) prepares the surface for painting, and reduces the incidence of peeling.

Remove wallpaper

Use vinegar to remove wallpaper. First remove the top layer of wallpaper. Spray vinegar on and let it set for a minute or two. Pull the backing away. Scrape any excess glue. Remove the remaining glue with vinegar and rinse with water.

Solvent for glue

White vinegar is a solvent for most glue. To dissolve any unwanted glue bonds, simply apply vinegar to the glued area and let sit until the bond becomes weak.

Wood stain

White vinegar can also be mixed with water-based inks to make a wonderful stain for wood. The resulting finish is the colour of the tint with a silvery sheen. Simply pour vinegar into a mixing jar, add the ink until the desired colour is achieved and apply to wood with a brush or rag. Wipe off excess and let dry.

Other uses for vinegar

Ants

Prevent ants and other insects crossing your door and/or window-sills, by 'pouring' vinegar across the threshold or opening sill.

Hems

When you 'let down' hems on children's clothes, get rid of the white mark that is left by taking an old toothbrush dipped in a little vinegar diluted with small amount of water, scrubbing the mark and pressing with a warm iron.

Ice-free windshields

When you have to leave your car outside overnight in the winter, mix three parts vinegar to one part water and coat the windows with this solution. This vinegar and water combination will keep windshields ice- and frost-free.

Keep flowers fresh

Keep cut flowers fresh longer by adding two tablespoons of vinegar and one tablespoon of sugar to each litre of water.

Set colours

Dip embroidery yarn in straight white vinegar and then air dry. This 'sets' the colours and you will not experience any 'running' of the colours.

Weeds

Kill grass or weeds by pouring hot vinegar onto the area. This might take a couple of times to work completely.

Deodorise with vinegar

Air freshener

1 teaspoon baking soda
1 tablespoon vinegar
2 cups of water

After it stops foaming, mix well, and use in a (recycled) spray bottle to spray into the air.

Carpets

Use diluted in equal parts with water to take pet odours out of carpets.

Fish smells

Warm a little vinegar on the stove when you cook fish or other strong- smelling food. It will help get rid of the odour.

Smoke smells
Put vinegar on white bread in various rooms of the house to get rid of smoke smell from a fire.

Unpleasant odours
Set shallow bowls of vinegar throughout the house to absorb unpleasant odours.

DIY cleaning
Bird droppings
Bird droppings on the car or on other paintwork need to come off quickly. They can cause enormous damage. Use washing-up detergent with plenty of warm water. Bird droppings can damage paintwork.

Brick fireplaces
Brick fireplaces can be cleaned with undiluted white vinegar on a wet cloth.

Cleaning and repairing wood
Candle grease
Put ice in a plastic bag and sit it over the candle grease for a few minutes. Scrape off as much as possible, rub the area with a few drops of eucalyptus on a soft cloth, then polish.

Cigarette burns
Cigarette burns are best treated with toothpaste.

Scratches
If you can't remove scratches, try hiding them. For dark wood, use iodine or a dark tan shoe polish. On light wood, use a shoe polish to match the colour, and if you can't get an exact match, use a lighter shade and keep repeating to build the colour up.

Wine and water
Wine or water on polished wood leaves a white, milky stain. Rub the area with Brasso, then polish.

Mildew on canvas
Moss, mildew and rust can all cause disintegration of the fabric. Mix:

2 cups of salt
1 litre of water
The juice of five or six lemons

Use this to rub on the mildew areas, and it will take it off.

Oil stains
Oil stains on concrete can be minimised by sprinkling sand to soak up the oil. Then scrub with warm soapy water.

Painting

- Before painting the woodwork around the windows, smear petroleum jelly on the glass. When you have finished simply wipe off the petroleum jelly and the paint will come with it.
- Use masking tape around the window and peel off for a similar result.
- To prevent paint getting into your pores, rub a little petroleum jelly on your hands before you start your project. It will cover your pores, making paint easier to wash off.

Rusty nails

Rusty nails may be cleaned of rust and made usable by placing them in a bag with sand and kerosene and shaking vigorously.

Woodworm and borer

Woodworm and borer can be treated with kerosene. Be sure to get the kerosene into all the little holes. When you are certain that all the little crawlies, and their eggs, are destroyed, fill the holes with wood filler and polish.

2
Cooking

The kitchen is the hub of the home. This is where pots and conversation bubble. Good food, good wine and good company are really what make life worth living. You need to achieve competence in the kitchen to enjoy these things, that is, unless you are very wealthy. Presentation of good food at your table is like making your family royalty.

Food needs to smell good, taste good and look good. Here are some hints and tips on how to make that kitchen sing!

Tools of the trade
Here are the essentials for every kitchen.

Bowls and dishes
A graduated set of mixing bowls has many uses. You'll need oven-to-table casserole dishes.

Cutting board
This should be thick and flat.

Essential utensils
- Potato peeler
- Three-pronged fork
- Basting spoon
- Potato masher
- Poultry scissors
- Egg slide
- Soup ladle
- Citrus squeezer
- Salt and pepper mills
- Colander
- Sieves
- Rubber spatula
- Beater
- Grater
- Rolling pin
- Can opener
- Mortar and pestle
- Draining spoons

Measuring correctly
For accurate measuring you will need a graduated set of cups, a set of spoons, a standard litre jug, and a 250 ml cup.

Saucepans
- Three good quality saucepans with heavy bases
- One milk saucepan with Teflon coating
- A thick frying pan

- An omelette pan
- A wok with a lid

Sieves
One fine, one coarse.

Steel knives
- Slicing and chopping knife
- Paring knife
- Boning knife
- Bread knife
- Fruit/vegetable knife

Store in a wooden block. Wipe clean after use. Keep sharpened.

Whisk
For sauces, omelettes, sponges and soufflés.

Wooden spoons
Wooden spoons and spatulas for stirring and beating.

Oven heat

Cool	200°F	90°C
Very slow	250°F	120°C
Slow	300°F	150°C
Moderately slow	325°F	160°F
Moderate	350°F	170°C
Moderately hot	375°F	190°C
Hot	400°F	200°C
Very hot	450°F	230°C

Staple foods and ingredients
Basmati rice
Basmati rice is a long fine-grained Indian rice. It is ideally suited to Indian curries.

Brown sugar
To soften brown sugar:

- Place apple slices in the container with the sugar.
- Place a slice of bread in the sugar container for twenty-four hours.
- Place a couple of marshmallows in a sealed container with the sugar.
- Substitute brown sugar with ½ cup white sugar, ½ teaspoon of maple flavouring and ½ teaspoon of molasses.

Delicious, crispy potato chips
Wash one large potato per person. Place in microwave and cook on 'potato' setting.

Allow to cool slightly and cut into generous chips. Heat oil. Drop chips into hot oil and cook until golden. Serve with fish.

Ghee

Ghee is clarified butter. It is able to reach higher temperatures than butter without burning. It can be bought at your supermarket in the dairy department.

Sauces

There are three main groups of sauces:

- White sauce
- Brown sauce
- Emulsified sauces

White sauce

The key to many dishes, every good cook knows how to make a white or 'béchamel' sauce. Here are two recipes.

White sauce recipe one:

40g butter
80g plain flour
500 ml milk
Seasoning to taste

The traditional European thickening agent for any liquid is called a roux. It is a mixture of flour and butter in proportions of one butter to two flour. The liquid is slowly worked in over low heat until it becomes a thin paste. It is then combined with the remaining liquid and heated slowly while being stirred, until thickening occurs.

White sauce recipe two:

2 egg yolks
500 ml milk
Pepper and salt to taste
You can also use egg yolks as a thickener.

Mix the egg yolks with the cold liquid and slowly heat over a double boiler. The protein in the egg causes the mixture to thicken. This method is fraught with danger as too much heat causes curdling.

Brown sauce

Brown sauces can be made in several different ways:

- In the cooking pan by scraping up all the juices.
- In a saucepan with the brown roux (see below) and brown stock.
- By thickening the liquid from stew with beurre manie (see below).

Emulsified sauces

These can be bought at your supermarket or grocer – packet sauces such as Gravox, etc.

Roux

This is a mixture of butter and flour which thickens a sauce. The colour of the roux depends upon the amount of time it has been cooked. It must be cooked over low heat and stirred constantly.

Creamy chilli sauce

Combine mayo, sour cream (or yoghurt), sweet chilli sauce and cayenne and stir well.

Beurre manie

This is made by blending one teaspoon flour and one tablespoon butter. It is added gradually to the sauce at the end of the cooking and stirred until it is blended. Do not boil once it has been added.

Egg yolks

Egg yolks thicken sauces. First mix a little of the hot sauce with the egg yolk and then quickly stir into the remainder of the sauce. Do not allow to boil.

Butter and oil

Mayonnaise is made when oil is dribbled onto egg yolks in a blender. Hollandaise and Béarnaise sauces achieve their body when butter is gradually stirred into egg yolks at a very low heat.

Adding wine to sauce

Only add dry wine to sauce. If you can't drink it, don't add it.

Salt

Be careful with the salt when making sauces. You can always add more, but it is not so simple to take it away!

Tartare sauce

1 cup favourite mayonnaise
½ cup chopped gherkins
1 tablespoon chopped capers
2 tablespoons French mustard
2 teaspoons finely chopped parsley
1 teaspoon finely chopped chives
3 black olives finely chopped

Combine all ingredients.

Lemon juice

Avoid adding too much lemon juice to sauces. A few drops is great, too much disastrous.

Keeping sauces

Prevent a skin forming on the top of a sauce by placing plastic wrap directly on the top.
    White sauce keeps covered in the refrigerator for several days.
    To keep brown sauce, pour a little sherry over the top and place in the refrigerator. It will keep for a week. If, at the end of the week, it is still not used, re-boil and restore. It will keep for another week.

Stock

Stock is the liquid obtained from simmering together meat, fish or chicken bones, trimmings and vegetables, seasonings and water. All stocks should be strained and chilled so that the fat rises to the top and is able to be skimmed off. It can be made up beforehand and frozen until needed. A good stock can truly make a dish.

White stock
500g of chicken or veal bones
3 litres cold water
2 onions
1 carrot
Bouquet garni, which consists of:
Celery, parsley, thyme, bay leaf and black peppercorns (tied together)

Place in large saucepan. Bring to boil, turn down and simmer gently for three to four hours. Strain, cool, refrigerate. The fat will rise to the top and seal the jelly underneath. Keeps for about a week in the refrigerator.

Brown stock
1 kg beef bones
1 carrot
2 onions
Bouquet garni
3 litres water
Peppercorns

Place in large saucepan. Bring to boil, then simmer for four to eight hours. Strain and refrigerate.

Fish stock
Fish heads and bones
5 cups water
1 cup white wine
1 onion
1 carrot
Bouquet garni

Place in large saucepan. Bring to boil, simmer for thirty minutes. Strain and refrigerate.

To clarify stock
Remove fat from the stock and place in a saucepan. Lightly beat two egg whites. Add egg whites and eggshells to stock. Simmer for twenty minutes. As egg whites cook they attract and hold the small particles of fat. Strain.

Essential cooking and kitchen tips
Almonds
Almonds bought with their skins on have a better flavour. To blanch almonds, cover with boiling water and allow to sit for a few minutes. Skins will come away easily.

Bread clips
The plastic clips that seal bread in plastic bags have many uses – to tie freezer bags, balloons, etc.

Brown sugar
In some weather, brown sugar lumps easily and makes measuring a problem. Put a piece of fresh bread in your sugar container to absorb the moisture, and after a few hours you should be able to shake the sugar freely.

Butter

To make the butter go further and spread more readily when you are making sandwiches, bring to room temperature, add a splash of milk and beat until smooth and creamy. Prevent butter from burning when you are sautéing by adding a small amount of cooking oil to the pan. (Olive oil is healthier and tastier.) Cottage cheese keeps better if you store the container upside down.

Cheese in the refrigerator

To store cheese, place in a covered dish with a lump of sugar on top. It will stay fresh and free from mould.

Chocolate

When melting chocolate, line the bowl with wax paper. Chocolate pours easily and none is wasted.

If you run out of cooking chocolate, substitute forty-five ml cocoa plus ten ml shortening for each square.

Coffee

To maintain the flavour and aroma of your ground coffee, store in an air-tight container in your refrigerator. Use purified water to enhance the taste of freshly brewed coffee. For a delicate taste treat, add vanilla extract to the water as the coffee brews. Cover left-over coffee with a lid and refrigerate. It will heat up in the microwave like a freshly brewed drop.

Egg substitute

If you are out of eggs when you go to crumb the chicken or fish, substitute the egg with two tablespoons of custard powder to make egg wash. It works like a treat.

Fresh breadcrumbs

To make fresh breadcrumbs, simply cut into cubes and use your vitamiser to break into crumbs. Add parsley and/or garlic or onions. Mix in some parmesan cheese. Freeze in a plastic bag until you are ready to use it.

Fruit cakes

Keep a wedge of apple in the fruit cake tin to prevent it from drying out.

Handy tips

- Save the vinegar from jars of pickled onions and gherkins and use it in place of ordinary vinegar for salad dressing or pouring over boiled beetroot.
- Use the left-over oil from sun-dried tomatoes to make salad dressing.
- When storing cooking oil, strain it through cotton wool to clear of residue.
- Make breadcrumbs by grating left-over frozen bread.
- To prevent pasta from clinging together while cooking, add a few drops of oil to the water.
- Baking soda will clean your oven door.
- When storing rice and other cereals add one teaspoon salt to keep the weevils away.
- To mix mustard use olive oil instead of water. The mixture will not dry out.
- Spiced vinegar and mustard makes an excellent addition to meat sandwiches.
- To soften hard brown sugar, put it in a bowl and cover with a wet cloth for five minutes. Lumps can then easily be removed.

Home-made baking powder
To make 'baking powder':

115g bicarbonate of soda
85g cream of tartar
30g tartaric acid

Sift together thoroughly and store in an airtight jar.

Honey
Sticky mixtures like honey will slide out easily and completely, if you first dip your measuring cup into flour.

Jam
Keep the mould from forming on home-made jams by storing the jar upside down.

Keeping a hygienic kitchen
Wash surfaces often
Cutting boards, dishes, utensils and counter tops should be washed with hot soapy water and sanitised after coming in contact with fresh produce, or raw meat, poultry or seafood. Sanitise after use with a solution of one teaspoon of chlorine bleach in one litre of water.

Don't cross-contaminate
Use clean cutting boards and utensils when handling fresh produce. If possible, use one clean cutting board for fresh produce and a separate one for raw meat, poultry and seafood. During food preparation, wash cutting boards, utensils or dishes that have come into contact with fresh produce, raw meat, poultry or seafood.

Lemon zest
Lemon zest can be added to flour when coating fish.

Luting paste
Luting paste is a thick flour and water paste, which is used for sealing lids on terrines and other oven-baked meats. Use one cup of flour and four tablespoons of water. Mix to a paste. Foil may be used, but the paste provides a superior seal and prevents shrinkage of the meat.

Manage mess
When baking a pie, casserole or similar dish, which might boil over, stand pie dish on a scone or oven tray. It is much easier to wash and there will be no mess in the oven.

Mixture to help you to put on weight
5 tablespoons of sugar
2 tablespoons powdered milk
1 tablespoon Akta-Vite
1 egg
1 litre of milk

Blend in the blender and place in the fridge. Drink as required. This quantity will probably last a couple of days.

Nifty hints

- When using ketchup, be sparing with the salt.
- One egg beaten well is worth two, not beaten.
- A stew boiled is a stew spoiled.
- Start roast meat in a hot oven.
- If you fill a dirty saucepan with water, it begins to clean itself.
- Wash your saucepans well but clean a frying pan with a piece of dry bread.
- Melt a teaspoon of oil in a frying pan before adding bacon.
- When the pastry comes out of the oven, the meat can go in.
- Green vegetables should be cooked quickly in the microwave.

Plate for cakes

Scratched vinyl records can be used as a cake plate for a stall. Simply cover in foil.

Pull-top rings

Save the pull-top rings on drink containers. Use them for placing in liquid paraffin wax when sealing jams and jellies. It makes the wax easy to remove when required.

Salt

In humid weather, salt gets quite lumpy. A little cornflour mixed with it will make it free-flowing. Or put some rice in the bottom of the shaker.

Sandwiches

Flavoured butters make delicious additions to sandwiches. Add lemon juice, anchovies, curry powder or chopped parsley.

Sauté

Sauté means to cook in an open pan in a small amount of hot oil, butter or fat. The fat should be free of moisture and, if necessary, clarified. Heat slowly at first to evaporate moisture and prevent sputtering.

Scissors

Always have a pair of kitchen scissors to cut meat, herbs and chicken.

Sponge cakes

The success of a sponge cake depends upon the amount of air that you manage to beat into the mixture. Use simple equipment – your hands, a whisk, a wooden spoon and get the feel of what you are making.

Tea

Enhance the flavour of your cup of tea. Add a mint to the pot and let it dissolve for a refreshing minty flavour. Dry an orange or lemon peel and put it in the caddy with your tea leaves.

Topping for ice cream

To make a quick and delicious topping for ice cream, simply melt a Mars Bar in the microwave and pour over the top.

To season a new frying pan

To season an iron frying pan, spread a tablespoon of oil in the pan and bake in the oven at 170°C for one hour.

Two handy measurements

2 cups breadcrumbs = 500g
1 tablespoon cheese = 15g

Using your vertical grill

To stop the fat that drains away from the meat from causing the grill to smoke place a slice of bread in the tray or add a cupful of water to the tray.

Stand the grill on a few sheets of newspaper to prevent the fat from splattering over your bench.

Walnuts
Keeping them

To keep walnuts, simply leave them in the shell and put them into an earthenware pot. Fill the pot almost to the top then cover about five centimetres thick with sawdust. Place the pot in a cool dry place.

Pickling walnuts

Place walnuts in a saucepan of brine and gently simmer for about thirty minutes. Pour off the brine then spread the walnuts flat to finish draining. Leave them in a nice dry place until they become black. Make up a pickle mixture by adding to every litre of vinegar:

30g black pepper
30g ginger
30g shallots
30g mustard seed
salt

Add the walnuts to pickle mixture and leave for four weeks.

Whipped cream

When whipping cream, make sure it is icy cold. Chill bowl and beaters and stand bowl over ice while beating. Well-chilled cream beats to a stiff consistency.

Condiments and garnishes
Crystallised violets

To crystallise violets beat an egg white slightly. Dip the violet into it, shake well to remove any excess, and gently roll in castor sugar.

Fake mint juleps

Small sprigs of peppermint can be frozen into ice cubes. They can be put into cold summer drinks. A nice added flavour.

Garnishes and accompaniments for soups
Melba toasts

Lightly toast thin slices of bread. Cut into triangles. Crisp in hot oven.

Croutons

May be bought. Or to make, remove crusts from six slices of bread. Lightly butter bread. You may add garlic, parsley, chives, cheese to the butter. Cut into cubes. Place on a tray in a hot oven until golden.

Fresh crusty bread

May be bought from the local bakery in a variety of forms.

Vegetable garnishes

- Julienne strips of carrot, celery, leeks, capsicum, zucchini, snow peas
- Chopped herbs sprinkled on top
- Noodles and rice cooked in the soup
- Sour cream spooned on top just before serving
- Chopped hard-boiled eggs added to soup
- Chopped strips of cooked chicken, meats, sausage, ham, bacon
- Tiny home-made dim sims
- Dumplings
- Grated cheese

Home-made seasoned salt

2 tablespoons pepper
1 tablespoon chicken bouillon powder
1 teaspoon onion salt
1 teaspoon onion powder
1 tablespoon garlic salt
1 teaspoon cumin powder
1 teaspoon dry marjoram leaves
1 tablespoon minced parsley
1 teaspoon paprika
½ teaspoon curry powder
1 tablespoon chilli powder
½ cup salt

Mix all ingredients together thoroughly, shaking until blended well. Keep at room temperature. Makes about one cup. Use within three months.

Jack Daniel's honey mustard

½ cup honey
½ cup dark vinegar
½ cup dark brown sugar – packed
2 eggs
2 tablespoons flour
2 tablespoons prepared yellow mustard
½ cup Jack Daniel's whisky
270 ml bottle Kraft horseradish cream

Blend honey, vinegar, sugar, eggs and flour for a few seconds on high speed in blender until smooth. Transfer to a large saucepan. Cook on medium-high, whisking to prevent it from sticking to bottom of pan. It will thicken just as it comes to a boil.

Quickly add mustard and whisky. Continue to cook and stir briskly for thirty seconds.

Remove from heat. Add the horseradish. Beat well. Cool completely. Bottle and cap tightly. Can store refrigerated for six to eight weeks.

Seasoned flour

Combine flour, paprika, garlic powder, pepper and cayenne. Place in a plastic bag and shake well.

Chicken
To baste a chicken

Spoon cooking juices over cooking chicken at intervals during the cooking process.

To truss a chicken

Pull the skin over the neck of the chicken. Secure by folding the wing tips under the chicken. Run a string around the wings. Cross over at the back. Turn the chicken and tie legs together, keeping them close to the body.

To test whether chicken is cooked

Pierce with skewer. If the juices run clear, it is cooked.

To carve a chicken

Use chicken-cutting scissors. Split chicken through the skin and along the backbone.

Turn and carve along the breastbone easing away the flesh. Turn and cut across the backbone. Trim away drumsticks and wings. Pull the flesh away from the rib cage. Arrange on a serving dish.

Grilling chicken

You may buy chicken for grilling with all manner of marinades from the butcher or chicken shop. Instructions may accompany them. If you are grilling drumsticks or thick pieces of chicken, half pre-cook in the microwave first and finish off on the grill. Cut breast of chicken into thin strips, marinade with your favourite marinade, and grill quickly. Serve with salad inside a pita bread.

Not-quite Kentucky Fried Chicken

1½ kilograms chicken pieces
2 serves Italian salad dressing mix
3 tablespoons flour
2 teaspoons salt
¼ cup lemon juice
1 cup milk
1½ cups pancake mix
1 teaspoon paprika
½ teaspoon sage
¼ teaspoon pepper

Make a paste out of the marinade ingredients. Coat chicken evenly. Stack chicken pieces in a bowl. Cover and refrigerate overnight or at least for several hours. Mix pancake mix with other seasonings. Dip pieces of chicken in milk, then in pancake coating. Dust off excess. Lightly brown in skillet with one centimetre vegetable oil in it. Brown for four minutes each side. Remove and place in a single layer on shallow baking pan. Seal with flour. Bake for one hour at 180°C. Uncover and baste again with milk. Return, uncovered, to oven heated to 200°C, to crisp for ten minutes.

Sweet and sour sauce for chicken nuggets

1 cup Apricot preserves
3 tablespoons Heinz 57 sauce
3 tablespoons Italian dressing
3 tablespoons soy sauce

Makes about two cups. Refrigerate for up to two weeks.

Mustard sauce for nuggets

1 tablespoon Dijon mustard
2 tablespoons French's prepared mustard
2 tablespoons Heinz 57 sauce
¼ cup mayonnaise
¼ cup sour cream

Mix all together. Cover and refrigerate to use within thirty days.

Meat

Boiled meats

Never boil meat: gently simmer. Use this method for cheaper cuts, which need long, slow cooking.

Carving boiled meats

Boiled and jellied meats should be cut with a sharp knife and are best cut into generous slices.

Never use a serrated-edged knife to cut boiled meats.

Storing boiled meats

Cool and store boiled meats in their own juices to keep them moist. Keep in an airtight container.

Grilling meat

Ideally the griller should be open as a closed-in griller does as much steaming as grilling of the meat.

- Preheat the griller so that it is as hot as possible.
- If possible grill outside on the BBQ as the fumes will not fill the kitchen with grease.
- Prime cuts are best for grilling.
- If you use cheaper cuts, tenderise with a marinade.
- Add flavour to grilled meat by brushing with oil and spices and allowing to stand for one hour before cooking.
- Turn grill meats with tongs.
- Don't pierce and release juices.
- Grilled meat is cooked when tiny beads of blood appear on the surface.
- Rare meat is firm, but springy when you touch.
- A dob of butter will improve most meats. It sizzles on top, glazing the surface.
- Serve grilled meats immediately upon cooking.

Beef cuts for grilling
Fillet steak

The most expensive, but also the most tender. A smaller serve is often preferable once you taste eye fillet. Scotch fillet as the name suggests is a cheaper cut with more fat.

Porterhouse and T-bone
T-bone is tasty as the bone is incorporated. Great for people who like to chew on the bone. Porterhouse is simply T-bone with the bone taken out.

Sirloin
Sirloin is cut from the ribs and is without any bone.

Rump
Rump is taken from the rump of the animal and is best cooked in a large piece and then cut into portions. Oyster blade/yearling steaks are often called BBQ steaks and are best marinated before grilling.

Grilling red meats
Select a cut about three to four centimetres deep. Brush with oil and grind pepper over surface.

Cut sinews between the fat to prevent buckling. Sear on both sides over high heat. Lower the heat and grill until rare medium or well done, however you like it.

Accompaniments for red grilled meat
Steaks do not need sauce. However, simply flavoured butter on top is delicious, Béarnaise sauce is good and mustards are excellent. Serve with a tossed green salad, potatoes done your favourite way, or vegetables.

Grilled lamb
Cuts suitable for grilling:

- Short loin chops
- Noisettes – boned lamb chops, rolled and tied with string
- Chump chops
- Cutlets
- Leg steaks/shoulder chops – not as tender as other chops and should be marinated for grilling
- Neck chops – deliciously sweet in the lambing season
- Lamb kidneys
- Lambs fry

Lamb is never served rare.

Serve with creamy mashed potatoes and a salad.

Ham
Once you use a ham, remove the outer plastic covering and wrap it in a damp cloth. Change the cloth every few days. This should keep the ham fresh for at least three weeks.

Hamburgers and rissoles
Avoid messy hands when moulding meat. If you rinse your hands in water the meat will not stick.

Home-made crumb coating
4 cups flour
2 teaspoons cayenne pepper
1 cup bran flake cereal, crushed
2 tablespoons parsley flakes

2 teaspoons garlic powder
1 tablespoon onion powder
2 teaspoons chilli powder
2 tablespoons taco seasoning
1 teaspoon season pepper
1 teaspoon curry (or more)
1 teaspoon sweet basil
1 teaspoon oregano

Mix all together in a plastic bag and store in the freezer. Use for coating any and all types of meat. Vary it according to taste. You may use fresh breadcrumbs if you wish.

Lamb's tongue
Tongue is usually soaked in brine by the butcher. The basic cooking for tongue is place in a saucepan with:

1 large onion, chopped
1 large carrot, chopped
2 or 3 stalks of celery, chopped
A few whole peppercorns and cloves
½ teaspoon of mixed herbs
Several bacon rinds
Enough water to cover

Bring to the boil. Reduce the heat. With the lid on, simmer slowly for 1½ hours. Remove the tongues, and as soon as they are cool enough to handle, peel and remove the fatty tissue and any cartilage. Put into a pudding bowl with weights on top to press. Leave overnight. Tongues can be served with a parsley or Madeira sauce, or cold with salad.

Sausages
To prevent sausages from oozing out at either end while cooking, put them into water, bring to the boil, strain immediately, and then cook in the normal manner.

Sausages done like this freeze very readily and can be used direct from the freezer, either for the pan, or for barbecue cooking.

Tenderising meat
Try one of the following methods:

- Brush with oil and garlic and allow to stand for one hour before cooking.
- Sprinkle vinegar over red meat and allow to stand.
- Marinade with your favourite marinade.
- Use a wooden mallet to tenderise. Place meat between two pieces of greaseproof paper and pound.

Thawing frozen meat or chicken
To prevent food poisoning when thawing meat, make sure you do so in the refrigerator, not outside on the kitchen bench. Frozen vegetables or fish may be thawed by placing the packet in cold water.

The roast
The perfect roast
There are two types of roast: the quick roast and the slow roast.

The quick roast
- Allow thirty minutes per 500g meat, plus thirty minutes.
- Sear the meat in a hot oven for the first twenty minutes.
- This sears in the juices.
- Turn oven down to moderate.

The slow roast
- Cook meat at a slow to moderate temperature for a longer time.
- Allow forty minutes per 500g plus forty minutes.
- Baste meat every twenty minutes using pan juices.
- This causes less shrinkage and meat is more tender.
- Meat should be at room temperature when put into the oven.
- Do not baste pork as it does not allow the crackling to crisp.
- Allow to rest for fifteen minutes before carving.

Roast lamb
Choose a lamb that is pinkish coloured and has some firm white fat. It may be either a leg or a loin, shoulder or a forequarter. For a small number, use a rack of lamb per person.

To roast lamb
- With a sharp knife make a few slits under the skin.
- Place slivers of garlic and sprigs of rosemary into these slits.
- Rub meat with salt and pepper.
- Place in roasting pan on a rack.
- Allow thirty minute per 500g plus thirty minutes.
- To make the gravy, use pan juices once the roast has been removed.

Improve the flavour of lamb by making tiny slits in it and filling them with either garlic as suggested above, or mint, before you put it in the oven.

Mint sauce for roast lamb
6 sprigs mint from garden
2 tablespoons boiling water
1 tablespoon sugar
2 tablespoons malt vinegar

Wash and chop mint leaves. Add sugar. Put into a jug and pour the boiling water on top. Place a cover on jug. Allow to stand for ten minutes. Add vinegar. Stir and serve.

Roast beef
Cuts for roasting
Good beef has a rich, red colour and a fine texture with a reasonable amount of firm white fat. A small marbling of fat throughout ensures tenderness and flavour. Sirloin, fillet, scotch fillet, rump, topside, silverside, bolar blade are all roast cuts.

To roast beef
- Cooking time thirty minutes per 500g plus thirty minutes.
- Rub with salt and pepper.
- Place on rack in a hot (200°C) oven for the first half hour.
- Reduce heat to 170°C.
- Baste every thirty minutes with pan juices.
- Make gravy with pan juices when roast is removed.

Yorkshire pudding

Yorkshire pudding can accompany any roast:

1 cup plain flour
½ teaspoon salt
1 egg
1 cup milk

Sift flour. Mix all ingredients together in a blender. Allow to stand for one hour in refrigerator. Spoon three tablespoons meat juices from around the meat and add to a smaller dish. Heat. Add batter and roast for one hour in the hottest part of the oven until light and fluffy.

Horseradish

Horseradish is easy to grow. Sauce made from horseradish is ideal for use with steaks or roast beef.

Horseradish sauce to accompany roast beef

To one cup of white sauce add:

A pinch each of mustard powder
Salt and sugar
2 teaspoons of lemon juice
1 tablespoon of cream
Then add 2 tablespoons of freshly grated horseradish

Roast pork

Buy pale pink flesh that is finely grained with pearly white fat and thin skin.
Leg and loin are preferred cuts for roasting.
    Fillet is often roasted stuffed with prunes, apricots or apples. It needs constant basting.

To roast pork

- Score the skin.
- Rub cooking salt into the skin.
- Place on a rack, skin up, in a very hot oven (260°C) for thirty minutes.
- Reduce heat to 160°C for remainder of time.
- Allow thirty-five minutes per 500g plus thirty-five minutes.
- Allow to rest before carving.

Easy apple sauce to accompany roast pork

1 tin baby food – strained apple. There you go!

Roast veal

Buy flesh that is very pale with just a hint of pink. The fat should be white and satiny and there should be no unpleasant odour.
    Roast veal can be very dry, and is best cooked in an oven bag. Before placing it in the bag, cover the piece of meat with oil and a little plain flour mixed with dry mustard, salt and pepper. Add a few bacon rinds to add flavour to the meat. When the meat is cooked, split the oven bag and use the juices to make gravy.
    If you are not cooking with an oven bag, here's what to do:

- Allow forty-five minutes for each 500g plus twenty minutes.
- Wrap bacon around the veal and secure with skewers.
- Place on an oven rack in a moderate oven (160°C).
- Baste every fifteen minutes.
- Allow to stand before carving.

Roast vegetables

Suitable vegetables for any roast are:

- Potatoes are essential. To ensure crispy potatoes one would die for, cook on medium in microwave for ten minutes before placing them in the dish with the meat.
- Pumpkin is highly desirable. Wash, remove seeds and cut into serving size pieces. Add to the pan with potatoes. There is no need to peel pumpkin. It cooks firmer and with more flavour in its skin.
- Carrots and parsnips, sweet potatoes and marrow can be halved lengthwise and added to the roast forty minutes before cooking is completed.
- Onions should be peeled and added to the roast for about an hour.

Gravy
To make a great gravy

Transfer vegetables and meat to the serving dish. Drain fat from roasting pan. Place pan over direct heat and sprinkle one tablespoon plain flour into juices. Stir over low heat until the flour mix is brown. Add 1½ cups stock into the pan. Bring to boil, stirring constantly. Simmer until gravy thickens. Season to taste.

Quick thicken

To thicken gravy quickly, add instant mashed potato instead of flour to the water mixture.

Using cooking bags

Cooking bags keep the juices in the meat. Less expensive cuts can be used. The oven remains clean.

Lightly oil and season food. Place in bag and then place bag in a roasting dish. Close bag securely. Puncture three or four holes in top of bag near the tie. After cooking, remove pan from oven, drain meat juices, remove meat and make gravy with juices.

Pot roast

1 rolled roast
6 small potatoes
6 carrots, cut lengthways
½ green pepper, cut into rings
1 medium onion
3 stalks celery
½ cup water or stock

Salt and pepper the meat generously. Place in a cooking bag. Add other ingredients. Cook in moderate oven for 1¼ hours.

Game
To cook wild duck

- Pluck and wipe the bird.
- Soak it in milk overnight to take away some of the gamey flavour.

- Stuff with forcemeat.
- Do not overspice.
- Roll in flour and brown in butter.
- Put it in a moderate oven and bake with the milk in which the bird was soaked.
- When nearly done, lift the bird out and place it in a casserole dish.
- Make gravy by browning equal parts of flour and butter and stirring over a low heat into the liquid in which the bird has been cooking.
- Strain the gravy.
- Add a glass of port wine and a dessertspoon of redcurrant jelly.
- Pour over the bird in the casserole and cook slowly until quite tender.

You may add:
- Cumquats soaked in brandy to the sauce just before you serve.
- Thinly sliced orange pieces.
- Thinly sliced lime and lemon.
- Drained tinned black cherries.

Venison

Venison is a very dry meat and if possible should be cooked in an oven bag. Alternatively:

- Lightly dust a joint of venison with flour, pepper and salt.
- Put onto the rack of a baking dish with pieces of bacon over the top of it.
- Put it into a hot oven for fifteen minutes.
- Reduce the temperature, and pour one cup boiling water into the pan.
- Cook until tender.
- Allow fifteen minutes to every 500g and baste every fifteen minutes.
- Serve with redcurrant jelly.

Cooking white meat

Pork and chicken should be cooked slowly under a moderate heat. This allows the colouring and cooking to take place at the same time. Baste the meat from time to time to prevent it drying out. When cooked juices will run clear. Never serve white meat rare.

Pork

Select chops that are at least two centimetres thick for if they are too thin they will cook too quickly and become dry and tough. Using a sharp knife cut through the skin at intervals to prevent the chops from curling. Brush with oil and season with pepper and rock salt. Cook on moderate grill, basting with oil every three minutes so that they stay moist. Grill apple slices at the same time. It is cooked when it releases clear juices when pierced.

Fish and seafood
When buying fish

Look for:

- Bright eyes
- Glistening scales
- Red gills

The fish should not have a strong smell. It should smell of the sea. Fillets should be firm to touch. They should never be slimy.

A good fish shop

Anyone who's ever smelled rotting seafood at the fish counter has a pretty good idea of what a poorly run seafood market smells like. But the absence of any strong odour doesn't necessarily mean that the seller is practising safe food handling techniques.

What's your general impression of the facility? Does it look clean? Smell clean? Is it free of flies and bugs?

A well-maintained facility can indicate that the vendor is following good sanitation practices.

- Employees should be in clean clothing or aprons.
- They should be wearing hair coverings.
- They shouldn't be smoking, eating or playing with their hair.
- They shouldn't be sick or have any open wounds.
- Employees should be wearing disposable gloves when handling food and change gloves after non-food handling tasks and after handling any raw seafood.
- Fish should be displayed on a thick bed of fresh, not melting ice, preferably in a case or under some type of cover.
- Fish should be arranged with the bellies down so that the melting ice drains away from the fish, thus reducing the chances of spoilage.
- Is the seafood employee knowledgeable about different types of seafood?
- Can he or she tell you how old the products are and explain why their seafood is fresh?
- If they can't, you should take your business elsewhere.

Cleaning your fish

- Scale the fish holding the fish firmly by the tail.
- Scrape the fish towards the head with a blunt knife.
- Remove the fins and head.
- Open the underside of the fish from head to tail.
- Remove the intestines and insides of the fish.
- Scrape the inside of the fish.
- Rinse thoroughly under running water.

To cut fish steaks

To cut fish steaks, cut across the fish in the thickness that suits you.

To skin fish

To skin, place a small cut across the tip of the tail. Slide the knife under the skin to separate it from the flesh. Dip your fingers in salt and grab a firm hold of the skin. Pull it towards you with your left hand and ease the flesh away using the knife with your right hand.

To fillet

To fillet, hold the tail and run sharp knife along the back bone.
Make a clean cut separating the flesh from the bone.
Turn over, and repeat on the other side.

Nana's method of frying fish

- Coat fish in seasoned flour.
- Whisk together 1 egg and 2 tablespoons of water.
- Run fillets through this mixture.
- Dip in either flour or breadcrumbs or batter.
- Allow to rest for thirty minutes in the refrigerator.
- Heat oil.

- Place fish in hot oil and cook until golden brown (three minutes approx).
- Drain and serve with crispy chips and salad.

To grill fish

Suitable for whole fish, fish steaks and fillets. Brush preheated grill with melted butter or oil. Slit the skin of whole fish at intervals to allow the heat to penetrate without bursting the skin. Grill three to four minutes on each side. Lower heat and cook until fish flakes easily. The larger the fish, the further it should be away from the heat.

To bake fish

Butter or oil foil wrap. Season fish with salt pepper and lemon. Bake in hot oven, allowing ten minutes for every 500g of fish. If the fish is stuffed it will take longer to cook.

Fish tips

- For a delightful crunchy extra, add raw diced celery to any fish mornay.
- For a crisp light batter use beer instead of water.
- It is easier to scale freshly caught fish if you drop it into hot water for a few seconds first.
- For extra flavour, add grated rind to the fish flour batter.
- Instead of serving lemon wedges with fish, make a sauce with the juice of two lemons, a teaspoon of sugar and parsley and pour it over the fish when it is cooked.

Fish batter

2 cups all-purpose flour
3 cups pancake mix
3 cups club soda
1 tablespoon onion powder
1 tablespoon seasoned salt
½ teaspoon cayenne pepper

Whip the pancake mix with the club soda to the consistency of buttermilk, add in the onion powder and seasoned salt.

Thai fish curry

500g ground, boneless white meat fish
1 teaspoon red curry
1 teaspoon minced kaffir lime leaves
1 cup minced ling beans
1 teaspoon salt
Cooking oil

Mix all ingredients together in a large bowl. Place cooking oil in a pan or wok and heat to a medium-low temperature. Take a portion of the ground fish-mixture into your hand and form into a ball approximately five centimetres in diameter. A helpful hint would be to keep your hands wet so the mixture doesn't stick to your hands and so the mixture forms correctly. Flatten the ball to form circular disks of about two centimetres in thickness. Fry the disks in the oil until golden brown in colour. Take the fish out of the oil when done. Place the fish cakes on a paper towel to absorb the excess oil. Serve with sweet chilli sauce and coriander.

Citrus prawn pasta

250g fettuccine
90g butter

½ cup chopped spring onions
¾ teaspoon cumin
¼ teaspoon hot chilli sauce
500g prawns, peeled and deveined
⅛ cup orange juice
¼ cup of chopped fresh coriander
1½ tablespoons grated orange rind
1½ teaspoons grated lime rind
¼ teaspoon salt

Cook pasta according to directions on packet. Melt _ butter in large frying pan. Add spring onions, cumin and chilli sauce. Cook about two minutes until the onions are tender. Add prawns. Cook, stirring until prawns turn pink. Remove prawns from pan.

Increase heat to high and add juices. Cook, stirring constantly until liquid is reduced to ⅛ cup. Remove pan from heat, stir in remaining butter. Stir in coriander, orange and lime rind. Stir in prawns. Serve.

The quick and easy way to peel prawns
- Place the prawns in a colander.
- Dip them in boiling water for five seconds.
- Grasp the legs and gently peel most of the shell.
- Hold the tail in one hand and tug to release the prawn from the rest of the shell and tail.

Barbeques
Tools
There are three essential tools for any barbecue:

- A long fork for toasting and for sausages.
- Tongs for turning meat.
- An egg slide for flipping tomatoes, eggs etc.

Always wear an apron to protect your clothes. A hat does nothing but it adds to the occasion and is therefore a good thing.

Flare-ups
- Avoid flare-ups by trimming excess fat from the meats and by not adding too much oil to the marinades.
- Keep a bucket of sand and a hose nearby in case fire flares up.
- Wait for the flames to die down before you start to cook.
- Charcoal takes twenty-five to thirty minutes to heat the plate to the required temperature and gas takes about ten minutes.

Aromatic BBQ
Soak fresh garden herbs such as rosemary in water and add them to your coals just before you cook.

Makeshift BBQs
To make a small impromptu picnic barbecue, punch holes around the side of an old biscuit tin. Fill the tin with heat beads and place a cake cooling rack or some chicken wire over the top. Light it, wait a while and the sausages will sizzle.

Pre-cooking

Make sure that meat and poultry are well cooked by pre-cooking them in the microwave before barbequing them.

Spicy butter

In a saucepan, melt a stick of butter over low heat. Stir in one or two tablespoons chopped fresh coriander and the juice of one lime. Add cayenne pepper, chilli powder, and cumin to taste. Spread on corn with a pastry brush before eating.

Meat and chicken on the BBQ
Minute-steak sandwiches

Pour marinade of your choice over minute steaks and allow to stand for one hour. Drain steaks and grill for three minutes each side. Sprinkle with salt and ground black pepper. Serve in warm buttered hamburger rolls with lettuce and tomato.

Pesto chicken

Brush chicken breasts with pesto to add flavour. Grill on the barbecue.

Apricot chicken

Save husks from sweetcorn and wrap chicken breasts stuffed with dried apricots.
Grill on the barbecue.

Mustard sausages

Slice thick sausages lengthwise and spread with mustard. Wrap with streaky bacon, secure with toothpick and grill.

Fish in vine leaves

Blanch vine leaves and wrap fish before grilling.

Filet mignon

Wrap bacon around an eye fillet steak. Secure with toothpick. Grill.

Hamburgers

1kg ground beef
1 onion, finely chopped
¼ cup water or evaporated milk
1 teaspoon salt
1 teaspoon Worcestershire sauce
¼ teaspoon pepper

Mix all ingredients together. Shape mixture into six large or twenty small patties. Broil or grill patties, turning once, ten to fifteen minutes. Serve on toasted buns with favourite toppings.

Vary the hamburger recipe by adding any of:
1 tablespoon horseradish
1 tablespoon mustard, prepared
1 tablespoon chives, snipped
2 tablespoon blue cheese, crumbled
2 tablespoon sesame seed
¼ cup ripe olives, chopped
¼ cup dill pickle, chopped or ¼ cup pickle relish
¼ cup nuts, chopped

Popular steaks for BBQs

Most popular steaks for the barbecue are:

- Fillet
- T-Bone
- Rump
- Porterhouse

Tips for BBQ steak

- If you use a cheaper steak it is a good idea to marinate it for twenty-four hours before cooking.
- To prevent steak from curling, slit the fat on the edges every three centimetres before placing on the grill.
- Always use tongs for turning steak as a fork will pierce the flesh and allow the juices to escape.
- Season steaks after you have barbecued them, for if you salt them before you cook, they tend to become tough.
- Turn the steak only once. The time depends upon the thickness of the steak. Estimate the time that it will take to cook to the required amount, rare, medium or well done. Divide that time in two and turn then.
- Rest steaks. Remove steaks from the barbecue when cooking is done and allow to rest a few minutes before you serve. In the case of rump, cut portions after you have cooked the whole steak.

Lamb chops

For chops that are three centimetres thick, allow six minutes on each side for searing and barbequing.

Poultry

Thaw whole chicken completely before cooking. Chicken pieces may be cooked straight from the freezer.

Pork

- The important thing to remember when cooking pork is to cook it well.
- Cook it slowly and turn it often.
- Belt the fat around a pork chop with a meat tenderiser before placing it on the grill. This helps it to cook through.
- Remember to baste spare ribs often as they cook. This prevents them from drying out.

Sausages

Par-boil before barbequing. Place in boiling water for five minutes, drain and cool.

Variations of sausages

Cut a slit in the sausage. Insert a slice of cheese. Wrap in bacon and secure with a tooth-pick. Grill.

Grill chipolatas (small sausages). Serve with BBQ sauce as a starter.

Spread a French roll with garlic butter. Add chopped chives and parsley. Add grilled sausage and a slice of cheese. Wrap in foil and heat until cheese melts. Serve with BBQ sauce.

Fish on the BBQ
Fish
Fish is delicious when done on the barbecue. Fish is cooked properly when it will flake easily. If you cook fish too much it will dry out.

Whole fish
- Scale and clean fish.
- Rub skin with melted butter and lemon juice.
- You may add other seasonings such as garlic, onions, dill, wine,ginger.
- You may fill the cavity with flavoured breadcrumbs or slices of lemon.
- Wrap in banana leaves or foil.
- Tightly fold in edges to seal.
- Turn two or three times during cooking.
- Allow eight minutes for every pound of large fish, fifteen minutes total time for small fish.

Basil paprika fish
Make a dry marinade of paprika, chicken salt, parsley and basil. Apply to fish steaks, let stand for thirty minutes and grill.

Vegetables on the BBQ
Bananas
Grill bananas in their skin. Remove and eat with icecream.

Eggplant rolls
Slice an eggplant lengthways, brush with oil, grill until tender, wrap around sticks of fetta cheese and basil leaves and grill again.

Garlic bruschetta
Grill whole cloves of garlic until tender. Brush slices of bread with olive oil and grill. Squeeze garlic onto the bread and sprinkle with basil.

Mushroom
Place about six mushrooms per person in foil. Add a knob of butter, salt and ground pepper. Wrap foil and cook on barbecue for eight minutes, turning halfway.

Onion
Slice onion into rings. Cook with meat on barbecue. Smells delicious and gets the digestive juices flowing.

Potatoes
Microwave potatoes for five minutes before slicing and placing on the barbecue. Microwave small new potatoes for five minutes, thread onto a skewer, brush with oil and grill for five to eight minutes.

Baked potatoes
Scrub potatoes. Place in the microwave, set on 'potatoes'. Serve with topping of butter, or sour cream and chives.

Barbecued potatoes

Scrub potatoes. Place in microwave and half cook. Remove and slice. Cook on barbecue with meat.

Cheesy potatoes

Scrub potatoes. Cook in microwave oven on 'potatoes' setting. Slice and sprinkle with mozzarella cheese. Bake in oven until cheese melts. Serve.

Sautéed potatoes

Scrub the potatoes. Place in the microwave and cook for half the required time for potatoes (about four to five minutes on medium). Slice and place in casserole dish. Season with salt and pepper. Sprinkle with home-made breadcrumbs. Melt two knobs of butter and pour over top. Bake in a moderate oven for forty minutes.

Roast corn on the cob

Pull down the husks without removing them and strip out the corn silk. Pull the husks back up and twist together the tops; soak in water for fifteen minutes. Roast the ears on a grill or directly on coals for eight to sixteen minutes. Serve with spicy butter.

Sweetcorn

Select tender sweetcorn in husk. Strip the husks to the end of the cob without tearing them off. Remove silk. Let stand in iced water for one hour. Drain. Brush the corn with softened butter. Sprinkle with salt. Bring the husks up around corn and secure. Cook on barbecue for ten minutes, turning once.

Tofu kebabs

Thread cubes of tofu onto skewers alternating with cherry tomatoes, mushrooms and zucchinis. Brush with oil and grill.

Tomatoes

Cut tomatoes in half. Place on foil. Sprinkle with salt, pepper and sugar. Drizzle olive oil and a few slivers of garlic over top. Place tomatoes back together as one. You may add sprigs of basil. Wrap foil and cook on barbecue for ten minutes, turning once.

Zucchini/capsicum

Brush with olive oil and garlic. Grill on barbecue for three minutes each side. Brush with balsamic vinegar when cooked. Serve.

Slice zucchinis, peppers, onions and eggplant, brush with oil and chargrill.

BBQ sauces

Barbeque sauce

1 cup of oil
2 onions, finely chopped
1½ cups brown sugar
5 tablespoons mustard
3 teaspoons salt
1 cup Worcestershire sauce
1 cup tomato sauce
5 stalks celery, cut fine
½ cup of vinegar
1 litre water

Sauté the onions and celery in the oil without browning. Add the other ingredients. Simmer for thirty minutes. Thicken with cornstarch, as desired.

Chilli tomato sauce
½ cup peanut oil
½ cup vinegar
1 tablespoon sugar
2 tablespoons tomato paste
1 tablespoon mustard
3 dessertspoons hot pepper sauce
Teaspoon of garlic salt

Combine ingredients and beat with a whisk until well blended. Use as baste for charcoal-broiled chicken.

Chilli barbecue sauce
½ cup chilli sauce
2 tablespoons vegetable oil
2 tablespoons orange juice
1 tablespoon brown sugar
1 dessertspoon Tabasco sauce

Combine all ingredients in a small bowl. Mix well. Use as a marinade or brush over seafood, chicken or pork in the last ten minutes of grilling.

Citrus barbecue sauce
1 onion, large, finely chopped
1 tablespoon ground red chillies
¼ teaspoon ground red pepper
1 tablespoon vegetable oil
1 cup orange juice
½ cup lime juice
2 tablespoons sugar
2 tablespoons lemon juice
1 tablespoon fresh coriander
1 teaspoon salt
1 capsicum

Cook onion, ground red chillies, red pepper and capsicum in oil for about five minutes, stirring frequently, until onion is tender. Stir in remaining ingredients.

Heat to boiling, reduce heat to low. Simmer uncovered, about ten minutes, stirring occasionally. Makes about 2⅛ cups of sauce.

Marinades for BBQ
Quick barbecue marinade
¼ cup finely chopped onion
2 tablespoons butter or margarine
¼ cup brown sugar, firmly packed
1 tablespoon Worcestershire sauce
⅛ teaspoon hot pepper sauce
1 clove garlic, finely chopped
1 cup tomato sauce
¼ cup of lemon juice
1 teaspoon mustard

Sauté onion and garlic in butter until tender. Add remaining ingredients; bring to a boil. Reduce heat; simmer uncovered fifteen to twenty minutes. Use as basting sauce for pork, chicken or beef. Refrigerate leftovers.

Pork spare ribs marinade
¼ cup honey
¼ cup sweet orange marmalade
½ teaspoon dry mustard

Mix all ingredients together. Heat and serve with pork chops or other meats.

Mexican barbecue marinade
⅓ cup dark karo syrup
⅓ cup strong coffee
¼ cup tomato sauce
¼ cup cider vinegar
¼ cup Worcestershire sauce
6 teaspoons chilli powder
1 tablespoon corn oil
2 teaspoons mustard
½ teaspoon salt
½ teaspoon pepper sauce

Mix well and allow flavours to blend for one hour or more.

Pickles and chutneys for the BBQ
Hot mango pickle
5 red chillies, chopped and seeded
2 green capsicum, chopped and seeded
2 red capsicum, chopped and seeded
4 large onions, peeled and chopped finely
12 green mangoes, peeled, seeded and chopped
1 cup sultanas
1 cup raisins
½ cup chopped garlic
½ cup chopped ginger root
½ cup chopped coriander
2 tablespoons black mustard seeds
75 ml malt vinegar

Combine all the ingredients, except vinegar, in a heavy-based saucepan. Add enough vinegar so that the other ingredients are covered in the pan. Bring to the boil then reduce heat and simmer until the mixture is thick and the fruit and vegetables are soft. Pour into sterilised jars. Seal with sterilised lids and store in a cool place.

If you like your foods really hot, then don't de-seed the chillies. Try this spicy pickle with Indian foods, salads, cold meats or sandwiches.

Salads
Bean salad
1 can kidney beans
1 can soy beans
1 cup chopped celery
½ cup chopped onion

1 chopped gherkin
½ cup chopped walnuts

Mix together and pour over vinaigrette dressing.

Coleslaw
½ finely shredded cabbage
½ green pepper, ½ red pepper, finely sliced
½ cup finely chopped celery
½ cup spring onions, finely chopped
1 medium sized grated carrot

Mix ingredients in bowl. Pour over coleslaw dressing. Refrigerate and serve.

Italian potato salad
½ cup Italian dressing
¾ cup mayonnaise
½ cup sliced green onions
2 tablespoons snipped fresh dill
1 teaspoon Dijon-style mustard
1 teaspoon lemon juice
⅛ teaspoon pepper
1½ pink or new potatoes, cooked and cut into large chunks

In large salad bowl, thoroughly combine all ingredients except potatoes. Toss with warm potatoes, cover and chill.

Layered antipasto salad
500g whole mild drained banana peppers
1 medium cucumber, thinly sliced
250g pitted ripe olives
1 tin Italian style tomatoes, quartered
250g zesty Italian dressing
4 cups torn iceberg lettuce
150g shaved hot pepperoni
1 can artichoke hearts, drained and halved
400g sliced mozzarella cheese
1 cup sliced fresh mushrooms
Reserve 2 banana peppers

Slice remaining peppers in half, and remove stems. Layer cucumber, olives, tomatoes, and peppers in a medium to large bowl. Pour ¼ cup dressing over layers. Top with lettuce, half of pepperoni, artichoke hearts, half of cheese strips, mushrooms, remaining pepperoni, and cheese strips. Pour remaining dressing over salad. Chill. Garnish with reserved peppers.

Layered salad
1 iceberg lettuce, finely sliced
1 cup frozen peas, blanched
2 tomatoes, chopped
3 eggs, chopped
Bacon, cut into bite-sized pieces and cooked

Beginning with the lettuce and in a glass dish layer the salad ingredients, finishing with the eggs. Add sour cream mayonnaise or dill ranch mayonnaise.
    Sprinkle bacon pieces on top and serve.

Mexican rice salad
6 chopped hard-boiled eggs
3 cups cooked rice
½ cup sliced green onions
1 cup sliced celery
1 cup grated cheddar cheese
¼ cup chopped canned green chillies
1 cup sour cream
1 tablespoon lemon juice
¼ cup piquant sauce (optional)
2 teaspoons salt
1 teaspoon seasoned pepper
1 large fresh tomato, chopped
Salad greens

Combine eggs, rice, onions, celery, chillies, and cheese in large mixing bowl. Blend sour cream, lemon juice, piquant sauce and seasonings. Pour over egg mixture; mix well. Chill. Serve over salad greens and top with tomato.

Potato salad
4 medium cooked and diced potatoes
1 small diced onion
2 hard boiled eggs
2 stalks chopped celery
¼ cup French dressing

Combine ingredients with exception of eggs and chill. Before serving, add mayonnaise and eggs.

Simple potato salad
Scrub potatoes. Cook in microwave until soft. Cut into bite-sized pieces. Pour over a dressing of olive oil, garlic and ground black pepper while still warm. Serve immediately.
    These potatoes can be reheated in the oven next day.

Tossed salad
Lettuce, broken into bite-sized pieces
2 tomatoes, sliced or quartered
Salad onion cut for rings
Cucumber, sliced
Avocado, sliced

Mix together. Just prior to serving, pour over your favourite dressing. Toss and serve.

Salad dressings
All-purpose Asian salad dressing
2 tablespoons white vinegar
1½ tablespoons soy sauce
1 tablespoon sugar
1½ teaspoon Asian sesame oil
½ teaspoon grated ginger
1 tablespoon chopped coriander
A few drops of hot chilli oil

In a small bowl, whisk together the vinegar, soy sauce, sugar, sesame oil and ginger. Just before serving, stir in the coriander and chilli oil. This all-purpose dressing is ideal for leafy greens, steamed vegetables and cold meats.

Avocado dressing

1 large ripe avocado
¼ teaspoon garlic salt
Juice of 1 lemon
¼ teaspoon onion salt
¼ cup mayonnaise

Put all ingredients into blender at high speed until creamy smooth. Garnish with paprika.

Balsamic vinaigrette dressing

8 tablespoons water
2 cups balsamic vinegar
4 tablespoons Dijon mustard
8 tablespoons lemon juice
3 cloves crushed garlic
2 teaspoons salt
2 teaspoons oregano
Black pepper to taste
2 teaspoons sugar
2 tablespoons chopped parsley

Mix all in a jar and shake vigorously.

Basic French dressing

1 cup oil
¼ cup wine vinegar
3 tablespoons water
2½ teaspoons sugar
1 teaspoon dry mustard
1 teaspoon black pepper
2½ teaspoons salt
1¼ teaspoon Worcestershire sauce
1¼ teaspoon Hungarian paprika
1 teaspoon grated onion
2 pieces blue cheese (optional)

Combine oil, vinegar and water and beat until blended.
    Add sugar, mustard, pepper, salt, Worcestershire and paprika and beat until blended.
    Add onion and beat well.
    If desired, stir in cheese.

Basic Roquefort dressing

1 cup Roquefort (or blue) cheese
1 tablespoon Worcestershire sauce
1 tablespoon lemon juice
⅔ cup salad oil
2 tablespoons vinegar

Mash cheese with a little oil. Add Worcestershire sauce, lemon juice, vinegar and balance of oil. Shake well until creamy.

Basic vinaigrette dressing
½ teaspoon salt
1 pinch black pepper
½ teaspoon sugar
½ teaspoon Dijon mustard
2 tablespoons red wine vinegar
6 tablespoons oil of choice

Add all ingredients to a shaker jar and shake very well just prior to use.

Variations
Lemon vinaigrette – Substitute lemon juice for vinegar.
Garlic vinaigrette – Add one or two cloves of minced garlic to dressing.
Herb vinaigrette – Add one or two tablespoons of chopped herbs.
Honey vinaigrette – Substitute one teaspoon of honey for the sugar.
Dijon vinaigrette – Add three tablespoons of additional Dijon mustard.

Blender mayonnaise
1 large egg or 2 small ones
1 tablespoon vinegar
½ teaspoon salt
¼ teaspoon dry mustard
⅛ teaspoon paprika
1 dash cayenne pepper
1 cup salad oil
1 tablespoon lemon juice

Put the egg, vinegar, salt, dry mustard, paprika and cayenne in a blender. With the blender *running slowly*, gradually pour half of the salad oil into the blender container.

When necessary, stop the blender and use a rubber spatula to scrape down the sides. Still with the blender running slowly, add the lemon juice to the mixture in the blender and slowly pour the remainder of the salad oil into the blender container.

Caesar salad dressing
½ cup mayonnaise
2 tablespoons white vinegar
3 tablespoons grated parmesan cheese
Fresh ground pepper

Thin mayonnaise with the vinegar. Stir in the cheese and black pepper.

Cajun mayonnaise
½ cup reduced-fat mayonnaise
½ cup non-fat plain yoghurt
½ teaspoon crumbled dried oregano
¼ teaspoon garlic salt
¼ teaspoon ground cumin
2 pinches cayenne pepper
2 pinches black pepper

Combine all ingredients in a small bowl. Refrigerate, covered, until ready to use.
Prepare twenty-four hours before using, for flavours to blend.

Dill ranch dressing
1 cup light sour cream
1 cup plain non-fat yoghurt
¼ cup reduced-fat mayonnaise
2 teaspoons sugar
1½ teaspoon dried dill weed
¾ teaspoon onion powder
½ teaspoon dried basil leaves
½ teaspoon pepper
½ teaspoon salt

Blend sour cream, yoghurt and mayonnaise in a small bowl using wire whisk. Add remaining dressing ingredients; mix well. Cover and refrigerate for a couple of hours to blend flavours.

Everyday salad dressing
½ cup rice vinegar
2 tablespoons olive oil
1 tablespoon soy sauce
1 tablespoon water
½ teaspoon Dijon mustard
1 minced garlic clove
¼ teaspoon dill weed or basil
Pepper
Sugar to taste

Combine all ingredients in a medium jar. With lid on, shake vigorously until well blended.

Fat-free honey Dijon dressing
¼ cup honey
2 tablespoons Dijon mustard
½ cup rice vinegar

Warm honey. Blend in remaining ingredients and refrigerate. It will thicken.

Gippsland dressing for iceberg lettuce salad
Two chopped hard-boiled eggs
½ teaspoon dry mustard
3 tablespoons vinegar
2 tablespoons sweetened condensed milk
½ teaspoon salt

Pound all dry ingredients together. Add liquid ingredients. Mix well.

Italian dressing mix
1 tablespoon garlic salt
1 tablespoon onion powder
1 tablespoon sugar
2 tablespoons dried oregano
1 teaspoon black pepper
¼ teaspoon dried thyme
1 teaspoon dried basil
1 tablespoon parsley, freeze-dried
⅛ teaspoon mustard powder
1 envelope Cup-A-Soup Cream of Chicken

¼ teaspoon celery salt
2 tablespoons seasoned salt
1 tablespoon dried grated lemon peel

Mix all ingredients together and force through a fine mesh sieve with back of a large spoon. Store covered and use within four to five months.

To use:
Combine 2 tablespoons of mix with :

¼ cup vinegar
⅔ cup oil
2 tablespoons water

Shake the mixture vigorously. Makes one cup.

Lemon garlic dressing
½ cup lemon juice
½ cup polyunsaturated oil
¼ teaspoon 'Lite' or table salt
¼ teaspoon ground nutmeg
2 garlic cloves, crushed
1 tablespoon lemon rind, grated

Blend oil and lemon juice. Add lemon rind, salt, garlic and nutmeg. Refrigerate for two hours to allow flavour to develop before using.

Simple tomato and lettuce salad dressing
½ cup vinegar
¼ cup olive oil
½ cup lemon juice
1 small minced onion
⅛ cup tomato sauce
⅔ cup sugar
½ teaspoon paprika
1 teaspoon salt

Put all ingredients together in a jar; cover and shake well.

Sour cream mayonnaise
¾ cup mayonnaise
¾ cup sour cream
⅜ cup sugar
3 tablespoons vinegar

Mix together and pour over coleslaw.

Tofu dressing
This recipe contains no eggs and very little oil and can be used in place of regular mayonnaise.

2 garlic cloves
1 tablespoon chives, roughly chopped
¼ cup vegetable oil
½ teaspoon mustard powder
¼ teaspoon sugar
1 lemon (juice only)

2 tablespoon parsley, roughly chopped
300g tofu, firm, crumbled
1 tablespoon white wine vinegar
1 pinch of salt and pepper

Chop garlic and herbs in a blender or food processor. Don't be over generous with the garlic or the dressing will taste of little else. Add the remaining ingredients and blend until the mixture is smooth and creamy. Refrigerate in a screw-topped jar for several weeks if desired.

Yoghurt pesto dressing
2 cups basil leaves, lightly packed
½ cup pine-nuts, toasted
½ cup parmesan cheese
1 cup natural yoghurt

Blend all ingredients in a food processor or blender, until at a pouring consistency.
    Serve on fresh salad greens.

Eggs
An egg is nature's fast food. It is a quick, easy to make and satisfying meal. It is full of protein and goodness.

To boil an egg
Bring the egg to room temperature. Place it on the end of a spoon and slip it into lightly salted boiling water.

Cooking times
Soft	2–3 minutes
Firm white/soft yolk	5–6 minutes
Hard boiled	10 minutes

To poach an egg
* Bring water to the boil in a wide-based saucepan.
* Add a teaspoon of salt and a teaspoon of vinegar.
* Take a wooden spoon and whirl the water.
* While it is still spinning, break in the egg.
* The whirling water will make the egg retain a round shape.
* Gently simmer the egg until desired hardness.
* Drain with a sieved spoon.
* Serve on buttered toast.

To scramble an egg
* Break and beat two eggs.
* Scramble with a fork.
* Add salt and pepper and a teaspoon of chopped parsley.
* Add a tablespoon of milk.
* Melt a knob of butter on the bottom of a milk saucepan.
* Cook over gentle heat until desired texture.
* Serve on hot buttered toast.
* May also serve with bacon and tomato.

To make an omelette
- Break two or three eggs.
- Scramble with a fork.
- Add a tablespoon of milk or cream.
- Season.
- Heat an omelette pan.
- Add mixture over medium heat.
- Omelette can either be flipped right over, or it may have fillings added.
- It will then be only half flipped with one side of the egg mixture being brought over the filling.
- When that side is cooked through, it can be turned and cooked on the other side.

Fillings and variations
- Ham
- Cheese
- Tomato
- Mushrooms
- Potato
- Herbs
- Salami
- Spinach

Egg tips
To avoid cracked eggs from spilling while boiling, add a teaspoon of salt to the water.

Add a teaspoon of vinegar to the water to prevent cracking.

If you have left-over egg yolks drop them into a pan and cook them to add to salads.

When slicing hard-boiled eggs, wet the knife before each cut.

Add breadcrumbs to scrambled eggs to make them go further and to improve the flavour.

To separate the whites from the yolk, break the egg into a funnel, allowing the white to slip through while the yolk stays there.

A few drops of glycerine added to egg white will make it firm.

Add a teaspoon of sugar and a dessertspoon of cold water to increase the quantity and make it froth more quickly.

Add a pinch of salt to egg whites when whisking.

Substitute one level tablespoon of milk and a level dessertspoon of custard powder for an egg when baking.

A little milk added to the water when boiling or poaching eggs will prevent the saucepan from discolouring.

To vary scrambled eggs try adding one of the following: chopped grilled bacon, chopped grilled mushrooms, chopped tomatoes, grated cheese, smoked salmon.

Hard-boiled eggs should be cooked gently for fifteen to twenty minutes and dropped immediately into cold water before peeling.

Prick the round end of an egg to lessen the chance of it cracking.

A bad egg will float in water.

Milk
Make your own condensed milk
Make your own condensed milk from powdered milk. In the blender mix for one minute:

¼ cup hot water
¾ cup granulated sugar
1¼ cups dry skim powdered milk.

Refrigerate for twenty-four hours. Keeps for five days. Always use skim milk powder in your cooking.

Useful dairy tips

Add honey to whipped cream instead of sugar. It stays firmer longer.

To prevent milk from burning, sprinkle one teaspoon of sugar over milk before heating. Do not stir.

When boiling milk, first rinse pan with cold water to avoid boilovers.

If cream refuses to whip, add one egg white.

When whipping cream with an electric mixer, set the bowl in the sink and whip. All the splatters are in the sink and there's no mess to clean.

Spoon dabs of left-over whipped cream onto wax paper and place in the freezer. They can be placed in a plastic bag and kept in the freezer to use for dessert toppings.

Make your own fruit yoghurt by adding fresh fruit to plain yoghurt.

Keep powdered milk in the cupboard in case you run out.

Quick and easy starters
Dolmades

Dolmades have a very special flavour when they are made from young grape leaves. Boil for two minutes and fill, placing leaves shiny side down.

Stuffed mushrooms

½ cup low-fat ricotta cheese or cottage cheese
½ cup finely chopped shallots
1 cucumber finely chopped
1 tomato finely chopped
1 teaspoon freshly ground black pepper, or to taste
2 tablespoon lemon juice
2 tablespoon fresh dill or chives chopped
8 large mushroom caps, 100g each

Mix ricotta, shallots, cucumber, tomato and pepper. Sprinkle mushroom caps with lemon juice and fill with the mixture. Sprinkle with dill or chives. Serve immediately or bake in oven for a few minutes. May be served raw or baked in oven for a few minutes only.

Omelette rolls

4 large eggs (53g each)
2 teaspoon soy sauce
2 teaspoon peanut oil
2 tablespoon water

In a medium bowl, whisk the eggs, water and sauce for two minutes. Lightly brush a non-stick frying pan with the oil. Heat pan on high. Pour one fifth of egg mixture evenly into pan (shake pan to spread). Heat for twenty seconds, or until almost set; remove from heat. With an egg slice, remove the omelette and roll it up. Place on a warm plate; cover with a tea towel. Repeat the process, using one fifth of egg mixture each time. To serve, slice rolls into one centimetres rounds. For extra flavour, spread omelettes with a filling of your choice before rolling (eg. pesto or sun-dried tomato spread).

Stuffed potatoes

250g packet frozen spinach, thawed and drained well
10 small unpeeled, washed potatoes (150g each)

¼ cup low-fat natural yoghurt
¼ cup breadcrumbs (30g)
¼ cup reduced-fat cheese (30g)

Prick the potatoes with a fork and bake at 200°C for one hour or until tender (or microwave on high for fifteen minutes). Cut the potatoes in half and scoop out most of the flesh. Combine flesh with spinach, yoghurt and pepper and spoon mixture back into potatoes. Top with combined breadcrumbs and cheese. Bake at 200°C until top is crisp and lightly browned. Allow to cool a little before serving as finger food.

Tips for serving starters
- To prevent pastries from going soggy, add the fillings just before serving.
- To prevent mess, make canapés small enough to be eaten in one mouthful.
- Serve hot and cold canapés in small batches over a period of about an hour.
- Make space for guests to put down their drinks so that they are not trying to juggle food and drink together.

Some simple serves
Avocado
Mash avocado with a little mayonnaise. Add lemon to taste.

Blue cheese
Mix equal amounts of blue cheese with soft cream cheese. Loosen with milk.

Cucumber
Grate cucumber, squeeze juices out, finely chop two cloves of garlic, add to yoghurt.

Fetta and peppers
Thread cubes of fetta onto a cocktail stick between a square of red and green pepper. You may cook the peppers first under the grill.

Ham with kiwi fruit
Wrap thinly sliced smoked ham around wedges of kiwi fruit and secure with a toothpick.

Mini meatballs
Pour sweet chilli sauce over mini meatballs and garnish with coriander.

Mini scones
Make small drop scones, the size of a dollar. When cool top with sour cream and a slice of smoked salmon or cream cheese and an olive.

Nacho bites
Spoon a little salsa or guacamole onto corn chips. Sprinkle with paprika.

Paté mushroom
Remove the stalks from small cup mushrooms and pipe paté into the hollows.

Pesto
Stir pesto sauce into Greek-style yoghurt.

Piped celery
Pipe cream cheese onto celery sticks.

Salami with melon
Wrap thin slices of salami around sticks of melon. Secure with a toothpick.

Simple dips
Serve plenty of crudités and savoury crisps for dipping. You may use Turkish bread cut into mouthfuls, rice crisps, potato crisps, all manner of breads, any crisp vegetable, washed and cut into bite-size pieces. Arrange attractively on a tray with the dip as a centrepiece. The dip can be put in a bowl, a hollowed out loaf of bread, a hollowed out melon or pumpkin, or a coconut shell. Use your imagination.

Snow peas
Pipe cream cheese into snow peas. Delicious!

Spicy tomato sauce
Mix salsa sauce, tomato sauce, Worcestershire sauce and a red chilli finely chopped.

Tuna
Drain a tin of tuna and mash with plain yoghurt. Add chopped dill, mashed boiled egg, sour cream and parsley.

Avocado dip
½ large peeled and stoned avocado (150g)
½ cup ricotta cheese (135g)
1 teaspoon tomato paste
½ teaspoon 'Lite' or table salt
3 drops hot chilli sauce (or to taste)
1 teaspoon freshly ground black pepper (or to taste)

Mash avocado with a fork until very smooth. Add ricotta cheese, tomato paste, salt, chilli sauce and pepper. Blend until smooth. This may be done in a food processor or blender. Serve chilled with mixed raw vegetables or small savoury biscuits. Best made a maximum of one hour before serving.

Vegetarian dip
2 cups soy drink
2 tablespoon margarine, milk-free
1 tablespoon flour
1 French onion soup packet
1 cob loaf of bread (23cm)

Cut the top third from cob loaf. Remove bread from inside leaving a four centimetre thick shell. Pre-heat oven to 180°C. Melt the margarine in a saucepan. Stir through the flour and soup mix. Cook for one minute. Remove from heat and gradually add soy drink. Stir over medium heat until mixture boils and thickens. Pour the mixture into a loaf tin. Heat in moderate oven for fifteen minutes, or until heated through.

Microwave directions
Melt margarine on HIGH 100% for forty to forty-five seconds. Stir through flour and soup mix.

Cook on MEDIUM for one minute. Remove from microwave and gradually add soy drink. Microwave on HIGH 100% for six minutes, stirring every minute until mixture thickens. Pour mixture into loaf. Heat in moderate oven for fifteen minutes, or until heated through.

Variations
Bread removed from inside a loaf can be dried out in the oven and served with the dip together with vegetable sticks. Garnish with steamed asparagus.

Chickpea dip
½ teaspoon dried cumin
1 tablespoon lemon juice
310g can chickpeas, drained
½ cup Greek-style yoghurt
1 teaspoon fresh coriander, chopped

Puree chickpeas and fold through remaining ingredients. Refrigerate until required. Serve with crunchy vegetable sticks and water crackers.

California sushi rolls
4 cups of rice
1 cup of rice vinegar
1 package roasted seaweed
½ avocado
Crab meat
Wasabi
Soy sauce

Wash the rice and put in a rice cooker (four cups rice, add four cups of water). After the rice is done put into a bowl. Pour one cup of rice vinegar, mix and let it cool. To begin making sushi: spread rice on top of the seaweed. Place seaweed on bamboo mat wrapped in plastic. Add above ingredients then roll. Cut into six pieces.

Vegetarian pizza
If using fresh tomatoes, place in a bowl and pour boiling water over. Allow to stand one to two minutes. Drain tomatoes and plunge into cold water. Skin should readily peel off.

300g tomatoes, fresh or tinned
1 Lebanese bread, large
3 spring onions, chopped
50g green capsicum (1 small), chopped
¼ teaspoon dried basil and oregano
1 teaspoon tomato paste
45g mushrooms, chopped
3 artichoke hearts, tinned
60g mozzarella cheese, grated

- Chop tomatoes roughly.
- Put tomatoes, spring onions, capsicum and spices in a non-stick pan.
- Bring to the boil and simmer for fifteen to twenty minutes.
- Allow sauce to cool. Spread sauce over bread.
- Add layer of mushroom and asparagus or chopped artichokes.
- Top with grated cheese.
- Bake for fifteen minutes in a hot oven.
- Serve hot, cut into bite-size serves.

Tomato, basil and zucchini low-fatmini muffins

2 cups self-raising flour
2 teaspoon baking powder
1 teaspoon bicarbonate soda
½ cup oat bran
1 cup apple sauce
½ cup skim milk
1 egg, lightly beaten
1 cup zucchini, grated
⅛ cup basil, chopped
2 tablespoon tomato paste
1 pinch of salt and pepper
1 tablespoon canola oil

- Pre-heat oven to moderate 180°C.
- Prepare a twelve-hole muffin tin with muffin papers.
- Sift flour, baking powder and soda in a medium bowl.
- Stir through oat bran.
- Make well in centre.
- Using a large table fork, stir in combined apple sauce, oil, egg, skim milk, zucchini, basil, tomato paste, salt and pepper until the mixture is just combined.
- Spoon mixture into prepared tin.
- Bake twenty-five to thirty minutes until golden brown and cooked through (use the toothpick test).
- Stand in pan five minutes before turning muffins onto wire rack to cool.

Leftovers

Don't throw food out. Leftovers are the great basis for a subsequent meal – and taste just as good, too!

For lunch

Take leftovers from the night before to work with you and eat them for lunch. They are delicious and cost effective.

Another meal

Freeze left-over pasta or curries and eat them another night when you get home late and cooking is out of the question. Simply remove from the freezer, microwave and you will be enjoying a tasty meal.

Breadcrumbs

Left-over bread can be made into bread crumbs that make delicious coating for your chicken or veal schnitzel. Great for eggplant slices also.

Cake

Slice left-over cake, wrap and freeze. It can be then used for lunches.

Cheese

Grate left-over cheeses and freeze for use in cooking.

Chicken bones
Use chicken bones to make a rich stock for soup.

Ham
Left-over ham can be used in omelettes.

Left-over sandwiches
A delicious way to use up left-over sandwiches, no matter how dry they are, is to make up a pancake batter, let it stand for half an hour then dip each sandwich in it, allowing it to soak well. Fry until golden brown in a small quantity of butter or oil.

Sandwiches can also be reconstituted by dipping in egg and milk and then shallow fried.

Looking ahead
Cook an extra couple of meals when you are cooking. Serve on a plate and wrap with plastic wrap. Microwave and serve when you get home late from work.

Nuts and potato chips
Left-over chips and nuts can be placed in sealed containers and frozen. They will stay fresh and crisp.

Pancakes
If you make too many pancakes and have some left over, you can layer a piece of wax paper between each and stack the pancakes on top of each other for freezing.

Basic pancake mix
Non-stick spray
1¼ cups all-purpose flour
1 egg
¼ cup granulated sugar
1 teaspoon baking powder
1 teaspoon baking soda
¼ cup cooking oil

Pre-heat a skillet over medium heat. Use a pan with a non-stick surface, or apply a little non-stick spray. In a blender or with a mixer, combine all of the remaining ingredients until smooth. Pour the batter by spoonfuls into the hot pan, forming twelve-centimetre circles. When the edges appear to harden, flip the pancakes. They should be light brown. Cook on the other side for same amount of time, until light brown. Makes eight to ten pancakes.

Salmon patties
Use left-over mashed potato to make salmon patties:

* Add a drained can of pink salmon.
* Sauté some onions and garlic and finely chopped parsley until soft.
* Bind together with a lightly beaten egg.
* Coat in breadcrumbs.
* Fry in hot oil until golden brown.

Shepherd's pie

Use left-over roast lamb to make shepherd's pie in the traditional way:

- Cut the meat off the bone and cube it.
- Grind it or put in your vitamiser to mince.
- Add seasonings and left-over vegies and gravy from the roast.
- Place in a casserole.
- Add mashed potatoes to the top.
- Cook in a medium oven for one hour.

Trifle

Use left-over sponge cake or jam roll to make a trifle:

- Simply, line the bottom of a glass dish with slices of cake.
- Soak with either fruit juice or your favourite tipple.
- Cover in creamy custard.
- Add a layer of jelly.
- Finish with piped cream.

Vegetables

Before shopping for the week, make way for fresh produce by grating and chopping all left-over vegetables. Make a rich vegetable soup that can be taken in a thermos for lunches each day.

Whipped cream

Left-over whipped cream can be made into rosettes with the piping bag and frozen.
Use as a decorative addition to float on coffees and milk shakes.

The freezer
Useful freezing tips

- You can make pancakes or crepes ahead of time, freeze, and then reheat in the microwave.
- Freeze baker's yeast to ensure that it lasts.
- Freeze coffee to keep it fresh and aromatic.
- Keep whole-wheat flour fresh by storing it in a freezer bag in the freezer.
- Use left-over bread to make up breadcrumbs and then place in usable quantities in plastic bags in the freezer.
- Brown sugar will remain soft if kept in the freezer.
- Store popcorn in the freezer – the pop will be louder and the corn juicier.
- Make your own baby food and store it in meal-size portions in freezer bags.

Liquids

- Freeze left-over coffee in ice cubes in the freezer. Great to add to black coffee to cool it down before drinking.
- Instead of ice cubes, freeze grapes and add to your punch. They have the same effect, but look great and add flavour.
- Freeze lemon peel in ice cubes, then use as an ingredient that will add zest to your favourite lemon dishes.
- Chop up left-over parsley and mint, add water, and make into tasty ice blocks.
- Freeze children's drink bottles for school on hot days.

Fruit

Fruit can be frozen raw, but remove the stones as they make it bitter.

Meat

Meat will be more tender if left to hang first. Avoid ice-burn by packing in airtight containers. Poultry must be thawed completely before cooking. Other meats may be left to thaw in refrigerator, but can be cooked semi-frozen. When freezing minced steak, put in a plastic bag, flatten until it spreads over the whole bag, and place on a flat shelf in the freezer. It will thaw very quickly when needed.

Do not freeze

- Hard-boiled eggs.
- Cooked potatoes.
- Any food that is set in gelatine or aspic, as they become rubbery.

Freezing meats

Buy meat in bulk. It is often cheaper that way. Meat should be prepared for freezing so that it is ready to cook when removed from the freezer.

- Pack in suitable sized quantities.
- Separate steaks, chops, cutlets etc by placing a sheet of plastic between each piece of meat.
- Dice stewing steak before freezing.
- Always move all the air from each package.
- Form flat packages where possible.
- Freeze meats that are over from a roast by slicing and adding the gravy.
- Place in plastic bag and flatten.
- Stews, casseroles and sauces can be cooled, then frozen. Place in a foil container and reheat as required. It will keep for two months.

Freezing vegetables

Blanching

Most vegetables need to be blanched with boiling water before they are frozen. Blanching kills the enzyme that causes vegetables to deteriorate.

Steam blanching

Blanche with steam by placing the vegetables in a steamer over a pan of boiling water. Steam for required time once the water has boiled.

Water blanching

Using a large saucepan, bring a pot of water to the boil. When the water is boiling rapidly, add vegetables. Leave for required time and drain.

Onions and capsicums do not require blanching. Simply freeze fresh.

Potatoes freeze better if they are boiled until they are soft.

Freezing requirements of some foods

Apples

Stew slightly. Pack in plastic containers, leaving head space.

Apricots

As for apples.

Asparagus

Remove woody portions. Cut into fifteen centimetres lengths. Blanche for three minutes. Cool in iced water. Pat dry. Place on trays and freeze for thirty minutes. Remove and pack in plastic bags. Keeps six months.

Avocado

Remove flesh from shell. Mash with juice of two lemons. Pack pulp back into shells. Wrap individually in plastic wrap. Pack in plastic bags.

Broccoli

Choose tender, young heads. Wash well in salted water. Divide into medium sized sprigs. Blanche for three minutes. Cool in iced water. Drain and spread on tray. Cover with plastic. Freeze for thirty minutes. Remove and pack into plastic bags. Keeps six months.

Butter

Over-wrap butter packaging with foil. Freeze. Thaw in the refrigerator for five hours.

Cakes

Bake and cool cakes. Package into plastic bags. Remove all air. Freeze.

Capsicum

Wash. Remove seeds and either leave whole or cut into rings. Spread on tray and freeze for thirty minutes. Pack into plastic bags.

Carrots

Wash and scrape. Cut into serving pieces. Blanche for three minutes. Chill with iced water. Drain, spread on tray and freeze. Pack into plastic bags.

Cheese

Although cheese does not lose its flavour, it does become crumbly. Grated cheese freezes better.

Corn

Remove husk and silk. Cut off the immature end. Wash and blanche for six minutes. Chill with iced water. Drain and pack several to a bag. Freeze.

Cream

Cream does not always freeze well as it tends to separate upon thawing.

Duchess potatoes

Boil potatoes in lightly salted water until tender. Drain and mash. Add one beaten egg, 125g butter, salt and pepper to taste. Pipe onto tray in rosette shapes. Freeze for thirty minutes. Remove and pack into plastic bags for freezing. Keeps three months.

Eggs

Break fresh, clean eggs into a basin and scramble slightly, making sure not to add air. Add a pinch of salt per egg to prevent glugginess. Package in commonly used quantities.

Egg whites and egg yolks can be frozen and stored separately as above.

Fish

Freeze only fish that you know to be freshly caught. Refrigerate no longer than twenty-four hours before freezing. Scale and fillet the fish before freezing.

Garlic

Separate cloves from bulb. Freeze in plastic bags. Run under hot water when needed. The skin will drop off.

Herbs

Pick sprigs or leaves. Wash well. Pat dry. Pack into plastic bags, removing air.

Lemons

Lemons are best frozen as juice. Peel can be frozen separately.

Milk

Only freeze homogenised/pasteurised milk. It can be frozen for three weeks before separating.

Onions

Pack onions in their skins in plastic bags. Remove air and freeze. Keeps for three months.

Passionfruit

Passionfruit can be frozen whole. Or remove the pulp. Freeze in ice cube containers. Remove from containers and place in plastic bags.

Peas and beans

Remove strings and snip off ends. Leave smaller beans whole and snap larger beans in two. Blanch for three minutes. Chill in iced water. Drain, pat dry. Spread on a tray and freeze for half an hour. Remove and pack in plastic bags. Remove the air and seal. Keeps for six months.

Pies and pastries

Pies and pastries can be frozen either before, or after, baking. Meat pies must have their filling cooked before freezing. Do not cut vents in pastry until ready to put in the oven. Cook straight from freezer.

Potato chips

Prepare chips in usual way. Drain well on paper towel. Spread on tray and freeze. Leave thirty minutes. Remove and pack into bags. Freeze. Keeps for three months.

Poultry

Pack chicken ready for cooking. Package in meal-size portions. Freeze crumbed chicken pieces on a tray initially. Remove and pack into plastic bags.

Remember . . .
Chicken pieces may be cooked from frozen. Whole chicken should be thawed in the refrigerator before cooking.

Scones, cakes and pastries
Cakes, scones and pastries emerge from the freezer in an excellent state. However, they do deteriorate more quickly and so should only be frozen in quantities that will be used immediately upon thawing.

Biscuits
Biscuits can be frozen, baked or unbaked.

Strawberries
Wash in iced water. Cut large ones in half. Pat dry with paper towel. Cover in light syrup. Pack into plastic containers.

Or sprinkle prepared fruit with castor sugar. Pack into plastic containers.

Sweet potatoes
Scrub and peel. Bake or roast until barely tender. Drain on paper towel. Cool. Pack into plastic bags and freeze. Keeps three months.

Tomatoes
Wash the tomatoes. Cut into halves. Pack into plastic bags. Remove air and seal. Use to add to cooked dishes.

Another method is to cook the tomatoes in a large pan until soft enough to push through a sieve, removing skins and seeds. Return to stove and continue to simmer until they are thick and reduced in quantity by half. Allow to cool. Pack into containers.

Freezer storage times
This table indicates the approximate length of time various foods can be safely stored in a refrigerator or freezer.

Food		Fridge	Freezer
Eggs	Fresh, in shell	20 days	Don't freeze
	Hard cooked	7 days	Don't freeze well
	Raw yolks, whites	2–4 days	1 year
	Liquid pasteurised eggs or egg substitutes (opened)	10 days	1 year
	Liquid pasteurised eggs or egg substitutes (unopened)	3 days	Don't freeze
	Mayonnaise	60 days (refrigerate after opening)	Don't freeze
Frozen Dinners		Don't refrigerate	Freezer: 90–120 days (keep frozen until ready to serve)
Deli Products ham, macaroni	Egg, chicken, tuna, salads	3–5 days	Don't freeze well
	Pre-stuffed pork & lamb chops, chicken breasts	1 day	Don't freeze well
	Store-cooked convenience meals	1–2 days	Don't freeze well
Soups & Stews		3–4 days	60–90 days
Hamburger, Ground & Stew Meats	Hamburger and stew meats	1–2 days	90–120 days
	Ground turkey, veal, pork, lamb (separate or mixed)	1–2 days	90–120 days
Hot Dogs & Lunch Meats	Hot dogs, opened & unopened	7 days	30–60 days in freezer wrap
	Lunch meats, opened	3–5 days	30–60 days in freezer wrap
	Lunch meats, unopened	14 days	30–60 days
Bacon & Sausage	Bacon	7 days	30 days
	Raw pork, beef, or turkey sausage	1–2 days	30–60 days
	Smoked breakfast links, patties	7 days	30–60 days
	Hard sausage (pepperoni, jerky sticks)	14–21 days	30–60 days
Ham & Corned Beef	Corned beef (drained)	5–7 days	30 days
	Ham, canned (label says keep refrigerated)	6–9 months	Don't freeze
	Ham, fully cooked, whole	7 days	30–60 days

Food		Fridge	Freezer
	Ham, fully cooked, half	3–5 days	30–60 days
	Ham, fully cooked, slices	3–4 days	30–60 days
Meats, Fresh	Beef steaks & roasts	3–5 days	6–12 months
	Pork chops, pork & veal roasts	3–5 days	120–180 days
	Lamb chops	3–5 days	6–9 months
	Variety meats (tongue, brain, kidney, liver, heart, chitterlings)	1–2 days	90–120 days
Poultry, Fresh	Chicken or turkey, whole	1–2 days	12 months
	Chicken or turkey, pieces	1–2 days	9 months
	Giblets	1–2 days	90–120 days
Poultry, Cooked Chicken Pieces	Fried chicken, plain	3–4 days	120 days
	Cooked poultry dishes	3–4 days	120–180 days
	Pieces, in broth or gravy	1–2 days	180 days
	Chicken nuggets, patties	1–2 days	30–90 days

Source: University of Florida, Institute of Food and Agricultural Sciences

Useful freezing tips

Coffee
Ground coffee and coffee beans freeze well and retain their flavour.

Decorative moulds
Make a decorative mould for your punch bowl by making a design with fruit and flowers on the bottom of a dish. Cover with water and freeze. Float in your punch bowl.

Drinks
Freeze strawberries, grapes or cherries in an ice cube and use in drinks.

Orange juice
Freeze oranges whole. They can be used for juice.

Ice trays
Ice trays can be used to freeze small amounts of food in convenient sizes.

- Meat and vegetable stock
- Tomato paste
- Soup
- Orange juice
- Lemon juice
- Apple sauce

- Black coffee for use in iced coffee
- Passionfruit pulp
- Puréed baby food

Do not consume ice that has come in contact with fresh produce or other raw products.

Icy poles
Cut into quarters and serve to children as ice blocks. Freeze fruit juices for healthy icy poles.

Jelly cakes
When making jelly cakes and lamingtons, freeze the butter cake first. The jelly sets more quickly and mess is reduced.

More tips when cooking for the freezer
- Potato should not be added until the dish is ready to be reheated as they tend to become watery and disintegrate.
- Peas lose their flavour so it is better to add them during the reheating stage.
- Wine tends to lose its flavour during freezing. Add wine during the reheating process.
- To prevent over cooking, reduce the cooking time of frozen food that will be reheated by 25%. This will prevent over cooking of ingredients in the reheating process.
- Cool foods to be frozen quickly before freezing. Stand in iced water and stir contents until cool.
- Toppings, such as cheese and breadcrumbs, should be added during the reheating stage.
- Large items such as casseroles should be thawed prior to reheating to reduce cooking time.
- Thaw items to be served cold in their packaging, in the refrigerator.

Prevent mould growth
Prevent fruit and jams from growing mould in hot weather by placing them in the freezer.

Sandwiches
Sandwiches can be frozen for lunches. Avoid using salad vegetables or hard-boiled eggs. Cut and pack in plastic wrap or sandwich bags in desired quantities.

Sandwich fillings suitable for freezing
- Seasoned chopped ham moistened with cream or mayonnaise.
- Chopped chicken, crispy bacon and mayonnaise.
- Minced ham with sour cream and horseradish.
- Chicken liver pate.
- Finely mashed sardines with lemon juice and seasoning.

Shopping for frozen foods
When shopping, shop last for frozen products. Take them home and return them to the freezer immediately. Check frozen commercial vegetables for goodness by feeling to see that they are free flowing in the packaging. If they are lumpy or icy, they have been thawed and refrozen. Shop from a supermarket that has a high turnover in order to avoid stale foods. Reject poultry with white patches as it has been burnt by the freezer and will have lost its flavour.

Perishable food
Danger zone
Perishable food is any food that will deteriorate and go bad if it is not refrigerated or handled in the appropriate manner. This is all fresh meats, fish, fruit vegetables, dairy. These need to be kept refrigerated and care needs to be taken when handling them. Exceptions are canned and preserved and dried foods, grains and pastas. These can be kept in the pantry.

Make sure perishable foods are not held at temperatures between 5°C and 55°C, the 'Danger Zone', for longer than two hours. Pathogenic bacteria can grow rapidly in the 'Danger Zone', but they do not generally affect the taste, smell, or appearance of a food. In other words, you cannot tell that a food has been mishandled or is unsafe to eat.

Shopping for perishable food
Fresh produce, meat and diary food deteriorate quickly. Care should be taken when shopping for them:

At the store
- Purchase produce that is not bruised or damaged.
- If buying fresh cut produce, be sure it is refrigerated or surrounded by ice.
- Use a cooler with ice or use ice gel packs when transporting perishable food, including cut fresh fruits and vegetables.
- While shopping, you should keep raw meat, poultry, seafood, and eggs separate from ready-to-eat foods in your shopping cart and your grocery bags.
- When the weather's hot, place the groceries in the air-conditioned compartment of your car rather than the hot boot.

At home
- Chill and refrigerate foods.
- After purchase, put produce that needs refrigeration away promptly.
- Fresh produce should be refrigerated within two hours of peeling or cutting.

Wash hands often
Hands should be washed with hot soapy water before and after handling fresh produce, or raw meat, poultry or seafood, as well as after using the bathroom, changing nappies, or handling pets.

Wash fruit
Wash all fresh fruits and vegetables with cool tap water immediately before eating. Don't use soap or detergents. Scrub firm produce, such as melons and cucumbers, with a clean produce brush. Cut away any bruised or damaged areas before eating.

Food parcels
When you receive a food item marked 'Keep Refrigerated', open it immediately and check its temperature. The food should arrive frozen or partially frozen with ice crystals still visible. Even if a product is smoked, cured, and/or fully cooked, it still is a perishable product and must be kept cold. If perishable food arrives warm, notify the company. Do not consume suspect food. Do not even taste suspect food.

Weevils
To prevent weevils from getting into any jar or packet and ruining good food, tape a few bay leaves to the lid of the container and the weevils will disappear. For dried fruit, add a twist of lemon rind into the jar.

When using dry ice
Don't touch dry ice with bare hands. Don't let it come in direct contact with food.

Refrigerators
Refrigerators should stay at 5°C or less. A temperature of 5°C or less is important because it slows the growth of most bacteria. The temperature won't kill the bacteria, but it will keep them from multiplying, and the fewer there are, the less likely you are to get sick from them.

Home-cooked gifts
For perishable foods prepared at home and mailed, follow these guidelines:

- Ship in a sturdy box.
- Pack with a cold source (frozen gel packs or dry ice).
- Warn the recipient of its use by writing 'Contains Dry Ice' on the outside of the box.
- Wrap box in two layers of brown paper.
- Use permanent markers to label outside of the box.
- Use recommended packing tape.
- Label outside clearly; make sure address is complete and correct.
- Write 'Keep Refrigerated' on outside of the box.
- Alert the recipient of the parcel's expected arrival.
- Do not send to business addresses or where there will not be adequate refrigerator storage.
- Do not send packages at the end of the week.
- Send them at the beginning of the week so they do not sit in the post office or mailing facility over the weekend.
- Whenever possible, send foods that do not require refrigeration.

Fruit
Crumble for fruit
2 tablespoons brown sugar
2 tablespoons melted butter/margarine
¼ cup plain flour
¼ cup biscuit crumbs*

Place in a bag and shake together.

*Wheatgerm, rolled oats, coconut or muesli may be used instead of biscuit crumbs.
　　To save time, when making your crumble topping for stewed fruit, make triple the quantity and place two quantities in freezer bags in the freezer for future use.

Apples
Stewing apples
When stewing sour apples, you don't need to use more sugar if you add a teaspoon of salt and a knob of butter.
　　When stewing any fruit, boil the sugar and water first before adding the fruit. This prevents the fruit from breaking up and becoming mushy.
　　To prevent apples from discolouring after peeling, stand in water until needed.

Apple crumble cake
A quick and easy sweet to make for a hungry family.

2 cups flour
1 cup brown sugar
½ cup quick cooking oats
¾ cup melted butter
1 cup sugar
3 tablespoons cornstarch
¼ teaspoon salt
1 cup water
1 teaspoon vanilla
6 apples, peeled, cored, sliced

Mix together flour, brown sugar, oats, butter. Spread half of mixture into medium cake tin. Pat down. Combine sugar, cornstarch, salt and water in saucepan. Cook over moderate heat, stirring until thickened. Add sliced apples and vanilla. Stir to coat well. Spread evenly over crumbly mixture in pan. Top with remaining crumbs.
Bake in 350° oven for about one hour. Serve with ice cream or cream.

Baked apples
To spare yourself mess, make a cup out of foil, place each apple in one, bake and simply turn out onto the plate.

Apple sauce
A can of apple baby food makes a great apple sauce for pork.

Bananas
A summer treat is to peel, wrap and freeze fresh bananas. Then coat them with chocolate sauce that hardens.
It's like eating banana-flavoured ice cream with chocolate on top, without the calories of ice cream!

Banana cake
2 cups unsifted flour
2 teaspoons baking powder
1 teaspoon baking soda
½ teaspoon salt
¼ cup apple sauce
1 cup sugar
1 large egg
1 large egg white
2 teaspoons lemon zest
1 teaspoon vanilla extract
500g ripe, mashed bananas
¾ cup light sour cream
1 teaspoon icing sugar (for dusting)

Preheat oven to 170°C. Grease medium sized baking pan and dust with flour. In medium bowl, combine two cups flour, baking powder, baking soda and salt; and mix well. In large bowl of electric mixer, cream margarine and sugar until fluffy. At medium speed, beat in egg, egg white, lemon zest and vanilla; and beat two minutes.
At low speed beat in bananas and add flour mixture and sour cream. Alternate so that mixture remains moist. Pour into prepared pan. Bake for thirty minutes or until done. Cool cake in the pan for ten minutes; run knife along sides and invert onto rack.
Cool. Dust with powdered sugar.

Jam making

Brush the pan with cooking oil before you make jam. It will stop the jam from frothing up.

To prevent jam from becoming sugary, add one teaspoon cream of tartar just before you remove it from the stove.

A few clean marbles in the saucepan helps prevent the jam from sticking.

Lemons

When you buy lemons, look for those that have the smoothest skin and no points on the ends.

Heat lemons for twelve seconds in the microwave oven before squeezing them. This will give you double the amount of juice.

If you love fried fish but not the smell, soak your fish in lemon juice for about twenty minutes before frying.

Brush meat with lemon to add flavour.

To tenderise steak rub with a mixture of lemon juice and Worcestershire sauce and allow to stand for a half hour before cooking.

To tenderise a boiling fowl, add lemon juice to the water.

To dry lemon peel, soak in salted water for thirty-six hours. Wash well and boil in a syrup of two cups water to two cups sugar until mixture is almost absorbed. Leave to dry on a rack.

Make a light pastry mix using equal parts of lemon juice and water.

Freeze the shells of spent lemons and they will grate easily for flavouring for cakes and desserts.

To make fluffy rice, add the juice of half a lemon to the water.

To keep lemons for a long time, clean with a dry cloth and roll in egg white and allow to dry.

Lemon rind

Wash fruit. Grate and dry. Mix rind with ½ volume of sugar. Store in a sealed jar in the refrigerator.

Lemon juice

Store lemon juice by squeezing the juice. Pour it into ice trays. When frozen, remove and put in freezer bags.

To store whole lemon

Cut lemons from the tree when they are almost ripe. Make a solution of one tablespoon household bleach to two litres of cold water. Dip the lemon in the solution. Leave for five minutes. Rinse. Dry thoroughly. Place on wooden racks in cool place, or place in fine sand, not touching each other, in polystyrene fruit box.

To make lemon/orange tea

Peel skin with potato peeler. Place on baking tray and dry for one hour at 100°C. Turn off oven and leave rind until it is cool. Store in sealed jar. To flavour tea, add a few strips to a caddy of tea, seal and leave for two weeks.

Lemonade

5 lemons
5 limes
5 oranges
6 litres water
1½ to 2 cups sugar

Squeeze the juice from four of the lemons, limes and oranges; pour into a large container. Thinly slice the remaining fruit and set aside for garnish. Add water and sugar to juices; mix well. Store in the refrigerator. Serve on ice with fruit slices.

California lemonade

1 shot blended whisky
Juice of 1 lemon
Juice of 1 lime
1 tablespoon powdered sugar
¼ teaspoon grenadine
Carbonated water

Shake all ingredients (except carbonated water) with ice and strain into a whisky glass over shaved ice. Fill with carbonated water and stir. Decorate with slices of orange and lemon. Add a cherry and serve with a straw.

Old-fashioned lemonade

1½ cups sugar, granulated
1½ cups lemon juice; 6-7 lemons
1½ cups water
1 lemon; sliced thinly
1 tablespoon lemon rind; finely grated
Mint sprigs

In small saucepan, stir together sugar, water and lemon rind. Bring to a boil, stirring constantly. Boil for five minutes, stirring. Remove from heat and let cool. Stir in lemon juice. Transfer to a jar; cover and refrigerate for up to three weeks.

To serve, place two ice cubes in each tall glass. Add ¼ cup (50 ml) of the syrup and ¾ cup (175 ml) cold water. Stir well. Garnish with lemon slice and sprig of mint. Yield: twelve servings.

Passionfruit

Put passionfruit in their shells in the freezer. They will keep all year.

Rhubarb

Add a banana to rhubarb when cooking to add flavour and thicken the juice.
A few drops of vanilla essence take away the tartness from stewed rhubarb.
Try adding a few sultanas to rhubarb when cooking.

Strawberries

To make a delicious sauce that can be drizzled over ice cream, pavlova, cheesecake or yoghurt. Take a punnet of fresh strawberries and three tablespoons of granulated sugar. Add the juice of one lemon. Place all ingredients in the blender and puree until smooth. Keep in refrigerator for up to three days.

Strawberries and ice cream

Take one punnet of strawberries, wash in colander and shake dry. Cut husks from them and slice into halves or quarters. Sprinkle with sugar and the juice of a lemon. Refrigerate. Serve with ice cream.

Strawberry ice cream
2 punnets strawberries
1 bottle cream
250g icing sugar

Blend in blender. Freeze.

Strawberry jam
500g strawberries, washed and husks removed
500g sugar
Juice 1 lemon

Place all the ingredients in the microwave. Cook on medium for fifteen minutes. Stir. Cook for another fifteen minutes. Bottle and seal. Keep in refrigerator.

Tamarillo
Known also as tree tomatoes, tamarillo trees will grow and bear fruit in moderate climates. Good water supply and drainage is needed in a frost-free area. The trees are decorative and grow to a height of about four metres. The fruit is most versatile and can be used for jam or chutney, as well as raw with cold meats, and as a fruit, either raw or cooked. The skin of the tamarillo is not pleasant to eat. Skin them by immersing the fruit in boiling water for a few minutes.

Vegetables
Cabbage and cauliflower
To prevent the ghastly odour of cooking cabbage add vinegar or a wedge of lemon to the water.

Cook cauliflower florets gently and mix with mayonnaise to make a delicious and easy salad.

Carrots
To curl carrots for a salad, peel long strips using a potato peeler, roll and secure with a toothpick. Remove the toothpick before adding to a salad.

To keep green-topped vegetables such as carrots, beetroot and turnips, remove tops before storing.

Store green-topped vegetables in a brown paper bag, never in plastic. The paper absorbs some of the moisture and the plastic can make them sweat and they quickly deteriorate.

Carrot cake
½ cup cocoa
2 cups flour
2 cups brown sugar
2 teaspoons baking soda
4 eggs
1 teaspoon vanilla
1½ cups vegetable oil
2 cups grated carrots
1 cup undrained crushed tinned pineapple

Preheat oven to 170°C. Combine cocoa, flour, sugar, baking soda and salt. In a separate bowl, mix together eggs, vanilla and oil. Add egg mixture to cocoa mixture and mix well.

Stir in carrots and pineapple. Pour into round greased cake pan. Bake for thirty minutes or until toothpick inserted in centre comes out clean. Cool cake.

Icing:
250g cream cheese
120g icing sugar
2 tablespoons lemon juice
1 cup chopped nuts

Combine cream cheese, butter, lemon and icing sugar, and beat well. Spread on carrot cake. Sprinkle nuts over top and around the sides. Refrigerate until ready to serve.

Grilled ratatouille salad

2 tablespoons extra-virgin olive oil
1 medium-large eggplant, sliced 1 cm crosswise
1 large red onion, sliced 1 cm thick
1 red bell pepper, halved and seeded
1 yellow bell pepper, halved and seeded
1 green bell pepper, halved and seeded
3 medium-size tomatoes, cut bite-size
3 tablespoons balsamic vinegar
2 tablespoons capers
Salt and freshly ground black pepper
¼ cup chopped Italian parsley

Brush all the vegetables, except the tomato, with olive oil, and grill until fork-tender. Set aside to cool. Place cut-up tomatoes in a large bowl. Add the basil, vinegar, capers, salt, pepper and parsley. When the grilled vegetables have cooled enough to touch, peel peppers and dice all vegetables into uniform bite-size pieces. Add to the bowl and toss to mix. Set aside for at least thirty minutes or up to two hours to allow flavours to marry. Serve warm or at room temperature.

Mung beans

To tone down the assertive taste of fresh mung beans, blanche in boiling water for ten seconds. Plunge into cold water. They retain their freshness and the flavour is not so strong.

Parsley

Fresh parsley, when mixed with meat, has a much better flavour than the dried variety.

Peas

Do not discard green pea pods after shelling. Boiled well, they make excellent stock which is full of flavour.

Potatoes

When mashing potatoes, boil until they are soft, mash with a fork, add salt, pepper and a knob of butter. Delicious.

If you have overcooked your potatoes and they have become watery, add powdered milk to soak up the moisture and to give a delicious and creamy flavour.

Potatoes and cauliflower will remain white if a dash of milk is added to the water when cooking.

To have crisp and light potato chips, soak for one hour in salted water, and then cook in hot oil.

Onions

To avoid tears, pour boiling water over onions before peeling.

To bake onions, prick all around with a meat fork and the centre will not pop out.

The aroma and delicate flavour of roasted onions is a vital ingredient in many dishes.

When buying onions, choose the firmest ones that you can find.

Use onions within ten days of purchase.

A cut onion, placed in the fridge, will absorb the bad odours.

Use purple onions for salads. They are a little milder than their brown cousins and the colour looks great in the salad bowl.

If you wish to sauté onions, add a clove of garlic. The aroma is heavenly and the garlic has health-giving properties.

Did you know that the garden lily is part of the onion family?

Spinach and bacon salad

3 cups torn spinach leaves
¼ cup bean sprouts
½ cup sliced mushrooms
½ cup sliced spring onions
2 tablespoons crumbled blue cheese
4 slices bacon
3 tablespoons granulated sugar
¼ cup cider vinegar

Divide the salad into serving sizes in separate bowls.

To make the dressing, cook the bacon. Drain on a paper towel. Add sugar to pan and stir until sugar is dissolved. Stir in vinegar. Cook for one minute. Crumble the bacon. Add to pan. Pour dressing over salad. Serve.

Tomatoes

Pulpy or over-ripe tomatoes may be made firmer by soaking in a basin of cold salted water with a tablespoon of sugar added.

To peel tomatoes

To peel tomatoes, plunge into boiling water and then quickly into cold water.

Hold them over heat on a long toasting fork until the skin wrinkles, then peel.

Recipe for dried tomatoes

Method one:
- Use roma or Italian tomatoes.
- Wash and dry tomatoes.
- Cut in half lengthwise.
- Sprinkle with salt.
- Sprinkle with ground pepper.
- Sprinkle lightly with sugar.
- Place out to dry on a drying rack in the sun for two or three days.
- Do not allow the tomatoes to become wet as they will go mouldy.

Then:
- Place on a baking dish.
- Dribble with olive oil.
- Sprinkle with finely cut garlic and oregano.
- Leave for two to three weeks to absorb flavours.

Method two:
- Use roma or Italian tomatoes.
- Wash and dry tomatoes.
- Cut in half lengthwise.
- Sprinkle with salt.
- Sprinkle with ground pepper.
- Sprinkle lightly with sugar.
- Dry for twelve hours in a very low oven with door slightly ajar.
- Place on a baking dish.
- Dribble with olive oil.
- Sprinkle with finely cut garlic and oregano.
- Leave for two to three weeks to absorb flavours.

Oven-dried tomatoes
- Cut Italian tomatoes lengthways.
- Place on oven tray.
- Sprinkle with sea salt, sugar and black pepper.
- Add chopped thyme, basil, parsley and oregano.
- Chop garlic and place on top of tomatoes.
- Dry in low oven for several hours.
- Allow to cool.
- Place in jars with garlic and cover with olive oil.

Traditional Italian tomato sauce
Ripe tomatoes
2 medium onions
2 cloves minced garlic
3 tablespoons olive oil
Chopped basil
Fresh oregano
Sugar and salt to taste
2 bay leaves
Chillies (optional)

- Cut tomatoes in half.
- Boil for ten minutes.
- Soften onion and garlic in olive oil over soft flame.
- Add chillies.
- Drain tomatoes, removing excess water.
- Push tomatoes through a sieve.
- Pour purée into pot with onions and garlic.
- Add seasonings.
- Fold in herbs.
- Bring to boil and simmer for one to two hours.
- Bottle.

Bottled tomatoes
Use firm, ripe tomatoes. Blanche the fruit in boiling water for three minutes, then plunge into cold water and peel. Make brine, using one dessertspoon of salt to one cup of water. Pour the hot brine over the fruit. Pack in jars. Fill right to the top with boiling water and seal immediately.

Tomato chutney
3 kg tomatoes
1½ kg onions

Slice and place in separate basins. Cover both with a small handful of salt and leave overnight. Drain. Put the onions into a preserving pan and just cover with brown vinegar. Cook for ten minutes. Add tomatoes.

Make a paste with:
1¼ kg sugar
6 tablespoons dry mustard
4 tablespoons curry powder
1 teaspoon cayenne pepper
brown vinegar

Add this to the preserving pan with the tomatoes and onions. Cook for about 1½ hours without the lid. Allow to cool and bottle.

Storing leafy greens
Leafy vegetables such as lettuce and cabbage should never be stored in plastic. Wrap them in kitchen paper and keep in the vegetable drawer of the refrigerator.

Vegetable stains
Ruined that dress or top, while making all these things up? Most vegetable stains can be removed by soaking in a mixture of two tablespoons of Borax to one litre of water.

Herbs
Parsley
Parsley will stay fresh for a couple of days if stored in a plastic bag in the fridge.
You can also freeze it in a plastic bag. Cut off the required amount when needed.

Sage
While quite a different flavoured herb, it is used in the same way as rosemary.

Savoury
Savoury is a herb which grows from either cutting or by seed. The finely chopped or dried leaves go with all kinds of cooked beans, either sprinkled over the beans or with a little melted butter, or in a cream. The fresh or dried herb can be mixed with breadcrumbs for coating fish, pork or veal fillets before frying. It is a good flavouring for seafood sauces and cocktails.

Sweet spice balls/pomanders
Choose a thin-skinned, unblemished orange or lemon. Begin at the stalk end and systematically press full cloves into the skin until the orange/lemon is totally covered. On a piece of tissue paper, mix together:

1 dessertspoon orisroot powder
2 dessertspoons of cinnamon

Roll the fruit in the powder, twist the paper around it, and store for several weeks. The cloves siphon the juice from the fruit that eventually hardens and shrinks. Shake off the excess spice powder, tie a ribbon around it and hang it in the wardrobe. The spice ball will impart a gentle aroma for two or three years.

Tarragon

Tarragon has strongly flavoured leaves and can be used in any meat, poultry, fish or vegetable dishes. The leaves can be blanched and deep frozen. It will grow from a cutting.

Thyme

There are numerous varieties of thyme but garden and lemon thyme are the two which have the most value in cooking. Thyme is probably the most versatile of all herbs for cooking. It can be used with meat, in stuffing, tasty sauces, marinades and pate. It gives a wonderful flavour to herb bread and many vegetables. Thyme is easy to grow, either in the garden or in pots. For drying, harvest the leafy branches just before they start to flower and make sure you gather them on a dry day before midday. Hang in bunches in a shady, airy place and when crisp, strip off the leaves and seal in airtight containers. The flavour and aroma of thyme are much more penetrating when dried.

Baking

Baking cakes, muffins, patty cakes, biscuits and so on, is a very rewarding experience.

There is nothing better than the welcome aroma of home-baking percolating through the house. But there are a few things you need to watch.

The flour

- Flour should always be well sifted to aerate it.
- With a metal spoon fold it into the basic mixture carefully in three parts.
- Beating after the flour is added toughens the cake and destroys the elasticity of the gluten in the flour, preventing the cake from rising.

The liquid

- The liquid content may be water, milk or fruit juice and is added alternatively with the flour.
- Make sure that the liquid is at room temperature.
- Some of the flour is always added first to dry the basic ingredients and to prevent them from curdling.

Adding the eggs

- When beating by hand, first mix the eggs lightly in a bowl or small jug and then gradually add to the butter and sugar, beating thoroughly in between each addition. If by chance the eggs curdle, stir a tablespoon of flour into the basic mixture.
- Eggs contain three parts water, which must be absorbed by the butter and sugar. Curdled mixtures give uneven textured cakes.
- If using an electric mixer turn it to the highest speed and add the eggs one at a time, beating well after each addition.

Preparing the cake tins

- Melt a little butter in a small saucepan.
- Using a pastry brush completely coat the inside of the cake tin.
- If the tin is to be lined, trace its shape on some greaseproof paper.
- Cut it out and fit into the tin.
- Brush with a little more melted butter.
- For perfect results, use the exact size tin mentioned in the recipe.
- The shape is important, too, and while you may get a satisfactory result from a different shaped tin, in some other cases it could be unsatisfactory.

Placing the cake in the oven
- Cakes that are cooked too near the top or the bottom of an oven tend to burn.
- Make sure the cake is always placed in the centre of the oven.

Testing the cake
After the suggested cooking time, or a few minutes either side:

- The cake will spring back when slightly touched in the centre.
- The cake will shrink from the sides of the tin.
- A fine skewer placed in the centre of the cake will come out clean.

When the cake is cooked it should be turned out on to a cake rack straight away, unless otherwise specified. The paper lining, if used, should be removed and the cake cooled.

Whipping cream
- Make sure cream is icy cold.
- Chill bowl and beaters if possible and stand bowl over ice while beating. These precautions are most necessary in the heat of summer.
- Well-chilled cream beats to a very stiff consistency, suitable for piping, whereas warm cream has a tendency to curdle before stiffening.

Finely chopped or ground nuts
- Nuts first have to be browned in a hot oven before being ground in a nut mill or electric blender.
- If the nuts have a skin, such as hazelnuts, rub in a tea towel after cooking.

Butter cakes
Butter cakes are made by first creaming the butter and sugar. Success depends on the proper creaming of the butter and sugar and a light hand when adding the dry ingredients.

To cream butter
- Remove the butter from the refrigerator at least one hour before using. It should be at room temperature.
- Beat the butter first, without the sugar, until it is soft and creamy.
- Add the sugar gradually and beat until it is soft and does not feel granular. This initial creaming distributes the butter as evenly as possible throughout the cake mixture, giving the cake an even texture. Insufficient creaming causes holes in cakes.
- Fruit rinds, spices and vanilla should be beaten in with the butter and sugar. This beating releases their flavour, and it is then distributed throughout the whole mixture.

Muffins
- When making muffins or cupcakes use an ice-cream scoop to measure out a consistent amount in each one.
- To encourage the muffins to exit the pan, place the bottom of the hot pan on a wet towel for several minutes.
- They will then slide out easily.

Cakes
- Add a teaspoon of jam to the cupcake mix for improved taste and moisture retention.
- To make cakes, pancakes, muffins and waffles stay moist longer, add two tablespoons of honey to the mixture.
- If you wish to double the mixture, only use the original amount of salt.

- When measuring honey, dust your measuring cup with flour or oil and the honey will slide out easily.
- To make cake flour, mix together two tablespoons of cornflour to one cup of flour.
- When creaming butter and sugar, add a tablespoon of boiling water to ensure a fine texture.
- If you are making a cake that requires you to mix the dry ingredients and then to add them to the mixture, a mess-free way to do this is to shake them together in a bag.
- Shake dried fruits in a bag with flour before mixing them into your cake mix. This prevents them from sinking to the bottom.
- Line cake tins with butter wrappers instead of greaseproof paper.
- For a delicious topping on freshly made scones, brush the top with butter and dip in cinnamon and sugar mixed together.
- Small patty cakes will not run over if they are placed on a tray so that they don't touch each other.

Biscuits

- Biscuit mixture handles better if it is placed in the freezer for ten minutes after it has been rolled.
- Before rolling out mixture on wax or foil paper, wet the bench that the paper will be placed on to prevent paper curling.
- Always sieve flour before adding to mixture as this keeps it light.
- Keep flour in an airtight tin as dampness spoils it.
- To keep fruit cakes moist, place a bowl of water in the oven while cooking.

Basic biscuit mix

This is the best biscuit mix you'll ever use. Make up three batches at a time, roll in Gladwrap and put in the freezer. When you wish to make a batch simply take out of the freezer, slice and put onto baking tray in a moderate oven for twenty minutes.

4½ cups all-purpose flour
5 teaspoons baking powder
1 teaspoon salt
3 tablespoons chopped unsalted butter

In a large bowl with an electric mixer whisk together dry ingredients on low speed.

Cut in fats until uniform in texture and fat particles are no longer visible. Remove from mixer. Divide into three airtight containers. Yields three batches of mix. Keep refrigerated for up to one month. Recipe is easily doubled/tripled.

Fruit cakes

- To darken and improve the flavour of fruitcakes, add one teaspoonful of coffee essence.

Toppings

- To make coloured coconut, add a few drops of food colouring to the loose coconut and shake together in a plastic bag.
- Clean an old mayonnaise or mustard container and use to dispense icing when you decorate your cakes.
- Make a disposable container to dispense icing by cutting the corner from an envelope.
- Sticky ingredients like honey or treacle will run off spoon if dipped in hot water first.
- Measure essences or colouring by using a dropper.
- A medicine glass is handy for measuring a small measure in a recipe.

Basic cake recipes

Now that you know the inside information on baking, here are some classic recipes gathered, devised, tested and refined by some great home cooks, and thoroughly enjoyed by family and friends.

Kathleen's banana cake

2 tablespoons butter
¾ cup sugar
1 egg
1½ cups flour
3 mashed bananas
1 teaspoon bicarbonate soda
1 teaspoon cream of tartar
1 tablespoon milk

- Preheat oven to 180°C. Grease and line a shallow tin.
- Cream butter and sugar.
- Add bananas and one beaten egg, and then add dry ingredients alternately with milk.
- Bake for thirty-five to forty minutes.
- Ice with cream cheese icing.

The cheat's bread and butter pudding

9 slices of raisin toast
4 eggs
1 litre milk
1 cup sugar
1 teaspoon vanilla essence
Cinnamon
Whipped cream

- Preheat oven to 180°C.
- Grease a casserole dish.
- Lay the bread on the bottom of the dish.
- Make custard by beating the eggs, milk, vanilla and sugar together until smooth. Pour custard mixture over the bread.
- Place the casserole dish inside a baking dish to which boiling water has been added.
- The water should come half of the way up the side of the baking dish.
- Bake in the oven for forty minutes or until the custard is set.
- Serve warm with cream.

Win's butter cake

280g butter
225g caster sugar
1½ teaspoons vanilla essence
4 eggs
225g self-raising flour
150g plain flour
185 ml milk

- Preheat oven to 180°C. Brush a deep twenty centimetre round cake tin with melted butter or oil and line the base with baking paper.
- Beat the butter, sugar and vanilla with electric beaters until light and creamy. Add the eggs one at a time, beating well after each addition.
- Using a large metal spoon, fold in the combined sifted flours alternately with the milk,

until smooth. Spoon the mixture into the tin and smooth the surface. Bake for 1½ hours, or until a skewer comes out clean when inserted into the centre of the cake.
- Leave the cake in the tin for at least five minutes before turning out on a wire rack to cool completely.

Storage time: Butter cake can be kept in an airtight container in the fridge for up to a week, or for three days in an airtight container in a cool dry place. Can also be frozen for up to two months.

Michelle's caramel slice
1 packet Marie biscuits
100g butter
3 tablespoons brown sugar
3 tablespoons condensed milk
1 tablespoon golden syrup

- Crush biscuits.
- Boil other ingredients together and add to biscuits.
- Press into slice tin.

Joan's carrot cake
½ cup cocoa
2 cups flour
2 cups brown sugar
2 teaspoons baking soda
4 eggs
1 teaspoon vanilla
1½ cups vegetable oil
2 cups grated carrots
1 cup undrained crushed tinned pineapple

Icing:
250g cream cheese
120g icing sugar
2 tablespoons lemon juice
1 cup chopped nuts

- Preheat oven to 180°C.
- Combine cocoa, flour, sugar, baking soda and salt.
- In a separate bowl, mix together eggs, vanilla and oil.
- Add egg mixture to cocoa mixture and mix well.
- Stir in carrots and pineapple.
- Pour into round greased cake pan.
- Bake thirty minutes or until toothpick inserted in centre comes out clean.
- Cool cake.

Icing:
- Combine cream cheese, butter, lemon and icing sugar and beat well.
- Spread on carrot cake.
- Sprinkle nuts over top and around the sides.
- Refrigerate until ready to serve.

Trina's carrot cake
150g self-raising flour
150g plain flour
2 teaspoons ground cinnamon

½ teaspoon ground cloves
1 teaspoon ground ginger
1½ teaspoons ground nutmeg
1 teaspoon bicarbonate soda
200 ml vegetable oil
230g soft brown sugar
4 eggs
125 ml golden syrup
500g grated carrot
60g chopped pecans or walnuts

- Preheat the oven to 160°C. Brush a deep twenty-two centimetre round cake tin with melted butter or oil. Line the base with baking paper.
- Sift the flours, spices and bicarbonate of soda in a large bowl. Make a well in the centre.
- Whisk together the oil, sugar, eggs and syrup. Gradually pour into the well, stirring into the dry ingredients until smooth.
- Stir in the carrot and nuts. Spoon into the tin and smooth the surface. Bake for one hour and fifteen minutes, or until a skewer comes out clean when inserted into the centre. Leave in the tin for at least fifteen minutes before turning out onto a wire rack to cool completely. Ice with cream cheese frosting (recipe below).

Storage time: Can be kept in an airtight container in the fridge for up to a week, or for three days in an airtight container in a cool dry place. Can also be frozen for up to two months.

Cream cheese frosting
375g cream cheese, softened
75g butter, softened
90g icing sugar, sifted
1 teaspoon vanilla essence

Beat the cream cheese and butter with electric beaters until smooth and creamy. Gradually beat in the icing sugar and the vanilla essence. Beat until thick and creamy.

Joan's chocolate cake
185g butter
330g caster sugar
2½ teaspoons vanilla essence
3 eggs
75g self-raising flour
225 g plain flour
1½ teaspoons bicarbonate soda
90g cocoa powder
280 ml buttermilk

- Preheat the oven to 180°C. Brush a deep, twenty centimetre round cake tin with melted butter or oil. Line the base with baking paper.
- Beat the butter, sugar and vanilla essence with electric beaters until light and creamy. Add the eggs, one at a time, beating well after each addition.
- Using a metal spoon, fold in the combined sifted flour, bicarbonate of soda and cocoa powder alternately with the milk. Stir until just smooth.
- Spoon the mixture into the tin and smooth the surface. Bake for 1½ hours, or until a skewer comes out clean when inserted into the centre. Leave the cake to cool in the tin for at least five minutes before turning out onto a wire rack to cool completely.

Storage time: Can be kept in an airtight container in the fridge for up to a week, or for three days in an airtight container in a cool dry place. Can also be frozen for up to two months.

Theresa's chocolate caramel bread pudding

9 slices of white bread
1 cooking apple
½ cup chocolate pieces
½ cup chopped pecans
12 vanilla caramels
3 cups milk
1 tablespoon butter
3 slightly beaten eggs
½ cup brown sugar
2 tablespoons vanilla
¼ tablespoon salt
Whipped cream

- Preheat oven to 180°C.
- Cut bread into cubes.
- Peel and chop apple.
- Spread bread cubes in a lightly greased two-litre rectangle baking dish.
- Sprinkle with chopped apple, chocolate and pecans.
- In a medium saucepan combine the caramels, one cup of the milk and the butter.
- Cook over medium heat until melted, stirring continuously.
- Add the remaining milk.
- Heat until mixture just begins to bubble around the side of the pan.
- Remove from heat.
- Slowly stir in the brown sugar, vanilla and salt.
- Pour over the bread mix.
- Press lightly with the back of a large spoon to moisten bread cubes.
- Bake in oven for thirty to forty minutes, or until a knife inserted comes out clean.
- Serve warm with cream.

Erin's chocolate crunch cheesecake

125g plain chocolate biscuits, crushed
60g butter, melted
250g cream cheese
¾ cup sweetened condensed milk
1 cup cream
1 tablespoon vanilla
3 tablespoons gelatine
¼ cup water
60g cooking chocolate, melted
1 Violet Crumble bar, chopped
1 cup cream, extra
Strawberries for decoration

- Combine biscuits and butter, press over base of twenty centimetre springform pan and refrigerate.
- Beat cream cheese and sweetened condensed milk until smooth.
- Beat in cream and vanilla.
- Sprinkle gelatine over water and dissolve over hot water.
- Cool.
- Beat gelatine into cream cheese mixture.

- Divide cheese mixture in half.
- Spoon one half over biscuit base, refrigerate until set.
- Add cooking chocolate and Violet Crumble bar to other half.
- Spoon over first half.
- Refrigerate until set and top with strawberries.

Jayne's chocolate fudge cake

85g soft butter
250g brown sugar
½ cup sour milk
2 small eggs
170g self-raising flour
¾ level teaspoon bicarbonate soda
3 level teaspoons cocoa

- Preheat oven to a moderate 180°C.
- Grease and flour a twenty-two centimetre round tin.
- Beat the butter, sugar, milk, egg and half the sifted dry ingredients for four minutes.
- Mix in the rest of the flour and beat for an extra one minute.
- Bake for forty minutes or until cooked.
- Ice with chocolate icing and serve with cream.

Linda's chocolate hazelnut slice

200g choc ripple biscuits
60g butter, melted
4 egg whites
¾ cup caster sugar
½ cup ground hazelnuts
2 tablespoons plain flour

- Preheat the oven to 180°C.
- Grease a twenty by thirty centimetre lamington pan, and then line the base and two opposite sides with a strip of baking paper.
- Process the biscuits until finely crushed.
- Combine one cup of the biscuit crumbs with the butter in a medium bowl and press over the base of the prepared tin.
- Refrigerate for ten minutes.
- Meanwhile, beat the egg whites in a small bowl with an electric mixer until soft peaks form.
- Gradually add the sugar, beating until dissolved between additions.
- Fold in the ground hazelnuts, remaining biscuit crumbs and the sifted flour.
- Spread over the biscuit base.
- Bake in a moderate oven for twenty minutes or until firm.
- Cool for twenty minutes while you prepare topping.
- Reduce the oven temperature to 160°C.

Topping:

125g butter, softened
½ cup caster sugar
4 egg yolks
1 tablespoon vanilla essence
200g milk chocolate, melted

- Beat the butter, sugar, egg yolks and vanilla in a small bowl with an electric mixer until the sugar is dissolved.
- Fold in the melted chocolate.

- Spread the topping over slice and bake in a reduced oven temperature for about fifteen minutes or until set.
- Cool in the pan and refrigerate until warm.

Patsy's chocolate mousse cheesecake

250g wheatmeal biscuits
¼ cup cocoa, sifted
125g butter, melted
500g cream cheese
¼ cup sugar
2 eggs
2 teaspoons gelatine
2 tablespoons hot water
300 ml cream
375g dark cooking chocolate, melted
1 punnet strawberries

- Crush biscuits in a food processor until fine crumbs are formed.
- In a large bowl, combine biscuit crumbs, cocoa and butter. Press firmly into base of twenty-three centimetre non-stick springform pan. Refrigerate until firm.
- Using electric beaters, beat cream cheese with sugar until soft and creamy. Beat in egg yolks.
- Sprinkle gelatine over water, stirring until gelatine is dissolved.
- Whip the cream until soft peaks form. In a separate bowl, beat egg whites until soft peaks form.
- Carefully fold chocolate into cream cheese mixture. It is important that both are at room temperature. If chocolate begins to set, place bowl with cream cheese mixture over hot water and stir gently until smooth.
- Gently fold in cream and egg whites. Whisk in gelatine mixture. Pour over biscuit base and refrigerate for several hours overnight until set.
- Remove cake from springform pan to serving plate. Serve with fresh strawberries.

Mary's chocolate mud cake that makes you look like a great cook

This cake looks as if you made it yourself, which you do, but you make it from a commercial cake mix. Buy two chocolate mud cake packs and follow the directions on the pack. Use a stainless steel roasting dish instead of cake pans. The result is a large chocolate mud cake, which looks impressive and tastes pretty good. The secret is not to tell anybody that it is a packet mix.

Joan's delicious chocolate cake with fudge frosting

2 cups flour
2 cups sugar
½ cup butter or margarine
¾ cup water
¾ cup milk
1 teaspoon baking soda
1 teaspoon salt
1 teaspoon vanilla
½ teaspoon baking powder
2 eggs
200g unsweetened chocolate, melted and cooled

- Heat oven to 180°C.
- Grease and flour medium pan.

- Beat all ingredients except fudge frosting in a large bowl on low speed for thirty seconds, scraping bowl constantly.
- Pour mixture into pan.
- Bake for forty to forty-five minutes or until wooden toothpick comes out clean.
- Cool, remove from pans.
- Cool completely.

Fudge frosting:
2 cups sugar
½ cup butter
100g unsweetened chocolate
⅔ cup milk
½ teaspoon salt
2 teaspoons vanilla

- Mix all ingredients except vanilla in a large saucepan.
- Heat to a rolling boil, stirring occasionally.
- Boil one minute without stirring.
- Place saucepan in a bowl of ice and water.
- Beat until frosting is smooth and of spreading consistency.
- Add vanilla.
- Spread over cake.

Nicole's creamy coconut ice
500g icing sugar, sifted
250g coconut
2 egg whites, slightly beaten
125g copha
1 teaspoon vanilla
Pink food colouring

- Mix dry ingredients with egg whites, melted copha and vanilla.
- Place half the mixture in a slice tin, then add pink colouring to the other half and place on top of non-coloured mixture.

Kathleen's easy-as-pie lemon meringue
180g crushed biscuits
90g melted butter
1 can sweetened condensed milk
½ cup lemon juice
Grated rind from a lemon
3 eggs
½ cup caster sugar

- Combine biscuits and butter.
- Press into a greased twenty-three centimetre pie plate.
- Chill.
- Pour sweetened condensed milk, lemon juice and rind into a bowl.
- Separate the eggs and pour the lightly beaten egg yolks into the lemon mixture.
- Save the whites for the meringue.
- Mix well.
- Spoon mixture evenly into the biscuit crumb base.
- Beat the egg whites until they are stiff.
- Gradually add the sugar as you beat.
- Spoon the meringue on top of the pie and bake in a moderate oven for fifteen minutes or until golden.

Sue's easy chocolate fudge

450g good-quality milk chocolate
395g can sweetened condensed milk
2 tablespoons butter
1 tablespoon vanilla essence

- Line a twenty centimetre square cake tin with foil.
- Break chocolate into pieces.
- Put chocolate, condensed milk and butter into a heavy-based saucepan.
- Stir over low heat until chocolate is melted and mixture is smooth.
- Remove from heat.
- Add vanilla essence.
- Pour into cake tin.
- Refrigerate until firm, then cut into squares.
- Store in an airtight container.

Caitlin's honey cake

1¾ cups self-raising flour, sifted
¾ cup caster sugar
½ cup honey
155g butter, melted
3 eggs, lightly beaten
¾ cup sour cream

- Preheat oven to 180°C. Grease a twenty-five centimetre fluted ring tin.
- Place sugar, flour and honey in a bowl. In a separate bowl, mix butter, eggs and sour cream until well combined. Add butter mixture to dry ingredients and stir until just combined.
- Bake in oven for thirty minutes or until cooked when tested with a skewer. Serve drizzled with honey and thick cream on the side.

Eloise's lemon cheesecake

250g plain sweet biscuits
50g melted butter
500g cream cheese
1 tin sweetened condensed milk
½ cup lemon rind
½ cup lemon juice
10g gelatine
1 packet of lemon jelly crystals
450 ml water

- Crush biscuits in a food processor until fine crumbs are formed. Add melted butter and stir until combined. If mixture is too dry, add extra melted butter. Flatten biscuit mixture on to the base of a twenty-two centimetre ring tin and refrigerate until needed.
- Using electric beaters beat cream cheese until smooth then add sweetened condensed milk.
- Place the lemon juice in a bowl and sprinkle on the gelatine in an even layer. Leave until the gelatine is spongy; do not stir. Bring a small pan of water to the boil, remove from the heat and place in the pan. The water should come halfway up the sides of the bowl. Stir the gelatine until clear and dissolved. Allow to cool slightly then blend into the cream cheese mixture. Add the lemon rind.
- Pour cream cheese mixture into prepared tin. Refrigerate until set.
- Boil water and add jelly crystals. Stir until dissolved. Cool slightly then pour over the cheesecake. Refrigerate again until the jelly has set.

Maureen's Mars Bar slice

3 Mars Bars
90g butter
3½ cups Rice Bubbles

- Place Mars Bars, cut into pieces, in a large saucepan.
- Add butter and stir over gentle heat until melted and mixed.
- Remove from heat.
- Add Rice Bubbles.
- Stir until well coated and place in a foiled eighteen by twenty-eight centimetre tin.
- Refrigerate.

Topping:

60g cooking chocolate
2 teaspoons butter

- To make topping, melt ingredients over simmering water.
- Pour over Mars Bar slice.
- Smooth top with knife and let set.
- Cut into small pieces.

Tess's orange and poppy seed cake

½ a cup poppy seeds
½ cup yoghurt
200g butter
1 tablespoon finely grated orange rind
1 cup caster sugar
3 eggs
1½ cups self-raising flour, sifted
½ cup plain flour, sifted
½ cup almond meal
¾ cup fresh orange juice

- Preheat oven to 180°C. Grease and line a twenty centimetre square cake tin with non-stick baking paper. Combine poppy seeds and yoghurt and set aside.
- Place butter, orange rind and sugar in a bowl and beat until light and creamy. Add eggs and beat well.
- Stir poppy seed mixture, flours, almond meal and orange juice.
- Spoon the mixture into the tin and bake for fifty minutes or until cooked when tested with a skewer.
- Pour hot orange syrup (recipe below) over warm cake and serve with thick cream.

Orange syrup

2 cups sugar
1 cup fresh orange juice
1½ cups of water
½ cup shredded orange rind

Stir sugar, orange juice, water and rind in a saucepan over medium heat until sugar is dissolved. Simmer for fifteen to twenty minutes or until slightly thickened.

Kathleen's pavlova

4 egg whites
3 cups caster sugar
2 teaspoons vinegar
2 teaspoons cornflour

3 teaspoons vanilla
6 tablespoons boiling water

- Preheat the oven to a moderate 180°C.
- Beat all ingredients together for twenty-five to thirty minutes.
- Spoon onto damp foil or brown paper.
- Bake forty-five minutes in moderate oven.
- Turn down heat to low and bake further forty-five minutes.
- Place on lowest shelf in oven and turn oven off.
- Leave till cool.
- Decorate as desired.

Mary's pavlova that makes you look like a great cook

Now this is impressive. Buy two pavlova mixes that come in the egg-shaped containers. Make them up as a double mixture as directed on the packet. Use baking paper on your oven tray. Shape the pavlova in a large circle. When the cooking time is complete, turn the oven off and leave the giant pavlova in the oven until you are ready to decorate it. Decorate with fruits in season and lashings of cream.

Maureen's peppermint slice

250g plain sweet biscuits
2 Peppermint Crisps
1 tin sweetened condensed milk

- Put the chopped Peppermint Crisps into a paper bag and crush with a rolling pin.
- Place broken biscuits into blender and blend until smooth.
- In a bowl mix the crushed Peppermint Crisps, biscuits and sweetened condensed milk until all the ingredients are well combined.
- Spoon into a foiled eighteen by twenty centimetre tin.
- Refrigerate.

Topping:
60g cooking chocolate
2 teaspoons butter

- Melt ingredients over simmering water.
- Pour over peppermint slice.
- Smooth top with knife and let set.
- Cut into small pieces.

Plain butter cake

1 cup butter
½ cup cooking oil
3 cups sugar
5 eggs
3 cups all-purpose flour
1 teaspoon baking powder
Pinch salt
1 cup milk
1 teaspoon each vanilla and lemon extract

- Cream butter, oil and sugar until very light and fluffy.
- Add eggs, one at a time until very creamy.
- Blend in flour, baking powder and salt mixture alternately with milk in small amounts, beating well after each addition.
- Blend in flavourings.

- Turn into greased and floured cake pan.
- Bake in preheated oven 180°C for one hour.
- Turn off oven heat and allow cake to remain in oven fifteen minutes longer.
- Cake is done when cake tester inserted in centre comes out clean.
- Cool ten to fifteen minutes in pan on cake rack, then remove from pan and finish cooling on rack.
- Decorate as you wish.

Kathleen's sponge cake to die for

¾ cup sugar
3 eggs
2 tablespoons milk
1 level breakfast cup plain flour
2 level teaspoons cream of tartar
1 level teaspoon of bicarbonate of soda
1 heaped tablespoon melted butter

- Preheat oven to 180°C. Grease and flour two sandwich tins.
- Put all ingredients in a basin and beat on high for three minutes.
- Bake in moderate oven fifteen minutes.

Kathleen's tia marie

¾ cup brown sugar
1 cup boiling water
5 teaspoons instant coffee powder
1 cup brandy
2 dessertspoons vanilla essence

- Mix with wooden spoon and cool.
- Add the brandy and vanilla essence.
- Bottle and let stand for at least two weeks, the longer the better.

Nana Tess's 4, 3, 2, 1 scones

4 cups flour
300 ml cream
2 cups soda water
1 pinch of salt

- Mix ingredients together.
- Spoon onto a baking tray and bake for fifteen minutes or until cooked.
- Serve with whipped cream and jam.

Scones like Nana Kate used to make

320g self-raising flour
80 ml low-fat milk
2 teaspoons 'No Egg' Egg Replacer
50g reduced fat margarine
20g cream
1 teaspoon salt
1 teaspoon baking powder
35g caster sugar

- Preheat oven to 225°C.
- Dry-blend flour, salt and baking powder.
- Soften margarine and add to mix.

- Add sugar and mix well.
- Gradually add the milk and mix to form a dough.
- Lightly roll out dough, stamp out into approximately sixty-five millimeter diameter circles using a crimped cutter.
- Bake for nine minutes.
- Serve with margarine or jam.

Quick and easy scones

2 cups self-raising flour
Pinch of salt
2 teaspoons of butter
About a cup of milk

- Sift the flour and salt.
- Add butter and rub into flour.
- Add sufficient milk to make a soft dough.
- Turn onto a floured board and knead very lightly.
- Roll out to two centimetres thick, cut into shape.
- Put on a hot, floured tray and bake for seven to ten minutes in a very hot oven.
- Scones may be glazed by brushing over with milk before putting into the oven.

Fried scones

1 cup flour
1 teaspoon baking powder
Pinch of salt
Milk to mix

- Mix ingredients into a soft dough.
- Roll out and cut into circles.
- Have the pan half full of very hot oil and fry until golden brown.
- Delicious served with bacon and eggs for breakfast.

Oatmeal scones made from left-over porridge

Left-over, cold porridge
Flour
Sugar
A dab of butter
Currants may be added to this mixture

- Make a stiff dough by adding flour to the porridge.
- Flavour with a few drops of vanilla essence.
- Roll out the dough to 1.3 centimetres thick.
- Cut into shapes and bake for about ½ hour in a moderate oven.
- Cut open, spread with butter and sprinkle with raw sugar.

Rum balls

400g sweetened condensed milk
250g crushed milk coffee biscuits
1 cup coconut
3 tablespoons cocoa
3 dessertspoons rum, alcoholic substitute or vanilla
Coconut, extra

- Mix all ingredients except for the extra coconut.
- Roll into small balls in extra coconut.
- Chill in refrigerator and store in an airtight container.

Elsie's patty cakes and variations

¼ cup (60g) butter
¼ cup (60g) caster sugar
1 egg, beaten
3 drops vanilla essence
3 tablespoons (60 ml) milk
¾ cup (115g) self-raising flour

- Preheat oven to 200°C. Grease patty pans. This recipe makes twelve.
- Cream butter, sugar and vanilla essence.
- Add beaten egg and mix well.
- Add flour and milk alternately, one-third at a time.
- Stir gently and thoroughly.
- Place mixture in pans, half-filling each one.
- Bake for twelve to fifteen minutes.
- Cool in pans for two minutes, then lift onto cake cooler.
- Ice with glacé icing (recipe below).

Glacé icing

1 cup sifted icing sugar
1 tablespoon boiling water
1 tablespoon butter
Flavouring (vanilla, lemon juice, vanilla essence etc.)
Colouring if required

- Place the icing sugar into a bowl.
- Make a well in the centre and add the boiling water, butter and flavouring.
- Stir until smooth and shiny.
- Colour if desired.

Orange icing

30g butter
1 tablespoon grated orange rind
1 tablespoon orange juice
2 cups sifted icing sugar

- Cream the butter with the orange rind and stir in the orange juice.
- Gradually add the sifted icing sugar beating until smooth.

Chocolate glacé icing

90g milk chocolate, chopped
4 tablespoons water
1¾ cups icing sugar
½ tablespoon oil
2 to 3 drops vanilla essence

- Melt chocolate over simmering water.
- As soon as it is melted and smooth, remove from heat.
- Allow to cool slightly.
- Beat in the icing sugar a spoonful at a time.
- Add the oil and vanilla and warm over low heat to enable it to spread easily.

Variations on patty cake recipe
Chocolate cakes
Follow the recipe for patty cakes. Add two teaspoons cocoa to the sifted flour.
Ice with chocolate glacé icing and decorate with nuts.

Cinnamon cakes
Follow the recipe for patty cakes. Add two teaspoons cinnamon to the sifted flour.
Ice with lemon glacé icing and decorate with nuts or chopped glacé ginger.

Coconut cakes
Follow the recipe for patty cakes. Add two tablespoons of coconut after creaming the butter, sugar and vanilla.
Ice with vanilla glacé icing.

Lemon cakes
Follow the recipe for patty cakes. Add the grated rind of half a lemon after creaming the butter, sugar and vanilla.
Ice with lemon glacé icing.

Orange cakes
Follow the recipe for patty cakes. Add the grated rind of one orange after creaming the butter, sugar and vanilla.
Ice with orange icing.

Baking bread
There's no nicer feel than walking into a house and the unmistakeable aroma of freshly baked bread is wafting through. It can pep up even the most jaded appetite.

Baking bread at home has become more popular with the introduction of home-bake machines, with their instructions to follow. These machines provide the easiest method of making bread. You can use your own bread recipe (such as the standard white bread recipe, below) or it is possible to buy manufactured bread mix.

With the manufactured bread mix, all you need to do is follow the instructions on the pack and add water and yeast, which is usually supplied. However, if you wish to make and bake bread the way your great grandmother used to, here is one method of doing it, followed by other simple recipes, hints, tips and troubleshooting ideas to make it work for you.

Standard white bread recipe
1¾ cups water
3 cups white flour
2 tablespoons butter
1 tablespoon dry milk
2 tablespoons sugar
1½ teaspoons salt
2½ teaspoons yeast

- Mix yeast with the liquid ingredients, put to one side.
- Mix the dry ingredients.
- Make a well in the middle.
- Add yeast and water mix to the well.
- Combine the wet and dry ingredients to make dough.

- Place on a marble or wooden work pad which has been lightly floured.
- Now you work the dough.
- Knead in a circle, folding the outside in as you go.
- Do this for a good five minutes.
- (This is an art and practice makes perfect.)
- Shape into a loaf.
- Place a damp tea towel over the top and put aside in a warm spot.
- Leave for forty minutes or until the loaf has expanded to reach the top of the bowl.
- Turn out onto a floured board.
- Knead again as before.
- Shape into a loaf and place in bread tin for cooking.
- Cover with damp towel for another forty minutes, and allow to prove.
- Cook in a medium oven for forty minutes, or until the bread is hard when you knock on the top of the loaf.

To add interest
- Sprinkle loaves or buns with sesame, poppy or caraway seeds.
- Top loaves with grated cheese for the last few minutes of baking.
- Glazes may be brushed over the loaf at any time, before during or after baking.
- For a matt finish, brush with melted butter or margarine.

Dough rising tips
- Use a well-greased glass mixing bowl to allow the yeast to rise or prove.
- Place the bowl in a warm, draft free area and cover with a cloth.
- A final rising should be after the dough has been shaped and placed on the greased baking tray. Cover the loaf with a damp cloth and leave in a draft free area.

To punch down the yeast dough
- Plunge fist into the centre of the risen dough to punch out excess air.
- Fold outer edges into the centre and turn dough onto a lightly floured board for shaping.
- Allow to rest for fifteen minutes.
- Use rolling pin to roll dough into a rectangle.
- Roll up like a Swiss roll.
- Flatten the edges with the sides of your hands.
- Place in a well-greased bread tin, seam side down.

Useful breadmaking tips
- Use flour that is labelled 'Bread Flour' or 'Better for Bread' as this flour has a higher gluten content and allows for greater absorption of moisture.
- Salt controls the activity of the yeast and keeps bread firm.
- Sugar adds sweetness. It also makes the crust brown and the bread softer.
- Butter enhances the flavour and makes the bread softer.
- Dry skim milk increases the nutritional value and enhances the flavour.
- When flour is mixed with water, gluten is formed and air is trapped, allowing the bread to rise. It needs to be tepid to activate the yeast.
- Home-made bread needs to be kept in an airtight container in the refrigerator.

Yeast
- Test baker's yeast by putting a teaspoon of yeast and a tablespoon of sugar in a cup of warm water. If the yeast bubbles in ten minutes, then it is OK.
- When using yeast to bake, prove the mixture in the oven with the light on. The temperature is perfect and it is out of drafts.

Make your own yeast
Method one:
Save about 1½ litres of stock from your boiled potatoes. When cold add:

1 tablespoon flour
1 tablespoon sugar

Pour into jug or preserving jar. Add one teaspoon compressed yeast (or old yeast). Make during morning, and by evening it should have frothy top, ready for use. Leave enough in jar each time you use it to start the next lot. Replenish with cool potato water and above quantities of flour and sugar each day. Do not add any more compressed yeast.

Method two:
Six breakfast cups of cold water
½ handful of hops
2 medium potatoes

Cut, but do not peel, the potatoes. Add the water and hops, and boil about half an hour. Have ready two tablespoons of flour, mixed with one tablespoon of sugar. Strain again through a fine sieve. Bottle when nearly cold, and put in a light warm place.

Method three:
30g hops
1 cup flour
2 tablespoons sugar
2 litres water

Boil hops for a few minutes in a small quantity of water. Drain and add sufficient water to make two litres. Add sugar, and when tepid also flour. Just shake it in and never mind if it seems lumpy. Grate in medium sized raw potato. Bottle. If you have a little yeast in the bottle to start working, it can be used the same night. With home-made yeast it takes longer for the bread to rise, than with compressed yeast. Divide it into three bottles, leaving sufficient room to work. Each bottle makes about 1½ kg of bread mix.

Problems with your loaf
Collapsed loaf
One of the following may help:

* Too much moisture in the mixture. Reduce water by half a cup.
* Remove bread promptly from the pan after baking as it will absorb moisture in the cooling down process.
* Try a lighter flour, as the flour was too heavy to sustain its shape.

Loaf not cooked in the middle
Use an extra knead step when working with heavier flours such as rye, bran or whole wheat.
You may have added ingredients which are too moist.

Bread has blown up like a balloon
May be one of the following:

* You have used too much yeast. Reduce yeast.
* You have used too much sugar which has caused the yeast to be over-active. Reduce sugar.
* Too much water. Reduce water.
* Flour is fine. Finer flours do not require so much yeast. Reduce yeast.

The bread does not rise
Did you add yeast? Is the yeast old and stale?

The bread smells bad
Did you use too much yeast? Were some of the ingredients stale?

Remember . . .
Humidity, temperature and quality of the water can all affect the bread. You may need to try variations to find exact ingredients.

General tips for bread
- Cut fresh bread with a hot knife.
- Revive stale rolls by spraying lightly with water, then wrap in foil and heat for five minutes in the oven at 180°C.
- Revive stale bread by wrapping in a damp cloth and heating in the microwave for sixty seconds.
- Use left-over crusts and bread to make breadcrumbs for stuffing or coatings. To make, simply whiz bread in the food processor and place in a plastic bag for freezing.
- Make your own croutons by buttering both sides of the bread, season, and then cut into cubes. Bake in a moderate oven for fifteen minutes or until lightly brown.

Alternative bread recipes
Soda bread
4 cups plain flour
1 teaspoon bicarbonate of soda
1 teaspoon salt
Milk

- Mix dry ingredients together and then add enough milk to make a stiff dough.
- Cook for one hour in medium oven.

Zucchini bread
3 eggs
2¼ cups caster sugar
3 teaspoons vanilla
1 cup oil
2 cups grated zucchini
3 cups plain flour
¼ teaspoon baking powder
1 teaspoon salt
1 teaspoon bicarbonate soda
3 teaspoons cinnamon
1 cup chopped walnuts

- Beat eggs until light and fluffy.
- Add sugar, vanilla and oil.
- Beat until thick.
- Stir in grated zucchini.
- Sift flour and baking powder, salt, soda and cinnamon.
- Fold into zucchini mixture with chopped walnuts.
- Pour into two greased loaf tins and bake in a moderate oven for 1¼ hours.

Glen's delicious home-made pizza

An extension of the bread-making process is to make dough for pizzas. Here is an excellent recipe.

Make dough by following our standard white bread recipe to the step of kneading, but then instead of shaping a loaf, roll it, and place it on a pizza dish.

* Brush with olive oil and garlic.
* Slice tomatoes finely and overlap on top.
* Sprinkle with salt, ground pepper and sugar.
* Add: Basil
    Bocconcini cut into thin slices
    Small pieces of anchovies.
* Place at intervals over the tomatoes.
* Place in a medium oven.
* When cooked add more slices of bocconcini and brush with a mixture of olive oil and balsamic vinegar.
* Slice and serve.

You may use the bread dough to make any of your favourite pizzas. Use any toppings that you like. Variety is only limited by your imagination.

Pastry
Standard pie pastry

For a single-crust pie:

1¼ cups flour
½ teaspoon salt
2½ tablespoons ice water
oil or butter

For a double-crust pie, simply double the above ingredients.

* Preheat oven to 210°C.
* Place shortening in a bowl.
* Over it, pour one cup of the flour (reserving half cup flour) and the salt.
* With your pastry blender, cut the flour and salt into the shortening until mixed.
* Mix the ¼ cup of reserved flour with the 2½ tablespoons in a small cup to make a smooth paste.
* Pour the paste over the pastry mixture and continue cutting in with the pastry blender until incorporated.
* Remember, the less you work the dough, the lighter and flakier the pastry.
* Form pastry into a ball, flatten and roll between sheets of waxed paper.
* Roll to a thickness of about half a centimetre and three centimetres wider than pie pan.
* Peel off top piece of waxed paper, invert pie pan on dough surface, turn over, centre dough on pie pan, and peel off second sheet of waxed paper.
* Trim dough to a three centimetres overhang, then turn under to make an edge.
* For a pre-baked pie shell, prick bottom and side of pastry with a fork to avoid bubbles. Bake in a 210°C oven for ten to twelve minutes until the crust is nicely browned.

* This recipe can be doubled or tripled.

Tips for better pastry
* When rolling out pastry, place a piece of wax paper at both the top and the bottom. When the pastry is rolled to the required thickness, simply remove the top sheet and invert over the pie pan, then remove the other sheet.

- To prevent the bottom of the pie from becoming mushy, simply grease the bottom of the pie dish with butter before you begin.
- For flakier pastry, add a teaspoon of lemon juice to the ingredients.
- Place sliced bread in the bottom of the pie shell for the first twenty minutes of cooking. This prevents the shell from blistering and the bread can be made into croutons for soup.
- Sprinkle sugar on a pie crust before adding a creamy filling. This prevents sogginess.
- Spread meringue mix right to the edge of the pastry.
- Short pieces of drinking straw inserted into the middle of the pie will prevent the juices from running everywhere.
- To ensure that the bottom cooks through and the top does not burn, always bake a two-crusted pie on the bottom shelf of the oven.
- Keep a plastic bag handy when working with pastry. Use it to slip your hand into if you have to answer the phone, open the fridge etc.
- A buttered knife slides easily through a pie when it is sliced.
- To tip shortbread pastry onto the pie plate, first roll between two pieces of greaseproof paper and slide onto plate.
- When reheating pies, place a small dish of water in the oven with them. This will keep the pastry fresh and moist.

Elsie's lemon meringue pie

1¼ cups sugar
½ cup flour
½ teaspoon salt
1½ cup water
3 eggs, separated
Zest from 1 medium lemon
Juice from 1½ medium lemons
1 tablespoon butter
1 baked, cooled 22 cm pie crust

- Preheat oven to 180°C.
- Combine the sugar, flour, salt and water in a heavy saucepan.
- Stir constantly over medium-high heat until mixture boils.
- Boil, stirring constantly and vigorously, for one minute.
- Remove from heat.
- Slightly beat the egg yolks in a bowl with a fork.
- Mix half the boiled mixture with the egg yolks.
- Put the egg yolk mixture back into the pan with the boiled ingredients.
- Cook for another minute, stirring constantly.
- Remove from heat, and add the butter
- Add the lemon zest and lemon juice.
- Stir to mix thoroughly.
- Pour into cooled, baked twenty-two cm pie crust and top with meringue, sealing meringue to edge of pastry.
- Bake in a 180°C oven ten to twelve minutes or until nicely browned.

Meringue

3 egg whites at room temperature
5 tablespoons sugar
½ teaspoon vanilla
¼ teaspoon cream of tartar

- Beat the egg whites on high speed of an electric mixer until soft peaks form.
- Add the cream of tartar.

- Gradually add the sugar, a tablespoon at a time.
- Beat until stiff peaks form.
- Beat in the vanilla.
- Pile on top of pie, and bake at 180°C for ten to twelve minutes, or until lightly browned.
- Be sure to seal the meringue to the pastry edge when spreading it on your pie. Also, remember that meringue pies cut better with a wet knife blade.

Wine

Wine can be broken up into four major categories – appetisers, sparkling wines, table wines and dessert wines.

Appetisers

These are sweet, medium and dry sherry, and vermouths. They are wines designed to leave the mouth feeling fresh and ready for food. They are high in alcohol and so are served in small glasses. Sweet sherry originated in Spain and well suits the spicy Spanish foods. Sherry is made as other white wines are, but a solution of extra alcohol and a grape essence is added. It is stored and turns to a light brown.

Sparkling wines

Sparkling wines, champagne and champagne-type wines: these are fun wines. They are generally sweetish with plenty of fizz. They can be served with food or by themselves. A dry sparkling wine can be served before food as it leaves the mouth feeling fresh and, because of the natural carbon dioxide content, gives the spirits a considerable lift. Nevertheless, champagne can be drunk any time. A good champagne keeps its bubbles right down to the last drop. Drink very cold to preserve the bubble.

True champagne

There are many ways of putting the sparkle into sparkling wines, and the more expensive the method the more expensive the wine. To the beginner wine drinker the difference will be hard to pick. However, it usually will tell in the morning. French champagne rarely leaves you with a hangover. Champagne is the perfect before-meal starter – it cleans off the tastebuds and lifts the spirit.

Champagne – which glass?

The broad, shallow 'coupe' glass is fine for drinking champagne, and has a nice look about it, but tends to release the all-important bubbles too quickly. The French devised the slender, deep 'flute' gas for champagne – the bubbles move about in the glass, but do not escape so quickly from the narrow mouth.

Did you know . . .?

The original champagne is made from a dry, rather acid wine, chardonnay or pinot noir, on the chalky soils of the Champagne district around Reims in Northern France. Champagne was discovered by a French monk, Dom Perignon, in the area, in the 17th century. He was making still wine, as usual, but by now had abandoned the traditional oil-soaked rag as a bottle stopper and replaced it with the new-fangled cork, which was becoming popular. During its second fermentation in the bottle, the carbon dioxide gas would normally escape through the rag-stopper, but this time it did not. When he uncorked this vintage, he discovered little bubbles in his wine. Champagne was born and the world has been a happier place in the 400 years since.

Table wines

Dry white, dry red, rosé. Table wines are bought for their taste and how they combine with food to improve the overall taste sensation. They are usually dry. The prime examples are:

Riesling is a dry white wine with a fruity palate.
Chablis is a sharp, acid very dry white with a flinty finish.
Moselle is sweet and easy for the beginning palate to drink.
White burgundy is a rounder and softer white wine.

Semillon

Most white Australian wines are made from semillon grapes, which produce a softer rounder wine than the European grapes.

Cabernet sauvignon

It all began in Bordeaux, it is the world's best-known grape variety, and it is right at the top of the vineyard hierarchy. Cabernet sauvignon vines have spread to most of the wine-growing world, especially South Africa, the USA, much of South America, and Australia. Local versions have developed from there. Some, such as in California, have slavishly followed the French model. Others, such as in Australia, have developed their own local interpretations.

Australia produces a quality cabernet sauvignon, in two versions:

- As a fine cellar-it-for-later type, produced in the cooler zones.
- As a very affordable drink-it-now type, grown in the warmer climes.

The French would probably raise their hands in horror, but cabernet sauvignon is such a class act and so well known that, in Australia, its name is shortened with sublime natural-ness to 'Cab Sav'.

Features of cabernet sauvignon

- The taste is predominantly blackcurrant, but variations include touches of redcurrant, plum or even blackberry, and, in the cooler climates, mint.
- The aroma is generally described as peppery.
- Cellaring for a couple of years softens the blend and eases the dry-mouth, tannin taste. But cabernet sauvignon is a very versatile wine. Don't hold back, it can still be enjoyed when young!

Perfect to enjoy with red meat, including steak, roast lamb, kangaroo, game.

Whites

White wines should be served chilled and drunk from stemmed glasses.
They can be drunk when they are young and fresh.
Fill the glass to only half full so that the bouquet may be trapped in the glass.

Reds

Claret is a dry, dark red with a firm flavour and a sharp furry finish.
   Merlot is a softer and more velvety dry red.
   Hermitage, shiraz, cabernet sauvignon and cabernet shiraz describe the grapes that those particular wines are made with. Red wines are made when grapes are crushed and fermented in their skins. The pigment in the skins of the black grapes produces the colour of red wine. The fermentation process converts grape sugar to alcohol and carbon dioxide. The liquid is then run off into oak casks and left to develop over twelve to eighteen months. It is bottled and left to mature. As they age, reds get rounder and softer.

Dessert wines

Sauternes, tawny port, vintage port, muscat. We drink dessert wines at the end of a meal to round it off.

Port

The name 'port' comes from the city of Oporto in Portugal. Portuguese wines – especially nice dry reds – were first exposed to the rest of the world when English soldiers stopped off there on their way to the Crusades. An export market was set up, and to ensure the wines travelled properly on the sea voyage to England, they were mixed with brandy. The fortified port was born. Portuguese ports are elegant and crisp, whereas other variations, such as Australian, are heavier and bolder. Port is shaking off its image as a cheap way of consuming a vast amount of alcohol quickly, and being respected for its integrity and taste as an after-dinner finisher.

Port types

There are three main types of port – ruby, tawny and vintage.

Ruby port is fresh and young, with a bright red colour that gives it its name.

Tawny port is kept longer in the cask after fermentation, picking up a tawny, woody colour from the oak barrel. It remains in good drinkable condition for about six months after the bottle is opened.

Vintage port is bottled after a year or so in the wood, the good ones then maturing in the bottle for anything up to twenty years. A true vintage port is like a table wine – once the cork is taken out, it will not last much longer than a few days.

A dash of tawny port in a dish such as a casserole adds to the flavour.

Try tawny port with fruit such melon, strawberries and pineapple. Marinade the fruit in the port for several hours and serve with cream.

Muscat

Muscat is one of the rare wines that was developed in Australia, rather than being a copy of the champagne from France, port from Portugal, or sherry from Spain.

A centre of muscat is Rutherglen in Victoria, making a dark amber, rich, high-alcohol wine, with great character, which is then fortified with brandy. It is sweet, without a sugary cloying taste.

A good muscat poured over ice cream and fresh fruit is an excellent dessert.

What temperature?
White wine

The better the white wine, the less you need to chill it. Chilling does things to your taste buds so that you do not detect the bad things in a cheaper wine. Take an ice bucket thirty minutes before the wine is to be served, put half a cup of water and half a handful of salt in the bottom, fill it with ice cubes, open the bottle and stick it in the ice. The salt and water reduce the temperature of the ice cubes, releasing the flavour, while the warm air around the open neck and the coldness around the bottom of the bottle activate the bouquet.

Red wine

French tradition says that red wine should be served *au chambre* or at room temperature. This works well in Europe, but not in the middle of an Australian summer or a Moroccan sand-storm. Considering that room temperature in France is roughly 18°C (about 65°F), it is not a social indiscretion, in very hot weather, to place a bottle of red in the fridge for half an hour to get it down to around 20° or thereabouts.

Cooking with wine

Wine softens the connective tissue of meat and improves the texture of cheaper cuts. Wine gives an extra tang to simple stews and casseroles, soups and sauces. Wine in food loses its alcoholic content. The heat evaporates the alcohol. As a general rule, white meats are best cooked with white wine, and red meats with red wine.

Wine and cheese party

For twenty guests for a drink-and-nibbles party (not a full meal) you will need:

- Forty wine glasses, 185 ml. Two for each person, one for the red wine, one for the white wine.
- Have 2.5 kg of cheese. This allows 125g per person. It is better to buy fewer but larger pieces of cheese, as they look more attractive and do not dry out so quickly.
- Twenty small plates and serviettes. Look for matched paper sets.
- Fruit to refresh the palate. This will depend on the season, but apples and pears are best with cheese.
- A selection of breads and water biscuits, dry biscuits, crackers. Here you have a great opportunity to provide a range of enjoyable, tasty products, including rye, wholemeal, black bread, cob, crusty, French, Turkish, etc.
- Spread – some people may like to spread butter or margarine on their bread/crackers before applying the cheese. You'll find 250g of each should be plenty.

Wine

Do not go overboard with a plethora of drinks that will mesmerise the guests, but try and provide a range that provides plenty of interest and conversation. Look at progressing it through from, say, a sparkling wine as a starter, to two/three whites and two/three reds, to a tawny and a vintage port to go with the stronger cheeses. Look at, for example, providing a quality champagne, a riesling, chardonnay, a cabernet sauvignon, a merlot, a vintage port, and a muscat. Other types to consider are Chablis, Semillon and shiraz. You might look around and find something intriguing such as Hungarian Tokay. A good wine to sample, now coming back in favour, is rosé, especially from Spain or France. The ports tend to go better with the heavier cheeses.

Cheese

Mild cheeses to consider include Dutch edam and gouda, English double Gloucester and Leicester, Welsh caerphilly, Italian erbo, Swiss gruyere, any of the fettas or ricotta. Stronger cheeses include English Cheshire, Stilton and Lancashire, Australian girgarre, Danish blue, Italian gorgonzola, New Zealand blue, NZ mainland cheddar, and any version of camembert and brie, especially King Island, Australia.

Make sure the cheese comes out of the fridge and stands in the room for about an hour before the party starts. Spread the food and wine across two or three tables so people can work through them in progression. And remember, they are there to savour the wines, not to get stuck into one type and hole up in a corner and talk about their bleak superannuation investments. Cater so they move along and enjoy the whole experience.

Teas

Tea was drunk in China before the birth of Christ. It was brought to Europe in the 17th century. Teas come in many varieties.

Orange pekoe – Selected blend of Ceylon teas.
Queen Mary – A fine Darjeeling tea with a muscatel aroma.
Earl Grey – A fragrant blend of selected oriental teas.
Prince of Wales – A Chinese keemun tea with a delicate flavour that has been likened to the scent of an orchid.
Russian caravan – A blend of keemun teas.
Irish breakfast – A blend of Ceylon and Assam teas.
Green tea – The whole leaves of the camellia bush.

To make an excellent cup of tea

Bring fresh, cold water to the boil. But just to the point where it starts to boil. This leaves nice bubbles of oxygen in it to give the tea a lively taste. Warm the pot. Measure the tea into the pot: one teaspoon for each cup and one for the pot. Taking the pot to the kettle, pour in boiling water. Allow to infuse for five minutes. Stir to allow the leaves to unfold. Pour. Apply a tea cosy.

Feeding young children

Keep it clean

Neglecting to wash hands could result in infant diarrhoea . Always begin formula and food preparation by washing your hands:

- After changing baby's nappy.
- After going to the bathroom.
- After handling raw meat.
- After petting animals.
- After gardening or working with soil.

Bacteria

Harmful bacteria from a baby's mouth can be introduced into food or bottles where it can grow and multiply even after refrigeration and reheating. If the baby does not finish a bottle, do not put it back in the refrigerator for another time. Likewise, do not feed a baby from a jar of baby food and put it back in the refrigerator for another time.

Saliva on the spoon contaminates the remaining food.

Perishable items

Perishable items like milk, formula or food left out of the refrigerator or without a cold source for more than two hours should not be used.

Feeding baby when out and about

- When travelling with baby, transport bottles and food in an insulated cooler.
- Place the ice chest in the passenger compartment of the car. It's cooler than in the boot.
- Use frozen gel packs to keep food or bottles cold on long outings.
- Do not keep bottles or food in the same bag with dirty nappies.
- Raw or unpasteurised milk should not be served to infants and children.

Manufacturer's recommendations

Follow the manufacturer's recommendations for preparing bottles before filling with formula or milk. Always observe 'use-by' dates on formula cans.

Honey

Honey is not safe for children less than a year old.

It can contain the botulinum organism that could cause illness or death.

Clean blender

If making home-made baby food, use a brush to clean areas around the blender blades or food processor parts.

Old food particles can harbour harmful bacteria that may contaminate other foods.

Wash

Use detergent and hot water to wash and rinse all utensils, including the can opener, which come in contact with baby's foods.

Safety button

If using commercial baby foods, check to see if the safety button on the lid is down.

If the jar lid doesn't 'pop' when opened, do not use.

Discard jars with chipped glass, or rusty lids.

Freezing baby food

To freeze home-made baby food, put the mixture in an ice cube tray. Cover with heavy-duty plastic wrap until the food is frozen. Then pop food cubes into a freezer bag or air-tight container and date it. Store up to three months. One cube equals one serving. Small jars can also be used for freezing. Leave about one cm of space at the top because food expands when frozen.

And finally . . .

The cook's philosophy

The best helping hand is the one on the end of your arm.

3
Gardening

Landscaping
Planning your garden
When planning a garden, take a walk around the neighbourhood and see what grows best in your neighbours' gardens. Once you have decided on the plants that you will have, make a plan for the layout of the garden, noting the paths and features. Remember to strata your plants so that you have the tall/larger ones at the back and the smallest/shortest plants at the front.

Carefully assess your own limitations and enthusiasm. Consult a local nurseryman or a local amateur gardener who knows the area, understands the conditions, and knows which plants do well in the area. Make notes and write down your thoughts and ideas. Assess limitations and features of the site – drainage, wind direction, mature trees. What water is available and of what quality is it? How much money can I spend? Identify the needs of the members of the household. Make a plan for your garden and how you would like to lay it out.

Make a plan
Have surprise corners, and try not to have a garden that can be seen all in the one glance. Plant the feature trees as soon as possible. Install paths and paving according to your plan. Allow for garden lighting. Create the garden by moving outwards from the house. Create the entertaining area first. Don't forget to include places to sit and enjoy your garden.

Choosing plants
Plant long-term flowering perennials and shrubs. Keep in mind that perennials spread quickly. However, it is better to plant closely and then you can thin out if required. When you are planting, keep in mind the garden features that you can't yet afford and leave space for them.

Be flexible
If you find that a plant is not suitable for the spot that you have planted it, wait until winter and shift it to another position.

Cooling blue
Blue, green and a dash of white are cooling on the eye and make a wonderful combination for a summer garden. Plants include jacaranda, hydrangea, the blue butterfly bush, delphiniums, white impatience, salvias, lobelia, blue spiraea, Russian sage, and agapanthus and lavender.

Bring colour to your garden
Aquilegia, candytuft, cosmos, English daisy, godetia, lobelia, marigold, verbena, viola, zinnia are colourful flowers.

Plants for a shady garden

For shadiest areas, select plants that have their peak growing seasons at different times and then become dormant while another plant has its turn.

Fences

The two most important reasons for building a fence are:

- To define a boundary line.
- For security.

Other reasons for building a fence:

- Fences can be used as climate modifiers for plants.
- They can be used to control wind and sun problems.
- Fences can be used to define outdoor areas for work, play and storage.
- Planting on both sides can help transform an ugly wall into an attractive addition to the landscape.

Wind

Before you build a fence to protect you from the wind, you should first understand the wind's behaviour in that area. Attach small flags to strategic points around the yard and observe the wind's behaviour.

Wind-break

A wind-break fence made of closely woven slats, or one with a slanting baffle on top, will break up the wind most effectively.

Noise barrier

For a fence to be an effective noise breaker, it should be solid and heavy. It should be more than a metre higher than the source of the sound that you are trying to eradicate. If you aim to create an outdoor room, you should use materials that harmonise with the total garden and house. Movable louvres offer many possibilities. They can be moved up and down to let the sun in, to catch the breeze and to protect the area from wind.

Repairing and replacing fences

When you are repairing or replacing a fence you must reach an agreement with your neighbour with whom you share the fence. The cost should be shared fifty-fifty. If you cannot agree as to the type or price of fence that you want, then you will have to take the matter to arbitration. The branches or the fruit of a neighbour's tree that overhang your property do not belong to you. You may ask the neighbour to prune the tree or you may do so yourself, but you must return the wood to the neighbour. Be careful not to damage anything on their side of the fence when you do so.

How steep is that fence line?

It is helpful to find out exactly how steep the block is before you start fencing. To do this:

- Run a string from a stake at the high point of your fence line.
- Tie the string to the stake at ground level.
- Stretch it to a tall stake at the lowest point.
- Draw the string taut.

- Hang a line level on the centre of the string.
- Move the string up or down until the bubble is centred.
- To calculate the drop, divide the height of the string above the ground on the tall stake into the length of line between stakes.

Spacing posts

When spacing your posts, it is a good idea to make the most economical use of standard lengths of rails (the classic 4by2s). Try to purchase rails at least twice the length of fence spacings so that you can nail the rails so that the end falls on alternate posts, thus making a stronger fence.

Digging post-holes

When digging post-holes it is a good idea to hire a post hole digger as this will save you time and your back won't suffer. The bottom of the post-hole should be wider than the top in order to provide a solid base in which to set the posts. Make the hole twenty cm deeper than the post needs to be set, in order to allow for rubble to be placed there for drainage.

Aligning the posts

The corner post method:

- Begin with two corner posts.
- Set one firmly in place.
- Secure the other firmly but so that it can be adjusted.
- Align and stretch string between them, both top and bottom.
- Mark where the centres of the intermediate posts will be.
- Use the plumb bob to transfer the marks to the lower line.
- Set each intermediate post in gravel with its face brushing the aligning string.
- Check to see that each post remains vertical as you work.

Preserve the wood

Before you begin to attach rails to posts, apply paint or preservative to all surfaces where the rails and posts touch.

Pickets

Pickets should not be allowed to touch the soil or they will rot. Before you attach pickets you should paint them to protect them against decay. Attach the pickets while the paint is still wet to create a weather seal. Use a picket, laid on its side, to regulate the space between each picket.

To age a redwood fence

Mix half a cup baking soda with two litres water. Stir. Brush or spray onto the wood. As it dries the acids in the wood combine with the soda to produce a dark weathered tone.

Fence maintenance

Repair or replace rotted posts early. You can buy post savers at the hardware store. They are iron posts which are inserted into the ground alongside the rotted post. The post is then securely attached.

Apron fence

An apron fence can be installed to keep dogs from burrowing under. Simply fold the bottom of a wire sleeve outward to form an apron. Stake it down onto the ground. In a few weeks the plants will conceal it and anchor it in place.

Plants for fence lines

For lightly constructed fences use vines that are light and airy. If they are too heavy they will pull your fence over.

A solid panel fence is an effective backdrop for a plant that you wish to highlight.

Keep fence plantings well trimmed to keep them from running wild.

Espalier

In narrow planting places along the fence, try espaliered fruit trees. Espalier is the technique of spreading the tree out against a fence, wall or trellis, so it is trained to grow flat. Leave space between the fence and the plants so that the plants do not burn in reflected heat.

Focal point

Add a birdbath, fountain or sculpture for a focal point. Enjoy.

Gates

Here's how to build a simple gate:

- Determine the gate size by measuring the space between the posts at both the top and the bottom.
- Plan your frame width for three cm less than this measurement.
- Build the frame, keeping in mind that when nailing the frame pieces together it must be kept at right angles using a square.
- Attach a diagonal brace at both ends by nailing through both the horizontal and vertical rails.
- Attach the siding. However, if the gate will be too heavy to handle, then this can be attached later.
- Prop gate in place with wooden blocks and attach the hinges to the gate and the loose ends of hinges to the posts.
- Fit the gate and trim so that it swings freely.
- Attach the latch.

If your gate doesn't swing

Check the hinges and replace loose ones with larger hinges. The screw may need to be replaced with longer ones. If the gate is more than 1.5 metres wide it should have three hinges. Check the post. If it is leaning, straighten it up. If it hasn't been set in concrete, then do it. It may need strengthening with a turnbuckle and heavy wire running to the bottom of another post down the fence line. Check the gate and if it is out of shape remedy this with a wire turnbuckle, which runs opposite to the diagonal wood brace. (Turnbuckle kits can be bought at hardware stores.) If the latch does not catch you may need to take it off and move it up or down until it catches again, and re-fix it.

Japanese gardens

Japanese gardens consist of three elements: plants, rocks and water. That's what makes them so interesting.

Let it evolve

A garden is a living, growing thing and is always evolving, allow it to have its head a little and to grow how it wants to grow by planting self-seeding plants that will pop up in the most unexpected places.

Lighting your garden

Proper lighting can create the right atmosphere for entertaining and relaxing in your garden. It is also important for safety reasons.

Plan your lighting properly

- Draw a plan of your garden, its features and landscaping. Include the paths and entertainment area and any water or other feature that you would wish to be highlighted.
- Mark in where you would like the lights and calculate how many you will need.
- Bring light to the dark spots and eliminate the danger of hazardous steps with backlights.
- Use bollards to highlight walkways and driveways.
- Eliminate dark areas around windows and doors by using spotlights for backlighting.
- Consider adding sensors, which can automatically turn on lights when movement is detected.
- Calculate the wattages of your lights and make sure that you buy a transformer that can cope with the load.
- You may need two to three transformers at different points.
- Calculate the length of cable that you will require.

Lighting effects

- Add warm, glowing upward lights to accent a garden area.
- Light a pathway with soft downward lights.
- Backlight from spotlights highlights walls and eaves.
- Use bollard walk lights to line a driveway.
- Use up-lights to dramatically highlight a beautiful tree.
- Down-light the steps at your entrance and backlight the shrubs to create an impressive entrance.

Installing the lighting system

If in doubt, have a professional do it for you. In some states you are not permitted to do electrical work yourself, as you must attain a Certificate of Safety. Always get a licensed electrician to install fixed wire products such as 240V outdoor lighting, switches and power points. You will need an outdoor power point.

Extra low voltage garden lighting does not have to be installed by a licensed electrician. You will need a transformer to reduce the 240V mains electricity to extra low 12V for the garden lighting. The transformer should have a higher rating than your lighting wattage. Remember to turn off the power when connecting, dismantling or cleaning lights.

Low-cost landscaping

You can do your landscaping yourself. Discover the plants that are suitable for local conditions. You can do this by asking at your local nursery about the hardiest plants it has for your soil and sunlight conditions. Draw up a plan as to where you are going to put significant trees, flowerbeds, grass, rockery, paving etc. Don't leave it to chance.

Stepping stones
Lay a few stepping stones for a path.

Paths
Paths are purposeful, frivolous, romantic, wild, domestic. Wait a while and watch where the paths make themselves as people move about the garden. Keep the curves flowing. Try not to allow the end of the path be seen from the beginning of the path. Lead to areas that will surprise.

Ponds
A pond can look great in your front or back yard, but will need attention to look clean and attractive.

- To stop the pond going green, it must have sufficient plant life – reeds are the best as they purify the water.
- Water lilies do not oxygenate the water. Only plants with foliage below the water are efficient enough to do that. It's best to mix lilies with other aquatic plants.
- Good depth in a pond is important to keep the water cool enough for fish. Shallow pools heat up very quickly on hot days.
- Symptoms of pollution include dying fish, plants turning yellow, water being discoloured, bubbles on the surface.
- Possible causes of pollution may be the run-off of nitrogenous fertilisers from gardens or farmland, over-feeding the fish, a build-up of methane, ammonia or nitrates.
- Symptoms of low oxygen levels in the pond include water turning black, fish gasping for breath at the surface, fish dying with no symptoms of disease.
- Possible causes of lack of oxygen include too many floating plants, too many fish, prolonged hot weather, excessive decomposing organic waste, excessive algae.
- Symptoms of poor pH balance in your pond are diminishing plant growth, fish prone to disease, diminished effectiveness of the filter.
- High alkalinity is likely to be caused by lime seeping through from cement, or perhaps the tap water.
- High acidity may be coming from the rainwater, fish waste, or decomposing plants.

Preloved garden
If you have inherited somebody else's garden because you have bought their house, then be patient. Wait and watch. If you wait twelve months before you plan your new garden you will have experienced the flowerings of the plants that already make up the garden. You may be pleasantly surprised.

Seats
Seats can provide a focal point in the garden. They are an essential feature in any garden and mean that you will be able to rest between garden-centred activities.

General gardening tips
At your back door
Hang a bunch of mint at the back door to deter blowflies.

Keep an aloe vera plant near the door. If you get burnt while cooking, break a piece off and rub over infected area.

Autumn leaves

Put in a bucket overnight with three tablespoons of salt to half a bucket of water. The next morning, stand in a mixture of:

- 6 tablespoons water
- 2 tablespoons glycerine
- 1 teaspoon Condy's Crystals

Leave for about twenty days and the leaves will be shiny and colourful.

Cut flowers

When gathering fresh flowers from your garden, always cut flowers in the cool of the evening, never in the heat of the day. Cut stems on a slant to give them the largest possible area in which to take in water.

Stand flowers in a bucket of water up to their necks for at least an hour before arranging them.

Making fresh flowers last

Wrap the stems of freshly cut flowers in a strip of foil to make them last longer.

Make sure your vase is clean and harbours no bacteria.

Spray blooms with hair spray to prevent them dropping. This is particularly effective with blossoms.

Hydrangeas will stay fresh indoors for a week if you make a split one cm long in the base of the stem and stand in hot water before putting them in the vase.

Keeping cut flowers fresh

Asters and all members of the aster family:
Add two tablespoons sugar and one tablespoon salt to the water.

Carnations:
One teaspoon sugar to the water.

Chrysanthemums:
One tablespoon sugar and five drops of oil of cloves to the water.

Daffodils and jonquils:
Do not arrange in too much water.

Dahlias:
Burn the ends of the stems and place in iced water.

Daisies and all members of the daisy family:
Add eight drops of peppermint oil to the water.

Evergreens:
Crush stems and add one tablespoon glycerine to the water.

Gladioli:
Add five tablespoons vinegar to the water.

Gardenias and camellias:
These flowers never take in water after being cut. Arrange in a floating vase or wrap stems in moist tissue paper.

Irises:
Add three drops of peppermint oil to the water.

Lilies:
Add half a cup vinegar to the water.

Poppies:
Burn the ends of the stems and add two tablespoons salt to the water.

Roses:
Add two tablespoons salt to the water.

Sweet peas:
Plunge into hot, then cold water.

Violets:
Submerge in water for a couple of hours after picking, then place in icy water.

Woody or semi-woody stemmed flowers should have their stems crushed before you put them in the vase, as this allows them to take in more water.

Add one of the following:

- an aspirin to the water to make flowers stay fresh longer
- one teaspoon of sugar to the water
- one tablespoon salt to the water
- half a cup of vinegar to the water
- five drops of peppermint oil to water

A splash of vodka in your cut flower arrangements keeps your flowers looking fresh several days longer.

Bananas are good for ferns

Don't throw your banana skins away. They make good food for staghorn ferns. Simply tuck in at the back. For potted maidenhair ferns, chop up banana skins and mix with the soil. For tree ferns, place in the top where the fronds emerge.

Bush fires

In the same way that drought is a normal occurrence in Australia, so too, are bush fires.

How can we minimise the risk?

Most houses adjoining bushland are built on ridges. Fire travels uphill at about four times the rate that it travels on flat land.

Embers often start fires well after the front has gone through. It is therefore important that you don't leave anything around the house that embers can catch onto.

- Keep gutters free, leaves off decks and from around the base of your house.
- Don't pile up paper, timber, lawn mower fuel under the house.
- Limit the possibility of a treetop fire by keeping trees to twenty metres from the house.
- Select smooth barked native trees, as rough bark catches the embers.
- Some native trees and shrubs are highly flammable as they have a high oil content.
- Climbing plants that hold a lot of dead wood, like potato vine, are bad.
- Privet is a good fire break as it doesn't drop its leaves and nothing else grows with it.
- Native rainforest plants also have fire retardant abilities.

Bushier plants

Pinch back annuals as you plant them to make them sturdier.

Buying new plants

If you are buying new plants on a hot day, get them out of your car and into a cool place as quickly as possible. Plant in the cool of the evening.

Digging tips

- Dig with a straight-edged spade. Scoop with a curved shovel.
- Don't dig when the soil is wet.
- Wait until it dries out enough to crumble in your hands.
- If your spade slides in nicely then it is right to dig.
- If the soil is hard and dry, water it well first before you dig.
- When digging, turn the soil in a 90° angle, not 180°.

Drying hydrangeas

Cut hydrangeas while in their prime. They should be cut on a mixture of hard and new wood. Cut the stems and plunge them into a container of water. Leave in the container for several weeks until they have absorbed all the water. Then hang upside down in bunches. They will dry out naturally and retain their colour.

Easy-care gardens

As you age, you can still enjoy the pleasure of the garden without the work.

- Reduce the area covered in lawn. Lawns are time-consuming, as they need to be mowed regularly.
- Limit the number of high maintenance plants and keep them to one or two specific areas.
- Choose shrubs with compact shapes that don't need much pruning
- Ground covers will prevent weed growth and will hold the soil together.
- Mulch well to stop the weeds from growing.
- Reduce the number of pot plants, as they require constant watering.
- Place all remaining pot plants in one location.

Eggs

Save the water when you hard-boil eggs and water your plants with it. It is full of minerals.

Put the eggshells in a container and soak in water for a few days. Sprinkle the shells on the garden to deter snails and water your plants with the mixture.

Save empty egg cartons to start your seedlings in. They can be transferred directly into the soil without disturbing the roots.

Eggshells

Instead of raising seeds in seed trays, plant them in eggshell halves. When it's time to plant them out, just crack the shell and put the plant and shell in the ground. The shell is a natural fertiliser.

A sprinkle of crushed eggshell will keep snails away from sensitive plants.

Eggshells make a good substitute for pebbles around houseplants. They add lime to the soil and promote drainage.

Flower parts

Bract
Is the leaf-like structure that grows below the flower cluster. They are most often green, but can be bright and more colourful than the flower itself.

Sepal
The outer circle of the flower parts. They may be either green or coloured. Grouped they are called a calyx.

Petal
The second circle of flower parts. If they are joined the structure is called a corolla.

Spurs
Spurs are projections from the rear of the flower which arise from the sepals or the petals.

Stamen
Stamens are the parts of the central flower that produce pollen. They are fragile stalks with pollen-covered swellings at the top. The stalks are filaments, the swellings are anthers.

Pistil
The pistil is the central part of the flower. It is a stalk-like tube with a moist sticky end. The tube is the style and the end is the stigma. The ovary is at the end of the stem and is the part that produces seeds and fruit.

Garden hose
If your garden hose springs a leak, make a clean cut either side of the leak and use a joiner to rejoin it. If you dip the hose ends into hot water for a few minutes you will find the joiner is easier to fit. Drive some solid pegs into corners so that the hose will not break delicate plants and shrubs when it is moved around the garden.

Gloves
When doing jobs in the garden, it is a good idea to always wear a strong pair of gardening gloves. It prevents bites from spiders and protects your hands from damage.

Uses for old garden hoses
Short lengths, slit sideways, can be slipped over sharp edges to make them safer.

Make soft cushions to tie tree stakes. Simply thread rope through them and tie.

Cut into smaller lengths they can be dangled from fruit trees at fruiting time. They look sufficiently like snakes to keep the birds away.

Going to seed
To prevent seeds from maturing, pinch off flowers as they fade. Flowering often slows when seeds ripen. If stems begin to yellow and look scraggly, you won't harm the plant by shearing it to half its size. Most perennials will reward you with fresh foliage and sometimes a second bloom.

Hand care
Rinse your hands with vinegar after working with garden lime to avoid rough and flaking skin.

Lawn

A properly fertilised lawn needs less water to keep it healthy than an unfertilised one.

Ground covers instead of lawn

Instead of re-seeding that patch of worn-out lawn year after year, plant shade-loving ground covers. Ground covers usually require less care than lawns. However they are not suitable for heavy-duty areas. When using ground covers consider:

- How much cold will it take?
- How fast will it grow?
- Does it need sun or shade?
- How far apart should the plants be spaced?

Lawn clippings

Lawn clippings, taken directly from the lawn mower catcher and laid on the garden as mulch, are not effective. When they break down they often form an impervious skin which inhibits moisture penetration. The water runs off rather than soaks through to the plants. Clippings are best put through your mulching cycle.

Lawn-mowing

- Mow lawns correctly to keep them healthy.
- Mow at a height of nothing less than six cm. By mowing too low we allow weeds to take over our patch.
- Use an old kitchen knife to remove weeds from lawn as you see them.
- Remove annual weeds such as capeweed and chickweed before they flower.
- Buttercup, dock and plantain have tap roots which should be removed totally.
- Oxalis and onion weed have bulbs and these should be removed entirely.
- Once you have removed weeds, re-sow the patch immediately.

Muddy feet

Plastic shopping bags are great covers for muddy feet when you have to go into the house for a telephone call or to get a forgotten item.

Music

Talk and play classical music to your plants, it makes them grow. It might spark whispered conversation among the neighbours about behaviour, but don't let that deter you . . .

Old hose

If your hose has sprung a leak, instead of throwing it out, punch a few more holes and block the end – you'll have a soaker hose for your lawn.

Potpourri

To make a nice potpourri:

- Choose flowers and herbs from your garden.
- Make sure that they are not damp or dewy.
- Separate petals and lay on absorbent paper in a warm spot for a few days.
- Lavender should be hung upside down and out of direct light to dry.
- If you want the petals for colour rather than scent, then they can be dried in the microwave for thirty seconds on high.
- Use orrisroot or oak moss, which are available from chemists and craft shops, as a fixative.

- You will need about two dessertspoons to a salad size bowl.
- Choose your favourite essential oils to add perfume.
- You will need two capfuls.
- Add a dessertspoon of sea salt.
- Add a few drops of essential oil every couple of weeks to maintain the perfume.

Protect your tree trunks

When you plant a tree that is a focal point, leave a circular area around its trunk for a small flowerbed. The flowers not only are attractive but also establish a buffer zone so lawn mowers and trimmers can't nick and cut the bark.

Recycle the broom handle

Don't throw away that old broom. Remove the head and drive a 7.5 cm nail into the end of the handle. Use it as an aerator for the lawn by pushing it into the grass. It will allow the water to penetrate instead of running off.

Sawdust

Before applying sawdust to your garden bed, let it sit in a mound for eight weeks, otherwise it will rob the soil of nitrogen as it breaks down.

Soil

Good soil, healthy garden

Keep loamy or clay soil in the best physical condition by digging, planting or generally disturbing it only when in the just damp state, never when it is wet and sticky.

Add copious compost and mulch to sandy soils to build up the nutrients.

All soils benefit from application of compost at least a couple of times a year.

In tough, caking soils, sow one or two radish seeds every few centimetres along the row of slower germinating seeds such as carrots. The robust and quick germinating radishes break up the soil crust which otherwise retards the growth of the carrots.

What soil do you have?

If you're not sure what type of soil you have in your garden, you can buy a soil testing kit which will tell you if it is 'acid' or 'alkaline'. Then you will know what types of plants to buy for your garden. Ask at your local nursery. Once you've followed the instructions you need to find out if you have sandy soil (which drains water quickly) or clay soil (which holds the moisture well).

Sandy soil

Use plenty of organic material to keep up the humus content.

It may be worked lightly into the surface soil, or used as a surface mulch.

Spray water

Of course, frequent sprayings from the hose (when water restrictions allow) or exposure to rain help the plant, and in addition, many insects are kept in control by a spray of cold water. But do not spray plants with water when the sun is directly on the foliage, or when it is cold. Some plants in flower and plants with hairy foliage are ruined by spraying with water, but all smooth-leaved subjects will respond to this care with a verdant appearance.

Sunshine

Sunshine and fresh air are the keynote to a healthy home. Open the doors and windows and let the sunshine, the perfume of the plants and the sounds of the birds in.

Tags

Always read the tags on the plants in nurseries for helpful planting and care instructions.

Topiary

If your topiary has sticky leaves it is being attacked by a sucking insect. Move it outside to a shady place and treat with Orthene following label directions. Repeat in seven to ten days.

Weeding the easy way

For a weed-free garden, just pull the weeds and till the plot thoroughly. Then, cover it with a six mm black plastic sheet and bury the edges to hold the sheet in place. Leave the garden plot covered for four weeks, then remove the sheet and let the soil cool a few days before planting. If you're killing grass, pin the plastic down with landscape-fabric spikes (available at garden centres) and let the grass 'cook' for two to three months. When you remove the sheet, turn the dead sod under so it can decompose.

Whipper snipper damage to trees

To prevent the whipper snipper cutting into your trees, take an old pot plant, remove its bottom with a Stanley knife, slit down one side and place around the tree.

It will spring back into place and protect the trunk from collar damage. As the tree grows, replace with bigger pots.

Garden tools
The garden shed
Keep your shed tidy

A well-planned shed should have a place for everything and everything in its place. The bench will be clear, the tools will be at hand and you will be able to navigate your way to the door without breaking your neck. Every shed needs a work-bench and that should be your first project. Use a mate's bench to build a bench. The world is then your oyster and you will have a place to make things and to twiddle.

Good storage in your shed will make life much easier and more pleasant.

- To store your bicycle on the wall, screw curtain brackets to the wall studs, high or low, wherever you have space. Line them with a soft material like felt or leather to protect the bike's finish.

You can even drop a shelf board on top to hold your helmet and water bottles.

- To pack away clutter from your bench tops, mount vinyl gutter sections along the open sides of your workbench. Cap the ends of the gutters to stiffen them and keep stuff from falling out.

- Jars are great for holding leftover paint as it is less likely to dry out and you can see the colour at a glance. To prevent the paint can sealing the lid permanently on, simply wrap Teflon tape around the glass threads and top lip.

- Screw the lid of a jar onto the underneath side of a bench that is at eye level. Put nails or screws in the jar and simply screw the jar into the lid.

A great way to keep nails and screws rust free and within easy reach. You can see at a glance just what is in each jar.

- An empty rectangular tissue box makes a convenient holder for small garbage bags, plastic grocery bags and small rags. Simply thumbtack it to the inside of a cabinet door.

- Get ladders, tree pruners, bikes, 2x4s and other unwieldy items off your garage floor with inexpensive PVC hooks.

- Store tall, thin stuff like dowels and tomato stakes inside PVC pipe standing on its end.

- Don't waste the roof space. Ladders and old doors and the like can be rested on the cross beams.

- Keep chemicals up high and right out of the reach of curious little hands.

- Make a shadow board where you can hang your tools. Simply get a piece of peg board, lay it on the bench and trace around your tools where you would like to hang them on the board. Mount the peg board on the wall, and hang the tools in their places with hooks. You will know at a glance if any tool is missing and you will be able to go looking for it before it is too late and the grass grows over it.

Garden tool maintenance

To clean the dirt off your garden tools while protecting the metal, shove the blade of your shovel or other garden tool in a bucket of sand mixed with vegetable oil.

The abrasive action of the sand will clean off the dirt, and the oil will coat the tool, thus preventing rust.

Hire your tools

You don't need to fill your shed with rarely used garden tools. You can save time and money by hiring equipment for special jobs. The following are tools that are available for hire.

Brush cutters	A large whipper snipper.
Fertiliser spreaders	For large areas or sowing seeds.
Lawn aerator	Saves water and keeps lawns alive.
Post-hole diggers	
Mowers	
Mulchers	Hire at pruning time to mulch your waste.
Rotary hoe	Use to churn up earth before planting.
Slashers	Good to cut grass on big blocks.
Trenchers	To dig out trenches to lay pipes, watering systems.
Water blasters	High pressure water cleaners to demoss or strip paint from house, clean boat, etc.
Whackers	Compactor used to compress sand, pavers or toppings.

Lawn mower

Care of your lawn mower

Always go over the lawn you are about to mow and remove any stones, sticks, nails, wire or other hard objects that will jam under the base plate and damage the mower or dull the blade edges.

Mechanical check

Before you start, check all major nuts, bolts and screws are tight, particularly holding the blades. Unhook the wire to the spark-plug before any inspection of the mower, particularly of the blades, to ensure that there is no way of it starting.

Fuel
Fill the tank with clean fuel, wellshaken, and to the correct two-stroke proportions. Fill the tank outside in the air, not in a confined space, such as a small shed, where the fumes could be dangerous.

Finishing up
When you have finished the lawn, do not turn the mower off at the controls, rather, turn the petrol tap off, and let it run itself out, using up all the fuel in the fuel line and the carburettor. Leaving oil-based fuel to evaporate in the carburettor makes the mower hard to start next time.

Maintenance
Regularly oil the drive mechanism – usually a chain – to minimise wear and ensure trouble-free, smooth operation. Check the spark-plug regularly – keep it clean, scrub it with a wire-brush, use a vacuum cleaner placed on reverse cycle to get rid of any dust. Keep the spark-plug gap to the manufacturer's specifications.

Replace blades on a rotary mower once a year. Replace both blades, even though one may look OK – having blades of different quality can unbalance the mower and put strain on the engine. Keep the motor mower clean, especially the area around the base plate.

Paint tools
Paint the ends of your tools in a bright, easy-to-spot colour – then it's easier to see where you've put them down.

Reduce blisters
Put foam over the handles of your garden tools to make them easier to grip and reduce calluses and blisters.

Secateurs
Make sure that your secateurs are clean and that disease does not spread in your garden, by wiping the blades with disinfectant before you use them.

Garden treatments
Bordeaux Mixture
Bordeaux Mixture is a dormant season fungicide spray. It is effective for fungal diseases and certain bacterial diseases such as fire blight of pear and apple. You may purchase Bordeaux Mixture as a 'ready to use' formulation at the local garden shop, or you may make your own supply. The mixture is prepared by combining hydrated lime or any type of finely ground lime with powdered copper sulphate (sometimes referred to as 'bluestone'). Both are available at garden shops.

While Bordeaux Mixture can be prepared in several strengths, the recommended for dormant season application is a four-four-fifty formulation. The standard formula for Bordeaux Mixture is 1.8 kg of copper sulphate, 1.8 kg of hydrated lime and 227 litres of water. Mix 1.8 kg of the lime in 18 litres of water. Do the same for the copper sulphate. Strain the lime mixture through cheesecloth, add to 191 litres of water, and then add the sulphate mixture. Use immediately.

The home gardener can make smaller amounts of spray mixture

3 tablespoons of copper sulphate
3 tablespoons of hydrated lime
4 litres water

Mix the lime with 500 ml water to make a 'milk of lime' suspension. Dissolve the copper sulphate in 500 ml of water. Strain through cheesecloth. Add copper sulphate solution to a two-litre container of water. Add filtered lime solution. Add remainder of water. For best results, use your Bordeaux Mixture the same day of preparation and keep the sprayer agitated. Do not add insecticides to the Bordeaux Mixture.

Compost

Recipe for a compost heap

- All waste material from spent crops, kitchen vegetable waste, leaves, weeds, etc. can be used to make a compost heap.
- Avoid using diseased plants, weeds that carry seed heads, heavy prunings and woody stalks.
- To begin, lay down a layer of material about fifteen cm deep.
- Fork in a sprinkling of lime.
- Add a couple of handfuls of complete fertiliser.
- Cover with five to seven cm layer of soil.
- On top of that place animal manure.
- Repeat the layers until the heap is one to 1.5 metres deep.
- Aerate by driving a stake into the heap several times.
- Keep the heap damp at all times.
- Decomposition takes from four to twelve months.

Compost bins

Any commercial compost bin may be used. It is better to have two small-based bins than one large-based bin as the compost will build up more quickly. You do not need to water. However it is useful to aerate the contents, occasionally forking it.

Compost tumbler

To get the best results out of a compost tumbler put in as wide a variety of materials as possible – kitchen waste, rice hulls, manure, straw, sawdust and plenty of fresh glass clippings to make it heat up.

Do not over-water material in a compost tumbler – add water only when it is very dry.

Environmentally friendly spray

To make an environmentally friendly spray that will discourage insects from eating your favourite plants, try mixing water with crushed garlic, chilli or onion. Don't make it too strong or it will make your homegrown vegetables unpalatable for you also.

Fertiliser

The best time to fertilise is spring and autumn. All fertilisers require a good watering in, because if you leave them to dry you may burn the plants.

Root plug fertilising

Make tube holes in a circle, about thirty cm apart and about sixty cm deep, just inside the drip line. Mix fertiliser with an equal amount of sand. Insert the tubes into the holes. Fill the plug holes with soluble fertiliser. Water in thoroughly. Use the water pressure from a hose inserted in the tube to force the fertiliser into the ground near the roots.

Natural fertilisers

Banana skins, placed just below the surface of the soil, rot and supply calcium, magnesium, sulphur, phosphorous, sodium and silica – great for all flowers but perfect for roses.

To grow the biggest and best tomatoes, sprinkle one teaspoon Epsom Salts into each planting hole. The magnesium works wonders.

To increase yields of tomatoes and cucumbers use one teaspoon blood and bone per plant every two weeks during the growing season.

Sprinkle a handful of ashes around each plant to keep the soil loose and to discourage cut worms.

Save all fruit and vegetable scraps to make humus.

Liquid fertilising

Make tube holes about thirty cm apart and about sixty cm deep, just inside the drip line. Insert the tubes into the holes. Insert soluble fertiliser. Use the water pressure from a hose inserted in the tube to force the fertiliser into the ground near the roots.

Surface fertiliser

Sprinkle complete fertiliser throughout the area that you wish to fertilise. Water in thoroughly.

Foliar fertiliser

Dampen the leaves by watering. Apply with a pressure spray to the leaves in the late evening or evening.

Home-made organic white oil

White oil is formulated to control scale and certain other insect pests on citrus, roses, daphne, other ornamental plants and indoor plants. It is also ideal for use as a leaf gloss for indoor plants. White oil can be made by mixing any light mineral oil with an emulsifier, a few drops of dishwashing detergent and a sunscreen to protect the plants from sunburn. Recent opinion is that if plants are sprayed without the sunscreen added (as in vegetable oil) apparently it is the sun, not the oil that can cause the burning. It should be sprayed on the effected plants in the evening.

Pour one cup cooking oil into blender. Add 1½ cups water and one teaspoon household detergent. Blend to a cream.

This mixture can further be broken down into one part white oil to fifty parts water.

Home-made plant food

4 litres water
1 tablespoon ammonia
1 tablespoon baking powder
1 tablespoon saltpetre
1 tablespoon sulphur
2 tablespoons Epsom Salts
1 rusty nail
2 tablespoons liquid soap

Use once a month to give your plants a lift.

For acid-loving plants
Add *one* of the following:
5 tablespoons black coffee
4 teaspoons vinegar
Leftover tea leaves

Camellias and azaleas
Empty your teapot on these plants.

Geraniums
Sprinkle Epsom Salts on the soil around the plant.

Ferns
Dissolve a birth control pill in two litres of water and use it to make your ferns grow stronger.

Verbenas
Dissolve one tablespoon sulphate of ammonia in eight litres of water and leave overnight before applying to your plants.
Dissolve an aspirin in a cup of tea and add to the watering can.

Liquid manure
Put a hessian bag of poultry (or cow) manure into a drum of water. Let stand for ten days. Mix one part liquid manure to three parts water. Water soil, apply liquid fertiliser, and water again.

Mulch
Mulch is a covering for the garden. Gardeners have used it for generations to retain water in the soil, to smother the weeds and to tidy the garden beds. Bare soil is not good for plant growth. It gets hot, does not hold water and encourages weeds.
Do not let mulch stand up beside the trunk of a tree or plant as it may cause it to rot.
Mulch should be dug in every couple of years and a new layer added.

Soot
Make a liquid mix by adding water to your fire ashes and water the roses with it. It clarifies their colour.
Soot as top dressing on plants deters snails and slugs.
Soot applied around potatoes kills wire worm.

Vegetable gardens
The best thing about growing your own vegetables is that they always taste better straight from the garden. Vitamins and minerals are at their peak when they are freshly picked and you know that they have not been sprayed with poisons and chemicals.

The vegetable plot
The vegetable plot must be as open and sunny as possible. Dig vacant beds early so that they can be ready for sowing in the spring. Dig in liberal quantities of soft grass, leaves and weeds so that they have time to rot down. Turn the compost into the top layer of soil

where it is able to do the most good. Poultry manure is excellent spread over the ground and dug in near to planting time. Spread it between the rows of vegetables. Ashes and blood and bone can be thrown on top of the poultry manure.

How to construct a no-dig vegetable garden

- Mow the grass where you're locating your patch.
- Spread out some heavy layers of newspapers and thoroughly water them so they don't blow away.
- Spread out thick layers of lovely organic matter. Use what's cheap and locally available. It may be sugar cane trash, straw, seaweed or grass clippings.
- Mix in lots of old manure like sheep, cow, horse or poultry manure.
- Sprinkle in some good handfuls of blood and bone.
- Add one part of sulphate of potash to ten parts blood and bone.
- After this is all mixed together, water it heavily and leave it for a few days to settle down.
- All the organic matter will help retain moisture (especially in summer) and the mulch will suppress weeds, prevent erosion, retain moisture and keep the plant roots from getting too hot.

Vegetables that tolerate acid soil
Potato
Radish
Parsley
Sweet potato
Tomato

Vegetables that like lime soil
Cabbage
Cauliflower
Beet
Onions
Parsnips
Beans
Peas

Companion planting
Companion planting is the name given when we plant certain vegetables, or herbs, together to ward away pests. Plant onions and garlic with carrots. The smell confuses pests, keeping them away from your carrots.

Sweet corn and beans
Sweet corn takes a lot of nitrogen from the soil. Beans and peas add nitrogen to the soil, so plant some climbing beans at the base of each growing corn stalk. You will then have a stake for them to grow up and the depleted soil will be re-nourished. Beans and other legumes (like peas) grow well with other nitrogen hungry vegetables, such as cabbages, broccoli and cauliflower.

Carrots and onions
When carrots and onions grow together, the onions' roots are very close to the top of the soil. Carrots, on the other hand, feed very deeply. By growing the two together you boost the productivity of your beds.

Tomatoes and . . . most things

Tomatoes are great companion plants. They grow well near asparagus, celery, parsley, basil, carrots and chives. Marigolds are good at protecting your tomatoes from pests as their smell confuses the insects. Parsley likes being next to capsicums and tomatoes. Basil works well with capsicums and tomatoes. Basil seems to help the growth of tomatoes and gives pleasant flavour when the herb is added to them in cooking. A few plants of basil planted among tomatoes will help to repel the white fly.

Pumpkins

Climbing beans, sweet corn and pumpkins (or squash) grow incredibly well together.
Try pumpkins with melons and cucumbers.

Plants which do not like each other

Among the most antagonistic neighbours are strawberries and cabbages, or their close relatives, broccoli and cauliflower.
Beans do not like onions and garlic, but get along famously with celery, beetroot, cucumbers and carrots.

Crop rotation

Crop rotation is about moving your vegetables around your little patch each year.
This way not only do you give your soil a rest from having specific nutrients depleted each year, you also help break the reproductive cycle of soil-borne diseases and some pests.

Mulch

Good organic matter on and in the soil is vitally important for vegetables. It shields the plant from the hot sun, seals in moisture, and cuts down on evaporation. It eliminates the sharp temperature fluctuations. Constant upward flow of humid air from the moistened mulch continually passes across the leaves and reduces the need for rapid transpiration.

Mixed gardens

Since many vegetable plants are as attractive as they are delicious, they'll accent and blend in with your landscaping, so try planting vegies in the flower garden or even among shrubs.
Or use trellises to grow climbing plants like pole beans . . .
You can edge a flowerbed in lettuces, or grow oregano, basil, onions, chives and many more herbs under your shrubs.

Strawberries and roses

Rose bushes appear shapeless and scraggly when they're not in bloom.
Underplant them with strawberries, which produce pretty white flowers in the spring, then red fruit in summer.
Roses and strawberries thrive under the same conditions, and strawberries spread on runners that don't compete with rose roots.

Planting by the moon

The theory is that planting by the moon works, just as it does by the phases affecting the tides – that is, it impacts on the rise and fall of moisture in the soil and within the plants. Therefore, a crop such as hay is harvested in the new moon, because it will dry faster. It is suggested that planting, propagating and harvesting your back-yard plants in the cycles of the moon will result in healthier plants.

The lunar month cycle

First Week (New Moon)

Plant leaf crops, such as cabbage, broccoli, celery, silverbeet, cauliflower; and herbs such as parsley, chives, basil, cress.

Second Week (Waxing into Full Moon)

Sow seed-bearing crops including peas, corns, tomatoes, beans, pumpkin, eggplant, marrow, squash, capsicum.

Third Week (Full Moon)

Plant root crops, such as potatoes, onions, carrots, parsnips, turnips and beetroot.

Fourth Week (Full Moon Waxing into New Moon)

Prepare beds for planting, cultivate the soil, remove weeds.

Full planting charts are available at health stores. Planting by the moon does not mean you are out in the back yard in the middle of the night – just stick to the schedule and plant in later afternoon.

All plants and seeds which bear above the earth should be planted when the moon is new, and all those plants that bear under the earth should be planted when the moon is full.

Vegetable garden tips

Scatter onions throughout the vegetable garden to prevent root maggots from travelling easily from plant to plant.

Plant radishes in the carrot and lettuce rows. They help to mark the slow germinating carrot row and help protect the lettuce from bugs.

Plant rows of fast-growing vegetables between rows of slow-growing ones. The quick-growing ones will be ready for harvest as the slow ones need more room.

When you plant mint, cut the tops from large juice cans and sink them into the ground around the plants. This will prevent the roots from spreading all over the garden.

Watering vegetables

It is harmful and wasteful to water vegetables in the hot sun. Wait until evening or water in the early morning. This allows the plants to engorge themselves with water while they are relatively inactive.

Beans

Beans do not germinate if the ground is too cold. If you want an early crop, sow them indoors and then plant out when the weather is warmer. In the springtime they need to be planted about two cm below the surface. In summer, plant the seeds three to four cm down to escape the heat. Beans need plenty of water. They yield more if you keep picking them when they are young and succulent.

Plant beans on each side of your sweet corn. The corn will provide a stake for your beans to climb upon. Soak seed in water for a few days before planting.

Tip

Mist foliage of beans with water in hot, dry weather, preferably late in the day. This not only improves the setting of flowers, but also deters the activity of red spider mites, which may otherwise cause the leaves to mottle badly and lose moisture during dry conditions.

Beetroot

A handful of common salt sprinkled on each side of the row will encourage beetroot to grow large and will prevent them from becoming woody in the centre.

Cabbages and cauliflowers

Plant in March for harvest in August or September. You cannot overfeed these vegetables and you must leave plenty of room for them to grow in well-drained soil and in a sunny spot. Slugs and snails need to be kept at bay and cabbages need to be dusted with cabbage dust every three weeks.

Carrots

Water ground well before sowing seeds. Simply push down into the ground around your young plant. Plant four cm deep. When first shoots appear dust with cabbage dust to prevent them being eaten by insects. Sudden rain or deep watering on dry beds can cause carrots to split in the ground.

Celery

To blanch bunches of celery, wrap newspapers around each bunch and tie. Leave for about three weeks before using them. If you do not need to use a whole plant, simply cut the required number of stalks off and leave the plant in the soil to grow. You can do the same with lettuce.

Garlic

Plant garlic bulbs between your vegetable rows and prevent disease.

Leeks

Cut the root part off and plant in good soil to produce spring onions.

Onions

Onion plants like to be planted close together. Never mulch onions as the bulbs will go mouldy.

Melons, cucumbers, pumpkins, zucchinis, marrows

These no longer need a large orchard area to roam over, as now there are restrained growers like butternut and compact bush types. Sowing time and cultivation are the same as for marrows. Pinch the leader of each shoot to induce lateral growths, which bear female flowers. The laterals can be, in turn, pinched to encourage further fruiting laterals. Zucchinis are best picked while still young and tender. Cucumbers are best if picked before they turn yellow. Soak seeds between a warm flannel, or in cotton wool for a few days before planting.

Picking pumpkins

When you are picking pumpkins and squashes for storage, leave the stem intact or at least six to eight cm of it. They then keep much better.

Parsnips

Parsnips need well-worked soil free from lumps and stones. They take five to six months to mature but can be harvested as needed over a three-month period. Always use fresh seed as parsnip seed is erratic in germination. Sow the seed thickly and later thin to stand three cm apart. Keep well watered and add liquid manure weekly. Sowing time: From early spring to early autumn in temperate areas or until late summer in cool districts. In the tropics, sowings are usually from late summer to early winter. Cultivation of parsnips is similar to carrots with improved results from well-composted soil. Seed needs firming down to ensure contact with soil moisture.

Peas

Peas need a well-limed soil prepared as for beans. For worthwhile cropping, sow dwarf types closely, preferably in a spade-wide furrow with seeds only three to four cm apart. In this case, fertiliser is sprinkled along the row base, then covered with a few centimetres of soil. Scatter the seed and cover with only two cm of soil unless the latter is light and very quick draining.

Climbing telephone, sugar, snow and snap peas are ideal for trellises where space is limited. Late sown peas are often inflicted with powdery mildew. Don't despair; harvest the whitened pods and you will find healthy peas inside.

Potatoes

To prepare the ground for potatoes, dig the whole bed over thoroughly and add a light dressing of blood and bone. Mark out rows and dig a shallow trench to plant the tubers in. Before planting, sprinkle more blood and bone along the trenches and work in with the hoe. Do not plant near the tomato bed.

Radishes

These are quick and easy to grow, and are excellent for children's gardens. They are best in a well-composted soil. Water regularly. Apply liquid manure or soluble fertilisers.

Rhubarb

Rhubarb should be divided and replanted every two years.

Silverbeet

In some areas these are referred to as spinach, but they are tougher, longer cropping plants with broad whitish stems and glossy rather than dull matt foliage. Six to eight plants are usually sufficient for the average family. Sow at any time except where winters are cold, which causes autumn and early winter plantings to run to seed in spring. Give silverbeet a well-composted, limey soil and, when established, fortnightly feeding with soluble plant food. Harvest by twisting and pulling leaves from ground level, leaving at least four near-mature leaves per plant. Over-picking weakens the plants.

Spinach

This has a softer texture than silverbeet. Sowing time: From late February to early spring to make its growth through cooler months or in cold districts. Cultivate as for silverbeet.

Sweet corn

Modern hybrids mature in a little over two months and are comparatively dwarfed

They are suitable for small gardens. Sow from early spring to midsummer. Prepare and cultivate as beans. Pollination is better in a block of short rows than a single long one. When sweet corn is about knee high, saturate the soil around the plants to ensure that the cobs are full and round.

Tomatoes
Allow them to ripen
The best tasting tomatoes are those that are allowed to ripen on the bush. Plant out seedlings when frosts are over. Plants set out when conditions are warm progress more rapidly than earlier plantings. Tomatoes prefer a well-composted soil with a dressing of complete plant food. Surface mulching maintains an even supply of moisture and when applied thickly encourages more roots to form. Set seedlings in several centimetres deeper than seed bed level. Taller types need staking and pruning to reduce excessive bushiness and improve fruit quality. Remove the laterals or side shoots that emerge from the leaf junctions. Use tomato dust frequently to combat fungus spot and tomato grub.

When buying young tomato plants
When buying tomato plants, try to get strong well-hardened off plants. The stems should have a bluish tinge to them. They should be about seven to eight weeks old and should have eight leaves, but not yet ten leaves. Plant the plants deeply up to the baby leaves as roots will form along the stem. Never plant tomatoes near potatoes. Special tomato powder or sulphur should be sprinkled on the plants to prevent disease.

When to pick tomatoes
Don't make the mistake of trimming off the leaves to expose tomatoes to the sun to hasten ripening. This will cause scalding of the skins. Pick as soon as they begin to redden, as if they are left on the vine to ripen they will lose most of their flavour.

Tomato tip
To encourage growth, thread copper wire through the stem about 3 cm from the ground. The bush will flourish.

Viruses on tomatoes
Tomatoes can be affected by certain viruses such as the mosaic virus (green mottling of leaves, sunken brown patches under the skin of fruit). They are spread during operations such as pruning, but are also on smokers' fingers, because most tobacco contains this virus. Smokers should wash thoroughly before touching the plants.

Problems will increase year by year if tomatoes or related crops are planted continuously in the same place. A four-year interval is a good idea.

Turnips
The turnip often suffers prejudice because of confusion with the stronger flavoured swede. White or purple top turnips are very sweet, especially when grown quickly through the cooler months. Sow in temperate and cool climates, in late winter.

Garden pests and diseases
Keep your garden free from pests the organic way
What is the best way to keep pests out of garden beds? The answer is easy – instead of fighting nature, make nature work for you. It just requires a little planning beforehand.

Monitor your pests
Early detection and diagnosis of pest infestations will allow you to make pest control decisions before the problem gets out of hand. Make weekly inspections of plants in all

sections of the garden and the greenhouse. Most of the insects considered common vegetable pests undergo a developmental process known as metamorphosis, which simply means that the insect changes form during its life.

Metamorphosis
Complete metamorphosis consists of four stages – egg, larva, pupa and adult.

Egg stage
The insect is immobile during this stage. A larva hatches from the egg. The larval stage is the growth stage and frequently the pest stage of insect life. This is especially true of moths, butterflies and true flies.

Larva
The insect changes into an adult and enters the pupa stage. The insect is immobile during this pupal or changeover period.

Pupa
Immature insects called nymphs hatch from eggs. Nymphs damage plants and reduce vegetable quality by sucking plant juices.

Adults
They may or may not feed in the same way and on the same plants as larvae. Beetles have chewing mouthparts and, like many grubs (beetle larvae), are capable of causing great damage to vegetables. Moths and butterflies, on the other hand, have mouthparts designed for siphoning and are unable to damage plants.

Identify pests
Correctly identifying the insects and other pests that attack vegetables is the first step towards controlling these pests effectively. Problems can be chronic unless recognised and corrected.

All-round non-toxic spray for insect pests
4 hot chillies
2 cloves garlic
4 large onions

Chop up ingredients and cover with soapy water. Leave for twenty-four hours. Strain liquid off. Add five litres water.

Another simple spray
Soak stinging nettles in boiling water and allow to soak for a couple of weeks.
    Place in spray container and use it on the pests.

Ant deterrent mixture
Place the following mixture in small flat containers around the garden. Ants will flock to it:

½ cup water
1 cup sugar
Boil for five minutes, stirring to make sugar dissolve.
Add one tablespoon Borax.

Bull ants
Pour kerosene down the nests.

Deter birds in the garden
Keep birds from seeds and seedlings and cats from uprooting them by covering the rows with wide strips of wire netting or chicken wire, bent into tunnel formation so that the centre is about twelve cm above the soil.

Deter pests in the garden
A combination of weak tea and a couple of drops of ammonia and dishwashing detergent sprayed on your plants makes an excellent pest deterrent.

Diseased plants
Never put diseased plants in your compost bin or heap. All you'll end up doing is bringing the disease back into your garden. So toss diseased plants in the disposal bin instead.

For your outdoor protection . . .
Mosquitoes
Wear light, loose, long-sleeved clothing to prevent them getting at you, especially at dusk. Citronella is the best organic spray to keep mosquitoes away, or an over the counter low impact personal spray.

Sandflies
A few dabs of citronella on the skin will help to keep sandflies at bay. If bitten, equal quantities of cold tea and methylated spirits will ease the itching almost immediately.

Wasps
Locate the nest and liberally sprinkle cabbage powder around the area so that the wasps will take it into the queen in the nest on their feet. When activity around the hive has ceased in a couple of days, dig the queen out.

Home-made insecticide that is safe for pets
Grind the rind of two or three lemons and add two litres of water. Bring your mixture to a boil for one minute. Cover it and let it stand at room temperature overnight. Strain the mixture to remove the rind and pour it into a spray bottle. Store the mixture in the refrigerator.

Insecticide
2 tablespoons soap flakes
4 litres water
½ teaspoon vinegar

Mix until soap flakes dissolve. Spray over affected plants.

Liquid spray
Pour boiling water over cut-up rhubarb and cabbage leaves. Leave to cool. It will counteract many diseases.

Aphids

Aphids, or plant lice, feed on most vegetables. These insects cause the greatest damage when they suck juices from and inject saliva into plants. They can transmit viruses that cause diseases. Adults are soft-bodied, pear-shaped, and may or may not have wings. Aphids may be green, pink, yellow or black. Nymphs resemble adults but are smaller and always wingless. These pests usually feed in clusters. A fast jet of water from the hose will dislodge aphids from the plant. Ants and ladybirds love to feed on these juicy morsels, so encourage them.

One of the best ways of keeping the aphid population to a minimum is to plant lots of garlic in the garden. It has the added advantage of producing an extra crop for kitchen use.

Garlic chives have similar effect, so two or three clumps of them could also be added to the garden.

Boil onions in water and when cold, sprinkle the strained water around the plants.

An effective natural spray for aphids:

1 tablespoon Epsom Salts
1 teaspoon Condy's Crystals

Add to a bucket of water. Spray a little around the plant every fortnight or so.

When aphids attack the washing on the clothes-line

Smear a yellow plastic bucket with Vaseline. Hang it on the clothes-line. The aphids are attracted to the yellow bucket. They will stick to the Vaseline. Spray off with heavy jet of water from the hose.

Or place the washing with the aphids on it in a pillowslip. Put it in the dryer for a few minutes. Run it on hot.

Woolly aphids

The aphids cover themselves with a waxy, cotton-like material and group together to feed. They congregate at the base of the tree, often along the graft line. Soak cotton wool in methylated spirits and wipe off.

Birds

Birds are a delight in most gardens, but they can be nuisances. They scratch at your seedlings and uproot young plants. Use strips of aluminium foil tied on string. The strips tinkle together as the birds flutter about. The combination of glittering and noise will often scare the birds away.

Hang Chinese or Japanese 'windsongs', a very pleasant way to keep birds from where they are not wanted.

To keep the birds away from plants, place streamers in the bushes near the plants.

Cabbage caterpillar

The cabbage caterpillar feeds on the underside of leaves of cabbage, lettuce, spinach, beets, peas and tomatoes. It chews large, irregular holes through leaves. Moths lay greenish-white eggs on the upper surface of leaves. Larvae, or worms, are 2.5 to four cm long when full grown. Larvae are pale green with four thin, white lines along the back and a wide, pale line on each side of the body. The adult is a white butterfly with one or two black spots on each wing. This pest winters as a pupa, either on old plant refuse or on nearby posts or buildings. There are three or four generations per year.

Dust with cabbage/tomato dust.

Cabbage butterflies
Sprinkle garlic powder on the cabbage leaves to deter cabbage butterflies.

Cat and dog repellents
When cats or dogs exercise their territorial claim by urinating on, in and around doorways, wash away with hot water and a good disinfectant. Allow to dry.

Spray with one of the commercial deterrents available from hardware stores and garden supply shops.

If you have trouble with your own pet, or your neighbour's pet urinating or defecating in a particular spot on the garden, causing your plants to die and the garden to smell, plant the herb, *Coleus caninus*, a small perennial which deters them. It is an attractive plant with blue spiked flowers. When bruised or brushed it lets off a pungent smell.

Spray the garden with diluted citronella oil. Cats find the sharp lemon smell is unpleasant and overwhelms their sense of smell.

Citrus bud mite
This mite makes the fruit distorted. Simply remove offending fruit and destroy.

Codlin moth
For the organic gardener, the only satisfactory method of ridding yourself of codlin moth is to spray with pyrethrum. To avoid wiping out the pollinating bees, do it after sunset. Spray programs for codlin moth should begin about the time that the apple blossom begins to fall. Make sure that the male moth is on the wing as this indicates that the female is active. Unless the female moth is in the tree it is a waste of time to spray, and one must be aware that the pyrethrum will not kill any eggs that the female has already laid, so a further two or three sprayings are required at fortnightly intervals to ensure a high percentage of clean fruit.

Cutworm
Clean up the garden in autumn and dig over the soil in early spring to reduce breeding spots.

Plant marigolds around the vegie patch. This will offer your cutworm friends a fragrant alternative to the vegetables.

Add three tablespoons dishwashing detergent to the watering can and water the affected area thoroughly. The cutworm will surface and dry out.

Add the wood ashes from your fireplace and dig into the soil. Cutworm do not like the roughness of the wood ashes so hopefully they go into the next door neighbour's place. But adding the ashes to the soil also enhances the soil particularly for lime loving plants such as azaleas and camellias.

Earwigs
Earwigs rage in your garden at night and can leave plants decimated. It is easy to trap them by placing folded newspaper or a cardboard box in the garden. They crawl in and go to sleep all ready for you to incinerate in the morning – earwigs and all.

Locusts
Lay straw and mulch around your vegetables; the locusts will feed on the dead matter and leave your lovely green seedlings alone.

Make a fly trap

Cut any yellow plastic container into strips and apply Vaseline to each strip. Place in the pot plant. Little flies are attracted to the yellow colour and will come in their droves and become stuck.

Mealy bugs

Mealy bugs are white and sticky to touch. To control mealy bugs dip a cotton bud in methylated spirits and dab it on. If there are large numbers spray with pyrethrum.

Mozzie repellent plants

Grow pelargonium citrosum, tansy or wormwood near the BBQ to deter mosquitoes.

Prevent pest infestations in a greenhouse by:

- Maintaining a clean, closely mowed area around the greenhouse.
- Keeping the greenhouse clean and free of rubbish.
- Removing all plants and any plant debris, and cleaning the greenhouse thoroughly after each production cycle.
- Keeping doors, screens and ventilators in good repair.
- Inspecting new plants thoroughly to prevent introduction of insect or disease infested material into the greenhouse.
- Watching for leaks or pooled water that can lead to fungus infestations.
- Avoiding wearing yellow clothing as it is attractive to insects which can be carried into the greenhouse from outside.

Red spider

Beans and tomatoes, eggplant, cucumber and celery may be severely damaged. Red spiders are more active during hot, dry years. Adults are usually red, but may be yellow, or even green, and have four pairs of legs. The body is oval. Adults lay eggs on plants. The eggs hatch into young mites and suck plant juices. Affected leaves curl and drop from the plant prematurely. They appear sickly. When an infestation is severe, fine silk webs may entangle an entire plant, and moving spider mites can easily be seen in the webbing. Many generations may occur each year.

Scale

To get rid of scale, spray in spring with a mixture of the following:

4 litres of water
2 tablespoons white oil
2 tablespoons malathion

Repeat every ten days if necessary.

Slugs and snails

Slugs are active at night, leaving silvery slime trails that can be seen the next morning.
Ashes, sawdust and eggshells keep snails away.
Encourage lizards, as they love snails.
Ducks and chickens love to eat snails.
Snails love a beer and can be enticed into a trap if you put out a bowl of stale beer into the garden. The snails will come in the dozens, drink up and fall in and drown.
Another method of killing snails without using poisons is to wait for a damp and wet night and then to take the family on a snail hunt with torches. Stomp on the poor critters. Great fun.

Snail bait

Many snail baits are poisonous to children and pets. Place snail bait in jam tins on their side. The poison will be out of harm's way and the rain will not dissolve the bait.

Sawdust

Snails find it difficult to get anywhere on sawdust and so they hate it. Use it as mulch.

Surround annuals and perennials with sawdust, which will prevent the growth of weeds, keep the roots cool and conserve water. Add sulphate of ammonia to keep up the supply of nitrogen.

Slugs

Put a band of sawdust around the plants you wish to protect. Or get a pet duck.

Thrips

Thrips cause most severe damage in hot, dry years. Damage appears as white flecks or streaks on leaves. Thrips vary in colour from light to dark brown. Wings are narrow and fringed, giving them a feathery appearance.

Wandering Jew

Collect your urine overnight, place in a watering can and sprinkle it on wandering Jew, the gardener's curse. It will shrivel up and die.

Common pests and diseases
Fruit trees
Deal quickly and efficiently with diseases on your fruit trees.

Leaf curl
Leaf curl occurs when the leaf buds open and the tiny leaves appear.
Spray with Bordeaux Mixture before the leaves appear.

Blossom blight
Blossom blight and brown rot make the fruit decay from the inside as they ripen.
Spray with a Bordeaux Mixture.

Mummies
Mummies are last year's fruit which whither and die on the tree. Prune and destroy.

Apple scab
The skin of the apple becomes disfigured with ugly brown and black spots.
Rake all fallen fruit and leaves and destroy. If you spot the spots, cut from tree and destroy. Spray with a fungicide before the leaves emerge.

Soft brown scale
The first sign that a citrus tree is infected with scale pests is a soft black sooty mould which covers the leaves. The tree must be sprayed or they will take over. Spray with white oil – one part white oil to fifty parts water. Ensure you spray beneath the foliage where the pests gather.

Weeds

Weeds in concrete paths

Pour boiling salted water or vinegar over weeds in concrete paths.

Weeding out the weeds

Encourage a canopy of shrubs and trees, as they reduce light and the less light the less weeds.

Plant a covering of ground covers close together, leaving no room for weeds to grow.

Use mulch to cover all open ground.

Remove weeds before they have a chance to flower and spread their seed.

Remember: the difference between a flower and a weed is a judgement.

Whiteflies

Whiteflies feed on a wide variety of vegetables. They can be found everywhere.

Host plants include beans, tomatoes, eggplant and cucumber. Adults are very small sucking insects with two pairs of broadly rounded wings. They look like tiny moths and may fly up in a cloud when disturbed. The wings and body are covered with a snow white, waxy powder. Eggs, which are almost microscopic, are laid on the underside of leaves. Young nymphs are small, flat, and hard to see. They cause the leaves to become discoloured and fall from a plant, which may become stunted. Whiteflies secrete honeydew on plants resulting in an unsightly black sooty mould.

Creatures great and small

Bats are good

Bats are one of the most beneficial creatures in nature. They are voracious insectivores with an appetite for mosquitoes and many other flying pests. Encourage them! In fact, the only thing that's better at getting rid of mosquitoes is a good cold spell.

Beneficial earthworms

Earthworms are a lawn and garden's best friend. If your yard has a lot of worms, avoid overworking your soil with a fork and spade. Instead, apply a layer of leaf mulch. Worms love it and they'll till the soil for you. They aerate it as they tunnel through, moving nitrogen and other nutrients down to the plants' roots.

Encouraging earthworms

Worms are very good for your garden. They:

- Redistribute lime, gypsum and fertilisers in the soil.
- Release plant nutrients.
- Aerate the soil.
- Allow roots and water to move more effectively through the compacted soil layers.

Each earthworm is both male and female and is very effective in reproducing. They each produce eggs which are stored in a cocoon. They look like small seed. Give plenty of food and moisture and let nature do the rest.

Encourage insects

Encourage insects that prey on pests into your garden, or which use pests as the host for their young. To get them into your garden, try growing herbs with umbrella-style flowers like coriander, fennel, parsley and Queen Anne's lace. Their flowers attract parasitic wasps (good wasps) that like laying their eggs into grubs, aphids and other pests in the garden. The eggs hatch, and the larvae feast on the host. These flowering herbs will also encourage ladybirds, which also enjoy chewing on aphids.

Make your own bird feeder

Back yard birds won't know the difference between a fancy, store-bought bird feeder and one that's home-made. Here's how to make one out of an empty milk carton:

- Cut openings on opposite sides of a clean carton and coat with non-toxic paint.
- Glue icy-pole stick shingles onto the roof.
- For a perch, poke holes below the openings and slip a dowel through the holes.
- Fill the bottom of the feeder with birdseed mix.
- You can make your own mix by combining a variety of nuts and seeds, such as sunflower seeds, millet, thistle seeds and yellow corn.
- Then hang the feeder with wire in a spot that's easy to view but far enough away from fences or posts to thwart predators.

Small animals

Chickens or ducks! Letting them loose in your garden will just about guarantee you'll have no snails or slugs left. Plus they'll dig up and eat other insect eggs on or just under the soil.

Gardening in small spaces
Container gardens

The rule to follow when planting in containers is—the more the merrier, the tighter fit, the better! Pots are for instant gratification. You don't have to worry about how big the plants are going to get next year. Just make sure you use a good potting mix, water once or twice a day, and fertilise weekly.

Pot plants

Pot plants have many advantages. They come in a variety of sizes and prices, they are easy to transport and they do not require immediate planting after purchase. Plants in large containers should have young and healthy foliage. The root system should not be protruding from the bottom of the pot. You should not be able to see the roots at the top of the pot. Choose a well-balanced and compact plant. Avoid plants with dead branches and leaves. Avoid leggy plants (with a lot of stem).

Watering plants in containers

Plants growing in containers can dry out much faster than those growing in open ground. It is best to check the top two to three cm of the soil's surface regularly, especially on hot or windy days. Frequent checking of the potting mix avoids the possibility of over-watering but if you leave it too long, you run the risk of the plant drying out and wilting. Dunk the plant in a bucket of water for a simple but effective way to revive it. Keep the pot under water until all the air bubbles have stopped coming up. The soil will then be saturated. Don't leave the pot standing in water as this may lead to root rot. A good soaking is much better for the plant than an occasional light sprinkling. The thinner the leaf, the more water the plant needs to survive.

Avoid using a strong jet of water from the hose as it will gouge out the soil. Use a soaker adjustment on your watering system. Soak plants in a large bucket until the bubbles cease.

When using a liquid fertiliser for your pot plants, hold the pot over a bucket – the water that runs through can then be used on the next pot, saving water and fertiliser.

If your soil is heavy, add peat moss, sand or mulch to make it light and help it to drain well.

Water pot plants in hot weather by filling a plastic bottle with water and turning it upside down. This will soak the soil and water the plant slowly. Only water them when they are dry. Test the soil by digging into it with your thumb.

Care should be exercised in watering plants confined to pots during winter, because evaporation is slow. When water is necessary, apply it during the warmest part of the day so that the excess is drained off before nightfall.

Repotting

Sooner or later the roots of the plant in a container fill all available space and the plant becomes potbound. Growth slows and the roots become entwined and coiled, the plant looses vigour and dies. The plant needs to be removed from its container and put in a bigger one, the next size up. If it is a large plant and it is not practicable to put it in a bigger pot, then the same effect can be achieved by root pruning and replanting in fresh soil.

Make your own potting mix

Blend equal parts good garden soil, well-rotted manure or compost, and vermiculite (available at garden centres). The manure provides the nutrients and the cork-like vermiculite keeps the soil light so that delicate roots get enough oxygen.

Azaleas

If you wish to plant azaleas in a cement tub, you need to treat the container before planting. Place 125g of alum into the tub. Fill the tub with cold water and leave it to neutralise the lime in the cement.

Orchids

If you leave orchids in a pot, they will eventually become overcrowded, exhaust the nutrients, and stop flowering. They will need repotting to restore flowering. An orchid is composed of a swollen part called a pseudo bulb which is full of moisture. The other swollen parts, which appear dead, but are not, are called back bulbs. Cut off as many of the dead roots as you can and divide the pseudo and back bulbs up. Tip the orchid out and tease apart the tough, large roots that the orchid uses to hang onto trees with.

Next drag the orchids apart with your hands. You may need to cut the woody part in the middle in order to separate the plants.

The potting soil is not really a soil but simply bark with a few nutrients, which is similar to the conditions they would grow in when on a tree trunk. To pot, place the pseudo bulbs on one side of the pot and fill around it with potting mix. Don't bury the pseudo bulb, just the roots. Dunk the pot in water for a couple of hours. Keep the plant out of direct sun. Remove any back bulbs that are soft and squashy. Cut off the good ones that have root systems and pot them in. They should start to shoot and flower after repotting.

Maidenhair fern

Epsom Salts sprinkled lightly around the surface after watering helps to keep maidenhair fern in good condition.

Staghorn ferns

Put banana peels or fruit into the centre of the plant, to add potassium. The brown growths on staghorns are spore-producing areas and are natural. The staghorn fern can get huge and weigh over a hundred kg and more. It is best attached to a strong tree, such as a live oak, in a shady location. If attached to a tree, the fern does not need food at all.

Geraniums and pelargonium

Geraniums make a colourful and easy-to-tend display and may be grown in pots, hanging baskets or in the garden. Geraniums, more correctly termed pelargonium, have adapted themselves superbly to many different habitats and climatic zones. Many are found in the winter rainfall area and prefer a Mediterranean climate.

Inexpensive houseplants

Grow your own houseplants from the seeds of avocados, orange pits, or carrot and turnip tops. Take an onion that has begun sprouting and plant it in a pot. It will continue to grow tops, which may be used in soups and salads. In autumn take your parsley and other spices from the garden and plant them in containers and take inside. You will have them for the winter.

Cement tubs

Cement tubs contain lime and not all plants like it. To prevent azaleas and camellias from dying in the pot, block the drainage holes and fill the pots with water to which 125g of alum has been added. Leave to soak for a week, empty, and plant.

Put as many plants as possible into a container

The rule for planting in containers is the more the merrier. You don't have to worry about how big the plants are going to get next year. Pots are for instant gratification.

Use a good potting mix, water once or twice a day, and fertilise weekly.

Keep pot plants clean and free from dust

The fresh, bright green appearance of well-grown pot plants may be attributed in a large measure to the practice of keeping the leaves clean and free from dust. The plant breathes through the pores in the leaves, much as we do through our skin. When the pores become closed, the function of the leaves becomes impaired, and the plant begins to look dull and eventually shows yellow leaves.

Wetting agents

Consider applying a wetting agent to your potting mix. It acts to open up the potting mix and allows water to be fully absorbed. Mix water-storing crystals into your potting mix. The crystals absorb the water, so you won't need to water as often.

Older plants versus young plants

The most likely cause of older plant leaves dropping is under-watering, whereas the most likely cause of younger plant leaves going yellow is over-watering.

Over-watering

Keep the pot well drained. There must be a certain amount of air in the soil if it is to be a satisfactory medium for the growth of plants, but when too much water is added, the air is driven out, and as a result the roots perish. A container that does not allow the surplus water to drain off after every watering will cause the soil to become saturated and turn sour, and as a consequence the roots will die.

Stand your pots in sand

It is bad practice to stand a saucer of water under potted plants. It prevents essential drainage. Instead, stand the pot in a saucer of sand. If the sand shows moisture, the plant has ample water. When the sand dries, water the plant again.

Dry leaves and faded blooms

Remove dry leaves and faded blooms from the plants. Do not be afraid to nip off the ends of branches that have grown so long that they spoil the shape of the plants. They may be used as cuttings and are easily rooted.

Indoor plants

* Plants growing indoors require plenty of fresh air.
* Rooms should be well ventilated daily.
* Foul air, lack of moisture, and a high temperature, should be carefully guarded against, especially in winter when doors and windows are closed and it is a temptation to over-heat the house.
* Dry heat from air-conditioning absorbs moisture from the plants, and fills the lung-like pores of the leaves with dust from the atmosphere.
* Under such conditions, house plants often perish.
* Prevent deadly dryness of the air by placing pots on sand-trays, the bottoms of which are covered with three cm of sand or moss that is kept damp.
* Sun-loving plants must be given the sunny positions, while the shade-loving ones can be placed in the shady places.
* Researchers believe pot plants are one of the cheapest and easiest ways to improve air quality.

Indoor pests

Red spider

Red spider in pot plants can be reduced by wiping the leaves, top and bottom, with a cloth dipped in soft soapy water.

Mealy bug

To reduce mealy bugs in pot plants, place moth balls under the plants.

Indoor plant food

Add a few drops of liquid detergent to the water when you water indoor plants.

To ensure that house plants get enough nitrogen, water once a month with a solution of two litres of water and an envelope of gelatine.

Plants as decontaminators

Outdoor plants are known to absorb air and soil pollutants and detoxify them. Plants and soil micro-organisms are used in the remediation of contaminated soils. Some indoor plants can reduce concentrations of air-borne contaminants. Indoor pot plants help to improve the quality of the indoor environment. They ensure that buildings have clean air and look beautiful. House plants could be the solution to 'sick classroom syndrome' because they turn the gas into oxygen, thereby improving the air quality. Research suggests pupils would do better in their exams and coursework if pot plants were placed in classrooms. In crowded classrooms, carbon dioxide levels are often high. High levels of carbon dioxide in classrooms impair a child's capacity to learn.

Shiny plant leaves

To make the leaves shiny, try one of the following:

* Wipe an indoor plant's leaves with a cloth dipped in milk.
* Rub leaves with castor oil or mineral oil.
* Mix one tablespoon of glycerine in with the water when you water the plant.
* Wipe leaves with a mixture of mayonnaise and water.

Yellow leaves

Put your plants out in the rain when the tips of their leaves turn brown. It is a sure sign that the soil has been kept too wet or too dry. Over-stimulating with manure will also bring about this state, but over-manuring induces a sickly (yellowish) appearance.

Hanging baskets

To water hanging baskets use a watering head with a long handle, or have a hanging line that can be lowered for watering. You can put hanging baskets on pulleys to make watering easy.

Watering hanging baskets

Be careful not to neglect plants grown in hanging baskets. As they are higher up where the air is warmer and the evaporation greater, they need more water than plants below. The most satisfactory way of watering them is by taking down the basket and letting it stand in a vessel of water until the soil has become thoroughly saturated.

Do not leave it to stand soaking in the water. Hanging baskets tend to dry out more quickly than conventional pots. Moss lined baskets are especially thirsty, and the more you water, the faster the soil loses nutrients. Fertilise hanging baskets every two weeks or so to keep the plants in them looking full and lush.

Old umbrella frames

An old umbrella frame can be used for garden decoration by stripping the cover from it, painting the frame to prevent rust, then planting the opened umbrella into a large pot of soil or in the garden. Grow ivy or a flowering creeper beside it and trail the runners up over the frame. This makes a spectacular display.

Small gardens

If you don't have enough space for a conventional vegetable plot, try planting vegies in the flower garden or even among shrubs, or use trellises to grow climbing plants like pole beans. Since many vegetable plants are as attractive as they are delicious, they'll accent and blend in with your landscaping. You can edge a flowerbed in lettuces or grow oregano, basil, onions, chives and many more herbs under your shrubs. Anything goes, as long as it looks good.

Compost for a small garden

Use a wooden box and keep it outside. Add peat moss. Add water. Add potato peels, vegetable and kitchen scraps. Add soil/peat moss. Repeat. Allow to rest until contents are crumbly.

Growing potatoes in a garbage bin

A productive way of growing new potatoes without taking up the whole back garden.

- Cut drainage holes in a plastic ten garbage bin.
- Add drainage and a layer of potting mix.
- Place two seed potatoes on potting mix.
- Add a layer of straw.
- Take a bag of mushroom compost, three or four spadefuls of topsoil and mix with well-rotted poultry manure.
- Add to container.
- Add seaweed if it is available.

- Container should then be about half full.
- As the potato foliage emerges and grows, add more straw.
- Harvest after the plants flower; you will be surprised at how many spuds you get.
- The soil in the garbage bin will be a rich addition to the compost heap.

Window boxes

Window boxes filled directly with potting mix, rather than soil, and planted straight to the box, give best results. The best-sized window box is about forty cm long, with a depth of fifteen to twenty cm. The plants need to have enough room to grow in the potting mix without drying out.

If you make a window box yourself, you need wood about 2.5 cm thick.

Hardwood is good, and pine is fine, although it will need to be painted with preservative, including the insides. Be careful of the choice of preservative so that it will not damage the plants. Always remember to drill drainage holes in the base of your window box, about five to ten cm apart, to ensure good drainage.

Leaving a gap of about 2.5cm between the top of the potting mix and the top of the window box is best for watering your plants. To have a permanent display in your window box, rotate lobelia, pelargonium and dianthus. Other long-flowering plants include nasturtium, petunia, impatiens, Sweet Alice, begonia and marigold.

Garden tasks

Hedges

To allow the sunlight to reach all the foliage of your hedge, and to prevent it from thinning out at the bottom, prune your hedge so that it's narrower at the top.

Mowing the lawn

In spring and summer, set your mower height so that the cut grass is at least eight cm tall. This will prevent the roots being exposed to the scorching sun and drying out.

Pruning

Pruning flowering shrubs in late autumn or early winter is not recommended, because it could make the plant more liable to be damaged by frosts.

When is the best time to prune?

Follow these green rules of thumb:

Spring bloomers: Prune spring-flowering shrubs immediately after they finish flowering. As these shrubs usually develop their flower buds throughout the growing season, a late-season pruning would remove buds and reduce the number of flowers the following year.

Summer bloomers: Prune summer-flowering shrubs in early spring. These shrubs bloom from new growth, so prune them before you see 'green' in the spring.

Pruning hydrangeas

Pruning hydrangeas in early winter will encourage strong leaf and flower growth for the next summer. Cut out all the dead and spindly wood, taking them as close to the ground as possible. Remove any superfluous canes so that you have an open plant with seven to ten canes for spring development. When cutting back canes, keep to two or three fat buds at the base of the plant, as these will provide the flowers next year. Spread half a cup of blood-and-bone at the base of the plant to encourage strong spring growth.

Pruning roses
When pruning your roses, keep the centre open to let the sunshine in and keep black spot out.

Pruning shrubs
Spring flowering
Prune spring-flowering shrubs right after they finish flowering, as these shrubs usually develop their flower buds throughout the growing season. A late-season pruning would remove these buds and reduce the number of flowers the following year.

Summer flowering
Prune summer-flowering shrubs in early spring. These shrubs bloom from new growth, so prune them before you see growth or 'green' in the spring.

Autumn and winter
In most cases, pruning flowering shrubs in late autumn or early winter isn't recommended, because it could make the plant more prone to winter damage.

Pruning variegated shrubs
Prune green shoots on your variegated shrubs as soon as they appear. If you don't, the green will take over and the tree will revert to green.

Shrubs and flowers
Annuals
To prevent seeds from maturing (flowering often slows when seeds ripen), pinch off flowers as they fade. If stems begin to yellow and look scraggly, you won't harm the plant by shearing it to half its size. Most annuals will reward you with fresh foliage and sometimes a second bloom.

Bulbs
Only buy bulbs in the correct planting season.

Planting bulbs
Till the soil to a depth of at least twenty cm. Dig a planting hole five cm deeper than the depth indicated on the planting instructions. Place a tablespoon of complete fertiliser into the bottom of the planting hole and cover with two cm soil. Plant two or three bulbs to a hole in a random way. Cover with soil. Water.

Storing bulbs
Store flower bulbs over winter in a dry place where the air is circulating in an old nylon stocking.

Dividing bulbs
Daffodils
Daffodils and jonquils can be left in the ground for three or four years and will still flower each year. It is time to divide the bulbs when the flowers become smaller or don't come up. Dig when the foliage has dried out. Separate only those bulbs that fall away easily from the mother bulb.

Common bulbs

Alliums
All members of the onion family, and a very large tribe.

Anemones
Brightly coloured, they make an impressive display and are wonderful cut flowers.

Bluebells
Arching stems of softly fragrant blue blooms. Plant in heavy soil and light shade. They need periods of cold to flower.

Crocus
The flower of saffron, the most expensive spice in the world. Do not do well in warm climates.

Daffodils
Come in a variety of colours from gold to white. Grow in a little shade and leave foliage to whither itself.

Freesias
The sweetest scented of all bulbs.
Plant in the sun on well-drained soil.
Easy to grow.

Hyacinths
Sweetly fragrant. Grow in pots or in the garden.

Iris
Need sunshine and good well-drained soil.
Come in all shades of blue, yellow and white.

Ixias
Corn lily. Warm coloured flowers on long, graceful stems. Flowers close up at night. Easy to grow.

Lachenalias
Soldier boys. Yellow, orange, maroon and green tubular bells, they flower late winter in warm climates. Good soil, sun or semi-shade.

Ranunculus
Kaleidoscope of colours. Need rich soil and sunshine.

Sparaxis
Harlequin flowers in brilliant colours. Prefer full sun. Close up at night.

Tritonias
South African cousins of the freesia, without the perfume.
Bowl-shaped bright orange flowers on six or eight stems, they flower in between the spring and summer bulbs.

Dahlias
In early winter when the foliage has turned brown dig and store your tubers. Allow them to dry out. To divide, use a sharp knife and cut the new tubers so that each part has a crown attached to it and at least one dormant eye. Store in sand in a dry place.

Naturalise your bulbs
Try naturalising your bulbs by planting them at the base of your deciduous trees. Make them look like they were scattered by nature, not by design. They can be left for years

undisturbed. Cast the bulbs about the ground by scattering and then plant them where they fall. Mulch lightly after they flower, but allow foliage to whither naturally.

Camellias and azaleas
White azaleas last longer than coloured ones.
If leaves turn yellow, a light sprinkling of sulphur helps

Chrysanthemums
Make chrysanthemums branch close to the ground by topping to about thirty cm. Pinch out as side shoots grow up. Don't allow them to get leggy. Feed and water well. When they have finished flowering, cut back to just above ground level to allow them to make plenty of side shoots, which can be divided and planted out later.

Gerberas
Gerberas come from South Africa and as such, love the sunshine. They are colourful and can stand alone as a single stem or look spectacular in a posy. They should be sown in the sunniest position in the garden. They need rich, well-drained soil which has been enriched with rotted manure. Plant in a sheltered frost-free position as they often go on to flower in the colder months. Sow in shallow drills when the soil has warmed up. Cover with seed raising mixture to about six cm. The plants are ready to transplant in about eight weeks. It is important that the crown is not covered at any time. Gerberas can be left in the same position for about three seasons. Old plants should be divided and replanted.

Hedges
Hedges are a cheap way of adding structure and form to the garden.
Plants with small leaves and naturally dense growth make good hedge plants.

Suitable hedging species
Buxus, camellia, cotoneaster, cupressus, murraya, oleander, photinia, plumbago, raphiolepis, rondeletia, viburnum.

Planting a hedge
Make a trench to the depth that you require in an area that has been fortified with organic matter. Space your plants at intervals about half of the width of the mature plant. Prune at planting time, the aim being to develop a compact bush with strong basal shoots. The aim is to produce a dwarf hedge that grows higher and wider as the years go by.

Hydrangeas
To make your hydrangeas blue, save old steel wool and throw them under the bushes.
To make hydrangeas pink, sprinkle a little lime on the soil.

Lilies
Did you know that the lily family includes onions and yuccas?

Native plants
Remember that native plants require less maintenance and less water.

Posies
Include some of the following flowers in your posy:

Friendship posy

Geranium	everlasting friendship
Larkspur	purity
Pansy	you occupy my thoughts
Zinnia	thoughts of absent friends
Ivy	fidelity

I love you posy

White camellia	perfect loveliness
Honeysuckle	sweet bonds of love
Rose	love
Forget-me-not	true love

Get well posy

Blue salvia	thinking of you
Rosemary	remembrance
Sweet basil	good wishes
Pansy	you occupy my thoughts

Good luck posy

Blossom	hope
Pansy	you occupy my thoughts
Violet	purple, the colour of triumph
Daisy (white)	good luck
Sweet basil	good wishes

Roses

Did you know that members of the rose family include cherries, pyracantha, roses and strawberries?

To stop mildew lightly dust with sulphur. Less is best.

Home-made fertiliser for roses

2 teaspoons of sulphur of ammonia
3 teaspoons super phosphate
1 teaspoon sulphate of potash
½ teaspoon sulphate of iron
½ teaspoon Epsom Salts

Mix together and scatter around the bush. Repeat every three weeks.

Blight-free roses

Prune roses, and keep the centre open, to keep them blight-free.

This lets in the sunshine which keeps out black spot and other such blights that love cool, moist, shady places.

Self-seeding plants

It is a good idea to have self-seeding plants so that you will be constantly surprised each year when the plants come up of their own accord in the most interesting places.

Growing plants
Basic potting mix
2 parts organic material such as bark, sawdust, humus
1 part sandy soil
1 cup complete fertiliser
1 cup lime

Mix together well.

Seeding mix
2 parts basic mix
1 part perlite or vermiculite

Acid mix
For azaleas, rhododendrons, camellias.

4 parts textured peat moss
1 part composted leaf mould

Bedding plants
Bedding plants are any plants that are grown in a garden bed. They can be seedlings of any type – vegetable, flower or herb. When choosing bedding plants, select compact plants with good leaf colour and vigorous appearance. Never choose those that are crowded and straggly. Plant after winter, when the soil has warmed up.

Planting
- Prepare soil by removing the weeds and turning over the soil. Rake.
- Remove plants from containers by carefully turning it over, pushing gently on the bottom, and being careful to keep the roots intact.
- Lightly separate the roots so that they will grow outward into the soil.
- Dig a generous hole and position the plant so that it is at the same level as it was in the container.
- Leave room for growth as plants will spread.
- Form a watering basin around each plant.
- Water each one in separately.
- Spread a mulch of shredded bark, compost or peat moss to reduce evaporation.

Cuttings
When you are striking cuttings in water use a small china or pottery container. Place a piece of charcoal in the water to help to keep it pure. The cuttings should be removed and potted up as soon as the roots are defined.

Accept cuttings and seedlings from other gardeners, as they will always remind you of that person when they flower, for years to come. Make your own cuttings and propagate your own plants to save money spent at the nursery.

Taking cuttings
Cuttings will produce plants exactly like those you took them from, whereas seeds may produce plants that are unlike their parents, and take longer to grow.

Share your garden with your friends and vice versa

Ask your friend if you can take cuttings from their plants and start your own. All you need are a few branch tips. Wrap them in moist paper and set them in a special potting mix. Keep all cuttings cool and moist until you can plant them.

Softwood cuttings

Softwood cuttings can be taken from spring until late summer during the active growing season. They are the easiest and quickest rooting of stem cuttings. Take them from soft, succulent new growth that has some flexibility but does break when bent sharply. Softwood cuttings root best if you can snap them off cleanly from the parent plant. If they crush or bend, the wood is too old.

Semi-hardwood cuttings

Semi-hardwood cuttings can be taken from the same plants, later in the season. They are taken after the active growing season or after a growth flush, usually in summer or early autumn, when growth is firm enough to snap when the twig is bent sharply. Look for normal, healthy growth. Avoid either fat or spindly branches. You should cut just below a leaf bud (node), but some plants can be cut between nodes.

Rooting cuttings

For both types of cutting (softwood and semi-hardwood), the procedures are the same:

- Start cuttings in a container of some sort, a pot, can, box or cup.
- Poke or punch holes in its bottom so excess water will be able to drain out.
- Fill the container with a blend of half sand and pre-moistened peat moss
- Firm it down slightly so that the surface is five cm below the top of the container.
- Remove cuttings from their moist wrapping.
- Make a clean, slanting cut with a sharp knife just below a leaf or bud.
- Dip individual ends in hormone rooting powder.
- If the leaves are very large, with scissors snip off about half of each leaf.
- Strip off any lower leaves so only the stem will be buried in the planting mix.
- Use a pencil to poke a hole in the sand and peat-moss mixture and set in the cutting.
- Firm the soil around the stem.
- Cover them with transparent kitchen wrap, a plastic bag, or a jar.
- Remove this cover once a day for a few minutes to allow air to circulate, then cover again.

It may take from a few days to a few weeks for the cuttings to root. To test, gently pull on the young plant, if it resists, then the roots are holding it into the soil. When new growth appears, the cutting has rooted. Gently lift each one out, carefully removing some of the soil until you see roots. Transplant the cutting to a slightly larger container to give the roots more growing room.

Carnation and rose cuttings

Split stems and place a grain of wheat between the split, place cutting in mouth for a few seconds, and then plant in the potting mix.

Daphne cuttings

Place the bottom of the cutting in rooting powder. Plant in damp, sandy soil and then transfer the whole lot into a plastic bag and seal. Plant out when roots appear.

Hydrangea cuttings

In late summer/autumn use hard-wood cuttings, about ten cm long. Remove the foliage, but leave the buds. Cut squarely below the bottom node and make a slanting cut above the top node. Plant the cutting in potting mix in a flowerpot. Place in a warm position and keep the soil damp. By the springtime they should be rooted.

Lavender cuttings

Take a cutting eight to ten cm from the tip. Remove the flowers and bottom leaves from the stem. Dip cuttings in hormone powder. Use an old pencil to make a hole in prepared propagating mixture. Place cutting in the hole about a finger's width apart. Place a plastic bag over the top of the pot to keep humidity high.

Mulch

Once the plants are in the ground, place shredded mulch around them to retain moisture and control weeds. Water new plants thoroughly for the first few days to help them settle in.

How to plant seeds in containers

Use a commercial potting mix or combine equal parts of light topsoil, fine ground bark or peat moss and sand. Sift the soil. Bake in the oven for thirty minutes in order to kill any weed, seeds and fungus in the soil. You may prefer to start seed in a sterile medium such as vermiculite.

- Fill the container almost to the top with the soil.
- Firm it with the palm of your hand.
- Check the seed packet directions for recommended planting depth.
- Sift a layer of soil on top (most fine seeds should not be covered).
- Lay a dampened piece of newspaper over the soil, unless seed packet indicates the seed need light to sprout.
- Water carefully.
- Place the container in a warm spot, but not in direct sun.
- Keep the soil mix moist, but not soaking wet.
- When the first sprouts appear, remove the paper and put the container in more light or filtered sun.
- When the seedlings have developed two sets of true leaves, transplant them to five cm pots.

Suitable containers

Almost anything that will hold soil and has provision for water to drain off will do for a seed-starting container. Your choice will depend on what you have available and how many seeds you have to plant. Plastic nursery flats will accommodate the largest number of seeds. You may also use:

- Clay or plastic pots
- Aluminium foil pans (the sort sold for kitchen use)
- Styrofoam or plastic cups
- Cut-down milk cartons
- Shallow wooden boxes
- Old ice cube trays

Remember to punch holes for drainage in the bottom of any container that will hold water. If you use containers that have held plants before give them a thorough cleaning.

Empty strawberry, cherry tomato and other berry containers make excellent propagating containers. They have holes in the base and the lids make the propagator complete.

Place a coffee filter in the pot before filling it with soil. This will prevent soil spillage from the drainage holes.

Always use moist soil when transplanting and repotting.

Newspaper
Line seed boxes with several thicknesses of newspaper before filling with soil. This prevents the moisture from drying out too quickly.

Egg cartons
Fibrous egg cartons can be used for raising seeds. Fill the lid section with seed raising mixture and sow your seeds. Lightly water. Keep damp. When seedlings are large enough to handle, transplant into the egg moulds. Make a few holes in the bottom of each to ensure good drainage. When planting out, plant the lot, mould and all, the carton will decompose and the plant will not be damaged in the replanting.

Planting plants
Planting in pots
- Dig a hole twice as wide as the container and half again as deep.
- Soak hole before planting.
- Add some complete fertiliser to the bottom of the hole.
- Mix the soil that you have removed from the hole – one part complete fertiliser to two parts soil.
- Use this soil mixture to half fill the hole.
- Set the plant in so that the top of the root ball is about two cm above the ground level.
- Continue adding soil until the hole is full.
- Form a watering basin with leftover soil.

Planting bare-rooted plants
Avoid shrivelled and dry, brittle-looking plants. These trees and shrubs should have firm, moist stems and roots. Late winter is the best time to plant bare-rooted plants.

Plant as quickly as possible after purchase. If you are unable to plant immediately, lay in a shallow trench and cover with damp sawdust or peat moss.

- Dig hole that fits roots.
- Spread roots evenly over the soil at the bottom of the hole.
- Use a shovel handle placed horizontally across the hole in order to place the plant so that the first branch is just above the ground.
- Add soil.
- Water around the plant, soaking the soil deeply, before you finish filling to ground level.
- Cover the plant with loose soil and when growth begins soak well and continue watering regularly.

Planting balled and burlapped plants
In autumn and early winter, large shrubs and trees are sold with their roots and soil intact, wrapped in burlap. Buy as soon as they appear in the nursery, and plant as soon as possible. These plants have an advantage over potted plants in that they do not become pot-bound. Be careful not to break up the ball of soil when you move the plant. If you are unable to plant immediately, cover the root ball with moist sawdust and place out of the sun in a shady, protected area of the garden.

- Dig a hole that is twice as wide as the root ball and ten cm deeper.
- Mix one part complete fertiliser to three parts soil and return to hole.
- Lift plant into hole. There is no need to take the burlap away altogether as it will rot.
- Add soil until the hole is half filled.
- Drive in a stake so that it is anchored in the firm soil and rests upon, but does not damage the root ball.
- Tie trunk firmly to stake.
- Soak the soil very deeply.
- Add remainder of soil, leaving a watering trough around the plant.

Planting seeds directly into soil

You'll have healthier plants and an earlier and longer bloom period if you sow seed directly in the open ground – especially with the faster kinds of summer annuals. The shock of transplanting is entirely eliminated. In choosing seeds, first check the instructions on the package for correct planting times. Spring is the best time to plant in most regions. Wait until frost danger is past and soil has begun to warm up.

Required conditions

Tender seedlings require perfect conditions to grow quickly and well. Soil should be just at the crumbly stage and not too wet. Count on a week or two for the seeds to sprout and another period of sparse growth before growth fills in and becomes sturdy.

If you want cut flowers, you may prefer to plant in rows. Seed tape is handy for this. Vegetables are often sown in rows, too.

Some flowers that do well sown in the open ground

Aster, coreopsis, gaillardia, marigold, nasturtium, phlox, portulaca, sweet alyssum, zinnia.

Planting seeds indoors

Indoor planting in pots or other containers is the best method to use for expensive or very fine seed, for seed that takes a long time to germinate and grow (including most perennials), and for some annuals and vegetables that you want to start early when the ground outside is still too cold or wet.

Advantages of nurturing seed inside

- You can control the soil mix.
- You can move the flats or pots around so plants get the right amount of sun or shade.
- Pest damage is more quickly noticeable and easier to control.

Transplanting seedlings

It will take about two months for the seedlings to mature enough so you can set them outside. If you sow them too early, the seedlings will be leggy and root bound when planting weather arrives.

To transplant, loosen soil around each seedling, gently grasp one of its leaves, and carefully pull out the plant. Use a pencil to poke hole in the new planting mix. Drop in the seedling, and gently firm the soil around it. Keep the plants in the shade for a day or two, then move them into the light again. Water plants occasionally. Water daily if weather is hot. Apply a light application of liquid fertiliser once a week.

When transplanting a small seedling, put a plastic bag over the pot to keep a moist ecosystem.

Protect your seedlings

Cut the top off plastic soft drink bottles and use to protect your young seedlings from frost, birds, insects, etc.

Kero protection

Soak carrot, peas and bean seeds in kerosene before planting. This will prevent them being eaten by worms.

Transplanting a shrub or small tree

- Cut the outer roots a few months before you plan to move the bush.
- Soak the roots a couple of days before you plan to do the job.
- Pre-prepare hole to where you will be moving the bush.
- Cut down with a spade or shovel at the base of the tree under the extreme canopy of the tree.
- Wrap root ball with chicken wire.
- Cut under root ball.
- Position the plant in pre-prepared planting hole.
- Water the plant well.

When planting a young sapling

When digging a hole to plant a tree, keep it as deep as the root ball is tall and twice as wide. The top of the root ball should line up with the existing ground level. Before you begin to dig, check for stormwater and drainage pipes. It is usually not necessary to support young trees with guide wires and stakes. If it is left to hold itself erect, then the young tree will develop stronger roots and trunk. If the spot you have chosen for the sapling is extra windy you may need to stake it. To prevent bruising, use old stockings to tie the tender trunk to the stake.

Herbs

Herbs are hardy and can grow in the most difficult and neglected of spots, but that is not to mean that you condemn them to a permanent struggle – well-drained sandy soil is the best spot, with the addition of compost.

Herbs love the sun. Give them a sunny position and they will thrive.

Aurium

The golden-leaved version of oregano, aurium, is not only a great herb but a wonderful ornamental plant, especially in flower in spring and summer.

Comfrey

Comfrey is used by naturalists as a treatment for bruises and cuts.

Feverfew

Feverfew is used for treatment of headaches, muscle soreness, worms, flatulence and even drug addiction.

Horseradish

Dig the long stools (roots) in winter and immediately replant the healthy roots with a crown. Peel roots and place in blender. Preserve pulp in vinegar. Use with mayonnaise or condensed milk to make up for accompaniment to beef.

Lavender

Despite its delicate fragrance and romantic name, lavender is a hardy herb and will survive difficult conditions.

Lemon balm

Lemon balm is strong enough to grow in part-shade areas.

Pelargonium

Pelargonium forms an excellent ground cover and therefore weed retardant.

Pineapple sage

Always keep pineapple sage under control with pruning, as it is vigorous and will take over the entire herb bed.

Thyme

Surround thyme by a thick layer of small stones or road metal to allow the air to circulate at the base of the stems. Thyme does not like organic mulch: it causes it to rot. Thyme is tough enough to be grown between the cracks of paving stocks – it looks good when it flowers and the scent is released when it is walked on.

Insect-repelling herbs

Sage
Dot sage plants through your cabbage patch to repel the white cabbage moth.

Wormwood
Wormwood repels fruit fly, and is effective around backyard trees and orchards.

Lavender
Dried lavender in a sachet hung in wardrobe not only smells nice but repels moths away from your clothes.

Tansy
Ants, flies and fleas do not like the aroma of tansy – a plant at the back door or in a window box is excellent for keeping flies out of the house.

Pennyroyal
The peppermint smell of pennyroyal is an excellent repellent of mosquitoes and ants.

Bay leaves
A few bay leaves around the pantry or kitchen will soon get rid of ants.

Citronella
The citronella smell of pelargonium drives mosquitoes away.

Garlic
Garlic grown among roses will drive off aphids.

Basil
Basil drives away flies and mosquitoes.

Gardening with children

Kids can be great gardeners. The key to successful gardening with children is to make sure that each of the kids has his or her own individual plants to care for. They like to see something grow and they like to see it grow fast. They enjoy watching a seed become a plant.

Depending upon the age of the children and their gardening experience, these simple projects may work for you.

Popcorn pies

Popcorn is just a seed. Fill a pie plate with potting soil and plant the kernels near the surface. Keep the soil moist. Within a week you'll see the first buds of popcorn pie. The kids will love it.

Bean seeds

Bean plants are hardy and easily grown. Egg cartons are a great container for these seeds. You can plant one per egg space. It will take about ten days to see a plant emerge. These seeds are planted near the surface, and you can watch the plant break out of the seed, shed the seed shell, and grow.

Grass people

Make a mix of grass seeds and potting mix. Take an old pair of pantihose and fill the mixture into the toe. Tie the foot off to make a head. Sew on two buttons for the eyes, a piece of cotton wool for the nose and a big red woollen mouth. Soak in a bucket of water for two hours. Sit on a half filled jar with the leg part of the stocking in the water. Leave in a sunny spot. It will grow hair and may need a haircut. Give it a name.

Carrot tops

The easiest path to a green, leafy creation is with a carrot top. Begin with carrots with the greens still attached. Cut off the leaves leaving about an inch of green. Munch the carrot leaving an inch of orange. Plant the carrot top in moist soil. Keep in a warm, sunny spot. Within two weeks you'll have a lacy kitchen plant.

Pineapples

Just like carrot tops, pineapple tops can also be planted to produce a lovely house plant. Pineapples, however, must be planted in sand and kept warm, imitating their natural climate. Cut off the top of the pineapple, leaving about two to three cm of fruit, and let the top dry on its side for five days. Plant it in a pot of damp sand. Bury the fruit completely, leaving the leaves uncovered. Keep the sand damp, but not too wet. In two or three weeks, when roots have grown, you can transfer the plant to a pot with potting soil. Pineapple makes an attractive house plant.

Humpty Dumpty

Take the shell of a hard-boiled egg that has been eaten. Gently fill it with damp cotton wool. Place half a dozen grains of wheat on the cotton wool. Draw a face on the egg and place it in an egg cup. Keep cotton wool damp and Humpty Dumpty will grow hair.

Cactus creatures

Invent your very own cactus plant by grafting the top of one small cactus, found at your local nursery, to the bottom of another. This project is best done in summer, when desert plants are in their growing season. You'll need a sterilised knife to slice off the top of the cactus that will be the bottom plant. Quickly place the sliced top of the other cactus on top. The top piece should be roughly the same size as the bottom one, and you can wash it off with water if there is a lot of sap running. Attach the parts with string, rubber bands or toothpicks. Keep your new creation in a shady place for two days. Resist the temptation to pull the pieces apart to check if they have grown together.

Potatoes

Find a potato with eyes sprouting in your own kitchen. To plant potatoes, cut one into pieces, making sure that each piece has an eye. You'll need a deep planter or bucket (with drainage) since potatoes are root plants and each eye should be planted about ten cm deep. Keep soil moist and sunny, and a green sprout will grow into a leafy plant producing yellow dotted flowers. Let the flowers bloom and fade. After about four months, pull up the plant and discover your home-grown tater tots.

Outdoor gardening for kids

A few basic salad ingredients, lettuce, carrots and radishes, make for easy planting, and may even make those vegies tastier to your kids.

Plan

Children can help draw a map of the garden on paper. A square metre of sunny spot will be plenty of room for a crop of these three vegetables.

Making the garden

First, you'll need to dig up the soil, break up the lumps and remove rocks and weeds. Sprinkle some commercial fertiliser on the soil, water it and let it sit for a day before planting. Then rake the ground and find some sticks to mark off straight rows. Set the sticks to mark the ends of three rows, ten cm apart, and connect the sticks with string.

You'll plant the seeds under each string, which will keep the rows straight. The kids can mark the sticks and label a row for lettuce, one for radishes, and one for carrots.

Lettuce

Lettuce likes cool weather and will do well early in the season. Plant the seeds four cm deep and five cm apart. Water daily. When the plants are five cm high, thin them out to fifteen cm apart. Lettuce will be ready to eat in forty-five days.

Carrots

Carrots have long roots that like to grow in deeply dug soil, and they take a little longer to grow. Plant the seeds shallow, just three to four cm deep and two to three cm apart. When the carrot-top plants are eight cm high, thin them to fifteen cm apart. Keep them watered. Carrots take about seventy days to grow. Check to see that the orange carrot top is about three cm wide.

Radishes

Red or white radishes grow very fast. Plant seeds three to four cm deep and five cm apart. Water daily. Thin in a week so that leaves are five cm apart. Radishes are ready in three weeks and you can plant another batch.

Cinderella's pumpkin

Dig a deep hole in a sunny spot, about thirty cm deep. Mix fertiliser with the soil and pile the mixture loosely back into the hole. Pat a small mound about forty-five cm across. Make three or four holes in the mound with your fingers and plant one pumpkin seed in each one. Keep the mound watered. When the plants are fifteen cm high, choose the best one and pull out the rest. The vines will blossom first, then produce pumpkins. Keep pinching off the fuzzy ends of the vine. Your pumpkin will be ready by the end of summer.

Sunflowers

For an easy summer treat, plant these seeds five cm deep and one metre apart in a sunny spot. Water every day.

Planting a butterfly garden

Attract butterflies to your garden by planting the types of nectar-producing flowers that butterflies love.

Site

Plant their favourite flowers in a protected yet sunny spot. Find a sheltered spot for the butterfly garden, ideally one that receives at least six hours of sun a day and offers shelter from the wind. When choosing the perfect spot make sure there is wind block nearby.

Flowers to plant

Plant nectar-producing varieties that would keep a flock of butterflies happy. Find out which butterflies live in your area to help you determine which flowers you should grow.

- Plant annuals – ageratum, impatiens, marigold, zinnia and cosmos.
- Add perennials – coreopsis, butterfly weed, purple coneflower, black-eyed Susan and bee balm.
- Choose plants with the nectar needs of adult butterflies in mind.

Butterfly larvae, or caterpillars, eat the leaves and seeds of other plants and herbs, such as milkweed, pussy willow, violets and dill. If you grow these as well, you may encourage visiting butterflies to breed and lay eggs.

Fruit trees
Espalier

Espalier is a good way of growing fruit or other trees when the space is limited.

The standard espalier consists of a central stem with horizontal arms tied along supporting wires. Apples and pears can be made to conform to almost any design, but stone fruits are best grown on a 'fan'.

- If the trellis is in open ground, the espalier should be trained north-south in order to attain maximum sunlight.
- If it is against the wall, it should run as near to east-west as possible.
- In hot districts a north facing wall will result in scorched fruit.
- The trellis posts should be three metres apart and two metres high.
- Five wires should be stretched tightly between the posts with the bottom wire fifty cm above the ground and with fifty cm between the wires.
- In the first winter after planting, the whipstick or single leader should be shortened to five cm above the lowest wire.
- When the growth starts, rub off all but the top three buds.
- During spring or summer, the two lower shoots are trained along the wire in opposite directions.
- If one shoot is weaker than the other, delay tying it down until it catches up.
- In the second winter, the upright shoot is again shortened, this time to five cm above the second wire.
- In the second summer, the lateral rods are continued outward along the wires and shoots are pinched back to about ten cm.
- This process is repeated each year until the top wire is reached.
- Once the fruiting wood becomes aged it will require pruning off the weak spurs.

Lemon trees
Tips for care of a lemon tree:

- Lemon trees have surface roots, so never dig around and under the tree. Instead, mulch under the tree to keep the ground moist and to discourage weeds.
- Trim regularly, as old trees that have been left unpruned grow weak and leggy and produce less fruit.
- Prune the lower branches less than a metre off the ground. This will improve ventilation and aid in pest control.
- Keep the middle of the tree free from growth, to allow the light to come through.
- To keep your lemon and all citrus trees free from pests, douse with sudsy water made with a solution of pure soap and water.
- Add a few drops of kerosene to every bucket of water. Do this frequently. It is a good idea to recycle all your waste water in this way.

A pick-me-up for your lemon tree can be achieved by driving nails into the trunk.

Peach trees
To prevent curly leaf, plant onions around the base.

Glossary of gardening terms
Acid/alkaline soils
Describes the concentration of hydrogen ions in the soil.

Acid soil
Is most commonly found in areas of high rainfall. It tends to be high in organic matter. Lime will help to neutralise the acidic content. Excessive acid conditions are not good for most plants. However, some plants prefer soils that are slightly acidic – azaleas, rhododendrons, camellias.

Alkaline soil
Alkaline soils are common in light rainfall areas. They have high levels of calcium carbonate (lime) and some other minerals. Most plants grow well in this soil. Gypsum may be added.

Annual
An annual is a plant that completes its life cycle in twelve months or less.
   Plant in spring after the last frost, enjoy it in spring, summer and autumn and pull it out of the soil before the first frost of winter.

Backfill
Backfill is the soil that is returned to the planting hole after the plant's roots are positioned. Often it is mixed with organic mix to improve its texture.

Balled and burlapped (b&b)
Shrubs and trees with a large ball of soil around the roots are wrapped in burlap to hold the soil and the roots together. They are sold like this in nurseries from late autumn to early spring.

Bare root
Deciduous shrubs and trees with all soil removed from their roots are sold in their dormant period in early winter. They must be planted immediately before they start to shoot.

Biannual
A biannual is a plant that completes its life cycle in two years. Plant the seeds in spring and trim back at the end of summer. They will flower again in spring before dying down.

Bolt
To grow too quickly to the flowering stage to the detriment of developing well otherwise.

This happens if you plant too late in the season or when the plant experiences unseasonably warm weather early in development.

Bonsai
A Japanese term for growing carefully trained, dwarf plants in containers that are carefully selected to harmonise with the plants. The bonsai artist carefully wires and prunes branches and trims roots in order to achieve the appearance of old and gnarled trees in a miniature landscape.

Bracts
Bracts are modified leaves that grow just below the flower or flower cluster. They are sometimes colourful and may be mistaken for the flower itself.

Broadcast
To scatter seed by hand over the soil surface.

Broad-leafed
A broad-leafed weed is any weed that is not grass. A broad-leafed evergreen is a plant that has green foliage all year but is not an evergreen.

Bud
A flower bud is one that develops into blossom. A growth bud may be at the tip of a stem (terminal) or along the side of the stem (lateral). These buds will produce new leafy growth. Also, a bud can be to propagate in a similar method to grafting.

Bulb
Any plant with a thickened underground structure is called a bulb. However a true bulb is rounded and composed of fleshy scales that store food and protect the developing plant that is inside. They bloom in spring. Once a bulb has flowered, pick off the dead leaves but leave the foliage, as the bulb needs to store the food and flower for the next year.

Cambium layer
The layer inside the plant's bark or outer layer.

Clay soils
A heavy soil that is easy to recognise, but difficult to work. It contains very little air and the drainage is poor. It holds water and nutrients well. Improve by adding organic material such as compost, leaf mulch or mushroom compost.

Chilling requirements
Many plants require certain amounts of cold weather to produce flowers and fruit. If your winter climate is warm sometimes you need to treat these plants with cold before planting.

Chlorosis
Chlorosis is a result of the plant being unable to obtain the iron it needs to produce its green colour. The leaf looks yellow. It is caused by an iron deficiency in the plant. This is not necessarily a result of iron deficiency in the soil, but rather because of the presence of some other element that renders the iron unavailable. It may be treated by spraying foliage with a special iron solution.

Complete fertiliser
Any plant food that contains the three primary nutrient elements – nitrogen, phosphorus, potassium.

Compost
A valuable additive to soil made up of decomposed organic material. As it decays fungus and bacteria grow, produce heat and break down the matter to a brown/black crumbly consistency.

Composite family
An enormous family of flowers that includes all the flowers known as daisies. A typical daisy is composed of many small flowers. There are two kinds – disk flowers (appear to be the

core) and ray flowers (appear to be the petals).

Conifer
Leaves are narrow and needlelike and produce seeds in a conelike structure.

Conservatory
A greenhouse for growing and cultivating plants.

Corm
A corm differs from a bulb in that the food is stored in the solid centre tissue.

Crown
Portion of a plant at the juncture of the root and stem or trunk. It is sensitive to rotting if kept too moist.

Cultivate
To break up the surface of the soil around plants, removing weeds as you go. The roughened surface retains water and allows the air to circulate.

Cuttings
Portions of the stem or root that can be induced to form roots and develop into new plants.

Damping off
A plant disease caused by fungi that makes small seedlings wilt and fall over in the ground soon after they break through the soil.

Deciduous
A plant that sheds its leaves in autumn.

Defoliation
The unnatural loss of the plant's leaves, usually to the detriment of the plant's health.

Die back
Death of the plant's stems which begins at the tips. Causes include lack of water, nutrient deficiency, unsuitable climate, severe insect, mite or disease injury.

Dividing
Easiest way to increase perennials, bulbs and shrubs that form clumps of stems with rooted bases.

Drainage
Movement of water through the soil in the plant's root area is vital in order that plants may grow. Fast drainage is typical of sandy soils, while slow drainage is typical of clay soils.

Drip line
The circle around the plant that is drawn under its outermost branches. Roots are concentrated in this circle and it is wise not to plant other plants closer to the tree than this. Rainwater tends to drip from the tree at this point, and so it is where we feed and drip water.

Dust
A chemical product in the form of a fine powder that is sprinkled on affected plants in order to eradicate insects or disease.

Epiphyte
A plant that grows on another plant but which does not receive nourishment from the host plant (orchids, staghorn ferns).

Espalier
A tree or shrub trained so that its branches grow in a flat pattern against a wall or trellis.

Established
An established plant is one that is firmly rooted and is producing good growth of leaves.

Evergreen
An evergreen is a plant that never loses all its leaves at the same time.

Everlastings
Everlasting flowers are those that hold their colour and shape when dried.

Eye
An underdeveloped bud on a tuber, which will sprout after the tuber is planted.
 Potatoes have many eyes.

Fertilise
To fertilise a flower is to apply pollen from the male element to the pistil or female element in order to set seed. It can also mean to apply fertiliser to feed the whole plant.

Family
Plants that share some characteristics even though they may look quite different. Sometimes members of the same family are prone to the same diseases.

Forcing
Forcing is causing a plant to grow or bloom more rapidly or earlier than is normal.
 Special techniques and manipulation of the environment are involved.

Formal
A garden that has a rigid, regular and geometric structure.
 They often contain formal hedges, standard plants and espaliers.

Foundation plant
A plant that you plant near the walls of the house.

Friable soil
Soil that is easily crumbled and ready for planting. It is neither too wet or too dry.

Frond
Foliage of ferns, but can include any foliage that appears fernlike.

Genus
The first name of plant classification by which a plant is named by the genus to which it belongs.

Grafting
A method of plant propagation, whereby a section of one plant is inserted into a branch of another plant.

Grasses
There are many types of grasses for home gardeners. They have two classifications – cool season, which grow all year and warm season, which die off in winter.

Harden off
To expose a plant over a week or more to the natural climate after it has been planted and grown in greenhouse conditions, so it does not become shocked when planted out.

Hardy
A plant's resistance or tolerance to frosts and freezing temperatures.

Heading back
A pruning term for cutting a branch back to the bud or side branch to change the direction of the growth or enhance bushiness.

Heeling in
A temporary storage of certain plants by burying the roots in soil or sawdust.

Herbaceous
A plant with soft, non-woody tissue.

Honeydew
A sticky, sweet substance produced by aphids and other related insects.

Humus
Vegetable matter which is in the final stages of decomposition.

Hybrid
A plant that has been genetically developed by crossing two species or varieties to produce a new and different plant.

Iron chelate
A compound that contains iron in a form that plants are able to use.

Lath
Any overhead plant-protecting structure that reduces the amount of sunlight that shines on plants and protects them from frost.

Layering
A method of propagating plants where you root a branch while it is still attached to the original plant.

Leaching
Pouring of water through the soil to dissolve and take away soluble minerals that might otherwise damage the plants.

Leader
The central, upward growing stem in any single-trunk tree or shrub.

Leaf mould
Partly decomposed leaf matter that can be dug into the soil and used as compost to add nutrients to the soil.

Leaf scar
A crescent shaped scar where once a stalk was attached.

Loam
Dark coloured soil that is rich in nutrients and drains well after watering.

Mulch
Loose, organic material that is placed over the soil to reduce evaporation and weed growth, provide insulation and to make the garden bed look attractive.

Naturalise
To plant out in a natural way so that there is no precise pattern.
    Many plants self seed and perform this task themselves.

Node
The joint along a plant stem where a leaf or branch may grow.
    The area in between is called the internode.

Nutrient deficiency
Most soils yield three major plant nutrients – nitrogen, phosphorus and potassium.
    If the soil is deficient in one of these elements then it needs to be added. Fertilisers are the most efficient method of doing this.

Offset
A new small plant that grows at the base of the parent plant.

Organic
Material that was once alive.

Organic gardening
Organic gardening is gardening without chemical sprays or fertilisers.

Parasite
A parasite is a creature that lives off another living organism.

Peat moss
The partially decomposed remains of any mosses, which adds to the acidity of the soil. It is highly water retentive.

Perennial
A non-woody plant that lives for more than two years. It usually dies down in winter and regrows the following spring.

Perlite
A mineral which has been chemically to form white, lightweight, porus granules useful in container soil mixes.

Perennials
Unlike annuals these flowers continue to bloom year after year. As a group, they are very hardy. They bloom from early spring to autumn with summer being their peak season. They make excellent ground cover and hardy pot plants. Most enjoy full sun. Divide the perennials in your garden every three or four years and do this job in autumn.

Pinching
To remove the twigs and branches by pinching with your index finger and thumb to make the plant bushy.

Plant classification
A standard system for grouping and naming plants.
> They include such descriptors as family, genus, species, variety, strain, hybrid.

Pleaching
A method of training a plant so that the branches are interwoven together to form a plait.

Pollarding
A pruning style that cuts back branches to one or two bud growths a season so that the tree produces a large, shady canopy in summer and has a knobbly gnarled appearance in winter.

Potbound
A plant that has remained in a container for so long that the roots have been forced to grow in a circle.
> Frequent repotting will prevent this.

Pseudobulbar
An above-the-ground modified stem found on some orchids.

Rhizome
A thickened modified stem that grows horizontally along or under the soil surface.

Raised beds
A great solution to continuing problem soils.
> The garden bed is built up using soil and organic material, above the ground.
> You can tailor the soil to suit the plants that you intend to grow.

Rock garden
A manmade landscape that contains natural looking rocky outcrops. They are drought resistant, low growing and spreading or matlike, and are suitable to the rocky terrain.

Rooting hormone
A compound containing growth hormones, which stimulates root growth when a cutting is dipped into it before planting.

Rootstock
A part of a budded or grafted plant that furnishes the root system.

Runner
A slender stem sent out from the bases of certain perennials and at the end of which a new plant develops.

Salinity
Excess salts in the soil. This is a widespread problem in arid and semi-arid regions.

It stunts plants, burns their foliage and finally kills them. It appears as white deposits on the surface of the soil. It is caused by too frequent and too shallow watering and the use of certain fertilisers. Slow, deep watering will help wash the salts below the roots.

Sandy soil
Sandy soil contains plenty of soil, but does not retain the water. Roots are free to find their own way wherever they wish. Improve sandy soil by adding humus and organic materials.

Shallow compacted soil
Roots cannot penetrate the hard layer of soil that sometimes develops near or just below the surface. It may be remedied with ploughing to a depth of at least one spade.

You may need to consider a drainage system that circumnavigates the area or you may make raised garden beds.

Shrubs
Shrubs and trees form the basic framework of the garden. Once you plant a shrub you may have many years of pleasure from it. There is a considerable variety of shrubs, many with pretty and colourful flowers and with a wide variety of foliage.

Scree
Fragmented rocks and pebbles used in landscaping.

Self branching
A plant that produces many side growths, that do not need to be pinched back to promote bushing.

Single flower
A flower that has the minimum number of petals.

Sphagnum
A moss with long fibres, which is sold dry to line fern baskets.

Spike
A flowering stem on which flowers are directly attached and which flower in turn, usually beginning at the bottom of the plant.

Spur
A short specialised twig on which blossoms and fruit grow on some fruit trees.

Standard
A plant that is trained into a small treelike form on a single upright trunk.

Stolon
A stem that creeps along the surface of the ground, taking roots at intervals and forming new plants where it puts down roots.

Strain
Plants in a strain usually share some growth characteristics but which vary in some way, usually colour.

Stress
A condition in which a plant is growing that is bad for its health; it may be temperature, drainage, heat, frost, wind, lack of water.

Sub shrub
A plant under a metre high with a woody stem, which is sometimes grown as a perennial and sometimes as a shrub.

Sucker
Sucker growth originates from the root stock.

Systemic
Any chemical that is absorbed into a plant's system either to kill organisms that feed on the plant or to kill the plant itself.

Taproot
A carrotlike root that grows deep into the soil searching for water.

Tender
A plant that is sensitive to cold temperatures.

Thinning out
To prune to make a plant or tree less dense. With seedlings, to remove as many of the small plants as is necessary for the remaining plants to grow to maturity.

Top dress
To spread organic material, compost or fertiliser onto the soil to enrich it.

Topiary
A technique to prune shrubs and trees into formalised shapes that represent animals and geometrical figures.

Truss
A cluster of flowers at the end of a stem, branch or stalk.

Tuber
A fat underground stem from which a plant grows.

Tuberous root
A thickened underground root that stores food and which is actually a modified stem.

Under planting
To plant one plant under another.

Vermiculite
A mineral that when puffed up retains water and air and is a useful additive in container soils.

Vines
Vines twine or spread and cling to structures such as fences and walls.
    Some vines produce flowers while others produce fruit or berries.

Wettable powder
Finely ground pesticide that can be mixed in water and sprayed onto plants.

Whorls
Three or more leaves, branches or flowers that grow in a circular formation from a joint or node.

4
Maintenance and
Decorating

Do it yourself

More and more, people are getting into DIY (Do It Yourself), especially with the prolif-eration of hardware chains offering the broadest possible range of products, materials and advice. But it is not as simple as that. Let's start with . . .

Home handyperson's ten commandments

1. Thou shalt make drawings and plans of the work that you plan to undertake. A good drawing is the beginning of a well-completed job.
2. Thou, who is a novice among you, should take your drawing to the local hardware store and have them cut the timber to size for you.
3. Thou shalt use the best of the timber in the places where it will be the most visible and the worst shall be hidden away.
4. Thou shalt group thine operations for repetition – the mother of efficiency and speed.
5. Thou shalt bore all screw holes slack in the shank and tight in the thread, thus ensur-ing a close and cosy fit.
6. Thou shalt leave all thine lines on until the job is complete.
7. Thou shalt fit intricate and difficult joints separately before thou assembleth the whole.
8. Thou shalt clean up surfaces as thou goest.
9. Thou shalt apply the glue only after thou hast prepared a truly level surface and hath made a trial clamping.
10. Thou shalt not sandpaper across the grain which is to be polished as this is a sin which will be evident to all those who view your work.

Using tools
Saw

To make a straight cut, place a length of wood over the piece of timber or board that you want to cut, clamp it in the position you need, then use the edge as a cutting guide.

For a straight saw line, use a knife to make a score line by running it along a ruler. Cut a small, triangular wedge along the score line and on the waste side of the wood, and start sawing in the groove.

To stop plywood and other fragile board from splintering when you saw it, put a piece of masking tape over the start of the saw line.

It is easier to saw a line when the board is lying flat than when it is on its side.

It is easier to saw a straight line if you rule two parallel straight lines and saw down the middle.

A hand-saw should glide through the wood, not be jabbed and jagged – if the cutting is getting hard, lift the saw, don't force it.

When using a coping saw, secure the work firmly – say with a brace to the bench – and work the saw with two hands to give firmer direction and control.

Sharpening your saw

If the teeth are uneven along the surface and shallow your saw needs a sharpening.

All points should be equal.

To drive a nail

Hold the hammer firmly with the thumb along the top for light nails or tacks and in the fist for heavy blows. Tap the nail lightly at first and then make sure that the hammer head falls firmly on the nail head in the direction in which you wish it to go.

Nails

A nail driven at a slight angle will hold more firmly than one that has been driven in straight.

A nail drives in more easily if the end is inserted into a bar of soap.

To draw a hard to move nail out, move forward and then back, then pull.

Screws

If you are working with a screw driver that constantly slips, grind the head to fit the screw. A screw that has lost its grip can be made to function by filling the screw hole with a wood peg, preferably glued in.

Hammer

A hammer head should be fitted snugly. A common screw will often fix a shaky head.

A rusty chisel will never cut straight. Oil it and sand it with fine sandpaper. Sharpen it on an oiled stone.

Hold your chisel as you would hold a pencil.

To bore a straight and clean hole bore from the first side until the point just shows through. Turn and nick the grain, then finish from the first side with the bit centred on a waste block.

The use of a wooden block under sandpaper tends to scratch. Instead use something soft such as cork or a rubber strip glue to a piece of pine.

Screwdriver

Undo a tight screw by turning the screwdriver fractionally in the tightening direction, and then immediately in the opposite direction.

If a screw on an appliance keeps coming out, apply nail varnish under the head and tighten it.

To fill up a screw hole made in the wrong place, insert a match-stick first. Later you can tidy it up, if need be, with putty, or other patching material and then paint or varnish over.

If the spot where you want to insert a screw is hard to get, rub some beeswax on the screw head and fill the slot, thus giving the screwdriver a firmer grip and keeping it in place as the screw gets started.

Nails and screws

To stop plaster from cracking or chipping when you put a nail in it, put a strip of clear tape over the spot first.

If a nail is too small to hold on to, push it through a piece of card (up near one corner) and use the card to hold into position for hammering. Once it is secure, tear the piece of card away.

To find the right size screw or nail among a can full of bits and pieces, top the lot on a piece of newspaper, sort through them, and then funnel the paper to tip the others back.

Nails and screws which have become rusted into the wood may be moved by dropping a small quantity of paraffin oil over them. Allow this to soak in, and after a short time the screws may be taken out.

Touching the head of the screw with a red-hot poker, or inserting a screwdriver into the head and tapping it firmly with a hammer, will often succeed in starting a stiff screw.

Repair kit

A stitch in time saves nine – repair or mend damaged articles as soon as you can.

Leaving problems only makes them worse. Keep a repair kit handy that is easily accessible, so that when you see something that needs to be mended, everything is at hand. The kit should contain:

- Gloves – Rubber and leather.
- Sandpaper – A supply of different grades that can be used for different jobs.
- Adhesives – Superglue and PVC.
- Solvents – Ammonia, methylated spirits and rubbing alcohol.

Store out of reach of children.
- Oil and polish – Linseed oil for wood and metal polish to remove scratches from glass and acrylic surfaces and will clean various metals.
- Brushes and wire wool – Clean, soft paint brushes, old toothbrushes for small corners and wire wool for applying and removing substances.

Sanding

Always wear gloves when sanding, to save damaging your fingers.

When sanding, wrap the sandpaper around a block of wood, or a cork block, to get a good grip.

To sand in an awkward spot, wrap the paper around an old pack of playing cards. The cards move around to suit the surface.

Workshop wisdom

Drilling a hole to insert a screw or nail, particularly on hardwood, can leave a burr on the edge of the hole, which stops a snug fit if the wood is being used in a join.

Use a countersink bit, or remove the burr with a hard chisel.

When sawing a moulding, cut from the face so that the burr from the saw will be on the back where it can be easily removed.

When using a mitre box, hold the piece to be cut against the side that offers the most support – usually the wide cuts in the box should be farthest from you.

When using an oil can, press the bottom after it is in position, not before.

Think first, measure twice, and saw afterwards.

Mark your cut mark clearly.

Trying to drive a nail into a board that springs or bends is tempting fate – bolster it behind, even with another hammer.

When installing a post and no spirit level is available, drive a nail in at the top, and hang a string from it with a weight on it, to test for uprightness.

If it's the one and only screw left and needs to be screwed back in but the slot is worn, you can deepen the slot with a hacksaw to get more purchase with the screwdriver.

If a screw is covered in paint or very rusty and proving difficult to get out, give it a sharp rap with the hammer to shatter the film of paint or rust.

A few drops of Penetrine or other available fluid will help loosen a rusty screw.

For a very obstinate screw, heat up a soldering iron and apply it to the head. An effective alternative is to use a red-hot poker.

A smear of soap or fat will help a screw go in easily – and assist later if it ever needs to be removed.

For a particularly obstinate screw that you want to remove, take a nail punch, hold it against the top left-hand corner of the screw and tap repeatedly with the hammer until the screw head starts to move.

Swearing at your screwdriver because it is too big for a job does not achieve much.

Take the time to find one that fits, or if there is no alternative, grind it down to fit the screw.

A hardwood block under sandpaper can sometimes scratch instead of smoothing the surface you are working on – use softwood, cork, or rubber glued to a wood block.

Make sure there is more than adequate lighting in your shed, garage or whatever location you do your handyman work – blundering around the gloom can lead to mistakes, accidents and injuries.

Words of wisdom
It is better to give than to lend, and it costs about the same.

Wood
Woods are generally classified under three headings – hard wood, medium wood and soft wood.

Softwood
Oregon
Oregon is used for shelving and cabinet making. It stains and varnishes well.

Baltic pine
Mainly used for weatherboards and flooring. Recycled Baltic pine is popular in cottage type furniture.

Western cedar
One of the most durable softwoods, it has few knots and is suitable for all types of furniture and cabinet making.

Huon pine
Pale yellow wood with straight grain. Durable and of oily character, it is one of the best woods for boat building. It stains and polishes well.

King William pine
Reddish when cut, it fades to pale pink. Soft in texture, it can be sawn and nailed easily. Suitable for all cabinet making.

Radiata pine
Plantation pine that is used for weatherboards, flooring and shelving.

Medium woods

Hoop pine and Queensland Kauri

Ranges in colour from pale yellow to light brown and has clean straight grain. Stains and polishes well. Great for all furniture making.

Celery top pine

White to light brown, straight grain.

Difficult to work, available only in short, thin lengths. Great for inlays for colour contrast.

Queensland maple

Pink to rose red in colour, it has figure which ranges from plain to ripple and ribbon effects which are really beautiful. Cleans up well, cuts easily and can be carved.

Pacific maple

Imported from Pacific countries. Cuts well and will take a high polish.

Red meranti

Malaysian timber, red colour and attractive grain.

Silky oak

Pinkish to light brown, straight grained and open texture with silver flecks. Easy to work and good for carving.

Hardwoods

A wide range of Australian hardwoods are selected seasoned timber suitable for joinery and furniture. It has usually been partially air dried and finished later in the kiln.

Queensland walnut

Colour ranges from reddish brown to black with striped, wavy figure. Hard on saws.

Silver ash

Yellow to light brown, straight/wavy grain. Blends well with all décors.

Tulip oak

Reddish brown, mottled wavy grain. Heavy. Attractive when finished in natural colour.

Blackwood

Golden to reddish brown, turns and bends well. Excellent cabinet wood. Polishes well.

Myrtle

Pink to pinkish brown with pale intermediate wood. Makes up beautifully for furniture with a natural finish. A favourite for carving.

Wood finishes

Gloss
Oil based and with a hard glossy finish. Suitable for all except resinous woods. Easy to retouch.

Eggshell
Can be oil based and has a semi-gloss finish. This is tough. Can be water based with a semi-sheen finish. This is not as tough.

Varnish
Oil based with finishes from matt to high gloss. Extremely hard wearing and suitable for all smooth planed wooden surfaces.

Woodstain
Oil based with low to high sheen. Has translucent finish and is hard wearing. Can be applied to all woods, but paint must be first stripped. Can apply several coats in one day.

Scandinavian oil
Solvent based, mid-sheen. Good for hardwoods. Low-wear areas.

Wax
Solvent or water based. Requires polishing. Can be applied over stains and dyes.

Care of wood
To protect your wooden furniture, position furniture out of direct sunlight, and humidify rooms with house plants. Here are some polish ideas to bring out the best in individual woods:

Mahogany
1 tablespoon linseed oil
1 tablespoon turpentine
1 litre water

Apply giving a good rub. Polish.

Teak
Apply a small amount of teal oil or cream once a year. Apply with fine wire wool. Buff to shine with a soft cloth. Keep dusted.

Oak
Make a polish of a pint of beer, a small square of melted beeswax and two teaspoons of sugar. Apply. Allow to dry. Buff with soft cloth.
   Wipe occasionally with warm vinegar. Allow to dry. Polish.

Ebony
Rub in petroleum jelly. Leave for thirty minutes. Polish.

Antique furniture

Antique furniture needs special treatment and care. Silicone polish gives antiques an unnatural shine and should be avoided.

Beeswax polish

- Warm 50g of natural beeswax for a few seconds in the microwave.
- Coarsely grate and place in a screw top jar.
- Add 150 ml turpentine and place lid loosely on jar.
- Stand jar in a bowl and pour hot water into the jar.
- Water should be hot, but not boiling.
- Shake the jar so that the mixture forms a paste.
- Leave to cool.

To use:
Apply using a soft cloth.
    Buff. If the mixture becomes hard, stand in a bowl of warm water to soften.

Other woods

Dust regularly. Polish regularly with a wax polish that matches the wood.

Removing marks from wood

Grease

Remove grease at once using a paper towel, because if left untreated it will leave a permanent dark patch. Then wipe over the area with a soft cloth that has been dipped in a solution of equal parts vinegar and water.

Alcohol stains

Blot up spill immediately. Rub the area with Brasso. Polish with a soft cloth.

Water marks

Mop up as soon as possible as water causes unvarnished wood to swell. Allow surface to dry and then rub with metal polish (Brasso is good) along the grain of the wood.

Heat marks

To prevent heat marks use table mats to protect the wood. However, if damage does occur, rub metal cleaner along the grain or apply a paste of vegetable oil and salt. Leave for a couple of hours and polish.

Slight burns

On veneered surfaces you may need to cut out the damage and insert a new piece but for solid wood proceed as follows. Rub the burn with metal polish, scrape and sand the surface. Place wet blotting paper over the mark, cover with gladwrap and leave over night.

Serious burns

May require professional treatment, but if you think you can do it yourself proceed as follows. Scrape out the burned part with a sharp knife. Fill scar with matching wood filler. Allow to dry. Sand with fine paper. Paint the area to match the grain with artist's paints.

Dents

Treat as soon as possible. Dented veneer may split and then will need to be cut out and replaced. Fill the dent with warm water and leave to swell.

Scratches

- Use a matching coloured wax crayon and rub into the scratch.
- Rub with beeswax polish with a drop of linseed oil and polish well.

To revive dull polish

2 tablespoons turpentine
2 tablespoons white vinegar
2 tablespoons methylated spirits
1 tablespoon linseed oil

Shake and apply with a soft cloth.

To remove surplus polish

Equal parts vinegar and water. Apply with damp cloth. Wipe off immediately.

Stuck paper

Paper that is stuck to wood can be removed by:

- Rubbing with baby oil.
- Leaving a few minutes.
- Peeling off.

Furniture tips
Cane chairs

If the seat of a cane chair is sagging, simply wet thoroughly with very hot water and leave in the sun to dry.

Framing

When framing pictures, for neat appearance and exclusion of dust, a sheet of brown paper should be damped and glued to frame edges over the backing. Gradually smooth out from the centre. Leave to dry until it is drum tight. Trim with a Stanley knife.

Long frames tend to bend under pressure. To avoid this insert a stretcher in the rebates before applying the cramp.

Glue and allow glue to dry before nailing. This will avoid damage from hammering.

French polishing

The art of French polishing lies in the preparation of the surface. The final test of the surface is to place it in a strong light and glance along it with the eyes on level with the timber. If no sign of a wave is visible, and there are no small white pits, you have managed to 'get it flat'. After the board has been smoothed for polishing, it should be damped on both sides and left to dry. Then, working with the grain, it should be finished with fine glass paper.

To make the polish

- 500g shellac.
- 2 litres methylated spirits.

- Mix together.
- Work with the grain, not across it.
- Before sandpapering, the whole surface of the timber should be dampened with a cloth wrung out in hot water so that any timber that has been bruised or crushed will rise.
- Allow to dry before sandpapering.
- Fill holes with beeswax and sand well.
- Ensure that the surface is flat and smooth.
- Wood dye to desired colour.
- Shake dye well and apply with brush.
- Use soft cloth to wipe off along the grain of the timber.
- Allow to dry thoroughly.
- Apply a coat of French polish with a soft brush.
- Allow to dry.
- Sand with No.0 sandpaper.
- Apply another coat of French polish.
- Allow to dry.
- Sand with No.0 sandpaper.
- Keep repeating until you have the polish you require.

Wobbly legs

If a table is wobbly because one leg is shorter than the others, cut a piece of cork to the right depth and width and attach to the bottom of the leg with woodwork adhesive.

Floors
Carpet protectors

Paint jam jar lids the same colour as the carpet.
> Place the lids under the feet of the heavy items of furniture.
> Use larger lids for larger pieces.
> OR
> Use mats and place them just inside all of the outside doors.
> OR
> Use rugs in the main thoroughfares to reduce wear on the carpet.
> Rearrange the rugs occasionally to distribute the wear on them.

Carpet on stairs

Before the stair carpet begins to wear in places, take it up and reverse it, top to bottom.
> It will double the life of your carpet.
> The treads will become risers and vice versa.

Ceramic tiles

As long as they are level ceramic tiles make an excellent base for a new floor and should be left undisturbed.

Cracks

Where a gap has opened up between floorboards, gently knock in a thin wedge-shaped sliver.
> Plane the wood until it is flush with the floorboards.
> OR
> Fill cracks with all purpose filler.
> Add a little wood dye to match the colour of your boards.

Cracks in floors

Fill spaces between floorboards with papier mâché made from newspaper and wallpaper paste.

Sand smooth when dry.

Creaking boards

To silence creaks, sprinkle talcum powder in the cracks between the creaking boards.

Kicker boards

Use leftover carpet tiles to make a kicker at the bottom of the door, which is often damaged by children and pets.

Simply glue to the door where little feet make contact.

Laying carpet tiles

Begin at the centre of the room. To locate the centre construct a line between the mid points of opposite walls. Use this line as a guide when laying your first tiles.

For difficult areas

Make a template exactly the same size and shape as the piece that you wish to put in. You can then try before you cut.

Kickboards

Remove kickboards and lay flooring underneath these fittings. Replace the boards and you will have a precise edge. Waterproof. Run a thin line of silicone around the flooring and skirting edges to make the surface waterproof and easy to clean.

Laying flooring

Laying flooring looks to be an easy job but poor laying can spoil the appearance of the whole room. If you are doubtful get in a professional.

Vinyl

Underlay sheets of hardboard. Begin in front of the window and lay the vinyl running away from it. Awkward bits can be tackled by making a pattern of the area on newspaper and using this as a template.

Cork

Easy to lay. Keep the grains all in the same direction.

Linoleum

Before laying linoleum, sprinkle sawdust on the floor instead of backing paper. It disappears into all the cracks and leaves no ridges.

Allow for the fact that it tends to stretch. Lay out on floor and leave for a time before beginning to cut.

Wood tiles

Allow wood tiles to acclimatise to the room for several days before laying.

Carpet on stairs
Leave a little extra carpet at the top and bottom of the stairs. You can then move it a little each year to even out wear.

Measuring floors
When measuring floors:
>   Allow an extra 10% for wooden floors.
>   Work in the direction that the carpet will be unrolled from to minimise wastage.
>   Allow 15% extra tiles to allow for cutting that will be required at the joins and on the edges.

Old flooring
*   Floors which have previously been stained, should be washed with warm water and washing soda and rinsed with clear water and thoroughly dried with a cloth.
*   When dry, sand with No. 2 sandpaper.
*   Remove all dust, finishing by wiping with a cloth that has been soaked in turpentine.
*   Fill cracks and nail holes with stained putty.
*   Touch up all bare patches with matching stain.
*   Apply stain and varnish as for new floors.

Preparing the floor
*   Remove lumps of concrete with a spade, a hammer and a chisel.
*   Fill gaps.
*   Soak hardboard by applying a coat of water and leaving for forty-eight hours.

This will prevent edge expansion and contraction after the floor is laid.

*   Arrange hardboard so that seams do not coincide with floorboard joints below.

Replacing old floorboards
Remove the area with the defective boards by cutting through the boards at the nearest joist to either side. Keep the angle to 45° as this will make the replacement section less obvious. Use a crow bar to remove the floorboard. Leaver it gently so as not to damage surrounding boards. Replace with new board.

Replacing boards
Use a good board from an area that isn't easily seen, like a board that is under the carpet and replace that with the new and different board.

To hide a badly pitted or grooved board, lift it out and turn it over so that the underneath side is on top.

Replacing carpet
Discard old carpet. Keep gripper boards as they can be reused. Underlay may also be reused.

Replacing vinyl
A hot air gun will soften adhesive. Slide a spade underneath and scrape it off the floor.

Sealer

Seal porus tiles with a sealer made of:

4 parts boiled linseed oil
1 part beeswax

Mix and cool.
Apply to tiles.
Buff.

Squeaks in floorboards

Shake talcum powder between the floorboards.
Use long nails, hammered in at an angle to refix loose floorboards.

Staining floors

- Do not confuse oil stains with varnish stains.
- Oil stains penetrate the wood and change the colour forever.
- Varnish is simply a layer that protects the surface and wears off.
- Most hardwood used for floors is machine sanded and kiln dried.
- When the floor is smooth and dustless the stain can be applied.
- To stain, simply sand with sanding machine to a smooth finish.
- Fill nail holes and cracks with stained putty.
- Sand again.
- Apply two coats of a good varnish.
- Finish with two coats of hard drying varnish.

Warped boards

Use screws rather than nails to hold down bulging boards as screws will hold them more firmly.

Wood tiles for floors

Lay out wood tiles and allow them to acclimatise to the room for several days before laying them.

Carpentry repairs
Boxes

Give ornamental wooden boxes a sheen and a perfume by rubbing them with lemon balm leaves.
A light sanding will return the natural scent to wooden boxes.

Clean your guitar

Remove dust from the inside of stringed instruments by pouring rice through the centre and then gently shaking it out onto newspaper.

Cedar chests

Restore natural scent by lightly sanding the interior.

Doors

- To prevent a wooden door from slamming, fit a sprung door closer or fit a door stop.
- To eliminate rattles, move the lock catch up or down.

- Fix a draught excluder inside the frame.
- Wedge a door before trying to work on it.
- A door can be shortened for carpet without having to take off its hinges.
- Lift a sagging door by tightening or moving the hinges.
- Find where a door is sticking by rubbing chalk down the edge of the door.
- Shut the door. It will leave a chalk mark on the frame at contact point. Plane that area, removing the paint first.
- If sliding doors stick, apply floor polish to the tracks.
- Repair wood rot quickly.
- Treat a sticking hinge by rubbing a pencil along the spine. Or smear a little light oil along the hinge with a cloth. Work the hinge back and forth until it moves freely.

Repairing and reupholstering chairs

- Drive out the old tacks with a chisel.
- Glue and nail angle blocks in front corners.
- Strain webbing with pincers and tack it.
- Fold webbing twice and fix with half inch tacks.
- Apply springs if necessary.
- Secure with stitches directly over the intersections of the webbing.
- Stuff with cushion stuffing fabric.
- Stitch hessian to seat.
- Push extra stuffing in as required.
- Cover with desired fabric.
- Secure with tacks.
- Cover tacks with braiding.
- Glue.

Shelves

It is important that you consider what it is that you wish to store in them as this will determine what supports you need and at which intervals. Construct quick and easy shelving by using piles of bricks with planks of planed wood laid at intervals between them.

Use strong brackets to support heavy equipment such as a music system or a television. Ensure that the walls are strong enough to support the weight.

Fix shelf brackets to the load bearing points of partition walls (studs). Tap the wall gently with a hammer and listen for the change of sound when you locate a stud. Alternatively a 'stud locator' may be purchased at your local hardware store.

To prevent items such as display plates from slipping from the shelf apply a thin strip of beading along the length of the shelf.

Stairs

It is best to treat creaking stairs from below. Glue a triangular block of wood into the corner of the tread and riser. Secure it with screws.

If it is inaccessible, take up the carpet and firmly screw the front of the tread to the top of the riser. Push a screw driver between the tread and the riser and insert a piece of card covered in woodwork adhesive. Leave. Repeat until squeak has disappeared.

You may need to replace the stair wedges. Clean off the old glue, reapply, then hammer the new wedges back into place.

Sticking drawers

If a drawer does not slide in and out easily, rub the runners with wax or soap. If it still sticks, take the drawer out, sand the runners with fine sandpaper and reapply the wax.

Wooden chopping boards

Eliminate splits from your chopping board by placing a damp tea towel on it overnight.

Soak new wooden cutting boards in cider vinegar overnight. This prevents them picking up food smells.

Coat your chopping board in vegetable oil when it begins to look dry.

Plumbing

It is good to know how to fix the plumbing yourself as in this area, small problems soon become big ones. Leaking taps can damage the walls and become dangerous if there is wetness near electricity.

Basic plumbing kit

Buy the best tools that you can afford as you will have them for life.

Store them safely in an accessible place in case of emergency.

Mole wrench
Sink plunger
Adjustable spanner
Resin
Insulating tape

Basics

Know where to turn off the water in the case of an emergency.

Turn it off from time to time to keep the mechanisms oiled and moving.

Begin the job early in the morning so that if a trip to the hardware store is required, it is still open.

Always have washers on hand. Buy several replacement washers at once.

Dripping taps

As a makeshift precaution to silence that annoying drip, tie a piece of string to the spout of the dripping tap. The water will flow quietly down the string.

Replace washers

Turn off the water supply.

Using an adjustable spanner place a cloth between the spanner and the tap to prevent scratching, then unscrew the tap cover.

Locate the large nut inside and remove with an open ended spanner.

Remove the valve mechanism.

Lift out the old washer.

Replace it with a new one.

Reassemble the tap.

Old taps

In old taps a leaking handle indicates the gland is worn and needs replacing.

Modern taps

Modern taps have o-ring seals instead of glands. You need to know the make of the tap to buy a new one.

Copper pipes
Temporary repairs
Cut a length of garden hose.
>Split it along the length.
>Enclose the pipe in it.
>Secure with hose clips.

Lead and plastic pipes
Squeeze petroleum jelly into the crack.
>Wrap a rag around the pipe until you can get it fixed.

Permanent repairs
Rub the pipe with abrasive paper so that epoxy resin will stick to it.
>Smear adhesive over the crack.
>Bind plumber's waterproof tape around the damaged area.
>Smear more resin over the newly taped surface.
>Leave to set hard before you turn water on.
>Open all faucets until water comes through to avoid airlocks forming.

If a pipe bursts
Turn off the main water and turn on all taps in the house to drain the water.
>If you have a water heater, turn it off to prevent damage.
>Turn off power.
>Try to find the source of the leak.
>Bind with cloth or waterproof tape.
>Place a bucket underneath.
>If ceiling is damaged, remove furniture from that room.
>Call a plumber.

Noisy pipes
Most noisy pipes are caused by pipes vibrating against each other, because they are not supported properly.
>Put foam rubber between them and the wall or secure them to a wooden batten.

Airlocks
Try tapping along the pipes with a mallet wrapped in cloth.
>OR
>Turn all the taps on full to run water through the pipes.
>AND
>If this fails, connect a piece of garden hose between the mains tap and the one that is faulty.
>Turn on the faulty tap, then the clear one.
>The pressure in the mains tap should push the air out of the pipe and back into the tank.
>Turn off the taps when the noise of the pipe stops.
>Remove the hose from the mains tap and drain it before disconnecting the other end.
>Reduce the pressure of the mains supply to prevent the airlock returning.

Blocked sinks and drains

Sinks become blocked with grease oil and food matter, which forms a solid barrier.
Keep drains clear with a mixture of salt, baking soda and cream of tartar.
Do not use caustic soda as this combines with grease to form a hard plug.
Use a plunger.
Smear the rim with petroleum jelly.
Place it over the plughole.
Run water until the cup is covered.
Pump the handle in an up and down movement.

U-bends

If the blockage is in the u-bend it will not respond to the plunger.
Place a bucket underneath the bend.
Unscrew the u-bend.
Carefully free the matter with a piece of wire.
Before replacing the u-bend, smear it with petroleum jelly around the threads.
Next time it will come off easily.

Smelly drains

Flush with washing soda and hot water.

Toilets

Stop flushing and let the water drain away.
Throw a bucket of water into the bowl all at once.
If the blockage remains, try a toilet plunger at the bottom of the bowl.
Pump up and down.

Overflowing cistern

Overflows may be caused by one of the following:

- Damaged ball float.
- Float arm at wrong angle.
- Worn washer in valve outlet.

If cistern is overflowing raise the ball float arm.
Tie to a wooden spoon and hold it in a raised position.
Get a new float.

Overflowing washing machine

Causes:

- Soap compartment may be wrongly installed.
- Filter may be overflowing.
- Wrong detergent.
- Too much detergent.

Solution for detergent problems:
Run machine through on rinse cycle.
Add a cup of vinegar about three minutes into the cycle.
If you can't see the problem, unplug the machine and call a mechanic.

General DIY tips
Battery power
If you have a job to do on the roof with your battery powered drill, always take a spare battery with you, as the battery is sure to run out while you're on the roof.

Left-over cork tiling
Left-over cork tiling can be used for:

Coasters
Draw around the top of a drinking glass. Cut out the shape to make a coaster.

Scratching post for cats
Stick the cork tiles onto an upright post. The cat will enjoy scratching on it.

Place mats
Glue a fabric that matches your kitchen curtains onto the cork tile. Use as a place mat.

Non-slip surfaces
Use the cork to glue underneath pottery vases and pots. Glue under the legs of chairs so that they won't scratch. Even up a wonky table by gluing a piece of cork to the shorter leg.

Notice-board
Glue cork tiles to a piece of wood. Hang on the wall for a notice-board.

Drill holster
To make an electric drill holster, cut the bottom off a bleach or similar container, nail the top half upside down, to the ladder.

Remote tidy
Attach one Velcro strip to the side of your TV and one strip on the back of the remote control. Then, when you have finished watching TV, put the remote onto the TV. You will always know where to find it.

Paving stones
Moving a heavy slab is easy if you manoeuvre the slab on to two poles.
Push the slab along as if it were on wheels.
Bring each pole to the front as it is left behind.

Soldering
Failures with soldering are due to one of three things:

* A cold soldering iron
* Dirty metal
* Cold flux

Aluminium cannot be successfully soldered by the amateur craftsman.

Stone and bone surfaces
To get tea, wine or coffee stains off marble, rub with a solution of one part hydrogen

peroxide to four parts of water. Wipe off. Repeat if necessary.

Salt is very good for removing stains from marble. Apply the salt, let it soak in, brush off and repeat if necessary until stain is gone.

A persistent stain in marble should be treated by pouring salt on, as described above, then adding sour milk. Leave the resultant paste for several days, then wipe off with a damp cloth.

Stains can be cleaned from alabaster with white spirit or turpentine.

Wash jade with water and a gentle soap, not abrasive cleaners. Wipe with paper towel.

Tortoise-shell hairbrushes can be cleaned with furniture cream.

Clean ivory hairbrushes with white spirit.

Bone handles on brushes, knives, etc. can be washed with methylated spirits.

Discolouration from bone handles can be removed by rubbing a paste of equal parts of hydrogen peroxide and whiting.

To clean ivory piano keys, use toothpaste on a damp cloth, rub gently, rinse with milk, and buff.

For plastic keys on a piano, dust regularly, and wipe occasionally with warm water and vinegar using a soft rag or chamois.

Washing machine stabiliser
Use left-over lino or vinyl to place under the washing machine. It cushions the vibrations.

Roofs
Ceiling stains
Get out on the roof on a rainy day and check where the water is going. Chances are that the leak will not be over the stain, but some distance away.

Iron or aluminium roofs
Sheets expand in the heat and loosen the nails. It may need a galvanised screw and washer to pull it tight. If the iron sheet has bent it will need to be straightened and secured.

Tiled roofs
To repair a cracked or broken tile or a badly fitting one, use a bitumen compound, which can be pressed in with a putty knife. It does not set hard but remains elastic.

Windows
Broken windows
- Always wear heavy gloves when handling glass.
- If you have to break glass, wear protective glasses.
- Dispose of broken glass by wrapping it securely in newspaper.
- If a window is broken and you cannot get a glazier straight away, board it up with chip board.
- Cover small cracks with plastic and masking tape.
- If the putty holding the window in becomes hard and falls out, chip it out with a chisel and replace putty.
- A build-up of paint may cause a window to stick. Remove the paint from window edges with stripper. Sand it to fit frame. Replace.

Window pane
To remove
To remove a window pane, carefully criss-cross pieces of masking tape over the pane.

Cover the glass with heavy cloth. Tap gently with a hammer to break away the pieces from the window, without splintering.

Replacing panes
Buy a sheet of glass that is 1.5 mm smaller than the window opening. Chip out the old putty. Clean out the recess. Paint it with primer. Lay a fresh bed of putty in the rebate window frame. Press the new piece of glass into position around the edges. (If you push in the middle, you could break the glass.) Insert glazing clips to keep the pane in place.

Sash cords
If sash cords have to be replaced, make sure that it is done with nylon cord, which will not rot.

Electricity
Electricity can kill so the greatest caution should be taken when dealing with it. If in doubt, call a professional. Before working on anything electrical, turn off the mains switch and remove the fuse that protects the circuit on which you are working. Check that the circuit is dead.

Appliances
Keep appliances in good repair. Faulty appliances can cause fires. If an appliance stops working check the manufacturer's handbook. Plug in another appliance to check if there is a fault in the socket.

Do not plug too many appliances into the one socket. You may overload it.

If an appliance gives out a shock, unplug it and either throw it out or have it repaired.

Basic electrical equipment
Keep all together in a box so that it is handy in case of a blackout. Keep candles in the freezer part of the fridge so you know where you can put your hand on them. You always need:

- Torch
- Screw driver
- Pliers
- Insulating tape
- Wire strippers

Lights
Clean lampshades regularly. Always use the recommended bulb for each lampshade. As dust reduces the light given out, keep it clean and dusted.

Lighting plan
Make a lighting plan for your house so that you have adequate and appropriate lighting in each area. Illuminate hazards such as outdoor steps with low level lights. Put luminous paint or stickers on all light switches so that you can see them in the dark.

Power failure

If several appliances in the one area fail, then it is most likely that the circuit has blown. Switch off each of the appliances. Switch off the mains and change the fuse.

Switch the appliances back on, one at a time. If the fuse blows again, you have overloaded the circuit.

During a power cut switch off all appliances except one light and the fridge and freezer as when the power comes on again, there may be a power surge, which could damage your appliances.

Safety

- Check all the plugs and flexes regularly for damage.
- Do not hammer nails into walls near sockets.
- Do not run flexes under carpets as they may become worn and the wires exposed.
- Do not touch anything electrical with wet hands. Always dry hands thoroughly.
- Do not use an adaptor plug to plug in more appliances than your circuit can accommodate.
- Avoid overloading your circuit.
- If a flex has worn, wrap it tightly in insulating tape to make it safe.
- Ensure that all metal appliances are earthed to prevent shock.
- Replace cracked or broken plugs before moisture can get in.
- Use a fire extinguisher.
- Never use water on an electrical fire. It will cause a short circuit and electric shocks.
- If you smell a fishy burning smell, turn the appliance off and remove the plug from the socket.
- It is an indication that the plug is over-heating.

Saving power

- Do not leave television on remote control when not in use. Switch it off.
- Buy energy-efficient appliances and choose the best that you can afford.
- Small appliances use considerably less power than ovens and stoves.
- Keep stoves clean to maximise reflective heat.
- Microwave ovens use less electricity than conventional ovens.
- Open the fridge or freezer as seldom as possible to save it having to work harder.
- Make sure saucepan lids fit tightly.
- Place lamps in corners to reflect light.
- Pale walls require less lighting than dark walls.

Warm plugs

Warm plugs spell danger. Take it out of the wall and remove the fuse from the circuit.

Heating and cooling

Heating

Turn down your heating and hot water by a couple of degrees to save 10% on bills.

Insulate

Insulate your home to keep it cool in summer and warm in winter. Double glazing is initially expensive but will pay for itself in the long run. Lag hot water pipes and cylinders. Clear plastic sheeting fixed to the window with tape will provide instant and cheap double glazing. Shrink it to fit with a hairdryer and peel off in summer. Insulate floors with rugs and carpets. Use sheets of plastic secured with strong tape. Insulate the roof space.

Block draughts in windows and doors

- Walk around the house with a lit candle.
- Where it flickers, there is a draught.
- Stuff an old jacket sleeve with wadding and sew the end and use it as a draft stopper.

Radiators

To stop the heat from radiators rising, fit a shelf directly above it and the heat will flow directly into the room. Tape aluminium foil to the wall behind the radiator with the shiny side out. It will reflect heat out.

Cooling

- Plant deciduous trees on the sunny side of the house. Ensure winter sun and summer shade.
- Fit outdoor canopies over sunny windows to shade them.
- Fit a sail cloth over a hot summer spot and take it down in winter.
- Install large fans that may be run on high to cool in summer, and on low, to draw heat down in winter.
- A solar hot-water service will pay for itself.
- Site air conditioners on the shady side of the house.
- Clean the air conditioner filters regularly.
- Use daylight as long as possible into the dusk. Avoid artificial lights as they generate heat.
- When showering open the windows to let as much moisture escape as possible.
- Draw curtains and blinds to keep the heat out.
- Reduce humidity by keeping the lids on saucepans firmly on.
- Don't use your oven in hot weather. Cook outside on the BBQ, and have salads instead of vegetables.

Electronic equipment

Dust is the killer for electronic equipment, so when computers, TVs, and so on are not in use, especially for long periods, keep them covered.

When cleaning any electrical or electronic equipment, make sure it is turned off at the power switch.

Telephones

Use methylated spirits to clean marks off the telephone. Clean the earpiece and mouthpiece of your telephone with a ball of cotton wool and antiseptic fluid or methylated spirits.

Televisions

Clean the television screen regularly with window cleaner or methylated spirits, and buff with a paper towel.

Occasionally spray an anti-static solution on the TV screen to prevent dust build-up.

Blank screen? No sound? Before rushing to the instruction manual or ringing the help hot-line, check that the power is on at both the wall outlet and the machine.

Emergency? If the antenna's gone down and the FA Cup is about to kick off, a coathanger hooked up and strategically placed could save the day.

Compact discs that are not playing properly can often be fixed by gently cleaning with toothpaste to get rid of dust and scratches.

If your room has high condensation, get silica sachets, available from a florist, and place them on top of your video player to keep it dry.

Run a video head cleaner regularly through your video player to maintain top performance and reduce potential tape damage.

Always store your camera in its case in between uses, and keep it clean. But leave maintenance and cleaning to a professional.

Set up your computer so it is out of direct sunlight and prevent over-heating.

Site the monitor so light and glare is not reflecting off it, causing you discomfort and interfering with your work or enjoyment.

Metals
Detecting cracks in metal
Clean the suspected part and then coat with a very thin paste made from red lead and petrol. The petrol will dry leaving the dry red lead which has been carried into the small cracks.

Brass
Clean brass with a lemon which has been cut in half and dipped in salt. If it has turned green rub with a solution of ammonia and salt. Wear gloves.

Bronze
Wipe bronze with a little shoe polish or vegetable oil to maintain the sheen. Marks can be removed with turpentine.

Chrome
- Do not use abrasives on chrome as they will damage the coating.
- Remove minor marks by wiping with water and liquid detergent.
- Wash with a cloth soaked in equal portions of white vinegar and water.
- Remove stubborn marks with a solution of bicarbonate of soda and water.
- To shine, rub on plain flour and buff with a soft cloth.

Copper
Copper reacts to food acids. You will need to have your copper pans relined when they show signs of wear.

Gold
- Wash gold chains in a bowl of soapy water, using a soft toothbrush to get into the difficult corners.
- Allow to dry on a soft towel.
- Polish with a chamois.
  To store:
- Wrap in chamois leather.
  Large gold objects:
- Clean with a silver cleaning cloth.
- Buff with chamois leather.

Iron

Cast iron must always be dried thoroughly after use.

Otherwise it will rust. Season well with cooking oil before the first use, and, after that, whenever needed.

Silver

- Silver keeps best if used.
- Wash your silver regularly in hot water to which dishwashing liquid has been added.
- Polish at the first hint of tarnish.
- Avoid over-cleaning.
- Treat silver-plated items as you would silver, but with more care as the coating can wash off.

To store silver

Place in a tarnish proof bag. Or wrap items in acid-free tissue paper. Place two sugar cubes inside a silver teapot or coffee pot between uses to prevent mustiness.

Enemies of silver

Salt, broccoli, fish and egg yolk are notorious for causing silver to tarnish. Clean as soon as possible after silver has had contact with any one of these.

To clean silver

- Do not rub hallmarks too hard as you will reduce the value of the piece by rubbing them away.
- Clean the silver in an open space where air circulates.
- Use a soft toothbrush to apply polish to embossed silver ware.
  To remove bad tarnish:
- Dissolve a half cup of washing soda in hot water in an aluminium dish.
- Place articles in solution.
- Leave until the tarnish disappears.
- Rinse thoroughly.
- Polish.

Use a paste made from salt and lemon juice.

To wash silver cutlery

- Wash silver cutlery as soon as possible after use to avoid damage caused by food.
- Place strips of aluminium foil along the bottom of a plastic bowl.
- Place silver cutlery on top.
- Cover with boiling water.
- Add three tablespoons baking soda.
- Soak for ten minutes.
- Dry with clean tea towel.

Never wash silver and stainless steel cutlery in the dishwasher together as the silver may cause the stainless steel to pit.

Home-made silver cleaning cloths

Soak cotton squares in a solution of:

2 parts ammonia
1 part silver polish

10 parts cold water

Leave to drip dry.

Useful hints for silver

Do not put salt directly into a silver shaker, fit a glass interior and remove salt after each use.

To clean the stain from the inside of coffee pots, rub with a piece of fine steel wool, which has been dipped in neat white vinegar and salt. Rinse thoroughly.

To clean the inside of a teapot, fill the teapot with boiling water and add half a cup baking soda. Leave overnight.

Remove wax from candlesticks by blowing hot air from a hairdryer over it.

Table napkin rings can be cleaned with a little toothpaste on a soft cloth.

Coat the posts of silver earrings with clear nail polish to prevent the tarnish causing infection.

Stainless steel

Dry stainless steel thoroughly after use. Rub with flour to give a good shine. Remove heat marks with lemon juice of a scouring pad.

Knives

Remove smells from knives by plunging them into soil. Keep knives sharp by storing them in a wooden block or on a magnetic board.

Pewter

To shine pewter objects, rub with cabbage leaves.

Immerse in left-over water that has been used to boil eggs.

Platinum

Immerse in a jewellery dip. Rinse and dry thoroughly.

Lead

Try one of these cleaning methods:

- Scrub with turpentine. Rinse in distilled water.
- Place in a solution of one part vinegar to nine parts water. Soak for ten minutes. Rinse.

Metal colouring

All colouring is done by immersion in water solutions.

Bronzing

Finish is generally a black blue colour on bright iron. This can be produced on small items by indirect heating over a gas flame.

For large pieces:

Dissolve 125g photographic hypo in a litre water. Mix 60g bog acetate of lead in one litre water. Combine and boil. Immerse bright clean iron in this. Stop when the desired shade is achieved. Vary the above portions for more or less solution.

French gold on brass

Coat highly polished brass with a transparent lacquer to which some orange dye has been added.

Antique brass or copper
Method one
Take three basins:

Basin 1 – weak solution of potassium sulphide in water.

Basin 2 – add tiny quantity of spirits of salts.

Basin 3 – clear water.

Dip clean and polished brass in these three basins successively in that order. Repeat until desired tone is achieved.

Method two
- Add small quantity barium sulphide to the water.
- Dip the articles to be bronzed into it.
- Wash clean.
- Dry thoroughly.
- Scrub with thin wire brush.

Coin bronze on copper
- Add a teaspoon potassium sulphide to ten litres water.
- Dip piece to be done in it.
- It will turn crimson, golden and brown.
- Finish with a fine wire brush to even out the colouring.

Verde green
Prepare a mixture of copper nitrate, chloride of lime and ammonia chloride in water. Better too much water than too little. Too little water will turn the copper black. Dip the work in the solution.

The solution may be brushed on work with soft brush. Allow work to stand for several days between coats.

Lacquering
Apply with soft muslin or soft brush. On no account use bristle brush.

Concreting
General concreting tips
Do not attempt concreting if it looks like rain.

If the day is hot the newly laid concrete should be prevented from drying out too quickly by covering with damp hessian.

As soon as the concrete is set hard it should be cured by sprinkling with water and covered with sand that should be kept damp for a week or so.

Satisfactory proportions for mixing concrete

Foundations	1 cement	3 sand	5 gravel screenings
Pavements/paths	1	2½	4
Floor surfaces	1	1½	2½
Mortar/topping paths	1	2½	
Mortar for brickwork	1	4	
Blocks for walls	1	5	

To harden concrete
- Add sodium silicate to the mixture to harden the surface of the concrete.
- Allow the concrete to partly dry out.
- Dilute sodium silicate with four times its volume in water.
- Mix well.
- Apply with mop or brush to clean concrete.
- Allow to dry.
- Repeat every twenty-four hours, three times.

Decorating furniture
Stencilling
Stencil images onto furniture. Create your own work of art by going over the stencil lines using an artist's brush and your own colours. Vary the design enough to personalise it.

Decoupage
- Customise the top of your table or the front of your cupboard with the decoupage of your choice.
- It may be family photos, which you have scanned and enlarged.
- It may be greeting cards that you have received for a special occasion.
- It may be magazine pictures that you like.
- Carefully cut out the images of choice.
- Stick them down using PVC.
- Brush more PVC over the top of them.
- Once the adhesive has dried, apply acrylic varnish to seal and protect the images.
- The more layers of varnish you apply, the more effective.

Useful tip
- You can also seal your decoupage with egg tempera.
- Use the white of an egg.
- Add 1 teaspoon distilled water.
- Add 1 teaspoon linseed oil.
- Apply with brush.
- Buff with cotton wool when dry.

Tablecloth
Paint a pretty tablecloth onto your garden table. It makes a pretty background for your table setting. It never has to be washed and won't blow away.

Store small brushes
To store small artist's paint brushes, clean thoroughly and tape them together.

Painting the house
Colour
Colour is the most fun to work with. You can change it inexpensively and you can mix and match. Add seasonal favourites or holiday hues. Nature colours are beautiful and interesting. Your favorite colours should be a major part of your scheme. Compromise always lends itself to peace on the home front. If you choose the main colour, let others pick the secondary colours.

Plan

Think through what you need to do, work out the paint and equipment, draw up a list, and go and get everything you need in one visit.

Equipment

Buy a range of small, medium and large brushes, including one with angled bristles to paint around window edges, etc.

Other equipment required may include rollers, and paint trays, a paint pad, sponge, scraper, masking tape and sandpaper.

Useful from around the house are old ice-cream containers, or, better still, old honey tubs with handles, to pour paint into and work from.

You can buy paint 'kettles' or buckets from your paint shop to use as your base-painting holder – these are especially good when you are buying paint in ten litres or bigger bulk cans.

To save cleaning up your paint kettle after each use, line it with aluminium foil and pour paint in.

Just throw the foil out when you have finished.

Cheap brushes will do that – give you a cheap, streaky result, and you will tear your hair out with the bristles pulling out and sticking on the paint.

Generally speaking, natural-bristle brushes, although more expensive, do not lose as many bristles as synthetic ones.

Safety

Safety first at all times – do not try and balance on chairs and tables.

When painting ceilings, use two sets of ladders and run a heavy plank between the two as scaffolding – make sure the plank is on the same step level for each ladder and both it and the ladders are secure.

If your stored paint brushes are stiff and dry from not being cleaned properly, simmer them in vinegar until they are soft.

No matter how small a job it is, don't try and paint in your best clothes and think you will get away spot-free – wear an old shirt, jeans, etc.

Wear safety goggles to prevent paint dripping in your eye or onto your glasses.

If painting internally, the job will be much easier, quicker and less frustrating if you move all furniture out, or shift it into one spot and cover it in plastic, canvas or dust sheets.

Prepare surfaces

Bare wood

Treat any knots with knotting solution; apply a primer according to the wood type. Fill holes – remove as much dust as possible from the hole with a dry paint brush, wet the hole. Apply the filler with a flat instrument such as a putty knife, scrape off the excess, leave to dry, then sand smooth.

Painted wood

Sand down surface to get rid off any flaky paint and to make sure surface is even. Use sandpaper wrapped around a block of wood. Wash with sugar soap, rinse and let dry.

Water-based paint

Wash with sugar soap. Scrub mould off with nylon pot scourer and water.

Wallpaper
Wet it well, one section at a time, and then peel it off. Wait until it is dry before sealing it and then painting.

Plaster, already painted
Sand down to get rid of any flaky paint and to make sure surface is even, using sandpaper wrapped around a block of wood. Make sure it is bone dry before sealing it with primer prior to applying the first coat.

Plaster, new
Brush down, and use a vacuum if necessary, to get rid of any remaining white dust. Smooth joins with sandpaper. Paint first coat with primer, or, as is becoming more common, with manufacturer-recommended first-coat paint.

Brick
Brush well, remove all mould with a wire brush, replace any missing or damaged mortar. Apply a sealer first.

Ceramic tiles
Clean with a solution of ammonia, sand down to key; always use enamel paint.

Home-made filler
An excellent, make-do filler for small holes in wood surfaces is a mixture of flour and the paint you are using. When it hardens it will match perfectly. Smooth off with sandpaper.

Types of paint include:
Primer
Use to prepare porous surfaces such as new plaster, bare wood, unpainted metal, etc.

Undercoat
Use to paint over the primer, before principal colour is applied.
    Can be specialist undercoat or first coat of colour chosen.

Water-based paint
This is generally a flat-surface paint for walls.
    However, its purposes are now expanding into a wider variety of applications, including wooden surrounds, etc.
    When using water-based paints, brushes wash up in water.

Satin or semi-gloss
This paint, with its sheen finish, is usually used for highlight areas or heavy traffic surfaces, can be water-based or oil-based.

Gloss
Gloss is usually used for wooden surrounds, etc, as it is very hard-wearing. It is usually oil-based and requires mineral turpentine for wash-up.

Paint coverage, approximately:

Primer – one litre covers 12 square metres (130 square feet).
Undercoat – one litre covers 16 square metres (170 square feet).
Topcoat – one litre covers 16 square metres (170 square feet).
Water-based paint – one litre covers 12 square metres (130 square feet).
Gloss – one litre covers 14 square metres (150 square foot).

Always paint a room in this sequence:

1. Ceiling, starting across from a window.
2. Walls, starting at right-hand top of a wall.
3. Doors.
4. Windows.
5. Skirting boards.

Hints to make your painting job easier

Use the blunt side of a knife to prise open cans of paint, making sure you dust it off first to ensure no foreign objects getting into the paint.

Stick masking tape around the rim of a can to reduce mess.

Stand cans on paper picnic plates to avoid getting drips on the floor.

To avoid drips down the side of the can, tie a piece of string across the middle of the can, securing it by either taping it or by tying it to the handle fixtures.

Use this to wipe excess paint off the brush, rather than as you normally do on the edge of the can.

To avoid brush marks showing, work your brush both vertically and horizontally when painting a section.

When using a roller, spread it evenly by rolling paint on the wall in the shape of over overlapping 'W's.

When using paint pads, smooth the pad over the wall in all directions without lifting it to get an even result.

When doing skirting boards, hold a thick piece of cardboard above the board as you paint to protect the wall.

When painting pipes, place piece of cardboard behind the pipes so that you won't paint the wall.

To get behind tricky spots, such as a radiator, pull a wire coat hanger apart and make a painting pad at one end by wrapping material around it.

If you stop to have a break, paint up to a corner of a wall, rather than stopping in the middle, so that you do not leave an obvious line which may be difficult to cover later.

If you stop to have a break, wrap all brushes being used in aluminium foil or cling wrap to keep them moist.

Another brush and time saver, if you are taking a break, is to put all brushes being used in a plastic bag and then immerse the bag in a container of water.

To cut down on the paint fumes in a room, leave half an onion, cut side up, in a dish in the room. Replace the onion each day until the odour of the paint disappears.

To avoid drips running down your hand when painting a ceiling, push the handle through a paper plate, so you end up with the painting equivalent of a protector on a sword.

When painting windows, it is wise to start early in the morning, so that they will be dry by night and you can close them without fear of sticking.

If you have to close a painted window at night, and the paint is not yet dry, rub the contact area with talcum powder.

When painting a door, start at the top left-hand quarter, and paint approximately the top quarter, then do the top quarter on the right. Move to the left again and do the next quarter down, and so on.

When painting doors, rub petroleum jelly on the knobs and hinges, so that any accidental paint spots or smears will wipe off easily.

Use masking tape around the edges of all glass – on windows and doors – so that you do not end up with spots and smears over the glass. Pull it away when it is dry to touch, but do not leave it too long as it may stick and you might end up pulling some of the paint away.

Do not apply paint in the early morning or on a surface that has been covered in frost or dew the previous night.

Always finish a stretch before stopping for lunch or the day.

Good work cannot be done with dirty brushes.

Allow plenty of time for the surface to dry.

To varnish woodwork

- Apply knotting seal to all knots, to stop any resin running, then rub varnish into the wood with a cloth. Go in the direction of the grain.
- After it is dry, rub it with extra-smooth sandpaper on a block. If there are still some knots leaking resin, apply more knotting seal.
- Dust surface well, and apply a second coat of varnish, either with a rag or a quality brush so that it does not shed bristles as you go.
- Work in line with the grain. Sand down before applying a final coat.
- Three coats is usually enough, but for that extra depth and sheen, apply as many coats as you wish.

To clean paint stains

- Fresh water-based stains on fabric – blot immediately, spot with cold water, then launder.
- Freshwater-based stains on carpet – dab at the stain with a sponge and cold water, working from the outside inwards so as not to spread it further. When as clear as possible, apply carpet shampoo.
- Fresh oil-based stains on carpet – blot as much up with paper towels as possible, then treat with carpet shampoo. If the stain is old and dry, try a solvent, or at worse, trim the top of the pile.
- Fresh water-based stains on clothes – blot with paper towels, then wash under a tap with soap and water. Launder as usual.
- Fresh oil-based stains on clothes – dab with white spirit, holding a pad underneath the stain. Repeat until all the stain is gone, then launder. Do not launder until all the paint is gone, as this will set the stain and leave it permanently.
- Dried stains on clothes – hold a pad under the stain, dab at the mark with methylated spirits or turps or other paint solvent until it comes out, then launder.

Cleaning up

Avoid fumes at all times, especially when cleaning equipment at the end of the day.

Rollers

To clean a roller, flatten out some newspaper pages and run the roller up and down those to get rid of excess paint. Wash the roller in warm, soapy water, then rinse again with cold water.

To do a quicker, better cleaning job on brushes and rollers covered in water-based paint, use warm water and detergent rather than simply cold water.

Brushes

With oil-based paint on brushes, give them a preliminary clean with newspaper, and then wash them in turpentine. Rinse off in warm, soapy water. Rinse again with cold water.

To soak a brush in turps, three-quarters fill an old jar with spirit. Drill a hole through the brush, just above the join to the bristles. Push a long nail through the hole, and rest it across the lips of the jar, thus balancing the brush with the bristles (a little like a gyroscope) in the turps. This not only saves the bristles from going hard but also stops them bending and becoming virtually useless.

Drill holes in your brushes to hang them up for storage. This keeps them straight rather than bending the bristles.

Rub a little oil into your brushes before you store them to keep them soft and pliable for next use.

Record the paints you use

Store some samples in jars of the paints you have used – especially if you used colours that are not ready-mixed – so they can be easily matched next time around.

Keep a log of what paints you used in an exercise book, in case you need to buy more later, for touching-up or revamping.

It saves racking your memory, digging out old tins, or slavishly going through all the colour charts again.

Make up some colour swatches, by applying samples of the paints you used to pieces of card, and take these with you when you go shopping for furniture and soft furnishings to make a match.

Cleaning gilt frames

Add a dash of ammonia to warm water. Sponge. Dry with a chamois.

Removing sticky varnish

Remove old varnish with paint remover. Stain with coat of one part linseed oil and two parts turpentine. Mix together. Allow two days to dry. Mix two parts linseed oil with one part boiled linseed oil. Brush in well.

Wallpaper
Hanging wallpaper

Use equipment of good quality. It may be a good idea to hire it. Always buy one more roll than you think you will need. Thick, good-quality paper may cost a little more but is easier to hang and will cover cracked or rough walls.

Tools you will need
- Sponge
- Paper hanging brush
- Pasting brush
- Scissors
- Wallpaper trough
- Bucket with handle
- Pasting table
- Plumbline
  (Make a plumbline by hanging any weight from a piece of string.)

Types of wallpaper

Lining
Is used for covering uneven walls before decorative wallpaper is hung.

Vinyl
Is good for kitchens, bathrooms and children's bedrooms as it has a wipe-clean surface.

Textured
Is used for uneven walls and must be painted over. Once on, it is difficult to remove.

Decorated
Is the common wallpaper and comes in a wide range of colour and patterns. Take a strip home and live with it for a week before you finally decide.

Remove old wallpaper
Peel off old vinyl. Begin at the bottom and carefully pull off the vinyl. You will find backing paper underneath which may either be removed or papered over.

Use a steamer
Hire a steamer machine. Dissolve the paste that glues the old wallpaper. Scrape the wallpaper off.

Do it by hand. Thoroughly soak a small area with a sponge. Make a few random slits in the area with the corner of the scraper. Scrape the paper, working upwards.

Tips for wallpapering
- Complete all painting in the room before you begin to paper.
- Cut paper to correct lengths, allowing ten cm before you start.
- Remember to match the pattern and allow for that in your measuring.
- Always paper the ceiling before you start on the wall so that the glue is not dripping on new paper.
- Apply paste to the wall as it reduces the absorbency of the surface and also allows you to move the paper around on the wall more freely.
- Use a roller rather than a sponge to apply paste more efficiently.
- In a bucket mix the paste following the manufacturer's instruction.
- Stir well and allow to settle.
- Paint any grease spots on the wall with emulsion before papering.
- This will prevent the stain going through onto the wallpaper.
- Lining paper provides a smooth surface for the top wallpaper. It also gives you prior practice in handling the awkward bits of your job.

Begin work
Begin work on the most important wall at a focal point. Work away from the starting point in both directions. To trim the edges push the paper into the top of the wall, crease, peel back and cut with scissors. Brush smooth with wallpaper brush eliminating all air holes.

Light switches
When papering around light switches cut a diagonal cross in the paper. Peel back the paper triangles and trim flush. Screw holes. Place a matchstick in the raw plughole and paper over. You will be able to see where the screws go.

Rectifying faults

Air bubbles
Remove air bubbles by slitting a small cross at the centre of the bubble with a sharp blade. Use a small narrow brush to insert wallpaper paste into the slits. Replace flaps. Smooth the edges down with paper-hanging brush. Wipe clean.

Lifting seams
Gently lift edges with craft knife. Apply paste. Sponge into place.

Shiny patches
Rub with white bread.

Uneven edges
Disguise uneven edges with a thin border. Crease. Cut along the crease. Apply the paste. Sponge flat.

Damp patches
Remove the strip. Apply another.

Interior decorating
It really doesn't matter how big or small your home is. Nor is it important that you own, rent, or live with family or friends. Your home is you and whoever else you may share it with. If everyone contributes and has a say then it becomes a 'family' home.

We also show pride in our heritage and backgrounds: Books, paintings, needlework, pottery or heirlooms. Whatever is important to you, display it proudly and let others admire it and enjoy it. Decorating where we live is really an extension of who we are.

Your home should be comfortable for you and your family. Rearranging, redecorating, or just adding or subtracting items makes our home fun, functional, enjoyable, and a pleasure to come back to.

Decorating styles
Wherever you live, and whatever style home you have, it should be a place that reflects who you are and where you want to be. You can create an atmosphere of comfort, relaxation and friendship. Decorating styles are typically grouped into the following:

Traditional
Formal, dressy, rich fabrics, cherry wood.

Colour combinations
Burgundy/taupe/sage green
Blue/yellow
Cream/white/beige
Purple/sage green/beige
Dark blue/paprika/sage green/gold

Country
Antiques, pine, collectibles, cosy warm feeling.

Colour combinations
Warm colours of similar hue.
Textures and patterns that differ but are in similar colours.

Contemporary
Clean lines and dramatic.

Colour combinations
White/maroon/black with stainless steel
Grey/black/cornflour with laminate surfaces, timber floors, big windows.
Aqua/rose/peach
Periwinkle blue/beige/white
Cobalt blue/lime green

Romantic
Soft, elegant, ruffles, lace.

Colour combinations
Pastel shades with white or cream.

Oriental
Antiques, dramatic colours, high style.

Colour combinations
Reds, yellows, blues, greens, shiny black surfaces.

Environmental
Earth tones, textures, taking advantage of the views and surrounds, artefacts.

Colour combinations
All of the autumn colours, sandstone, wood, brick.

Transitional or eclectic
Mixes of any style.

Colour combinations
Sage green/rose/pink/beige
Terracotta/sage green/purple
Moss green/rust/camel
Yellow/green/rose/blue/peach (equal multi-colour)

About colour
There are three primary colours – red, yellow, blue. All other colours are derived from these.

White is a combination of all colours.

Secondary colours are made by combining two primary colours. All other colours are known as tertiary colours. They are formed from many and varied combinations of colours. Shades and tones are achieved by lightening with white and darkening with black. They are placed at equal intervals around the colour wheel. On either side of each primary colour there is a range of tones.

Complementary colours are directly opposite each other on the colour wheel.

Emotions

- Colour produces different emotional responses in people.
- Strong, hot colours make a comment or draw attention.
- Warm colours are welcoming and comforting.
- Strong, cold colours are calming.
- Cool colours are invigorating, but soothing.

When choosing colours

Ask yourself these questions:

- What sort of mood do I wish to create with this room?
- Who is going to be using this room?
- For what purpose will this room be used?
- How does the light fall on this room?
- Do I wish to create a feeling of space?
- Do I wish to create a feeling of cosiness?
- Select your main colour with these aims in mind.
- Which features in the room do you wish to accentuate?
- Is this a rest room or an activity room?

Create your colour scheme around one main colour and then consider which other colours combined with that will give the effect that you desire.

Contrasting shades

You may use various hues of the same colour. If you limit the differences of shade so that they are very subtle, the room will be more calming. If you use pale colours and subtle differences the effect will be better.

Complementary

Use colours directly opposite each other on the colour wheel. Light and dark. Use a colour that is a direct contrast to the main colour to highlight.

White

White has the ability to show off all other colours. An all-white room gives you great licence with your choice of accessories.

If you use subtle colours for the walls and woodwork, you are more able to make statements with your furniture pieces and placements.

Warm colours

Oranges, pinks, warm yellows.

Warm colours tend to close the walls in and add to the feeling of cosiness. Choose these for a room on the cold side of the house.

Cool colours

Blues, greens, lemon.

Cool colours give a greater feeling of spaciousness. Choose these colours for a room that gets plenty of sun, a small room that you wish to make look bigger, or passageways.

Dark colours

Dark colours close the walls in and make the room look smaller. They can be used to 'lower' the ceiling, create a feeling of intimacy, and make the space cosy.

Light colours

Light colours create a feeling of space. They can be used to make ceilings look higher, create a feeling of spaciousness and to make a sunny room feel cooler.

Using other colour already in the room

When creating a colour scheme, look at the other colours in the room that you are unable to change – the carpet, the curtains, the woodwork, masonry. Consider using hues of these colours to balance your room. Perhaps these colours may need to be played down. Use your colour scheme to do this.

Choosing colours

- Repeat each colour in your scheme at eye level, mid level and floor level to achieve good visual balance.
- Repeat any pattern and/or textures at least twice in the room.
- Paint and wallpaper/borders go a long way in updating and freshening a room and usually cost very little.
- View colour sand patterns in your home during daylight hours before making a purchase.
- The colour that you choose will be a combination of many things, including culture and individual experiences.

Accessories

Link the features of your room by matching colours or patterns. Use texture to vary colour subtly.

Less is best

Too many colours only make for confusion and clutter. Limit the colours that you will use.

Colour charts

Many manufacturers offer free colour charts where they give you examples of modern colour schemes for different rooms.

Take these and adapt them to suit yourself.

Some manufacturers offer a CD Rom that you can buy and take home and try the colour scheme that you choose on your computer. This is an excellent way to check for liveability.

Buy a sample pot of the colour that you have chosen from the chart and try it on the wall. You will be surprised at how much stronger the colour is when painted in a large area on your wall.

A good rule of thumb is to choose your colour and then take it back three or four shades lighter. You can always add more colour, but you can't take it away.

Use one of the manufacturers larger sample sheets and throw it on the floor next to the carpet/tiles/curtains. Check to see if it clashes.

Once you have decided on your colour, buy a colour sampler and live with it on your wall for a week or so.

If you are hiring a painter

- Get three quotes.
- Avoid painters who have big teams of painters who come and do the job quickly. It is often a case of too many chiefs and not enough Indians. No one takes the responsibility for a well-done job.
- Ask to see other jobs that the painter has done in your area. Talk to the home owner.
- Have your painting done in small, manageable lots – inside downstairs, inside upstairs, outside.

- It is a mistake to have too much done at once as the disruption is unbearable and it is almost impossible to see that the job is well done.
- For example, if it rains the outside crew will come inside without finishing outside, so you end up with pandemonium.
- Do not be afraid to insist that the job be completed properly.
- Hold back final payment until it is.

There are eight steps to home decorating
1. Walls
2. Flooring
3. Furniture
4. Window treatments
5. Lighting
6. Artwork
7. Accessories
8. Plants/floral

How do I know what I want?
Use home decorating magazines. Flip through them, find photographs of rooms you really like and which appeal to you. Make note of them or set the magazines aside.

Borrow decorating books from the library and do the same thing.

Check out other people's homes. Eventually you will see a pattern emerge of rooms you like and styles that represent the kind of home you want. Knowing basic style categories will further help define your style preferences. Shopping for your home can be extremely frustrating if you don't know what you are looking for.

Budget
Once you find your style, work out a budget, and the rest falls into place. Decide on a budget so that you can pace your decorating. Include money for accessories.

Decide on one room at a time and designate a priority within your room.

Have a plan, colour scheme, style and atmosphere that you wish to create. Have a target date for completion.

Plan to scale
Measure your room to scale. Show windows and doors. Decide on a focal point. Measure furniture, rugs and other accessories before purchase. Draw your furniture to scale and cut out the drawings. Place these on your floor plan, moving them around until you get an arrangement that you like. This procedure will help you decide if the items are proportionately correct for your room. Think too about ceiling height and traffic flow.

Accessories
If you do not plan to be in your home for a long time, invest in accessories (artwork, area rugs, decorator pillows) that you can take with you to another home.

Remember . . .
Money doesn't buy taste and you do not need a lot of it to achieve good interior decoration.

Questions to ask before you begin to decorate
The answers to these questions will determine where you should begin decorating your home.

- Who are you and how does your home get used?
- Do you entertain a lot?
- Do you only entertain a few times a year for family and friends?

- Do you have large dinner parties with business associates?
- Do you like to read?
- How many people are in your family?
- Do you have small children?
- Do all the kids in the neighbourhood come to your house?
- Do you prefer to have a home where jeans and T-shirts are considered formal wear?

Which rooms shall I do first?

Focus on what area you plan to do – first, second and third. If you don't define the order of work, then you will become very overwhelmed by all the things you need to accomplish. Break it down into smaller pieces and get it done. With your lifestyle in mind, decide what rooms are most important to finish first, while, at the same time, keeping an overall eye on your whole house.

- If you are a person who loves to entertain formally, then you should consider working first on your living room and dining room.
- If you like to entertain informally with friends and family, work on your family room and kitchen spaces.
- If you are a cook and everyone congregates in your kitchen, then, by all means, do that room first.
- If you are a homebody and just love relaxing in your bedroom, do that room first.
- If you are a busy professional and are rarely home, then the bedroom theory from above may be the best for you as you will be in that room more often.

Windows

Windows can be a decorating opportunity for setting the room's mood and style.

Or, they can be merely a feature that blends into the whole room. Whether you treat windows as a background element or as focal point, always remember that the purpose of a window is to provide light and air.

A well-designed window suits not only the window but also the room. It harmonises with the rest of the room and adds to the sense of unity. It is in scale with the room and its furnishings. It is well proportioned.

When deciding how to treat the windows in the room ask the following questions:

- Does the room face north, south, east, west?
- What degree of privacy do you need?
- Do you want to maintain the view?
- Do you need the window for ventilation?
- How much light control do you want?
- Is energy efficiency a concern?
- Do you want easy access to the window for cleaning?
- Are there any interfering factors such as security buttons, window cranks, window air conditioners, baseboard heaters, etc.?
- Are there light switches or wall sockets that need to be considered?
- Are there any interfering architectural features such as crown mouldings, beams, chair rails, built-in cabinets, etc.?
- Is the window located close to a corner of the room so that extension of the treatment may be prohibited or operation of a traverse treatment limited?
- Is there a combination of doors and windows in the room that needs to be treated?
- Is the door used frequently?
- What about cleaning and maintenance of the treatment itself?
- Will children be in the room?
- Will pets be in the room?

French country style
French country makes creating pieces to furnish your rooms easy and affordable. If you like this style, take a moment to curl up with a cup of coffee or tea and browse through some lifestyle magazines. Note accessories and furnishings you like. Shop at flea markets, boutiques, and garage sales or dig in attics and basements for pieces that you can refinish to reflect your French country theme. You'll be well on your way to creating a fashionable look for a reasonable cost.

French country style walls
Inside a typical French farmhouse, the walls are finished in coarse plaster, often with exposed beams on ceilings and walls. Whether left white or painted in warm hues with the soft patina of age, the effect is unmistakably rustic. You can easily re-create this textured plaster look.

Paint old furniture French country style
Paint a distressed trunk or an old cane chair so that it looks old and used. Use the distressed look that you can mimic. Simply ask at your paint store.

Make a topiary. Create topiaries that can be enjoyed both as a unique porch decoration and as a buffet-table or serving-table centrepiece.

Feng-shui
Feng-shui (pronounced *fung-shway*) comes from the Chinese words FENG (wind) and SHUI (water). It is an ancient Chinese art of placement of furniture or objects to create balance in one's life. In other words, creating a harmonious environment.

It is said that energy is carried by wind and is retained when it hits water. Feng shui is also the study of time, space and people. Feng shui is increasingly becoming popular. Many people consult feng shui experts when they are decorating.

Welcome
A simple wooden or metal 'Greetings' sign by your main entrance will let others know that you welcome their visit and are extending a hand of friendship.

Name your home
A name on a house reflects the people who live there.

- It may be a name that the previous owners had: Avon, Tipperary, Korumburra.
- It may be a native bush or flower that grows in the area: Buttercup Cottage, Wisteria, Heath.
- It may be a play on words, designed to amuse. Yworry: Thisisours, Homelea.
- It may be the place that you met and fell in love with your partner: Venice, Mildura, Alaska:

Planters
- Planters make great catch-alls for everyday items.
- A small one on a desk can make an attractive container for pens, markers and scissors.
- A larger planter by the front door can catch umbrellas, wet mittens or mail.
- Try tucking a planter under a side table to hold magazines and books.
- Place rolled-up towels in one for your guest room.
- Silverware, nuts, seasonal candy or anything else you might put in a bowl can also be placed in a planter.

Making something from something else

Loose slipcovers, tailored slipcovers, pillow covers and duvets are all the rage . . . even chic! It's great to know that one can refresh an old outdated chair, footstool or couch with just a few yards of fabric. Sometimes, to get a sofa or a chair recovered costs almost as much as to buy a new one. Here are just a few ideas as to how you can make slipcovers and napery cheaply.

Painters canvas/unbleached calico

Try unbleached calico for simple, natural coloured covers, drapes and cushions.

Cover the front of a wardrobe or closet with it. Either drape or attach to a simple frame. Cheap and effective.

Heavy duty, unbleached, cotton duck canvas from the hardware store costs a fraction of the cost of material from the decorators. With a few tucks, hidden safety pins and ribbon ties to gather everything up under the arms of the couch, you can have a loose slipcover that can be washed and dried easily.

If you just don't like plain canvas or fabric, try stamping or stencilling with fabric paints to customise your own look. Paint straight lines, flowers, or transfer photos to the canvas to make your own custom fabric. You'll have a conversation piece.

Tablecloths

Try using tablecloths for smaller slipcover projects like chairs, seat covers, footstools or ottomans. They come in all shapes and sizes, colours and textiles. Buy them at sales, flea markets, thrift stores. Use a new tablecloth to 'gift-wrap' chair cushions.

You don't need to sew. Simply wrap the cloth around the cushions and pin with safety pins. Lace tablecloths can be used as an overlay for solid cushions or fabric that you just want to tone down.

Clothing

Be inventive in your use of outdated and old clothing. Sometimes the fabric is perfect for the type of effect that you require. Make cushion covers, laundry bags, use the lace as trimming.

Use the cotton, linen, velvets, silks, organza, or other expensive fabric you have lurking in your closet and which will never be worn again. Turn them into something special for your home.

Sheets

Rather than purchasing an expensive doona cover for a comforter, buy a couple of flat sheets in the size and colour you need and sew them together on three sides.

Old curtains, draperies and sheers

Shop at the op shop for fabrics that catch your eye. They may come in the form of clothes, but they may also come in the form of old curtains, drapes, bedspreads, doona covers and the like.

Quilts and bedspreads

Chenille and matelasse bedspreads are the best finds when it comes to making slip covers for your furniture. Handmade quilts can be some of the most unique treasures you'll find. Some you may be able to use whole, some you will only be able to salvage bits from. They may come from your own cherished memories or maybe they were found at a garage sale.

With a little imagination, you'll find the perfect slipcover fabric in all sorts of places and things, and each one will have a story to tell.

Furnishings

Furnishings also should be stamped with your personal touch. They can be simple, exotic, or handed down from previous generations. Whatever your taste in furniture, let it be comfortable and friendly. If you give an impression of 'Don't Touch', people will not want to stay. They may admire, but they won't visit. If you have valuables, place them in curio cabinets, on shelves, or in unique places where they will come to no harm, but others may still enjoy seeing them.

Add your own personal touches

Pillows, pictures, quilts, flowers, and so on give colour, texture, and speak for the people who live in the house.

Marbles

When your child grows out of playing with marbles, place them in a clear glass bowl and stand where they catch the light and it can filter through to give a lovely effect.

Paintings

The best way to store paintings is to hang them on a wall. If they must be packed make sure the storage area is dry and airy so that mould will not grow. Don't stack paintings. Air should be allowed to circulate between them. Oil paintings should be dusted only with a soft brush. Do it regularly. Never rub an oil painting with a cloth.

Decorating a home office

A home office should provide a pleasing area to work that is efficient and well lighted.

It should not be cluttered, it should be professional but it should also be inviting and reflect your personality.

Strive for a look that is somewhere between residential and commercial by choosing patterns that are soothing and warm rather than harsh, stark or cold.

Choose a base colour that the rest of the home is painted to tie your office to the residential part of the house.

You may choose to paint the walls in a darker tone than the rest of the home or add a glazing technique over the top to promote the reflection of additional light.

Storage

Computers, faxes and scanners are necessities for the home office. Your decorating and storage budget should be geared around suitable housing for those items. Integrate office technology with the style of your home by choosing storage options that look more like furniture than stark office equipment. An efficient workspace has adequate and attractive storage. Some desks and work centres allow the computer to be concealed inside the desk top or have built-in cabinet doors to close when it is not in use. A rolltop desk is an attractive alternative for the computer centre as well.

Furniture

Choose furnishings that can perform double duty jobs. If your home office needs to accommodate drop-in houseguests you may need to decorate around a hide-a-bed couch as well. Use large screens to disguise unsightly equipment. Accessorise professional items in a wide variety of colours and materials that can soften a utility workspace.

Lighting

Add warmth to your workspace with well-placed lighting options. An adjustable desktop lamp reduces glare to your computer screen while looking decorative and inviting.

Windows in the home office

Choose window shade and fabric treatments that allow you to control the amount of light coming into your workspace. Make sure you do not close yourself off to the outside world. Use soft, translucent window shades to reduce glare but give you a view outdoors.

Accessories

Employ the principles of feng shui to make your home office prosperous and inviting.

Hang inspiring artwork. Use mirrors to keep your energy flowing while you work and to reflect any interesting focal points of the room. Have a bowl of fish to act as a balance and to dissipate tension. Large houseplants or trailing vines in a basket can also help bring nature in to your office space. A comfortable chair and couch adds a space to read up on a report or review your work and looks inviting. Add a chenille throw or a couple of pillows to create a cosy warm setting.

Decorating kids' rooms

- Kids need a flexible environment that will grow and change as they grow.
- It needs to be safe and secure.
- It needs to be fun and appeal to the child's imagination.
- It needs to be utilitarian.
- A child sleeps, plays. reads, does his/her homework and entertains friends in the bedroom.
- Kids' room décor needs to be less expensive and easily changeable.

Space

Younger kids need floor space to spread out while playing.

All kids need separate areas for sleeping, playing and studying.

They need more elbow space compared to adults.

Furniture

A typical kids' room needs a bed, study table and storage. When buying these staple furniture pieces, buy the best you can afford and they will last all of your child's youth.

Pre-schoolers

Pre-schoolers and toddlers love primary colours. These bright colours and complex patterns engage them for a longer time. The most inexpensive way to decorate their room is using paint. Keep the walls and furniture in a neutral colour. Add:

- Large murals on poster boards with complex patterns and colours and hang them.
- You can use colourful prints, wrapping paper, pictures from early childhood shops, pictures from greeting cards and magazines or you can paint them yourself.
- You can also hang posters.
- Add a colourful area rug or play mat.
- Create a cosy corner with a rug and lots of pillows.
- You can place a bookshelf next to it.
- Kids of all ages love something like this.

- Add decorative shelving to add functionality and charm.
- They are great for displaying books and soft toys.
- Make temporary storage from coloured storage boxes that can be bought at department stores and can be stacked away when not in use.

Storage

- Storage in a kid's room should be accessible to them.
- If you have less floor space vertical storage becomes necessary.
- Then you can store all less frequently used items on top.
- Inflatable furniture is a quick and inexpensive furniture.
- It comes in a variety of colours and designs.
- It is easy to store away when not in use or when more floor space is needed.
- Hang a large black board or white board on the wall at their level.
- This satisfies their need to write on the wall without actually doing so.

School-age children's rooms

Children who are at school will need a space and a desk to do their homework. The homework area should be well lit and have storage space for books, pens and pencils. They will need storage and display for their collections and sporting and other medals. A cupboard that is accessible and allows the child to hang and look after his/her own clothes provides good training.

Teenagers' rooms

A teenager's room is his/her refuge. Don't even think about decorating your teenage son's/daughter's room without having him/her on the job with you. They will have very firm ideas about what is needed and what is cool. Go along with what they want.

You can always change it when they leave home to go to university.

Decorating bathrooms and small rooms

Bathrooms should not be an afterthought. We do spend some of our time in these usually small rooms, and sometimes they are places to relax and hide from the world.

Decorate them with everyone in mind. Gear the accessories to everyone. Choose some rugged and handsome and others pretty and feminine. If there are children, adding a whimsical touch here or there gives a child the feeling that it is their home too and they are an important, contributing resident.

Small spaces

Living in a small space can be quite a challenge, but with a little creativity you can make living in a small space as comfortable as living in a castle.

Declutter

The first thing to do is to let go of unnecessary items. If you haven't used an item in six months to a year, you probably won't use it again. Check your closet. Go through each piece of clothing. If you haven't worn it in the past year, it's time to get rid of it. Donate all your unused clothing and items to your local charity. Your trash will be somebody else's treasure.

Less is best

When living in a small space, it's all about storage. Consider multi-function furniture such as chests and ottomans that are useful for storage of blankets and clothes and can be used as tables or seats. A futon can serve as a couch during the day and a bed at night. With the things that you do have, it's best to try and store as much as possible so as to make the room appear uncluttered. Less is definitely more in the case of small space living.

Bigger is better

Small furniture does not make the room appear bigger. Rather, larger, bolder pieces of furniture draw the eye to them, creating the illusion of a bigger room.

Storage solutions

Create a wall of shelving to store all those books and knick knacks. Group most of your belongings in one place rather than scattered around the room.

This frees up space to move around. Place baskets on the shelves for stray items and papers. Baskets can also be used to hold magazines and placed next to the couch or a chair.

Light

Light is important in a small room. Hang a big mirror opposite the window to reflect light into the room. Keep the walls and fabrics used in the room a light colour. Accent with coloured cushions and accessories. Remember that dark colours absorb light and light colours reflect light.

Designate areas

You can divide space in a room by using screens or bookcases. Screens or bookshelves can be inexpensively purchased or made. They can be covered with fabric or painted to add a personal touch. Area rugs are also a good way to create division in a room.

Recycling waste
Paper logs

Recycle newspapers into bricks for burning in the fireplace is fun. Fill a large plastic bin with cold water and torn up newspapers. Leave a few days until the paper is thoroughly saturated. Drain the water and make the soggy paper into rough bricks. Apply weights to squeeze out excess water and compact paper into a brick. Leave bricks to dry.

Pull-top rings

Save the pull-top rings on drink containers. Use them for placing in liquid paraffin wax when sealing jams and jellies. It makes the wax easy to remove when required.

Plastic clips

The plastic clips that seal bread in plastic bags have many uses – tie freezer bags, balloons etc.

Vinyl records

Scratched vinyl records can be used as a cake plate for a stall. Simply cover in foil.

Marbles

When your child grows out of playing with marbles, place them in a clear glass bowl and stand where they catch the light and it can filter through to give a lovely effect.

Seashells

Shells tend to lose their lustre when they are removed from the water and become dry.

Keep in a jar with salt water to retain the colour. Spread the shells on old newspaper and coat them with clear varnish or lacquer to retain the lustre and the colour.

Old CDs

Use old CD discs to make a colourful and stimulating ceiling mobile for your young baby. They catch the light and whirl around and will keep baby going happily for a time in his/her cot.

Uses for planters

Planters can be easily turned into an impromptu table by stacking a large book, suitcase, or a piece of wood or glass on top.

Fill it with interesting objects – seashells, large pinecones, firewood, balls of yarn, or pumpkins, leaves, gourds or corn.

If the planter is too deep and you don't have enough items, try filling half or two-thirds of the pot with a piece of cloth, crumpled up newspaper or other filler material.

Top with your chosen objects and no one will ever know the difference.

Add an arrangement of spiral branches, and local shrubs that won't need watering and will look great.

Weave holiday lights inside the contents of the planter – the hole on the bottom makes a great exit for the cord.

Small planters can be used to make wonderful and unique table centre pieces.

Fill it with plants, flowers or candles, or other objets d'art.

Handy tips

- Give new life to dented ping-pong balls by dropping into a boiling kettle for two minutes.
- Restore bounce to an old tired tennis ball by wrapping in foil and heating in a 200°C oven for thirty minutes.
- Save wax paper from cereal containers and use them to wrap family size pies for the freezer. They are the perfect size.
- To restore old playing cards dust with talcum powder.
- When tying a parcel with string, dampen it first. It won't slip and will tighten as it dries.

Conserve water

Save on your water bill and protect the environment:

- Use a tap timer. A forgotten sprinkler can waste more than 1000 litres an hour. A timer makes sure you never forget.
- Installing a drip system will put the water at the root system. The soil will absorb the water preventing run-off.
- Water roots, not leaves.
- Water less frequently and give your garden a good watering twice a week.
- This encourages roots to spread deeper.
- When mowing, leave grass longer to protect it from the burning sun.
- Group plants into high and low water users. Windbreaks also reduce the drying effect of the wind.
- Mulch around your plants and trees keeps the moisture in the soil longer. That means less watering.
- Avoid watering during the heat of the day. Water can evaporate before it reaches the roots.

- Broom it, don't hose it. Sweeping the drive with a broom is much quicker and more efficient than using a hose.
- Wash your car on the lawn and the grass also gets a good drink.

Home-made chamomile shampoo
1 tablespoon of Borax powder
1 tablespoon pure soap, grated
30g of powdered chamomile flowers
500ml of hot water

Mix in blender. Let it cool before using.

Car care
Do it yourself
Do you know your way around under the bonnet of your car? It is often cheaper and more convenient to do it yourself.

Safety first
If the engine has been running for any length of time, it will be hot. All checks, with the exception of checking the oil level, should be done while the engine is turned off. If the engine is running, do not put your hands near any belts or fans.

The following items should be checked periodically:

- Engine oil level
- Transmission fluid
- Brake fluid
- Power steering fluid
- Coolant (antifreeze) level
- Battery
- Windshield washer solvent
- Belts and hoses
- Windshield wiper blades

A good way to begin to be a home mechanic is to read your owner's manual from cover to cover.

When to do checks
An under-the-bonnet checks should be done once a week or when refuelling.

Oil change
- Oil change should be done every 5000 km or when manufacturer specifies.
- Regular oil changes are the best way to ensure longer engine life.
- If you frequently take short trips where the car doesn't always completely warm up, then oil changes are even more important because acid and moisture build-up does not have a chance to burn off.
- Some new engines normally run very hot and are very hard on oil.
- Modern oils contain detergents and additives that are designed to protect against sludge formation.
- Missing a single oil change can cause an engine to develop sludge, which can cause engine damage in as little as 20,000 km.
- Sludge problems are not covered by the warrantee.

Washing

- Washing should be done once a week.
- Garaged cars can go longer.
- Environmental pollution will take its toll on your car's finish.
- The best way to protect the finish is to keep it clean.
- Hand washing is best.
- If you use a car wash, find one that relies upon high pressure water or attendants that soap the car by hand.
- Bird droppings should be removed as soon as possible as they can damage the finish.
- If you have retractable headlights, make sure you clean them regularly.

Waxing

Waxing should be done every six months with a good quality non-abrasive wax.

Once a year put some wax on the door jams and the underside of the boot. For more detailed instructions on car washing and waxing, see the next section.

Tyres

- Buy a tyre gauge and keep it in the car.
- Always check tyre pressure when they are cold.
- Tyre pressure tends to rise as you drive due to heat build-up.
- Manufacturers have this in mind when they set the recommended cold pressures, so do not let air out when the tyre gets hot.
- Always use the manufacturer's recommended tyre pressures.
- Bad tyre pressure can affect tyre wear, as well as ride and handling. Have the car checked every 20,000 km for alignment and balance.
- Also have it checked if you notice unusual steering behaviour or a vibration at highway speeds.
- Rotate your tyres every 10,000 km, following the manufacturer's rotation recommendation.
- If you have a matching spare, include it in the rotation.
- To find out if you need an alignment, first check each tyre and look for uneven wear patterns.
- At each tyre, take a coin and insert it in the tread at the inside, centre and outside.
- If the tread is deeper on the edges than in the centre, the tyre is over-inflated.
- If the tread is deeper in the centre than the edges, the tyre is under-inflated.
- If the tread is deeper on one side than the other, have your wheel alignment checked soon.

Check your engine oil level

This is the most important under-bonnet check you can do. An engine cannot run without oil even for a minute without serious engine damage or total destruction!

To check

Turn the engine off. Locate the engine oil dipstick and remove it. With a paper towel or rag, wipe off the end of the stick and take note of the markings on it. You will usually see a mark for 'Full' and another mark for 'Add'. Check your owner's manual to be sure. Push the stick back into the tube until it seats, then immediately pull it out to see the oil level. You should not add oil unless the level is below the 'Add' mark.

Never add oil to bring the level above the 'Full' mark.

Main concern

Your main concern is that oil consumption is not rapidly increasing. If it is, take the car to a repair shop as soon as possible and have it checked out. It is acceptable for the oil to be dark as long as you change it at the recommended intervals. It should never be foamy and should never have a strong gasoline smell. If either of these conditions exist, have it checked out soon.

Handy hint

Keep a pair of old gloves and a roll of paper towels in the boot to use in an emergency.

Transmission fluid

Most automatic transmissions should be checked while the engine is running.
  Check your owner's manual to be sure.

- Ensure that the car is on a level surface and fully warmed up.
- Pull the transmission dipstick out, wipe off the end and note the markings on the end of the stick.
- The usual markings are 'Full' and 'Add'.
- Push the stick into the tube until it seats, then immediately pull it out to see the fluid level. Transmission fluid should be pink or red in colour.
- If the fluid is a muddy brown or has a burnt smell, have it checked by a mechanic.
- As with the engine, never add fluid unless it is below the 'Add' mark.
- Never bring it above the 'Full' mark.
- Make sure you use the correct transmission fluid for your vehicle.
- If you plan to add transmission fluid yourself, you should know that fluid usually comes in litres, but the level may not be low enough to take the full litre.
- You will need a special funnel to get the fluid into the small tube that the dipstick came from.
- Check your owner's manual for the right type of fluid and do not substitute anything else.

Any noticeable transmission oil consumption should be checked out at a repair shop.

Brake fluid

The brake fluid reservoir is under the bonnet right in front of the steering wheel. Most cars today have a transparent reservoir so that you can see the level without opening the cover. The brake fluid level will drop slightly as the brake pads wear out. This is a normal condition and you shouldn't worry about it. If the level drops noticeably over a short period of time or goes down to about two-thirds full, have your brakes checked as soon as possible. Remember:

- Never put anything but the approved brake fluid in your brakes. Anything else can lead to brake failure.
- Keep the reservoir covered except for the amount of time you need to fill it and never leave a can of brake fluid uncovered.
- Brake fluid must maintain a very high boiling point.
- Exposure to air will cause the fluid to absorb moisture, which will lower that boiling point.

Power steering fluid

The power steering fluid reservoir usually has a small dipstick attached to the cap. Remove the cap and check the fluid level.

- The level should not change more than the normal range on the stick.
- If you have to add fluid more than once or twice a year, then have the system checked for leaks.
- These systems are easily damaged if you drive while the fluid is very low.
- Another warning that you have low power steering fluid is a buzzing noise when you turn the steering wheel at slow speeds.

Coolant (antifreeze) level

Never open the radiator of a car that has just been running.

The cooling system of a car is under high pressure with fluid that is usually hotter than boiling water.

- Look for the cooling system reserve tank, somewhere near the radiator.
- It is usually translucent white so you can see the fluid level without opening it.
- (Do not confuse it with the windshield washer tank.)
- The reserve tank will have two marks on the side of it. 'FULL HOT' and 'FULL COLD'.
- If the level frequently goes below 'full cold' after adding fluid, you probably have a leak, which should be checked as soon as possible.

Today's engines are much more susceptible to damage from overheating, so do not neglect this important system.

Battery

Most batteries today are 'maintenance free' which simply means that you can't check the water level. This doesn't mean however, that there is nothing to check. The main things to check are the top of the battery which should be clean and dry, and the terminal connections which should be clean and tight. If the top of the battery continuously becomes damp or corroded soon after cleaning, then have the charging system and battery checked by your mechanic.

Windshield washer solvent

Windshield washer solvent is cheap and readily available by the half-litre in auto supply stores and supermarkets.

Belts and hoses

In most cases your mechanic can check your belts and hoses when you bring in the car for an oil change. However, if you get your oil changed by some quick lube type centres, belts and hoses may not be on their list of items to check in which case you're on your own. Belts are used to drive a number of components on an engine including:

- Water pump
- Power steering pump
- Air conditioner
- Alternator
- Emission control pump

These checks are best done while the car is cold.

Some later model cars have a single 'serpentine' belt that handles everything. This type of belt looks flat on one side with several ribs on the other side. You should check the ribbed side for signs of dry and cracked rubber. Serpentine belts are usually self adjusting and very durable. They should last about 50,000 km.

The other type of belt is called a 'V' belt and is adjustable. There is usually more than one to an engine, sometimes three or four. Check each one for cracks and tightness and have them replaced if you find any problems. Some V belts are hard to reach but no less important so if you can't reach it to check then have your mechanic do it periodically. In most cases your mechanic can check your belts and hoses when you bring in the car for an oil change.

Hoses should be checked visually and by feel. You are looking for dry cracked rubber, especially at the ends where they are attached. You should also check the ends for any signs of ballooning.

Filters

There are a number of replaceable filters in a car. They are listed in your owner's manual along with recommended replacement intervals. If you live in a dusty area or in a big city, then you should replace them more frequently.

The following filters are common to most cars

Air filter – used to filter the air going into an engine. This filter is usually easy to replace yourself.

Fuel filter – found either in the engine compartment or near the fuel tank. This filter is best left to your auto mechanic to change.

Breather – works with the PCV valve to allow clean air to be drawn into the crankcase to purge moisture and acids from the engine.

PCV valve – works with engine vacuum to draw fumes from the crankcase and burns them in the combustion chamber.

Windscreen wipers

Your car's windshield wipers should properly remove the rain from the windshield to ensure optimal vision during driving. Wiper blades will tend to streak when they are dirty. Take a paper towel with some window cleaner and clean the rubber blade whenever you clean the windshield. Wiper blades should be changed regularly, at least once a year.

Spark plugs

Follow the manufacturer's preventative maintenance recommendations for spark plugs, fuel metering system and ignition timing. The only items that need to be replaced on a regular basis are the spark plugs and certain filters such as the air filter, fuel filter, and some emission control filters. When the spark plugs are replaced, the technician should check the ignition wires and the cap and rotor if your car has them. Some new cars are even equipped with platinum-tipped spark plugs some of which last for more than 100,000 km!

Fuel

Use the fuel type recommended by the manufacturer. Get regular annual tune-ups. Service should be performed by a technician, who understands modern emission control systems.

Save fuel

Avoid long idles. Park instead of using the drive-through.

Drive smoothly

- Accelerate and slow down gradually. This saves fuel and wear and tear.
- Maintain steady speeds. Use cruise control on highways.
- Don't rev the engine.

Open the windows

Only use the air conditioner when necessary. Open the window or use recirculating air instead.

Travel lightly
Avoid carrying unnecessary weight in the boot.

Stop filling when bowser clicks
Don't 'top off' the gas tank. Fuel expands in warm weather and can cause an overflow.

Keep track of distance
Set the trip meter each time you refuel. You can keep a log to track your mileage. If mileage is less than you expected, the vehicle may need service.

Tyres
Keep tyres properly inflated. Check the pressure in all four tyres every two weeks.
    Check the owner's manual or the label on the inside of the driver's door, for proper inflation guidelines.

Air filter
Check and periodically replace the air filter, vacuum and coolant hoses, oil, oil filter, fluids and belts.

Emergency kit
Keep these items in your car, in case of emergency:

* First-aid kit
* Flashlight with extra batteries
* Jumper cables
* Hazard signs
* Gloves
* Boots
* Blankets
* Flares
* Bottled water

Environment and your car
Oil and other toxic chemicals which leak from your car can kill fish and other wildlife in the bay and ocean. When your car is not well maintained, toxic fluids often leak onto streets and driveways. The rain washes them into the street drains, which ultimately carry them to the bay and ocean.

Prevent pollution
You can prevent water pollution from your car by:

* Fixing leaks promptly.
* Keeping your car in tune.
* Following the proper disposal methods.
* Never putting any automotive product into street drains, inside drains, or into the garbage.

Also:
* Recycle used motor oil at petrol stations and auto supply stores.
* Recycle used antifreeze.
* Recycle your old battery! Exchange it when you buy a new one.

Spills
- Clean up spills immediately.
- For small spills, use absorbents, such as kitty litter.
- Sweep up absorbents and take to the hazardous chemicals checkpoint.
- Do not store used absorbents because they can become a fire hazard.
- For large spills, capture as much fluid as possible for recycling or hazardous waste disposal, using a squeegee and dustpan.

More car tips
Blocked filters
Fluids running through your car are only as good as they are clean. Engine oil, transmission fluid and fuel are three systems that all have filters. These need to be replaced on a periodic basis. If your car is not running properly, get it checked out. One of these blocked filters might not be helping matters.

Tyre safety
Safety in your car begins with tyres – they are in constant contact with the road. Have your tyres rotated every 5000 to 8000 km, and balanced at least every 16,000 km.

Can't see out?
Maybe that is because the rubber on the windshield wiper is as thin as a cigarette paper. Wiper rubber should be changed at least once, and better still, twice a year. As winter comes on this is essential.

Flat battery
There is no great 'joy' in life standing beside the road with a flat battery. Monitor the water level yourself, and regularly have the battery checked, especially if it is more than two years old.

Deflating tyres
Tyres at incorrect pressure, especially under-inflated, are not only dangerous but can lead to increased fuel consumption by as much as 10%! Remember, in cold weather, tyres deflate as the temperature decreases.

Air conditioner
It is good to run your air conditioner at least once a month to keep the compressor-seal lubricated and in good running order.

Hinges
Regularly check and, if necessary, lubricate moving parts such as door, bonnet and boot hinges and latches. It can save your ears from horrible squeaky noises, and your wallet from paying up big money later.

Cooling system
Have your car's cooling system checked once a year. When needed have it flushed and drained and replace the antifreeze.

Misfires

Is the car hard to start? Misfires? Is it sluggish during acceleration? Have your ignition system checked out. Have the battery tested. Examine spark-plug wires for corrosion or cracks.

Radiator

The radiator works hard at all times. Occasionally flush dirt, leaves and insects from the front of the radiator with a brush/hose and head off any cooling system problems.

Audio system

A good audio system can be expensive, especially if you want a system that ensures that the neighbourhood can hear you from four blocks away. You don't have to buy the absolute latest model. New designs come out in this business all the time. So have a good look around for discounts, and end of line sales. You will be pleasantly surprised with the cheap buys that are around.

Be prepared

Read everything about car audio you can get your hands on. Buy the specialist magazines and books, pick up the brochures, and read the weekly features in the daily newspapers.

Specialist magazines

Car audio magazines examine all installations, product reviews, and questions and answers about 12-volt products. Before you buy anything, decide what features you need. CD? CD stacker? Cassette with CD changer controls? Know what you want.

Highs and lows

Many retailers/manufacturers will claim that their speakers can reproduce sound through the frequency range from as low as fifty Hertz right up to 18 000 Hertz.

Technically true, but what they don't say is how loud the low bass notes or high-pitched singing will be compared to the middle range. You think you are getting sound that covers all ranges, but in fact you discover you can hardly hear the bass guitar or bass drum because, while they are there, they are too soft. If you don't want to miss out on the highs and lows, the solution is three specific speakers:

* One to reproduce the lows (woofers).
* One to produce the middle frequencies (mid-ranges).
* And the other, the highs (tweeters).

A two-way system has the mid-range, plus a tweeter and a woofer linked.

Head unit

The head unit is the source of audio. If the head unit is not to your liking, and doesn't sound right to you, then nothing in the rest of the system will sound OK. You need a head unit with decent internal power.

Features

Car audio often leads the way in sound design and innovation. Many of the features we take for granted in our home CD stereo were dreamed up first in the car audio field and incorporated later into domestic systems. The latest development is a CD-transport that does not come into contact with the surface of the CD.

Loudness

More watts does not necessarily mean more loudness. A 200-watt speaker may not necessarily be 'louder' than a 100-watt speaker. The output level depends on the power of the amp driving it, the speaker's sensitivity, and how it's mounted.

Sensitivity

Sensitivity is a measurement of how loud the speaker will be for a given input of electrical energy. You could, for example, need only a smaller, and therefore cheaper, wattage amplifier to get the same loudness out of a speaker than is first suggested, thus saving you big bucks.

Sound is made up of vibrations, which travel through air. The very lowest sound frequency you can detect is about twenty vibration waves per second. That's called twenty Hertz, and is something of the order of an earthquake rumble. The beauty of the audio technology of today is that a CD player and its amplifier can reproduce sound all the way from twenty to 20,000 Hertz!

Woofers

Woofers are tricky things. For a variety of reasons, getting down and reproducing low frequencies is the hardest challenge for a speaker system. You need to speak to an expert if you are a bass fan, and want that big zoom-zoom thumping noise coming through the car without having the entire boot taken over by a brace of woofers.

Beware car thieves

Car thieves love cars with expensive sound systems.
They either take some of the system, or all of the system, or the entire car.
Car thieves love unlocked cars in dark places.
Take precautions:

- Park in a well-lit area.
- Lock the car doors.
- Use a steering wheel lock if your car does not have anti-theft devices or alarms.

Cleaning your car

When washing and waxing your car:

Do:

- Make sure your vehicle's surface temperature is moderate to cool before washing and waxing.
- Clean the wash bucket prior to each wash.
- Wash the vehicle in sections starting from the top surfaces and working downwards.
- Remove debris from a painted surface with a wet, clean, soft cloth only after the surface has been allowed to cool.
- Wax your vehicle at least once every two months.

Do not:

- Wash or wax your car in direct sunlight.
- Scrub your vehicle when washing it. Light pressure is all that is needed. Use a wash mitt on wheels or tyres.
- Allow bird droppings, leaves, dew, grease, road tar, or other debris to remain on your vehicle's paint for an extended period of time.

- Apply heavy amounts of wax to your vehicle's paint surface. It will only make the wax more difficult to remove and will not increase paint protection.
- Use dirty, stiff or rough rags on your car's paint. Clean cotton rags are recommended.

Looking good?

Some cars will always look better than others. This can be due to:

- Colour. Dark colours tend to show more blemishes, unremoved wax, scratches and swirls than light colours.
- Geographical location. If the car is garaged in a dusty or dirty spot, opposite the sea or left out in the street, it will get dirty more quickly.
- Other reasons:
  Exposure to sunlight.
  Exposure to heat.
  Exposure to cold.
  Exposure to acid rain.
  Exposure to dew.
  Exposure to salts (airborne and road).
  Exposure to rainfall (transports airborne toxins to your paint).
  Exposure to high humidity.
  Exposure to harmful rays.
  Exposure to your partner's jealous ex . . .

Protect your paint

Protect the paint finish on your car by:

When washing
- Wash frequently, the more the better.
- Wash at least once per week, even in winter.

When waxing
- Wax frequently, the more the better. It is a common misconception that once or twice per year is adequate. Only if your car is in a garage and under a cover for half of the year! Wax at least once every two months.

Washing tips

- Do not wash in direct sunlight. Do it in the morning, evening, or in the shade.
- It is better to let your paint cool first, as it is better for the paint. Warm paint will also cause the water beads to dry on the paint.
- It is better to use cool water for above reasons.
- Wash from the top down, the bottom is closer to the road, and is dirtier.
- Hose from the top down, so you push more dirt off the car, instead of spreading it around.
- Establish a pattern. For example, I do the roof, boot area, bonnet, rear top, left top, front top, right top, rear bumper, left bottom, front bumper, right bottom, in that order. This way, you have less of a chance of missing any spots, and will wash faster as the pattern becomes habit.
- Avoid automatic car washes. They aren't your friends.
- The best way is to do it by hand, so do it that way. Protect your investment.
- If your drive your car in a winter-weather area, and it is driven through salted roads, it is recommended that the car have a power washing of the undercarriage at every wash.
- Do not use household detergent to wash your car. Use a high-quality car wash.
- If there is an annoying spot where you just can't get some dirt off, try using undiluted car wash.

Drying

Now that you've washed the car, dry it.

- Dry in the same pattern you used to wash. This will speed up your drying time, therefore allowing no water beads to dry.
- Avoid using a chamois or synthetic dryer. These will strip the wax from your car. Use 100% cotton (soft) towels.
- Make sure your towels are clean.
- Using one of your towels, quickly (one minute) go over the car, getting the big beads. Don't be perfect or meticulous here; just get it a little drier.
- Take another towel, and dry the car completely. Remember to use the same pattern you did to wash.
- Now open the bonnet, doors and boot. The fuel door wouldn't hurt either. Dry the door jambs, weather-stripping, and all of the places in these areas that get wet.

Interior

- Clean the interior on a regular basis, it will make it less of a chore. Do it every other wash.
- If something spills, clean it right away. If you don't you'll give it a chance to set in, and it will be much harder to remove.
- Read product labels before using it on your car. Always follow directions exactly.
- Test new products in an out-of-sight place. Moving the seats forward all the way will reveal a nice test area.
- Don't use too much water. The interior will get that famous musty smell. Also be cautious of the water your feet track in, as it will produce the same ill effect.
- Always use clean water and cleaning supplies. Best results will be produced if you rinse your cloth/sponge, and squeeze out all excess water.
- When using solvent-type cleaners, use as little as possible, and keep windows/doors open to allow odours to leave.
- Brush your carpet with a soft, but relatively stiff brush to loosen dirt and debris before vacuuming.

Waxing

That car looks great washed and dried. Now let's wax it!

- Use a high-quality polish before you wax. The polish is what makes the car really shine, the wax is the protective coating.
- Use a high-quality wax.
- The wax is designed to protect your paint, as mentioned earlier. Wax frequently, and especially before bad seasons, like winter. Wax is also a good protectant for when the car is wet and in sunlight. The water beads on the car act like magnifying glasses, and the sun will shine on these beads, magnifying the heat, and etching your paint.
- Wax indoors if at all possible. If not, find a cool, shady spot.
- Break out the wax. Apply either with a small towel, or a small random-orbit buffer.
- If using a towel, apply and remove in straight lines, not in circular motions. Circular swirls stick out from any angle, but you have to search hard to find straight ones.
- If using a buffer, make sure you spread the wax around a little before turning the buffer on. If you don't, wax will fly everywhere.
- If using a buffer, don't sit in one place for a long time. Keep it moving.
- Wax in the same pattern you used to wash and apply all wax at one time.
- Remove wax with a clean towel or a buffer with a different pad.
- If using a towel, remove in straight lines for reasons mentioned above. Change sides/spots of towel frequently, and never use the same part of the towel twice. You'll get wax-dust everywhere.

- It's better to use too many towels, so don't hesitate. Don't forget, 100% cotton (soft) towels.
- If using a buffer, follow same rules as before. Keep the buffer moving so you don't burn swirls in the paint.

Warming up the engine

In almost all circumstances you should *not* warm up your car before driving. This is the most destructive time for the engine and its related parts. The quicker it warms up the better. Your car will warm up much faster driving than just sitting there idling and you will save a lot of fuel.

Jump-starting another car

Always make sure the cables are connected positive to positive (red to red) and negative to negative (black to black).

If the engine compartment smells like a rotten egg (sulphur) do not connect the engine as the battery may explode.

Do not leave your car running when you are trying to jump start another car. It can cause damage to both cars. This common mistake can be dangerous to both of your cars. Your good battery should be able to start their car without running your engine.

If it does not, call a tow truck, as they usually handle bigger problems. Damage to the charging system is possible.

If water gets in your fuel tank

Sometimes water gets into the fuel tank and an alcohol-based additive is sold on the promise that it will allow the water to mix with the alcohol, then this will permit the water to be passed harmlessly through the fuel system. This only works when the water volume is so small that it doesn't matter anyway. The best solution is to drain the water out of the tank.

Electronic equipment
DVD player

What does DVD stand for? Digital Video Disc is a term that people often use. And we have seen it given sometimes as Digital Variable Disc. The correct version is Digital Versatile Disc.

These discs can be loaded with any digital information such as music, data backups and so on, and are not restricted to storing videos only.

Things to look for when buying a DVD
Connections

A DVD player is not a stand-alone component that will do any good by itself. That is, it is not an island. It has to be connected to a TV, hi-fi, or home theatre system. Most DVD players have composite, S-VHS, and component video-out connections, but check what your TV can handle. Most players will output Dolby Digital and DTS audio for home theatre systems. Check your hi-fi's audio inputs if you plan to connect a DVD player.

Regions

DVD players are sold matched to world geographical regions, which allows the movie studios to control releases around the world. Australia is in Region 4. Coding can be removed from players, but it's not meant to be done, and immediately voids your warranty. Discs without codes will play on any player.

Format
Like VHS, DVD suffers from differences between the PAL and NSTC TV formats. Many players will handle both formats, but if you've never heard of them before, don't get too stressed about it.

Audio/video performance
Because DVD players can play CDs, don't discount audio performance. Look for at least a 10-bit video converter and a 24-bit audio converter. Something of the order of 96kHz audio will give a better dynamic range. Seek multi-disc capability if you play a lot of CDs. Three-D stereo simulates surround sound using a standard two-speaker hi-fi, which is worthwhile if you have no intention of buying a six-speaker home theatre system.

Enhancements
There is a myriad of DVD audio and video enhancements (jitter reduction, noise reduction, etc), and the only way to understand it all is get into a shop and experiment. Rule of thumb – if your ears and eyes don't notice the difference, don't bother.

Construction
Look for a solid unit, especially the disc tray. One of the guidelines is to try and match it with the finish of your other video/audio components. A complete set in the same look and colour looks much better than a composite collection of bits and pieces.

Extras
Handy features include picture zoom during playback; parental lock from DVD nasties; multiple speeds for slow motion; and multiple simultaneous subtitles.

Some units also play CD-Recordable and CD-Recordable/Writable discs, and Karaoke for the home exhibitionist.

Exploding discs
Old or damaged compact discs can explode, causing damage and injury. Check your discs thoroughly for any flaws. Ensure home-made CD labels are properly centred before sticking them on. Check your CDs for cracks before you put them in your computer drive. Always remove CDs in the computer drive when they are not in use. Beware old discs as they may not be able to cope with the speed of new machines.

Mobile phones
Mobile telephones are constantly getting smaller and more efficient. Each day they offer more features. We can now access the Internet on a mobile phone. Read and ask questions before you make a decision. Choosing the right plan and handset is getting cheaper. But it is also getting more complicated!

Some guidelines to help you through the mobile maze:
Plans
It's all in the plans. Buying the right handset is important, but the plan dictates what you'll pay each month. Don't trust the carrier's ideas of which plan suits you. Estimate how many calls you will make per day and calculate the cost from the published rates. Don't forget the cost of accessing voicemail. Buy only what you need – you can easily upgrade later.

Coverage
Coverage in the major cities is generally very good, but can be restricted to major roads once you leave the big smoke. Check coverage maps from the carriers for details. Consider other options if you live in rural Australia.

Weight/size
Small and light is not always right
Several mobiles are less than 100g, but minuscule keys can be difficult for long fingernails and small phones often mean short battery life. Judge how you will usually carry the mobile. In your pocket? In a handbag? Then decide.

Battery life
This varies significantly from phone to phone, so match performance against your mobile lifestyle. Standby times start at about two days and grow to over ten days; talk times can be as low as one hour and increase to over five hours.

SMS
Short Message Service is the email of mobile phones, and a great way to avoid call costs while still staying in touch. SMS is booming. Check each carrier's SMS charges. Some phones have 'predictive' input that makes typing text on the keypad much easier. Some have plug-in keyboards as accessories.

Dual band
A dual band phone has the ability to switch between two frequencies. This is good insurance against congestion on the network as more people join.

WAP
Wireless Application Protocol is the Internet on your mobile.

It's tempting to see WAP as a technology looking for a useful application, but services are growing. You can get email, news, weather, personal banking, stock quotes, movie sessions and now take photos, email them to your friends and talk to people face to face, all in the palm of your hand.

Controls
Main functions should only be a couple of button presses away. Control options include Nokia's Navi Roller, and voice recognition on some Philips handsets.

Extra features
A clock and calculator are useful; built-in games less so. A vibrating alert could be useful for those trapped in those long, boring meetings. (See how to control a meeting in our Finance chapter.) Every day extra features are being added.

Accessories
Apart from the colour covers, there is a wealth of car chargers, leather pouches, etc. If you buy 'non-original' accessories, be careful of quality and fit.

Personal computers and notebooks
With every new model, PCs and notebooks get faster, smaller, lighter. And, fortunately, cheaper! Here's some detail in deciphering the specifications.

PCs
Many people buy a PC the way they buy a house. That is, getting the most expensive they can afford. Instead, ask yourself how you'll actually use it, and then buy what you'll need. There's a huge variety of CPUs – to give it its proper name it's a Central Processing Unit, the 'brains' of the computer – from Intel and AMD, plus the models from Apple. So the best way to find the model for you is to try them, try them, try them.

Find a way to run the programs you'll use regularly on the system you want to buy. But remember: a PC is the sum of many parts, not just a CPU.

All-in-one

Thanks to the popularity of Apple's iMac, several vendors have released PCs with the CPU and monitor in the same case. They're great space-savers but stick to the bigger vendors, such as IBM with its NetVista range, to avoid models that are just riding the marketing wave.

Memory

256MB is the bare minimum, and many models will come standard with twice that.

Hard drive

Bigger and faster is better. You'll never put your head in your hands and lament: 'I wish I bought a smaller hard drive.' Remember the evil-doers that take up most of your hard drive space are video clips, graphics files and games.

Ports

Go with USB (Universal Serial Bus) ports. They're fast, convenient and almost all peripherals come in USB flavour. If you have serial-connected peripherals already, get a PC with one or two serial ports as well. Or buy new peripherals!

Monitor

The actual viewable screen of a monitor is measured diagonally, is usually less than the quoted size, and varies from vendor to vendor. As a guide, a 15' model gives you about an A4-sized display. 17' and 19' monitors are becoming standard, but you'll pay extra. The same goes for flat, TFT displays.

Graphics and audio

A PC primarily for playing games and doing heavy-duty graphics will benefit most from the latest and greatest video card with gobs of video memory. Check the compatibility of your favourite games with the graphics chipset. Weak, tinny PC speakers are rare these days, and there are some excellent units from companies such as Altec, Lansing and JBL.

Bundled software and hardware

Products included for 'free' with a computer are always tempting, but think long and hard whether you really need them. Read the offers very carefully. Many a buyer has assumed that 'Word' is in the package only to find dear old 'Works' pops up on the screen.

Service

Check whether service is on-site – at your place. Or back-to-base – down at their place. And whether their place is on the other side of the country! Or, for that matter, is in the country. You'll usually pay the freight costs for back-to-base deals.

Also, does the warranty cover parts and labour?

Notebooks

Ease of use

Not all notebook keyboards are alike.

Make sure it 'feels' right to you, and the keys aren't too flimsy.

Most notebooks use touch pads for pointing; some use track points; and a few use both.

Battery life

Always go for the latest battery chemistry, currently lithium ion.
Be realistic about how often you will be away from a power outlet.
Running DVD movies drains a lot more power than word processing.

Weight

Not many laptops ever make it onto a lap, so weight is usually only an issue if you are frequently on the move.
Expect from 1.5 to over three kg.

Multimedia

If your notebook is destined for multimedia glory, make sure it has a fast CD-ROM/DVD drive, a TV-out connection and/or VGA-out.

Peripherals and ports

Do you want your floppy and CD drives inside or out?
Do you want a floppy drive at all?
Do you want to swap in a second battery without powering down?
Again, let the way you work decide the best configuration.

Personal digital assistant

PDAs are certainly 'handy' devices, containing a lot of information, and despite their size, also displaying a lot of information. You can cradle your world in the palm of your hand.
The Palm company has more than 70% of the worldwide market, so you can expect to come across plenty of its pocket-sized wonders. But there are also PDAs from Compaq, Hewlett-Packard and Casio, running Microsoft's new slimmed-down Pocket PC (formerly Windows CE). Don't discount the Psions from the UK, especially if you want a real, albeit tiny, keyboard.

Display

It's surprising how much useful information you can get onto a small screen. More models are appearing with colour displays, which look great but can reduce battery life. For any PDA, make sure it has backlighting for less than perfect ambient lighting.

Battery life

PDAs outlast even mobile phones, using standard pen batteries or rechargeable cells. Performance ranges from one week to three months of 'average use' between charges. So shop wisely.

Connectivity

Check that the PDA will talk to your PC-based PIM (Personal Information Manager) software. With a compatible mobile phone and PDA modem, you can send email, SMS messages, and faxes and even do a little Web browsing. PDA-to-mobile and PDA-to-PDA connections are now available, via infrared. But watch out for Bluetooth technology, connecting PDAs, phones and notebooks via radio waves.

Audio

CD-quality MP3 support is the latest for hand-helds, so your PDA can double as a personal stereo. Most models are capable of simple voice recordings, which is handy for quick notes on the go.

Memory

The Palm PDAs are wonderfully efficient users of memory. Gauge your RAM requirements from the number of extra applications you might install – there are hundreds available. Some PDAs use Compact Flash cards for extra storage.

Size/weight

PDAs are essentially shirt-pocket-sized, except for the Psions that are more like an average novel in size. They are an impressive 200g and under.

Data entry

Some have an inbuilt keyboard, while other PDAs use a form of pen-based character recognition. You just write on the screen. The Pocket PCs accept basically normal handwriting, whereas the Palms require you to learn letter-like symbols. All models also have on-screen 'tap' keyboards, and Palm sells a fold-out, laptop-sized keyboard accessory.

Internet Service Providers

Are you on the hunt for the best deal from an Internet Service Provider (ISP)? They make a myriad of offers, guaranteed to jam your mind. Just remember: Some features are non-negotiable, others you can do without.

- Access. Not all ISPs are reachable everywhere. Check that you can connect via a local call.
- Free! Many ISPs are converting to a free access model. You pay nix but you get extra online advertising. Free accounts are great for 'light' Net users, but there can be drawbacks: timed logouts after a couple of hours; big city access only; no Web space; and limited Net applications. If you have a POP (Point Of Presence) email address with another ISP, make sure the free service can access it.
- Speed. For dial-up access, 56Kbps is mandatory. For prices about twice that for dial-up, you can surf at cable speeds of 400Kbps and higher from Telstra Big Pond and Optus@Home. Now, of course, broadband and ADSL is spreading, providing much faster speeds for access and downloads. The best way to test an ISP's real-life performance is with a trial access offer, often advertised in computer magazines. Just make sure to cancel the account at the end of the trial period if you don't want to continue . . .
- Facilities. You'll almost always get one email address with your account, with some ISPs offering more, which is handy for families. Space for a Web page should also be included – 5MB is plenty for a personal site. But think about whether you'll really use it. And keep it updated. For the full Net experience, an ISP should support chat and instant messaging.
- Billing. Automatic billing by credit card and online payments are great, but make sure you can access your usage details online. Most ISPs sell usage plans, just like getting a mobile phone; check that you can move between plans without penalty.
- Support. Often overlooked. Technical support from an ISP can be vital. Phone support is a must, not just via the Net, although some ISPs charge high call rates. Also, what software will the ISP provide for free?
- Extras. Larger ISPs have value-added services only available to subscribers, such as OzEmail's StockWatch sharemarket site. For frequent overseas travellers, local call access in foreign cities, called 'global roaming', is a boon.

5

Health

A healthy body, a healthy mind, a healthy spirit and a positive outlook. These things make good health. We are all given a certain amount of each when we start out on life's journey. What we do with them is up to us.

How is your body operating?
Do you have a problem with digestive function?
Does your stomach often feel uncomfortable after eating?
Do you often get digestive problems after eating certain foods?
Do you crave salty, sugary or processed foods?
Can you never satisfy your craving for food no matter how much you eat?

What can you do?
- Eat slowly. Chew your food.
- Eat plenty of fresh, organic fruit and vegetables.
- Sit still for ten minutes after you have eaten to give your body a chance to begin the digestive process.
- Avoid fast food or overly processed foods.
- Drink at least eight glasses of water a day.
- Substitute caffeine drinks with herbal teas.
- Exercise daily.
- Sleep at least eight hours a day.
- Find a leisure activity that you really enjoy.

Do you suffer from adrenal malfunction?
Is your concentration poor?
Do you suffer from mood swings, anxiety attacks, nervousness or anxiety?
Have you ever experiences incontinence or bladder problems?
Are you constantly tired or fatigued?
Do you have high or low blood pressure?
Do you suffer from insomnia, cold sweats, migraine or fainting spells?
Does alcohol go straight to your head?
Do you suffer from skin disorders?
Are you constantly thirsty?

What can you do?
- Pay attention to your diet.
- Eat regular meals.
- Reduce salt intake.
- Cut out refined carbohydrates.
- Reduce spicy foods.
- Stop smoking, reduce alcohol intake.
- Drink eight glasses of water a day.
- Relax, yoga is good for you.
- Proactively reduce work stress.

Liver function

Have you ever had hepatitis, cirrhosis or diabetes?
Are you overweight?
Are you in your job constantly exposed to chemicals?
Do you drink alcohol more than four times a week?
Do you react adversely to foods that contain high sugar?
Do you gain weight easily?
Do you suffer from constipation or wind?
Are you always tired?

What can you do?
- Drink ginger tea twice daily.
- Drink plenty of fresh fruit juice and vegetable juice to help you cleanse your liver.
- Cut down on your intake of saturated fats and oils.
- Decrease your consumption of caffeine drinks.
- Limit alcohol consumption to two standard drinks for women and four standard drinks for men per day.
- Have at least three alcohol-free days per week.
- Let your liver repair itself by reducing stress and sleeping regular hours.

Thyroid function

Do you always feel tired, no matter how much sleep you actually get?
Do you feel cold all the time?
Is your skin very dry and your hair very brittle?
Do you suffer from water retention in your eyes and face, or have swollen feet, ankles and hands?
Do you suffer from muscle twitches or cramps at night when you are in bed?
Do you find it difficult to lose weight?
Do you have erratic bowel movements?
Do you suffer from short-term memory loss, poor coordination and a likelihood to fumble objects?

What can you do?
- Eliminate all sugars and foods sweetened with sugar or sugar substitutes.
- Eliminate all processed flour.
- Peanuts, soya, and members of the cabbage family block the absorption of iodine, which is essential for a healthy thyroid. Avoid these foods completely.
- Eat foods which are high in iodine – shellfish and any deep-sea fish.
- Eat regularly and avoid snacking.

Hypoglycaemia

Do you need to urinate often?
Do you always feel thirsty?
Do you always want to eat when you are nervous or anxious?
Do you have an excessive appetite?
Do you eat to relieve shaking?
Do you have mood swings or moments of depression?
Do you wake up in the early morning craving for a snack?
Are you seemingly always sick with viruses and infections?

What can you do?
- You must balance your sugar intake throughout the day.
- Meals must be on time.
- Never go for more than three hours without a meal or a snack.
- Keep snacks such as nuts, rice cakes and seeds to hand.
- Avoid alcohol and caffeine.

Minerals and trace elements
Sodium
Function in body
Along with potassium, maintains balance of fluids, especially water, and pH in the body; function of nerve and muscles.

Sources
Common salt, baking powder, cured and smoked fish and meats, kelp, beets, artichokes, coconut, figs.

Effects
Deficiency can cause heat prostration, dehydration, low blood pressure and indigestion.
Excess causes high blood pressure, heart disorders and oedema (fluid retention).

Sulphur (trace element)
Function in body
Synthesis of protein; promotes healthy skin, hair and nails; combats bacterial infection.

Sources
Meat, fish, dairy products, eggs, pulses, cabbage.

Effects
Deficiency can cause skin diseases.

Zinc (trace element)
Function in body
Formation of insulin in body; release of Vitamin A; healing; healthy reproductive organs; functioning of growth and development enzymes.

Sources
Red meat, liver, egg yolks, dairy products, whole-wheat products, oysters, brewers yeast.

Effects
Deficiency can cause infertility, enlarged prostate gland, acne and skin disorders, slow healing of wounds, and slow physical, mental and sexual development.
Excess can cause nausea, diarrhoea, dizziness and dehydration.

Fluorine (trace element)
Function in body
Strengthens teeth and bones.

Sources
Fluoridated tap water and toothpastes, fish (especially those eaten with bones), meat, tea, cereals.

Effects
Deficiency causes tooth decay, osteoporosis.
Excess causes mottled and discoloured teeth, increased density of bones in the spine, pelvis and limbs and calcified ligaments.

Iodine (trace element)
Function in body
Production of hormones in the thyroid gland which control metabolism; promotes growth; promotes energy; mental alertness.

Sources
Iodised salt, Irish moss, kelp, seafood, fruit and vegetables grown in soils containing iodine.

Effects
Deficiency causes goitre, weight gain, lack of energy.
Excess can cause thyroid diseases.

Iron
Function in body
Production of haemoglobin; distribution of oxygen and removal of carbon dioxide in body tissues; production of myoglobin (red pigment in muscles).

Sources
Red meat, liver, kidney, oysters, kelp, pulses, dried fruits, nuts, oats.

Effects
Deficiency causes anaemia.

Magnesium
Function in body
Healthy teeth and bones; functioning of the nerves, muscles and metabolic enzymes.

Sources
Whole-wheat cereals and products, eggs, meat, nuts, pulses, seeds.

Effects

Deficiency causes muscle cramps, tremors, tics, loss of appetite, nausea, insomnia, irregular heartbeat.

Manganese (trace element)
Function in body

Functioning of the nerves, muscles and many enzymes, bone strength.

Sources

Dairy products, eggs, fish, fruit, vegetables, grains.

Calcium
Function in body

Growth and maintenance of healthy teeth and bones; nerve function; blood clotting; muscle contraction; metabolises iron.

Sources

Fish (especially those eaten with bones), soybeans, dairy products, almonds, sesame seeds, sunflower seeds, watercress, fortified cereals.

Effects

Vitamin D facilitates uptake.
Deficiency can cause rickets, osteomalacia, osteoporosis.

Chromium (trace element)
Function in body

Functioning of skeletal muscles; storing and metabolising sugars and fats.

Sources

Unrefined wholegrain and cereal products, fish and shellfish, brewers yeast, beef.

Effects

Deficiency can cause depression, confusion, irritability.
Excess can be toxic.

Cobalt (trace element)
Function in body

Component of vitamin B12 which prevents anaemia.

Sources

Meat, liver, kidney, shellfish, green leafy vegetables.

Effects

Deficiency causes lack of vitamin B12, leading to pernicious anaemia; bowel disorders; weak muscles.

Copper (trace element)

Function in body

Formation of red blood cells; growth of bones; absorption of iron; pigmentation of hair and skin.

Sources

Shellfish, nuts, liver, kidney, pulses, brewer's yeast, tap water from copper pipes.

Phosphorus

Function in body

Conversion and storage of energy; healthy bones; function of muscles and nerves and some enzymes; intestinal absorption of certain foods.

Sources

Meat, poultry, fish and shellfish, nuts, seeds, pulses, dairy products, eggs.

Effects

Deficiency causes bone pain; stiff joints; disorders of the central nervous system; weakness.

Excess can interfere with intestinal absorption of calcium, iron, magnesium and zinc.

Potassium

Function in body

Maintains balance of fluids and pH in the body; disposal of body wastes; aids in sending oxygen to the brain; function of nerves and muscles.

Sources:

Fresh fruits and vegetables, whole grains, dairy products.

Effects

Deficiency can case muscular weakness and paralysis, low blood pressure; thirst; loss of appetite; sensitivity to noise.

Excess can aggravate some heart conditions.

Selenium (trace element)

Function in body

Functioning of the red and white blood cells, along with vitamin E works as an antioxidant; detoxifies metals including cadmium, mercury and lead; may protect against some cancers; prevents dandruff and some skin disorders; healthy liver function.

Sources
Garlic, onions, whole wheat and products, fish and shellfish.

Effects
Deficiency causes premature ageing, cardiovascular disease and asthma and may be a factor in cancer.

Excess can cause neurological disorders.

Women's health
Menstruation
A normal cycle can be from twenty-four to thirty-five days. Bleeding can last between two and seven days. The amount of blood lost can range from 10 to 80 ml with about 35 ml being the average.

Keep a diary
So that you know what is normal for you keep a menstrual diary, then you will be aware if your pattern changes.

Heavy periods
Heavy periods can be caused by a number of things: fibroids, pelvic inflammation, hormonal disturbances, tumours and IUDs. Seek professional medical advice if your periods become heavier.

Menstrual cramps
There are two types of period pain:

- Primary dysmenorrhoea is related to the uterus contracting under the influence of hormones.
- Secondary dysmenorrhoea extends outside the actual time that you are bleeding and is caused by cysts, fibroids, polyps, infections and tumours.

You should consult a doctor if you are experiencing the latter.

Remedies
Not all women suffer from menstrual cramps, but if you do, here are some remedies:

- Improve your overall feeling of health and wellbeing by eating regular meals, getting plenty of fresh air and exercise, and staying happy.
- Keep your system in good shape by eating fibre and fresh vegetables and fruit.
- Take a daily vitamin supplement of vitamin B6.
- Have sex. The muscle contractions do wonders for a cramping stomach.
- Abstain from alcohol.
- Cut out the caffeine. Instead drink chamomile tea and warm lemon juice.
- Take a relaxing bath to which you have added half a cup Epsom Salts.
- Take a brisk walk in the fresh air.
- Stretch your body in slow movements to relaxing music.
- Take a pain reliever.

Premenstrual tension
Be positive about menstruation. It is a good and natural thing. If you are menstruating then you are healthy. If you stop menstruating, then that is cause to worry. It is part of being a

woman. Although it is not always convenient, its onset is a cause for rejoicing as it means that your body is capable of enjoying sex and giving birth to new life.

Eat a balanced diet. Eat fresh fruit and vegetables and whole grains. Restrict salt as it holds fluid in your body and may cause bloating. Destress your environment. Be calm and tranquil. Exercise. If all else fails, there are over-the-counter medications that are devised especially for your problem. Take one and soak in a hot bath with your favourite music on in the background.

Pregnancy
Are you having a boy or a girl?
Here are some popular ways to guess:

Have your partner hold a needle on a thread loosely over your swollen, pregnant tummy. If the needle swings back and forth, then it is a boy child within. If the needle goes wildly off in oscillating circles, then your baby is a little girl.

If you are carrying to the back, you have a little son in there. If you are carrying to the front, then it is a damsel fair.

If you are having a dog of a pregnancy, it is a boy. If your pregnancy is a dream, then it is a sweet little girl. (She is probably saving all her disruptive behaviours until she is a teenager!)

Remembering it all
A way of immortalising the wonderful shape you achieve during pregnancy is to make a plaster or paper casts of your pregnant belly and hanging it on the wall.

Not only does it bring back memories, but in the teenage years it is always available and visible for you to point at and say, 'And after all I have been through for you . . . !'

Natural medicine
Herbs, vitamins and mineral supplements can play an important role in childbirth preparing the mother's body for conception, nourishing her throughout the pregnancy, preparing her for the birth and assisting with recovery and with breastfeeding. Care should be taken when ingesting any substance during pregnancy and women should note that several herbs, which are of great benefit at particular stages of reproduction, can be dangerous to the baby if taken at the wrong time. Some herbs, which are uterine stimulants, and others, which contain chemicals that will cross the placental barrier, should be avoided in pregnancy. Please check with your doctor before you take anything. Follow all instructions carefully. Consult a medical practitioner if you have any doubts at all.

Well in advance of conceiving
A woman is advised to give up smoking and drinking, eat well and exercise regularly.

The inclusion of nutritious red clover, nettle or ginseng tea in the diet is safe and beneficial for the woman waiting to conceive. If conception proves difficult, consult a health professional. A supplement of folic acid can help as can an increased intake of vitamin B2, also known as riboflavin.

Morning sickness
Morning sickness is the name given for the nausea resulting from the destabilisation of the gastric juices. About 60% of women suffer from morning sickness. Morning sickness does not necessarily come upon you in the morning. It can happen at any time of the day and as a result of any trigger. To some women the very sight of red meat in a butcher's window can bring on nausea, and the vomiting and resulting loss of nutrients can be debilitating.

Some women suffer morning sickness for the entire nine months of the pregnancy, but this is not common and most get over it by the beginning of the second trimester. Some women never experience morning sickness at all. Morning sickness is natural and is a good sign that everything is going well and that the body is producing the hormones that the foetus needs to survive in the womb. So rejoice!

Remedies for morning sickness

For most women morning sickness is mild and lasts only a few weeks. Ginger is highly effective in reducing nausea and the tablets, powder or fresh root can be taken safely at this time.

A widely prescribed remedy for mild morning sickness is raspberry leaf, taken as a tea or a tablet.

Both peppermint and chamomile teas are helpful. It is recommended that you drink no more than three cups daily.

Other helpful tips:

- Eat the way that baby eats – constantly and in small amounts. Fruit is absorbed easily and quickly.
- Never let your stomach get empty, as the stomach acids will react against you.
- Avoid fatty foods which take a long time to digest.
- Snack on raw almonds.
- Have your partner bring you a cup of tea and a biscuit before you get out of bed in the morning.
- Drink lots of fluids – fruit juice and water and some sports drinks.
- Try peppermint tea.
- Ginger ale settles the stomach.
- Massage helps you to relax.
- Listen to your body, and eat what appeals to you.

Reasons to see your doctor

If you lose weight.
If you do not urinate and feel dehydrated.
If you are unable to keep anything down at all.

Remember, remedies are many, and what works for one woman may not work for another. The one sure remedy that always works is time. No morning sickness lasts more than nine months . . .

Nutrition

Care should be taken with the diet to include the consumption of plenty of protein and carbohydrates. The most common nutrients found to be deficient in pregnant women are:

- Zinc (from brewers yeast, wheatgerm, green leaf vegetables, eggs and legumes). Zinc deficiency is thought to result in increased birth defects and increased stretch marks on the mother.
- Folic acid (from yeast, green leaf vegetables, nuts, milk, and mushrooms). Folic acid, a B group vitamin, assists with the production of red blood cells.
- Calcium (from dairy foods, nuts, green vegetables and fish). Calcium gives strength to teeth, bones and cartilages.

Listeria

To protect your unborn baby, eat hard cheeses instead of soft cheeses while you are pregnant. As a pregnant woman, eating for two, you should be aware that certain soft cheeses can become contaminated with bacteria called *Listeria*. If you become sick from *Listeria*, the baby you're carrying could get sick or die.

Ailments

During pregnancy, normally healthy women are prone to ailments such as indigestion, constipation, fluid retention and backache. Most of these can be safely treated with natural remedies.

- Take slippery elm for indigestion.
- Take psyllium seeds for constipation.
- Seek advice on gentle exercises you can do to relieve backache.
- Consider a gentle spinal manipulation by a qualified chiropractor if backache is severe.

Labour

Raspberry leaf tea, rich in a citrate of iron, can be taken throughout pregnancy and helps to prevent miscarriage and strengthen the uterine and pelvic muscles for the birth. It can help control the pain when administered during labour. Feverfew will regulate contractions and help to hasten the expulsion of the afterbirth.

After the birth

After the birth, the mother's milk flow can be encouraged by:

- Keeping the atmosphere serene and calm.
- Obtaining plenty of rest between feeding.
- Eating a balanced diet which includes dairy.
- Maintaining a general feeling of wellbeing.

Milk flow can be increased safely with the help of herbal preparations such as raspberry leaf tea, dill or fennel oil or milk thistle seeds.

Raspberry tea is soothing when dabbed on sore nipples.

Cabbage leaves relieve breast soreness.

If you are unable to breastfeed, don't stress. Some women can, some can't. Just love and enjoy your baby and give him/her a bottle. It is not the end of the world.

Naming baby

A baby born to the Amhara people of Ethiopia is given as its name the first word that its mother utters after the birth.

See the Family and Home chapter for more on naming baby.

Tell your baby 'I love you' in nine languages

Ek het jou lief	Afrikaans
Ngyiya kuthanda	Zulu
Ikh hob dikh tib	Yiddish
Phom Rak Khun	Thai
Aishite imasu	Japanese
Mi amas vin	Esperanto
Je t'adore	French
Amore	Italian
Mina rakastan sinua	Finnish

Rubella (German measles)

Rubella infection in the first few weeks of pregnancy can cause abnormalities in the baby. Most women will have been vaccinated against rubella in their teens – but this doesn't necessarily give lifelong immunity. It's therefore important to check a woman's immunity with a blood test before she tries to conceive. If you are not immune, vaccination is advisable. There may be a risk that vaccination itself can cause damage to an early foetus. Therefore you should have it done early in your menstrual cycle (before you could have conceived) and take contraceptive precautions until a repeat blood test eight weeks later to check that vaccination has been effective.

Toxoplasmosis

This isn't common (typically one in 50,000 pregnancies) but it can cause severe damage to the brain, eyes and other organs if it is passed from a mother to her unborn baby. It is sometimes carried by cats, dogs and sheep that pass the parasites that cause the infection in their motions. If you have a cat which uses a litter tray, it's sensible not to handle or change soiled cat litter in pregnancy unless you use rubber gloves and wash thoroughly afterwards. No matter how clean and healthy your pet is, wash your hands after handling it and before preparing food.

Miscarriage

The risk of miscarriage exists with every pregnancy, but there are some things that can be done to reduce this risk:

- Cease smoking.
- Avoid alcohol.
- Consult your doctor about medications that you may be taking.
- Drink raspberry tea.
- Avoid eating new green potatoes.
- Eat a balanced diet.

If spotting occurs seek medical advice immediately.

Menopause

Menopause is when a woman's ovaries no longer function, and monthly menstruation becomes irregular, ultimately stopping altogether. It is also known as 'the change of life'. The average age of menopause is fifty-one years, but it most commonly takes place between the ages of forty-five and fifty-five years. It takes anywhere from three months to three years to go through menopause.

Some symptoms include:

- Lowered sex drive
- Vaginal dryness
- Highly charged emotions
- Sleeping problems
- Hot and cold flushes
- Excess bleeding
- Depression

Getting the better of hot and cold flushes

Your face and upper body reddens and feels hot. Your skin temperature rises about 3° to 4°C. Most women feel a hot flush coming on and can therefore put things in place to minimise them.

- Relax and go with your body.
- Control those factors that trigger a hot flush for you.
- Limit your alcohol.
- Wear natural fibres.
- Wear layers that can be added or subtracted.
- Carry a fan.
- Eat six small meals a day instead of three big ones.
- Drink lots of water.
- Cut down on caffeine.
- Carry a purse-size moist towel with you.
- Open the windows and let in the fresh air.
- Continue to have regular sex.

Adrenal glands

Adrenal glands take over some of the ovary's functions at this time and produce oestrogen. It is important that the function of these glands is kept at a premium. Vitamins B5, C and E as well as zinc all help adrenal activity. Citrus fruits, onions and tea are a good source of these.

Exercise

Exercise regularly and eat a diet with a high proportion of raw foods. Anthropologist Margaret Mead coined the term PMZ which stands for postmenopausal zest. 'This,' she said, 'is freedom.'

Keep a healthy sex life

- Talk to your partner and discuss feelings and needs.
- Lubricate your dry vagina with any non-perfumed vegetable oil or KY jelly.
- Experiment and employ new positions and new ways of showing that you care for each other as sexual beings.
- Try mutual massage and new ways of touching.
- Practice pelvic floor exercises daily to keep all of your muscles in good working order.

Remember, regular sex helps to minimise the symptoms of menopause.

Yeast infections

Yeast infections are caused by an imbalance of the bacteria that live in the intestines of both men and women, and in women's vaginas. It causes burning and itching in the vaginal area, has a yeasty smell, and causes a yellow white discharge. It reoccurs.

Causes

- Pregnancy.
- Hormonal medicines.
- Chemical douches.
- Antibiotics.
- Spermicides.
- Lack of lubrication during sex.
- Damage to the vaginal walls by tampons.
- Intercourse with a partner who has the yeast infection.

Cures

- Limit your sugar intake as sugar promotes the growth of yeast.
- Avoid foods that contain yeasts and moulds – bread, beer, cakes and doughnuts, wine, pickles, cheese, mushrooms and fruit juices.
- Sleep naked to allow your body to air.
- Wear loose clothing and underpants.
- Throw away the talcum powder.
- Use a lubricant for sexual intercourse.
- Eat yoghurt to encourage good bacteria.
- Keep away from perfumed toilet paper, tampons and sanitary pads.
- Use a hand held shower to wash your nether regions with plain water.
- Wear cotton undies.
- Use uncoloured toilet paper.
- Wipe from front to back, not vice versa.
- Wash before intercourse.
- Keep chemicals out of your vagina, including spermicide. Put spermicide inside the tip of the condom where it is meant to go.
- If you must douche, use a solution of water and vinegar.
- Urinate before and after sex.
- Make a bath and add one cup of salt and one cup of vinegar and sit in it with knees apart until it gets cool.

Stay safe while out and about

While it's good to be aware of your surroundings at all times, it's especially important when it's dark outside. Here are a few stay-safe tips:

- Park in well-lit areas or as close as possible to the front door of wherever you're going.
- Keep your hands free to be able to fight off a potential attacker.
- Walk with confidence so you don't look like an easy target.
- Get some training in self-defence.
- Trust your instincts and immediately go to a crowded or well-lit area if you don't feel safe.

Men's health
Beer belly

As the years go by, a man's metabolism slows and he needs fewer calories. However, his calorie intake often stays the same as it's always been, or even increases, while his levels of activity generally decrease. The fat likes to settle on the stomach first and it's the last place it wants to leave. The result is the 'beer belly'.

Diet

Diet should be low in fat and include lots of carbohydrates (bread, rice, potatoes, pasta, fruit and vegetables). Snack on a piece of fruit rather than a bar of chocolate.

Posture

Poor posture accentuates the appearance of a beer belly. Reduce this by keeping your belly sucked in when you are standing or sitting. Hold it in for five seconds, releasing, and repeating this ten times every couple of hours during the day for a quick and simple way of improving the abdominal muscle tone.

Alcohol

Many men enjoy a drink or two. It is part of the culture and is sociable, relaxing and enjoyable. Alcohol eases the inhibitions. A moderate amount of alcohol may actually help protect the heart and circulation. However, one in four men drink too much alcohol, and do this too often. If you regularly go over the top with your drinking then you will damage your body. Drinking too much alcohol is also often responsible for accidents, poor work performance, relationship problems, and crime. Never drink and drive.

How much?

Sensible levels of alcohol for a man are up to twenty-one units each week. That is, no more than three to four units a day. One unit is:

- Half a pint of ordinary strength beer or lager.
- A glass of wine.
- A pub measure of spirits.

If your belly is growing out of control, then, as part of your healthy diet, reduce your alcohol intake to no more than fourteen units a week.

A can of extra strong beer or lager is equal to two pints of ordinary strength beer and is equivalent to four units of alcohol.

Too much alcohol

Too much alcohol causes:

- High blood pressure
- Indigestion and stomach ulcers
- Obesity
- Malnutrition
- Nerve damage
- Memory loss
- Depression

Think you need help?

If you answer 'yes' to two or more of the following questions, then you may have alcohol-related problems and should seek help and advice from your doctor or Alcoholics Anonymous (AA).

- Have you ever felt you should cut down on your drinking?
- Have people annoyed you by criticising your drinking?
- Have you ever felt guilty about your drinking?
- Have you ever had a drink first thing in the morning to steady your nerves or to get rid of a hangover?

Male suicides

The number of men committing suicide is increasing. It is estimated that more than three times as many men than women commit suicide per year. Young men in particular, between the ages of fifteen and thirty-four, are increasingly ending their lives. Many young men choose to hang themselves or to gas themselves in the family car.

Who is at greater risk of suicide?

- People who already have a mental health illness are at a greater risk of committing suicide.
- People who are depressed.

- Teenagers are at risk because the teenage years can be difficult at the best of times. Emotional and physical development brings with it the turmoil associated with body changes and a desire for independence.
- People addicted to drugs and alcohol. Problems with drugs and alcohol, the law, and at school, are common at this time in life and associated with a higher risk of overdose and subsequent suicide.
- Older people are a risk group. Ageing brings much loss. Loved ones and friends pass on. Ill-health causes loss of independence and social isolation as older people are forgotten and ignored.

Testicular cancer

Testicular cancer is the commonest cancer that affects young men. Testicular cancer affects one in 450 men before the age of fifty and is most common between nineteen and forty-four years of age.

Self-examination

Regular self-examination is the best way of detecting testicular cancer early. This is best done in or after a bath or shower, when the scrotum is relaxed. Hold the scrotum in the palms of the hands and use the fingers and thumbs to examine the shape, consistency, and smoothness of the testicles. It's not unusual for one testicle to be slightly smaller than the other or for one to hang lower than the other. If something doesn't feel right then don't ignore it, get it checked out by the doctor.

Signs to look for
- The first sign is usually a swelling of one of the testicles, or a pea-sized hard lump on the front or side of the testicle.
- There may be a dull ache or a sharp pain felt around the testicle or in the scrotum.

Those at risk
- Men who have had undescended testicles.
- Those with a close male relative who had testicular cancer.
- All men have some risk and should examine themselves.

There are no guaranteed ways of preventing testicular cancer. However, if undescended testicles are corrected before a boy is ten years old, his risk of developing testicular cancer drops back to the average level. Regular exercise may also reduce the risk.

Treatment

Testicular cancer is one of the most curable cancers with around 90% of men making a full recovery. The affected testicle is removed surgically. If the cancer has not spread then further treatment may not be necessary. If it has spread then chemotherapy is usually given. Sometimes radiotherapy is used in the early stages.

Having a testicle removed shouldn't affect a man's sex life or the chance of becoming a father.

Prostate cancer

Prostate cancer usually affects slightly older men. One in twelve men develop it. The prostate gland lies tucked away below the bladder, and thus changes to it may go completely unnoticed. As cancer of the prostate is often very slow-growing, men can have the tumour for years without realising it. Symptoms include:

- Difficulty or pain passing urine.
- Passing urine more often or at night.
- Waiting for long periods before urine flows.
- Feeling you have not emptied your bladder fully.

Take a prostate screening test
Men over the age of forty-five to fifty should consider having a blood test called PSA (Prostate Specific Antigen) done every year, which can indicate if they are at high risk.

Sex
Most men find it difficult to talk even to their own GP about sex and related problems, whether it's a matter of performance or worries about infections. Personal questions to ask yourself:

- Am I practising safe sex?
- Is sex good for my partner and I?
- Could I be at risk from a sexually transmitted disease?

Sex therapy
Sex therapy offers help for people with sexual problems. It's been around for over forty years or so. Sex therapists are trained counsellors or medical professionals who've undertaken additional training in the physical and psychological issues associated with sexual functioning.

What sort of problems do therapists deal with?
Some sexual problems are purely physical. For example, as a result of disability, illness or a side-effect of medication. Some are purely psychological, originating in negative childhood messages or sexual trauma or stemming from relationship difficulties. The majority of problems have a combination of physical and psychological elements:

- Erection difficulties
- Premature ejaculation
- Difficulty reaching orgasm
- Problems with penetration
- Disinterest in sex

Who is it for?
You can go to therapy on your own or with your partner. You may be gay, straight or bi, in your teens or an octogenarian. But, in reality, sexual problems affect pretty much everyone at some stage in their life. For some the problem resolves itself over time, for others – it's time to call in the experts.

How does it work?
Your therapist will work with you to help you identify if the cause is physical, psychological or a combination of the two. If you're in a relationship, you'll also explore if there are any unresolved tensions or anxieties that are significant. You may decide that relationship counselling would be useful to resolve some particular issues. Your therapist will put together a personalised plan of exercises for you and your partner to do at home. These exercises will help you grow in self-awareness, sexual knowledge and sexual skills. At the same time, it will help to reprogram your body to respond to sensual and sexual stimulation and overcome your specific problem. Remember that sex is meant to be fun. If your sex life isn't fun anymore – think about going for some help. You'll be glad you did.

Male fertility

Infertility is not just a female thing – men are just as likely to have problems.

Maximise your health

The healthier you are, the greater your chances of conceiving. A healthy well-balanced diet is important, and make sure you are getting plenty of fresh fruit and vegetables and all the micronutrients (minerals and vitamins) you require.

Smoking

Smoking by either the man or the woman reduces a couple's fertility. It's been estimated that if a person smokes, the chances of conceiving are reduced by a third. Smoking also increases the risk of miscarriage, so women should give up before you try to conceive.

Alcohol

Alcohol has been shown to damage a man's fertility by a direct toxic effect which lowers the sperm count. Restrict your alcohol intake as soon as you want to try for a baby, to a maximum of twenty-one units a week for men. In particular, avoid binges.

Exercise

Regular exercise, at least three times a week, is important for maximising your fertility. Aim to get slightly out of breath during each session!

Drugs and medicines

A number of drugs are known to reduce fertility. It is thought that some pain relievers may affect fertility. Recreational drugs such as cocaine also reduce fertility. Avoid them.

Stress

Stress can be a major factor in infertility. Take a look at your life, spot the stress and try to find ways to deal with it.

Risks to fertility

Some risks to fertility can't be avoided – but being aware of them now will keep you alert to the possible need for extra help. Make a note if you have had any of the following, and talk to your doctor if you're worried:

- Mumps
- Trauma to the testes or an undescended testis
- Serious major illness
- Exposure to toxic chemicals
- A family history of infertility problems

Major illnesses such as diabetes or an over/under active thyroid reduce fertility.

Test your sperm count

It's possible to test a man's sperm count and sperm mobility. Unfortunately sperm counting is only really useful if there is a severe defect and the counts are zero or extremely low, because it can tell little about sperm *function* (how they work), which is what really matters. Some men with normal sperm counts in semen are infertile, and some with low counts are fertile.

Getting sex right

Maximise your fertility. It is vital to have sex at the right time – around the time when the woman ovulates.

When does the woman ovulate?

The time of ovulation will vary depending on the length of the woman's menstrual cycle. A woman usually ovulates fourteen days before the next cycle begins. Record the starting date of the woman's period over a number of months. Count back fourteen days from then, as this will be when ovulation occurs. The woman's most fertile time is the two or three days around the date of ovulation.

When is a woman fertile?

If a woman has a twenty-eight-day cycle, ovulation occurs roughly between days thirteen and fifteen. If she has a thirty-two-day cycle, she will ovulate around day eighteen. A woman with a short cycle – about twenty-five days long – will ovulate around day eleven. Just before ovulation, a woman has a mucous surge. This lasts only two to three days. Most women can learn to recognise it themselves. They are often randy around this time. This is the ideal time to have sex if you wish to have a baby.

Frequency of sex

Having sex frequently around the time of ovulation maximises your chances of conceiving. Sperm deteriorate in quality and motility once they have been made, so abstaining from sex for long periods of time might actually decrease your chances of pregnancy.

Impotence

Impotence, or erectile dysfunction to give it its proper name, means that a man's erection does not stay hard enough for long enough for him to have satisfactory sex.

Men of any age might be affected, although it becomes more likely with age. Impotence is now more commonly known as erectile dysfunction (ED). Men find that they are unable to achieve or to sustain an erection adequate for sexual intercourse.

Many lose interest in sex. Men with ED may feel angry, guilty and become depressed. Relationships often suffer. Most men experience occasional erectile failures at some time in their lives as a result of fatigue, stress or excessive alcohol consumption. For many men, erectile dysfunction is a persistent problem. It's believed that 70% of cases have physical causes and that the remaining 30% are due to psychological causes.

Physical causes include:

- Diabetes
- Thyroid problems
- Kidney problems
- High blood pressure
- Blood vessel damage
- Nerve damage
- Pelvic surgery or trauma
- Heavy smoking
- Side effects of medication

Dealing with impotence

There are some aspects to consider which could help a lot next time around.
Relax. It is important to be in a relaxed frame of mind. It's a complex issue relating to

nerve ends, but basically if you are tense and in 'fight or flight' mode, all your blood is being taken away from unnecessary spots such as your digestive system and penis and sent over to bolster up the muscles. If you are relaxed, the blood will flow to the penis, it will expand, and more will flow in, and so on.

Don't go for broke. It's not a 100 metre sprint, and in fact one of the great problems is the anxiety levels heightening in an effort to make things happen. Focus on intimacy, enjoy each other, play with tactile spots and let Mr Erection worry about himself. A light touch of the hand across your partner's skin is a beautiful sensation, and will bring on other responses and gradually lead to where you want to go.

Feel good about your body. Make an effort with diet and exercise to develop a body you are proud of, thus giving you the necessary confidence when with your partner.

Get over any illnesses or pain. No use searching for Nirvana if you feel jaded or ill. Pain produces body opiates, which can undermine and negate sexual stimulus.

Check that cholesterol. As you get older, the arteries to the penis start to narrow anyway. High cholesterol can block them even further. This is a significant impotence issue.

Be careful of the stimulants. People will tell of great passionate experiences hinging on caffeine, oysters, chocolate and all sorts of stimulants. Might be helpful in very tiny doses in the early stages to help people unwind and relax, but can rebound badly on you if done to excess.

Be very wary of alcohol. A few drinks may develop the ardour, but can do terrible things to the performance. While you think it is going to be the night of nights, they don't call it 'brewers droop' for nothing.

Put away the ciggies. Inhaling cigarette smoke inhibits relaxation of the penile muscle and tissue. Nicotine blocks the blood vessels.

Put away the drugs. You'd have to be a mug to be on them, anyway. But rather than heightening the experience, as some of their proponents will tell you, cocaine, marijuana, amphetamines and barbiturates can cause further grief.

Solve your problems. A lot of impotence issues are in the head – worrying about work, anxious about the relationship in the first place, concerned about family issues. A good partnership will be discussing these issues anyway, but if they are not in the open, make them. Even discuss in the bedroom with your partner what is worrying you. A problem shared is a problem solved and a good talk can do wonders.

Psychological causes include:
- Stress
- Depression
- Sexual or relationship worries

A vicious cycle can start whereby the more a man worries about the problem, the less likely an erection is to happen, and so on. Relationships are harmed, sometimes destroyed with each partner thinking it's their fault. Why does it happen? Temporary failure of the erection, such as in the case of 'brewers droop', after drinking too much alcohol. Recreational drug use can cause temporary and chronic impotence.

Treatment of ED depends upon the underlying cause
- Avoid smoking and too much alcohol.
- Eat a healthy diet.
- Take regular exercise.
- Take time to relax.
- Get plenty of rest.
- Talk to your partner about the problem.
- Sexual counselling may be necessary.

Other treatments

- Vacuum pumps – The first one was apparently invented by an American mechanic in his garage while he played around with a tyre pump. Good for a temporary display of penis power.
- Penile implants – These are surgically implanted in the penis and are semi-rigid rods or devices that can be inflated when the moment arrives.
- Medication – This can come in injection, intra-urethral pellet, and most recently tablet forms.
- Herbal therapy – Ginkgo, biloba, ginseng or Muira Puama are popular.

Illnesses and conditions more common in men
Colorectal cancer

Colorectal cancer, more usually known as bowel cancer, is the third most common form of cancer. It is more likely to develop as a man gets older. If caught early enough it can be successfully treated. It affects the lower part of the bowel, the large intestine and the rectum.

Symptoms

- Rectal bleeding
- Change from normal bowel habit
- Unexplained weight loss
- Abdominal or rectal pain

Some men feel tired, or dizzy, or breathless because they have become anaemic from microscopic bleeding from the bowel. For some men the first sign of a problem is bowel obstruction, constipation, severe abdominal pain, vomiting and a swollen abdomen.

Men at risk

Men at risk of developing bowel cancer include those with:

- A strong family history of bowel cancer.
- An inherited condition called adenomatous polyposis which causes small non-cancerous growths to develop in the bowel. In time these growths can become cancerous.
- Ulcerative colitis.
- Men are thought to be more at risk of developing bowel cancer if they have a high fat, low fibre diet that contains lots of meat and alcohol.
- Being overweight increases the risk.

Prevention

A high fibre diet with plenty of fruit and vegetables and carbohydrates (pasta, bread, rice) is believed to lessen the risk of developing bowel cancer.
Eating at least five portions of fruit and vegetables each day is believed to protect against this and many different cancers.

Symptoms

The most common symptom is rectal bleeding and should never be ignored.

Colour blindness

Colour blindness is the reduced ability to distinguish between certain colours.

- Vision itself is not affected, only the ability to distinguish between certain colours.
- Colour blindness is hereditary and is usually due to an abnormal gene inherited from the mother.
- Genetic colour blindness only affects men.
- It is usually inherited and present from birth.
- It affects around one in twenty men.

The most common form involves the confusion of red and green. This has two forms:

Different shades of red appear dull and indistinct, and men are unable to distinguish between greens, oranges, pale reds, and browns. These colours appear as the same hue only being distinguished by their intensity. In one rare form of colour blindness, blues and yellows cannot be distinguished. In another all colours are seen in black and white.

Why does it happen?

To see colours properly, colour detecting vision cells, called cones, are needed in the retina of the eye. Three types of cone cell exist, each being sensitive to red, blue or green light. If one or more of these types of cells is faulty then colour blindness results. Sometimes colour blindness occurs because of diseases such as macular degeneration or from side effects of medicines. Overall colour blindness is a harmless condition. It does not prevent someone from driving since traffic lights can be distinguished by the position of the lights. No treatment is possible for the inherited forms of colour blindness.

Constipation

Many men think that constipation means 'not going at all'. Medically speaking, constipation is when the stools are hard and being passed less often than they usually are. It's a strain and a struggle. If you're passing stools less often and they are like hard rabbit pellets, or if producing them is a strain and painful, then you're probably constipated. If you're spending more than a minute on the toilet then this is another sign that the motions are not moving as easily as they should be. Straining to pass hard stools can also cause small tears in the sensitive lining in and around the back passage that may bleed. It may also cause piles.

Causes of constipation

Ignoring the urge to go to the toilet because you are too busy or because it's inconvenient is a common cause of constipation. This may result in a loss of the reflex sensation that tells us that we need to go to the toilet. For the bowel to function well it needs people to move around and to be active. Stools need to be soft and bulky. Not eating enough fibre in our diet means that the stools are not bulky enough. Fibre is also needed to hold liquid in the motion that makes it soft to pass. Everyone should be drinking around two litres of water a day. If the body is starved of liquid then it squeezes as much as it can out of the motion to absorb into the body. This leaves the motion hard and dry.

Preventing constipation

Prevent constipation by:

- Drinking more liquid.
- Becoming more active.
- Eating more fibre.
- Going to the toilet when you feel the urge.

Medical advice should be sought

A man should seek advice when he:

- Notices any change in bowel opening pattern, and is over the age of forty-five.
- Passes blood when evacuating the bowel.
- Loses weight without trying.
- Feels unusually tired and fatigued.
- Is on medication where a side effect may be responsible for the constipation.

Laxatives

Laxatives are good for relief in the short-term but should not be relied upon.
They stimulate the bowel directly, making the motions more bulky and increasing the amount of liquid in the motions.

Hair loss

Hair loss is probably the one thing that causes men more anxiety than anything else in their life. The receding hairline and the arrival of the bald patch are the fear of men all over the world.

How does it happen?

Hair may start to disappear from the temples and the crown of the head at any time.

For some men this process starts as early as the later teenage years, for most it happens in the later twenties and early thirties. Initially it may just be a little thinning that's noticed. Then, the absence of hair allows more of the scalp to become visible. Some men are not troubled by this process. Others, however, suffer great emotional distress, lack of confidence and depression.

Why does it happen?

Male pattern baldness is hereditary. The hair is usually lost at the temples and the crown. This happens because an over-sensitivity of the hair follicle to normal levels of testosterone switches the hair loss gene on. Not every hair follicle has this gene which is why some hair falls out while other hair doesn't.

Reversible hair loss is caused by:

- Iron deficiency
- Anaemia
- Under-active thyroid
- Fungal scalp infection
- Some prescription medicines
- Stress

Haemophilia

Haemophilia is a blood condition in which an essential clotting factor is either partly or completely missing. Only boys get it, but it is passed through the mother's genes. Haemophiliacs bleed more, and for longer than normal. Minor cuts and grazes do not usually cause any problems. The main problem is internal bleeding, which may be spontaneous, into joints, muscles and soft tissues. This can cause pain and severe joint damage leading to disability.

Haemophilia types

There are two types of haemophilia:

Haemophilia A – Clotting Factor 8 is lacking.
Haemophilia B (also known as Christmas disease) – Clotting Factor 9 is lacking.

Genetic counselling and antenatal screening of those families with haemophilia provides an opportunity to prevent these diseases being passed on to children. There is no cure for haemophilia and no permanent way of replacing or increasing the clotting factor level. Haemophilia is treated by regularly replacing the missing clotting factor by injections or by injections at the time a bleed occurs.

Hernia

A hernia appears as a lump when the internal organs (intestines) protrude through a weakness in the abdominal muscle wall. The most common place for hernias to appear is in the groin. If they appear here they are called 'inguinal hernias'. Other places are in and around the umbilicus (belly button) and where a scar is present. In bad cases hernias can strangulate an organ and cut off its blood supply. This needs emergency treatment to avoid permanent damage.

What happens?

Many men describe a feeling of 'something giving way'. This is followed by a little groin pain. Later, the pain disappears and the lump comes into view. The lump disappears when you lie down, and gets bigger if you cough, sneeze, strain or exercise vigorously. In some cases hernias can be as large as a football.

Why does it happen?

The following activities can increase the pressure within the abdomen causing a hernia to be pushed out:

* Heavy lifting
* Straining on the toilet
* Coughing
* Vigorous exercise

Can I stop it?

Unless you can completely avoid coughing, laughing, sneezing, becoming constipated, lifting heavy weights or having vigorous exercise or sex there is no sure-fire way of avoiding a hernia.

The following will help however:

* Lift correctly
* Eat plenty of fibre
* Stop smoking
* Maintain your ideal weight

You should always get a hernia checked by a doctor, especially in cases of strangulated hernias. Hernia repairs are, in fact, the commonest male operation undertaken. Simple operations to repair the weakness are recommended.

* A hernioplasty involves putting special mesh material over the weakened area. The operation is done under local or general anaesthetic. Most men can go home the same day.

- A herniorrhaphy involves cutting the skin, pushing the protruding tissue back into place and sewing it back up to prevent the hernia from recurring. This may require a short stay in hospital.

HIV

The human immunodeficiency virus (HIV) causes infection that can lead to acquired immunodeficiency syndrome (AIDS). HIV infects and gradually destroys immune system cells, reducing the body's protection against infection and cancers.

How do I get it?

HIV is most often transmitted through unprotected sex. Sharing contaminated needles for drug use can also transmit it. The majority of HIV infections in the UK occur in gay men and the number of infections in this group has remained steady. The number of heterosexually acquired HIV infections has increased steadily and since 1999 has been greater than the number acquired through sex between men. The number of people becoming infected through injecting drugs appears to be falling.

Symptoms

The first symptoms of HIV infection can appear within six weeks of the virus entering the body. When this occurs some people have a flu-like illness with sore throat, fever, swollen lymph nodes, muscle aches and a rash. After a few weeks these symptoms usually disappear. Many people who are HIV positive do not have any symptoms for many years after initial infection. Others may have persistent swollen lymph nodes, mouth infections, persistent herpes infections such as cold sores or extensive genital warts, or weight loss.

AIDS

AIDS may develop at any time from one to ten years from the original infection, and in some cases, does not develop at all. A person may develop severe weight loss over a short period of time, severe and persistent infections, and cancers such as Kaposi's sarcoma and lymphoma. Since combination therapy has become available the number of people dying from AIDS has fallen. Practising safer sex by using a condom for vaginal and anal sex, and oral sex with a man, and using a dental dam for oral sex with a woman, and not sharing needles reduces the risk of infection. There is no vaccine or cure for HIV. Anti HIV drugs are available and taking a combination of these can slow down the damaging effect of HIV on the immune system. Medication is used when needed, to treat infection, for example. Maintaining a healthy lifestyle to keep the immune system as strong as possible is very important. The person with the HIV and those around them need emotional support.

Legionnaire's disease

Legionnaire's disease is a bacterial disease that can cause pneumonia. It is caused by the bacterium called *Legionella pneumophilia*. The disease and the bacterium were discovered following an outbreak at an American Legion convention in Philadelphia in 1976. Legionnaire's disease is not contagious. It can only be transmitted from contaminated water systems when a person breathes in the contaminated water droplets.

Common sources

- Cooling towers of air conditioning systems
- Communal whirlpools
- Fountains and ponds
- Communal showers where the bacterium is usually found in the showerhead

Symptoms
- Flu-like illness with fever
- Headache
- Muscle aches
- Dry cough
- Chest pain
- Shortness of breath
- Pneumonia
- Abdominal pain
- Vomiting
- Diarrhoea
- Hallucinations

It is more common in late summer and early autumn. Men are affected more than women, particularly middle-aged men. Smoking, alcohol misuse, chronic lung disease and weakened immunity all increase the risk of a person developing the infection following exposure. Antibiotics are effective in treating the disease.

STDs
STD, VD or 'a dose of something', they all mean the same thing – that a person has had unsafe sex and ended up with a sexually transmitted infection. It needs medical attention and any partners need to be traced, tested and treated too. Always practise safe sex and use a condom.

Supraspinatus tendonitis
Supraspinatus tendonitis is responsible for around six out of ten cases of shoulder pain. The supraspinatus muscle is one of the shoulder muscles and has a tendon that attaches it to the bone, called the supraspinatus tendon. Inflammation of this tendon is called supraspinatus tendonitis and is usually caused by repetitive strain that causes tiny tears in the supraspinatus tendon. The most common symptom is pain, which is often felt over the top of the shoulder and may come on suddenly or gradually. The shoulder is often stiff and moving the shoulder makes the pain worse.

Causes
Trauma is responsible for one in three cases of supraspinatus tendonitis. Overuse is another common cause. It can occur at any age but is most common between twenty and forty years of age. It's difficult to prevent supraspinatus tendonitis. However, regular exercise to keep the shoulder muscles strong and not over-using the shoulder joint can help to prevent it developing.

Treatment
- Painkillers and anti-inflammatory medication
- Rest
- Heat and cold treatment
- Physiotherapy
- Osteopathy
- Acupuncture

Joint injections may be recommended, and in severe but rare cases surgical treatment may be necessary.

Exercise

Aerobic exercises such as running, tennis and swimming help to burn up unnecessary calories and fat. As with any exercise the best results come from doing it regularly. Don't forget to warm up and warm down by stretching gently before and after exercise.

Common excuses for not exercising and their rebuttals:

'It's not cool.'

Try telling that to David Beckham, Tiger Woods and Cathy Freeman. We can all be fitter. People who tell you it's not cool are pretty uncool themselves.

'No one in my family/among my friends does it/respects it.'

Sport is also a good way of making new friends. It is fun. Maybe your example will get your family moving.

'It's a boy thing.'

It's true more boys than girls take exercise but that's not because girls can't enjoy sport. Many girls don't think competitive sports suit them but there are things to try outside school like dance, martial arts, swimming, social tennis, golf.

'It's sore/uncomfortable/sweaty.'

Feeling a bit stiff after activity is natural. Activity does make you sweat. If you're enjoying yourself at your activity you tend not to notice and everyone else is sweaty too. The great part is the rewarding shower afterwards.

'I don't want muscles.'

Getting fitter and getting big bulgy muscles don't necessarily go together. If you take regular exercise your body will tone up and you'll find you don't put on extra weight. To get big muscles you would have to do a program of specific exercise.

'I'm overweight/skinny/disabled.'

Don't worry about what you think you look like – get in there and enjoy yourself. If you are genuinely very overweight, not just a few kilos over, then have a chat with your doctor and tell them what you want to do. If you're disabled, don't let yourself be cut out of the action. Getting fitter benefits everyone.

'I don't like joining in teams.'

If teams leave you cold, activities you can do by yourself or with a friend are:

- Walking
- Swimming
- Golf
- Sailing
- Jogging
- Bushwalking/hiking
- Aerobics
- Walking the dog
- Bicycling
- Ten-pin bowling
- Wind surfing
- Surfing
- Flying a kite
- Orienteering
- Skipping

'I'd rather play with the computer/watch TV/talk to mates.'

It doesn't have to be either/or. You can do both. When there's nothing on TV and you're fed up with your current computer game, sporty activities can be fun.

Benefits of exercise
Make friends/meet up with friends

Get out and be with your mates or make new friends while playing.

Improves your health
As well as general fitness, exercise helps strengthen growing bones and muscles.

Stops you putting on weight
If you eat a lot and sit about doing nothing you will, eventually, get unhealthily overweight.

Achievement
It's fun to win competitions and be better than the others. It's fun to beat your record at skipping or cycling, to make up a complicated dance routine or score a goal against a mate at the park.

Fun
Exercise is fun. Get over that first feeling of 'I can't be bothered' and do it. Afterwards you'll be thinking, 'That was fun, I'll do it again.'

Meditation
Meditation is known to cause beneficial physiological and psychological changes to the system.

These include lowering of the rate of respiration, a decrease in the consumption of oxygen and the decline of the amount of blood lactate.

There is an increase in the alpha brain waves which are associated with peace and tranquillity.

It decreases stress.

Find more time to exercise
Extend your waking day. If you normally set the alarm clock for 7.30am, set it for 7.00am instead, and use the extra half hour to go for a walk or take part in some other form of physical activity that you enjoy.

Use any free time you have in the evening to increase your activity patterns. Find a gym that is open twenty-four hours a day.

Buy some home exercise equipment that enables you to exercise while watching the television or listening to the radio.

Listen to your body
Our natural twenty-four-hour biological cycle (circadian rhythms) mean that we experience exercise differently at different times of the day. We know if we are the 'morning type' or not. If you find it hard to get up in the morning, then don't try and exercise then, as you will naturally find it hard to stick to your new routine and won't enjoy what you are doing. It is important to find a time to exercise when you feel at your best for physical activity. Experiment with exercising at different times and find out what suits you.

Some tips to improve your exercise timemanagement
- Put your exercise times in your diary.
- Prioritise it by making it an appointment.
- Record what you did in your diary, so that you can keep track of your activity achievements.
- Make an appointment with a friend, colleague or relative to exercise together.
- Set your computer to send you reminder messages to take a walk or go for a swim.
- Keep an exercise kit handy in the boot of your car so you can exercise in different places if you get an unexpected free fifteen minutes, or a sudden wave of motivation.

- Say 'no' to people who ask you to do things that aren't your responsibility or don't even need doing, and which take up your valuable time.
- Protect your free time so that you can use it for sport, exercise or physical activity.
- Use your computer skills to save time on a range of mundane activities, and then try and use the free time you have created to be physically active.
- Take all of your holiday entitlement, and consider taking active holidays like cycle touring or trekking trips.
- Leave your car at home as much as possible and walk or cycle to the shops for those small things like milk or a newspaper.

Skip your way to good health

You can skip anywhere. The only equipment needed is a rope that is easy to transport anywhere. With just fifteen minutes of skipping a day you are well on the way to better health and fitness. Skip in the morning and your energy will flow all day. It is important to work up a sweat. Make sure that your shoes are suitable for skipping. The fifteen minutes does not all have to be achieved at once.

Rules for skipping
- Breathe only through your nose.
- Skip lightly on your toes.
- Keep your eyes forward.
- Skip in front of a mirror.

Four basic skipping steps

1. Rest jump
Jump over the rope with your left foot. When the rope is over your head skip again on your left foot, moving your right foot slightly. Repeat this, alternating your feet. Use only small steps.

2. Direct jump
Jump with your feet together onto your toes, knees slightly bent to soften the landing. Jump as often as you can.

3. Running jump
Alternate your feet when the rope passes under them, lifting your legs as high as possible. Skip as though you are running but without moving from the spot.

4. Stamping jump
Jump on your toes, placing your left foot in front of your right and vice versa. Then jump with your feet together.

Exercise for the older person

Sport, exercise and fitness are all things we tend to associate with younger people.

Statistics show that we all take less and less exercise as we get older. By the time we are over fifty few of us take regular exercise. Whether you're fit or not – and no matter what your age – you *can* take exercise and get lots out of it. You'll be surprised at what counts as exercise too.

Why it's good to be fit
- Physical exercise is good for our bodies in many ways – keeping muscles, ligaments and other soft tissues supple, providing aerobic exercise for the heart and lungs, counteracting obesity, and improving blood supply to vital organs including the brain.

- It's effective in bringing down high blood pressure and has even been shown to reduce the risk of bowel cancer and breast cancer.
- It is also a good way to counteract feelings of lethargy and helps tension, digestion and sleep and, as part of balance retraining, helps prevent falls in the elderly.

Start by warming up gently

Take some deep breaths. Stretch and relax the muscles. If the exercise causes pain or severe discomfort at any point, slow down and stop. If you are unable to do the exercise you want or find your movements restricted, see your doctor for more specific advice or to consider physiotherapy.

Remember:
- You don't need to belong to a gym or have any expensive equipment.
- You don't need to buy weights – improvise.
- Walking is the simplest, cheapest form of exercise and it benefits most of your muscles and bones as well as your heart, lungs and brain.
- Involve the whole household, even if they consider themselves fit.

We could all do with a bit more exercise, and it makes the routine more fun!

Should I eat before exercise?

Many top-class athletes do better when they have snacked before, or even during exercise. Food will restore and maintain blood sugar levels.

Some people feel worse for food

During moderately paced activity, the body is able to carry on digesting food and the chances of nausea or discomfort after eating are much less. But with more intensive sports, such as aerobics or running, the blood supply to the gut is reduced in order to send blood to the muscles instead. In this case the food is much more slowly digested, so it is more important not to eat (especially a large meal) for several hours before action.

Good pre-sport snacks

Carbohydrates are the key – they provide energy in an accessible form to maintain blood sugar and glycogen levels, and are easily digested. Try some of the following, ideally about thirty minutes before exercise:

- Cereal bars
- Sandwich
- Bananas
- Muffins
- Raisins
- Fruit juice

Exercise after a hip replacement

Sports that one can resume on a regular basis after hip replacement include golf, swimming, cycling, sailing, hiking, walking, tennis, swimming, ballet and aerobics.

Activities which can damage the new hip or cause loosening of its parts

Karate, football, water-skiing, basketball, rugby, running, squash, hockey.

Exercise is important

Exercise is important after a hip replacement. It can help to reduce joint pain and stiffness. It increases flexibility and muscle strength. Follow a suitable exercise plan as recommended by your surgical team. The initial focus will be on low impact activities which will safely encourage a good range of motion and strengthen muscles. After a few weeks, once the wound is healed, swimming will be introduced. This will be followed by walking and stationary bicycling. These exercises can increase muscle strength and cardiovascular fitness without injuring the new hip.

Six months out

If things are going well after about six months, you can start recreational bicycling and light sports such as golf or ballroom dancing. You should be careful about putting too much pressure on your new hip for at least a year. This advice varies depending on your own fitness and general progress after the operation, as well as the type of new hip you have.

Be aware

If you have one made of polyethylene bearings (rather than metal-on-metal) the more you use it the faster it will wear out, and heavy sports can shorten the lifespan of the implant. If you do play golf it may be worth investing in smooth, spikeless shoes to minimise the rotation stress on the lead leg and hip. Or you can simply change your lead leg to avoid using the new hip.

Sex after a hip replacement

Advice on sex varies. Some say wait until six weeks after the operation while others say you can start again as soon as comfortable. Be careful to take all the usual hip precautions.

Older person's health
Avoiding falls

- Install safety devices in your bathroom, such as grab-bars near the toilet and in the shower and bathtub.
- Use a non-slip mat when you shower or bathe to help avoid falls.
- If you don't have non-skid carpets, use double-sided tape or non-skid underpads under your rugs and mats to ensure they won't slide under your feet.
- Make sure stair rails and banisters are sturdy and attached properly to walls, so they won't come loose if you pull on them.
- Keep your floors tidy.
- Move or remove anything you might trip over, such as small pieces of furniture, electrical cords, handbags, etc.
- When the grandchildren visit, have them keep their shoes and toys in a safe place.
- Make sure your home is well lit.
- Use night-lights, especially in areas that tend to be dark, or where you might want to go during the night, such as bathrooms, stairwells or the kitchen.
- In the kitchen, laundry room or storage area, keep the items you use most often on the shelves you find easiest to reach.
- Avoid climbing on chairs or stools.
- Think about wearing pyjamas instead of long nightgowns or robes that might cause you to trip.
- For the same reason, beware of overlong skirts, dresses or pants. Avoid long shoelaces.
- Wear boots, shoes and slippers with soles made of rubber or other non-skid material.

Assisted living

As you age, it is wise to be aware of the options that may be available for you when you get to that stage in life where you are unable to stay in your own home. If you are wise you will take control now, while you still can, and still have some say in what your fate may be. Look around your local area and discover what accommodation there is for the elderly. Make decisions now and let your children know your wishes.

Choosing assisted living

Call or visit assisted-living facilities in your area to determine what services they provide and whether these services will be suitable for you or your loved one. The definition of 'assistance' can be vastly different in various facilities. Similarly, the 'age in place' promise at some assisted-living facilities (meaning that you will not need to move as your needs increase) can have limits or strings attached. Find out about all the terms and conditions for staying in the residence of your choice.

Compare homes

You need not accept a room or apartment in the first facility you see. You can take your time and find a new home you or your loved one will enjoy. Visit as many facilities as possible, keeping in mind the services required and how easily these can be provided. Your first visit should usually include a meeting with the administrator and a tour.

Research

Another source of information on assisted-living facilities is your doctor or local council. They will have basic information on any facility's supportive living services such as meals, medication assistance and personal care, and on its social and recreational activities.

Visit more than once

Once you have created a short list of possible facilities, go back to visit each one at least once more. You may wish to visit at different times, such as mealtimes, evenings and weekends. In this way you will get a true picture of the way the facility is run and determine whether the day-to-day atmosphere is pleasant. Be sure to speak informally to the staff, other residents and/or their family members.

Ask a lot of questions

You are the client/buyer in this situation and should be as cautious as you are with any major purchase. Ask about prices and when and why your costs might increase.

- Do the rates quoted include every service you want?
- If not, how much will these extras cost?
- How is an assessment made of each resident's needs?
- How often is this assessment reviewed and compliance monitored?
- Also ask questions about refunds, transfers and discharges.
- What if the residence were to close?
- What provisions exist to secure the rights of the people living there?
- If a resident is unhappy with some aspect of the facility, how are complaints handled?

Brochures and documentation

You want to make an informed choice, so get all the information you can. Check marketing materials used by the facility, or its parent company, as well as the resident contract agreement. Ask for survey information about the facility, which can usually be obtained by contacting your state's health care ombudsman. Other government agencies may have consumer information brochures that can help you come up with appropriate questions to ask.

Documentation

The residence contract should formalise all the agreements and promises made to you. Be sure you read it through carefully before you sign it. Consider having an attorney who specialises in seniors' issues review the contract, especially if you find any part of it confusing or ambiguous.

What will it cost?

Assisted living is often expensive, so get all the information you need to compare each facility's charges for the care you need now, and what you might need later on.

Can you afford it? Decide early on what you will be able to afford and plan accordingly. Will your adult children be able to help you finance your long-term needs? They may wish to discuss this aspect among themselves.

Family involvement

When an elderly person moves to an assisted living residence, it is often because their adult children have suggested the time has come to do so; and they are often involved in choosing the senior's new home. However, adult children should avoid making the final choice of residence for the senior. They should keep in mind that the senior's comfort, interests, needs and wishes – and not their own convenience – must take precedence. No matter how pleasant the environment and no matter the efforts made to preserve the senior's autonomy and dignity, moving into an assisted living facility can be traumatic.

Hints for life
Written by a woman in a nursing home for her carers

What do you see, nurses, what do you see?
What are you thinking when you are looking at me?
A crabby old woman, not very wise,
Uncertain of health, with faraway eyes,
Who dribbles her food and makes no reply,
When you say in a loud voice, 'I do wish you'd try',
Who seems not to notice the things that you do,
And who is forever losing a stocking or shoe,
Who unresisting or not, lets you do as you will,
With bathing and feeding the long day to fill.
Is that what you're thinking?
Is that what you see?
Then open your eyes, nurse, you're not looking at me,

I'll tell you who I am as I sit here so still,
As I rise to your bidding and eat at your will,
I'm a small child of ten with a father and mother,
Brothers and sisters who love one another.
A young girl of sixteen with wings under her feet,
Dreaming that soon now, a lover she'll meet;
A bride soon at twenty – my heart gives a leap
Remembering the vows that I promised to keep;
At twenty-five I now have young of my own
Who need me to build a secure, happy home;

A young woman of thirty, my young now grow so fast,
Bound to each other with ties that should last.
At forty my young sons have grown and are gone,
But my man is beside me to see I don't mourn;
At fifty once more, babies play round my knee,
Again we know children, my loved one and me.
Dark days are upon me, my husband is dead,
I look to the future, I shudder with dread.
For all my young are rearing young of their own,
And I think of the years and the love I have known.
I'm an old woman now and nature is cruel –
Tis her jest to make old age look like a fool.
The body is crumbled, grace and vigour depart
There now is a stone where there once was a heart;
But inside this old carcass a young girl still dwells,
And now and again my battered heart swells.
I remember the years, I remember the pain,
And I'm loving and living life over again.
I think of the years, all too few – gone too fast,
And accept the stark fact that nothing can last.
So open your eyes, nurses, open and see,
Not the crabby old woman, look close – see me!

Alcohol and older people

Drinking 'in moderation' is not considered very harmful for most people.
In fact, it can be beneficial. On the other hand, we all know that drinking too much alcohol is not healthy. As we age, so too, should we be careful of how much alcohol we take. A fall for an older person can be catastrophic. Drinking alone or drinking too much can alienate you from family and society. It can take away your motivation and can make you feel terrible in the morning.

Do you drink too much?

Ask yourself these questions:

- When you are alone and feeling upset about something, do you have a drink 'to calm your nerves'?
- Has your drinking ever made you late for work or a social engagement?
- Have you ever had a drink after thinking you shouldn't, or telling yourself it was time to stop?
- Have you ever forgotten what you did while you were drinking, or wondered how you got home?
- Do you ever have headaches or a hangover the morning after you have been drinking?
- Has anyone in your family expressed concern about the amount you drink?

If you responded 'yes' to any of these questions, it's possible that you have a drinking problem. Have an honest talk with your doctor. He or she will help you decide what you should do about it and how to go about making any necessary changes in your life.

Cutting back on alcohol consumption

If your doctor has told you that you should drink less, here are twelve hints that can help make it easier.

1. Make a list.

Make a list of your reasons for not drinking or for drinking less. There will probably be many.

2. Keep a diary.

Over three or four weeks, record your drinking. Write down the time, place and circumstances of every drink. You may be surprised at the amount you drink, or you may detect a pattern you hadn't noticed before – such as drinking when you've had an argument, or when you are with certain friends.

3. Set a goal.

With your doctor's advice, decide how much you can safely drink. That could mean nothing at all, or that you'll allow yourself one drink at a social event. If you are a senior or have certain medical problems, you should not drink too much. Once you have decided that you want to cut back or stop drinking, and you've set a goal, there are various helpful strategies you can try.

4. Avoid having alcohol in the house.

If you have nothing to drink you may be less tempted to imbibe. Keep only a small amount or no alcohol at home.

5. Drink slowly.

If you still plan to have the odd drink, make sure you drink each serving slowly. Have only one drink every hour. Between times, or once you have reached your limit, ask for soda, water or juice. Do not drink alcohol if you have not eaten for a while, or drink without having at least a small snack at the same time.

6. Take a break.

If you've been in the habit of drinking daily, stop drinking for a day or two every week. If you feel increasingly healthier as you cut back, that can be your motivation.

7. Just say 'no'.

Take the advice adults give to teens: you don't have to do anything, including drink alcohol, just because others are doing it. Neither must you drink something just because it has been offered.

8. Avoid temptation.

If you kept a diary you'll probably have found that being with certain people or being in certain places or situations make you drink or crave a drink. The simple solution is to avoid people who drink to excess or places where you used to go to drink.

9. Find another activity.

Use the time and money you once spent drinking to do something fun with your family or friends. Take up a new hobby, see a film, go sightseeing, or renew an old interest in sports.

10. Seek emotional support.

Altering a habit can be difficult, and reducing your alcohol consumption is no exception. Seek support from family members and friends or a professional.

11. Give yourself a chance!
Not everyone can succeed immediately. Cutting back or quitting may take longer than you planned, or you may have a relapse before you succeed.

12. Do not give up.

Don't be an easy target
Burglars, muggers, sometimes even kids, see older people as a soft target and perfect for robbery or just making life difficult. Don't be an easy target. Here are some tips to keep safe:

Before you answer the door
When the doorbell rings or someone knocks at your door, try to find out who your visitor is before you open the door. If you don't already have a peephole or a safe window, have one installed.

Ask for identification
Seniors are often targets for criminals who go door-to-door claiming to be servicemen. Ask any stranger at the door to tell you his or her name. If he claims to represent a company or group, ask for proof or a telephone number you can call to confirm that the visit is legitimate. If you are not sure someone can be trusted, it is perfectly all right to keep your door closed and locked.

Install locks
To protect against crime such as a break-in, the locks on your doors and windows should be good ones. An alarm system is ideal. If you are not sure what other changes you should make to increase your home's security, most police departments have a crime prevention unit that can advise you.

Thief-proof possessions
Many police departments can lend you a tool that allows you to mark your name or a permanent identification number (such as your driver's licence number) on valuable property. Keep an inventory of all your possessions, especially those that have value such as jewellery or silver. One simple and effective way of doing this is to take a photo or video image of the valuable item(s). The picture or videotape should be stored in a safe place, such as a safety deposit box. If you don't use your valuable items frequently, they might be better off in the safety deposit box, too.

Be alert when you are out
No matter whether you are far from home or near your front porch, try not to travel alone. Stay away from dark parking lots or alleys.

Go cashless
Avoid carrying cash; and if you must carry a handbag, avoid keeping your money and credit cards in it. Put these items in an inside pocket or consider using a money belt.

- Don't dress in a way that signals you might be carrying money.
- In other words, unless you know for sure you will be safe, don't wear your best jewellery or your fur coat.

- If you do have the misfortune to be stopped by a robber, the best way to minimise your risk is to hand over any cash you have.
- Your monthly pension or any other funds you receive regularly should be deposited directly to your bank account rather than sent by cheque.
- If you go to the bank frequently, don't always go at the same time of the day or week.

Don't be conned

- Never withdraw and hand over money from your bank account if a stranger asks you to do it.
- Do not give your credit card or bank account number to a stranger who has telephoned you to sell a product or ask for a charitable contribution.
- If a deal sounds too good to be true, it probably is. Stay away from it.
- In particular, avoid any scheme in which you have to provide money up front, even if you are promised a large or valuable prize.

Remember, quick fixes or miracle cures for most health problems do not exist. But advertisements and promotions for these products, such as cures for arthritis, baldness, or even cancer, can be persuasive and tempting. Always ask your doctor about these products first, because many can do as much harm as good.

Tips for carers
Reduced cognitive abilities
Some helpful hints for people who are caring for a senior with reduced cognitive abilities. If you are already a caregiver you know the job takes a great deal of your time and energy.

- Try to look at the positive. There can be much fulfillment and pleasure in letting your loved one remain a part of family life.
- Recognise your abilities and limitations and take time for yourself.
- Avoid putting pressure on yourself.
- Set reasonable goals.

Learning to cope with your new role
- Nothing will stay the same forever and you must be flexible.
- Your goals and the person's needs will change over time.
- You'll probably become very observant about the person's condition.
- Don't hesitate to report any changes to his or her doctor or other health care practitioner. They will usually appreciate any details you can provide.
- If you have never done it before, you'll have to learn how to coordinate (such as make appointments, organise visits, etc.), delegate (let others help you!) and plan ahead.
- Because theirs is a twenty-four-hour job, caregivers often neglect their own health and emotional needs.
- Care for yourself or else you will become ill or exhausted, and then everyone is in strife.
- Taking care of yourself doesn't mean you are neglecting your loved one – just the opposite, because their health depends on your own.

Be realistic about the person's illness and your abilities
You will want to make sure the person is safe and comfortable, has a tranquil environment and can be as independent as possible. Ask the person's doctor or other health care provider to give you as much information as they can about the person's illness, or point you to other sources of information. In this way you'll have a better understanding of what symptoms to expect and what the person can and can't do, and for how long.

Don't take it personally

People who are sick, and especially those who have had a stroke or head injury or suffer from Alzheimer's disease, often cannot control their behaviour or their speech.

You may have to remind yourself of this periodically so that you don't feel angry, wounded and frustrated.

Allow the patient autonomy

Give the person as much freedom and independence as is practical, even if this simply means letting him choose whether to wear a red or a blue shirt. Too many choices can be confusing, so limit them.

Allow time

He may take a long time to accomplish a task independently or semi-independently, but may be happier for having done so. For example, try setting out toothbrush and toothpaste and letting the person take up the task from there.

Keep directions short and simple

It may be necessary to give directions in short, simple steps. Rather than telling the person 'Put on your jacket' you may have to cue her with 'Pick up your coat; put your arm in the sleeve; now the other arm; now let's zip it up.'

Be positive

Be positive: tell the person what to do, not what she should not do.

Avoid burnout

The person for whom you are caring has limitations, but so do you. You cannot do everything and you should not attempt to.

Share the burden

- Let friends and family help out – in fact, don't wait for them to offer but ask for their assistance.
- Even if they simply sit and chat or watch television with the person, or read the newspaper to him, it will allow you to leave the house to do something pleasant or take care of your own health.
- Accept that others won't do everything just the way you do.
- Even children can help care for the ill senior; the experience can be beneficial for them. Ask them to help you out with small tasks or chores such as cooking, or to play cards or a game with the person or to discuss something they've learned in school.
- Include other family members in discussions and decisions about your loved one and his or her illness.
- If possible, include the person being cared for.
- By providing information you can probably improve communication and cooperation among family members.
- Think about sending your loved one to an adult day centre for at least a couple of days a week. Such centres often provide transportation.

Take care of yourself

Recognise that you will feel stress and learn to manage it. Take time to relax. If your loved one often calls out at night, have someone else stay over sometimes to ensure you can have an uninterrupted night of sleep.

Music

Put the stereo on or sing. Elderly people especially enjoy music that helps them recall 'the old days'. Music can be very powerful: even those with Alzheimer's disease can often remember song lyrics even if they can no longer hold a conversation. And music can have a calming effect.

Support groups

There are other people in your situation, and there may be a caregivers' support group you can join. Try attending a meeting. You may discover that sharing your problems can help you find solutions, or that you can help others cope.

Tap into services

If your loved one's illness becomes too much for you, it may be time to consider placing him or her in a nursing home or other facility. Other services that may be as close as a few phone calls away:

- Some nursing homes offer temporary or respite care.
- With respite service your loved one can stay for a short period, usually two weeks or less, while you have some time off.
- You'll likely need to book in advance and may require a doctor's note.
- Some church and fraternal groups will send volunteers to care for your loved one while you have a few hours off.
- You may be able to hire a nurse or nursing assistant occasionally by calling a home health agency.
- There are many resources for seniors that can be of assistance.

General health
Allergies

Most allergies fit into three basic categories – contact, food and inhalants. It is almost impossible to avoid allergy triggers altogether, but there are things that we can do to minimise the pain and suffering.

- Avoid carpets on the floor. Instead, have boards or tiles and throw rugs that can be shaken out.
- Air-condition your house. This keeps humidity low and filters the air. It reduces dust mites and moulds.
- Air-condition your car.
- Keep your bathroom and wet areas free from mould.
- Keep your pets outside.
- Wear a face mask when you are doing anything that is likely to expose you to irritants, such as when you are cleaning or gardening.
- Hire a cleaning service if you are allergic to cleaners and the vacuum cleaner.
- Use synthetic pillows and doonas.
- Wash mattress and pillow protectors regularly.
- Make your bedroom a mite-free area and keep the door to the rest of the house firmly shut.

Antihistamines often work wonders on dripping noses and sore red eyes. They are available over the counter from chemists. If symptoms persist for more than five to seven days see your doctor who will be able to give you allergy shots.

Bad breath

Testing for bad breath

Test your breath by cupping your hands and breathing into them with a long breath. If it smells bad to you, then it is horrible to those around you.

Floss your teeth and sniff the results of your probe. If it smells bad, it is.

Dealing with bad breath

- Carry a toothbrush with you and use it after you eat.
- Remember to brush your tongue to remove food and bacteria.
- When you are unable to brush, swish your mouth clean with water.
- Gargle with a mouthwash.
- Eat parsley, as it is a natural breath freshener.
- Eat three regular meals a day as bad breath can be caused by eating irregularly or not eating enough.

Beware bad breath

Persistent bad breath may be an indicator of more serious medical conditions.

Bed wetting

Most children will grow out of wetting the bed in time. Be patient and don't make an issue of it. If your child has not grown out of it by the time he or she goes to school, then it may be time to get help from the experts.

- Be patient and supportive. No child wants to lie in a wet cold bed and suffer the embarrassment of waking up wet yet again.
- Remain neutral. Just change the bed without making a fuss. Don't praise when the bed is dry. Children do not wet the bed on purpose. If they could control it they would. So don't make a big thing of it.
- Boost bladder capacity by training the child to put off going to the toilet for as long as possible during the day.

It has been shown that 98% of children grow out of bed wetting by the time they reach puberty.

Black eye

- Minimise swelling and bruising by holding a cold can of soft drink up to the eye intermittently until you can ice the wound.
- If your vision is impaired, see your doctor.
- Avoid aspirin as it stops the blood coagulating and you may end up with an even bigger bruise.
- Refrain from blowing your nose as you may cause even more damage.

Body odour

Body odour is caused by a combination of perspiration and bacteria. Keep body odour under control by adopting some of these principles:

- Wear clean clothes, especially natural fabrics rather than synthetics.
- Give yourself a good wash with soap and water, especially around the armpits and the naughty bits.
- Be careful of what you eat. Garlic, fish and curry spices can come up through the skin for days.
- Purchase a good deodorant or antiperspirant.

- Keep in control in potentially romantic situations – body odour is linked back to sexuality.
- Handle pressure scenarios – getting nervous only makes you perspire and sends the odour-meter into turbo-charge.

If all else fails: Try using pine soap. Or pour two cups of tomato juice into your next bath. No one is sure why, but it seems to work.

Boils

A boil is a pus-filled abscess which erupts from the skin. It can be treated at home, but be aware that an infected boil can cause blood poisoning.

Do not squeeze a boil that is on your lips or nose as the infection can be carried to the brain.

Also be wary of squeezing a boil that has developed in the region of the armpits, the groin or on the breast.

To treat a boil

Apply a warm compress over the boil for half an hour, three or four times a day until the boil breaks. Try one of the following:

- Continue the compresses for several days after the boil opens as it is important that all the pus is drained from the tissues.
- Apply a heated slice of tomato as a compress.
- Compress with a slice of onion.
- Apply a paste of mashed garlic to the boil.
- Wrap boil in the outer edge of a cabbage.
- Apply a teabag to the boil.
- Make a poultice of warm milk and bread and apply.

When the boil has come to a head, sterilise a needle over a flame and make a hole in the head. Gently squeeze the pus out. Keep the boil draining and keep the skin around it clean.

Bruises

- To reduce the size, discoloration, swelling and general impact of a bruise, immediately apply an ice-pack.
- The most immediate and easiest ice-pack is a pack of frozen peas straight from the freezer! But you can make up a pack using ice and cloth.
- Apply the pack every fifteen minutes.
- Do not, as is often thought, mix and match ice with heat.
- Keep the ice treatment going for anything up to twenty-four hours. It restricts the blood vessels and prevents blood flowing into the tissue, which is the major cause of the black discoloration.
- Ice eases the pain by causing numbness on the area.
- Ice helps to keep the swelling to a minimum.
- After a day, apply the heat. Heat improves circulation in the injury zone by dilating the blood vessels.

You can apply heat by a cloth in very hot water, or applying heat treatments, such as arthritic or injury-repair creams from the pharmacist or supermarket. If you have bruised your lower limb, prop it up on a pillow or chair. Otherwise the blood will collect like a reservoir and lengthen the recovery period.

Why is it so?

Regular or easy bruising from simple impact could be a sign of age, but also could indicate a health issue worth checking with your doctor. Bruising might happen more easily, too, if you are on medication such as anti-inflammatory or blood thinners, and you may have to reconsider the dosage of these. A good diet helps prevent or minimise bruising, especially adequate vitamin C intake via fresh fruit and vegetables.

Burns

How to gauge the seriousness of a burn:

1st degree burns – Red and painful like sunburn and scalds.
2nd degree burns – Blister, ooze and are painful.
3rd degree burns – Charred, white or cream coloured. The nerve endings are destroyed and they always require medical care.

Burns that require medical attention:

3rd degree burns:

- Burns to the face, eyes, hands, feet and pubic areas.
- Any burn that shows signs of infection – blisters filled with brown or greenish fluid, or a burn that turns hot and red again.
- Burns on children under twelve months or older people over sixty years.
- Any burn that doesn't heal in ten days.

Treatment for burns that require medical assistance:

- Douse the flame.
- Stop the burning process by running the burn under cold water for twenty minutes.
- If a child is burnt badly turn on the shower to cold water and stand under the shower with him/her.
- Do not attempt to take off clothing that is sticking to the wound. Leave that to your doctor.
- Gently wrap the burn in a clean dry cloth and seek medical aid as soon as possible.

Treatment for burns that can be dealt with at home:
- Run the wound under cold water for twenty minutes.
- Wrap in a clean dry cloth.
- Leave for twenty-four hours to allow the body to begin its own healing process.
- After the burn is beginning to heal, rub on aloe vera or an ointment containing vitamin E.
- Leave blister intact as they are nature's own bandage.

Chapped dry lips

The old statement is true – do *not* lick chapped lips!

Comforting as it may feel, you are not doing the situation any good. What little moisture you apply only evaporates, taking you back into the cycle of lips feeling drier than before.

Before you know it, a sore has developed, or even worse, an ugly red ring of dermatitis around your mouth.

Once lips are chapped, the only solution is the doctor and/or pharmacist to get anti-bacterial and hydrocortisone ointment.

The best solution is prevention.

A good starting point is your fluid intake. Keep up the water, and increase it in climatic situations that are likely to lead to chapped lips, especially dry, cold weather.

Your ability to moisturise areas such as your lips decreases as you get older – the answer is to moisturise from within.

Consider your diet, too, especially levels of vitamin B.

To stop getting dry or chapped lips in the first place, regularly apply lip balm in dry (either hot or cold) weather.

Sunscreen, too, is a valuable deterrent against chapped lips, so use at least 15-plus sunscreen or the special lip products that contain sunscreen.

Zinc cream certainly is a great protector of your lips, especially in hot weather. Not the most glamorous looking though, unless you are a Swedish tennis fan at a Grand Slam event.

Don't forget lipstick, either. It is not necessarily aimed at preventing or curing chapped lips, but at least provides some form of covering and does help. Lipstick is a bonus for women, and an opportunity to be considered by men brave enough to care about their health or with a dramatic flare for the fashion statement.

Cold sores

Cold sores are caused by the *Herpes simplex* virus. They are highly infectious and once you have the virus in your system, you have it for life, and cold sores are liable to pop up around your mouth and lips whenever you are run-down, stressed or tired.

How can you minimise the damage?

- Leave it alone. Keep the area clean and dry and seek medical attention if the sore becomes infected.
- Get a new toothbrush as your old one could harbour the virus. Once the sore has healed, throw away that toothbrush and start out again with a new one.
- Keep your toothbrush out of the warm, moist environment of the bathroom. Store it in a clean dry place.
- Use small tubes of toothpaste that can be replaced regularly.
- Use a fresh cotton swab and apply petroleum jelly to your cold sore.
- Apply zinc cream the minute you get that initial tingling feeling.
- If you have more than three doses of cold sores a year, supplement your diet with lysine. Pregnant women and nursing mothers should speak to their doctor first.
- Identify the trigger for your cold sores and endeavour to avoid that situation. If you find the trigger take lysine when you are most prone to cold sores.
- When you feel the first sensation, ice the area.
- Dab on witch hazel or pure alcohol.
- Protect lips from the sun and wind.
- Reduce stress-prone situations.
- Relax.
- Exercise.
- Remember that cold sores come and cold sores go and that having one does not ruin your life. Learn to live with it.

Constipation

Constipation is the result of an intricate mix of how you treat your body, what you feed it, and how you go about your life. Here are a few tips that can help make those visits to the toilet less of a strain.

Don't worry

A tense response to situations brings on a number of effects – your heart beats faster, your blood pressure goes up, and your lips dry up. But your bowels also tighten up. Loosen up, and so will your bowels.

Be happy

The state of play of your mind can have a lot to do with the resultant action in the toilet. Laughter truly is the best medicine, massaging your intestines and reducing your stress levels. Smile all the way to the dunny.

Try to get into a daily routine

You were toilet-trained as a baby, but the rhythm has probably been lost in the sands of time. It's a busy, crazy world, and that is probably half your problem – not going when you need to, and only going when time allows but when you actually don't want to! Determine that you will go after a particular meal each day, and sit there for fifteen minutes with a good book. Eventually, after several days of doing this, some consistent action will occur and you will be on the way to wellness.

Drink plenty of fluid

Drink lots of fluids such as water and juices, between six to eight glasses a day. Water is the best, and it helps things come to pass.

Take in plenty of fibre

Whole grains, vegetables and fruit provide plenty of fibre and aid your system. Prunes, raisins, figs, pears are good for you, as are flax and oat bran. You need about 25g of dietary fibre a day. As an example, an apple will give you 3 to 5g.

Exercise

Exercise is all important. Walking, aerobics and gym can do wonders for the bowels.

Go for smaller meals

Eating-wise, don't gorge yourself to a standstill. Remember what happened to Elvis? He died on the can, his colon stuffed chockablock by a virtually unmoveable substance with the consistency of putty, built up by poor diet accelerated by a massive binge of fatty foods. Work out what food is good for you and what is not. Some people get constipated by foods as seemingly innocent as milk.

Medicines?

Carefully evaluate what medicine or treatment you need. Laxatives might solve your problem in the short-term but then do you really want to spend your life hooked on these? They vary from chemical versions to the natural type such as psyllium. Herbal remedies include cascara sagrada, senna, dandelion and rhubarb. Avoid, if you can, medicines such as antihistamines, antacids, sedatives and anti-depressants. While they may be solving one problem, they could well be making your constipation worse and only serving to make your life miserable.

Can the can . . .

Avoid, too, being a hero and letting rip on the toilet at all costs. Apart from the determined grunts of desperation being heard throughout the house, you could bring on haemorrhoids or tiny anal fissures. Worse still, your heartbeat could drop, your blood pressure could go up, you could black out, and the next thing you know, you are waking up in the old folks' home.

The final solution

Of course, there is the final solution – the suppository or the enema. This will bring short-term relief, but don't make a habit of it. Your colon will think it doesn't have to do anything at all anymore, and will start to go on strike, and you will be in a more precarious situation than before. If you have reached the point where you think the only solution is to have a saline-solution enema, then it is time to take stock, get over what ever it is that is making you worried, and lighten up.

Diarrhoea

First up, annoying and debilitating as it may be, the fact that you have diarrhoea may be a good thing. Diarrhoea is seen by many physicians as a defence technique. It is getting something bad out of your body, and so the only real solution is to hang in there and see it through.

Lactose intolerance is a major cause of diarrhoea. It does not necessarily start out with you as a baby – for unknown reasons it could strike you in adult life. A lactose intolerance test involves eliminating all dairy products from your diet for up to two weeks. If the diarrhoea disappears then you know you are onto something. By slowly bringing back dairy products into your diet you will learn which are the major causes for concern. You can then establish whether these need to be eliminated totally or what levels you can take on board before discomfort starts. The aim is to work within your levels. The solution, once it is verified, could mean cutting down or eliminating dairy products from your diet including milk, butter, cheese, and so on. However, not all cheese is a culprit, nor is yoghurt.

Antacids, taken for heartburn, and other medications such as antibiotics and quinidine, can cause diarrhoea.

It's important to keep eating during an episode of diarrhoea, but stay away from foods that will overload the bowel and take it easy with jelly, chicken soup, and lots of water or rehydration fluids that contain salt and sugar.

When things are feeling a little more stable move up to a banana, rice or yoghurt.

A pinch of salt and some honey in a glass of fruit juice is an excellent rehydration drink when you have diarrhoea.

It is not advisable to eat prunes when you have diarrhoea! For fairly obvious reasons – you want to dampen this thing down, not start it up again with a bang.

Stay away also from pears, peaches and apples (one of the rare times in this chapter that you will see advice against eating fruit) and don't touch wheat products such as bread and pasta or other grains such as corn and oats, as well as ice-cream.

Bubbly drinks, such as soda and lemonade, are not a good idea, either. They only add to the situation.

While 'binding' the bowel sounds a good idea – and there are many old-fashioned suggestions including Swiss cheese, carob and barley – you are only delaying the diarrhoea coming to its logical end. Remember, this has come upon you for a reason – to expel whatever it is that is not good for you – and the sooner you get it over and done with, no matter how discomforting it gets, the better.

Above all, be very careful. Wash your hands, and stay out of the kitchen, so as not to pass the diarrhoea on to others.

First aid for cuts and scrapes

Medical attention is needed if:

- Bleeding spurts and is bright red. You may have damaged an artery.
- You are unable to wash all the gunk out of the wound.
- The cut is on the face or in an area where it is important that you minimise scarring.
- You have lost a digit or a limb.
- The wound is large.
- If any sign of infection develops – red streaks, pus or redness.

Otherwise:
- Stop the bleeding by placing a clean absorbent cloth or towel over the wound and applying pressure by pressing firmly against it.
- If the pressure doesn't stem the bleeding, elevate the wound so that it is above the level of the heart.
- Clean the wound by gently washing with water and mild soap.
- Bandage the wound.
- You may need a tetanus shot.

Flatulence and farting

Everyone farts – men fart on average about thirty times a day and women about twelve times. So if this is your level you have nothing to worry about. Just be discreet.

Some people have limited tolerance for dairy products. If you fart more than average, this may be the cause. Reduce dairy consumption and reduce wind levels.

Other gas promoting foods are beans, legumes, cabbage, broccoli, Brussels sprouts, onions, curries and highly spiced foods.

Studies have shown that soaking legumes in water reduces gas-producing properties. Soak and then cook well.

Activated charcoal tablets are effective in eliminating gas.

Food poisoning
Symptoms of food poisoning
- Cramps
- Nausea
- Vomiting
- Diarrhoea
- Dizziness

See your doctor if symptoms include:
- Difficulty swallowing, speaking or breathing
- Changes in vision
- Muscle weakness
- Fever
- Severe vomiting or diarrhoea that lasts for more than two days
- Bloody diarrhoea
- Persistent localised stomach pain
- Dehydration

To avoid food poisoning
- Wash hands before handling food.
- Heat or chill raw food. Heat to above 65°C, chill to below 4.5°C.
- Don't use cracked eggs.
- Cook red meat until the pinkness disappears.
- Defrost chicken in the bottom of the fridge and cook until all traces of blood disappear.
- Use a separate chopping board when preparing raw meat.
- Disinfect kitchen surfaces where you have chopped chicken of fish.
- Make sure all surfaces and utensils are washed with hot soapy water.
- Use paper towel to wipe surfaces.
- Don't leave food out for longer than two hours.
- Refrigerate leftovers immediately even if they are still warm.
- Never pick and eat wild mushrooms.
- If in doubt, throw it out. Chuck out any food that doesn't smell or look right.

How to deal with a bilious attack

- Try to rehydrate your body by slowly sipping a little water or soft drink.
- Mix fruit juice, a teaspoon of honey and a pinch of salt and sip slowly to replace minerals that you have lost by vomiting.
- Don't take antacid tablets as they weaken your defence against the bacteria in your stomach.
- Go with the flow. Allow your body to flush out the toxins.

There's no need to induce vomiting. Your body will do that if necessary. Go easy on the spicy foods after the attack is over. Help the body to renew itself by introducing small amounts of bland food.

Growth

Boys stop growing when they are about eighteen years old. Girls cease to grow at about sixteen and a half years. The greatest rate of growth is that experienced by an infant from zero to two years. Our skull stays much the same size throughout our lives. Our legs grow the most. Ears and noses never stop growing.

Haemorrhoids

Haemorrhoids strike anything up to 80% of the population at some point in time. So don't be coy about 'piles' or whatever you wish to call them.

Prevention is better than cure, so watching your diet and weight is all-important if you want to have a haemorrhoids-free life.

Overweight people tend to have more problems with haemorrhoids than people who keep an eye on the kilograms.

Just as it puts pressure on your joints, the excess weight puts stress on areas in lower extremities, such as anal veins.

Pregnant women often get haemorrhoids. One technique is to lie down for about twenty minutes every few hours – but only on the left side. The uterus sits directly on the vessels that drain the haemorrhoidal veins. By lying only on the left, you lessen the pressure on the main vein draining the lower half of your body.

Salt exacerbates the effect of haemorrhoids because it retains fluid, causing veins to bulge.

Spicy foods and too much of a good thing like caffeine create itching as they pass through.

The key is to always aim for soft and easy bowel movements. Drink lots of fluid, eat lots of fibre. Otherwise you end up with hard stools, lots of straining and groaning, and enlargement of the veins in your rectum.

At all times, resist the urge to scratch – even though your haemorrhoids might be itchy and giving you hell. You could damage the veins and make things worse.

If you are a fitness type, you might have to give our exercises a rest for a few days or modify your routines so as not to put strain on them as if you are on the toilet.

Same goes with heavy lifting. Repel that urgent desire to shift that eight-drawer oak sideboard from the lounge to the dining room and put it off until things have calmed down.

A dab of Vaseline or other petroleum jelly to lubricate just inside your anus will help a lot.

After you have been to the toilet, don't scrape your bottom with Number 6 Grade Industrial Strength sandpaper. Use soft, non-perfumed, white-only paper.

Dampen your toilet paper to make things even smoother and gentler. Or instead of toilet paper use the facial tissues that are seeped in oil such as aloe vera or lavender.

In that vein, excuse the pun, a dab of witch hazel works wonders.

Warm water is good, and the best way is the 'sitz' bath. Put about ten cm of water in the bath, and sit in it with your knees raised. The warm water increases blood flow and eases the pain.

You will get some relief from products purchased at your local pharmacy. It is not up to us to notate the exact effectiveness of each brand, but they will at least provide a localised pain-killing agent.

Creams probably work better than suppositories, as they go straight to the problem. Critics of suppositories say that they go too far up the rectum to be of any value, particularly to external haemorrhoids.

Incontinence

Incontinence, the inability to control the bladder and the involuntary urge to wee when you don't want to, is not inevitable. Just because you get old, it doesn't have to happen to you. Nor is it irreversible. You can do things to reduce it, resolve it, or eliminate it.

Keep a diary for your doctor. Over a fortnight note what food you had, what liquids you consumed, when you deliberately went to the bathroom, and when it involuntarily snuck up on you. This will help your doctor plot out a program to ease or solve the issue.

Depending on the results of the diary, begin to balance your fluid intake. Drinking six to eight glasses of water each day is generally proposed as good for your health. You might have to cut back on the fluids a little, especially in the evening when you are preparing for bed.

Alcohol is one fluid you may have to seriously consider curtailing or abandoning if you are genuine about resolving the incontinence issue. Beer, wine and spirits with mixers only keep heading you towards the bathroom. After a strenuous sporting performance in a hot atmosphere, athletes often have to be given a couple of cans of beer to stimulate them to provide a urine sample for a drug test.

Cut down on the coffee and other drinks or foods with caffeine. It's a diuretic and will only add to your problem.

Stay away from the grapefruit juice, too. It's another diuretic. Drink cranberry instead, it has less acid.

Give up the cigarettes. For starters, notice how sometimes a hearty cough can spark off a leaking episode. As well, nicotine irritates the surface of the bladder.

Lose weight. Less kilograms mean less stress and less impact on the bladder and therefore less little accidents.

Always go to the toilet when you have to. When asked for a bit of good advice that people could take with them through life, King Edward VIII, so used to royal occasions, ceremonies, speeches and travelling, replied: 'Always go to the toilet at every opportunity.'

Develop a routine to eliminate as much urine as you can under your control. This could mean going every hour initially, and then gradually increasing the interval to two and then three hours.

When you go, make sure you eliminate as much as you can. Void the bladder, then before you exit, double-up and have one more go.

Talk to your doctor about exercises to tighten pelvic muscles and regain control of the flow.

Be prepared with pads purchased from your pharmacist and maybe even a bedpan under the bed. Old-fashioned maybe, but it could save a lot of disasters!

Ingrown hair

An ingrown hair sounds innocuous enough, but it can cause mayhem when the infection starts to spread.

To get it out:
- Use tweezers to pull ingrown hairs out. Don't give them a second chance.
- Prepare the area with warm water on a cloth.

- Locate the hair with tweezers (or perhaps a needle) and pull it out.
- Clean it after with water, rubbing alcohol or antiseptic.

Ingrown hairs often occur among men with curly hair. Growing a beard, or shaving to give the permanent five o'clock shadow (once trendy in the eighties) helps prevent ingrown hairs.

For women, consider how you shave your legs. Most women, understandably, shave up, starting at the ankle and going to the knee. This is against the grain and can promote the growth of ingrown hairs. Even though it is not as convenient, it is better to shave downwards, from knee to ankle.

Ingrown nails

The butt of numerous jokes, and, like ingrown hair, sounds innocuous. But an ingrown nail, usually the big one, can cause a lot of pain, discomfort and make your lifestyle miserable.

Ingrown toenails can come from poor cutting of the nails, badly fitting footwear, and accidents such as stubbing your toe.

Soak your feet in warm water before you cut your nails – it makes them easier to handle and prevents splitting.

Always cut your nails straight across, and not in the curved shape of the toe, and especially not deep into the corners and the skin.

Do not cut your nails too short. The idea of the nail is to protect the toe, especially the tip. Do not trim the nail any deeper than the tip.

If a nail splits or breaks when cutting, smooth it down and tidy it up with an emery board so you will not damage the surrounding skin.

Do not cut a v-shape wedge in the middle of your toenail, in the misguided belief that it will reduce the likelihood of an ingrown nail forming. The theory is that cutting a wedge from the middle will mean that the sides will grow towards the centre and therefore away from the edge. It does not work that way. All nails grow from the back to the front, so you are achieving nothing other than having people at the beach stare at your big toes in astonishment and conclude that you are a worshipper in some strange big toe cult.

Be careful when buying footwear. Styles come and go, and you do not want to be wearing something out of date. But do not let fashion ruin your health, especially tight or pointed shoes that impinge on the toes.

If you do start developing an ingrown toenail, you can soften the nail and toe area by using any of the specially made products from the foot-care section at your pharmacist. This helps ease the pain.

Iodine and antibiotic creams help, too.

If you want to try a home remedy before having to go to the doctor, and ultimately end up on the operating table, soften the toe by bathing it in warm water or using one of the softening products. The idea is to get the nail to grow out over the skin folds at the side of it, rather than grow through or into them. With the nail softened, lift the burrowing edge away from the tender skin and insert a few cotton strands under it. This holds the edge away from the skin. Repeat this process for several days, until the nail has grown past the skin, rather than digging into it.

If your toe becomes red, raw, sore and infected, go and see your doctor. After all, if you let it go too far, apart form the extreme discomfort, you could be developing gangrene.

Insomnia

Lack of sleep can have a terrible effect on your life. There is nothing worse than getting out of bed in the morning feeling as if you have already done a day's work.

If you are waking at night, or struggling to get to sleep, or only get a restless sleep, here are a few pointers to consider:

The main aim is get enough sleep at night so that when you wake in the morning you feel refreshed and ready for the day and not drowsy and put off by it already.

There is no clear-cut amount of time that a person should sleep. For some, five hours is enough, for others, ten is not enough. Babies need eighteen hours.

Most people need about seven to eight hours sleep a day, although it is noticeable that as you get older, you need less sleep.

The worst scenario is going to bed at a reasonable time, say 10pm, and discovering that you are awake five to six hours later.

The answer? Go to bed at one, wake up at six and see how you feel.

If you believe you need more sleep, start adding fifteen-minute increments. So, next night, go to bed at a quarter to one, and so on, until you find the right balance of sleeping right through and feeling energetic when you get up.

It is good, also, to try and keep to this pattern every day, seven days a week.

If you do wake up in the middle of the night, don't get stressed, don't fight it, and don't try and force yourself back to sleep. It won't work.

Sleep comes in waves, of about seventy-five to ninety minutes apart. The art is to patiently wait for the next wave. You can do this by turning over, turning on the radio, and letting it wash over you.

An alternative is to get up and do something – but make sure it is not too exciting and likely to get your energy levels up so high that you can't get back to sleep. Stay away from computer games or deciding to do the housework. Just watch a bit of telly, read the paper or a Do It Yourself catalogue – not a book that will get you engrossed.

Go back to bed and if you still cannot get back to sleep, get up again until you do. But the important issue is to get up at your scheduled time again in the morning.

Have 'quiet time' before you go to bed. This might sound a bit crazy – after all, you could not get a more quieter time than in bed. But in fact, very often your whole day is full-on until that point when you hit the sack. This is the first moment you have had to unwind and think about the day's events. The adrenalin may well be still running and sleep is the last thing on your body's agenda. An hour or so before going to bed, sit down for ten minutes and think through the day, resolving any issues.

Fix things that need to be fixed. It is no use going to bed with a problem on your mind that can be resolved, and let it nag at you all night. Either fix it, or determine a strategy for the morning to resolve it, and then forget about it until then.

Then again, think about this. Say you have a little challenge on your minds that needs a solution. Think about it once before you go to sleep and leave it at that. You will be amazed how, during the night, a solution develops in the back-blocks of your brain, and is there, waiting for you in the morning.

If you find that you are constantly thinking about the office, and in a very stressed state, then seriously re-examine your workload, your schedule, the support you are getting from the people around you, and the whole aim of the job. You might come to the conclusion that you are not sleeping because this job is not for you.

Make things as comfortable as you can – with the décor of the room, and perhaps even the mood music. Devise pleasant distractions to stop your mind wandering back to things that get it racing.

Earplugs and eyeshades can help block out unwanted noise and light.

Coffee, alcohol, chocolate and sugar are delicious delights but can impinge on your sleeping. Caffeine is a stimulant, and while alcohol depresses the central nervous system, its effects will wear off in the middle of the night, your body will move into withdrawal phase, and you will wake up.

A light snack an hour or so before bedtime works well – particularly fruit, and, yes, the famous glass of warm milk.

Exercise is not only good for you, it can also help achieve a good sleep pattern. Exercise such as, for example, a walk around the block, raises your body temperature. Later, when your temperature starts to lower, it helps induce a sleepy feel.

Your temperature dropping after you have had a warm bath will also help you get off to sleep.

Remember, the bedroom is exactly that – the room containing the bed, the object being to sleep. If you use it as an office, a sound studio, a TV viewing room, or a restaurant, that is all very well, but it will distract you from the principal target of getting some sleep. There is only one good alternative for using the bed – having sex. Having done that, you might find you get a great night's sleep, too!

Mouth ulcers

Recurring mouth ulcers are sometimes caused by:

- Intolerance to the fluoride in toothpaste.
- Intolerance to gluten in the diet.
- Being generally run-down.
- Poor oral hygiene.

To treat mouth ulcers

Try one of the following:

- Apply a tincture of myrrh.
- Gargle with sage tea.
- Gargle with a couple of drops of tea tree oil and warm water.
- At night, before bed, drink milk to coat the ulcer and prevent further inflammation.

Nail biting

The medical term for nail biting is onychophagia. It is caused by stress. About 25% of Westerners bite their nails. Willpower is the best treatment, but there are over-the-counter medications which, when applied to the fingers, turn them into a turn-off. Very often, chewing nails is an indication of low self-esteem, or concern about problems.

Night blindness

Night blindness is the inability to see clearly in dim light. It can be dangerous, particularly when driving. Usually it indicates a vitamin A or beta-carotene deficiency. It can be corrected by dietary measures. Include more:

- Carrots
- Dark green leafy vegetables
- Tomatoes
- Butter
- Cream
- Eggs

Nose bleeds

First aid:
- Give one big almighty blow to remove any clots.
- Plug the nostril with damp cotton wool or gauze.
- Apply pressure with the thumb and the index finger to the fleshy part of the nose.
- Sit up straight.
- Apply an ice-pack.
- Apply an antibiotic/steroid ointment to the inside of your nose two or three times a day.

To remove a Band-Aid without too much trauma

Try one of the following:
- Using a pair of nail scissors, separate the bandage part from the sticky part, gently remove the bandage and then pull away the sticky part.
- Soak the area in salt and water and wait. The adhesive will eventually let go.
- Use a cotton swab soaked in baby oil to moisten the adhesive and then quickly pull in the direction that the hairs are growing.
- Avoid scabs by applying a plastic bandage of food wrap to trap healing moisture into the wound, as cells regenerate more rapidly when moist.

Snoring

To cure your snoring:
- Lose weight. Snoring is often related to being overweight.
- Don't take alcohol before bed.
- Don't use sleeping pills.
- Give up smoking.
- Don't sleep on you back.
- Sleep on your side.
- Get rid of your pillow.

How to cope with a snorer in your bed.
- Use earplugs at night.
- Sew a tennis ball into the back of the snorer's PJs. Then when he rolls over onto his back he will roll back onto his side.
- Put a couple of bricks under the top of the bed to elevate it.

Urinary tract infections

Avoid urinary tract infections by some of the following techniques:
- Drink lots of water to flush out the bacteria in the bladder.
- Drink cranberry juice.
- Soak in a hot bath.
- Increase your vitamin C intake.
- Wipe from front to back, not vice versa.
- Empty your bladder before intercourse.
- Empty your bladder after intercourse.
- Use pads instead of tampons.
- Wear cotton underwear.
- Avoid tight underpants.
- Practice good hygiene.

If there is blood in the urine seek medical attention immediately.

Vertigo

Vertigo is the fear of heights or dizziness when confronted with the situation of being in a very elevated position. It is usually the symptom of one of a number of disorders affecting the inner ear. An attack of vertigo usually involves the sensation of the head spinning around and around, and a loss of balance. The patient may suddenly fall right over. Sweating, nausea and vomiting may also occur. It is best to calm the patient, and devise a method of getting him or her back onto the ground.

Meniere's disease

The most common condition behind attacks of vertigo is Meniere's disease, or Meniere's syndrome, a degenerative condition of the middle ear usually affecting people for the first time in their fifties. Apart from the dizzy spells and periodic loss of balance, a person with Meniere's may experience ongoing ringing in the ears, called tinnitus, and gradual hearing impairment. The cause of Meniere's disease is little understood but believed by some medical practitioners to be caused by congestion of the lymphatic system. While medications such as Dramamine help manage the vertigo, they will not cure the disease and will not prevent the loss of hearing.

Other vertigo causes

Simple motion sickness can lead to vertigo as can bacterial infections of the inner ear and viral infections such as influenza. The sensations may continue even after the patient appears to have recovered from the more acute symptoms of the flu. Recurrent attacks of vertigo may also be caused by the pressure of a tumour or non-cancerous growth on the auditory or acoustic nerve. High blood pressure or hardening of the arteries may also be responsible. Strokes can bring on vertigo in the elderly. If attacks of vertigo are unexplained and recurrent, you should seek medical advice.

Aches and pains
Acute pain

Acute pain is experienced suddenly and intensely and is usually a result of a movement such as bad lifting. It can be caused by strains, sprains or pulling on muscles. Although it can be very debilitating for a few days, it is possible to limit damage.

- In the first couple of days after your injury, ice the injured area twice a day for seven to eight minutes each time.
- Moist heat reduces muscle spasms. After Day Two, apply heat to the area. Wet a towel, place it in the microwave to heat, and apply this to the injured area.
- Apply heat for thirty minutes and then ice for thirty minutes. Alternate.
- Gently stretch your sore back.
- Rest your back, but beware of staying in bed too long.
- To get yourself out of bed, roll onto your side and gently roll over the edge of the bed.
- Remember, if you don't move it you will lose it, so begin exercising as soon as possible. Listen to what your body is telling you to do.
- Swimming is great exercise for a bad back as the water takes the weight from your spine.

Back pain

There are two types of back pain, acute and chronic. They are both debilitating in their own way.

Chronic pain

Chronic pain is usually one of the following:
- Back pain that comes upon you suddenly and for no apparent reason.
- Back pain that is accompanied by other symptoms – fever, chest pain, breathing difficulties, stomach cramps.
- An attack that lasts for three days without subsiding.
- Back pain that radiates down your leg.

You should see your doctor if you experience any of the above situations. For some people, chronic back pain is a part of everyday life. They must learn to deal with it, but there are things that can be done to minimise discomfort.

- Never sleep on a sagging bed. Sleep on a firm bed. You may need to make a wooden base for your bed.
- Never sleep on your stomach as that puts added pressure on your back.
- The figure 'S' sleeping position is the best for somebody with a bad back. Put a pillow under your head, curl up into the foetal position and place another pillow between your legs to keep your hip from rotating during the night.
- An aspirin helps to reduce the inflammation around the site of the pain.
- A water-bed will equalise the pressure on various segments of your body and take the pressure off the spine.
- Try Tai Chi, an ancient Chinese discipline of slow fluid movements that stretches your body, enhances your breathing, and fosters harmony within you.
- Surround yourself with well and happy people. Keep busy and have a positive attitude.

Earache

Most earache does get worse at night. This is because you are lying down and your ears do not drain properly. Other causes of earache are infections, irritation of the ear canal by foreign substances, atmospheric causes and referred pain from teeth, nose and throat. If your ear aches, then you need to visit the doctor, but until then:

- Sit upright and drain the Eustachian tubes.
- Swallow hard.
- Chew gum.
- Yawn.
- Sip a glass of water as this also helps the Eustachian tubes to drain.
- Use the hair-dryer to blow warm air into the ears from a distance of about forty cm.

A dose of over-the-counter decongestant before bedtime will dry up fluid inside the ears. Over-the-counter painkillers bring relief from aching ears.

In an aeroplane

Hold your nose to equalise the pressure inside and outside of your ear. Don't sleep during the aeroplane's descent.

Ear wax

Never put anything in your ears. You may think that you are cleaning them out, but in reality you are just ramming the wax further down the ear canal to wrap itself around the ear drum. Soften ear wax by adding a drop or two of warm oil or glycerine into each ear, then turn your head on the side and squirt water which is body temperature into the ear. Leave a few seconds, turn your head on the side and let run out.

Swimmer's ear

Swimmer's ear is often a result of spending lots of time in water – swimming, showering, washing hair, and so on. It is made worse by endeavouring to clean or dry your ear after with a towel, cloth or cotton bud. This only serves to strip off the outer layer of 'good' bacteria from the skin in the ear canal, and allow the 'bad' bacteria to take over. The result is otitis externa. Itchy, red, annoying, and ultimately, if it is let to go too far, infected and very sore. The best idea, especially for enthusiastic swimmers, is to use ear plugs when you swim to keep the water out.

A good way of keeping ears dry is to make a cotton ball plug dipped in petroleum jelly, mineral oil, baby oil or lanolin.

Don't swim in poorly maintained pools or muddy, unclean water.

Blow-dry your ears with your hair-dryer rather than a towel. This gives a better result, without causing damage to the skin and opening up the opportunity for infection. But keep it on cool or warm and hold it fifty cm away, and do it for about thirty seconds.

Dry your ears after swimming and kill any germs by carefully putting in two or three drops of such solutions as rubbing alcohol or white vinegar.

If an infection develops, eardrops from your pharmacist will help, especially if you catch it early.

Aspirin will help to deaden the pain.

Apply a warm towel, a hot-water bottle wrapped in a blanket, or a micro-waveable grain pillow to the ear to ease the pain and provide comfort.

As mentioned before, it is better to keep earwax in, rather than stripping it out or pushing it further down the canal. Ear wax is there for a good reason – to harbour 'good' bacteria and keep your ear in good shape. (See Ear wax.)

Eye strain

Eye strain has long been a part of life, especially into the forties and beyond. This has become even more so as we become computer-dependent and spend hours in front of a monitor.

Rest your eyes. When any opportunity arises, close your eyes and give them a break. A prime opportunity is when you are talking on the phone. If you think about it, it means you could give your eyes anything up to an hour or more of extra 'rest' each day.

Correct lighting can do a lot to help reduce eyestrain. If you read a lot, us a soft gentle light, rather than one that glares.

Turn down the brightness on your computer screen.

Put a shade over the top of your computer screen – you can buy them, or make something original yourself which will have the whole office floor talking.

Take the mandatory breaks from the screen. If you are using one all day, get up and walk away, at least ten to fifteen minutes every two hours.

Blinking is good for you – blinking cleanses the eyes.

You may have reached the point where, despite your best efforts, you are going to need glasses for reading. The off-the-rack glasses at your local pharmacist are a good starting point, but it may be you need to get prescription lenses from an optometrist.

Fatigue

There is nothing worse than starting the day feeling as if you have reached the end of the day already.

Here are some simple suggestions to shake off fatigue and make the day more enjoyable:

First up, fix all ongoing personal matters that are nagging at you and probably causing you to lose sleep and wake up tired already. Family situations, work problems, relationship difficulties, all combine to drag you down – don't let them hover around any longer, resolve them now, talk to those who have to be spoken to, and get them off your mind. (See also Insomnia.)

Develop a regular sleeping pattern so that you get between six and eight hours continuous sleep each night. If you can sleep from 10pm until 6am, and get eight hours, that's good.

But for some people, going to bed at midnight and waking up at 6am refreshed is better than going to bed at 10pm, hoping for eight hours sleep, and waking up at four in the morning, tossing and turning for two hours, and then – when it is time to get up – falling back to sleep!

Too much sleep, or oversleeping, leaves you feeling tired and disoriented, and therefore, unproductive for the rest of the day.

Similarly, with rare exceptions, trying to exist on four hours sleep each and every day will only make you feel exhausted. You might think you are a hero, but the wild-eyed look and erratic behaviour gives it away.

Regain control of your life by getting up fifteen minutes earlier, and getting ready in a calm, prepared way, rather than rushed.

Set goals for the day. List them out, if need be, so that you are in charge, rather than letting things overwhelm you. Then, if something unaccountable does crop up, you will be feeling fresh, energetic and in control enough to fix it.

Writing down a daily list of things to do works wonders. Listing things eliminates that thought: 'I've got so much to do, I don't know where to start', which only emphasises the feeling of fatigue. At the end of the day, a diary page with a list of tasks and big ticks beside them showing that they have been achieved is a very comforting thing.

Eat a decent breakfast. While a non-filter cigarette, a cup of jet-black coffee, and a philosophic look out the kitchen window has a raffish air about it, it is not setting you up for the day. Your body needs energy and the best source is a good breakfast – a combination of protein, carbohydrate and fats.

Did we mention a cigarette? No, no, no, butt it out. Apart from the serious long-term consequences, smoking reduces the flow of oxygen to body tissue, bringing on fatigue.

Do some exercise. Regular physical endeavour, ranging from a walk, to ten to fifteen minutes exercise on the floor, to a full gym workout will make you feel fitter, happier and ready for any challenge.

With exercise, take it slowly at first, and don't expect miracles overnight. But when it does start to kick in, you will feel great.

If you can, spread your exercise out during the day. Walk away from the computer and do some stretching. Or take fifteen minutes off to go for a brisk walk around the block.

Watch your diet. Eat the right mix of the famous 'triangle of foods' to ensure a healthy, energetic approach.

Eat regularly. Have three meals a day, as close as possible to the same time every day. Rushed meals with long hours in between only increase fatigue, heighten irritability, and bring on mistakes.

Make the midday meal nice and light. Salad, sandwich, fruit, juice, plenty of water. A big meal only bogs you down for the rest of the day.

Alcohol during the day is not going to help. If you are in a situation where drinks are de rigueur, limit it to one or two, and sip plenty of water in between.

Coffee can be a drain on your day, too. One cup might get you started, but many cups during the day, while they give the feeling that they are giving you energy bursts, are actually doing the opposite and slowing you down. Enjoy coffee, but limit it.

The best drink during the day is water. Water, water, water. Six to eight glasses is the best defence against fatigue.

Reduce the weight. We are not talking fashion here, just common sense. Your body frame and genetics dictate what your weight should be, not stick-thin models bouncing down the catwalk. But you will find that just trimming off a few kilos can make an extraordinary difference.

Remember, it took years to pack those extra kilos on, so don't expect them to strip off in a few days on some gung-ho military diet. It will only make you more tired, and the kilos will only come back, yo-yo style, to haunt you. Do it moderately and over time.

Go down the vitamin trail if you must. But at least be consistent – if you are going to have a supplement, take it each day, every day.

Do not take a sudden handful of vitamin pills, expecting that a rapid-fire vitamin burst will boost your energy levels and make you feel better. It won't.

Don't overload your day – especially with little things that consume vast amounts of time for no great gain. The happiest people are those who surround themselves with people who are very good at their job, confidently delegate to them, and who know when to say 'No!'

Don't waste emotional energy on things that do not deserve it. Get over it, and convert your emotions such as anger or alarm into energy directed at more constructive issues.

Be upbeat, motivated, confident, switched-on. You will not only get your tasks done, but encourage those around you.

Unlike their Mediterranean counterparts, a lot of high-tech Western cultures are not built around the 'siesta' concept, but are starting to recognise that a little mid-afternoon nap can do wonders for the energy levels. How you can conspire to sneak one in each day is up to you.

A desk-top alternative to the nap is the breathing technique. Three big, deep breaths restores oxygen to the brain, relaxes you and restores energy levels. Use the ten–ten–ten technique. Breathe in across ten seconds, hold it for ten seconds, breathe it out across ten seconds. Do this two more times and you will be ready to go again.

For an instant energy charge, go to the bathroom and splash cold water over your face.

Change your environment – brighten up the house, rearrange the furniture, go out and buy some new music.

Tidy up your desk, throw out all the clutter, have only on your work-station the project you are working on at the time.

Change your routines – make different meals, go on spontaneous walks or visits, try new places to eat or go to the movies.

Take time off. Holidays are there to be taken. Regular vacations get you away from the desk and the workload. Don't hoard your holidays thinking you are some sort of corporate macho type – you are only doing yourself damage and probably boring all those around you who are waiting for you to give them a break, too.

If all else fails, get a new job . . .

Hangovers

It was fun last night drinking everything in sight, but this morning you are paying the price – your tummy is queasy, your legs are shaky, and the percussion division of the musical 'We will rock you' is rehearsing inside your head.

Time to get back on the recovery road.

There are three sure-fire things that will make you feel better – time, rest and lots of non-alcoholic fluids. Dull as they sound, they are your best bet, and if you can find the wherewithal and opportunity to get all three, you are on the road to recovery.

Drink lots of water. The alcohol has dehydrated your body cells, so rehydration is important and will start making you feel better. The canny types take time out to drink lots of water the night before, after all the drinking has been done, and just prior to hitting the bed.

Drink lots of fruit juice. The fructose in the juice helps burn up the alcohol still in your system. Tastes good, too!

Eat honey. Honey also contains fructose, and this will help purge the alcohol. Try it on toast or even dry biscuits.

Take two aspirin. Not necessarily the super-strength ones, but enough to dull the incessant drum beats inside your brain. But don't make too much of a habit of this – you do not want to end up an aspirin junkie.

Take a seltzer or similar fizzy drink to settle your stomach. Warning – this may take you down the character-testing path of upsetting your stomach further, leading you to, how shall we put this delicately, involuntarily reproducing all that has gone before. Best to hang around the bathroom zone for a while until things become clear as to which way they are heading.

Have some coffee. Yes, coffee does have a technical reason for working. Your headache partly comes from the swelling of the blood vessels, and the coffee reduces the swelling. But don't drink too much – before you know it, you'll be getting a buzz from the coffee and opening up a whole new can of worms.

Take vitamin B complex. It will push your recovery along and help bring things to a happier conclusion sooner. Berocca is the age-old popular version that many people swear by, but there are more of these vitamin B and multivitamin products coming on the market.

Take amino acids. These are the building blocks of protein, and are diminished by the alcohol. They need to be restored. Health stores sell them in capsule form.

Try and eat something. Your body is crying out for the salt and potassium you have burnt off. Just what you eat depends a lot on personal taste. Soup is a good starter – thin soup made from a beef cube. Being thin it is easy to take, helps settle your stomach, and contains the salts that you need. (See also Hair of the dog and other 'cures'.)

Get some rest. Rest is the best thing you can do – lie down and let it all go away. But that is not always possible. If you can't lie down or stay in bed because you have to go to work, or have a very important engagement – like, your wedding! – then you have been bad, bad, bad. Suffer, suffer, suffer, and stick it out all the way through the long day until you can hit the cot, have a good night's sleep, and bounce out next morning as if nothing has happened. Hopefully by then all the others will have forgotten your disgraceful behaviour on the night in question, too.

Hair of the dog and other 'cures'

Over the years, all sort of ideas have been developed as a hangover cure – with many people insisting that they work. Very often there is no physical or chemical reason to justify them, but people still swear by them. Consider some of these from the past:

- Chinese have cured hangovers for more than 2000 years using tea made from a vine called kudzu.

- In America's wild west, cowboys drank a cup of rabbit pee tea.
- Heavy drinkers in the Middle Ages ate a meal of almonds and eel.

Here, for your interest and without prejudice or verification, are some solutions we have picked up over the years.

Hair of the dog
A long-supported theory that if you start the next day with a glass of what has done the damage the night before, it will start you well on the road to recovery. The theory is that it takes you back to where you were before. But be warned – you need a firm constitution and to be stout of heart, mind and stomach to knock down a stubby of beer at nine in the morning. Well recommended by old dossers living around the streets. Mightn't cure you but will certainly make you feel better for a brief glorious moment.

Bloody Mary
This has the perfect mixture for the road to recovery – the soothing, healthy, qualities of the juice, the zing of the Tabasco to revitalise those jaded taste buds, and a shot of alcohol to jolt the body back into action. The ice and pepper helps, too.

Bloody Mary with raw egg
See above, but with an additional component to really put your constitution to the test.

The Mongolian version
This is not so much a Bloody Mary but a 'bloody hell!' The Mongolians down a cocktail of tomato juice and pickled sheep's eye . . .

Gazpacho
The cold Mediterranean soup, gazpacho, with its tomato base, and therefore a link to the Bloody Mary, is said to be a great cure by its proponents.

Raw egg, oyster and Worcestershire sauce
This has to be seen to be believed – an old-fashioned remedy. Even if you don't take it, just watching someone break an egg into a glass, drop one or two fresh oysters, squirting Worcestershire sauce into it, sprinkling it with salt and pepper, and swallowing it, bang, in one go, is going to sort you out one way or the other. Some types give it a Bloody Mary-type aspect by putting in some tomato juice. Serious punters put in a hair-of-the-dog dash of what it was that you were enjoying so much the night before.

Coca-Cola
The young buck's elixir of life. The story goes that Coke was originally invented in Atlanta as a hangover cure to be sold through drug stores, and its legacy lives on. Many a young bloke will swear by a 600 ml Coke slammed down – the caffeine sparks the senses, the sugar lifts the spirits, and the bubbles do wonders for that queasy stomach. A portable cure, and one of the best.

Sports drinks
These fluids were originally devised to get the salts and electrolytes back into footballers and athletes after extreme exertion, and help them see out the contest. Some drinking enthusiasts swear that the same process works very well on a hangover, which, after all is some sort of contest, is it not? But, oh, the taste of some of them . . .

Aminos
Aminos, a natural health supplement, helps break down alcohol in the liver and get you back into shape quicker.

Vegemite on toast
An Australian product, salty, yeast-based, Vegemite is slowly gaining acceptance around the world. Aussies swear by it, scraped over buttery toast, to get all those salts back into your system. A backpacker's lifesaver.

Greasy chips
There's something about French fries and lots of salt that contributes well to the recovery process. The medicine men will say the grease is not good for you, but in tough times you have to make tough decisions. Hard-core punters will tackle a hamburger with the lot as well, including double cheese and extra beetroot. Throw down a Coke, and, hey, you're ready to rock again.

Mashed potatoes
The Irish swear by this – especially with plenty of butter, salt and pepper.

Cold pizza
Last night's pizza seems to work well on a hangover, especially the spicy, pepperoni kind. But cold, for some reason, is best, not reheated.

The Puerto Rican Cure – El Lemon
Simply rub a lemon that has been cut in half under the armpit of your drinking arm. Not sure how or why, but they swear by it.

Rose oil
No, you don't drink it. Dab rose oil on that throbbing temple, and it will ease the hangover headache.

Herring
The Germans call a hangover 'having a bubble in your head'. They go for a cold pickled herring. Pickled herrings help to prevent liver damage. For serious recovery aficionados only.

Curry
When the British ruled India, Sunday lunch began with a hot, hot, hot mulligatawny soup to help sweat out the previous night's excesses, and a cold, cold, cold gin-and-tonic as a hair of the dog. This was followed by an even hotter curry, a couple of glasses of chilled white, and a nap. At that point the sun never set on the Empire, so there must be something in it.

A final note: South Africans tackle the problem before it happens. Before a big night out they make a paste of swallow's beak and myrrh. The poor swallow . . .

Headache
About 90% of headaches can be classified as tension headaches and these are generally caused by the stresses of work and living. They are a result of muscle contraction. Not all people who suffer from stress get headaches. Many people inherit genes that make them more prone to headache. The two major types of headaches that cause the most distress are migraine headaches and cluster headaches.

Cluster headaches
Generally come in the form of localised pain around and behind the eye. They may come every day for a week or a month and then disappear for a couple of years. Unfortunately, they almost always come back at some stage. About 90% of sufferers are men and many of these are smokers.

Ice-cream headaches

People develop an ice-cream headache when the cold of the ice cream touches the roof of the mouth. The headache can come on very quickly and for a few seconds be painful almost to the point of being unbearable. Then it will start to go away. They can be avoided by licking your ice-cream and slowly savouring the flavour. The same headache response can come from drinking a crushed iced type drink too rapidly. Slow down!

Migraine

Migraine headaches are headaches that continually reoccur. They are a chronic problem. Typically they are a severe throbbing pain, often accompanied by nausea and vomiting. Many people can predict that a migraine is about to descend upon them as they experience pre-migraine sensation. About 70% of migraine sufferers are women.

Migraines are caused by the tight constriction of blood vessels in the head. The vessels then suddenly dilate, resulting in a throbbing headache, light sensitivity, nausea, numbness and vomiting. They may come in groups and at intermittent intervals. They are known to be brought on by stress and food allergies.

Migraine headaches and allergies

Common allergies that can spark migraine attacks include:
- Coffee
- Chocolate
- Alcohol
- MSG
- Oranges
- Hard cheeses
- Fried and greasy foods

Diary allergy

To work out what foods could be causing the problem, keep a diary and then refer back to it to note the foods eaten just before an attack. Eliminate these foods from your diet. Eventually you can work out a balanced diet which lets you enjoy life but reduce or even eliminate migraines. The herb feverfew is known to limit attacks. Prevention is better than cure.

Dealing with headache

Recognise the factors that bring headaches on, and then try to eliminate them from your life.

Aspirin and Paracetamol are effective over-the-counter medicines which relieve the pain of headache. Take it as soon as you feel a headache coming on.

Lie in a darkened room. Relax. Take forty winks and your headache may just disappear. However, napping may cause migraines.

Relieve stress by getting out in the fresh air and exercising. A tension headache is often relieved by exercise at onset. This does not work for migraine.

Breathe deeply with your hand on your stomach to feel the air being inhaled and exhaled. This will relieve stress.

Pay attention to your deportment. Sleep on a firm mattress and avoid sleeping on your stomach.

Use a compress on your forehead. Some like it hot and others prefer it cold.

Be aware of your body and be conscious if you feel yourself tensing up.

Try acupressure. Squeeze the webbing between your index finger and your thumb.

Have your partner apply pressure to the bony area at the back of your neck.

Wear a tight headband to decrease the blood flow to the scalp.

Triggers for headaches

- Excessive noise. Seek quietness.
- Bright light. Wear sunglasses outside and take breaks from staring at the computer screen.
- Perfume. It may be what you are wearing or it may be what another person in the room is wearing.
- Caffeine. Limit coffee to two cups a day.
- Chewing gum. The repetitive motion can tighten muscles.
- Salt.
- Nitrates in food – cured meats especially.
- Food allergy. Be aware of the foods that set off a headache for you and avoid them.
- MSG in food. A definite no-no.
- Chocolate and aged cheeses. These contain tyramine which triggers headache in some people.
- Smoking in confined places.
- Alcohol in excess. Definitely not good for the head.

Preventatives

- Reduce your expectations of yourself and of others.
- Laugh, instead of growling, and release the muscles in your face and neck.
- Use relaxation imagery to imagine your head and neck muscles all loose and easy.
- Eat regularly and well.

Muscle pain

The golden rule for exercise is that even though it is good for you, don't overdo it.

Soreness means damage. If the pain doesn't get better after a few days, see your doctor as there may be other underlying problems. Don't abuse your body.

First aid for sore muscles

Give your muscles time to heal themselves. Think RICE:

Rest
Ice
Compression – Be careful not to wrap too tightly
Elevate

After a couple of days using the RICE theory then it is time to try heat or a heat penetrating rub.

- Take an anti-inflammatory such as aspirin to reduce pain.
- Stretch the affected muscle.
- Massage the muscle.

Repeat the activity that made you sore the next day, but with less intensity. If a certain activity always makes you sore, then that is not the activity for you. Find something else to do. Warm down after exercise. In cold weather wear warm clothing when you exercise.

A pain in the neck

For relief from neck pain – becoming more and more prevalent as more of us spend our lives hunched over a computer – try one or more of the following:

- Wrap ice in a towel and drape it around your neck.
- Heat a heat bag in the microwave and drape it around your neck.
- Massage your neck with a heat rub.
- Stand up, walk around and change your position.

- Use a chair with a good back support.
- Keep your head level and your chin tucked when you are working.
- If you are working at a computer, have the screen at eye level.
- Exercise your neck muscles when you have been bent over working for a while.
- Sleep on a firm mattress.
- Don't sleep on your stomach.
- Get rid of your pillow or buy a special pillow.
- Never sleep on two pillows.
- Sleep in the foetal position.
- Wear a scarf.

Nocturnal cramps

Nocturnal cramps are a result of your calf muscle contracting and remaining contracted when you turn over or stretch in bed. Things you can do:

- Push your foot against the wall, at right angles to your body, and push hard.
- Use an electric blanket to keep your calf muscles warm.
- Wear roomy PJs, not tight ones.
- Loosen the bed covers.
- Get out of bed and stand up.
- Drink plenty of fluids.

Pain due to misaligned jaw

A misaligned jaw produces a variety of symptoms including:

- Headaches
- Toothaches
- Neck aches
- Shoulder and backache
- Clicking noise when you open your jaw

To relieve symptoms
- Take a holiday from hard and chewy foods. Limit yourself to soft foods and liquids for a time.
- Wear a mouth support. Have one made by your dentist to fit you exactly.
- Get rid of your pillow.
- Keep jaw movements to a minimum.
- Take an aspirin.

Things that you should not do
Do *not:*
- Sleep on your stomach.
- Lie on your back with your head propped up.
- Sleep on two pillows.
- Prop your chin on your hands.
- Carry a heavy shoulder bag.
- Wear high heels.
- Cradle the telephone between your chin and your shoulder.
- Do anything that requires prolonged looking up.

Get treatment
If you are unable to open your mouth, are having sharp headaches, or can't brush your teeth, then see your doctor.

Stitch

A stitch or sharp temporary pain in the side is caused when the diaphragm is starved of oxygen and your breathing becomes uneven.

If you have a stitch
- Stop what you are doing.
- Press on the area where the pain is worse with three fingers.
- Breathe out slowly.
- Breathe in, breathe out, breathe in . . . keep this going until the stitch goes away.

To prevent stitches
- Massage your diaphragm before you exercise.
- Try to have a bowel movement before exercise.
- Belly-breathe when you exercise.
- Breathe deeply and evenly all the time you are exercising.
- Release wind if you need to.

Tired red eyes

Red eyes are dry eyes and the easiest way to fix that is to moisten them. And the simplest way to do that is get some sleep. Eight hours will rehydrate your eyes and reduce or eliminate the redness.

A good short-term remedy is a wet cloth laid over your closed eyes. The moisture rehydrates the eyes and the coolness shrinks the blood vessels that are giving you that red-eyed, tired look.

Drops are effective, but do not go overboard with them. They shrink the blood vessels, and heighten the whiteness of your eyes. But once their effectiveness wears off, you are back to where you started, or even worse.

There are solutions called artificial tears, which moisten the eyes but do not have the impact of shrinking the blood vessels, as eye drops do.

Sometimes the problem is caused by a low-grade infection on the eyelids, which can be resolved by washing your eyes with warm soapy water and getting rid of the day's dust, make-up, and bacteria.

As you get older something like a patch of blood might appear in the white of your eye. This generally is okay. It is not usually associated with pain, swelling, or impact on your vision, and should disappear over a couple of weeks.

But a red spot over the pupil is more serious and you should get medical attention immediately. It could lead to damage or loss of sight. Generally it is associated with some pain, blurring of vision, or seeing pink. If this is happening, get to a doctor.

Toothache

Until you are able to see a dentist there are some things that you can do to relieve the pain.

- Rinse your mouth out. You may dislodge a foreign body.
- Floss gently between your teeth.
- Take a shot of whisky or brandy in your mouth and hold it over the sore tooth.
- Drop clove oil onto the sore tooth.
- Rub an ice cube into the V shaped area where the bones of the thumb and forefinger meet for five to seven minutes.
- Take an aspirin or a Panadol.

Sensitive teeth

There is a saying to describe somebody who is ageing which says that he is getting 'long in the tooth'. This is because, as we age, the gum can draw back from the base of the tooth, exposing more of it, and the tooth appears to be getting longer. When this happens it is often accompanied by sensitive teeth that react to heat and cold. People with this condition should use an over-the-counter toothpaste especially made for sensitive teeth.

Two arthritis treatments

Bruise and soak twenty hot chillies in a cup of brandy for three days. Remove chillies and bottle liquid. Add five drops to your cup of tea or coffee. You won't know yourself.

Wash and remove pips of three grapefruit, three lemons and three oranges. Put them all through the blender. Add 200 ml water and let stand overnight. Add 1½ litres boiling water, 50g Epsom Salts, 50g cream of tartar. Allow to cool, mix with citrus solution, and refrigerate. Take two dessertspoons each morning on an empty stomach.

Psychological problems
Anxiety and depression

Everybody gets sad or anxious occasionally. The people who don't succumb to depression are the ones who have the ability to 'get over it'.

Do something proactive

What do you enjoy doing? Do it.

- Visit a friend.
- Go for a walk.
- See a movie.
- Read a book.
- Do some charity work.
- Telephone a family member.
- Talk it out with a friend.
- Have a good cry.
- Consider your options.
- Don't be too disheartened if you have tried your best and it just hasn't been good enough. Shit happens!
- Get some exercise.
- Do something. Anything as long as you are busy. Clean a cupboard, wash out the bath.
- Spoil yourself with a warm bath or a massage.
- Be respectful to others. Just because you are feeling down that doesn't give you the right to be rude.
- Avoid making major decisions while you are feeling this way.
- Go to a secluded spot and let out one almighty scream.

Professional help

Seek professional help if:

- You have difficulty concentrating or remembering.
- You are constantly restless and irritable.
- You constantly feel fatigued.
- You suffer sleep disturbances.
- You lose interest or pleasure in ordinary activities, including sex.
- You feel helpless, worthless or guilty.
- You have feelings of pessimism and hopelessness.
- You are persistently anxious and feel 'empty'.

Stress

Stress happens as a result of being alive and simply living. To achieve the ultimate state of stress-free being you will need to be dead. Now that's a stressful thought!

Stress is not so much caused by what the problem happens to be, but by the way that you react to it. So change the way that you think and view a 'problem' as a 'challenge'.

Break the stress chain by distracting yourself. Take yourself out of the situation, either mentally or physically, regroup, and tackle it in a different way.

Be a positive thinker. Take the positive angle on every situation. Give yourself positive intellectual messages: 'I can do this. This is OK. I only need to tackle one piece at a time. It will get done.'

If you feel yourself tensing up, consciously make a decision to relax all over. Talk out loud and say to yourself: 'Forehead, unravel. Neck, unknot. Breathe deeply in and out. Stomach be still. Legs just hang there. Toes hang off those legs. I am calm.'

Get out and go for a walk and think your problem through.

Let loose with an almighty yell. Careful of the cat!

Cry, it will do you good.

Put your favourite music on and lay on the floor and listen to it for five minutes.

See your doctor if you experience sudden and unexplained stress and if it interferes with everyday living.

Basic meditation

Practice this daily. Sit in a comfortable position in a quiet room and place all your intellectual focus on a mantra. The mantra could be any word or thought. Relax, breathe in and out slowly, speak the mantra each time you exhale. Do this for fifteen to twenty minutes. If your thoughts wander, bring them back by saying your mantra.

Phobias

A phobia, or fear of something, can be very debilitating. Here are some of the phobias and their technical names:

Selachophobia	Sharks
Pogonophobia	Beards
Pteronophobia	Tickling with feathers
Ereuthophobia	Blushing
Coulrophobia	Clowns
Gephryophobia	Crossing bridges
Categelophobia	Being ridiculed
Doraphobia	Skins of animals
Rhytiphobia	Getting wrinkles
Didaskaleinophobia	Going to school
Stygiophobia	Hell
Philmatophobia	Kissing
Chionophobia	Snow
Enochiophobia	Crowds

Being bullied

Bullying is when one person picks on another. The bully might call a person names, tease them, push, hit, or attack them. A bully may also spread rumours, take money or possessions from someone, or ignore and leave a person out of activities and games. Bullying occurs at school, on the way to and from school, on the bus or train, in fact it can happen anywhere. Bullies pick on others because they want to show off, or because they are scared, or because they have their own problems.

Someone being bullied can be harmed both physically and emotionally. They may suffer cuts and bruises, broken bones, and even loss of consciousness. Emotionally they may become frightened to go to school or to go out at all. This affects their education and can make them socially withdrawn. Many people who suffer bullying become depressed. Boys and girls can be bullies. Sometimes adults are bullies too. It's important that someone being bullied understands that it is not his/her fault. Speaking to someone about the bullying can help to prevent more serious problems.

Anorexia nervosa and bulimia

Anorexia and bulimia are often symptomatic of psychological problems and psychological counselling is really the only way to address the problems.

Anorexia nervosa

Anorexia nervosa is an eating disorder where dieting is carried to extremes. The extreme weight loss causes hormonal imbalances within the body, and if not treated, can lead to death.

Bulimia

Bulimia is an eating disorder whereby the sufferer binge eats. He/she then induces vomiting or uses laxatives to purge the body. It is often more difficult to pick than anorexia as appearance is not so affected. It can lead to serious imbalances in the body chemistry and irregularities in the heart rhythm.

Hair
Is it dandruff or dermatitis?

It is dermatitis, and you need to see your doctor, if:

- You have scalp irritation.
- You have thick scale despite attempts to eliminate it.
- You have yellowish crusting.
- You have red patches along the neckline.

Dandruff is scaling of the scalp and is an interactive condition. The scaling causes itching, causes scratching, causes scaling, causes itching, causes scratching, causes scaling.

Wash your hair daily. The more often you wash your hair the easier dandruff is to control. Wash in this sequence:
- Use a mild shampoo diluted with an equal amount of pure water.
- Gently massage it in with you fingertips to help loosen scales and flakes.
- Rinse.
- Apply a conditioner.
- Rinse again.

If this doesn't do the job, then it is time to switch to an anti-dandruff shampoo.

For stubborn cases, try a tar-based formula and alternate it with regular shampoo. However, if your hair is blonde or grey avoid the tar-based formula as this will darken your hair.

Apply baby oil at night and cover with a plastic shower cap. Wash off in the morning.

Rinse hair in a solution made with four tablespoons thyme and two cups of boiling water. Allow to cool, and then pour over your head.

Spend time outdoors, as the sun's ultra-violet rays have an anti-inflammatory effect on scaly skin conditions.

Counteract stress with exercise and meditation.

Oily hair

The more hair you have the more oily your hair is likely to be. Blondes tend to have the oiliest hair while redheads rarely have oily hair. Curly hair does not appear oily. Hormonal changes can cause oiliness.
Avoid oily hair by:

- Shampooing daily with a clear, see-through shampoo.
- If your hair is excessively oily double shampoo and leave the first lot of shampoo in for a few minutes before rinsing it out.
- Do not use a conditioner.
- Go easy on the brushing as this stimulates oil production.
- Rinse your hair with lemon, beer, apple-cider vinegar.

Oral hygiene
Gingivitis

Gingivitis is swollen, red gums. They bleed when they are cleaned. If it is allowed to go on, it will cause you to lose your teeth.

Toothbrush choice

Use an electric toothbrush. They do an excellent job and remove 98% of the plaque as compared with 48% for a manual toothbrush. Brush the gum line as well as the teeth. Brush for at least five minutes, twice a day. Using an icy-pole stick scrape your tongue. Massage your gums with your thumb and your index finger. Use a good mouthwash. Eat a raw vegetable or crisp fruit daily. Excessive smoking and drinking can drain your body of vitamins and minerals.

Baking soda and oral hygiene

To clean, polish, neutralise acidic bacterial wastes and deodorise all at once. Mix plain baking soda with water and apply to your gum line with your fingers. Then brush your teeth.

Tartar and plaque

Plaque is a sticky film of living and dead bacteria that grows on your teeth. If it is not removed, it hardens and this is known as tartar. Tartar and plaque cause gingivitis and periodontal disease.

To remove plaque

If possible use an electric toothbrush and brush for the length of a pop song. Pay attention to the back of your mouth as well as the smiley bits.

- Always brush your teeth before you go to bed.
- Be gentle on your mouth and gums. Brush gently and slowly.
- Use dental floss to finish off the job.
- Chew on an apple or a carrot every day to scour your teeth and gums.
- Swish with water after a meal during the day.
- Chew on sugarless gum to give you a cleaner healthier mouth.
- Use baking soda on your brush to give your teeth a scrub.
- Use a mouthwash.

Feet and legs
Bad knees
If you damage your knee in any way, ice it and see a doctor or physiotherapist..
The word to remember for any knee injury is RICE:

Rest the area
Ice
Compression
Elevate

Choosing your shoes
Choose shoes that fit well, are not too high and which stay on without effort from you.
Save high heels for special occasions, wear medium heels for work.

- Have your shoes fitted properly.
- If a shoe is too big the foot will slide about and cause other problems.
- If the shoe is too small it will pinch your feet.
- Make sure it is the proper length – you need a thumb's distance from the end of your longest toe to the toe of the shoe.
- The shoe should be broad enough across the ball of the foot to avoid cramming.
- The toe box should have enough room to prevent pressure across the toes.
- Buy natural materials that breathe.
- Have a shoe repairer stretch your shoes and then apply a leather stretching solution. This allows your shoes to move with your feet.

Corns and calluses
Catch the corn before it begins to cause you grief by massaging the area with lanolin to soften the corn, then pad the area to remove pressure. Take pressure off a callus by padding the area with gauze and absorbent cotton. Change daily.

Separate your toes by placing a little piece of foam rubber between the offending ones. Or use a piece of lamb's wool to loosely wrap the toes. Remove to bathe.

Soak your feet in Epsom Salts or a brew of chamomile tea. Then use a pumice stone to rub away the callused parts.

Crush half a dozen aspirins and make into a paste with lemon juice and water. Apply this paste to hard spots on the skin, put the entire foot in a plastic bag and wrap a warm towel around the lot. Leave for fifteen minutes, unwrap and rub away the rough skin with a pumice stone.

Dos and don'ts
If you suffer from diabetes, never tend to your own feet. Always have a professional to do it for you.

Be very careful not to treat your own feet by cutting at your corns and calluses with sharp instruments. Avoid it if you can, as it can end in disaster.

Be wary of corn plasters as they may eat away at the corn but they don't differentiate between corn and healthy skin. If you do use them make the doughnut opening into a horse-shoe by cutting away one edge. Then your foot can move about without putting pressure on the area surrounding the corn.

Some calluses are good and develop to protect your feet. For example, if you often go barefoot, you shall most probably develop calluses on your heel and the base of your feet. These calluses are rarely painful and are good in that they protect the feet from hard ground and sharp objects.

Buy a pumice stone and gently exfoliate feet during each shower. This is a great habit to get into.

Dancing legs syndrome

You're in bed, you're ready to fall asleep and then your legs suddenly go into an uncontrollable, restless 'dance'. No one is sure why it is, although it may have something to do with a slight imbalance in the chemistry of the brain. It is believed to affect about 5% of the population. As soon as it strikes, get up and walk. A stroll around the house will satisfy your legs' needs and you should be all right.

A pre-emptive solution is to go for a walk first before you go to bed. This reduces incidence considerably. Soak your feet. Some people find cool water (but not freezing cold) works well, while others find warm water assists. Eating a big meal just prior to going to bed is a big no-no. There is a thought the syndrome is brought on by the body working hard to digest so much food.

Massage your legs before going to bed. Quit smoking, cut out alcoholic drinks before bed, and cut down on the caffeine.

Feet

Be kind to your feet

- Try wearing thick shock absorbing soles.
- Keep your shoes in good condition.
- Wear walking shoes to and from the office.
- Change heel heights from high to low during the day.
- Wear insoles that suit your feet.

Do your feet smell?

Make sure your shoes suit your feet. If your feet muscles don't have to work so hard, they will not get hot and sweaty. Wash your feet with warm soapy water as often as needed. Dry thoroughly. Apply foot powder or anti-fungal spray. Use a foot deodorant. Change your socks often. Avoid synthetic socks. Wear shoes made of natural material.

Footbath

Use a footbath and add one of the following to it:

- Vinegar
- Sodium bicarbonate
- Sage leaves
- Coarse salt

Foot massage

Fill a basin with warm water and rock salt. Add ten marbles and roll your feet over them. A great way to massage your feet with little effort.

Sore and aching feet

Painful burning in the feet can be a sign of poor circulation, athlete's foot, diabetes, anaemia, thyroid disease or alcoholism. But at the end of a day on your feet they may simply be tired.

Treat your feet kindly

Elevate them. Soak them in a tub of warm water and one of the following:

- 2 teaspoons of Epsom Salts
- 6 drops of rosemary oil
- 6 drops of lavender oil

- A strong brew of peppermint tea
- A strong brew of chamomile tea

Wrap a few ice cubes in a towel and rub that over your soles. Massage them by rolling your soles over a golf ball.

Tendinitis

Tendinitis is inflammation in or around the tendon. It tends to stay with you but there are things that you can do to prevent flare-ups. Give the affected area a rest, but don't rest it for too long, as muscles will begin to atrophy. Change the exercise that you are doing to cause the tendinitis. You may have to change sports.

- Soak in a warm spa bath.
- Warm up with simple stretching exercises before heavy exercise. Apply ice to the affected area.
- Wrap the area up tightly.
- Elevate.
- Take an aspirin.
- Work with light weights to strengthen the area.
- Vary your routines so that you are not using the same muscles all the time.

Toenails

Always cut nails straight across above the tip of your toe. Never cut below your toe or around your nail as this can cause ingrown toenails.

Fingernails and toenails are made from a specialised kind of skin cell. Nail cells are living when they have not yet emerged from under the skin but are dead from the 'moon' of the nail outwards. This dead cell material can vary in texture, strength and flexibility depending on the condition of the original living cells, the nail bed, a person's general health and environmental factors.

- Weak, splitting, discoloured or ridged nails tell us much about our nutrition and overall health.
- White spots can indicate zinc or vitamin A deficiency.
- Ridging and brittleness can point to a sluggishness of the thyroid or poor circulation.
- White pits or grooves can result from anaemia or calcium imbalance, and spooning can indicate low iron levels.
- External factors such as detergents, solvents and manicure preparations cause damage to nails.

These deficiencies can be overcome with dietary adjustment and vitamin or mineral supplements. Some tests have shown that taking gelatine or silicon helps increase the flexibility of the nail.

Varicose veins

Varicose veins come in the form of either swollen lumpy veins or spider veins in your legs. They are inherited and more women have them than men. The condition is not life threatening, but is usually accompanied by tired sore legs at the end of the day.

To relieve the symptoms:
- Elevate your legs.
- Wear support hose.
- Wear sensible shoes.
- Wear loose underwear.
- Keep your weight under control.

- Quit smoking.
- Walk regularly.

See your doctor if you develop a sore, red, tender lump on your vein. It may be a blood clot. Beware of veins around the ankle that may rupture and cause you to lose lots of blood.

Skin
You and your skin
The skin is a complex part of our bodies. It is the largest organ in our body. Throughout our lives it needs constant attention:

- Babies get nappy rash, birthmarks and eczema.
- Children suffer measles, chicken-pox, warts and impetigo.
- Teenagers endure acne, pimples, cold sores and blisters.
- Adulthood brings athlete's foot, dermatitis, allergies and psoriasis.

As we age the skin dries, varicose veins develop, and wrinkles appear. In old age, the skin may break down and unfortunate bed sores occur.

Rules for healthy skin
- Eat a balanced diet with plenty of fresh fruit and vegetables.
- Reduce fats.
- Supplement your diet with vitamins if you think you are stressed.
- Vitamin A, vitamin E and zinc are vitamins and minerals which help your skin.
- Drink eight glasses of water a day.
- Dramatic weight loss over the age of forty is very ageing to the skin. If you need to lose weight, do it slowly and get daily exercise to tone your skin to the change. Baggy skin or stretch marks are the result of rapid weight changes.
- The best exercise for skin is outdoor brisk walking. It stimulates the circulation, builds up sweat to clear the pores, and leaves the skin looking pink and healthy.

Aromatherapy for skin
Normal skin
1 drop of rose oil
I drop of chamomile oil
2 teaspoons of almond oil
Massage into the face.

Oily skin
Wash the face with a mild soap. Apply an astringent. Massage with:

1 drop of cypress oil
I drop of juniper oil
2 teaspoons of sweet almond oil

Dry skin
Wash the face with mild soap. Rinse in a cool wash of chamomile tea. Massage with:

1 drop of lavender oil
1 drop of sandalwood oil
1 drop of rose oil
2 teaspoons of carrier oil

Acne

Acne is genetic and tends to run in families. If both your parents had acne then the chances are that three out of four of the offspring will get it also. Acne is classified in four grades ranging from Grade 1 which is mild to Grade 4 which consists of whiteheads, blackheads, pustules, nodules and cysts. If you suffer from Grade 4 acne, then you should see a dermatologist who will prescribe Accutane or similar.

There are some factors that can aggravate acne

Stress, exposure to the sun, seasonal changes and climate can aggravate the situation.
   If your acne is of the teenage kind there are rules to live by when dealing with it.

- Leave well alone.
- If your acne is mild, try to refrain from squeezing and poking.
- Keep fingers away from your face unless the pimple has a central yellow pus head.
- It is then better to pop this out and the pimple will heal more quickly.
- You need to get rid of blackheads by squeezing them, as a blackhead is a blocked pore.
- Wash make-up off thoroughly every night using a mild soap and lots of clean water.
- Exercise daily.
- Avoid foods that contain iodine – salt, shellfish, tortilla chips, wheat germ, potato chips, turkey, liver, butter, cheese, asparagus, Brussels sprouts, onions, broccoli.
- Eat plenty of other fresh fruit and vegetables.
- If you are on the Pill it may be the brand that you are using. Speak to your doctor and ask him to change your prescription.
- Over-the-counter medications and creams are effective in the fight against acne. Water-based gels are probably the best.
- Acne medications may cause adverse reactions to the sun.
- Don't mix treatments.
- Use one at a time.
- Treat an area that is more than the affected area as this will help to keep the acne from spreading.

Acne and make-up

Less is best. Oil-based make-up is a no-no for acne sufferers. Use an oil-free make-up. Test your cosmetics for oil by spreading a big dab on a piece of paper towel and leaving it to spread overnight. You can then see the ring of oil that forms around the circumference. Avoid cosmetics that contain lanolin.

Dermatitis and eczema

Dermatitis and eczema can be very discomforting. Here are some basic rules:

- Beware air conditioning and central heating. Dry air causes and aggravates dermatitis. Central heating dries the air out.
- Avoid water that is too hot or too cold.
- Keep your skin moisturised.
- Use oatmeal soap. Soak in a bath to which two cups of oatmeal has been added.
- Avoid antiperspirants.
- Use cotton underwear.
- Avoid fake nails as clinical studies have shown that they cause frequent and obvious cases of dermatitis.
- Soothe with cool, wet dressings that have been soaked in milk.
- Apply calamine lotion to relieve itching.
- Avoid rapid changes in air temperature.
- Avoid using printed toilet papers as the dye in them can irritate dermatitis.
- Baby lotions can cause more harm than good. Avoid them.

- Rinse laundry thoroughly to remove all traces of detergent.
- Try elimination diets to eliminate any food that may cause allergy.
- Breast milk contains antibiotic and can relieve eczema in a baby if squirted on the offending area.

Dry skin

The rule of thumb for dry skin is 'bathe less and use cooler water'.

Do not dry yourself too well before you apply moisturiser. Dab dry with a towel.

Petroleum jelly or any vegetable oil are by far and away the best moisturisers.

Make a bag, the size of a coin bag, with a piece of muslin and fill it with oatmeal. Dampen it and dab this on your skin.

Use pure soaps such as velvet, Dove or Neutrogena, and use them sparingly.

Dry heating in winter aggravates dry skin. Place a bowl of water near the heating outlet to keep the room humidified.

Cooler air is better for you. Turn the thermostat down a couple of notches and wear more clothes inside.

Use the skin of a banana or kiwi fruit to soften and smooth the skin.

Face masks for dry skin

Face mask one

Add a few drops of any vegetable oil to a whipped egg white and apply to face, avoiding the area around the eyes. Allow to dry. Rinse off with clean water.

Face mask two

2 egg yolks
2 tablespoons glycerine
1 tablespoon cream

Apply to face and neck. Leave for ten minutes. Sponge off with warm cloth.

Hives

Hives are itchy red wheals that appear on the skin as a reaction to allergies, and physical and emotional stress. To relieve symptoms:

- Buy over-the-counter antihistamines.
- Apply an ice bag.
- Calamine lotion.
- Relax and drink a herbal tea – peppermint, chamomile, valerian.
- Make a paste of cream of tartar and water, and apply.
- Cover with cabbage leaves.

Lupus

Lupus means the attack of the wolf and is so named because sufferers often experience a red mark on their faces similar to that which a wolf would leave if he attacked. It's a blotchy red mark shaped like a butterfly on the cheek or the bridge of the nose. As one patch heals another one forms. The person may also suffer from arthritic pain, fever and lung inflammation. If these symptoms appear, then you need to see your doctor.

Nappy rash

Most cases of nappy rash disappear within twenty-four hours – but it can last up to a week. The best solution is to give the baby's bottom plenty of air. Air does wonders, so lie baby on the floor on towels or a waterproof sheet, and leave him/her as long as is possible – allowing, of course, for being able to keep an eye on things, and being prepared to accept that at some point you might have to do a little clean-up job!

Blow-dry his or her bottom with a hair-dryer rather than a towel, which could irritate skin. But keep the dryer on the lowest temperature.

Give your cloth nappies a final rinse in vinegar. This reduces the high pH rating to something closer to that of the baby's skin, reducing rash.

For older babies, a little cranberry juice introduced to the diet also helps reduce the pH rating.

Nappy technology is improving all the time, and the gel-based versions are better than ever at soaking up moisture and at the same time being smooth on skin.

When it comes to ointments, zinc oxide-based ones are the best to reduce the redness and chapping.

Natural skin toners

Honey leaves skin as soft as a baby's bottom.

Apply a raw egg which has been lightly scrambled. Leave to dry. Wash off. It tightens the skin in the same way as a face mask.

Apply a mask of oatmeal and water. Leave to dry. Wash off.

Rub on the peel of a cucumber for a cooling effect.

Nickel rash

Nickel dermatitis is often triggered by ear piercing which also causes rashes in other areas of the body.

Newly pierced ears should be studded only with steel posts until the earlobes heal.

Jewellery brings on a contact rash, too. Buy the highest carat gold jewellery that you can afford. The higher the carat, the less nickel in it.

Oily skin

Oily skin is inherited. The up-side with oily skin is that it tends to wrinkle less and to age better than its drier counterpart.

To reduce oiliness:
- Use a mud facial mask.
- Use hot sudsy water to clean your skin.
- Use an astringent.
- Use water-based cosmetics.

Citrus fruits are toning, astringent and antiseptic. To reduce oiliness, rub on tomato, strawberry, apple or cucumber.

Face masks for oily skin

Face mask one

1 teaspoon honey
90g oatmeal
4 drops almond oil

Make a paste. Apply. Leave for twenty minutes. Rinse off with clean water.

Face mask two

1 egg yolk
Juice of 1 lemon
1 teaspoon honey

Mix to paste. Spread on face and neck. Leave ten minutes. Rinse with fresh clean water.

Psoriasis

Skin usually replaces itself every thirty days. That is, across a month a new skin cell works itself up from the innermost layer to the outermost, and then it dies. But sometimes things go wrong and a cell will rise to the top in as little as three days. This is psoriasis. As a result, raised, red and often itchy sections of skin develop, called plaques. They turn white when the cells flake off and die. It is not a good look, is very uncomfortable, and seems to be difficult to resolve – especially as it comes and goes. Just when you think it has settled down, it flares again. Sometimes it disappears for months or years on end, giving the impression that it is all over, but then returns to haunt you. Flare-ups often occur in winter.

Skin with psoriasis is very dry. Emollients help your skin retain water and go a long way to alleviating the dryness. Petroleum jelly, menthol, camphor, or other body oils should be tried until you find the one that works for you.

Sunlight is excellent for psoriasis. More than 90% of cases show improvement with controlled exposure to the sun and its ultra-violet rays. But make sure you wear plenty of sunscreen. No use swapping psoriasis for skin cancer.

If you don't fancy sitting out in the sun, you can purchase an ultra-violet lamp to treat individual areas.

Coal tar is a long acknowledged and accepted treatment for psoriasis, whether applied directly to individual spots or as an overall coal tar bath. There is also coal tar shampoo.

Similarly, cortisone, in a cream form, also provides relief and a diminution of the plaques. But it is not advisable to keep this up as a full-strength long-term treatment because it gradually weakens in its effectiveness and when you stop, the psoriasis can come back with a vengeance. Use it to a point where significant gains have been made then slowly go on a weaning program to get off it.

A novel but very effective method of treating psoriasis plaques is to apply cream normally used to treat mastitis among cows. It can be purchased from a veterinarian surgeon, and while it sounds 'out there', plenty of sufferers swear by it.

Ice is an excellent short-term itch reliever. Make up an ice-pack with cubes in a plastic bag and hold it against the plaques.

A cold-water bath also provides relief, as does a swim in a heated pool. But it is generally felt that hot water only tends to exacerbate the itching, rather than relieve it.

It may look odd, but many patients have found that covering the raw red skin with kitchen plastic wrap for several days helps clean it up, especially if you put a bit of cortisone ointment on it first. But this is preferably for small lesions only, not large areas. The point is, it makes the area moist, and slows up spreading of the plaque. But moistness can lead to infection, so be careful.

Establish a disciplined diet, especially one with lots of fish oil in it. Fish oil is available in capsules, and contains a fatty acid EPA, and helps to reduce redness and itching in many, but not all cases.

Chill out. This is probably the easiest thing to say, but the hardest thing to do. Research, folklore and general word of mouth will tell you that psoriasis often strikes a young person as a result of stress, unhappiness in life, or a traumatic episode, such as the death of a parent or mum and dad splitting up. It varies enormously, but outside pressures – which could well be solved by some intuitive questioning and follow-up counselling – could be a major cause in the first place.

Repairing scars

Scars can not only change a person's visual appearance, they can also alter how people perceive them, and therefore have a dramatic effect on their lifestyle.

How you treat an injury effects what, if any, scar results.

- Make sure the wound is immediately and properly cleaned. Keep it moist with an antibiotic cream. The quicker the wound heals, the lesser the scarring.

- If the cut is so big that it warrants stitches, get to a doctor immediately.
- If you feel that it can be treated without surgical help, get 'butterfly' bandages from your pharmacist. Make sure the wound is clean, first. These help close the wound properly for better healing and therefore minimal scarring.
- Keep the lacerated or scarred area covered at all times with a skin cream to protect from any further damage.
- Leave scabs alone. Picking at them will only make the final scar worse.
- Watch your diet. The better and healthier the diet, the quicker you will respond to any injury and the less permanent scarring you will suffer.

Shingles

Shingles is a virus, varicella zoster, and it affects the nerves. The result is bumps, reddish blisters and pain.

- Take strong painkillers to reduce the pain.
- Boost your system with vitamin B-complex and vitamin C.
- Cover the infected area with calamine lotion. You can add phenol and a dash of menthol to help.
- Make up a paste of aspirin and chloroform and apply it.
- Cool the worst of the eruptions with a damp towel.
- Throw a handful of corn starch in to a bath and hop in. This is an excellent treatment just before bedtime because, while only temporary, it provides enough relief to let you go to bed relatively pain-free and hopefully off to sleep.
- Use hydrogen peroxide on infected blisters.
- An ice bag on the affected area – sometimes the pain lingers after the blisters have gone – works well.
- Try and work out what is going wrong. Like many on-again, off-again skin disorders, shingles often indicates a deeper emotional problem that needs to be identified and resolved.

Skin cancer
Melanomas

There are numerous forms of skin cancer, but the most lethal is the malignant melanoma. It is linked to over-exposure to the sun's damaging ultra-violet rays, particularly in the early years of life. There may be other factors involved. There is almost certainly a genetic predisposition in some families towards developing melanoma. While fair-skinned people of all races can develop melanoma, it is those of Celtic origin, with their fair, red-toned skin, red hair and blue eyes, who are particularly prone. There may be some truth in the theories linking our high rate of skin cancer with a deficiency of antioxidants such as selenium in our soils and diets.

Through the chemical contamination and over-processing of our food, we may be either ingesting substances which increase our sensitivity to light, or killing off substances which might have increased UV protection such as vitamin B6. If detected early, and if removed or burnt off the skin, it may not cause further problems.

Inspect the surface of the skin regularly. Be doubly vigilant if you have a family history of melanoma, or have yourself been treated for skin cancer previously. Make sure somebody else looks at the danger zone on the shoulders, back, and back of the neck. Note:

- Any change in the size or colour of moles.
- New growths.
- Sores which are slow to heal.
- Any change in the size or colour of marks on the skin that are wine coloured, and irregular shaped.

Remember: Waste no time! Anything that worries you should be shown to a doctor immediately. Early detection and swift action are crucial to stop the spread of the cancer through the body.

Do not place all your trust in sunscreen preparations. Good as the protection they give is, they may be dangerous in themselves. They encourage us to stay out in strong sunlight for extended periods of time without warning signals such as sunburn.

Little is known about the risks associated with the absorption of these chemicals through the skin over a prolonged period of time. Many people suffer from allergic reactions to ingredients in sunscreens. Opt instead for a patch of shade, a large sunhat which protects both the face and the back of the neck and light, sun-protective clothing.

Never sunbake intentionally. If using sunscreens, the best protection is found in the ubiquitous zinc cream, because it blocks the sun on the surface of the skin, rather than being absorbed through the pores. Allergic reactions to zinc creams are rare.

Sunburn

Always wear a sunscreen. Apply thirty minutes before going out. Avoid being in the sun in the middle of the day. Keep out of the sun between the hours of 11am and 3pm. Wear protective clothing. Wear a hat. Don't lie in the sun and bake yourself.

If you are caught without protection and suffer sunburn here are some things that you can do:

- Take two aspirin every four hours until the pain and itching go out of the burn.
- Cool down the burn by standing under a cold shower, or jumping into a cold swimming pool, or soaking in a cool bath.
- Drink plenty of fluids.
- Elevate your legs if they are burnt.

Make a compress dab on the burn for fifteen to twenty minutes at a time. Repeat every four hours. Try one of the following:

- One cup skim milk and four cups water, add three or four ice cubes.
- Moisten a cloth with witch hazel.
- Wrap oatmeal in cheesecloth, run cool water through it, discard the oatmeal and keep the liquid.
- One cup of vinegar to one jug cold water.
- Sprinkle baking powder onto skin, spray with tepid water and let sit on skin.
- Break a leaf of aloe vera and apply the juice.
- Wrap ice cubes in a cloth.
- Plain yoghurt. Leave and rinse in shower.
- Cucumber peel.
- Cold teabags over eyes if they are red and sore.

Remember that sun exposure damages skin and accelerates ageing.

Warts

A wart is a pale, skin-coloured growth that has a rough-to-touch surface. They are surface growths and are caused by a virus. Before you treat them, make sure that it is a wart, and not a corn, callus, mole or cancerous lesion. Most warts disappear of their own accord, so leave them alone unless they begin to multiply rapidly. Ways to treat your wart:

- Apply vitamin A directly to the wart.
- Break off a dandelion and apply the milk from the sap.
- Cover and deprive it of air.
- Paint the wart in castor oil twice daily.
- Keep the wart dry.

- Count your warts, place the same amount of thin sticks under the house, and wait.
- Take garlic capsules.
- Rub with raw potato.
- Rub with chalk.
- Tape a banana skin face down to the wart.
- Use an over-the-counter wart paint.

To make warts disappear very quickly, break off a thistle and use the milk that runs from the stem on the wart.

Another cure for warts is equal parts of kerosene, lemon juice and castor oil. This mixture should be applied three times a day for a week.

Wrinkles
Avoid looking old before your time
- Stay out of the sun.
- Keep away from solariums.
- Don't frown.
- Wear sunglasses and a hat.
- Exercise regularly.
- Eat good healthy food.
- Don't smoke.
- Don't overdo the alcohol.
- Moisturise dry skin.
- Don't yo-yo diet.
- Massage your face.
- Be happy, talk and laugh your way through life.
- Avoid stress.

Respiratory illnesses
Asthma
Asthma means twitchy airways. It may be triggered by an allergy or by some form of lung disorder. It can cause death and if your symptoms alter and you are using your medication more frequently, then you should see your doctor. There are many things that you can do to minimise or reverse your asthma.

- Stay away from cigarettes and smoke-filled rooms.
- Stay away from wood and solid fuel fires.
- Take an antacid tablet at bedtime to cut down on your stomach's acidity. Asthma can sometimes be caused by stomach reflux where acid backs up into your oesophagus from your stomach. Prop yourself up with pillows to avoid stomach contents dripping down into your airway.
- Cover your mouth and nose when you go outdoors with a scarf. You then breathe warm, humid air.
- Keep your air-conditioning system serviced.
- Know what foods you are allergic to and don't eat them.
- Cut down on salt.
- Beware of food additives. Read the labels.
- Stay clear of aspirin and aspirin products.
- Use your inhaler correctly, making sure that it gets to your lungs.
- Strong coffee has beneficial effects on asthma. In an emergency when you do not have your medication, two strong cups of coffee will buy you time until you can get help.
- Vitamin B6, taken as directed, can have beneficial effects.
- Listen to your body. Be aware of the early signs of asthma for you and act immediately.

Exercise-induced asthma

- Keep your mouth closed and breathe through your nose. When you gasp for air through your mouth you dry the back of your throat and it becomes cool which triggers your asthma.
- Swim. This is the ideal exercise for asthmatics.
- Other exercise which is good is any sport that requires short bursts of energy – tennis, golf, cricket, baseball.
- Take time to warm up before exercise. Pace yourself.
- Always take your asthma medication with you in your gym bag.

Common cold

Yes, the cold is common, and no, there is no true cure. Antibiotics won't kill it, and lozenges, tablets and syrups will only pacify the symptoms with varying degrees of success. But while you sniffle on, there are a few options that might help.

- First up, be positive. It might get you down, it may be annoying, it might be distracting you from your work or family life, but being upbeat and positive can help make life a lot easier and bring the cold to an earlier conclusion.
- Direct your energy towards getting better. Rest and relax, get things prioritised, ease up on the schedule, particularly socialising.
- Partying is out, but a soothing glass of wine before you retire at night will help you get a good night's sleep, which is what you really need.
- Take plenty of vitamin C, whether by supplement or plenty of fruits such as oranges, grapefruit, and the hero of the moment, the cranberry. It will help the coughing and sneezing and might cut the duration of the cold by a couple of days.
- Boost your zinc intake, via a change in diet, or if necessary zinc supplements or lozenges. Zinc can help reduce the length of a cold.
- Drink plenty of fluids, particularly water, tea, and juices to flush out the germs and impurities and replace lost fluids.
- Feed a cold, they say. But maybe it's time to change tack. Look to cutting out fatty foods, which may have weakened you in the first place and helped bring on the cold, and go for more healthy stuff, particularly fresh vegetables and fruit. Chicken soup is not only good for you, it helps open up those nasal passages.
- You probably don't feel like it, but doing a bit of exercise – even a walk around the block – helps a lot. Rug up to keep out the cold.
- Gargle with salty water to ease a raw throat, apply Vaseline or petro-leum jelly around a red nose, and clear congestion with a steaming hot shower.
- As for medication, you can go down the chemical path – aspirin, antihistamine, nasal sprays and drops, syrups and medications. Or the natural route with herb teas, lots of garlic (worry about the body odour problem when you are well), or the current darling of the naturopaths, Echinacea.
- If you are a smoker, and keep lighting up at your usual rate, it's not going to help.

How can you tell the difference between a cold and the 'flu?

- A fever always accompanies the 'flu, whereas it seldom accompanies a cold. It comes on suddenly.
- General aches are severe with the 'flu whereas with a cold they are mild.
- The 'flu leaves you fatigued for two or three weeks.
- A runny nose accompanies a cold, but rarely the 'flu.
- A sore throat is a common symptom of a cold and only occasionally accompanies the 'flu.
- A severe cough often accompanies the 'flu, whereas a cold only brings a mild to moderate cough.

How to avoid a 'flu virus that is going around.

- Get a 'flu shot at the beginning of the 'flu season.
- Avoid crowds.
- Keep up your strength by sleeping regularly, eating well and staying fit.
- If your spouse succumbs to the 'flu, sleep in another room and don't kiss him/her until he/she is over it.
- Know when to come in out of the rain as prolonged exposure to wet, cold weather lowers resistance.

If you contract the 'flu

- Stay home from work. Your colleagues do not want your virus.
- Get plenty of bed rest.
- Drink plenty of fluid.
- Take two aspirin every four hours to reduce fever and alleviate pain. Do not give aspirin to children.
- Humidify the air with a humidifier to ease sore and raspy throat.
- Suck on a cough lolly.
- Stay warm.
- Make sure you take in some fresh air.

Symptoms that mean you should see your doctor

- Your voice is hoarse.
- You develop chest pains.
- You have difficulty breathing.
- You cough up green or yellow phlegm.
- Prolonged vomiting.

Blocked nasal passages

Malformation of the nasal passages can make breathing through the nose difficult, particularly during sleep. This can be remedied by:

- An operation, in which a small portion of the soft palate is removed to keep the air passages open.
- Contraptions which fit the mouth but these can be uncomfortable.
- Machines which keep the nasal passages open.

Laryngitis

Laryngitis is a condition that occurs when you lose your voice for whatever reason – upper respiratory infection, allergy, misusing your voice, cold air. What should you do?

- Don't talk. Don't even whisper.
- Humidify the air.
- Take a steaming bath.
- Drink plenty of warm fluids.
- Breathe through your nose.
- No cigarettes.
- Avoid mint and mentholated cough drops. Use honey-based ones.
- Check that your medication is not the cause.
- Respect your voice and employ electronic aids if you need to project.

If your voice does not return to normal in three or four days, consult your doctor.

Mucus eliminators
- Garlic
- Horseradish
- Cayenne pepper

Beware nasal sprays, as they often cause more harm than good.

Sinusitis
Sinusitis is a condition where the sinus cavities around your eyes and nose become infect-ed which produces pressure and pain, as well as a good serve of mucus. Your sinuses get clogged up.

The best treatment for blocked sinuses is steam. Solutions include:
- Stand in a hot shower.
- Make a steam bath with hot water and a few drops of eucalyptus oil in a tub. Cover your head with a towel and inhale the steam.
- If you are at work get a hot cup of tea, cup your hands over the top and breathe the steam.
- Use a humidifier, which can be bought at chemists, in your bedroom.
- Flush out your nostrils each day. Make a mix of saline water, cover one nostril, breathe in the saline, then blow your nose. Repeat on the other nostril.
- Blow one nostril at a time.
- Drink plenty of fluid.
- Sniffle your stale secretions down your throat.
- Use over-the-counter medication such as Sudafed.
- Massage your sinuses to bring fresh blood supply to the area.
- Exercise.
- Apply a warm wash-cloth to your cheeks and eyes and leave until it cools.

Snoring
The vibration of the soft palate at the back of the mouth during sleep is not serious in itself, but can be symptomatic of breathing problems. It only occurs if a person breathes through their mouth. This can be out of habit or can indicate nasal or mucus congestion or enlarged adenoids.

Sore throat
Sore throats are often the first sign that you may be in for a dose of cold or 'flu. To relieve sore throat:
- Suck on a lozenge.
- Gargle with salt water.
- Clear your airways and breathe through your nose.
- Moisturise the air you are breathing.
- Sip a mixture of lemon juice and honey.
- Eat a teaspoon of honey.
- Make yourself a shot of brandy and gargle it.
- Take garlic capsules.
- Change your toothbrush.

Indigestion
A normal meal takes about twenty-four hours to digest. A meal of soft, processed food may take a week to pass through the gut. Heartburn, flatulence, cramps, belching are usually a result of eating too quickly or overeating. Eat smaller amounts. Take your time. Avoid eat-

ing for at least three hours before sleeping. Antacids, available from the chemist, may alleviate the problem.

Crohn's disease

Crohn's disease is an inflammatory condition of the digestive system which restricts the absorption of nutrients. It can delay puberty and stunt growth in childhood. Its symptoms include diarrhoea, severe abdominal pain, nausea, weakness and weight loss.

Foreign objects

If you swallow a foreign object, especially small things with smooth edges, such as a button or bead, etc., it will simply pass through your stomach and intestines and will be passed out of the body in a motion.

If it has sharp edges it may cut the lining of the bowel and therefore may need to be surgically removed.

Hiccups

Scientists think that the hiccup is a reflex from prehistoric times. No one knows why they come and nobody really knows what makes them go. The general aim is to stop the nerve impulse that causes them in its tracks and to increase carbon dioxide levels.

Some cures that are said to work
- Take one teaspoon sugar, dry.
- Suck on a lemon wedge.
- A glass of water drunk upside down. How you do it is up to you!
- Take a deep breath and then, as slowly as you can, release it.
- Gargle with water.
- Take a deep breath, and when you feel the hiccup coming on, gulp, repeat two or three times on that breath and do it again.
- Suck on ice cubes.
- Have somebody tickle you while you hold your breath and try not to laugh.
- Hope that someone will come up and frighten the daylights out of you. Your bank manager is a good choice . . .
- Take a brown paper bag, and blow into it, in and out, ten times, as fast as you can.

Heartburn

Heartburn is mostly caused by acid reflex where digestive juices find their way into the esophageus and cause a burning sensation.

Foods to avoid if you are a heartburn sufferer
- Milk stimulates the stomach to secrete acid. Just what you don't want!
- Mints relax your lower esophageus sphincter whose job it is to keep the acid in your stomach. You don't want that either!
- Caffeine irritates an inflamed esophageus.
- Chocolate contains fat and caffeine. Not good for you.
- Fizzy drinks expand your stomach and have the same effect as over-eating.
- Greasy foods sit in the stomach and foster surplus acid production.

If you suffer from heartburn
- Avoid eating too much, too fast. Heartburn is most often caused by over-indulgence.
- Stay upright to keep the acid in your stomach.
- If you do need to sleep, elevate your head.

- Take an antacid.
- Avoid tobacco smoke.
- Do not eat hot, spicy foods.
- Loosen your belt.
- Lift with your legs, not with your stomach.
- Review any prescription drugs that you may be on with your doctor.
- Eat three hours before bedtime to give your stomach time to digest your food.

Irritable bowel syndrome

Also known as spastic colon.

This is an extremely common complaint and there are many things that can be done to alleviate the problem.

There is a strong connection between stress and irritable bowel syndrome, so if you can relieve the stress then you have gone a long way towards solving the problem.

In the short term:

Stay calm. You are not going to die. People don't die from this complaint.

Take a Panadol.

Lifestyle changes you can make to alleviate the problem:

- Hold a hot water bottle against your stomach.
- Find a hobby or activity that helps you to unwind.
- Take up yoga or meditation.
- Try visualisation, where you imagine that you are in a wonderful place and the pain is flowing over your body and up into the air.
- Keep a stress diary and learn to recognise those situations that are stressful and keep away from them.
- Eat regular meals.
- Keep a food diary and learn to recognise those foods that cause you grief.
- Eat more fruit, wholegrains, vegetables and bran.
- Drink lots of fluid.
- Eat a low-fat diet.
- Avoid gas-producing foods such as beans and members of the cabbage family.
- Be wary of spicy foods.
- Some people react negatively to acidic foods such as citrus, tomatoes and vinegar.
- Beer and red wine are often the culprit.
- Smoking is a no-no.
- Exercise strengthens the body and helps to relieve stress.

Lactose intolerance

Lactose intolerance is the inability to digest lactose, a natural sugar found in milk and other dairy products. Symptoms are abdominal pain and diarrhoea. Avoid all dairy products.

Nausea

To control nausea:

- Sip warm herbal tea or fruit juice.
- Sip dry ginger ale.
- If you must eat, eat dry toast or dry biscuits.
- Apply pressure to the webbing between your thumb and index finger.

It might not sound nice, but allow yourself a good vomit as it rids the stomach of the substance that is making you queasy.

The liver

The liver is the largest internal organ. It is one of the few organs that has the ability to repair itself. If a person has up to half of their liver removed through damage or trauma, it will grow back to its original size within four weeks. In a healthy adult it weighs about 1.5 kg. The liver is the link between the digestive system and the circulatory systems and it performs over 500 functions. It is worth looking after.

Ulcers

Stomach acid is said to be the prime cause of ulcers, but another theory suggests bacteria may be involved. High stress levels are seen by many as the foundation, or at least aggravation, of an ulcer. Whatever the cause, an ulcer can be a very painful exercise, and if it starts to bleed, then it is potentially lethal.

If something that you eat consistently causes you burning pain, then don't eat it, simple as that. This may well be the generally acknowledged hot and spicy foods, such as pizza, but it varies from person to person. Ulcer sufferers have been known to be set on fire by ice-cream. Milk, as has long been traditionally held, might act as a soother and initially buffer the acid and ease the discomfort.

But, don't go overboard, as it then stimulates more secretion of acid in the stomach, causing you more grief. Aspirin might ease the pain, but too many can have an adverse effect on the stomach lining, heightening the impact of the ulcer. Iron is good for you, but too much iron can be a gastric irritant, which does not help an ulcer.

Food neutralises stomach acid, so rather than have the usual three meals, have six smaller meals during the day. By spreading out the ingestion of food, you are neutralising the acid for more of the day.

Alcohol does not necessarily irritate an ulcer nor start a new one. As with all things, be moderate. Give up the cigarettes. Look at your lifestyle, and consider, are you getting too stressed? Consider your job and relationships – are they causing you concern? Take up exercise, deep breathing, relaxation techniques.

Heart
Heart problems

To avoid heart problems:

- Stop smoking.
- Avoid being in a room with somebody who is smoking.
- Less is best when eating – less salt, less fat, less calories.
- Eat only meat that is lean and trimmed of all fat.
- Remove the skin from poultry before cooking.
- Eat no more than six ounces of meat, seafood or poultry daily.
- Use only monounsaturated or polyunsaturated oils and then use them sparingly.
- Do not eat offal.
- Use low-fat dairy products.
- Increase your daily intake of fruit and vegetables.
- Begin an exercise program and stick to it.
- Learn to relax and resolve your conflicts.
- Take an aspirin daily to thin your blood. Speak to your doctor first.

Magnesium

Magnesium is vital for healthy heart and muscles, and a proper intake is vital. Magnesium is used to convert sugars in the blood to energy and is essential for vitality. It influences levels of fertility and is important in the production of the female hormones of oestrogen and progesterone. It also regulates the levels of calcium which is helpful for both the prevention and treatment of osteoporosis. It is found naturally in leafy green vegetables, seafoods, soybeans, milk, wholegrains, apples, lemons, grapefruit, some nuts, seeds and molasses.

Blood pressure

To reduce high blood pressure:

- Lose weight.
- Reduce salt.
- Reduce alcohol.
- Boost potassium intake by increasing fresh fruit and vegetable intake.
- Increase aerobic exercise.
- Avoid isometric exercise such as weight lifting, which tends to increase blood pressure.
- Monitor your blood pressure at home.
- Avoid stress and worry.
- Talk less, as talking has been shown to increase blood pressure.
- Owning and fondling a pet reduces blood pressure.
- Check your partner's blood pressure as studies have shown that the longer a couple are together the more similar their blood pressures become.

Cholesterol

There is good cholesterol and bad cholesterol. There are different types of cholesterol, so how do you tell them apart?

Dietary cholesterol

Dietary cholesterol is what is contained in food. It is recommended that you keep your dietary intake of cholesterol to 300 milligrams.

Serum cholesterol

Serum cholesterol is what is in your bloodstream and is what is measured with a blood cholesterol test. A reading of under 200 milligrams is desirable.

High density lipoprotein

High density lipoprotein (HDL) has artery-scouring ability and the higher your levels of it, the better.

Low density lipoprotein

Low density lipoprotein (LDL) is an artery-clogging cholesterol and the lower your levels of this, the better.

How can you control your cholesterol levels?

- Reduce your weight if you are overweight.
- Increase your daily intake of:
    Niacin (start on low doses and gradually build up)
    Vitamin C and pectin (contained in citrus fruits, tomatoes, potatoes, strawberries, spinach).
    Vitamin E supplement
    Calcium
- Reduce saturated fats in your diet and increase monounsaturated fats (vegetable and olive oil)

- Limit your egg intake to three a week.
- Eat more beans and legumes.
- Eat a variety of fruit and vegetables.
- Drink tea. Cut back on the coffee.
- Use lemon grass oil in your cooking.
- Make and eat barley broth.
- Exercise regularly.
- Change to low-fat dairy products.
- Use garlic in your cooking often and regularly.
- Don't smoke.
- Relax and enjoy life.

Rapid heartbeat

Rapid heartbeat, or tachycardia, can come on very quickly – your heartbeat suddenly accelerates from the normal seventy-odd beats a minute to beyond, even up to 200-plus. This may bring on sweating, perhaps a feeling of being sick, or a feeling of tiredness and an inability to perform at normal capacity.

With children, parents will notice their child become very lethargic and drowsy. The first time around, this can be very alarming, and obviously it is best to seek immediate medical attention to establish what is wrong.

The full title is paroxysmal atrial tachycardia. It is not life-threatening and can be controlled and maintained. But it is important to establish that that is exactly what it is. There is another rapid heartbeat syndrome, ventricular tachycardia, which is life-threatening.

Tachycardia means a heartbeat of more than 100 beats a minute. The chambers in your heart – the atriums, or atria, which take the blood from your veins and pump it into the ventricles – get out of control and start going faster. It is as if their inbuilt regulatory device suddenly stops. The beat actually remains consistent – it does not get out of rhythm, which is another problem altogether – but beats very rapidly.

Means of calming down paroxysmal atrial tachycardia include:

- Rest. Calm down, stop whatever it is you are doing, and rest. Clinicians all agree that in the first instance, rest is the best solution to an attack.
- Cold water. Fill a sink with icy cold water and splash it on your face. Sometimes the shock of this has the reaction of interrupting the attack.

The pace of your heartbeat is controlled by two sets of nerves – the sympathetic nerves and the parasympathetic (vagal) nerves. The vagal nerve is the braking mechanism, and to stimulate this, take a deep breath, and bear down as if you were making a bowel movement on the toilet.

Another vagal movement is to gently massage the right carotid artery. The best point is approximately where it connects in the neck as far underneath the jaw as possible. It is best to check with your physician to be shown exactly the point to massage.

As a preventative, it is worth noting that stimulants such as coffee, chocolate, diet pills, and so on, increase the risk of paroxysmal atrial tachycardia attacks.

Magnesium and potassium levels are important, so a well-balanced diet is a guard against tachycardia, combined with exercise.

A common link with tachycardia sufferers is they are often goal-oriented A-types, anxious for success at all costs and who rarely relax. They have to bring a more balanced, tranquil approach and routine to their life.

Raynaud's Syndrome

Raynaud's Syndrome is exhibited by a coldness at the end of the fingers – they go pale, maybe with a tinge of blue, and sometimes even numb. It may be a minor moment of no inconvenience, but it can also affect your sense of touch and strength of grip. This has been caused by the blood flow being restricted to the end of the fingers, generally caused by the cold, but sometimes by injury, or reaction to drugs.

Eat plenty of foods containing iron, such as lean red meat, fish, poultry and lentils.

Swing your arms like a softball pitcher to get the blood moving. Dress in layers to keep warm. Wear a hat – 60% of heat loss goes through your head, so wearing a hat does wonders for retaining heat.

Drink plenty of water – dehydration actually aggravates chills. Give up the cigarettes. Smoking restricts blood vessels and aggravates the situation.

Red wine

A glass or two of red wine a day is good for you. It's the thirty-seven beers beforehand that cause the problem . . .

Red wine contains 200 natural chemicals, many of which are antioxidants. Antioxidants increase tissue blood flow and protect cells from injury. They enhance the blood flow to your heart, brain, and organs such as the kidneys.

Red wine is the virtual equivalent of a cholesterol medicine, a blood thinner, a metabolism tuner and a cell repairer.

Alcohol raises the level of HDL, the good cholesterol, which scours blood vessels free of fatty plaques in moderate drinkers by 10%, and in heavy drinkers by even more. Running five kilometres a week increases HDL by only a fraction of that. Researchers estimate that half the heart benefits of moderate drinking stem directly from the HDL gain.

Alcohol decreases blood proteins that promote clotting, and allows the blood to flow more freely. It does this by keeping the platelets – the tiny blood cells – from adhering to one another and forming a clot.

The antioxidant activity in a glass of red wine is equal to seven glasses of orange juice, or twenty glasses of apple juice.

Alcohol may also prevent diabetes. When healthy post-menopausal women were given two drinks per day for two months they become sensitive to insulin, their metabolism became more efficient, and their risk of diabetes was reduced.

Smoking
To help you to quit
Preparation is paramount. Set a date to quit, and stick to it.

Remember the four Ds:
1. Drink water.
2. Deep breathe.
3. Delay having your next cigarette if you feel compelled to have one.
4. Do something else, distract yourself.

Myths about quitting smoking
- Cigarettes relieve stress and help you to relax. (False)
- Smoking actually increases blood pressure and increases your heart rate. (True)
- Aunty Vee smoked like a chimney all her life and lived to be eighty. (False)
- One half of smokers die prematurely, half of them in middle age. Aunty Vee may have lived to be eighty, but she had two heart by-passes and her legs weren't good. (True)
- A few cigarettes a day won't cause any damage. (False)
- There is no safe level of smoking. Every cigarette takes eleven minutes off your life. (True)
- I will put on weight if I quit. (False)
- Regular exercise and sensible eating will ensure that weight gain is minimal. (True)

Techniques to try

Nicotine patches. The claim is that nicotine patches double the chances of you quitting. Worn on the upper arm or body, Nicabate QC and Nicorette release a controlled dose of nicotine into the body. They are rated to last between sixteen to twenty-four hours, and some are produced in three levels of strength. Taking the patch off and having a smoke and putting the patch back on is showing a considerable lack of commitment. Smoking with the patch still on is not a very good idea at all.

Buffer drops. NicoBloc is a relatively new product available from your pharmacist, aimed at helping smokers gradually cut down. The drops are applied to the cigarette filter before you light up, and act as a buffer, trapping up to 99% of the nicotine, tar and chemicals. Good if you want to wean off gradually rather than abruptly.

Lozenges. These release nicotine slowly through the lining of the mouth, the aim being to reduce some symptoms of withdrawal. They do not contain the tar or carbon monoxide of cigarette smoke. But be warned, if you have an angina condition or have suffered stroke or heart attack, it is not advisable to take these.

Gum. Sugar-free gum such as Nicorette Gum 2mg is probably best for people who smoke less than twenty cigarettes a day, but stronger doses and flavours are available for heavier smokers. They are aimed at controlling the cravings.

Natural gum. Nicrobrevin is a chewing gum made of natural substances, chamomile and passiflora. These are herbs acknowledged for their ability to relieve stress and anxiety. Natural gum's action on the body can help relieve withdrawal side effects.

Herbal cigarettes. These provide the continuance of the habitual act of smoking – which some people find as hard to give up as the cravings – but do not contain the nicotine. Some herbs ease the physical craving by blocking nicotine receptors in the brain. But a herbal cigarette can cover the lungs in as much tar as a mild traditional cigarette.

Spray. Smoke Eze is a homeopathic spray providing a natural alternative to the chemical-based substitutes.

Supplements. Herbal supplements, such as Nico Free, also provide a natural alternative to the chemical-based substitutes.

Antidepressants. Antidepressants such as Zyban are available only by prescription and help lessen the desire to smoke. But be careful, you must wait a fortnight before quitting to allow the drug enough time to take effect. Side effects are also possible, including mood swings, aggression and insomnia.

Acupuncture. This has become popular over the last thirty years, with research supporting the claims that the traditional needle technique can double your chances of giving up the smokes.

Hypnotherapy. Claims of up to a 60% success rate are made for hypnotherapy. The practitioners say that it puts you into a state of deep relaxation, and therefore makes you receptive to messages about giving up. You must have the willpower too.

Will Power. He is not only part of your make-up, but he exists, too. Will Power is the character creation of one of the most consistent and successful anti-smoking campaigns, Quit, run by health authorities in the Australian state of Victoria. He lives on your computer desktop and reads messages from the Quit website, www.quit.org.au, and helps you purchase anti-smoking quit packs.

Facts to encourage you

- Twelve hours after you have stopped, almost all of the nicotine is out of your system.
- After twenty-four hours, the level of carbon monoxide in your blood has dropped dramatically.
- After a few days, your senses of taste and smell will have improved dramatically.
- Within a month, your blood pressure should be back to near normal, with your immune system showing continued recovery.
- By three months the blood flow to your feet and hands will be considerably better.
- After a year, your risk of heart disease is half that of a continuing smoker.

Alcohol

There are physical side effects to drinking too much alcohol. They include restlessness, agitation, the shakes, sweating, nausea, high blood pressure and rapid heart beat.

Alcohol increases the risk of breast cancer. Studies have shown that a woman's chance of contacting breast cancer increases by 6% for every drink that she has each day.

Indicators of alcoholism

- Drinking only one type of alcoholic drink or brand of drink.
- Exhibiting drink-seeking behaviour, that is, only going places where there will be a drink.
- Having to drink increasingly more alcohol to achieve the same level of wellbeing.
- Drinking to relieve or avoid withdrawal symptoms.
- Craving for alcohol.
- Being unable to quit drinking alcohol.

Itches and bites
To relieve itching

- Apply an oral antihistamine.
- Apply calamine lotion.
- Apply an ice-pack.
- Apply salt moistened with water and made into a paste.
- Dissolve one teaspoon of baking powder in a glass of water and apply to the bite.
- Dissolve one tablespoon Epsom Salts to a litre of hot water. Chill and apply to bite.
- Rub an aspirin onto the bite.

If bitten by a spider

- Wash and disinfect the bite.
- Apply an ice-pack.
- Rub in an aspirin.
- Seek medical help.
- Capture the offending spider if possible and take it along with you to the doctor so that it may be identified and the correct anti-venom used.

Ticks

Irritate the tick and make it loosen its grip by dabbing petrol, kerosene or alcohol on it. Remove the tick by gently pulling it out with a pair of tweezers. Suffocate the tick by covering it with a dab of fingernail polish. Once the tick is removed wash and disinfect the area.

Dog bites
- Assess the damage and seek medical attention if needed.
- Thoroughly wash and disinfect the wound.
- Cover with a sterile cloth to stem bleeding and to protect the wound.
- Take patient to the doctor for a tetanus injection.
- Report the matter to your local council.
- Regularly check wound site for signs of infection.
- Be aware that large dogs can cause internal damage without breaking the skin.

Stings
When stung, it is important to identify the source of the injury – whether it is a bee, wasp, spider and so on, to know what you are dealing with. Always act quickly.

Don't waste precious time determining what happened and taking remedial action – especially where children are involved.

If it is a bee, or some other insect that leaves stinger, remove that first, as the longer it stays there, the more venom is injected into the skin. Don't try and pull the stinger out – scrape it out using a fingernail, or a smooth straight edge like a nail file, business card, credit card, something like that.

Clean the sting area with water, or water and soap, if it is handy. Provide some aspirin to deaden the pain if it is really strong. Provide an antihistamine, either tablet or syrup. It helps with sedation and calms the pain and swelling.

Use one or more of these alternatives to rub on the affected area to help deaden the pain:

Cold – using an ice-pack. Frozen peas are excellent, or ice cubes in a plastic bag or rag. It has a soothing effect.

Heat – using a hair-dryer. The heat neutralises chemicals that cause inflammation.

Baking soda – either rubbing the crystals direct onto bite, or using water to make up a paste or poultice to put on it.

Ammonia – dab it on the sting. Use one of the ammonia-based household cleaning products, or the over-the-counter anti-sting sprays or ointments, which are often ammonia-based. It should relieve the sting quickly.

Meat tenderiser – an enzyme in meat tenderiser breaks down the proteins that make up sting venom.

Mud – when you are out in the middle of nowhere, with limited resources at hand, make up a poultice of mud, water and a scarf or handkerchief.

When all else fails, be like the father in *My Big Fat Greek Wedding* and spray Windex on it. It worked for him.

Avoidance
Avoid getting stung in the first place by wearing white or lightly coloured, long-sleeved loose clothing, and spraying on a chemical or natural repellent. Interestingly, research shows that insects are attracted by people whose zinc reserves are down, so make sure you always have – as with many things in this book – a balanced diet.

Turpentine is a guaranteed insect repellent – ask any painter.

Jellyfish
Jellyfish are in a special stinging category of their own, with predators such as the box jellyfish in northern parts of Australia potentially lethal. Acting very fast is very important

with jellyfish stings – including summoning lifeguard, medical or other professional help immediately.

- First remove any attached tentacles. It is important you do not touch them, so cover your hands with a towel or rag; or cover the spot with sand or mud, or something like shaving cream. Scrape the tentacles off with a razor blade, credit card, emery board, knife, etc.
- Rinse the area immediately with any of the following if they are at hand – ammonia, vinegar, meat tenderiser, alcohol.
- Offer aspirin, antihistamine, or cortisone cream.

Memory

Is your memory 'playing tricks' on you? Are you getting concerned that you seem to be forgetting things that once were locked in the memory bank to be easily accessed?

Consider these words:
I hear it, I forget.
I see it, I remember.
I do it, I understand.
– Confucius, 450 BC.

'I am more likely to remember something that I understand, and forget things that I do not understand.' (Anonymous)

We all have incredible capacity for memory. For most of the time we are not even aware that our memories are at work. It is only when it fails us that we sit up and take notice. We have more stored memory in our brains than we will ever want or need to use. Remembering and forgetting are essential attributes of the mind. If we didn't forget some things our brains would be so clogged up that they would cease to function.

Age and memory

- All people forget things at different stages of life.
- It may be that there are many things going on, then there is brain overload.
- You may be distracted because you are stressed, not feeling well, or have other things on your mind.
- Most forgetting occurs because we do not record it properly in the first place.
- Short-term memory can suffer from overload. It can only hold a certain amount.
- After fifteen minutes, short-term memory lets go of those things that have not been repeatedly learned.
- Your memory does not have to be perfect to be OK.
- A certain degree of forgetfulness is desirable.

Factors influencing memory

Alcohol

Alcohol is a natural memory inhibiter. Even one glass of alcohol measurably influences our ability to recall.

Stress

When we are stressed we are unable to concentrate for long enough for our brain to retrieve the information from stored memory.

Mental alertness

Keep your brain active by using it for problem solving. Studies have shown that people who do crosswords, read and keep active, retain brain function.

See the doctor

It is time to see a doctor if:

- You forget things such as what your partner's name is, where you live, or what meal you just ate.
- You are unhappy or uncomfortable about your memory lapses.
- Memory lapse is affecting your professional work.
- Memory lapse is affecting your family.

Exercises to improve your memory

- Make as many connections as you are able about a topic.
- Reduce the material that you wish to remember to keywords. Use acronyms, anagrams, chunking things together.
- Use more than one scenario when you wish to commit something to memory. For example: 'The car keys are on the sideboard in the kitchen, the radio is on, there is a cake in the oven.'
- Talk to yourself, tell yourself what it is that you wish to remember. 'There you go, keys, you're there on the sideboard.'
- Make a camera. You do this by making an imaginary camera with your fingers and take an imaginary photograph of the object you want to remember, such as the keys on the sideboard.
- Give yourself a prompt. For example, an elastic band around your finger to remind you to buy something.
- Make lists. Wherever possible make lists to free your short-term memory so that you can remember more.
- Groupings. Put things together in groups, like we do to telephone numbers.
- Make the things that you wish to remember into a story.
- Make associations.
- Think of faces when you think of names.
- When you are introduced repeat the person's name. 'Pleased to meet you, Paul.'
- Be selective. Remember what is important. Discard the rest.
- Read, do puzzles, keep your mind alert.
- Avoid stress, remain calm.
- Check your medicine cupboard. It may be the medication that you are taking that makes you forgetful.
- Alcohol can make you forget things and not even worry about forgetting them.

Marijuana and memory

Also known as cannabis, marijuana has been used for pain relief for chronic pain sufferers. There are, however, many detrimental effects of the drug, especially if used heavily. They include deficiency of the immune system, disruption of the reproductive system, and impaired short-term memory.

Ginkgo and memory

The leaf of the ancient ginkgo tree increases blood flow to the brain and is a recognised memory stimulant.

Rosemary for remembrance

Increase awareness and improve recall by rubbing the oil of rosemary onto the temples.

Learning to forget

There are some things that we need to forget because, if we remember them, they are too painful. When we receive bad news and feel 'out of it', this is the body's way of helping us to cope by forgetting for a time. Women forget the pain of childbirth and go back for more because the body releases endorphins which inhibit the memory of painful experiences. Time also heals, and we know that if we can just get through the present, then one day we will look back and things will not hurt so much. Expressing your emotions is good for the soul and helps you to talk the memory away.

Face your pain and deal with it

- Seek professional help.
- Look for the positives in the experience that you wish to forget.
- Project through the pain that you are suffering to a better time when you will be pain free.
- Use your imagination to make the reality better.

For the memory bank

Sentences containing every letter of the alphabet

The quick brown fox jumped over the lazy dog.
Waltz, bad nymph, for quick jigs vex.
We promptly judged antique ivory buckles for the next prize.
Sixty zippers were quickly picked from the woven jute bag.

Words with all the vowels in alphabetical order

Facetious – jocular.
Arsenious – containing arsenic.
Abstemious – sparing.
Abstentious – self restraining.
Caesious – greyish green.

Chinese medicine

Chinese medicine is one of the oldest medical systems in the world. It is practised by practitioners who have skills which are married to a belief in the cosmos. It is part of a whole belief system – philosophy, religion and a healing system. The human is a part of the universe and each organ is a universe within a universe.

Three aspects

Chinese medicine concentrates on three aspects – Tao, Yin/Yang, The Five Elements.

Tao

The universe, life before, life after, heaven, earth, gods and demons are interwoven and there must be understanding of the cosmos before healing can be attempted.

Chi or Qi (pronounced 'chee') is a difficult concept to translate. It's usually left untranslated because there is no single English word that conveys all parts of the Chinese concept. The word that comes closest is 'energy'. Like energy, Chi is the fundamental stuff of the universe.

The Taoist creation theory isn't actually a theory. It's more a statement of fact than speculation. 'From nothing came something.' From Yin and Yang came the Five Elements (metal, wood, water, fire, earth). From the Five Elements came the Ten Thousand Things, all things in creation. Neither Chi nor energy can be destroyed. They can only be changed.

Yin/Yang

Yin and Yang are the negative and positive energy flows. They are life and death. Yin/Yang are complementary opposites that must remain balanced in order that the whole is in harmony. The body is divided into Yin and Yang. There is Yin within Yin, Yang within Yang, Yin within Yang, and Yang within Yin. Disease can only be cured by balancing the harmony of a disturbed Yin and Yang.

The five elements

The five elements – metal, wood, water, fire, earth – help to create one another, but can also destroy each other. They must co-exist.

Metal creates water – Metal melts to create liquid.
Metal destroys wood – An axe fells a tree.
Earth creates metal – There is metal in the earth.
Earth destroys water – Water becomes mud when mixed with earth.
Water creates wood – With water forests grow.
Fire creates earth – Within the earth there are molten metals.
Fire destroys metal – Heat makes metal molten.
Water destroys fire – Water extinguishes fire.
Wood creates fire – Humankind creates warmth by rubbing two sticks together.
Wood destroys earth – Trees take water and minerals from the earth.

Holistic approach

Chinese medicine is a holistic approach to healing – physical, emotional, spiritual.

Everything is composed of Chi:
- Our bodies
- The earth
- Water
- Sound
- Light

'Every birth is a condensation of Chi, every death is a dispersal.'

Chi flows throughout the body in currents or conduits called channels. There are fourteen main channels and these possess the most commonly used acupuncture points. Twelve of these channels connect to a Yin or Yang organ from which they derive their name.

Six functions

Chi has six main functions. These are:

- It produces motion within the body and moves the body.
- It transforms.
- It transports.
- It warms.
- It protects.
- It contains.

When you have the proper amount of Chi and it is flowing smoothly, you have health.

Acupuncture

Acupuncturists diagnose human illness in terms of traditional Chinese medicine. They perceive the human organism and its processes as flows of energy or Chi, somewhat like the currents, eddies and swirls in a stream or lake.

The major currents are called channels or meridians, or in Chinese, 'jing luo'. Twelve of the channels connect with organs in the trunk. Each of the twelve is named for the organ with which it connects. The organ channels and two other channels which follow the front (Ren channel) and rear (Du channel) along the midline of the body contain the acupuncture points.

Proper rate of flow and amount of Chi in the channels is the definition of health. The acupuncture points are needled to restore or maintain the flow. Each of the acupuncture points has specific effects on the different currents and/or organs of the body.

In traditional Chinese medicine, there are at least seven very commonly used groups of acu-points. There are five transporting points on each channel. They begin at the fingers and toes and stop at the elbows and knees. The Five Elements points begin at the fingertips and toe tips. Each set of points begins with the names of Wood or Metal and continues up the arm or leg until all Five Elements are represented. The Five Elements relationships are the keys to the selection of the points in treatment.

There is one Yuan-Source point on each organ channel. This point will release Source Chi in the system when needled.

Mu points
A Mu-Front point is on the front of the body and located close to the organ with which it has a diagnostic relationship. Mu translates as Alarm.

Shu points
The Shu-Back points are on the back, on both branches of the bladder channel. They are each named for an organ or body part and have the same diagnostic relationship with those parts as the Mu points have with the organs. Window to the Sky points are all in the upper third of the body. This third of the body is likened to Heaven. If there is poor Chi flow between the upper third and lower thirds then a window must be opened to restore communication between Heaven and Earth.

Significant diagnostic information includes:
* Visual examination
* Obtaining certain reactions when pressing the point
* Spontaneous sensation at the point

Needles
Acupuncture needles range from half-inch to several inches in length (0.6 cm to 15 cm) and a few thousandths to several thousandths of an inch in diameter. The vast majority of needles used are stainless steel but copper, gold and silver are still in use. Gold is thought by some to tone and silver to disperse Chi. Sterile needles are designed for a single use.

Herbal medicine
Aloe vera
Aloe vera is well known for its first-aid properties. The mildly antiseptic transparent gel inside the fleshy leaves is used to treat a range of skin disorders:

* Burns and sunburn
* Bruises
* Insect bites

Apply directly to the skin after treating with cold water.
It can be taken internally for:

- Colitis
- Peptic ulcers

Two teaspoons mixed with fruit juice, up to twice daily. Do not take for any complaint of which diarrhoea is a symptom.

Aloe vera in cosmetics
Helps reduce excessive oil in the skin and on the hair.

Anaemia
Anaemia is characterised by a reduction in the number of red blood cells. Symptoms vary between tiredness, pale skin and a general feeling of being out of sorts. The body has become deficient in vitamins B12, B6, folic acid and iron. Vitamin C is essential so that the iron may be absorbed. Preventing anaemia is vital in pregnancy.

Necessary vitamins are found in:
- Leafy green vegetables
- Eggs
- Lean red meat
- Shellfish
- Whole grains
- Yeast

Herbs
Plants have powerful healing properties. Herbs contain active chemical constituents. Each herb is treated in a different manner and may be taken in different forms.

The most common forms are:
- **Liquid extracts** – This is a highly concentrated form of the herb formed by a process of evaporation under high pressure.
- **Infusions** – Infusions are made by pouring boiling water over a dried form of the herb and letting it stand, then draining the liquid off.
- **Decoction** – Decoction is made by boiling the herb, cooling the mixture and then straining it.
- **Percolation** – Percolation is where the soluble matter of the plant is strained off through repeated movement of boiling water.
- **Tinctures** – Tinctures are made with spirits where the herb cannot be heated.

Poultices
A poultice helps to treat and make a boil disappear. To make a poultice:

- Mix the herb that you need to use with cornflour.
- Stir it to a paste with apple cider vinegar.
- Place a plate over a pot of boiling water.
- Place a piece of muslin on the plate and cover half of it with the poultice mixture.
- Fold the remaining muslin over it.
- Place another plate over the top of this and allow to steam.
- Apply to the area as hot as is bearable.
- Cover with plastic wrap and secure.
- Leave overnight.
- Repeat process in the morning.

Continue this treatment until the boil has broken or healed.

Compresses

Compresses are excellent for speeding up the healing of wounds. To make a compress:
- Boil 50g of required herb in half litre water.
- Strain and soak bandage in the mixture.
- While it is still hot apply to affected area.

It is a good idea to have two compresses going at once – one on the wound and the other in the pot.

Herbal baths

- Use two litres of herbal infusion in the hot bath.
- Soak for no more than ten minutes.
- Shower after you have finished treatment.

Douches

- Use only mild herbs and make a fresh mixture every day.
- Boil and strain through coffee filter paper.
- Add apple cider vinegar to douche.
- Lie in the bath, insert the douche.
- Turn on the tap to flood the vagina.
- Repeat until all fluid has gone.
- Pregnant or post-natal women should never use a douche.

Herbal teas

Herbal teas are therapeutic and a pleasant substitute for tea and coffee. Use either fresh herbs or tea bags. Do not add milk.

Aromatherapy

Aromatherapy is the use of natural oils – variously as rubs, rinses, massages, applications and gargles – for therapeutic purposes. As well as the natural healing powers of the oil, the aroma provides a pleasant sensation, which can be variously uplifting, energising, calming or relaxing.

Pregnant women should only use lavender oil.

Some health uses for oils

Acne – Tea tree, lavender, sandalwood, eucalyptus applied on the skin.

Antiseptic – Dilute eucalyptus, tea tree, rosemary, pine or lavender oil in water.

Bad breath – Gargle lavender, tea tree, peppermint or parsley oil in water.

Concentration – Apply peppermint oil to the temples.

Deodorant – Rub sandalwood into the armpits.

Hair – Rinse with diluted rosemary oil.

Headache – Rub lavender or rose oil into the temples.

Herpes – Dilute eucalyptus, tea tree or thyme in water and apply to affected area.

Insect repellent – Apply citronella or lavender oil directly to the skin.

Relaxation – Spray lavender, neroli or rose oil.

Thrush – Make a bum bath of ten drops of eucalyptus, tea tree or lavender oil and water and sit in it twice a day.

Varicose veins – Mix two drops of geranium and two drops of cypress in two tablespoons carrier oil and gently massage the area.

Rheumatism – Dilute eucalyptus, pine, thyme or wintergreen one part to twenty with a carrier oil, and massage into area.

Menstruation – two drops cypress, geranium or clary sage into ten drops carrier oil and massage tummy.

The effects of travelling
Bali Belly

There's a variety of names for traveller's diarrhoea – Montezuma's Revenge, Delhi Belly, Bali Belly, or the Kathmandu Trot. But you can get it anywhere, depending on your response and reaction to different diet, the impact of fatigue, the way local food is prepared, and so on.

Bacteria is preventing you absorbing the water that you take on board in food and fluid – and it has to come out somewhere!

Not everyone gets it. Sometimes the most cautious of people, who have it at the forefront of their minds and take all the necessary precautions get it – yet others who never even think about it, stroll in unaware and eat the local food, don't!

Nevertheless, in terms of prevention, there are things to consider:
- Avoid uncooked vegetables, uncooked raw meat, ice cubes, raw shellfish, and fruits you can't peel.
- Drink only water that you know has been boiled for three to five minutes, or bottled/canned water.
- Use bottled/canned water for personal hygiene such as cleaning your teeth. The less likelihood of ingesting local water – even when showering – the better.
- Orange juice, and even acidic drinks such as cola, are good for keeping the bad bugs at bay.
- Where possible use only dishes and cutlery that have been cleaned in boiled or purified water.
- Drink plenty of water. You risk dehydration, which could make matters worse. Make sure it is purified water.

Rehydrating is essential. Try an oral rehydration solution, ORS, which contains the sugars and salts that you have been so rapidly losing. This can be bought at a pharmacist, or you can make up this one:
- Glass of fruit juice, teaspoon of honey, pinch of salt.
- Glass of purified water, half teaspoon baking soda.
- Take alternative swallows from each until finished.

Remember:
- The more yellow your urine, the more fluid you need.
- Alcohol only dehydrates you and makes matters worse.
- Avoid milk products and solid stodgy foods.

Opium-based anti-diarrhoea products and some antibiotics will help the situation, depending on availability.

Taking natural laxatives at this stage, such as Metamucil, might sound crazy, but in fact they also help with diarrhoea.

Fight fire with fire and take a yoghurt drink such as Yakult. It contains lactobacillus bacteria which will knock out the bad micro-organisms that are causing you grief.

Deep vein thrombosis

When travelling or sitting for long periods, there is a risk that you may develop deep vein thrombosis, or DVT as it is becoming popularly known. A clot can form, particularly in the lower limbs, which can be dangerous and if left unchecked, fatal.

Your risk of getting DVT is increased:
- If you have suffered from DVT before.
- If you have recently undergone surgery.
- You have been in bed for a prolonged period prior to travelling.
- If you are an older person who is prone to blood clots.

Before you travel
- Take an aspirin a day for the previous week to thin your blood.
- Get up and walk around the cabin of the plane every hour.
- Exercise your legs and feet by stretching while you are sitting.
- Wear support stockings for the journey.

Jet lag
Jet lag can be debilitating, especially after a long flight. Here are some suggestions to reduce its effects:

- Minimise jet lag by changing your body clock before you travel.
- Keep a routine in your life and don't party right up until the last minute before you get on the plane.
- Make sure you have plenty of sleep before you go.
- Try to arrange your flight so that you fly by day and arrive in the evening. You can then have a light meal and go to bed.
- Change your caffeine intake so that you are only drinking it when it is morning at your destination.
- A couple of days before set a watch to the time of your destination and remain mentally active in the time immediately preceding breakfast time at your destination.
- By-pass meals on the aeroplane and eat the next meal that the locals are eating when you arrive at your destination. Adapt to your new environment as quickly as possible.
- Try not to sleep until evening at your destination.
- If you wake up in the middle of the night, relax and remember that a sleepless rest is better than a restless sleep.
- Avoid alcohol on the flight but keep up your fluid intake.
- If you are feeling tired in the middle of the afternoon, socialise. Other people keep you awake.
- Get some sunshine and help your body realise that your biological clock is out of wack.
- Exercise at your destination, out in the sunshine if possible.

Motion sickness
Travel sickness is a result of the over-stimulation of the canals of the inner ear which regulate the body's balance system. There is an imbalance between the inner ear and sight, and the terrible feeling of queasiness comes on when the body gets the wrong messages about the environment. Children are more susceptible to motion sickness than adults. It is more likely to occur in an enclosed space. Once you begin to be nauseous it is very difficult to stop motion sickness taking over.

There are some things that you can do to prevent it from getting to that stage:

- Before travelling take an over-the-counter medication for travel illness.
- Stay in the fresh air, as odours can bring motion sickness on.
    - At sea, get up onto the deck.
    - In a bus or car, open the window.
    - In an aeroplane, keep the ventilator on full.
- Think positive. Motion sickness can be psychological.
- Ignore those who are being sick around you.
- Don't smoke, as cigarette smoke will only aggravate the situation.
- Travel at night.
- Be careful of what you eat. Avoid alcohol, rich foods, tobacco.
- Suck on an olive or a lemon.
- Nibble on a dry biscuit.
- Take a bottle of ginger ale, or a flask of ginger tea, with you and sip on it regularly. Ginger settles the stomach.

- Do not read.
- Focus your eyes on an object around or in front of you.
- Sit still.
- If possible, you be the driver.

Did you know?
Always remember . . .
God made wrinkles to show where the smiles have been.

Always remember . . .
You don't stop laughing because you grow old; you grow old because you stop laughing.

Astrology
Your star's key phrase
Each star sign has a key phrase, which is very representative of the person's attitude and approach to life. The key phrases are:

Aries: 'I am.'
Taurus: 'I have.'
Gemini: 'I think.'
Cancer: 'I feel.'
Leo: 'I will.'
Virgo: 'I analyse.'
Libra: 'I balance.'
Scorpio: 'I create.'
Sagittarius: 'I perceive.'
Capricorn: 'I use.'
Aquarius: 'I know.'
Pisces: 'I believe.'

Belly buttons
No two belly buttons are the same. The belly button, or navel, is the scar left after the umbilical cord drops off. Sometimes it is a pop-out version, and sometimes it is inverted, but they are all individual.

Beware of too much exercise
For every minute you exercise, you add one minute to your life. This allows you to spend extra quality time laying around in a nursing home . . .

I joined a gym last year. It cost me $500 and I haven't lost an ounce. Apparently you have to turn up . . . !

I think I may take up exercise just so that I can hear heavy breathing . . .

My grandmother began walking five km a day when she was sixty-five. She's ninety-seven now, but we don't know where the hell she is . . .

I like to exercise early in the morning so I get it over and done with before my brain realises what I am doing . . .

Brain power
The human brain produces enough electricity to power a toy train.

Breakfast cereal
In 1894, Will Kellogg boiled wheat and fed it through a roller. He then baked it to create thin and tasty wheat flakes, a new product was born, and the world has never been the same since.

Crocodile tears
Crocodile tears, that is, tears or crying that is only put on for show, are well named. Crocodiles do cry. And so do elephants and seals. But they only do it to remove the salt from their eyes.

Can you say 'R'?
With the increasing emphasis on the ability to speak English, many Chinese are having the fraenum or the flap of tissue under the tongue snipped so that they are able to say 'r'.

Did you know . . . ?
The British Journal of Plastic Surgeons has warned enthusiastic male suitors to beware the fumbling finger that can end up damaged in the endeavour to remove the bra of a loved one. 'It can be a nasty injury,' warn the surgeons, 'one that is more commonly associated with rock climbing.'

Diet advice
If you're thin, don't eat fast.
If you're fat, don't eat – fast.

Famous last words
'Don't pull down the blinds. I feel fine. I want the sunshine to greet me.'
— Rudolph Valentino.

'I've had eighteen straight whiskies. I think that is a record.'
— Dylan Thomas.

'Nothing but death.'
Jane Austen when asked if there was anything that she required.

'Either that wallpaper goes, or I do.'
– Oscar Wilde.

'Good night, my darlings. I shall see you in the morning.'
– Noel Coward.

'Oh, I am so bored with it all.'
– Winston Churchill.

'Does nobody understand?'
– James Joyce.

It just goes to show . . .
In 1911, Bobby Leech survived a fall over the Niagara Falls in a barrel. Several months later he died after slipping on a banana peel.

Long walks
I like long walks, especially when they are taken by people who annoy me . . .

Middle age
Middle age is when a broad mind and a narrow waist change places.

Organisations
Almost every organisation has four sets of bones:
>   **Wishbones** – they spend their time wishing that somebody else will do it for them.
>   **Jawbones** – they do all the talking and very little else.
>   **Knucklebones** – they knock everything that everyone else does.
>   **Backbones** – they hop in and do the work.

Our body
- The heart beats about 2.8 billion times in the average lifetime.
- It beats about seventy-two times a minute.
- The heart pumps enough blood to fill a petrol tanker each day.
- Our bodies contain twenty-five billion red blood cells and thirty-five billion white blood cells.
- It takes about sixty seconds for blood to make a complete circuit of the body.
- Each cell lives long enough to pass through our bodies 100,000 times.

Painkillers
Men generally tolerate pain better than women, but painkillers work better on women.

Saliva
Human beings produce about a litre of saliva a day.
Cows produce sixty litres a day.

The biggest and the tallest
The heaviest person in medical history was an American, Jon Brower Minnoch.
He weighed 635 kg. He died at age thirty. The tallest man in medical history was American, Robert Pershing Wadlow. He was 2.72 metres tall (8ft 11 inches). He died aged twenty-two years.

The kidneys
The kidneys take the waste products from the blood and regulate the amount of fluid in the body. Our two kidneys filter 1700 litres of blood a day and produce 1.5 litres of urine.

The stomach
Over a seventy-year life span the stomach processes thirty tonnes of food.

Tip of the tongue
The tip of the tongue phenomenon is that feeling we get when our brain knows the thought that it wants to express, but cannot find that right word at the right time.

Wisdom teeth

Wisdom teeth are a third set of molars, developed by prehistoric humans, when food was seldom cooked and much grinding needed to be done by the teeth. They appear in our mouth in our teenage years, and nowadays with much better dental care, it is more a matter of whether they need to be removed if they are causing pain and compacting of the other teeth.

6
Family and Home

Parenting
Parenting is not an easy job
Unlike other jobs, it just gets harder as the children get older, and you become more experienced. The overwhelming majority of parents give their all for their children. We all make mistakes because there is no such thing as a practice run. However, we all do the best we can with what we know at that moment in time. Time and hindsight may prove us wrong. But the secret is to just stick in there and do our best. Read this, and you will feel better.

Sharing the workload
Common sense says that if one person tries to do it all, overload will result. As a household member, everyone has a responsibility for helping with work.

Hire someone to do the job
Pay a household member or someone outside the household to wash windows or clean the garage. Having a cleaning service come in every week may be just what everyone needs to keep the home intact and operating.

Don't do it
Apply the motto 'Less is best', so you have fewer possessions to manage.

Lower standards if health and/or safety are not threatened. If the carpet is not vacuumed or the living room not dusted, chances are no one will notice. Learn to live with comfortable clutter.

Give the job away to other household members
Keys to the successful giving away of a job include:

- Teach the person how to do the job, including short cuts.
- Have the best tools, supplies, and equipment for doing the job.
- Consider what household work a person already does.

Set Friday night or Saturday morning as house cleaning time for everyone. Develop a flexible cleaning schedule so everything eventually gets done. All family members over the age of five are responsible for their own bedrooms. Use shelves instead of cabinets or drawers for storage; it's easier to put something away if you don't have to open a drawer or door. In each room have either all or no carpeting. Decorate with darker colours especially in high traffic areas.

Accept the job as done
If you don't accept the job as done and fix it up, you'll get the job back. Realise others may not meet your standards. But accept that your standards no longer apply. Praise people; let them know their work is appreciated. Don't demand help, but do expect it.

Running a household smoothly
Bedroom
Use quilts or sleeping bags for easier bed-making. Make the bed as soon as you get up.

Bathroom
Wipe the bathroom sink after each use. Clean the tub or shower after you get out of it.

Rugs
Use throw rugs with rubber backs in heavy traffic areas.

Filters
Change filters on the heating/cooling system frequently to cut down on the amount of house dust.

Supplies
Keep multiple sets of cleaning supplies and equipment especially if the house has more than one level.

Multi-task
When supervising baths or homework, do other tasks as well. Clean cabinets, checking supplies, mend, plan events and make lists, iron, wash the dishes, or do personal grooming.

Laundry
- All family members above the age of five should put away their own laundry.
- Have separate baskets coded for whites, colours, darks, towels.
- Locate laundry baskets near the bathroom or the kitchen.
- Put away coats and boots as soon as possible when entering the house.
- Have pegs in the hallway for coats, jackets, scarves and hats.

Ironing
When the ironing has been sorted and done, then each person is responsible for putting his/her clothes away neatly. Ironing can be a chore that is shared around. Make it a more enjoyable task by allowing the person whose ironing duty it is, to have his/her favourite music or television program on while he/she does it.

Make it a rule that all adult members, or anyone over twelve years old, does his/her own ironing.

Food
Develop and use a rotating menu system, which can include complete meals or just main dishes. Photocopy a master shopping list so you just have to check off needed items.

Buy and cook in quantity
Do only one large shopping trip each fortnight or each month for basics and staples.

Breakfast
Prepare quick and easy but nutritious breakfasts only. Let everyone get their own breakfast and put their bowl or plate in the dishwasher or sink.

Food preparation
- Use food preparation and storage equipment to the maximum such as a slow cooker, freezer, microwave, food processor and pressure cooker.
- Prepare as much in advance as possible.
- Prepare lunches for the next day or the next week.
- Cook on the weekends.
- Make double portions and freeze one for another night's dinner.

Dishwashing
Get everyone in the habit of rinsing dishes immediately after use.

Appointments
Group routine medical/dental/haircut appointments for household members, so that you all go together. This cuts down on the running around.

Childcare
Organise back-up childcare before you need it for when the child or primary care giver is ill.

Schedule
Use a master calendar to schedule chauffeuring of family members. If the older family members need to be taken somewhere on a certain date, it is their responsibility to write it on the calendar. This method avoids double booking and the stress that ensues.

Pets
Keep a medical record for family pets.
    Find a pet care alternative for those times when you are away, before you need it.

Shopping
- Save your shopping expeditions until you have multiple tasks to do.
- Run several errands at the same time.
- Carry a list of current sizes for everyone in the household when shopping.
- Buy when you see a bargain or an item that is needed. You will have information at hand.
- Buy an entire season's clothing in one trip.
- Do as much routine shopping (bedding, underwear, footwear, etc.) as possible by telephone or mail.
- Buy duplicates of gifts, cards, etc. Put them away and you will not have to make a special trip for that birthday party your child is invited to.

Stop the panic
Organise an area in the home where backpacks, briefcases, papers, money, etc are always kept. This will avoid that awful early morning panic when everyone is trying to get out of the house and things are lost.

Safe papers
Organise important papers and records in a filing system.
    Be meticulous about putting papers away after you read them and before they get lost.
    Develop a one-touch system, where you only deal with a piece of paper once. Read it, do what is required and either file it or throw it out.

Reminders

Use 'sticky notes' on the bathroom mirror or by the door to remind someone of something they tend to forget. Use magnets to hold notes on metal surfaces. Have a noticeboard in the kitchen near the phone for messages to each other and from other people.

Time wise

Buy alarm clocks and make each person responsible for getting him/herself out of bed on time.

Be rigid and if they don't make it to school or work or an important appointment one day, that is bad luck. They'll soon get out of bed on time.

Of course, this has to be started well before they reach their teenage years, when it still matters to them that they are late for school.

Garden

Simplify landscaping; consolidate several flowerbeds into a large one.
Use low maintenance plantings.

Keep lawn care equipment in topnotch working order.

Car

Schedule the next routine car service appointment each time you pick up the car left for servicing.

Develop a car care calendar for routine service and seasonal maintenance.

Baby
Chinese birthing chart

The Chinese birthing chart claims to be able to predict the sex of your unborn child with 99% accuracy. The chart was buried in a tomb near Beijing for 700 years. The original can be found in the Institute of Science in Beijing. In order to predict the baby's sex, you need to know the month the child was conceived as well as the age the mother will be when she gives birth.

Cradle cap

To help remove 'cradle cap' from a baby's head, mix a paste of bicarbonate soda and water and spread over the affected area. Leave overnight then wash off.

Goodbye odour

When travelling with a baby take a packet of bicarbonate of soda with you. If the baby vomits a sprinkle on the baby's clothes with the bicarbonate of soda will take away the odour when brushed off.

Make your own baby wipes

1 roll of paper towels cut in half, using a non-serrated knife
2 cups of warm water
2 tablespoons of baby wash
2 tablespoons of baby oil
1 airtight container

Place half the roll of paper towels in the container. Mix the last three ingredients. Pour the mixture over paper towels and let stand an hour. Refit the lid and use as needed.

Naming the baby

The baby's name should be associated with pleasantries. The definition should also be meaningful. A baby's name has a strong first impression. Imagine the child using the name not only on the playground, but also as an adult.

Baby name tips

- You will say this name thousands of times.
- You will say it lovingly and in anger.
- You will whisper it when the child is asleep and yell it when dinner is ready.
- Try it out by going to a busy playground and yelling the name across it.
- If you feel uncomfortable yelling it (people may look at you strangely) or if several children answer you, then rethink that name.

Same first letter

Often, first and last names with the same first letter do not sound well together. If the last name ends with a vowel, the first name usually should not. The first name should not end with a syllable that rhymes with the first syllable of the last name.

Rhythm

The baby's name should have a rhythm that is pleasant to the ear. Usually, it sounds better if the number of syllables in the given name and the number of syllables in the family name differ. Say the first, middle and last name several times to test the rhythm. Say the first name and last name together, too.

First and last names

Be conscious of what the first name and last name together say. If your last name is Land, please don't use the first name Scott. If your name is Crapp, don't use Hugh . . .

If you have a common or easy-to-pronounce last name like Smith, Jones, Brown, you might find that an unusual or long first name can complement the last name nicely.

Check the first initial of the first and last names. Do they stand for anything? How about when you include all the middle name? If the initials are not satisfactory, then the first and middle names can be switched. The child can still use the middle name on a day-by-day basis.

Pronunciation

If you use an unusual pronunciation, your child will need to continually correct it.

The same applies to spellings. Don't put your child through the annoyance of having to spell his/her name for the rest of his/her life, for the sake of being different.

Family variations

Check with your parents or grandparents to collect as many family names as possible. You can use the same name, or a variation of the name. It's good to keep up the family tradition, but works well if you modernise it and use a variation. For example:

- Caitlin for Kathleen.
- Tess for Theresa.
- Jack for John.
- Mitchell for Michael.

Outside input?

If you do not want input from anybody else on the final selection, do not announce the name until the baby is born.

Make a rule in the family: 'If you are not pregnant, you cannot claim a name.'

That way, all the family names are up for grabs until there is a baby to be named.

Famous person

One avenue is to name the baby after a famous person.

- It can be somebody that you admire greatly.
- It may be somebody who does something particularly well.
- It may be a figure from history that is universally admired.

When the child is old enough to understand, explain whom you named her/him after. He/she will love to hear the story over and over again.

It is a great feeling to be connected to the past.

Sons/daughters of celebrities

An interesting source of names has been the selection of names because someone famous has used it. For example after soccer star David Beckham and singer/wife Victoria named their first son Brooklyn, it became very popular.

Middle name

The middle baby name can be used to honour a family member when it is not desirable to be used as a first name. It can be a way to settle the name selection between parents. If needed to keep the family happy, the child can be given two middle names. Some families leave the middle name blank, then the child can pick a name later in life. Some families like to use the middle name for naming the child after the mother or father. The child has his/her own first name, yet has mum's or dad's name as the middle name. You can also use the mother's maiden name as the middle name or other family member's last name as the middle name.

Create a new name

You could use the letters of family names to create a new name. You can choose two or more words to create a unique baby name. By separating each word into syllables and combining the syllables, you can create new baby names. You can even scramble a word to create a new baby name.

Instead of using a family name, you can use family geographical location. You may use the name of the church in which you married, the place where you met, the place where you conceived or just a place that you find beautiful.

Another way to find a name is to use a version of a name that relates to a different ethnic group or an ethnic group from which your family derived.

Meanings

Use names that mean other things, like Amy for love, Beau for beautiful, Felicity for happy, etc.

Nickname

You may select a baby name that can have many nicknames and variations. This will enable the child to have more control of his/her name when older. The disadvantage is that childhood nicknames can linger into adulthood and be uncomfortable.

Teething

You have trouble getting them, you have trouble while you have them, and you have trouble getting them out.

By the time baby arrives on the scene all twenty primary teeth are in his/her mouth, ready to sprout. They make their appearance sometime between the ages of about three and ten months. The gums become red and swollen, and the baby will often be irritable and restless. Some babies suffer earache and colds with every tooth that they cut and some will get a nappy rash. If your baby has a temperature, then see a doctor.

Teething is often the cause of unsettled babies and is a great excuse if your baby is grizzly and cantankerous. 'Oh he/she is teething.' You don't need to make any other excuse.

To ease teething troubles for baby

Buy a teething ring and cool it in the refrigerator. It will cool baby's gum when he/she bites on it. Massage baby's gums with your finger. Buy an over-the-counter teething rub to rub on baby's gums.

When does baby begin to eat solids?

About twenty-five years ago, it was commonly recommended that babies be given 'solid' food beginning at six weeks of age or sometimes younger. Today the common recommendation is that babies should receive only breast milk or infant formula until they are at least four to six months old. Reasons for this are several:

- Solid food does not make a baby any more likely to sleep through the night than a diet of only formula or breast milk.
- The nervous system needs to mature so the baby can recognise a spoon, coordinate swallowing, and signal if hungry or full.
- Feeding solids before the baby has these skills is really a kind of force-feeding. Introducing solids too early may contribute to overfeeding and result in food allergies, which can cause gastrointestinal and other problems.
- The biggest concern with feeding solids too early is that the solids will replace breast milk or formula in the baby's diet.

Exactly when solid foods are introduced depends on several factors:
- Babies should be able to sit up and turn their heads away.
- They should be able to communicate that they're not ready for the next spoonful or just not hungry anymore.
- Another factor involves the disappearance of the involuntary action called the extrusion reflex. Before this reflex disappears, feeding solids usually involves putting a spoonful in the mouth and scraping most of it off the baby's face as he or she spits it back out.

First food

The first food recommended is a single-grain, iron-fortified, infant cereal.

Starting with single-grain cereals makes it easier to pinpoint any allergic reactions.

Children
Chewing gum

If chewing gum is tangled in a child's hair use olive oil, peanut butter or cold cream to soften it and make the removal process less painful.

Children's shoes

You should never try to economise on children's shoes as it could result in damaged feet, which will give trouble in later life. Promote healthy feet by encouraging your child to run around barefoot in the summer months. Children love it and you save the wear and tear on shoes.

Cracked plastic

Cracked plastic on children's toys can be mended by heating an old steel knife over a gas flame, and running it over the crack. This melts the plastic and seals the crack.

Gumboots

Sprinkle the inside of children's gumboots with talcum powder. Their feet will slide in without any trouble.

Icy drink

When going on a picnic or barbecue, freeze a large bottle of mixed-up cordial.

Place it in the car fridge with your picnic and it will keep cool, while at the same time, provide a refreshing drink.

Naming pencils

When marking children's pencils with their names, use a potato peeler instead of a knife to remove the outer layer.

Safe play area

A bed sheet provides a clean play area on a motel room floor or outdoors when travelling.

Safe sleeping

Put pillows on the edges of the bed (under the mattress; atop the box springs) to help keep a toddler from falling off the bed while sleeping.

Scuffs on shoes

A little raw egg white rubbed on the toes of children's shoes will conceal scuffs in the leather. Dry and then polish.

Apply clear nail polish over the stitching on children's school shoes. It will stay intact for longer.

Seat belts

Tired of nagging your child about buckling up every time you get in the car? Make him or her your family's official Seat Belt Police, the one who checks to make sure everyone is safe and secure before you leave the driveway. Together brainstorm creative ideas for citations and penalties for seat belt slackers.

Splinters

Using a compress of baby oil or olive oil on a splinter will make it slide out easily.

Sticking on Band-aids

To avoid bandages sticking, rub baby oil or olive oil all over the bandage and it will come off more easily.

Wet bike seats
On a wet day give plastic sandwich bags to your kids to put on their bike seats while in school.

Wet cloth storage
A sandwich bag or small baby food jar in purse or car provides a place to keep a wet cloth.

Which foot?
To teach your youngster which foot goes into which shoe or slipper, simply paint a toenail on the right foot with red nail polish and put a dab of the same on the right shoe.

Children's parties
Children's birthday parties will change as the years go by and the child matures. They will vary depending upon the interests and personality of individual children. Some children will be more than happy to entertain the same group of friends with a similar type of party every year. Our youngest has a summer birthday, and so has had a pool party every year from when she was five. There are two or three guests who have enjoyed all ten parties and they never tire of the musical beach towel game that *must* be played every year. (It's played like musical chairs except instead of chairs we place beach towels on the ground for the children to dance around.) Our daughter's birthday party has become a tradition in our neighbourhood, and it probably won't stop until she and her friends split up to go to college or university.

On the other hand, the more adventurous type is always on the lookout for a different type of party, and will stretch his/her parent's imaginations in their attempt to conduct one for him/her.

Keeping children's birthday parties safe and happy
* Restrict the party proceedings to a contained area so that it can be supervised adequately.
* Make sure that you have enough adults on hand to always have somebody with the children.
* Keep the numbers manageable.
* Keep electrical appliances and sharp implements up and away from curious little fingers.
* If you need to drive to the party venue, arrange that parents drop off and pick up their own children.
* Make sure that gates are shut so that little people cannot get out onto the road or into the pool area.
* If you are having a pool party have a parent attend with each child.
* When organising a treasure hunt or a game, make sure everyone gets a reward. This will avoid unscheduled tears.
* Banish the dog or cat from the party.
* Don't serve small candies, peanuts, popcorn, or even raisins. Children can pick them off the table and choke on them.
* Put a stop to rough or dangerous play as soon as it starts.
* Have plenty of activities planned to keep the children busy and happy.
* Put a time limit on the length of the party.
* If you remain unstressed, then the kids will be happy.

Birthday party timetable
Three weeks out
- Choose a party theme.
- Create the guest list.
- Pick the party date and time. Parties are generally 1½ to 2½ hours long.

Two weeks out
- Order party supplies, decorations, party favours, activities and prizes for games.
- Send the invitations.
- It is best to ask guests to RSVP to get an estimate of how many children to expect.
- Let siblings invite a special friend over for the day so they won't feel left out.
- They can either play apart from the party or they can be helpers.
- Decide on activities and games to play.
- Plan more games than you expect to use in case you run out of activities before the party is over.
- Plan your menu.
- Arrange for extra help on the party day from friends or relatives.

One week out
- Order a cake from a bakery if you are not baking your own.
- If making your own, bake a cake and freeze it.
- Make any other foods that can be made ahead of time and store foods in the freezer.
- Buy party favours and prizes for games.

Two days before
- Buy remaining food for the party.
- Check batteries for the camera and/or camcorder. Buy film and/or videotape.
- Get an exact guest count.
- Call those who haven't responded.
- Arrange to have balloons for the day of the party.
- It is fun to have each guest go home with a balloon.

On the day before
- Defreeze cake and other foods.
- Finish decorating the cake, or pick up the cake from the bakery.
- Make sure you have plenty of candles and matches.
- Prepare the props, etc. for the games you have planned.
- Childproof the party area.
- Decorate any indoor areas.
- Save outdoor decorating for the day of the party.
- Prepare food that can be made ahead of time.
- Prepare party bags for each guest to take home.

On party day
- Prepare foods and beverages that could not be made ahead of time.
- Finish the decorations.
- Put out the food, have the games prepared, and open the door to the first guest.
- Enjoy celebrating your child's birthday with him/her.
- Remember that parties are supposed to be fun.
- Take plenty of pictures and videos to commemorate this special day.
- Pat yourself on the back when it is all over and be happy that it is twelve months before your child's next birthday.

First birthday parties

This is really a party for you to celebrate getting through the first twelve months unscathed.

- One-year-olds won't remember anything about a party, so you can invite your own friends or family members.
- This party may well be an adults' only affair. That's OK, your baby won't care.
- Plan the event for immediately after baby's sleep time when you know he/she will be happy to be passed from person to person.
- If you plan an adult meal, schedule it during baby's nap or bedtime so you can enjoy yourself too.
- Take plenty of photos to record the event.

Toddlers parties

One-to-threes are happy with a short, simple party. They will enjoy having a few friends present.

- Limit the number of guests to the birthday child's age plus one (e.g. three for a two-year-old's party).
- It's a good idea to ask parents to stay with their child, as separation anxiety can still be an issue with this age group.
- For toddlers, the best time of day is usually mid-afternoon, when kids have napped and are in good moods.
- Avoid lunch times.
- A toddler party needs to be only one hour, and shouldn't go longer than an hour and a half.
- Don't even try to get toddlers to play organised games.
- Instead, plan a simple activity that they can do side by side or even a trip to the park.
- A half hour of play followed by cake and gift opening is all kids want at this stage. Getting a 'party bag' is a highlight for toddlers.
- Make sure that all gifts are identical and that items are safe.
- A cake is essential.
- Keep it simple and stick to basic choices like a plain white cake and milk or apple juice.

Pre-school parties

These are the most exciting and most looked-forward-to birthday parties of all. It is still a good idea to limit the number of guests, but groups of up to eight kids are manageable. Parents need not be invited, but be sure to enlist at least one adult helper.

- If most of the children are in pre-school or kindergarten, schedule the event for the weekend.
- Saturday morning is recommended as it takes advantage of kids' high energy levels and gives the host's parents the rest of the weekend to recover.
- Four- and five-year-olds love mastering the rules of games and dances. Play games like musical chairs/cushions, pin the tail on the donkey, hokey pokey, treasure hunt.
- Have small prizes available for games.
- Make sure that each child wins at least one prize. Children this age like to win something to take home and show mum.
- Cake and ice-cream are what count.
- Kids may enjoy getting involved in decorating individual cup cakes or making their own ice-cream concoctions.
- Simplicity is the key. If you offer a meal, keep it simple. Keep the party simple, the competitive games to a minimum.
- It's possible to have the theme your toddler wants and find creative ways to include older children! When playing games, pair up an older child with a younger one so they work together as a team.

- Most older children enjoy reliving their 'youth' and can really get into the games they remember playing when they were younger.
- Just remind them not to overwhelm the younger child.
- Older children can also be a great asset, assisting the younger ones while making crafts, decorating cookies or helping with any activity you have planned.

Early school years

Your child will want to invite her whole school class, and this is OK as long as you can handle it. Whatever you do, don't exclude only one or two children in the class.

Perhaps you can take a cake or some treats up to the school to share. Otherwise be firm about limiting numbers.

Children of this age love games so make sure there are enough players. Play general party games and games with music. After school is a great time to have your party.

Two to three hours is plenty of time for kids this age. Enlist your child to help in planning activities, as this is a major part of the fun. School-age children love theme parties. Take-home favours are essential. These are little packets of goodies for your guests.

Let the kids take part in the cooking. Cook a sausage sizzle, make individual pizzas or ice-cream sundaes. Anticipation and planning is most of the fun so keep your child as involved as possible. Since at this age children love to be creative in the kitchen, a wonderful party activity is to bake biscuits and have the guests decorate them. Simply set out bowls of coloured icing and an assortment of colourful sprinkles, and let the kids decorate their own biscuit. They will love decorating and then eating their own handiwork!

Late primary years

Peer pressure is beginning to become important. It is best to keep the party small with a few best friends. The amount of time you allot depends on the number of guests and the planned activity. Saturday and Sunday afternoons work best for activities with larger groups, while Friday is the top sleepover night. This is the prime age for sleepovers and a pyjama party with a pizza and video. Children still love a party bag to take home. Stock up on midnight snacks if a sleepover is planned.

Twelve and older

Your teen will most certainly want a weekend evening bash. If plans call for a late night, be sure to discuss curfews and rides home well in advance to avoid conflict. Allow your child to plan the activities, and count on lots of music and dancing. Teenagers enjoy excursions to the cinema, to the football, to an amusement park, the blue light disco, etc. Arrangements for drop-off and pick-ups must be concise.

Food depends upon the occasion and may vary from take away pizza to sit down dinner party. Always have a cake. Parents don't have to be invisible, but avoid being intrusive. Allow them the freedom to have fun without being watched.

Just because they are older doesn't mean your pre-teens and teenagers have grown out of the excitement of receiving favours or a small gift themselves.

Party themes

Choosing a theme will make your child's party special and it will help you to coordinate the birthday party. Use the same theme for:

- The invitations
- The decorations
- The birthday cake
- The games
- The food
- The treats to take home

Once you decide on a theme, let your imagination run wild. If your little one loves rainbows, ask your toddler guests to make rainbows on your sidewalk with chalk! If it's fairies, make a magic tree in the garden for the children to explore. If it's dinosaurs, make the back yard into a dinosaur forest for the day.

Suggestions for party themes

Here are some suggestions for themes that you could consider. However listen to your child and use your imagination as new ideas are always popping up.

Little princess party

A little princess party is great for little girls. Make a castle out of a large box and hide the party girl inside. When everyone has arrived she comes out of the castle and is crowned princess for the day.

Story-book people

Children dress as characters from story-book land. Decorations are story-land.

Colours

Children dress in their favourite colour. Alternatively you could suggest a colour and everyone could come in that colour.

Alphabet

Come as your favourite letter of the alphabet. Decorate the room with letters. Make the food in the shape of the letters.

Teddy bears' picnic

Bring your teddy for a picnic.

Dolls tea party

Bring your dolly for tea and cake.

Pyjama party

Come in your pyjamas with teddy in tow.

Bad taste party

Come in anything that is of bad taste.

Other themes

- Monster party
- Friday the 13th party
- Dinosaur party
- Mask party
- Clown party
- Swimming pool party
- McDonald's party
- Day at the zoo party
- Mini-golf party
- Ice-cream shop party
- Party in the park
- Party at the beach
- Make-up party

Party preparation
Party balloons
Balloons and streamers will brighten up any room and add a festive spirit to a special day!

- Decorate and add colour to your party room by using streamers and balloons.
- Gather different coloured streamers, twist them and attach them to the ceiling in the centre of the room.
- If you have an overhead light fixture, attach your streamers to the fixture and add a small bouquet of balloons.
- Use colourful ribbon to tie the balloons together, and curl the ends of the ribbon.
- If you don't have a light fixture, attach your streamers to the ceiling in the centre of the room, tie a small bunch of balloons together and attach the balloons to the ceiling where your streamers meet.
- You can also use balloons on your mailbox to mark the party spot; arrange them as a decoration at the door; or tie them to your daughter's chair to mark the seat of honour.
- For an extra-special touch, make a balloon arch and anchor the ends to the floor beside the doorway.

Trinkets
Purchase cheap plastic tiaras for the girls to be princesses, and swords and shields for the boys so they could be knights in shining armour.

Make a birthday banner
Purchase a large piece of white butcher paper from your local arts and crafts store.

At the top of the banner, write 'Happy Birthday (your child's name)'. Mount the paper on a wall within easy reach of your guests. You can also lay the paper on the floor if you're worried some of the artists may mistake your wall for their canvas. Provide a variety of crayons and waterproof markers and let the children create their own masterpieces. Don't forget to ask each artist to write their name and age beside their drawing. You can even encourage them to write a special message to the birthday child.

Party games
Always have a few more games ready than you expect to play. You don't have to spend a lot of money to create a special party for your child. Kids love the competition that goes along with playing games that don't require a lot of props. It's a good idea to have other parents, grandparents, or older kids on hand to help supervise the various games and activities.

Treasure hunt
A treasure hunt is always a favourite. Hide little trinkets, gems, pearls, gold coins, lollies, and lots of other fun treasures for an exciting treasure hunt.

Personalised T-shirts
This is a craft activity that both boys and girls will enjoy. Purchase inexpensive T-shirts at a discount or thrift store. Before painting, line the inside of each T-shirt with cardboard or waxed paper, so that colours don't bleed onto the other side of the shirt. Use sponges dipped in fabric paint or fabric pens to decorate the shirts. Lay the shirts in a safe place to dry, and heat-set painted shirts in the dryer if necessary.

Search for the birthday cake

Kids love to hunt for surprises! So on your child's big day, create a special hunt for the birthday cake! You will need the help of a few family members, neighbours, or friends. Let the children separate into teams and give each team a set of clues and party favours to find. Give each child a bag to put his/her favours in, and make sure that each guest has at least one favour so nobody feels left out. The clues and favours should lead them to the location of the cake. The first team to locate the cake gets served first.

Guess the jelly beans

Before the party, fill a jar with jelly beans. Count the jelly beans before you put them into the jar. As your guests arrive, have each one guess how many beans they think are in the jar. Write down each person's guess. At the end of the party, the person who guesses the closest number is the winner and gets to take home the jar of jelly beans.

Jungle knots

This game will make your party guests tumble about with laughter. Instruct your guests to stand in a circle facing inward. To begin, everyone extends his or her right hand into the ring and takes hold of someone else's hand. Then, they do the same with their left hands. The object of the game is to see if they can untangle the 'knot' by stepping over, ducking under people, or turning around. Whatever else happens, they can't let go of hands!

Balloon tennis

This is a fun and easy way to start or end any party! Pass out a large balloon to each guest. Let them blow up their balloon and offer your help tying each one securely. The object of this game is to hit the balloons up into the air and keep them afloat for the longest period of time.

Balloon race

Children stand in two single-file lines, facing forward. Place a balloon between the knees of the first child in each line. When the race starts, the first child on each team turns to face the next person in line. The second child must grasp the balloon with his or her knees and turn to pass it on to the third person, and so on. If the balloon falls to the ground, the team must start over. The first team to successfully pass the balloon down the line, wins!

What's on my back?

Pair up your party guests and put a sticker or a picture of a bug on each child's back. Have the guests try to guess what the bug is by asking questions that can be answered with only 'yes' or 'no'. For example, 'Do I have legs?' 'Can I fly?' and 'Am I Green?'

Ha, ha, ha!

The object of this game is to keep a straight face while the other players try to make you laugh. All players form a circle and one player begins by saying, 'ha'. The next player says, 'ha, ha', followed by the next player who says, 'ha, ha, ha', and so on around the circle with each player adding another 'ha' to the string. Each player must pronounce their 'ha ha' as solemnly as they can, to avoid laughter as long as possible.

Any player who laughs or makes a mistake must drop out of the 'ha ha' circle. However, that player then gets to try to make the remaining players laugh in any way they can (except by touching them or talking). The player who keeps a straight face the longest, wins!

Duck, duck, goose

This classic children's game is perfect for any party. Gather your guests to sit in a circle and let the birthday child begin as the 'Goose'. He/she walks around the circle tapping each child on the head, saying, 'Duck', with each tap. When he/she is ready to choose the next person to be the Goose, he/she says 'Goose' when tapping that person on the head. That child gets up and chases the birthday child around the circle.

If the new Goose does not tag the birthday child before he/she makes it all the way around the circle and sits in the open spot, then the new Goose becomes 'it'. If the new Goose tags the birthday child, then the birthday child remains 'it' for the next round and the game continues.

Roundabout relay

Your guests will jump for joy during this fun relay. Before the party, cut four large shapes out of cardboard. For added fun, make the shapes theme-specific to your party (i.e. flying saucers for an Alien or Star Wars party). At the party, divide your guests into two equal lines and give the first person in each line two of the cardboard shapes. These become the only thing they can step on as they travel from the front of the line, across the room, around a chair and back to the line again. The game begins by having the first child on each team place one cardboard shape on the ground and step on it. Then, they place the other cardboard shape on the ground in front of the first and step on it. Next, they pick up the first cardboard shape and place it on the ground in front of the other, etc. When they reach the finish line, they hand the two cardboard shapes to the next player in line. The team to make it all the way around the course first, wins!

Pin the tail on the donkey

This game can be made theme-specific by pinning any object that is relevant to your party's theme (i.e. for a Pirate party, you can draw a treasure map and have your guests try to pin treasure chests nearest the area where 'X' marks the spot). When it's time to play the game, mount your poster on the wall and place a piece of tape on the back of each object the children will be pinning on the poster. Before each child takes a turn, apply a blindfold, spin him/her around, and point him/her towards the poster. The child who pins their object closest to the designated spot, is the winner! You may want to play this game several times to give your guests more chances to win.

Jelly-eating contest

Make one bowl of jelly for each child (plus have a few extra on hand). Line the bowls along the ground. It's a good idea to place a tablecloth or other protective covering on the ground for easy clean up. Put a cartoon dog's name (Rex, Sally, Spot) on each bowl; it'll make calling the race more fun. Each player places their hands on the ground beside their bowl and must keep them there throughout the game. When the command is given to start, all the contestants begin eating their jelly.

The first one to clean their bowl completely, wins.

Bean bag throw

Purchase bean bags suitable for tossing, or create your own with dried beans, socks and rubber bands. Draw a character (or image) relevant to your theme on the side of a cardboard box. Cut a hole in the box, large enough for the bean bags to be thrown through easily. Place the box about three metres away and give each child several chances to toss the bean bags through the hole. Most through wins the prize. This is a great activity for kids of all ages.

Pass the parcel

This pass-around activity requires a small amount of advance set-up time. You will need a small prize, scissors, tape, wrapping paper and music. First, wrap the prize.

Cut a small piece of wrapping paper and again. Repeat wrapping individual layers around and around. Make enough layers so that each guest has the opportunity to unwrap at least one layer. At the party, seat your guests in a circle, start the music and have the children begin passing the wrapped ball quickly from one person to another. Stop the music. The guest holding the ball removes a layer. Continue until you find the prize. The person who unwraps it last, wins the prize.

Fire-fighters

Divide your partygoers into two teams, and line them up next to each other. Give the first person in each line a small bucket or cup full of water. About ten metres away, place an empty cup or bucket for each team. When you say '*go!*,' the first person runs down to the empty bucket, pours the water from his or her container into the bucket, and races back to their team with their empty container. The next team-mate must then race down to the full bucket and pour the water from the bucket into his or her empty container, and then return it to the next person in line. Your guests will have fun trying to keep as much water as they can in their buckets. The game ends when each team member has run down and back once. The team with the most water in their bucket wins.

Fire alarm relay

Sound the alarm and put on the gear – there's no time to waste! Your fire-fighters will need to dress as fast as possible, run to the blazing fire, attempt to put it out, undress, and return to their team line. Before the party, collect two sets of fire-fighter's clothing – boots, oversized jackets, hats and gloves. Use masking tape to mark the start/finish line on the floor. Put chairs across the room with an empty wrapping paper tube on them. This serves as the location of your fire and the hose to put it out. Divide your fire-fighters into two equal groups and have them stand in two lines. Either you or the birthday child should demonstrate what you want them to do. They will need to put on the fire-fighter's clothing, run to the chair, pick up the hose, run around the chair with the hose spraying the fire, set the hose back on the chair, return to the dressing station, take off the clothes, and go back to their line. The next person in line then repeats all these actions until all team members have taken a turn. The team that completes the relay first, wins!

Blind man's bluff

Blindfold one person who will be the 'it'. (It usually works best to let the birthday child be the first.) Spin the blindfolded player around several times. The other players move around the blindfolded 'it', making car and truck noises. 'It' tries to locate the players. If they are tagged they must sit out of the game. The last person tagged becomes 'it' and the game continues.

Water pistols

This is a game for outdoors. Set up a number of plastic soft drink bottles about three metres from where the kids will be standing. Place a jump rope on the ground to designate where the kids should stand. Give the kids squirt bottles or water pistols and let them try to knock down as many bottles as they can. For younger children, decrease the distance between the bottles and the shooting line.

Bobbing for apples

Purchase a small apple for each child who will be in attendance and tie a string to the stem of each one. Then either hang the apples from a fixture in your home, a tree branch, or a swing set. Be sure that the apples hang low enough so the children can reach them with their mouths. To play the game, the children must try to take a bite out of their apples without using their hands. The children will have a challenging time keeping the apples still long enough to take a bite.

Edible jewellery

You will need at least twenty cm of string for each guest. Choose lollies or sweet cereal with holes in them. Have small bowls to put them in. Fill the small bowls with the lollies or cereal and place them within easy reach of your guests at the party table.

Give each child a length of string, and let them create a necklace, bracelet or anklet. They'll have lots of fun creating their own yummy, edible jewellery!

Cinderella's ball

Your party girls are ready for a magical ball, they just need a little dressing up! Collect dresses, skirts, blouses, scarves, high-heeled shoes, ribbons, shawls, hats, gloves and costume jewellery, to create your own beauty box. Encourage the girls (it won't take much) to make themselves even more beautiful than they already are by donning the clothing and accessories of their choice. If possible, provide a mirror so the girls can admire themselves in the party room, or allow them to use one in a nearby room. Play music to set the mood while the girls dress. Once the girls are elegantly attired, give them the opportunity to dance around to the music.

Find the buried treasure

This is a perfect game for someone who has a sandpit. Hide a number of small toys in a sandbox and let your guests dig through the sand in search of fun treasures.

Balloon wrestling

Before the party, insert a small, lightweight party favour into the opening of a balloon. Inflate the balloon. Have a balloon for each guest. Decorate the party area with the balloons as you normally would. When the party is almost over, give a balloon to each guest. Tell the children that they must pop the balloon by sitting, jumping, kicking it, etc. in order to win the match. They'll love the great surprise they find inside and will have a lot of fun trying to pop the balloon!

Cattle dogs

You will need two brooms, a long string to mark your course, six balloons (and a few extra in case any should pop). Set up an obstacle course in your party area using boxes, chairs, bushes, trees, etc. Mark the path of your obstacle course with string. Divide your party guests into two teams and line up both teams at the starting line. Give the first person in each line a broom and three balloons. (Be sure to use different coloured balloons for each team.) They must use the broom to herd their cattle (balloons) through the course. Each player must herd their balloons through the entire course to complete their turn. The first team to finish the course, wins! If a balloon pops during a player's turn, he or she must take a new balloon to the starting line and begin again.

Indian whispers

Seat your guests in a circle. Help the birthday child think of a message related to your party's theme. The birthday child then whispers the message to the person on their left, and so on. When the message has travelled all the way around the circle, the person on the birthday child's right tells the message out loud. Then the birthday child tells the original message. Expect the unexpected when you hear the final mixed-up message. Try again with another player starting the message and continue until your guests are ready for a new activity.

Fill the bucket

This game can also be played in a sandbox. You will need:

- 2 buckets or bowls of equal size
- One spoon or small shovel for each guest
- A pile of sand next to each bucket (make sure you have enough sand to fill each bucket)

Divide your guests into two teams. Have each team sit around their bucket. When you say 'go', each team must try to fill their bucket with sand, using only their spoons or shovels.

Racing cars

Play this game outdoors, so that you have more room for a racecourse. You don't need cars for this game. The children act as both cars and drivers. Divide your guests into two teams and line them up next to each other. Place an object, or choose a landmark, ten metres away so that each player must drive their car to, go around, and come back. When the game begins, the first person in each line becomes the car and carries the second person on his or her back around the track. When car and driver return to the team, the driver becomes the car for the third person in line, etc. The game continues until every player has 'driven' around the racetrack. The team who finishes first, wins!

Leap frog

This game is best played outside where there's lots of room to leap. Show your guests how to get into a frog position by bending down and dividing their weight evenly between their hands and feet. Instruct the children to form a line and remind them to keep their heads down. The frog at the end of the line begins by placing their hands on the back of the frog in front of them, jumping in the air a little, and sliding their legs around the body of the frog they're leaping over. They continue jumping over all the other frogs in line. The person who is now at the end of the line, does the same thing, and so on, until everyone has jumped through the line several times. Try mixing up the order of the frogs and keep leaping!

Tag

For this popular game, you need to be outside where there's room to run. Let the birthday child be the first 'tagger'. The tagger tries to tag all the other guests. If a player is tagged, he or she must freeze. Players who are not frozen can 'melt' frozen players by touching them. The first player to be frozen three times becomes the next tagger.

Red light-green light

Before the game, lay two lengths of rope, about eight metres apart in your play area to make start and finish lines. The birthday child stands in front of the finish line (they're the Police Officer), while the others stand behind the start line.

The game begins when the Police Officer turns his/her back on the other players and shouts, 'Green Light!' He/she then turns around and counts to five. While the Police Officer is counting, the other players try to run or walk quickly towards the finish line.

When the Police Officer has finished counting to five he/she shouts, 'Red Light!' and turns around quickly. The other players must freeze instantly. If the Police Officer catches anyone moving, that player must return to the starting line. Play continues until one of the participants crosses the line while the Police Officer's back is turned. That player then becomes the Police Officer.

Let's go fishing
You will need a helper for this activity. Tie a string across the room and lay a sheet over it so no one can see what is on the other side. Use an old fishing pole, or make one using a stick and some string. Attach a peg on the end of the fishing pole's string. Let each guest take a turn 'casting' their line over the sheet. Have your helper stand on the other side and attach small gifts, favours or treats to the peg. When they're done, the helper gives a slight tug on the line. When the kids 'reel' in their lines, they'll be delighted to see what they've caught!

Story time
Invite your guests to sit in a circle to hear a wonderful story! While the children listen, you can also have them colour a picture related to your party's theme. This activity will not only keep the children entertained, but it will also help calm everyone down as the party comes to an end.

Toddlers
Little helper
Allowing a toddler to help pack the car when taking trips makes them feel more involved and less apprehensive about long trips.

Games adults can play with pre-schoolers
Cubbies
Make a cubby under the dining room table by hanging some sheets over the side. Make chairs out of cushions and invite the dolls and teddies in to play.

Bath time
Bath time is a good opportunity to play with measuring jugs and spoons and plastic containers. By pouring water from one to another your child is learning all about volume while he/she plays.

Make play dough
Play dough is great fun to play with and very easy to make. Store in an airtight container in the fridge and you will get many plays from the one batch. Make lots of different things and help your child to cut out shapes using plastic forks and biscuit cutters. Use plastic forks and spoons to cut the dough, use scone cutters to make cakes and use the rolling pin to roll it out.

Here's a play dough recipe:
2 drops food colouring
2 cups boiling water
½ cup salt
2 tablespoons oil
3 cups flour

Boil until it forms into a ball. Knead and keep in refrigerator.

Help with housework
Little people can play while you go about your work. They love to help at the clothes-line while you are pegging out the clothes. Begin by asking him/her to pass the pegs. Move on to having them pass the clothes from the basket to be hung. Eventually your child can stand on a garden bench and help to peg.

Play hide-and-seek
You hide while your little one looks for you. Give hints by sneezing or some such. The little one will think it is hilarious. When he/she has found you, then it is your turn to find him/her.

Shopping
Take your child shopping with you at your local shops, and make it a fun, exciting adventure. Before you go make a little list of two or three things for him/her to get. Draw the pictures of the articles as very likely your child can't read yet. When you get to the shops, your little one will search out the items. Give him/her a $5 note to hand to the shopkeeper. Wait for the change and the docket.

Water play
Little ones love to play with water. What better way than the pretence that he/she is helping with the washing up. Fill the sink with warm sudsy water. Place in some unbreakable utensils. Draw up a chair for him/her to stand on. Away she/he goes and will play happily for quite some time.
   Supervision is essential to avoid accidents.

Plant a garden
Plant flowers or seedlings together and then watch them grow. Your child can water the plant each day. See the Gardening chapter in this book, for lots of ideas for children gardening.

Bake
Baking together is great fun. Ice plain manufactured biscuits. Sprinkle with hundreds and thousands.

An animal never before seen
With markers, paper and a vivid imagination, your kids can invent and draw unusual, never-seen-before creatures. First, help them brainstorm for ideas by asking questions about the animal. What is its name? Does it fly or swim? What does it eat? Does it have feathers? Antennae? Twenty-five fingers? Then, have each child draw a picture of his or her creature, being sure to write in the animal's name, habitat and physical characteristics. When the pictures are done, your kids can tape the wild, new zoo on the refrigerator.

Make jelly
It needs lots of stirring and is fun to eat.

Tidy up time
When storing toys, it is much easier to keep them together and in good condition if they are put away after each use. Train your child to pick up after him/herself by making a game of it. Do it to music, see who can put away the most things, suggest that after the toys are put away that you will go on to do such and such that the child likes doing.

Board games

Little kids love to play cards and simple board games with an adult. You'll enjoy it too.

Toys and games

Bubbles

To make bubbles to blow:

2 tablespoons washing powder
1 tablespoon glycerine
1 cup hot water
2 drops food colouring

Mix well and blow with straws.

Dress-up box

A dress-up box is fun to play with and simple to assemble. Put old outdated clothes in a basket. Add some hats and bags from the op shop. Make some simple costumes like fairy outfit, Superman, a Star Trek character.

Finger paints

Sure it's messy, but in the summertime, cleaning off finger paints can be as simple as dashing through the sprinkler. Here's a recipe for washable paints:

2 tablespoons of sugar
½ cup of cornstarch

Mix together in a saucepan. Slowly add two cups of cold water. Cook over low heat for five minutes, stirring constantly until the mixture is a clear, smooth gel. When cool, stir in half a cup of liquid dishwashing soap. Scoop into plastic containers, and stir in food colouring drops or tempera paints. A fun and sensory experience.

Limit toys

It is easier to keep the toys together and tidy if you limit the number of toys that your child has at a time to play with. You will find that each time you bring an old toy out in the rotation system that there will be new excitement about it.

Making a collage

To make a collage:

- Grab a stack of old magazines and mix some home-made glue made from water and flour.
- Cover the table with old newspapers or a plastic garbage bag and let them create some amazing pictures.
- Don't throw away the cardboard tubes from empty rolls.
- Your child can transform them into great puppets by painting or drawing faces on them and by making clothes with scraps of fabric.
- Wool can be stuck on to make hair.
- Use baking paper as tracing paper for re-creating designs and drawings.
- Use used yoghurt containers to store play dough and plasticine to stop it from drying out.
- Take a favourite drawing, add the services of a copy shop, and you'll be amazed at the results.
- Your child's art can be copied, laminated, and cut into all sorts of useful gifts, allowing even the youngest person to create a treasured present.
- Simple designs with clear lines work best.

Toy library
Join a toy library and allow your child to experience the joys of a big variety of toys.

Support for Mum
Don't neglect play groups
They are great therapy for mums. The children play and you get to compare how you are going with other people who are in the same situation as you are.

Local parks
The local park is a great source of fun. And that is where the other mums hang out too. You will most probably get to talk to adults while your child plays. Add variety – have several local parks that you visit.

Local library
Check out the program at the local library. They generally have book reading time for toddlers and pre-schoolers.

Learn to be alone
Incorporate some quiet, wind-down time into the day. It gives your child a rest and you some time out.

Teenager
Adolescence is the time when children stop asking questions and begin questioning answers.

Conflict
Conflict is a part of dealing with teenagers. They continually contest the boundaries – it's scheduled into their biological time-clock – and know exactly how to make you feel bad. Conflict is simply a part of the growing-up process. A certain amount of conflict with your teenager is inevitable.

- Develop selective deafness and withdraw from the conflict.
- Never try to sort things out when emotions run high.
- Keep positive in your relationship with your teenager.
- Establish a pattern, in early adolescence, of having special time with your teenager. It may be going to see a movie with your daughter or stopping off at a fast-food outlet with your son, it may be coffee and cake after school every now and then, or a football match on a Saturday.
- Embrace the role of taxi driver for your child and friends. Even though it is often inconvenient, this is a time when a smart parent finds out much about what is really going on in their child's life.
- Remember that your bargaining power with your adolescent is a good one. You control the money and the taxi service, two things that a teenager values highly. Make full use of this advantage. Set limits that are understood by both of you. Be aware that you should allow enough freedom so that your child can experience independence in a friendly and safe environment.

In the end, always remember that even if we do make mistakes, most parents try to do the best that they are able, with what they know at the time, and in the circumstances that they find themselves.

The teenager's view
'When you demand total and absolute obedience and loyalty from me, you are turning me into a robot and taking away the one thing that makes me, my individuality.

'When you praise and encourage me, you give me dignity and make me try harder to contribute more.

'When you consult me you make me feel useful and valued.

'When you make me a partner in decisions you give me dignity and I will try to live up to it.'

Teenage parties
Ten tips for when the party is at your house
- Keep the numbers to a manageable size. Do not let the word get around that it is an open-house bash.
- Talk to your child. Discuss expectations, concerns, limits, consequences. Agree that you will cooperatively solve problems that arise.
- Establish a starting and an ending time, and make it clear those times will be adhered to.
- Warn your child that it is illegal for an under-aged person to use alcohol or illegal drugs and that you will be enforcing that law.
- Share with other parents your guidelines for behaviour when they call to confirm details regarding the party.
- Make sure that either you or another adult is in the house when the party is to be held. You could ask two or three other parents to keep you company.
- Consider removing your personal supply of wine or beer from the refrigerator, and prescription medications from bathrooms and bedrooms.
- If there is to be more than twenty people, have an adult at the front door to greet guests, check the invitation list, collect heavy coats and backpacks, and generally keep an eye on things.
- If a guest becomes ill while at the party, it is better if you, not your child, handle the situation. Take the guest aside to a quiet, separate place. Call the parents, or have a responsible adult take him or her home.
- Do not hesitate to call parents if any problems arise.

Seven rules for when the party is elsewhere
- Establish a time to be picked up/or to be home.
- Be available so that you or another responsible adult will pick up, no questions asked.
- Be aware of your child's plans: where, with whom, and who's driving (both ways).
- Contact the parents of the party giver.
- Don't be afraid to ask if the parents will be home to supervise and whether there is zero tolerance to alcohol or drugs.
- Do not try to solve controversial issues on the night, when emotions are high. Send your child to bed and wait until the next morning when it will be easier to remain calm and listen.
- You may want to agree on a 'code word' ahead of time, which means, 'Mum, please come get me'. This will make it easy for your child to leave a party if s/he is uncomfortable.

When it is time to fly the nest
Leaving home
This is always a watershed in a parent's life. For twenty years you have been guiding, nurturing, encouraging and paying the bills! And now it is time for your young person to begin their own independent life where you are not central to all that happens.

Trust in what you have produced

This is the time for the testing of your parenting methods. Good parenting is the art of gradually and lovingly moving the child from the intimacy of the womb to the independence of the outside world. This is done over a period of twenty years. It moves the child from being completely and utterly dependent upon you for its every need, to being an adult person who rejoices in life and in life's challenges and who is not relying upon you for emotional or physical support.

The human baby develops from seed to adult:

• In vitro

The embryonic child is totally dependent upon the mother for its every need.

If the mother dies, so, too, does the baby. It cannot exist outside the mother.

• Babyhood

Babyhood is when baby breathes by itself but is dependent upon you for almost everything else. His/her social group includes immediate family.

• Toddler

Toddler time is when the young child begins to learn about the world and to branch out for him/herself. His/her social group increases to include family and significant others. The toddler sometimes spends time away from home and mother.

• Primary school

School days are spent forging new friends and experiencing new things.

The parent's role changes. The child becomes less dependent on the parent for his every need. His/her social group is extended to include peer group and family of peers, teachers and community people. He/she spends considerable time away from home each day.

• Secondary school

While in secondary school the child spends less time at home with the parents and more out in the world discovering life. This is a time of transition from childhood to adulthood and it is also a time for the parent to wean him/herself away from being constantly needed by your child. The parent should be there in the background, encouraging and supporting the child's learning, socialisation and maturation.

The child should be learning to take responsibility for his/her own decisions. It's difficult to step back and allow your loved son/daughter to take risks and make decisions, but that is what must be done. You are there to cushion and council.

• Post-school

When your child moves out of home your relationship will change, and if it is a happy move, you and your child should relate on an adult level. You will always be the parent, but you should now become parent/friend.

Things to do to make the transition easier

• Prepare your child for independence from an early age. Let them take responsibility for their actions and decisions while you are there to help them through. Little children, small consequences.
• Make the teenage years learning and growing years for your child. Enjoy the journey together. Allow them to get out there and do things on their own.
• Even though your child has left home, reassure them that you still love them and that they are still a very important family member.
• Trust that they will survive in the world out there, but be available for support when necessary.

- Don't make the mistake of continuing the mother/servant role once your child has moved out. Let them cook their own meals, do their own washing, clean their own flat.
- Instead, meet for coffee and a chat.

Specialised family care
Caring for a parent or partner with Alzheimer's disease

Being the caregiver for a loved one who has developed Alzheimer's disease (AD) takes a great deal of patience and tolerance. Keeping the person safe is of utmost importance, but on the other hand, he or she should be encouraged to do things independently.

Here are some tips that may be of assistance for caregivers:

- Reduce stress and problems by keeping the person's surroundings and routines familiar, as much as possible. That includes putting a limit on the number of new people in the environment.
- Crowds, unfamiliar faces and noise can be a cause of stress and anxiety and can lead to unusual behaviour.
- If you know what the person liked to do in the past, try to keep their routines as similar as possible.
- Avoid letting them become inactive or overly dependent. Do only those tasks for them that they can't do for themselves. Often they will be able to complete at least part of a task successfully and should be encouraged to do so.
- Avoid asking questions that involve too many choices.
- However, offering two choices can sometimes help to direct the person's behaviour. For example, rather than asking 'Can I brush your teeth now?' you might ask 'Will you brush your teeth, or shall I?'
- Look at the positive, such as activities they can do well, rather than what they can't or can no longer do.
- Especially, do not remind them of what they used to be capable of.
- If the person can't avoid or stop certain unwanted behaviours, try diversion. Say, 'Let's move over here and do x instead.' This is usually much more effective than telling them their behaviour is inappropriate.
- Do not let the person become overtired.
- Include time for amusement and togetherness in the present, even if the person prefers to focus on the past and forgets quickly.
- Avoid baiting, teasing or quarrelling with a person with AD.
- Listen to what they are saying – not just the actual words or content but the emotions behind them. Try to respond accordingly, and avoid arguing with the content of their thought or speech. For example, if the person says she wants to speak to her mother, don't say that her mother is dead.

Rather, say, 'You miss her, don't you? What would you say to her, if she were here?' Then gradually move on to a new topic.

A child with special needs

- Get help and advice right away if you have a concern about your child's development and learning. It may prevent some developmental delays.
- Start by talking to your child's, doctor or teacher.
- Make notes and lists of questions for meetings.
- Bring a friend or relative with you to give support when meeting with doctors and teachers.
- Keep good records of shots, tests, letters from doctors and teachers, and notes from meetings, and put them in a file.

- Learn all you can about your child's special needs.
- Try to learn as much as you can about supports and services that can help you and your child.
- As a parent or caregiver it is important to make sure that your child's education and environment meet his or her special needs.
- Ask for changes if something is not working.
- Imagine goals and dreams for your child and talk about them with others who know your child.
- Your child has special abilities and talents. Use your child's abilities to create a plan to make the dreams come true.
- You know your child best; set goals you believe your child can reach.
- Keep notes of your child's progress.
- Get the support you need by joining a support group, or by talking to other parents, friends or family members you can trust.
- Brothers and sisters of children with special needs require support and attention, too.
- Include your child with special needs in activities with all children, both with and without special needs.
- Gather as much information as you can about programs your community offers children your child's age.
- Be sure to look at your whole child: your child's strengths as well as the areas for which your child needs support and services.
- Do not give up when you know you are right!

Pets
Cats
Which is the cat for you?
Abyssinian
Short-haired. Gentle and affectionate. Shy and reserved. Nervous with children.

Angora
Long-haired. Gentle. Highly strung. Nervous. Loves to swim. Needs daily grooming.

Birman
Long-haired. Placid. Friendly. Affectionate. Demanding. Needs daily grooming. Good with children.

Burmese
Short-haired. Intelligent, affable and adaptable. Affectionate. Loves attention. Good with children. Withdrawn around strangers.

Himalayan
Long-haired. Gentle temperament. Outgoing personality. Very noisy. Needs to be groomed daily.

Persian
Long-haired. Placid and gentle temperament. Not demanding. Quiet and usually well adjusted. Needs daily grooming.

Rex
Short-haired. Intelligent, extrovert, inquisitive. Highly strung. Moody. Noisy. Does not shed hair so may be good for a household where there is a person who is allergic to cats.

Siamese

Short-haired. Sociable and out-going. Becomes strongly attached. Demanding, needs attention and affection. Active and playful. Intelligent but can tend to be neurotic. Miaows in a loud penetrating voice and is not afraid to let you know when he wants something. Can be hard to take. Observe the parents very closely before buying a kitten, as genetics play an important role in this breed of cat.

Tokinese

Short-haired. An affectionate cat. Not as demanding as a Siamese and less dependent than a Burmese. The best of the Siamese and the Burmese breeds, without the eccentricities. Intolerant to milk.

Choosing a kitten

See the whole litter together. Look for a playful and alert kitten. Does the kitten take an interest in you when you approach? A kitten that approaches you first is likely to have a dominant personality. Select this one if you want a strong-willed, independent cat. A kitten that holds back or shies away will need patience and gentleness. You will need to spend time gaining his confidence. This one will not be suitable for young children or for a person who moves houses a lot. Avoid aggressive kittens, as they will grow into aggressive cats.

If a kitten has a pedigree, take it to a vet who will examine it for evidence of inbreeding. Choose a kitten with clear eyes and a shiny coat. Look at the ears and feet for signs of ringworm.

Bringing your kitten home

Collect the kitten when you have time to spend to help him settle in. Shut all windows and doors. Select the area where you want the litter tray and where you want the kitten to eat. Keep these constant. Give the kitten time to explore and get to know his new home. When the kitten relaxes it will begin to groom. This is your cue to offer food.

On the first night, give the kitten a hot water bottle wrapped in an old jumper for warmth, and give him a soft toy to snuggle up against. A ticking alarm clock will add some comfort as it will be like the ticking of his mother's heart beat.

Do not let the kitten out at night. It may be harmed by roving cats. When the kitten has eaten, put him in his litter tray. Praise him when he urinates.

Training your cat

Choose a name for your kitten as soon as possible. Use this name whenever you stroke it, give it food or when you greet it. Use short, simple commands: No, Down, Out.

Use positive reinforcement. Reward good behaviour by petting and a kind word. Never feed a cat after it has misbehaved. Never let the kitten sleep on your bed, bite you or scratch the furniture.

Every time you see the cat engaged in an unwanted activity, use aversion therapy. It could be a water pistol, a rolled-up piece of paper thrown at it, or your car keys dropped loudly on the ground near the kitten. Remember it is best to nip things in the bud before they become innate behaviours.

Diseases transferable from cats to humans
• Roundworms
• Ringworm

Wash your hands after handling your pet.

Does your cat drink from the toilet?

Cats don't like tap water because it is too heavily chlorinated. They search out a place where the water has been standing and is still and the chlorine has evaporated.

Giving your cat a pill

Grab your cat by the scruff of the neck. Tilt its head right up so the bottom jaw is slack. Drag the bottom jaw down and drop the tablet down the cat's throat. If the pill doesn't go straight down, blow gently on your feline's nostrils. Give the throat a downward rub.

Wrap stroppy cats in a towel to perform the above operation.

Clipping the cat's nails

Press down on the cat's pad and the nail will come out of the shaft. Then just trim the hook off the end. Clip the nails, one at a time.

Toilet-training your cat

Cats never soil their own beds. So confine your cat to one small room. The laundry is good. Give him a nice warm bed and a litter tray close by. When the cat is using the litter tray regularly, then expand his horizons gradually.

Cat urine

Never clean up cat urine with ammonia, as a cat will perceive that spot as a toilet spot as cat's urine contains ammonia. Scrub the affected area with methylated spirits.

Litter tray

A cat will be very reluctant to use a litter tray if it is in an open space. Put it in a quiet corner. A closed-in litter tray will stop litter being spilled out everywhere and will give the cat privacy.

Training your kitten

Put the kitten in the litter box immediately after feeding. Hold the front paws and make a digging action. Litter should be cleaned daily. Praise the kitten for correct toilet habits. If you catch the kitten soiling on the floor, use an aversion technique.

Fur balls

Cats usually regurgitate fur balls. Add two teaspoons of butter to the cat food every week to prevent fur balls. If in trouble, give a little olive oil.

Include a tin of sardines in oil on your cat's menu.

Mix one teaspoon paraffin oil to food each week.

Aggression

Cats can learn to manipulate their owners. They must not think that they are leader of the pack. The owner must assert dominance. Only pet the cat when it suits you and ignore the cat if it lashes out. Put it down and leave the room.

Famous cat owners

The Kennedys	'Tom Kitten'
10 Downing Street	'Humphrey'
John Lennon	'Elvis'
Winston Churchill	'Margate, Jock'
Mark Twain	'Beelzebub'
The Johnstones	'Madge', 'Morrie'

Scratching cats

To stop your cat from scratching the furniture, either make or buy a cat tree. A cat tree can be easily made by nailing a log to a piece of board, so that it will stand upright. Cover tightly with left-over carpet.

Cat deterrent

To deter unwanted cats from your garden, mix:

1 whole garlic, crushed
1 tablespoon cayenne pepper
1 teaspoon Tabasco
4 cups water

Let stand overnight. Using a watering can apply to area where needed.

Dogs
Which dog is for you?
Border collie

Active, intelligent dogs with surplus energy and a constant need for mental stimulation. These are working dogs. They are easy to train. If left by themselves for too long they will quickly become bored and start to dig. They have an instinct to herd everything and anything. This breed needs a good lot of exercise and plenty of stimulation. They are not suitable for a small suburban back yard.

Cocker spaniels

Cheerful and loving. Cocker spaniels like a big back yard and plenty of walks. They are easily trained, gentle, protective and devoted to their family. They are great with children and make wonderful companion dogs. They like to travel in cars. The ideal cocker owner would be home most of the day and have plenty of time to spare for grooming and ear maintenance.

Golden retriever

Very good with children. Loyal, easy to please, and a delight to train. They are very tolerant of children and extremely protective of their family. Need regular walking and a good-sized back yard.

Maltese terriers

Lively and alert, they are devoted to their owners. Can be over-protective and snappy. Good dog for flats and townhouses, the elderly and the disabled. They need daily grooming, washing and clipping.

Miniature bull terrier

Generally love people and are intolerant of other animals. They are small and easily handled, but can be cunning and determined. They are curious and lack road sense. They make an ideal house dog. They are too nice to people to be a guard dog. They don't demand too much exercise.

Mongrel

Mongrels need a home and so are popular pets among those who have a soft spot for the underdog. Because they are a mixture of breeds, they are usually very healthy and easy to get along with. Makes an ideal family pet.

Pugs
Friendly, docile and very good with children and old people. They are great to be around. Eye injuries are a worry as the eyes protrude. The wrinkling above the nose needs to be maintained by wiping with a tissue and smearing with Vaseline. They do not have good road sense.

Schnauzer
Alert, intelligent and daring. Excellent with children. Good watchdogs. They are clean and considerate house dogs.

Shih Tzu
Devoted to owner. Determined and arrogant. You must have their respect and cooperation if training is to be successful. Ideal for suburban-sized blocks.

Terrier
Like their Scottish masters they are dour, faithful and fiery if provoked. Bright and alert, they are good watchdogs. Protective of owners and territories. A dog that is unused to children should not be left alone with them.

Bringing your dog home
There are many things to consider before bringing a dog into the household.

- Is the locality where you live suitable to the breed of dog that you wish to have?
- You must be able to provide a big dog with enough exercise.
- Have you the means to keep the dog happy and healthy?
- Are you willing to pick up the dog's bowel motions and take them home with you?
- Terriers are diggers and must be allowed to do a certain amount of digging.
- Consider the conditions that the dog you choose needs to be able to live happily. For example, a bulldog hates the heat, and a long-haired dog in the country will pick up ticks, burrs and mites.
- Can you provide your dog with enough company so that it will not be bored?
- Are you willing and able to train your dog so that it is not a nuisance to you and to others?

Kennel
Make the dog a home. It must be warm, dry, cosy and away from perceived danger. Like Snoopy, all dogs love a vantage point and if a dog can spend a lot of time on top of his kennel he will. Make the roof of the kennel flat so the dog can lie up there.

Chains
Avoid chaining your dog unless absolutely necessary. If you must chain your dog, do so in a humane way. Allow a run whereby the leash is tied to an overhead wire, along which the dog can freely run.

Feeding your dog
One good and satisfactory meal a day is sufficient to keep a dog in good health. The greatest danger to a dog's health is that of constant feeding. Save money by cooking up your own dog food, using a mixture of meat, vegetables and rice. Give your dog a good-sized chewing bone a couple of times a week.

Vary the diet with a combination of dried, canned and fresh foods. Cooked meat is easier to digest, but raw meat is acceptable. Cooked meat kills parasites in the meat.

Add fresh vegetables at least twice a week.

Collie nose

Collie nose is a large scab on the tip of the dog's nose, plus ulcerated nostrils. Keep the dog out of the sun in the middle of the day. Apply sunscreen each day.

Vaccination

An annual booster shot to vaccinate your dog will give you peace of mind and will ensure that your pet has an annual check-up from the vet.

Grooming your dog

A dog's coat is one of the main indicators of his condition. A dog should be groomed regularly. Brush your dog with a wide-toothed comb to remove all the dead undercoat without damage to the animal.

Bathing

Use warm water as the dog won't shake his coat as much. To save shampoo, apply with a kitchen sponge. Use an old lead to tie the dog up during bath time. Experiment with shampoos until you find one that best suits your dog.

Flatulence

Change the dog's diet. Add carbohydrates in the form of rice, pasta or potatoes. Add a couple of charcoal tablets to the evening meal.

Arthritis

If your dog is old and has arthritis give him aspirin. The dosage is ten ml aspirin per kilo of body weight.

Bitches on heat

Spray bedding and areas frequented by a bitch on heat with a deodorising spray. This will reduce odours.

Wounds

Bloodied footprints will tell you that your dog has a cut foot.

- Clean the wound with a hose and remove glass and dirt.
- Bathe the wound gently in warm water and Dettol.
- Dry the wound and apply methylated spirits.
- Place a pad between the toes with cotton wool.
- Bandage the foot with a pressure bandage.

Hydatids

Hydatids is a disease that can be passed from dog to man and is capable of causing death.

- Always wash your hands after handling your dog.
- Never feed your dog raw offal from sheep.
- Dispose of dead sheep properly.
- Treat your dog with a good worm product regularly.

A dose of castor oil will often solve the problem if the dog is out of sorts. Keep your dog wormed.

Training your dog

Rule number one: you are the boss and your dog must know this. You are king. He is servant. Reward good and acceptable behaviour. Punish unacceptable behaviour. You are boss.

Keep commands simple so that the dog understands what it is that you want. Food rewards are a valuable resource when training a dog. Gradually adapt your dog's behaviour by using small and incremental learning tasks. Do not do anything that allows the dog to think that he is your equal. For example, do not feed him scraps from your plate, don't allow him to sleep on the bed with you, make him wait for a command to begin eating. Do not let him go through a door or opening first. Remember, you are the boss, he is a dog.

Symptoms that require treatment by a vet

- Blood in the stool.
- Bleeding from the mouth or rectum.
- Vomiting.
- Diarrhoea that continues unabated.
- Difficulty in breathing.
- Abdominal swelling.
- Any seizure.
- Frequent drinking and urination.
- Difficulty giving birth.

Dog fights

Male and female dogs fight for different reasons.

A male dog's aggression is 'display behaviour' and fights between two male dogs will result in only flesh wounds.

A female dog fights to protect her young or herself and will fight till the death.

Stop that fight

A dog fight usually begins with one dog making an aggressive lunge towards its opponent. Jerking the leash and shouting only adds to the excitement, and will only make matters worse. Distract the dog from its intention to attack by spinning around on the spot and heading in the other direction. In the process bump into your animal, step on its toes and generally confuse him.

Useful hints

Mix vegetable water with your dog's dry food to add vitamins and flavour.

Store bulk dog food in a plastic garbage bin with a lid.

To prevent fleas, rub brewers yeast on your dog's fur.

If your kids are begging for a dog, have them take care of a neighbour's dog for a month to see whether they like the good parts as well as the cleaning up of droppings and the responsibility of regularly taking care of it.

A dog's letter to God

Dear God,

Are there leads in heaven?

When I get to heaven and the saints throw sticks, do I have to retrieve them and place them at their feet?

Are there posties in heaven? If there are, do I have to apologise?

When I get to heaven, am I allowed to sit on your couch?

Or is it the same old story?

When I get up there to the Pearly Gates do I have to sit and shake hands in order to get in?

Can I go out and have fun chasing cars in heaven?

In heaven, do I have to wait for you to come home before the fun starts?

If I go out into the middle of the bush and bark until I am blue in the face, am I still a bad dog?

How come people love to smell roses, but don't like to smell one another?

Where are their priorities?

Are there dogs on other planets? Do they howl at the moon too?

A cat's letter to God

Dear God,

Do you really exist? I don't really care, I'm just curious.

Fish
Keeping a goldfish
Rule for stocking the pond: three cm of body length of fish to every four litres water. Keep cats away from the pond.

Food for your fish
Pellets available from aquariums. Cut up earthworms. Mosquito larvae.

Too much feed contaminates the water, as a fish will only eat the amount of food that it needs.

Healthy fish
A fish that is in good health will swim quickly through the water keeping its balance. The dorsal fin should be in an upright position.

Fish fungus
The most prevalent disease of fish is caused by fungus that affects the tail and the fins. Bath your fish in one part sea-water to five parts fresh water. Never leave the fish in this solution for more than a few hours.

Feathered pets
Budgies
Budgies are colourful pets and may be kept individually inside or in a group in an aviary. If kept individually, ensure they don't get bored by providing playthings in the cage – a mirror, a ladder, a swing.

Scaly face
If your budgie is suffering from 'scaly face', treat it with liquid paraffin. Dip a cotton bud into liquid paraffin and smear it all over the area where you see the scale building up on the bird's skin. Do this weekly until clear.

Canary
A piece of apple a day will keep your canary in good condition.

Cockatoos

Cockatoos are very affectionate birds. They live a long life so often they belong to two or three generations of the one family. They love human contact. They are intelligent and are excellent mimics. If tamed before the age of three months they are very loyal and loving.

Ducks

A duck makes an excellent pet. They will keep the snails and slugs down in the garden. They will provide eggs. They need water and it must be clean. The water needs to be deep enough for them to get their heads right under. This will prevent them developing a condition called 'white eye'.

Hens

A bantam or two wandering about the garden make good pets. They will scratch and forage, aerating the soil. Their droppings make excellent fertiliser. They lay eggs.

Check with your council as some municipalities do not allow them.

If you keep chooks purely for eggs, they should be allowed two laying seasons and then disposed of.

Wild birds

If you like to attract parrots and other wild birds to your garden by feeding them, then bell the cat so as to give them a fighting chance.

Horses

Horses can cost a lot of money if you don't have your own grazing land. Agistment is available, including exercise and training if required. If you do have enough room for a horse, be aware that you may need to provide additional feed during the dry summer months and sometimes through winter. However, a grass-fed horse can be quite low maintenance.

You will need to handle, exercise and groom your horse frequently, and regularly have his hooves filed and shod. Give him (or her) rock salt, and keep him wormed regularly to avoid internal parasites. Keep water troughs clean.

A small horse can be an efficient lawn mower, and horse droppings make excellent fertiliser.

When buying your horse, have a vet do a health check prior to purchase. The vet will provide you with a report to help you make your decision.

Famous horses:

'Silver'	The Lone Ranger
'Marengo'	Napoleon
'Black Bess'	Dick Turpin
'Copenhagen'	Lord Wellington
'Haizum'	The Archangel Gabriel
'Rosinante'	Don Quixote
'Blackie'	Chief Sitting Bull
'Phar Lap'	Australian racehorse preserved in the Melbourne Museum
'Bucephalus'	Alexander the Great
'Trigger'	Hopalong Cassidy
'Champion'	The Phantom

Other furry friends
Guinea pigs
Rabbit food pellets are good food for guinea pigs.

Move the cage around the lawn every three or four days and you will find that they will do the lawn mowing for you.

Ferrets
An old, above-ground swimming pool makes a great place to keep ferrets and they will thrive on the environment. Fill the pool half full with garden soil, making a hill(s) in the middle and allowing the soil to fall away at the sides, so that the ferrets cannot simply step out into the big wide world. It is a good idea to apply a chicken wire cover fifty cm wide around the circumference of the pool to prevent escapes. Sprinkle grass seed over the soil in order to bind it together. Initially pieces of storm water pipe can also be joined together to create tunnels under the soil, but your ferrets will also like to create their own tunnels once they are acclimatised to their new fun park.

A constant supply of fresh water and food is required; if placed in heavy bowls the ferret will not be able to tip them over. Ferrets do well on cat food. In addition chicken wings can be given weekly to help clean teeth. Place a large water dish and feeding station in an area that is easily accessible by you. This will encourage the ferrets to come out to feed so that you will be able to pet and bond with them. Ferrets are playful and love toys. Dog and cat toys, balls and wheels are suitable as long as the ferret cannot bite pieces off them.

Frogs
Raise some tadpoles and have a frog for a pet. Collect tadpoles from a fresh water pond or creek. Take them home and watch them grow. Remember to provide rocks or branches so that young frogs can leave the water when they want to. Tadpoles eat the algae on the lily pad or fish food. Overfeeding causes water pollution. Underfeeding results in cannibalism. Frogs eat insects.

Useful tips
Baths
Dry cornmeal or baking soda can be used as dry shampoos for any furry pet. Rub it in well, and then brush it out. The good news is that your pet will not only be cleaner, but deodorised as well.

Place a bath mat in the tub to help your pet feel sure of his footing and therefore enjoy the bath more.

Using baking soda in the rinse water will help make your pet's coat shinier and softer – plus the deodorising effect will make him smell better.

Natural flea control for pets
Groom your dog daily. Bathe your cat or dog in an anti-flea bath regularly. Keep bedding clean and aired. Use rosemary or mint to ward off the little blighters. Sprinkle the crushed fresh rosemary or mint in the bedding or bunch and hang from the inside of the kennel. Add garlic or brewers yeast to your pet food.

Animal smells
Nilodor or a similar product, sprinkled onto cotton balls and left in unobtrusive spots around the room, will chase smells away.

Matted fur

To avoid leaving gaping holes in the pet's coat, trim the matted hair vertically, not horizontally. De-mat the hair with your fingers while you are grooming your pet. Spray on quick and easy cooking oil and let it stand for a few minutes before you begin the de-matting process.

Ticks

When searching for ticks on your pet, concentrate on the head and neck region. When you find one, dab kerosene on it to make it loosen its grip. Grab the tick with a pair of tweezers as close to the skin as possible and pull. Dab eucalyptus oil on the wound.

Burrs

If your pet comes home with burrs or other tangling plants in his coat, crush the objects with pliers or oil them and they'll be easier to remove.

Pet hair

Remove pet hair from upholstery with a slightly damp cloth or a strip of adhesive tape.

Protect your territory

Placing mothballs under the sofa cushions will discourage your pet from spending any time in your favourite spot.

A slice of raw onion will remind your pet that the place where their 'mistake' occurred is not the place for a repeat calling.

To discourage dogs or cats straying into your garden, crush mothballs to a powder and sprinkle it about in small quantities. They do not like it.

Study

Study is all-important, whether at school, or furthering your education in the workplace. There are ways and means of achieving your goal without too much stress.

- Make boring tasks into a puzzle so that you will enjoy them more.
- Don't try to achieve everything at once.
- Arrange the information that you gather in manageable chunks and then deal with it.
- Simple information is often hidden among a huge pile of words. This makes it appear more difficult than it is.
- Underline key words.
- Then step back and see the meaning in simplified form.

Special place

Have a special place where you study and complete assignments.

- It should be well lit.
- It should have a desk and a good chair.
- There should be access to fresh air.
- You should have all the materials that you need close at hand.
- It should be quiet and away from the hustle and bustle of the house.
- Keep it tidy and well organised.

Never bring other books and magazines into your study zone, as they will only distract you.

Put a 'Do not disturb' sign on the door and study alone. If another person studies with you, the exercise becomes a social activity.

Prioritise so that the important stuff is attended to first.

Give equal time to all your subjects, even those that you like least.

Use a study diary to organise your blocks of time.

Subject files

Make subject files and file all your notes into the correct area the day that you get them. Take notes, do the research required and do the assignments. Then file the notes away so that they are easy to find.

Set realistic targets

Set realistic targets for what you want to achieve in each study session. When you reach that target, take a break, make a phone call, get a snack.

Get organised

Organise your time so that there is time for work and time for play. List the tasks that you will need to do for the week. Put them in order of importance and urgency. Write the expected amount of time that they should take next to each task. List the extracurricular activities that you wish to take part in, and when they occur. Slot them into the timetable for that week, beginning with the urgent tasks. Once you have a homework/study plan, try to stick to it. However, be adaptable and be willing to change if need be.

Correct posture prevents aches

If you spend most of your day in a chair, chances are your posture's not so great. That's because the spine is pulled out of its natural alignment when you sit. Continued bad posture, sitting or standing, can lead to back problems, fatigue and muscle strain, especially around the shoulders and neck. To avoid the sit-and-slouch routine, try out these steps for regular posture checks:

- Sit up straight with your hips, shoulders and ears in alignment.
- Make sure your lower back is touching the chair and your shoulder blades are back.
- Lift your chest.
- Keep your feet flat on the floor, or on an angled footrest.

Just do it

Studying at high school, university, TAFE, or at a mature-age college all comes down to one thing – you have to sit down and do it. There is no easy way out. Here are a few hints and tips that might help.

Study at secondary level

Carry a copy of your timetable with you until you know it by second nature. You'll always be in the right place at the right time, and not exiting strange classrooms looking all red-faced and flustered.

Make friends in every class. Good mates are important so that you can have a happy time at school, and there will always be someone to help you with study queries and homework problems.

Never be afraid to ask for help if you're getting behind because you don't understand something.

Get involved in extra-curricula activities such as music, sport, debating, rock eisteddfod, drama. It means more friends and helps you develop in other areas that could lead to a career.

Don't go looking to embarrass, start a fight with, or upset teachers. It might be fun at the time, but you will rue the consequences, and you will be missing out on the help of the person you need most.

If you believe a teacher is ignoring you, or giving you a hard time unnecessarily, ask for an opportunity to talk it out. Don't keep grudges.

Keep a diary and take it everywhere with you. Write down your homework and the dates when it is due.

Never start homework until you have consulted your diary first and worked out exactly what needs to be done and when.

Don't get caught up in school corridor gossip. It's a waste of time, only hurts other people, and means that inevitably one day you will be the subject yourself.

If you're having a tough time at home or school or socially, find someone you can trust to talk to and help you through it. Talking can make a big difference.

Set realistic goals for what you can achieve in one study session. There's no point attempting several tasks and running out of time for the most important one.

Know how you work best. Whether that is having music in the background, the TV blaring loudly, or total silence. We all have different ways.

Don't shut out the world. Ignorance will only show up in your work. The more exposed you are to other ideas, thoughts and views, the better your material will be.

Find something that intrigues you, or that you appreciate, in every subject.

Give yourself a chance to get into your work. If you find it hard to apply yourself to the task, tell yourself that you will sit at your desk for, say, forty-five minutes. And do it.

If you can't believe in yourself or trust yourself enough to work as you know you should, give your schedule to someone else before you start, and get them to monitor you and check your output at the end.

Join study discussion groups. Being part of a group keeps you working to schedules, and helps when trying to resolve difficult issues, projects, subjects, etc.

Study alone, but phone a fellow-student if you're having trouble with a subject, a concept or question. However, don't spend two hours on the phone talking about sport or nail-polish.

Water! Drink lots of water at regular intervals. It is well established that your body, brain and memory work better when properly hydrated.

Study at tertiary level

Buy all your books well before the year starts. If you don't, then time, lack of finances and inertia will set in, and suddenly the year is almost gone.

Your social life is important, but try to keep expeditions to the pub down to an enjoyable minimum. Might be fun, but many a young undergraduate's star-studded career has disappeared down the bottom of a schooner glass after the first joyous visit to the local hang-out opens up a whole new world.

Go to all lectures and tutorials. The information you need to get through is pretty much handed to you on a plate. May not feel trendy being there all the time, but lectures and tutorials are what it's all about.

Break the ice and make friends. It's often very hard going from a tiny school of a few hundred to a campus of thousands of varying ages and from an extraordinary range of backgrounds. It's easy to get lost, or be surrounded by people and yet be lonely. There are lots more like you, so it only takes a simple 'hello' to find someone similarly looking for friendship and support.

When choosing subjects and courses, pick those in which you have the most interest. You will always get a better result when you can bring passion to your work.

Living on beer, nachos and pizza sounds great, but will bring you undone in the end. Enjoy things in moderation and eat well.

Use the library extensively, not just for your reading list. The extra resources you find there can make the difference between a Pass and a High Distinction.

At lectures and tutorials, be sure your pen works, you have a spare, and you have plenty of paper. Being prepared is vital.

Sharing a flat or house with others is often an economic necessity, and can be exciting after all those years of living at home with Mum and Dad. But it can turn into disaster. Look for like-minded housemates, and establish house rules right from the start.

Make full use of university sports clubs, dramatic societies, political clubs, music groups, counselling services, careers support and so on.

Don't try to write everything the lecturer says. Choose key concepts for headings and make clear points underneath. Use a highlighter.

If lecture notes are distributed, don't waste energy writing down information that's in the notes.

Sit up the front. You can hear better, see better, pick up the nuances more clearly. And your questions are more likely to be answered.

If a lecturer goes to the trouble of writing something on the board or using an overhead or PowerPoint presentation, you can bet it's important – so write it down.

Be sure you can read your own writing. There's really not much point priding yourself on how much you managed to write when you can't read it at revision time.

Prepare for the lecture by doing the required and suggested reading. It's much easier to know what is relevant when you know what the lecturer is talking about.

Taping the lecture is never a substitute for note-taking. Often it can be difficult to hear, and you are repeating the whole process of going through the entire lecture again! Not to mention when the batteries go flat . . .

Don't take notes in pencil. It can be very difficult to read late at night when revising and is more likely to fade over time.

Don't just aim for a Pass. Because that's all you will get. Set your aim high and be happy knowing that you did your best.

Preparing for exams

Get a good night's sleep before the exam – studies show that we operate at our peak capacity with ten hours' sleep. Every hour less than that reduces mental efficiency dramatically.

Know what to expect. Be sure you know the exact structure of the exam and the percentages that will be allocated to each area of study.

Study at the time of day that your exam is set. That way, for example, if your mathematics exam is at 2pm on a Tuesday, your mind will be tuned into mathematics at that time.

Look at past exams that you have done, and work out where you went wrong. Pay plenty of attention to those areas, but don't forget to revise your strengths as well.

Get a friend or family member to ask you questions.

If you have quotes, facts, formulas or equations to remember, devise a rhyme or song so they will stay in your memory bank. If it's a 2½-hour exam, and your maximum study effort has never been more than forty-five minutes, then get used to working hard and uninterrupted at your desk for 2½-hour hours.

Take a positive attitude in. Don't fear it. You know what you know at this point, and you will do the best you can with that knowledge.

Don't panic. Panicking clouds your thinking completely. Breathe deeply, count to ten, and take it one question at a time.

Read all the instructions on the paper. They are there for good reason. The examiners are telling you what it is they want.

Plan your time and stick religiously to that plan. There's no point getting to the end regretting what you didn't get a chance to write.

Take time to plan your answer in an essay question. Underline the key words and make topic headings on scrap paper. Under those, write points. Only then begin your essay.

Memorise that which you're sure you'll forget and write it down on scrap paper as soon as you're allowed to write.

Pay no attention to those writing furiously around you. They might know more than you – then again, they may be writing a load of ill-considered rubbish!

Attempt all questions. There are marks to be gained in every question and examiners are usually looking for reasons to reward rather than penalise.

Try to leave time at the end to read over your answers and resolve any things that are not clear, questions you have not fully finished, or elements that you have missed.

Do as many practice exam papers as possible.

Always go to the final class before the exam. You often get some of the best tips and thinly veiled hints as to what questions are actually likely to be on the paper.

Write your own summaries rather than relying on those given. It will mean you have thoroughly explored the material yourself, committed it to your memory bank, and it should pop out at the exam table.

The last-gasp study surge sounds tempting, and there are legions of stories of students pulling out a great mark allegedly due to cramming. Take those yarns with a grain of salt. Pre-exam, late-night, last-minute cramming probably does more harm than good. It only confirms in your mind what you don't know, and sets you up to go into that exam room bleary-eyed, tired, and unable to concentrate fully.

Coping with it all

Eat properly. When time pressures mount you'll often grab what's easiest. You might crave the instant hit of junk food. Don't. You're only putting more stress on your body.

Plan in advance what needs to be done when, and stick to your schedule. Stress builds in direct correlation to time running out.

Make a little time each week to do something just for you. Walk along the beach, spend an hour in the park, dance like there's no tomorrow.

Schedule regular exercise into your diary. Make it something you like. No point swimming if you hate water. If exercise disgusts you, a brisk walk will do the trick.

Watch TV or feel-good movies occasionally. An afternoon soap of mindless entertainment will take your mind off things for a while, and make you realise that things aren't so bad after all.

Find a mentor who can help you organise a realistic schedule and who will give you that pat on the back that you sometimes won't allow yourself.

Don't worry. Be happy. Be careful not to start fights with your family, friends or housemates because you're feeling stressed. They'll just bite back and then you'll feel worse.

Be realistic about what you can achieve in a set time period. If you schedule in more than is practical you will only add to your stress.

Find a release for your emotions. Something that brings you sheer joy or makes you laugh. Conversely try a sad movie to cry with or a football game to yell at.

Get a planner for your wall. The bigger the better. Put all assignment and exam dates up, and then schedule the work you plan to do for each.

Get up from your desk – stretch your legs, have a drink – every forty-five to sixty minutes. Neck and back problems will creep up on you. They are painful, annoying and often hard to get rid of.

Make sure you are prepared for what it is you will be studying. Be sure to have all the books, notes, etc. with you at your place of study.

Appropriate temperature is very important to effective study. Don't overheat the room, as it will make you sleepy. If it's too cold you won't be able to concentrate.

Try to ensure that you have an area to yourself in which to study, where you won't be interrupted by the activities of others.

Let your friends and family know when you will be studying and ask them not to interrupt you during these hours.

Don't leave research until the last minute – you can guarantee that Murphy's Law will strike and your Internet connection will crash superbly at the critical time, the library books you need are all out (because everybody else is panicking at the last minute, but got in faster than you did), and the research materials you had carefully built up have disappeared. You find them three weeks later under the bed . . .

Physical comfort is essential. Lying in bed is not the answer, as you will fall asleep! But be sure you have a comfortable, ergonomic workspace in which to study.

Practise good time management. When you get an assignment, use your diary to input the dates that research will begin and conclude, the date of first-draft completion and the date of final-draft completion.

Work out if you're a morning person or a night person and study then. There's not much point going against your natural rhythms unless your schedule demands it.

Sewing, knitting and fabrics
Fashions and age
Teenage years

Your teenage years are fun years and are a great time to experiment with clothes and fashions. Young girls are beautiful and can get away with anything. The clothes that you buy are disposable and throw-away fashions. You can change your style by the season and buy your clothes from the factory outlets and department stores. The fashion world is your oyster and it is through experimentation that you will begin to learn what looks good on you and what you feel good in. Go for it.

Twenties

You are now well on the way to developing your own style. You are still young and free enough to experiment with clothes and to wear disposable clothing. However, by now you should be learning to adapt the fashion to your style and body shape, rather than following it slavishly. You should have decided by now what colour suits you.

Thirties

Your style is now well set. Your wardrobe is well coordinated with basic pieces that you can build upon. You stick to three or four colours that you know look great on you. Girly clothes have gone to the op shop and you are beginning to buy classic pieces that will look good for several seasons. You buy quality accessories. You own a little black dress. You own well-cut black pants as well as your jeans.

Forties

You know what suits you and what doesn't. You buy for quality, not quantity. You dress to please yourself and for what makes you feel good about yourself. Buy classic pieces and enjoy them for years. Accessorise well to add a dash of panache.

Fifties

Buy the best cut and quality of outfit that you can afford. Wear only what you know suits you and in the colours that complement your skin. Get down off those high heels, you don't need to fall over and break a hip. Buy swanky high-quality court shoes and matching bags. Base your wardrobe around well-cut pants and skirts and jackets. Don't cover yourself in jewellery; there is nothing that ages you more.

Sixties

There is no reason why people in their sixties, seventies, eighties and nineties can't be stylish. By now you know what you like to wear and what suits you.

- Always wear clothes that make you feel confident, comfortable and stylish.
- Wear good comfortable shoes that fit well so that you will avoid falls, which can be very debilitating at this age.
- Go for classically designed clothes, which will not date.
- Invest in your clothes. Buy the best that you can possibly afford and they will last and always look good.
- Try to keep your wardrobe colour coordinated.
- Choose the colours that you like to wear and buy mix and match items.
- Use one or two basic colours and accessorise.
- As you age and your hair whitens, the pastel colours are very flattering.

Sewing and alterations
Alter clothes to flatter your figure

When wide-leg pants are combined with a boxy jacket, they make the person look blocky. Bought pants that fit 'around' the waist and hips are generally cut for a taller figure and so do not fit the shorter person well. Once the tummy, hip and thigh area are covered by the third layer, the pants can be narrowed considerably and a much slimmer look is the result. If pants are too big and you alter them, a higher crotch line looks better because it has been adjusted for the figure's height.

Darts

After cutting your pattern, clearly mark seams and darts with dressmakers chalk. They are the road maps of sewing and make assembly simple.

Fitting a garment

Although you can do it yourself, it is a good idea to have another person help when you are fitting a garment for yourself. It makes life so much easier.

If you do a lot of sewing, then a dressmakers dummy is a good investment. You will have a replica of your body shape and size always on the ready for fitting.

True dressmakers make a pattern with cheap calico fabric before they move onto the real garment. That way you are able to fit and adjust the pattern. Once you have it right, simply use the calico pattern to make the final garment. That way you will know that you will have it perfect all the time.

Hems

It is false economy to pay somebody to take up a hem. The best way is to sew the hem, but if that is too difficult for you, then you can buy hemming tape. You simply iron the hem up with a hot iron.

When taking up or letting down a hem, always use cotton that is the same colour as the fabric. The stitches won't show through.

Iron

If you are doing any mending or sewing at all, always have the iron heated and at your side ready to use. It makes any sewing job much easier and neater.

Tacking

Tacking is a loose stitch that joins fabric in a quick and easy way. Tack before you sew. It saves many headaches and hours of unpicking.

Mending clothes and materials

Repair a tear in a sheet by placing a sheet of paper under the tear and darning back and forth with the sewing machine. When the sheet is washed the paper dissolves, leaving the tear neatly darned.

When sewing new elastic into a garment, stitch the new end to the old one, and pull in the new elastic as you pull out the old one.

Instead of the thimble, attach a piece of adhesive tape to the finger that is usually pricked. This is much more comfortable.

Use left-over bunny rugs to make cot sheets.

Sew four together and then turn a small hem around them.

Babies will love them.

When sewing on buttons, double the cotton when threading the needle, using four strands instead of two.

Zippers

If a zip fastener becomes stuck, talcum powder liberally sprinkled over the teeth often helps to free it.

Lead pencil is also effective, but take care it doesn't mark your clothes.

Zippers sometimes stick because of fabric from the inside hem folding back into the zip. Try to jiggle it loose rather than cut it.

Knitting tips

To avoid casting off too tightly, change to a larger sized needle when you are casting off.

Reusing wool

To straighten wool before reknitting, roll it around the ironing board, cover with a damp cloth, and iron.

Another way is to roll the wool into balls and put them into the pressure cooker for two minutes.

Storing woollens

Wash woollens before storing. Silverfish are attracted to unwashed garments. For hints on washing and drying woollens, see the Cleaning chapter.

Add a few cakes of unwrapped, highly scented soap in among the woollens to assist in keeping moths and silverfish away.

Powdered sulphur deters silverfish. It is a good idea to take the garments out to air about once every two months.

Furnishings

Patches

Patch holes and worn areas as soon as they appear. Fade the replacement fabric first by exposing it to sunlight. To patch upholstery, cut a piece of matching fabric to the required size. Fold or tuck edges under. Sew the patch in place with tiny stitches.

Cut patches from similar fabric, being careful to match pattern. Iron edges straight. Glue on with craft glue.

Slip covers

Arms of chairs and sofas wear out first. Protect them by making a slip cover to place over the work area.

Cover sofas

Disguise worn-out sofas by covering with large throw overs, or sheets of fabric.
  Make replacement loose covers to go over existing ones.
  Dye existing covers and replace.

Curtains

Boil curtain rings in vinegar to make them bright again.
  Rub soap onto curtain rods to make them run smoothly.
  To lengthen curtains for a longer window, simply add a ruffle to the bottom.
  To keep curtains hanging well, place a coin in each corner at the bottom.
  To prevent sheer curtains from snagging when you put them on the rod, place the finger of a rubber glove over the end of the rod.

Linen

Rotate your linen so that it is all used regularly. If some linen is kept for guests it deteriorates and attracts moths. Duvets/doonas keep longer if they are aired outside on a regular basis. Bed linen can be repaired and recycled. If the middle of the sheet begins to look worn, cut down the middle and rejoin with the worn areas at the sides.
  Patch holes in linen bedding.

Clothes
To make your pantihose last longer

To prevent your new pantihose from snagging when you are putting them on, wear disposable rubber gloves.
  Freeze your pantihose before wearing them. Wet, wring and place in a plastic bag in the freezer. Remove, dry and wear.
  Buy two pairs of pantihose at a time – same colour and texture, and then mix and match legs if one runs.
  Use hairspray on the heels and toes of pantihose to reinforce them.
  Add one teaspoon vinegar to the rinse water to help pantihose retain elasticity.
  If hanging pantihose on the clothes-line, put a spoon in each toe to stop them blowing up over the line and snagging.

Men's clothes
Suits

It is best to own at least two suits so that they can be worn on alternate days.
  After wearing, remove suit and hang in the steam of the bathroom. This will ease out the creases. Allow to air before hanging in wardrobe.

Extra trousers

An extra pair of trousers is a good idea. The trousers wear out before the jacket. Purchase an extra pair when you buy your suit. Use clip hangers for trousers.

Shiny suit

A suit that has become shiny in parts, can often be restored. Wring a cloth out in water. Add a dash of brown vinegar to the cloth. Sponge the shiny area. Press with a warm iron, using a brown paper bag to protect fabric.

Shirts

Shirts can be restored by the application of bias binding or ribbon around the collar.

If the collar is worn, simply remove and sew back on inside out. You will get twice the wear. The same can be done for cuffs.

If a white business shirt has lost its brightness, simply dye another colour. Lots more wear to be had here.

When major stores have their sales, they almost always include top brand business shirts in their stock. Keep an eye out for business shirts on sale. Buy as many as you can afford then, and save heaps.

Shoes and leather

Never leave wet shoes next to a fire or radiator. Direct heat dries out the leather. Pack them with newspaper that will absorb the moisture at the same time keeping the shoes in shape.

Avoid storing shoes in plastic bags. They sweat and can become mouldy.

To store leather shoes, handbags or boots:

Ensure they are clean. Rub with a dry brush to get dirt and dry grit from the seams.

Don't forget underneath the heel. Apply methylated spirits to both the upper and the sole. Dry thoroughly. Apply liquid paraffin, which is obtainable from chemists or hardware stores. Leave twenty-four hours. Rub with a soft cloth. Polish.

Cracks in white leather

For cracks in white leather, touch up with a dab of typist's white correction fluid.

Shoes made from denim

Shoes made from denim, or similar material, can be washed or scrubbed with a wool mix or detergent.

Black marks on shoes

Black marks on shoes can be sponged off with kerosene on a soft cloth.
You can also try rubbing marks off with an eraser.

Suede shoes

Use a good powder carpet cleaner. Rub the powder into the shoes with the palms of the hands. Brush off with a soft cloth.

Smelly shoes

Sprinkle with specially formulated foot powder that can be bought from chemists. Leave overnight. Shake the powder out lightly next wear.

Here are two more recipes for treating smelly shoes:
Mix 2 tablespoons powdered Borax
1 tablespoon bicarbonate of soda
3 drops Nilodor

Divide the powder mixture onto two pieces of tissue paper. Lightly roll the tissue and push into the toe of each shoe.

Sift together:
2 cups of bicarbonate of soda
4 dessertspoons of talcum powder
4 tablespoons of powdered Borax

Add:
20 drops lavender oil
20 drops lemon oil
10 drops cinnamon
10 drops pine oil

Stir and store in a glass jar with a lid. Sprinkle into shoes about three times weekly.

Shopping for bedding
Bedding is best shopped for in person, as the quality checks need to be hands-on.

Sheets
Hold up a sheet to the light to determine its quality. Light will not shine through a high-quality thread-count sheet. Higher-quality thread-count sheets will not fuzz or pill.

Scratch the sheet with your fingernail to see if any pill comes off. If it does, this is a lesser-quality sheet.

Purchase a full flat sheet to use instead of a queen flat sheet on your bed. Not only is a full sheet less expensive, but there's much less material hanging over the edge when you make the bed.

When purchasing flannel sheets, make sure that the label says 'pre-shrunk'. Otherwise the flannel will probably shrink, causing your fitted sheet to no longer fit.

Cotton sheets are described by thread count. This means the number of threads in the cloth. Most sheets are in the 200 range. Expensive sheets can go from 250 to more than 300. The higher the thread count, the softer and more durable they will be.

Blankets
For the summer months, purchase easy-care cotton or thermal blankets. These will allow air to flow through them.

The finest-quality wool blankets that can be purchased are merino wool. They are also the warmest. Synthetic blankets, however, are non-allergenic, less expensive and easier to wash.

Doonas
With doonas it's not the weight that is important, it's the fill power of the down. Fill power is a measurement of the quality of down products. Down comforters with great 'loft' (fill power) have 'fluffy' clusters of down that have the power to fill the comforter with less grams than inferior types of down. Down comforters with higher fill power listed on the package are lighter and warmer than down comforters, where there is less fill power or the fill power is not stated at all.

Mattress
If you want to give your current mattress a 'pillow-top' look and feel, buy either a feather doona or a polyester fibre doona. They're soft and luxurious and give your bed that 'lofty' look. It's also less expensive than buying a new mattress.

Modern mattresses

When purchasing a new mattress with a pillow top, it's important to buy fitted sheets that are deep enough so they don't 'pop off'. Deep fitted sheets run anywhere from 32 to 55 cm depending on how 'thick' your new mattress is. If you own some wonderful sheets, which you have bought prior to purchasing your deeper mattress and you want to continue using them, buy 'suspenders' for the fitted sheet. This will keep it from popping off. Flat sheets will fit standard or deeper mattresses.

When buying a new mattress, it is advisable to take your partner and to go to a bedding shop and to lie on a few beds to try them out. You will be surprised at the differences.

Care of the mattress

Turn your mattress regularly. You should turn it over and flip it sideways so that all corners are in a different place.

Every now and then vacuum your mattress. This will remove the dust and dust mites.

If your mattress becomes stained, attend to it immediately. Soak up the excess moisture with paper towel. Gently sponge with warm water and vinegar. Put in the sun to dry.

An old mattress that doesn't give proper support can be responsible for sore backs and knobbly knees. A good mattress equals a good night's sleep.

Pillows

Pillows are such a personal thing. Some like them high, some like them low, some like them soft, others hard. They come in many shapes and sizes. Some people carry their pillow around the world with them and others can sleep on their rolled-up jumper. Once you have found a pillow that suits you, take note of its brand and stick with it.

When filling a decorative pillow case, always buy an inexpensive queen-size pillow.

It fills the pillowcase completely right out to the corners. This will give your bed the beautiful full look.

Handy hints and tips
A new broom

To give a new broom longer life, soak it in hot salted water.

Annoying neighbours

You have a problem with something that your neighbour is doing? Here are some simple rules on how to solve it without ill will:

- Choose the right time to speak to your neighbour about the problem.
- Attack the problem, not the person.
- Indicate the extent of the problem and how it affects you.
- Approach it as a mutual problem that you both can work on.
- Look first for solutions that you have control over before making demands of the other person.
- Be prepared to compromise.

Bag store

Store plastic carry bags in empty tissue boxes.

Card system

- Keep a card system of names and addresses.
- It is easy to change when addresses change.

- Use a recipe box and file names alphabetically.
- You may recycle card from pantihose packets etc.

Eyeglasses screws
Apply clear nail-polish to the screws on your eyeglasses to keep them in place.

Get-well cards
When posting a get-well card to a person in hospital, use the patient's home address instead of your return address.

If the patient is released from hospital before the card arrives it will be sent to their home.

Kitchen glasses
If kitchen glasses stick together when stacked, fill the top glass with cold water and put the bottom glass in hot water.

Lining cupboards
Use left-over wallpaper to line shelves and cupboards.

Paste postcards on a sheet of paper, have it laminated and line shelves with it.

Old pantihose
- Store onions in the legs of old pantihose.
- Store bulbs that have finished blooming.
- Store bulbs of garlic, tie end and hang in a dry place.
- Use the elastic tops from old pantihose to keep lids on big boxes, packages etc.
- Make a strong and flexible yarn for sewing on children's buttons by cutting a thin strip around the pantihose and threading onto a darning needle.
- Wash old pantihose and use them to stuff cushions and toys. They are easy to wash and they dry quickly.
- Strain paint with old pantihose.
- Tie plants to stakes using old pantihose.
- In an emergency a pair of pantihose may substitute for a fan belt on the car.

Outside tables
When eating outside secure the tablecloth at each corner with a peg to stop it blowing around.

Peg bags shut
Use a peg to clip shut chip and nut bags to keep the contents fresh.

Rubbish
Rinse out empty milk containers and use as mini-waste bins on your sink.
Use plastic garbage bags as bin liners.

Storage of magazines
Make a storage system for magazines and recipes by cutting the top off detergent boxes at an angle, covering with coloured paper and contact and storing them together on a shelf.

Storing important papers

When going away for a period of time store important papers in the freezer of refrigerator. In case of a fire they will survive.

Wake-up tip

If you set your alarm clock on a tin plate it will make enough din to wake the dead.

Wrapping gifts

Use wallpaper ends to wrap presents, cheaper and prettier.

Wrap wedding and kitchen tea presents in tea towels. Wrap baby gifts in a bunny rug. Other gifts in T-shirts, scarves, table napkins. Decorate with hair ribbons, balloons and dried flowers.

Use recycled sheets, towels and skirts to make drawstring gift bags.

Health
Living with arthritis

If arthritis makes it difficult for you to hold a pen, push the pen through a small rubber ball.

Barbeque tongs make an ideal pincher to pick things up.

To loosen bottle tops and jar lids, use a nutcracker.

Patron Saints

St Louis	Barbers
St Joseph	Wine growers
St Anthony	Lost things
St Jude	The hopeless
St Brendan	Fishermen
St Ambrose	Beekeepers
St Gabriel	Broadcasters
St Giles	Horses
St Cecilia	Singers
St Stephen	Bricklayers
St George	Syphilis sufferers
St Venerius	Lighthouse keepers
St Mary Magdalene	Sinners

Gambling

People who gamble responsibly . . .

- Expect to lose.
- Think of the money lost as money spent for an evening's entertainment.
- Consider that if they are lucky enough to win something, that's a bonus.
- Decide how much they can afford to lose.
- Set a limit before they go and don't let anyone or anything persuade them to go beyond it.
- Know exactly how long they are going to stay out gambling.
- Leave when the time is up.

- Don't stay because they are winning or because they are losing and feel certain the tide will soon turn in their favour.
- Never borrow to gamble.
- Have a balanced life, with activities besides gambling and friends apart from those met while gambling.
- Don't use gambling as a way to escape discomfort or difficulties.

When gambling is a problem

A preoccupation with gambling doesn't occur suddenly, but develops over time.
Here are some of the signs:

- Is the person going to the casino or bingo hall more frequently, spending longer periods there, and betting larger sums?
- Does he only talk about how much he has won, and never about losing?
- Does he try to hide or avoid talking about the losses?
- Does the person continue to gamble even though the habit is causing conflict with the spouse or family, or has lost significant sums of money?
- Has he denied going to gamble even when you know he did go?
- Has she been dipping into savings or capital to fund gambling outings?
- Has the person sought to borrow money for gambling debts to allow him or her to continue gambling?
- Is he having trouble paying for rent, food or other living expenses that previously were not a burden?
- Has anything from the home, especially something of value, disappeared recently?
- Has the person borrowed or even stolen money from friends or family?
- Did he/she begin gambling as a social outing, but now prefers to go alone?
- Or has gambling become his/her sole social activity?
- If the person moved recently, has he made any effort to make friends who do not gamble?
- Does she say there's nothing else worth doing or that life is boring without gambling?
- Has the person tried to gamble less, and been unsuccessful?

Gambling addictions have often led to people getting divorced, embezzling money, contemplating suicide and going bankrupt.

Is there a problem gambler in your family?

You may not have the gambling problem but you and your family suffer from it. The more you understand about problem gambling, then the better you are able to handle the situation. You may need to get help and support for the problem before the gambler will seek help. Don't pay for gambling debts, or debts created by problem gambling. The more you bail out the problem gambler the worse the situation gets.

The gambler must take responsibility for his/her own actions. Recognise the problem.

A problem gambler often uses subterfuge to cover his/her tracks. He/she can be abusive, controlling and isolated. They tend to plan their whole life around opportunities for the punt. Whose problem is it? Do not take responsibilities for your partner's gambling. The only reason a gambler wants to gamble is because they want to. To gamble, or not to gamble, is a choice – nobody can make a person gamble.

The more support the better

Avoid secrecy and enlist help and support of others. Keep in mind that the best strategy is to be aware of the facts about problem gambling. The more you understand it the better you can handle it.

Find help
- Family members.
- Understanding friends.
- Support groups of other people who are affected by problem gambling.
- Counsellors and spiritual leaders.
- Self-help books, website information, documentaries.
- Community self-help: Gam-anon (self-help group for family members of a problem gambler/s).
- Professional help.

Guidance, clarification and motivation are common reasons for seeking extra help. A visitor or even a telephone call to a counsellor who is trained to help problem gamblers may make all the difference.

Injuries, allergies and conditions
Cuts
A small cut or nick will stop bleeding if covered in paper.

Swollen knee
To drain fluid off a swollen knee caused by a sports injury, put 'washing soda' into an old sock. Place it around the knee and bandage. Leave overnight and in the morning the knee should be back to normal size. Repeat if necessary.

Itching skin
If you're suffering from eczema or psoriasis, shake a good covering of cornflour over affected area for relief from the terrible itch.

Hay fever
If your child is affected by hay fever, rub petroleum jelly around the inside of nostrils before going outside. This catches the pollen and should stop a lot of sneezing.

Weight problems
Have you got a weight problem?
Are you half a metre too short on the weight-for-height chart?
What do you look like naked? Are there extra bits of you?
Do you weigh much more than you did in your twenties?

Where does it come from?
- Do you overeat from habit?
- Do you get enough exercise?
- Do you drink a lot of alcohol?
- Do you nibble all the time?
- Do you eat business lunches or entertain frequently?
- Do you eat a lot of foods that contain fats and sugar?
- Have you had your blood fats checked?

Why do we get too fat?
Weight gain is generally caused by over-eating and lack of exercise.

We eat too much because:
- We are tempted by the good food we enjoy in this country.
- We enjoy our food and drink and our over-indulgence eventually catches up with us.
- Over-eating becomes a habit.
- We are bored, frustrated or depressed.
- Our social customs encourage us to eat more.

There are times in our life when we are inclined to put on weight.
- Leaving school
- Getting married
- After an operation
- After giving birth
- During puberty
- When giving up cigarettes
- Menopause

Weight maintenance
Weight maintenance refers to keeping your current (target) weight reasonably constant. This can be achieved when the number of calories (kilojoules) that you eat is equal to the number of calories (kilojoules) your body uses.

Energy In (Food) = Energy Out (Basal Metabolic Rate + Activity) = Body weight remains stable.

Weight fluctuations
For most people, weight maintenance means weighing within one to two kg of their current (target) weight. The weight on the scale can fluctuate even when you have reached your target weight and there are a number of reasons for this:

- Normal body fluctuations related to eating and elimination.
- Consuming a high salt (sodium) diet.
- Temporary weight gain due to fluid retention for women near the time of menstruation.
- Decrease in physical activity.

Diets and dieting
To reduce weight you need to do two things:

- Change the quantity and type of food that you eat, while maintaining a nutritionally balanced diet.
- Increase your physical activity.

Dieting tips
Tips for dieting and for keeping off the weight include:

- Anticipate when it will be difficult to diet and plan accordingly.
- Don't reach for food when your emotions dictate.
- Eat only when you are hungry.
- Keep busy. Substitute a walk for a snack.
- Take time to eat. Eat slowly and eat small pieces.
- Don't buy snack foods. Save some of your meal for a snack later.

- Don't eat food that is left over, put it in the bin.
- Cut up raw fruit and vegetables and keep them in the fridge for when the munchies strike.
- Don't eat when reading or watching TV.
- Avoid shopping when you are hungry.
- Keep all food out of sight and in the kitchen.
- Avoid 'fad' diets. They are not healthy. Rapid weight loss is often followed by rapid weight gain.
- Beware of drugs that promise to help you to lose weight. They can cause more harm than good.
- Even a modest loss of weight is beneficial to your health if you are overweight.

Winter weight
It is harder to control weight during winter. Make a hearty pot of vegetable soup and enjoy a bowl between meals to keep hunger pains at bay.

Lunch
Lunch is a dangerous time for someone trying to lose weight. It's easy to go overboard, but you really do not need a big meal at lunch time.

- Take your lunch from home. (Apart from knowing what you are getting, you will be amazed at the money you save.)
- A sandwich is a good basic lunch.
- Add a couple of pieces of fruit and a cup of tea or coffee and you will be more than satisfied.
- When using a moist filling there should be no need to use a spread on the bread.
- A lunch box full of salad is a great summer lunch.
- You can have as many vegetables as you wish.
- In winter a thermos of hot home-made soup is warm, nutritious and filling.

Vegetarian meals
Vegetarian meals are nutritious, high in fibre, low in kilojoules and fat, and also economical. They are an excellent way to assist you in your mission to trim off the kilos.

Diet desserts
Don't deprive yourself of dessert altogether, even though you are trying to trim off the kilos. You can have:

- Fresh fruit
- Fruit salad
- Low-fat yoghurt
- Cottage cheese
- Low-calorie jelly
- Custard made with skim milk

Garnishes
Garnish your food to make it look more attractive. Use herbs, lemon and other fruits.

Vegetables for the dieter
Steam vegetables for just a few minutes, so that they retain their crispness.

Vegetables can be made more interesting by the clever use of herbs. Try adding:

- Nutmeg to cauliflower
- Sesame seed to cabbage
- Lemon juice to carrots
- Oregano to tomatoes
- Orange rind to peas

Salads for the dieter

Make salads more interesting by using vegetables and fruits other than the traditional salad vegetables. Instead of using manufactured salad dressing, make your own using olive oil and vinegar or lemon juice. Experiment with herbs and spices to make it interesting.

Other tips for the dieter

- When a recipe calls for cream or sour cream use plain low-fat yoghurt.
- Small amounts of alcohol can be used in cooking to add flavour, as the alcohol evaporates with the heat.
- Thicken stew by using vegetables instead of flour or a commercial thickener.
- Chill stews and casseroles and remove any fat that rests on the top before you put it back into the oven to heat.
- Trim excess fat from all red meats. Trim skin from poultry.
- Gravy is high in fat and should be avoided. Instead use mustard, mint sauce or tomato paste.
- When you are dieting cook meats and poultry by any method that does not involve adding extra fat.
- Don't assume that just because a beer is a light beer that it is not fattening. It contains lots of sugar and some alcohol.
- Vegetable salts – garlic, onion, sea salts – have the same amount of sodium as table salt.
- Beware of 'health bars'. They are often high in sugar and sometimes high in fat.

Double chin

A good exercise for a double chin is to roll a pencil between your teeth with your chin held high.

Reduce fat and cholesterol in your diet

- Steam, boil bake or microwave vegetables rather than frying.
- Season vegetables with herbs and spices, instead of fatty sauces or butter or margarine.
- Use flavoured vinegars or lemon juice on salads or use smaller servings of oil-based or low-fat salad dressings.
- Try whole-grain flours to enhance flavours of baked goods made with less fat and fewer or no cholesterol-containing ingredients.
- Replace whole milk with low-fat or skim milk in puddings, soups and baked products.
- Substitute plain low-fat yoghurt or blender-whipped low-fat cottage cheese for sour cream or mayonnaise.
- Choose lean cuts of meat, and trim fat from meat and poultry before and after cooking.
- Remove skin from poultry before or after cooking.
- Roast, bake, broil or simmer meat, poultry and fish rather than frying.
- Cook meat or poultry on a rack so the fat will drain off.

- Use a non-stick pan for cooking so added fat is unnecessary.
- Chill meat and poultry broth until the fat becomes solid. Remove the fat before using the broth.
- Limit egg yolks to one per serving when making scrambled eggs. Use additional egg whites for larger servings.
- Try substituting egg whites in recipes calling for whole eggs.
- Use two egg whites in place of one whole egg in muffins, cookies and puddings.

Keep a food diary

Prevent 'calorie amnesia' and weight rebound by keeping a diary of your food and exercise. Studies show that people who keep a food diary, not only lose more weight, they are also more likely to keep it off. For maximum awareness, record your food intake before or as you eat.

Healthier tricks

Try these tricks for healthier eating:

- Store pre-cut carrots and celery sticks in clear plastic containers on the top shelf for fast-and-easy snacking.
- Shove tempting desserts or high-calorie casseroles in the back.
- Place water bottles in front of pop cans.
- Put a note with the words 'Open Me!' on the drawer full of good-for-you greens.
- Keep low-fat condiments, such as spicy mustard, balsamic vinegar, salsa and soy sauce, handy to give food a tasty kick.
- Store leftovers in the freezer so you're not tempted to eat them as a snack instead of a meal.

Read labels

It is important to read labels and to be aware of what goes into commercially produced foods.

Positive body talk

Here are a few tips for positive body talk:

- Avoid making negative comments about your own or someone else's appearance.
- Compliment people around you who are smart, kind and thoughtful, not just those who are pretty.
- Make sure your kids know that not eating or eating a restricted diet can be detrimental to their health.
- Watch movies together and discuss the fact that Hollywood digitally retouches bodies to unrealistic sizes and shapes.
- Throw away the scales. If your child eats healthily and is fit and well, then weight is irrelevant.

A balanced diet

A balanced diet contains:

Breads and cereals	three to four serves daily
Vegetables and fruit	four serves daily
Meat and protein	two small serves daily
Milk and dairy	300 ml per day
	600 ml for children and women who are breast-feeding.
Fats	15g per day

Reduce fat intake

Eat fish, poultry, lean meat, legumes and grains.
Trim fat from meat.
Trim skin from poultry.
Avoid fried foods – grill, steam or boil.
Choose low-fat milk and dairy.
Limit intake of snack foods, cakes, biscuits, confectionary.

Eat foods high in fibre

Foods that are high in fibre are:

- Wholegrain breads
- Vegetables
- Wholegrain cereals
- Fruit
- Cereal products
- Lentils
- Seeds
- Nuts
- Legumes

Eat less salt

Foods high in salt are:
- Cured
- Canned and corned meats
- Salami and luncheon meats
- Cheese and cheese spreads
- Vegetable extracts, commercial sauces, pickles and soups
- Take away and snack foods such as nuts, crisps
- Crackers

Eat less sugar

Reduce intake of:

- Sugar
- Honey
- Jams
- Biscuits
- Desserts
- Soft drinks
- Beer
- Sweet wine

Alcohol

Reduce alcohol intake as alcohol contains empty calories.

Physical activity

Exercise controls weight. It helps relieve boredom that sometimes leads to overeating. It improves the function of your heart muscle, lungs and other muscles.

Increase activity

Here are some tips for increasing your level of activity:

- Walk instead of using the car.
- Get off the bus or train a couple of stops early and walk the rest.
- Use the stairs instead of a lift.
- Give yourself ten minutes of floor exercise each day.
- Play a social sport – golf, tennis, swimming, squash, netball, volleyball.
- Take a walk. Start at ten minutes a day and increase your time.
- Get out in the garden and enjoy making it grow.
- Walk to the local shops instead of driving to a shopping centre.
- Play with your children or grandchildren.
- Do something for somebody else in your neighbourhood who could do with the help.
- Volunteer with a charity organisation near you.

Overweight children
Overweight tendencies during infancy and childhood should be taken seriously as they often lead to problems in later life. Contributing factors are:

- Anxiety by parents if the child does not seem to be gaining weight.
- Use of food and drinks as a reward.
- Family eating patterns that are fixed, regardless of hunger.
- Insufficient exercise.

Helping children
Parents can help their children by not having biscuits, sweet drinks, ice-cream etc. available. Unless they are extremely overweight, children should not lose weight. Instead they should maintain their weight as they grow. Children should be encouraged to participate in physical activity. They should learn skills that will carry over to adult life so that exercise becomes a way of life.

Kids and media
Make your children aware that not all media images are real. While you can't erase all the cultural and media-related factors that lead to unrealistic expectations as to body size and shape, watching what you say around your kids goes a long way towards helping them love their body.

Putting on weight
Changing your shape does not always necessarily mean losing weight. There may be a time when you need to try the following:

Mixture to help you to put on weight
5 tablespoons of sugar
2 tablespoons powdered milk
1 tablespoon Akta-Vite
1 egg
1 litre of milk

Blend in the blender and place in the fridge. Drink as required. This quantity will probably last a couple of days.

Personal wellbeing
Essential oils
Known and used for centuries, essential oils are now being revisited and appreciated for their healing, relaxing and soothing capabilities.

Sexy ylang ylang
The alluring and exotic fragrance of ylang ylang arouses the senses and uplifts the spirits. It soothes fears and anxieties. Ylang ylang essential oil is reputed to be one of the best aphrodisiacs available, increasing sensuality and enhancing passion.

Miraculous tea tree oil
Tea tree oil is one of the most effective substances for use against infections – bacterial, viral and fungal. This tree is grown in Australia and New Zealand, and is appreciated worldwide for its healing properties. Use, neat, as a cure for:

- Acne
- Cuts
- Infections
- Tinea
- Ringworm
- Insect bites
- Cold sores

Mouth ulcers
Dilute tea tree oil with water, as a gargle for inner mouth problems (do not swallow).
Apply to handkerchief and inhale or steam inhalation for colds and flu.

Thrush
Add a few drops to the bath as a douche for thrush.

Harmonious geranium
Geranium was used once to protect one's home from evil spirits. Today it is thought to have special healing properties for women and women's problems. It is a rosy scented oil with a rich bouquet.

Invigorating peppermint
Peppermint possesses a powerful menthol perfume, which can clear nasal passages and relieve jet lag and nausea.

Antiseptic eucalyptus
Eucalyptus is sweet smelling and purifying. It is without peer as an antiseptic and decongestant and can be used many ways:

- Relief of symptoms of colds and respiratory problems, bronchial coughs and congested sinuses – vaporise and steam inhalation.
- Skin infections and wounds – direct application (five drops in ten ml of carrier oil).
- Cystitis – topical application.
- Temporary relief of arthritis and rheumatism – massage, bath.
- Temporary relief of headaches – temple and head massage.

Inhaling steam from a bowl of steaming water with eucalyptus oil will clear a stuffy nose and relieve a sore throat.

Soothing lavender

Lavender has many wonderful and health-giving properties. It is a general healing oil which appeals to people of different ages for emotional calming and physical healing. Use it for:

- Relaxing when stressed, tense or mildly anxious – bath, massage, vaporiser
- Burns and sunburn – gentle light massage
- PMS/PMT – massage on abdomen in clockwise strokes
- Psoriasis, dermatitis and eczema – massage
- Hyperactivity and restlessness in children – bath, massage
- Insect bites and stings – topical undiluted
- Headaches – massage on temple, cheeks, neck and shoulders
- Insomnia – put one drop onto pillow, vaporiser, bath
- Headache – in a vaporiser, blend lavender, rosemary and peppermint to use as a massage on the temples

Luxurious rose

Rose aroma is intense and enriching. It can only be produced in small amounts and so is very precious. This oil can alter the emotional state, indulge your femininity and support the system medicinally.

Stinging nettle

The common or stinging nettle, which causes burning sensations when brushed upon .the skin, will relieve the pain of mild burns when made into a poultice and pressed on the affected area. Itching skin conditions can be soothed by washing with a nettle infusion.

Essential oil combinations

Some beneficial combinations of essential oils are:

To make us smile

Sweet Orange + Benzoin + Nutmeg + Oak moss
Lemon myrtle + Geranium + Ginger

To achieve tranquillity and relaxation

Lavender + Sweet orange + Oremis flower
Mandarin + Rosewood + Lavender + Roman chamomile
Lavender + Sweet marjoram + Clary sage + Lemon
(don't use this one if you have low blood pressure.)

Lavender is the main oil used to help us to relax.
Sweet orange and geranium relieve stress and aid enjoyment.

For when we are feeling down

Grapefruit + Sweet orange + Frankincense + Rose

Romantic oils

Ylang Ylang + Geranium + Sandalwood + Patchouli
These make a sensational blend that will help to give that loving feeling and your will smell irresistible.

Confidence and courage

Spike lavender + Sweet marjoram + Ginger + Black pepper

Relieve stress and muscle tension
Lemon eucalyptus + Benzoin resinoid + Bay + Ylang Ylang

Keep your mind and memory sharp
Lemon + Grapefruit + Rosemary + Ginger + Ylang Ylang
Lemon helps to clear the mind. Grapefruit is to focus. Rosemary is to remember. Ginger to stimulate. Ylang Ylang is to relieve stress.

Body and hair treatments
Avocado sunburn soother
1½ medium sized avocados
2–3 tablespoons fresh aloe vera gel
2–3 tablespoons natural yoghurt

Blend ingredients together in a food processor and slather onto sunburnt skin. Wrap yourself in cling wrap and cover yourself in towels. This will help the avocado absorb into your skin. Shower to remove twenty minutes later.

Banana hair mask
1 ripe banana
1 tablespoon olive oil

Mix the ingredients for the mask together and smooth onto hair. Massage the scalp. Wrap your head in cling wrap or a hot towel for fifteen minutes. Rinse and shampoo as normal.

Beetroot lip and cheek tint
1 teaspoon glycerine
4-6 drops beetroot juice

Firstly, as beetroot can stain quite badly, slip into an old dark shirt. Grate a raw beetroot and strain the juice. Put the juice into a saucepan and simmer it to a quarter of its original volume. When cooled, add the juice to the glycerine in a glass bottle, using a dropper and shake. Dab onto cheekbones or lips and blend quickly.

Carrot and honey hair mask
2 carrots
1 tablespoon thick honey
2 tablespoons oatmeal
1 tablespoon sweet almond oil

Grate the carrots. Mix all the ingredients together to form a thick paste. The mixture should smell sweet and feel sticky. Apply to hair, leave on for a few minutes and then shampoo out. The carotene in the carrots will nourish your hair and leave it shiny.

Fizzy footbath
2 drops geranium essential oil.
2 drops lavender essential oil
100g sodium bicarbonate
3 teaspoons citric acid or a Berocca tablet

Dissolve all ingredients in a bowl big enough to use as a foot spa. When your feet are soft and ready for scrubbing, use a foot file to gently remove tough dead skin.

Hair fruit salad
½ banana
1 teaspoon lime juice
2 tablespoons coconut milk
1 tablespoon papaya juice

Mix the ingredients well and apply to towel-dried hair. Comb through, put on a shower cap and wrap your head in a towel. Aim a hairdryer at the towel to warm it up.

Leave the mixture on for one minute. Shampoo twice and rinse.

Hair spray
20g sugar
80 ml water or strained lemon juice

Dissolve the sugar into the water or lemon juice then pour the mixture into a spray bottle and use as normal hairspray.

Home-made chamomile shampoo
1 tablespoon of Borax
1 tablespoon pure soap, grated
30g of powdered chamomile flowers
½ litre of hot water
Mix in blender.
Let it cool before using.

Honey lips
½ teaspoon honey
12g ghee butter

For sweet-tasting lips, melt the ghee butter in the microwave for ten seconds then stir in the honey.

Insect repellent
For an insect repellent that really works, mix:

500 ml baby oil
25 ml eucalyptus oil
25 ml Dettol

Mix together. Put into a spray bottle.

Lemon cuticle soak
1 egg yolk
1 tablespoon pineapple juice
5 drops lemon juice
1 drop lemon essential oil

Mix the egg with the pineapple juice, then combine the lemon juice and the lemon oil.

Soak your nails in this mixture for fifteen minutes, then push your cuticles back gently with an orange stick.

Lemon oily skin saver
1 teaspoon lemon juice
50 ml purified water

Mix the ingredients together and keep in the fridge for up to four days. To use, pour some onto cotton wool and wipe over your face.

Orange face mask
Clay masks will help absorb oil, deep clean and heal your skin.

1 teaspoon green clay
1½ teaspoons fresh orange juice

Mix the clay and orange juice together to form a thick paste. Apply the mixture to a damp face, leave on for one minute then rinse.

Orange oil body moisturiser
1 orange
2 tablespoons jojoba oil
2 drops orange essential oil

Use a vegetable peeler to remove the orange skin (coloured part only, not the white pith). Combine with the oils in a bowl and leave at room temperature to infuse for twenty-four hours. The next day, remove the peel and pour into a bottle. To use, just pour some into your hand and slather all over your body after showering.

Parsley
Chew on a few sprigs of parsley to take away the smell of 'garlic breath'.

Paw paw skin scrub
Removes dead skin cells and leaves your skin tingly clean. Paw paw contains natural exfoliating enzymes, and the semolina granules help to exfoliate.

1 teaspoon semolina
2 teaspoons mashed paw paw

Mix the semolina and mashed paw paw together. Massage the smooth paste over a damp face and rinse off with warm water.

Oats
This grain, common in the Western diet, has become fashionable in recent years for its bran's ability to control cholesterol levels in the blood. It is the inositol in oat bran, a B-complex vitamin, which helps to increase the blood's ratio of high density lipoproteins to the cholesterol-rich low density lipoproteins. While the miraculous properties of oat bran may have been exaggerated, a deficiency of inositol can certainly lead to a significant increase in blood cholesterol levels. As a source of fibre, oat bran is considered superior to wheat bran, as it will not scour the bowel. In cases of severe bowel irritation however, laxatives such as psyllium should be used instead. Oats in their wholegrain and rolled forms are an excellent source of protein, vitamin B1, calcium, iron and silicon. Inositol also aids the body's absorption of zinc.

A tea made of oat straw is sometimes recommended for chest and skin complaints.

The skin toning properties of oats are widely recognised and oatmeal is an ingredient in many natural facial scrubs and face packs.

Bran and oatmeal scrub
1 cup bran
1 cup oatmeal
2 tablespoons whole milk

Mix the bran and oatmeal together then add the milk little by little. It should be moist enough to apply, but not sticky. Take handfuls of the mixture and massage onto your face or body. Rinse off in the shower.

Hair removal
Waxing
Apart from the ritual of the shave, the common form of removing excess hair on a semi-permanent basis is waxing. Waxing has been around for centuries. But if plucking your eyebrows makes your eyes water, ripping out hundreds of hairs simultaneously from tender areas will challenge your senses.

The main advantage of waxing over shaving is that it totally removes the hairs instead of cutting them. Regrowth is therefore much slower and the hairs tend to come back finer than with shaving, which only inspires thicker regrowth. Repeat waxing is recommended every four to six weeks.

You can get a waxing job done on:
* Leg
* Half-leg
* Bikini
* Underarm
* Chin
* Eyebrow
* Lip
* Chin
* Back
* Chest

Bikini waxes vary, including the Brazil and the 'Intimate Wax'.

Electrolysis
The principal alternative is electrolysis where a needle-like probe is inserted into the follicle and an electrical charge sent down the hair.

* This method is expensive and painstaking as each hair has to be treated individually over numerous visits.
* Permanency of removal cannot be guaranteed.
* Electrolysis can be effective in the treatment of small areas and is often used on unwanted facial hair.

Laser
Using a similar theory to electrolysis, laser technology treats a large number of hairs at once.

* The laser's fully qualified operator is able to treat a whole area in one session.
* Most clinics recommend four to six treatments, each of about ten minutes, four weeks apart.
* The beam creates a hot sensation which is accompanied by the smell of burning hair.
* Laser clinics are unable to guarantee that the hair will not eventually grow back.

First aid
When approaching a trauma scene be aware of the following.

Remember DRABC

D - check for **DANGER**
- to you
- to others
- to casualty

R - check **RESPONSE**
- is casualty conscious?
- is casualty unconscious?

A - check **AIRWAY**
- is airway clear of objects?
- is airway open?

B - check for **BREATHING**
- is chest rising and falling?
- can you hear casualty's breathing?
- can you feel the breath on your cheek?

C - check for **CIRCULATION**
- can you feel a pulse?
- can you see any obvious signs of life?

Only after you have checked the above should you begin first aid.

First aid kit

A simple first aid kit should at least comprise:

- Antiseptic
- Bandages – two or three different sizes
- Bandaids
- Scissors
- Tweezers
- Cold pack
- Disposable rubber gloves
- Face mask
- (Paracetamol is not really 'first aid' but is often included in household packs)
- If there is an asthmatic in your family, include a puffer.

Bites and stings

Following a bite or sting, try to capture the animal or insect – if it's safe to do so – for identification purposes in case antivenom is required.

Bees

Remove the sting by sliding or scraping your fingernail across it, rather than pulling at it. Wash the area and apply ice to reduce the swelling. If the person has an allergy to bee-stings, they can fall into a life-threatening state of anaphylactic shock. The only treatment is an injection of adrenaline. Immobilise the person, apply pressure to the bite and seek immediate medical help.

Blue-ringed octopus

A bite can cause paralysis; seek immediate medical help. You may need to resuscitate the person.

Box jellyfish
Seek immediate medical help. Stop the tentacles from stinging by pouring vinegar over them. Immobilise the limb and bandage firmly. You may need to resuscitate the person. Antivenom is available.

Funnel web spider
Seek immediate medical help. Bandage the wound firmly. Use a second bandage to wrap the arm or leg and splint the affected limb. Antivenom is required.

Jellyfish
Wash the tentacles off with water. Use ice-packs or anaesthetic cream to reduce the pain.

Redback spider
Wash the affected area well and soothe the pain with ice-packs or iced water. Don't bandage the area. Seek medical help.

Snakes
Seek immediate medical help. Not all snakes are venomous; however, you should follow the basic first aid techniques, just in case. Don't wash the skin, as traces of venom left behind might be needed by medical personnel to identify the snake. Bandage and splint the limb. (The old tight tourniquet technique is out.) If the person was bitten on the torso, make sure your bandaging doesn't restrict their breathing.

Stonefish
Seek immediate medical help. Bathe the area in warm water. Antivenom is available. A tetanus injection might be needed.

Tick
If a tick has burrowed into the skin, douse it with alcohol or methylated spirits then carefully pull it out with tweezers, making sure you remove the entire body of the tick. In the case of the Australian paralysis tick, antivenom is available. A tetanus injection might also be needed.

Wasps
Wasps can sting a number of times. If the sting is left in the wound it must be removed. Mix a solution of baking powder with water to relieve the pain.

Removing adhesive bandage
To remove without pain, soak a cotton ball with baby oil and dampen the sides of the bandage. In about ten minutes, the adhesive will be softened and the bandage will lift off painlessly.

Splinter removal
Apply a thin layer of white glue over the splinter, spreading it around the area. Let dry. Peel off the glue and out comes the splinter.

Genealogy
Searching for your ancestors – where to start

You do not have to move far to begin – start at home! Search records and items that may be in your own, or a relative's home.

- Look in attics and chests.
- Search for old family photographs and letters, photographs, baby books, important papers brought over from the old country.
- Another great source of information is family records of births, marriages and deaths.
- Books that mourners sign at the funeral home will tell you who was alive at the time of the death.
- Cards sent to congratulate a couple on their wedding and birthday cards will also tell you who was alive then and sometimes the spouse's name.

Standard searches

Once you have gleaned all you can from home sources, you then proceed to standard places to search, which can easily be done at your local Historical Society or local genealogy library.

Obituaries

Obituaries will tell you who survived the person, and often give biographical data.

Cemeteries and tombstones

Cemetery records and/or tombstone inscriptions can often be helpful, as there may be other family members in the plot who did not have a headstone. Many immigrants, especially Irish, stated a place of origin on their tombstone.

Census

This will tell you things like:

- Who was living with them?
- Who was living near them?
- What were the occupations?
- What information does it give on naturalisation and year of arrival?

Naturalisation

This may give you information on exactly where they came from and whom they married.

Certificates

Obtain birth, death and/or marriage certificates. Try and obtain corresponding newspaper notices, which may add details to this information.

Shipping arrivals

Helpful information may be in them, and it is interesting to see if the family travelled together to this country. It is a nice addition to your family history to have a copy of the ship manifest in your records, or even obtain a picture of the ship they arrived on.

Military records
These can have a wealth of information:

- Medical records
- Service records
- Marriage certificate
- Death certificate

Church records
Records of church ceremonies and membership can give you information on the family, and on the witnesses to the events.

Court records
Court records can tell you a lot about your ancestors:

- Wills
- Probate
- Divorce
- Child custody
- Criminal records

Wills and interstate records can often give you death dates and information on minor children that cannot be obtained from other sources.

Social security records
These can give you:

- Parents' names, including the maiden name of the mother
- The person's birthplace

This is especially good for females in your line, as information is generally filed under her married name, but will give her maiden name, name of her father, and also her mother's maiden name.

Other sources for information
- Samplers done by female ancestors
- Monograms
- Yearbooks
- Report cards
- School records
- Alumni lists
- Fraternal organisations
- Passport applications
- Scrapbooks
- Other family

Often the family records were given to the oldest male child, so try and track down his descendants. Online phonebooks and directories can give you addresses of people, then you can do a bulk mailing and hope for responses.

Good luck with your search.

When researching genealogies
Be kind to others. You will probably find digging up relatives, tracing ancestors, and discovering links with the famous, the infamous, the not-so-famous, and the downright

notorious, all very fascinating, but not everyone has the same attitude. Some members of the family, for varying reasons, might not want a lot of this dredged up, and lots of people prefer to look forward rather than back.

When you do find your way back to Bonny Prince Charlie, have mercy on the poor soul sitting next to you on the train. He is not the least interested in your family tree. In fact, by the time you go back that far, there may not be one person in your world who wants to hear about your ancestors!

Moving house
A fresh start
Moving house is a big job, but look on it as a chance to throw away the flotsam and jetsam of your life and come out the other end with only the possessions that you need or love.

Be brutal
Make three piles, the items that you will take with you, the good stuff that goes to charity, the rest to the tip.

The golden rule of chucking things out
If you haven't used it for more than twelve months, get rid of it.

Cartons
Whether or not you choose to use a professional removalist, it is a wise investment to buy proper cartons for packing. Supermarket boxes tend to fall apart or collapse. They are not designed for heavy use.

- Before you start packing, line the bottom of the boxes with butcher's paper.
- Label each carton with its contents and the room it is to go in.
- Clothes can be used to cushion articles.
- Pack heavier items into smaller boxes and light articles into bigger boxes.
- Don't wrap in old newspapers. They stain your hands with ink and it goes everywhere. Use butcher's paper instead.
- When packing and labelling boxes, write the room in the house in which the contents belong. Upon arrival at the destination they can then be placed in the appropriate room.

Packing crockery
The strongest point on crockery is the edge. Don't lay the plates flat. Stack them on their sides.

When packing your good crockery, place paper plates between large plates. This will prevent chipping.

Place mugs and glasses upside down in the box. You can get special boxes for this.

General moving tips
To move heavy furniture easily, place foil pastry cases under furniture legs. The heavy pieces will then slide easily over the carpet.

After disassembling the furniture, keep nuts and bolts together in a snap lock bag.

Wrap table legs with packing paper.

Tape microwave shut and wrap its glass plate.

Measure the width of your larger items before moving day to check that they will fit through the doors of your new home.

Clean belongings before you move.

If your belongings are being moved to different locations, use different coloured tags.

Allow forty-eight hours for your gas, water and electricity to be disconnected and reconnected.

Check to see if your home contents insurance covers you in transit.

Computer equipment

If you are not familiar with setting up the computer yourself, as you unplug each cord, wrap it and use masking tape to secure it, and label both the cord and the port into which it was plugged. For example, 'printer' at one end and 'printer port' at the other end of the printer cable. Label the power supply cords 'computer power' and 'printer power', and so on. This way, you won't end up with a roomful of electrical spaghetti without a clue as to where anything should go!

Packing truck

When loading the truck, use heavy gloves.

Pack the truck tightly and fill the spaces with boxes, cushions and blankets.

Hire a professional

If it is all too much for you, there are professionals who will do the whole job, from whoa to go, for you. You can do it from your computer. Try www.movinghome.com.au or www.telstra.com.au/movinghome.

If hiring a removalist check if the removalist you have chosen is a member of a society who will guarantee the job.

Moving house timetable
Three months before moving
- Three months out from the move pack up all those things that you will not be using in day-to-day living.
- Place them in boxes and clearly label.
- If you haven't used something for two years or more, put it aside for a garage sale or send it to charity.

One month before moving
- Begin to pack those items that you do not need for everyday living.
- Write the name of the room to which it belongs on the outside of the box.
- Pack the clothes for the season that has just gone. Label boxes.
- Fill out a Change of Address form, available from the post office.
- Fill out a tax office Change of Address form.
- Make arrangements with a moving company or reserve moving truck.
- Make travel arrangements, if necessary, with airlines, buses, car rental agencies and hotels.
- Transfer memberships in clubs and organisations
- Obtain medical and dental records, x-rays and prescription histories.
- Ask your doctor and dentist for referrals and transfer prescriptions.
- If moving to a new city, arrange the transfer of your bank account.
- Take inventory of your belongings before they're packed, in the event you need to file an insurance claim later.
- If possible take pictures or videotape your belongings.
- Record serial numbers of electronic equipment.
- Make arrangements for transporting pets.
- Start using up food items, so that there is less to pack and spoil.

Two weeks before moving

- Have children pack up the toys that they cannot live without. Label boxes.
- Have appliances serviced for moving.
- Clean rugs and clothing and have them wrapped for moving.
- Plan ahead for special needs of infants and pets.
- Arrange for help on moving day.
- Arrange for a cleaner to come in and clean after you have gone.

One week before moving

- Pack all clothes and personal items except those that you will require in the next week.
- Inform the following utilities of your move:
  Electric company
  Water company
  Gas company
  Newspaper/magazine subscription
  Telephone and cable companies
- Confirm travel reservations
- Speak to your bank and have your signature wired to your new bank.
  Check there are no outstanding cheques or automatic payments that haven't been processed.
  Collect valuables from your safe-deposit box.
- Make copies of any important documents, and then mail or hand carry them to your new address.
- Check with your insurance agent to ensure you'll be covered through your home-owner or renter's policy during the move.
- Defrost the freezer and refrigerator. Place deodoriser inside to control odours.
- Give a close friend or relative your travel route and schedule, so you can be reached if necessary.

On moving day

- Leave a welcoming note and a box of chocolates to the person who will be coming into your old home.
- Double-check closets, drawers, shelves, attic and garage to be sure they are empty.
- Carry important documents, currency and jewellery yourself, or use registered mail.
- Make sure that linen for beds and towels for the shower are easily accessible. Organise the bedding first when you begin unpacking, as everyone will be tired after a busy day and will fall into bed exhausted.
- Keep the kettle, tea and coffee out and pack them last so that they are easily accessible when you arrive at your destination.

Arriving at your new home

- Have the boxes put into the rooms where they belong.
- Don't try to do it all at once.
- Set up beds first so that you will have a comfy bed to sleep on at the end of a tiring day.
- Unpack the kitchen things that you will need immediately. Leave the rest.
- Ring the local pizza place and order dinner. Bottle of champagne, optional.
- Locate the hospitals, police stations, veterinarian and fire stations near your home.

Moving pets

Cats

Everybody knows a tale of a cat that returned to his old home 300 km away when the family moved to a new house. Cats are particularly sensitive to stress and are therefore well known for getting into trouble during the moving process because:

- Cats like sameness.
- Cats don't like events to be unpredictable.
- Cats don't like to be out of control.

When you move, you have a high degree of all three. Try to maintain your cat's normal routine. Transport your cat in a well-constructed cat carrier large enough to have room for food, water and a small litter box.

Prior to the move

Before moving, acclimatise your cat. Keep him confined to one room with food, water, a litter pan, some favourite toys, and the carrier you plan to use so your cat can get used to it.

Upon arrival

- Upon arrival at your destination, place the cat and carrier in one secure room with at least two doors between the cat and the outside world.
- The door should be locked or have a large 'Do Not Open' sign on it, so the movers won't inadvertently let the 'cat out of the bag'.
- Open the door of the carrier and let the cat decide when to come out in its own time.

Gradually does it

- Allow your cat to become used to the one room before releasing him to the rest of the house.
- If the cat scurries for cover when you open the door, wait a day or two longer, then try again.
- Only when your cat meets you at the door, let him explore the other rooms of the house.
- If your cat is accustomed to going outdoors, wait several days after arriving at your new home before letting the cat out. Stay with him.
- After a couple of these excursions, you can begin to let your cat out on its own.
- Remember that cats are territorial creatures and the other cats in the neighbourhood will surely be displeased that another feline has turned up to share their turf.
- There will be an initial settling in period where dominance is determined and honour secured.

Dogs

Dogs are not as affected by the stress as cats are, and so are generally easier to move than cats. If you have a small dog and plan on flying to your new home, he may be able to fly with you. Check with the airlines for details. If you are transporting a larger dog by plane, try to book a direct flight to prevent your pet from having to spend long periods in a distant airport.

Have someone scheduled to pick up your dog at the other end. Never leave any pet in the car for more than a few minutes by himself. This is especially important during warm weather. If you are carrying your dog with you in the car and plan to stop overnight, be sure to call ahead to find a hotel that accepts pets.

Your dog will be unfamiliar in his new surroundings, but will be happy to be where you are and so won't take so much settling in as the family cat will. Reassure him. Take him for long walks in your new neighbourhood.

Clean up after your dog at rest stops
Be prepared to clean up after your dog at rest stops.

* Carry a roll of paper towels and disposable plastic bags.
* Place a piece of paper towel over the solid matter, and your hand in one of the plastic bags.
* Pick up the towel and solid matter and pull the bag down over your hand and towel, turning it inside out.
* Twist, seal and dispose.

Birds
* Well before you pack up, check with your vet that your bird is healthy and able to travel.
* If you will be taking your bird in the car, maintain a warm, constant temperature since birds are particularly sensitive to temperature changes.
* It is possible to carry the bird in its cage as long as you have a cover for it to prevent draughts and keep the bird in a darkened setting to reduce the bird's anxiety.
* If you have an excitable bird, it may be necessary to cushion the cage or crate with a soft material to reduce self-inflicted trauma.

Reptiles
* For a venomous snake, it must be placed inside two sturdy boxes or a box inside a wooden crate.
* Non-venomous snakes only need to be packed in one box.
* Ensure the containers are well insulated and contain air holes for ventilation, and are clearly marked with both the common and scientific name of the species.
* If you are transporting your snake in your car, be sure not to leave it in the car overnight.
* Keep the surroundings of all reptiles moist but not wet. Dampening a cloth and placing it inside the container is the best way to do this.

Other pets
The easiest pet to move is a turtle.

* It can be carried in a well-ventilated box with you.
* Alternatively it can be overnight-expressed in a well-cushioned, insulated box with air holes.
* Be kind to your little friend and be sure to write 'Fragile, Live Cargo' and 'this side up' on the outside of the box.
* Also place leaves or grass inside the container for added cushion and to give the box a homier environment.

Note: there are some governmental regulations regarding the shipment of reptiles, so be sure to consult with the relevant authorities.

Small mammals
* The best way to move small mammals such as mice, gerbils, guinea pigs and hamsters is to keep them in the car with you and in their normal container.
* Take their water bottle out to avoid it leaking and soaking the bedding.
* At rest stops, check the animal and place the bottle back in the cage so it can drink.
* Be sure to maintain a comfortable, steady temperature.
* They are comfortable at about the same temperatures people are so if you are cold or hot, they are too.

Moving your plants
A couple of weeks before you move
Prune plants to facilitate packing and to relieve the stress load on the plant. Less foliage, less work for the plant to do.

Some plants can be dug up and transplanted. You will need to do this well ahead of time. Wrap root ball in hessian and keep damp in a cool area in the garden until moving day.

A week before you move
Kill any pests on the plant or in the soil. Place your plants in a black plastic bag, along with a bug/pest strip, conventional flea collar or bug powder. Close the bag and place in a cool area overnight.

The day before you move
Place the plants in cardboard containers. Hold them in place with dampened newspaper or packing paper.

Use paper to cushion the leaves. Place a final layer of wet paper on top to keep them moist. If you must leave your plants behind, take cuttings and place them in a plastic bag with wet paper towels around them. You can plant them at your new place.

On the day of your move
Close the boxes and punch air holes in the top before loading into your car. Or set the boxes aside and mark 'Plants, Be Gentle' so the removalists will be careful with them on the moving van.

Upon arrival
Unpack the plants as soon as possible after arrival. Remove plants through the bottom of the box to avoid breaking the stems. Do not expose the plants to much sunlight at first. Let them gradually get accustomed to more light.

Moving garden equipment and plants
Seeds
Gather seeds from your garden when your favourite plants go to seed, and store in an air-tight container.

Bulbs
Dig up bulbs during their natural dormant season. Store in old onion bags in a dry cool place.

Garden tools
Sharpen blades, oil lightly, and apply a thin layer of oil.

Protect the environment
Our environment
The world doesn't belong to us. We belong to the world. We are part of the environment. We are part of the ecosystem and we have a part to play, no more or less important than the role that is played by the other species on the planet. The state of the forests, the oceans and the atmosphere, all have a direct affect upon us and our wellbeing.

How can we help to protect our planet for future generations?

* Raise awareness in the family.
* Start at home and do little things that make a difference.
* Raise awareness in the community.
* Write to politicians, asking them what is being done to make a sustainable future.
* Write letters on local issues to the papers bringing attention to concerns in your community.
* Make buying and investing decisions based upon what you know about the companies involved.

House design makes a difference

* If building or renovating pay attention to site layout, window placement and air flow.
* Use verandas and carefully planted trees and shrubs to protect the building from the summer sun, and to cut down on summer heat.
* Concrete floors covered in tiles are good insulators.
* Insulate the walls and ceilings, use curtains to keep heat in or out.
* Heavier materials are better insulators. Choose materials such as brick or concrete.
* Place windows that make the most of the winter sun, but are shaded in summer.
* Awnings, pergolas and carefully planted gardens cut down on summer heat.
* Insulate the ceilings and the walls.
* Make the best use of natural lighting.
* Fluorescent lighting is more energy efficient than incandescent lighting.
* Consider installing a solar hot water system.

In the home
Appliances
Before you buy an appliance ask: do I really need this? Can I do the job quite easily manually?

* Buy appliances that have a high energy efficiency rating.
* Wash clothes in cold water.
* Only wash clothes and dishes when the machine is full.
* Use an electric kettle, wok and frying-pan, as they use less energy than cooker top appliances.
* When boiling the kettle, boil only the water that you need.
* Use the old-fashioned way, not the electrical way, to squeeze your juice, grate your cheese, and open your cans.
* Do not preheat the oven when cooking casseroles or meat dishes.
* For foods which require lengthy cooking time, use the oven. It is more economical than using the cook top.
* If using the oven, try to cook the whole meal in it and conserve energy.
* A microwave oven uses half the power that a conventional oven uses.
* Don't use the dryer. Hang clothes out on the line to dry.
* When drying clothes in the dryer, put a dry towel in with the load and the clothes will dry faster.
* Only partially dry towels in the dryer. Complete the drying on the clothes horse.
* If you do use the dryer, keep the lint filter clean. As well as putting pressure on the motor, there is a high risk of it catching a flame and starting a fire.
* Encourage your children not to continually open and close the refrigerator. Especially the great male teenage technique of opening the door, staring at the contents for several minutes, and then claiming in despair: 'Mum, there's nothing to eat.'
* Defrost regularly.

- Make sure that the door is tightly sealed. There are businesses that specialise in fixing refrigerator seals – saves you buying a whole new fridge.
- Keep drinking water in the refrigerator. It saves turning the tap on and running it every time somebody wants a drink of water.
- Buy a refrigerator that is only as large as needed.
- Keep it well stocked as it operates better that way.

Heating and cooling

- Turn down the heating. Wear more clothing.
- Bathroom fans remove warm air in winter. Use sparingly.
- Turn down the thermostat on your central heating if you are out for the day.
- Turn down the thermostat when you retire for the night.
- Close off all doors to rooms that you don't use. Heat only the rooms that you are using.
- Keep wardrobe and closet doors closed. There is no need to heat inside cupboards.
- Open curtains when the sun is shining and close them at night to retain heat.
- Make sure that windows and doors are well sealed in order to conserve heat.
- In summer keep the house closed and the blinds drawn during the day, shade windows and install ceiling fans.

Hot water

Use less by:

- Having shorter showers and not having baths.
- Repairing dripping taps.
- Using washing machines only with full loads.
- Installing a solar powered hot water system.

Lighting

Reducing our energy consumption in the home can make a difference in slowing the greenhouse effect, as 50% of all carbon dioxide emissions arise from the generation of electricity. Every kilowatt hour you save can reduce the amount of carbon dioxide released into the atmosphere by nearly one kilogram.

- Turn off the light as you leave a room.
- A dimmer switch will save electricity.
- It is more economical to use one large bulb than lots of smaller ones. A 100-watt bulb gives as much light as six 25-watt bulbs and uses only half of the power.
- Dust the light bulbs, as a dusty light bulb does not give off as much light.

Water

- Replace washers on dripping taps.
- Place a block in the cistern to displace some of the water that would be normally used.
- Do not put oils of any description down the drains, sinks or toilet.
- Install a rain water tank.
- Take a shower, not a bath, and make it short.
- Turn down the thermostat on the hot water service to save on bills.

In the garden

Make a compost heap and recycle food scraps. Put cooking oil on the compost and motor oil to be recycled. Give unused clothes to charity. Reuse plastic shopping bags. Share newspapers and magazines with family and neighbours.

Be an environmentally friendly shopper

At the supermarket ask yourself:

- Do I really need this?
- What is it made of?
- How was it made?
- Can it be recycled?
- How many times can I use it?
- What will become of it when I throw it away?

When buying for the family

- Avoid excessive packaging.
- Do not use plastic bags. Instead take your own hessian bag and if you do take plastic bags home, recycle them.
- Remember that aerosols are a wasteful form of packaging and cannot be recycled. Instead buy pump action packs and roll-ons.
- Avoid polystyrene products, which are bulky and non-degradable.
- Avoid chemically based insecticides which have a serious impact on the environment. Instead use fly swatters, mosquito coils, plantings of herbs near the barbecue area, citronella oil.
- Chemical air fresheners are also a non-contributor to our wellbeing. Instead, burn natural oils and incense. Clean the toilet bowl with vinegar and bicarbonate of soda.
- Opt for glass packaging over plastic packaging.
- Never shop when you are hungry. You will buy things that you do not need.
- Always try to buy in bulk.
- Read all product labels carefully so that you are aware of exactly what is in them.
- Make your own cleaning products using natural ingredients. (Recipes are in this book.)

Environmental shopping list

- Phosphate-free soaps and detergents.
- Handkerchiefs instead of tissues.
- Cloth towels instead of paper towels.
- Cloth napkins instead of serviettes.
- Recycled toilet paper. Or, at least, non-chlorine bleached products.
- Recycled writing paper and envelopes.
- Unbleached coffee filters.
- Feminine sanitary products that are 100% non-chlorine bleached pulp.
- Dolphin-safe tuna and salmon.
- Free-range eggs and chickens.
- Fresh, seasonal produce whenever possible.
- Organic fruit and vegetables whenever possible.
- Cosmetics, shampoos and toiletries that have not been tested on animals.
- Rechargeable batteries.

Cars and the environment

Transportation sources contribute more than half the total amount of air pollution. Motor vehicle emissions account for approximately 77% of the carbon monoxide, more than 35% of the volatile organic compounds, including hydrocarbons and 45% of the nitrogen oxides in the air. It is in yours and everyone's interest to limit use of the car and to use public transport wherever practicable.

Following the tips described and having your car tuned up regularly, will go a long way towards reducing air pollution, improving your car's performance, conserving energy, and saving you money on repairs.

Carbon monoxide

Carbon monoxide emissions are a result of incomplete fuel combustion. Carbon monoxide is a colourless, odourless gas which limits the blood's ability to transport oxygen to body tissues. This places a strain on people with weak hearts and respiratory diseases, the elderly, and pregnant women. High levels can also cause dizziness, headaches, impaired coordination and, at very high levels, even death.

Nitrogen

Nitrogen oxides are the result of high temperature combustion. These pollutants can damage lung tissue and aggravate chronic lung diseases such as asthma. In addition, they can lower the body's resistance to respiratory infection.

Ozone layer

Volatile organic compounds are another product of incomplete combustion, and when exposed to sunlight are involved in the chemical reactions which lead to the formation of a hole in the ozone layer. This causes skin cancers and melanomas.

When using your car

• Avoid long idles

Idling wastes gas and pollutes more. Turn your engine off if you're waiting for an extended period of time. Park instead of using the drive-through.

• Drive smoothly

Accelerate and slow down gradually. Only use the air conditioner when necessary. Open the window or use recirculating air instead.

• Maintain steady speeds

Over-accelerating and braking quickly are hard on your car. If you can drive smoothly, you'll save up to two miles per gallon (1.5 km each litre). Fast starts use up 50% more gas than slower starts. The average car loses almost 2% in fuel economy for every mile per hour over 55 mph (90 km/h).

• Use cruise control on highways

Driving at high speeds also causes tyres to wear out sooner because rubber breaks down faster at higher temperatures. Don't rev the engine.

• Avoid carrying unnecessary weight in the boot.
• Don't 'top off' the petrol tank.

Fuel expands in warm weather and can cause an overflow.

• Check your mileage

Set the trip meter each time you refuel. You can keep a log to track your mileage. If mileage is less than you expected, the vehicle may need a service.

• Keep tyres properly inflated

Keep your wheels aligned and your tyres properly inflated to increase fuel efficiency and make them last longer. Check the owner's manual or the label on the inside of the driver's door, for proper inflation guidelines. Check the pressure in all four tyres every two weeks.

- Fuel

Use the fuel type recommended by the manufacturer. Contrary to popular belief, using a higher octane fuel does not necessarily increase engine performance. Octane is not a measure of the fuel's power or quality. Using leaded petrol in a car that requires unleaded petrol reduces spark plug and oil filter life and damages both the exhaust system and the catalytic converter. It makes economic and environmental sense to use the proper fuel. Lead replacement fuel, which contains significantly less lead than original standard fuel, but still works efficiently in the car, is becoming more readily available for older cars.

- Keep the car serviced.

Components that aren't functioning properly on your car, like spark plugs, fuel metering system, ignition timing, etc., can also increase air pollution emissions and decrease fuel economy. Follow the manufacturer's preventative maintenance recommendations for spark plugs, fuel metering system and ignition timing. Get regular tune-ups performed by a technician who understands modern emission control systems.

- Make fewer trips.

Do several tasks at a time when you go out in your car. Your car burns more fuel and pollutes more in the first few minutes after a cold start.

Do your bit
Help to reduce global warming by:

- Driving your car less, and using public transport.
- Organising a car pool.
- Riding a bicycle.
- Not discarding old motor oil, but recycling it.
- Keeping your car well serviced and running smoothly.
- Keeping fuel consumption low by not accelerating or braking suddenly.
- Ensuring tyres are at the correct pressure.
- Recycling old batteries and tyres.
- Keeping the litter in your car.
- Planting more trees.
- Installing a solar hot water system.
- Avoiding products containing CFCs (chloro-fluorocarbons).
- Endeavouring to consume less of everything.
- Reusing and recycling.
- Writing to governments asking them to invest taxpayers' money in alternative sources of power.
- Reducing your personal and family consumption of electricity wherever possible.

Recycle your used car products
The exhaust isn't your car's only environmentally harmful by-product. Most fluids from your car are toxic and must be handled carefully. You can dispose of many used and unwanted car products properly at a household hazardous waste facility. They'll recycle them or dispose of them safely. Batteries, tyres, antifreeze, gasoline, motor oil and oil filters, diesel fuel, brake fluid and automatic transmission fluid can be recycled.

Antifreeze
Is toxic to pets and harmful to humans. Don't pour it down the drain. Store used antifreeze in its original container.

Batteries
Contain lead and acid that can be recycled. These materials can contaminate ground water if not disposed of properly.

Used motor oil
Can be recycled. Pour the oil into an unbreakable, see-through container with a screw-on lid like a milk jug. Oil will travel directly into streams and underground water sources if poured down a household or storm drain.

Tyres
Can be recycled for a dollar a piece off the rim. Large piles of tyres in a landfill are a fire hazard. Tyres emit toxic smoke when burnt.

Ocean and atmosphere
Enjoy the ocean, but protect it by:

- Disposing of old fishing tackle carefully as it could entangle birds, dolphins and fish.
- Disposing of rubbish on land, not at sea.
- Not applying toxic paint to boat hulls, as it will poison crustaceans.
- Being careful, when filling the engine, not to spill petrol or oil overboard.
- Trying other means of locomotion rather than the engine. Sail or row.
- Boycotting shipping companies that you know to cause pollution.
- Taking home from the boat and the beach all plastic bags and plastic six pack rings, which are a danger to birds and sea life.
- Disposing of polystyrene packages carefully, as they break up and look like food to a number of creatures. It is known that some turtles have eaten so much polystyrene that they are unable to dive under the water.

Protect the atmosphere
- Avoid polystyrene packaging and anything that comes in it.
- Refuse to buy furniture and fittings made with foam rubber.
- Service your car air conditioner regularly at a service operator who recycles the CFCs.
- Buy clothes that you can wash yourself and that don't need dry-cleaning.

Protect the earth
- Never dispose of chemicals or pesticides down the drain, the toilet or the sink.
- Put paint cans and other chemical containers out for collection when your local council organises a hazardous waste collection. It they don't do this, lobby them to do so.
- If possible, buy goods that are produced locally, thereby cutting down on the fossil fuel that is needed to transport them.
- Buy organic fruit and vegetables.
- Grow your own fruit and vegetables.
- Use non-chemical methods such as companion planting to avoid using pesticides in your own garden.
- Leave dead trees standing, as native birds and animals use these for their homes.
- Plant native trees and bushes. They are more suited to our climate.
- Buy second-hand or antique furniture.
- Do not buy furniture made from native rainforest wood.
- When building or renovating, buy recycled wood and fittings from second-hand shops.
- When in the country, be aware of the danger of fire and act accordingly.

An environmentally friendly office
- Make the best of natural lighting and reduce lighting costs.

- Recycle office paper.
- Turn the air conditioner up a couple of degrees in summer and down a couple of degrees in winter.
- Use the backs of photocopier discarded paper or fax sheets for notes.
- Use lavender oil or eucalyptus oil in a dehumidifier to keep the air fresh and sweet.

Other ways to help the environment

- Where possible, walk, or ride your bicycle, to the shops and on errands.
- Use vinegar for environmentally friendly cleaning.
- Use toilet paper made from recycled paper.
- Take unused clothing and household goods to the opshop.
- Avoid using plastic bags if possible.
- Share newspapers and magazines with neighbours and work mates.
- Give old magazines to schools and kindergartens to cut up and use in educational activities.
- Plant as many trees as possible. They add oxygen to the air at night, take carbon dioxide out of it during the day and shade the house in summer. They keep your family healthy.
- Recycle food waste by making a compost heap to fertilise your garden with.
- Allow the pests in your garden to evolve their own eco-system. A natural balance will emerge if you stop pouring on the chemicals.
- Reduce the area that you have under lawn. Grow natives instead.
- Plant natives, which will attract birds which will eat the pests.
- In summer, water the garden early in the morning or late in the evening to avoid evaporation.
- Add worms to your compost. They will aerate the soil and speed up decomposition.
- If the council allows, keep hens. They provide eggs, dispose of waste, eat bugs and provide fertiliser for the garden.
- Build a pond to attract frogs, which will eat the snails and insects.

The workplace
You know it's a bad day when . . .

- You turn on the news and it is showing emergency routes out of the city.
- You go to put on the clothes from last night's party, and can't find them.
- You put both contacts in the same eye.
- You put your bra on backwards, and it fits better.
- You walk to work and find your dress is stuck in the back of your pantyhose.
- Your car horn gets stuck, as you draw up behind a group of Hell's Angels on the motorway.
- Your boss says, 'Don't bother taking off your coat.'
- Your pay cheque bounces.
- Your wife says, 'Good morning George', and your name is Frank.
- That fabulous blind date you have been looking forward to all day turns out to be your ex-boyfriend. The one you put the restraining order on . . .

Choosing a career
Goal setting
Ask yourself what do you really want? A goal is a dream that you have. It may be something to do with your studies or it may be something that you aim to do with your life.

Set your goals. Make them long term and short term. What is it that you want in the end? What do you need to do along the way to achieve this?

Obtaining information and advice
Sources of information could be:
Libraries
Internet
Telephone book
Teachers
Magazines and newspapers
Films and videos
Encyclopaedias
Family
Gossip

Use the information that you have gathered to make a decision.

- How much time will it take to achieve a relevant qualification?
- Will it cost much money?
- Do I need training?
- Do I need equipment?
- Are there entry requirements?

Interviewing well for a job
You will be sure to be asked to talk on at least three things:

- The past – your previous jobs, experience, early life and education
- The present – your current views, attitudes, opinions and judgments
- The future – aims, ambitions, long-term career goals, where you see yourself in the future

Topics for discussion in job interviews
Often employers have a plan and it will cover such things as:

- Personal achievements
- General intelligence
- Special talents and aptitudes
- Physical and psychological makeup
- Interests
- Disposition

Before the interview
Confirm the time and date of the appointment. Have clear directions on how to get to the interview. Be punctual. Make sure that you leave sufficient time and a bit more to get there. Look good. Be dressed appropriately and be well groomed. When you go into the interview, walk confidently, smile, give eye contact and shake the interviewer's hand. Be aware of your posture. Don't slump, but try to be relaxed.

Speak up when asked a question. Be thoughtful and measured in your answers. Speak freely, openly and relevantly. Endeavour to put your case clearly and well. Try not to give simple 'Yes' or 'No' answers.

Once you get the job
Be organised
If you are unable to manage yourself, then later on you will be unable to manage other people. Chaos is contagious. If you are not organised then the people around you will be also in disarray. Your lack of organisation will be a constant source of disruption to them.

Make a time management plan

Without planning you will not have time for anything. You need to make time to make time. Time is a resource and you need to decide what you will do with it. How are you going to spend it most effectively?

You cannot know how to plan if you don't know what to plan. Make a list of all the jobs that have to be done. When you have the list study it and decide which of those items will help you best achieve your goal. Time for everything means time for nothing.

Identify active and reactive tasks

Being busy does not necessarily mean that things get done. There are two sets of tasks you have to work on.

* Active tasks are those that need to be done in order to achieve your goals.
* Reactive tasks are those day-to-day tasks that you do simply because they are imposed upon you by somebody else. (For example, reading through emails, replying to unrelated correspondence, checking messages, etc.)

Prioritise

Schedule your tasks.

* How long will the task take?
* What is the deadline?
* When does the task need to be done?

Deal with the urgent tasks immediately. Deal with the important tasks next. Slot reactive tasks into your day after you have taken care of the priorities. Make sure that the people you are working with recognise the priorities. Give yourself time and opportunity to think. Use your diary effectively to organise chunks of time to achieve goals.

Business letters, faxes and emails

A business letter, fax or email clearly provides a permanent record of the message that you wish to get across. Unlike the telephone, there can be no argument as to what exactly was said.

* Clarity, simplicity and brevity are hallmarks of a good business letter.
* Be clear and concise.
* It is essential that the person to whom you are writing, understands your message.
* Make sure spelling and punctuation is correct. Others judge you by how and what you write.
* Punctuate for meaning.
* Keep sentences short.
* Takes notes before you start so that your thoughts are organised and your words are logical.
* Clearly state name and job title, return address, and copies sent to.
* Avoid trade jargon.

Make your business stand out from the rest

Do it in style!

Make sure your company maintains a professional image on and in all marketing material. Have business cards, letterhead, and envelopes professionally printed in a consistent style and colour. It's worth the investment. What you send to others is a reflection of you and your company. It gives them their first impression of you, so make it good.

Management material

If your planning, hard work, success and loyalty see you moving up the ladder, remember that the manager who does not know his/her job confuses those around him/her.

Leadership in the workplace

Don't let yourself be tricked into believing that managing means being responsible for someone else. You may be responsible for the work and the deadline, but not for the people. You are not responsible for the motivations of others. And you don't have to like it when people you're counting on are not doing what needs to be done. You can lead by:

- Listening to your people without judgment.
- Helping them identify the problems and roadblocks they insist they're experiencing.
- Helping them find reasons to commit to the success of whatever projects you share with them.
- Telling them they need to get the agreed-upon work done! No excuses!

Don't do the work for them

- Ask them what they need to complete the task.
- Ask them what they can do to remove the obstacles they face.
- You can help them get started. But don't do the job.

Delegate

- Decide which jobs you will delegate.
- Decide to whom you will delegate.
- Brief and train the person to whom you delegate.
- Inform others that you have delegated.
- Delegation is not about giving out tasks, it is about achieving a common goal.
- Don't interfere with others who are working with you towards a common goal.
- Be available for advice.
- Actively check on progress.

Making a decision in the workplace

The decision to take a decision is a decision in itself. Never make a decision that you are unable to implement. Before taking a decision:

- Establish whether the decision is yours to take.
- Establish whether the decision is to be taken alone or in conjunction with others.
- What is this decision supposed to achieve?
- Are there limiting factors such as time or money?
- Does this decision encompass a larger picture?
- Consider all options.
- What are the pros and cons for each option?
- Give yourself time to think and to 'sleep' on it.

The decision-making process

All decisions should be worked through in the following stages:

- Gathering of facts.
- Consultation with the people who have an opinion. Never be afraid to draw on the expertise and experience of others.
- Making the decision.
- Communicating the decision.
- Following up.

Involve other people

Nothing disenfranchises or frustrates people more than a boss or company taking decisions that directly affect them, and which they know a lot about, and there has been no consultation. If this happens over a period of time, then staff become antagonistic to the boss and to any change that he or she may suggest.

Communicate your decision

You must 'sell' your decisions. It is vital that you brief the team collectively so that you avoid gossip and supposition.

Call the team together

- Tell them what you have decided.
- When the decision will take effect.
- Where the changes will take place.
- How the decision will be implemented.
- Who will be affected?
- Why you have chosen this solution to the problem.

Once the decision has been taken you must be totally committed to it.

Take responsibility

- Be a leader and lead.
- Make sure that everyone in the team knows the common goal.
- Conduct regular team meetings where team members can feel valued for their contributions.
- Ensure that every member of the team knows exactly what is expected of them and where they fit into the bigger picture.
- Reduce the opportunity for the 'grapevine' to thrive by keeping staff well informed.
- You must be sensitive to problems in your team.
- Spend at least part of the day walking around and being accepted as part of the everyday activity. You will then be aware when the normal atmosphere is different and something is not quite right.
- Group morale is undermined when team members feel resentful.
- Loyalty must operate both upwards and downwards.
- Establish regular on the job training programs, which show your competence at the job, and transfer skills to team members.

Let your boss know what is happening in your department. Communicate and give complete information about the progress of the team you lead, the strengths and skills of the members and any weaknesses you may perceive.

An appraisal

An appraisal is conducted against the background of a job description, the standard of performance and short-term goals. The four questions that need answering are:

- What is expected?
- How am I going?
- Where am I going?
- What can I do to improve?

An appraisal is an excellent opportunity to discover your boss's opinion of you and the job that you do. Try to find out:

- How can you work more effectively?

- What is your future within the organisation?
- How does the boss see your career developing within the company?

Meetings

Meetings have become a huge part of the business process over the last twenty years. They can be productive, but they can also be a great waste of time. It's up to you to make meetings work for you.

A good meeting is a cross-flow of discussion and debate.

Functions of a meeting

A meeting defines a group, a team or a unit. It is the forum whereby a group revises, updates and adds to what it already knows as a group. It reinforces the collective aims of the group, and the manner in which each member contributes to the workings of the whole. All of those present at a meeting become committed to the decisions that it makes and the objectives that it pursues. A meeting designates the status of each person in the group in relation to the other.

Start on time

Latecomers will soon learn that meetings begin when scheduled. They will not wish to look silly by being late. Consider listing latecomers, and early leavers in the minutes. This is legitimate as decisions may be made when they are absent. Nobody will want his/her name circulated as a latecomer.

The agenda

When it is properly drawn up, an agenda facilitates the speedy and efficient functions of a meeting. It should be circulated in advance so that the people attending will have time to consider and think about items presented. It is useful to head each agenda item either 'For decision' or 'For information'.

The chair

The chair is not the master of the group, but rather the servant. His/her role is:

- To assist the group towards the best decision in the most efficient manner possible.
- To move discussion forward.
- To interpret and clarify.
- To resolve issues in a manner that the group understands and accepts.

The chair should let others contribute and discuss ideas and should be there to summarise, mediate, probe and stimulate. In order to get a wider spread of opinion and ideas, work up the pecking order, rather than down it. Senior members of staff speaking out too soon inhibit younger and more timid members.

Chair's summary

At the end of a discussion of any agenda item, the chair should give a brief and concise summary of what has been agreed upon. If that conclusion involves action by a member then that member should confirm that they understand what is expected of them.

Recording the meeting

Minutes should be brief, but should include:

- Time and date of the meeting.
- Where it was held.

- Name of the chairman.
- Names of all present.
- Apologies.
- All agenda items discussed and decisions reached.
- Action agreed upon.
- Name of the person responsible for that action.
- The main arguments leading to decisions.
- The time at which the meeting concluded.
- Date, time and place of the next meeting.

Types of meeting

Daily meetings
People who work together on a common project with common goals meet to reach decisions informally by general agreement.

Weekly or monthly meetings
People who work on different, but parallel projects meet. The chair often makes the final decision.

Special meeting
People are united only by the project that the meeting exists to promote and the common goal is the achievement of that project.

Using the Net
In your job, it well worth it to be up with the events of the world – news, business, social, sport, and so on. It's always productive to be wellarmed with what is going on around you, especially in meetings or company social situations. The days of having to go through the paper have been overtaken by all the major media outlets setting up their websites to provide you with the latest happenings across the world.

Here are some of the best sites to browse:

Australian Broadcasting Commission<http://www.abc.net>	
London Times	<http://www.telegraph.co.uk/>
New York Times	<http://wwwNYTimes.com>
IJ St Petersburg Press	
(Russian)	<http://www.spb.su/sppress/>
USA Today	<http://alpha.acast.nova.edu/usatoday.html>
Wall Street Journal	<http:/ /dowvision.wais.net/>
San Francisco Examiner	<http:/ /sfgate.com/examiner/>
CNN Headline News	<http:/ /biomedd.nus.sg/MOE/sch/news1.html>
CEC Radio News (Canada)	<http:/ /debra,dgbt.doc.ca/cbc/news.html>
Time/Warner (Time, Vibe,	<http:/ /www.timeinc.com/pathfinder/
Virtual Garden, Money)	Watch)Welcome.html>
Hot Wired	<http:/ /www.wired.com>
PC Magazine	<http:/ /www.ziff.com/~pcmag/>
Nine msn	<http:/ /www.ninemsn.com.au>
Fairfax newspapers Australia	<http:/ /www.Fairfax.com.au>

Finding a job on the Net

Seek	<http:/ /www.seek.com.au>
Mycareer	<http:/ /www.mycareer.com.au>
	<http:/ /www.aus.jobs.com.au>

Computer graphics

Discussions about computer generated art, animation, image processing, hyper-realism, raytracing and more:

<http://www.comp.graphics>

The arts

All variety of the arts from dance to fine art to sculpture etc:

<http://www.rec.arts.fine.com>
<http://www.rec.arts.fine>
<http://www.rec.arts.folk-dancing.com>
<http://www.rec.arts.misc.com>
<http://www.rec.arts.theatre.com>

Sports

<http://www.football.Australian>
<http://www.rec.sport.baseball>
<http://www.rec.sport.basketball>
<http://www.rec.bicycles.misc>
<http://www.rec.boats>
<http://www.alt.rec.camping>
<http://www.rec.climbing>
<http://www.rec.sport.cricket>
<http://www.abc.net/sports>
<http://www.rec.equestrian>
<http://www.rec.outdoors/fishing>

Choosing a mobile phone plan

Competition in the mobile telephone market is strong, and any network should be offering serious inducements for you to join them. The answers to the following questions should help you decide which mobile phone is right for you.

- How will you use your phone?
- When will you use the phone most?
- Does the area covered suit you?
- Do you want a contract or prepaid calls?
- How much will it cost?
- Are there extra services?
- What plans are your friends and family on?

7
Events and Travel

Christmas
The Christmas tree
When buying Christmas trees, check for freshness by rubbing your finger across the cut side of the base. If the stump is gooey with sap, it is a fresh tree.

To keep the needles greener longer, cut an extra inch or two from the bottom of the tree and stand the tree in a bucket of cold water in which one cup of sugar, molasses, syrup, or honey has been added. Let the tree soak for two to three days prior to decorating.

Cards and gifts
Cut the pictures from last year's Christmas cards and use as gift tags.

When you purchase gifts, come home and wrap them immediately.

Don't wait until the last minute to do all of your wrapping at once.

Wrap as you go.

If you are purchasing gifts for those outside your city or state, choose gifts from the Internet or from direct sell catalogues, and have them shipped directly to the recipients. It will save you having to queue at the post office to post holiday packages.

Make out a list of those who you are going to buy presents for and take time to think and to decide what is a good present for each person. Buy early and enjoy the peace and calm prior to Christmas when everybody else is racing around doing last-minute shops.

Gifts to make it special
Bon bons
Make simple lolly-filled cardboard tubes from plastic wrap tubes. Fill them with lollies, a joke and a treat. Cover them with gift wrap tied with a bow. Your child can personalise them by adding mini handwritten notes or drawings along with the sweets, or adding noise by tying a jingle bell on one end.

Children's art
Your child's art can be copied, laminated, and cut into all sorts of useful gifts, allowing even the youngest person to create a treasured present: take a favourite drawing, add the services of a copy shop, and you'll be amazed at the results. Simple designs with clear lines work best.

Coffee break
For teachers, neighbours and friends, make a special gift for the sweet-tooth: Buy a coffee mug and fill it with delicious, home-made biscuits.

Funky picture frame
Make a funky foam frame. Use foam to cut a rectangular square. You can experiment with shapes. Attach a photo of the child. Grandparents and favourite aunties will love this.

Garden ornaments

This project is perfect for elves of all ages: clay or craft sculpturing material is easy to shape into creepy critters, small signs, and other adorable plant markers. Your child can gift-wrap a couple of them together with a few seed packs, or present them in a small potted plant.

Knitting needles

Craft decorative chopsticks for a relative who knits, or a long-haired friend.

Mittens

Sew a pair of colourful mittens from an old jumper.

Mosaic flowerpot

Make a mosaic flowerpot from old crockery.
Preserve old treasures and create a useful gift in the process.

Notebooks

Cover notebooks with embossed fabric for easy, yet fancy, gifts.

Stationery

Feature kids' artwork on envelopes and cards for one-of-a-kind stationery.

Trinket boxes

Present collectors with handy decorated boxes to house their trinkets.

T-shirt

Your child will love making whimsical tie-dye T-shirts. Just be sure all elves involved wear rubber gloves and use caution during the dyeing process.

Make Christmas easier

Get a babysitter for your kids. The time you save by shopping more efficiently will be well worth the price.
Say no to parties that you don't want to attend!
You and your family come first. Create your own family traditions. They don't have to be elaborate. They can be as simple as going to church or to Carols by Candlelight on Christmas Eve. It may be watching a certain holiday movie as a family on the same night every year. It doesn't matter how small or how large, how elaborate or how simple they are. It only matters that *they are*.

Share the load

To alleviate some of the stress of preparing Christmas dinner, pass around the holiday hat. Ask each guest to take a slip of paper on which is written a job to be done, eg, mash the potatoes, set the table, fill glasses, make gravy, carve the turkey. Children may be included too. Just place the easier jobs in a different container for them.

The Christmas table

For beautiful candleholders, insert red, white or green tapered candles into shiny, red, cored apples. Cut a flat base in the apple so they don't tip, then tie with a pretty ribbon, and group on a sideboard or beside each plate.
Melt the bottoms of long red candles and stick them firmly to the base of a glass flower bowl. When they are firm, add water to the vase and float flowers in it.

Use your old candles

Melt them down and pour into Christmas moulds, add a wick while still wet and once they have set, float in a glass bowl. The more colourful the candles are, the prettier they look.

For a centrepiece for the table

Buy a very small evergreen tree in a pretty pot and decorate it with tiny ornaments or candies. Place small wooden blocks, dolls and toy cars around the bottom.

Place cards

Make place cards using silver and gold pens. Decorate with silver and gold stars.

Make gingerbread men and tuck them into small envelopes with the guest's name on it.

Cut biscuit dough into festive shapes and cook. Write the person's name with piped icing on it.

If you are short of time, write the guest's name on a gift tag.

Spray apples, pears and lemons with gold paint and attach a name-tag with each guest's name on it.

If you do not have enough matching tableware for all of your guests, then mix and match, combining colours and styles. Layer contrasting colours on top of each other.

Napkin rings

Weave straw or raffia into napkin rings.

Simply tie colourful ribbons around the napkin.

Use strings of imitation pearls or old costume jewellery.

Make them up with curtain braids and tassels.

Thread small shells onto fine wire and wrap around.

Tuck sprigs of herbs or herb flowers into rings.

Bend florist's wire into a ring and thread small flowers into it. Bind with fine wire.

Select long flat leaves from plants such as iris and simply loop and tie in a bow.

Make edible napkin rings by threading colourful sweets such as liquorice allsorts onto cotton and making a loop.

Instead of bread rolls, make bread rings, glaze with egg, and sprinkle with poppy seeds and slip a napkin through.

Menu

Use a stencil to make a border on the menu card. Make a handwritten menu then attach to a slightly larger, coloured sheet of cardboard. Attach the card and menu together with a furnishing cord.

Write the menu on a paper plate. Your children can decorate the plates. Make a plain menu look festive by cutting up last year's greeting cards and decorating.

Decorations

Purchase half-price wrapping paper and decorations during the after-Christmas sales for the next year. Make a note of what you have purchased so that you don't forget!

Small children love Christmas

Small children love to be a part of the holiday preparations. They can help by creating a memorable family Christmas card. Let them pick out a favourite family photograph to include inside the cards that you mail out!

Simple Santa

To make Santa out of a toothpaste box, simply cover with red paper.

Add cotton wool for the beard, make arms from red pipe cleaners, paint a black belt, paint a happy face and there you have the old fellow!

The table

Get the children to help decorate a plain tablecloth for Christmas. Use stencils and fabric paint. Stencil a border on each place setting and add people's names. Spray paint colourful, abstract designs.

Scatter rose petals or other edible flowers over the cloth. Add sparkle with gold and silver festive stars.

Make posies with aromatic herbs, tie with ribbons and attach to the corners of the cloth.

Cut out pictures from previous years' cards and papers and spread over a plain tablecloth.

Place a single rose across each plate.

Decorate the chairs with red and green Christmas bows.

Christmas cakes and puddings

When cooking the cake it is a good idea to place an ovenproof bowl of water in the oven with it. This keeps the cake moist.

When cooling, leave your Christmas cake upside down to redistribute the moisture.

The cake will stay moist longer if an apple is finely grated and added to the fruit mixture.

To further moisten your fruitcake, make holes in the top with a skewer. Each day for five days pour over brandy, sherry or some other alcoholic beverage. Store in an airtight container, and on the day you will have everybody asking for your recipe.

To stop dried fruits and nuts from sinking to the bottom of your cake, simply roll in cornflour before you add to mixture.

To prevent the fruit from sinking, add the fruit before the flour.

To prevent the fruitcake from burning on top, place brown paper over the top before placing it in the oven.

To store a large Christmas cake it is sometimes less awkward to put it on a board and wrap tightly with glad wrap. Seal in a plastic bag and store. Then when you cut it you simply need to unwrap and cut on the board it is stored on.

Joan's Christmas cake

480g butter
480g sugar
9 eggs
480g plain flour
120g self-raising flour
480g currants
480g sultanas
480g raisins
240g dates
120g almonds
60g cherries
180g mixed peel
1 teaspoon essence of lemon
1 teaspoon essence of almond
½ teaspoon nutmeg
1 teaspoon ground ginger

1 teaspoon cinnamon
¼ teaspoon crushed cloves
½ cup brandy, sherry or rum

- Prepare fruit, blanche and slit almonds, chop peel, put into a bowl and add spirits.
- Cover and leave for at least two hours.
- Line the cake tin with one layer of brown paper, foil or greaseproof paper.
- Cream the butter and sugar, then add eggs, one at a time, and beat well as each egg is added.
- Add the peel and essence.
- Sift in the flour and spice, mixing well.
- Two thirds fill the cake tin, making a shallow hollow in the centre of the cake.
- Bake in a slow oven for five to six hours.
- Leave in the tin until the cake is cold.
- This mixture can be divided and cooked in two tins, in which case it will take three to four hours to cook.

Economy Christmas cake

3 cups plain flour
1 cup butter
1 cup sugar
1 cup milk
2 eggs
2 cups raisins
2 cups currants
1 piece lemon peel
1 teaspoon bicarbonate soda
2 teaspoons cream of tartar

- Beat the sugar and butter together until quite smooth.
- Beat the eggs thoroughly.
- Warm the milk and dissolve the soda in it.
- Add it to the mixture.
- Beat well.
- Sift the flour with two teaspoons cream of tartar.
- Put the fruit into the flour and add to the mixture.
- Bake in a moderate oven for about one hour.

Connie's Christmas mince

240g each of raisins, sultanas, currants and apples
120g chopped peel
The rind and juice of 1 lemon
1 cup brown sugar
1 tablespoon golden syrup
1 teaspoon each of nutmeg, allspice and cinnamon
½ teaspoon salt
30g butter
3 tablespoons rum or brandy

- Peel and grate the apples and put them into a basin with the dry ingredients.
- Add the lemon and syrup.
- Melt the butter with the spirits and thoroughly mix with all the ingredients.
- Store in screw-top jars in a cool dark place, or in the refrigerator.

Freeze leftovers

If you decide to freeze any of your holiday leftovers, make sure your containers aren't too big. If you put a small amount of food into a large container, the captured air may allow ice crystals to form. Instead, allow only enough space for the food to expand when it freezes.

Conversation ice-breaker

Some sure-fire conversation starters for those Christmas parties you'll be attending?

Try these:
- Compliment the other person on something he or she is wearing.
- Wear an unusual hat or pin that will encourage questions.
- Breeze through the day's news before you go so you can comment on a current event.
- Prepare a few opening lines, such as 'How do you know [hostess' name]?'; 'Have you seen [latest popular movie] yet?'; 'What are your holiday plans?'.
- And the sure-fire pipe opener, 'My, you're a handsome man. Tell me about yourself'. Three hours later you will still be there!

Weddings
Some useful tips

Choose colours that allow easy-to-find matching decorations.

A wedding is a family affair and always an emotional event.

If a couple is paying for their own wedding, they do perhaps have more autonomy and may be able to do things exactly as they wish.

Even if you have been living together for some time, a wedding is a public acknowledgment of your commitment for each other, and is therefore a huge event.

Plan well in advance, leave nothing to chance, and make this a day to remember.

Make sure your partner is in no doubt that you are both fully involved in the planning of the wedding.

On the day, gather people together that you love and who love you, and who wish you well in your future life together.

Remember, everyone loves a wedding and if you have planned it well you will certainly have a wonderful day to remember.

Tradition
Who pays for what?

The bride's parents traditionally pay for the wedding reception, but these days, there are all manner of arrangements made to pay for the wedding. Discuss it with your partner and your families and come to an arrangement that suits you.

Rings

The groom traditionally pays for the wedding rings. However, there are always exceptions. The couple may choose to wear family heirloom rings or the bride may buy the groom's ring as a gift. These need to be ordered well in advance of the day.

Suits

The groom's parents sometimes offer to pay for the suit rentals as a gift. Asking the individuals to pay for it themselves, however, is expected and therefore acceptable.

Groom's family

Often the groom's family offers to pay half the cost of the wedding. Or they may offer to pay the bar bill or they may simply offer to pay for some aspects of the wedding, such as the flowers, band or photography.

The guests

The groom's family should give a list of people they want to invite to the bride's parents. They should find out from their son approximately how many people he and his fiancée wish to entertain and then create the list appropriately.

Wedding rehearsal dinner

Normally the groom and his family will pay for a dinner for the wedding party prior to the wedding, often on the night of the rehearsal.

Keep it affordable

A wedding is simply a celebration to herald the beginning of a long and lasting relationship. Do not let it begin badly by unwise spending. Have the wedding that you can afford with the people who love you and wish you well. Even a couple who plan to keep the day simple and informal will find themselves caught up in the hopes and expectations of other people. Delegate jobs to friends and family.

Trappings and lavish spending do not a happy day make. If your budget is really tight, work with it. You can enlist the help of family and friends to keep costs down.

- Have one of your friends or relatives do the photography or video.
- You could either have a printer do the invitations for you or you could do it yourself with the computer.
- Do the flowers yourself.
- Make your own gown.
- Borrow friends' or relatives' cars to take you to the church/reception.
- Shop around for catering.
- Consider having the wedding in a park, or at home.

Invitations

Word the invitations in a manner that is most appropriate for you and the kind of celebration that you wish your wedding to be.

If you are having a theme wedding it will be in the same style as the theme you have decided upon.

The invitations should be sent out at least six weeks prior to the wedding.

You must make a decision as to whether you wish to have parents' names on the invitation. It is traditional to include the bride's parents on the invitation. It is very rare to include the groom's parents on the invitation.

If the bride's parents are divorced it may complicate things, especially if there are new partners involved. If you do not wish to mention the parents you could write, Joe Blow and Mary Brown request the honour of your presence at . . .

It is a good idea to send out the hotel information in the same envelope as the invitation. If you are including children on their parent's invitation, say so. Most people don't usually assume their children are invited.

Include children if you can

Experience has taught me that children from about age five up just love a wedding and get so excited about going to one. It is an event that they will remember until they go to the grave, so invite the children and your wedding will be remembered forever.

The dress
The type of wedding gown you choose says something about you as a person.

Your mother's dress
Many brides really do want to wear their mother's gown. However, this is not always possible, as the gown may have discoloured. The gown may not fit the modern bride.
However, the mother's gown can be put to good use.

- Cut it up!
- Make a ring bearer pillow.
- A flower girl dress.
- Use the fabric and lace in the bridal bouquet.
- If there is an abundance of fabric, create a beautiful overlay for the bridal table.
- Bows for the bride and groom's chairs.
- The possibilities are endless.

Traditional
If you choose a traditional dress you are likely to have a traditional marriage with roles clearly defined – the wife, the mother and home-maker and the man, the father and bread-winner. The woman will do the inside work and the man will do the outside work. The woman will sew and the man will make things in his shed.

Traditional but with modern styling
Yours will be a marriage that upholds the sacredness of marriage and the exclusivity of the partnership, but will be a modern marriage with less clearly defined roles and both partners sharing the domestic and bread-winning roles.

A dress that has been worn before
If a bride wore the dress, and went on to have a happy and fruitful marriage, this can be a very lucky dress. If it belonged to a close relative and has happy connotations, then this is extremely lucky.

A bohemian dress
This dress will signify that your marriage will not be conducted according to any rules but those made by the two of you. You will not be tied down to tradition and you will do things in your own way with your own style and others can like it or lump it. It only matters what you, your partner and your group of friends think.

Casual gear
Perhaps you haven't put enough thought into the significance of your wedding day.
It is not just a day like any other, it is a day above all others, when you tell the world that this is the man that you love and plan to spend the rest of your life with. Casual gear suggests that you are entering into this union with not much thought. It may be unlucky.

A special street dress
Your wedding day is intensely personal and you do not really care about what anybody else thinks. The only person in the world for you on this day is your beloved and you dress to please him without spending a fortune. This augurs well for your relationship.

Storing your wedding dress

Your gown should be cleaned as soon as possible. The most important thing about storing a wedding dress is to make sure it is clean. Dry-cleaning by a specialist dry-cleaner is best.

Stains

The longer that stains set on the gown the harder it will be to remove them, creating a risk to the fabric or colour. Any stains such as food, grease, cake, hemline soil, grass and especially champagne should be noted and discussed with the cleaner. Champagne and any sugar-based stains are often the most difficult to remove unless pre-treated before cleaning.

Beads

Beads should be secured and sewn on before cleaning. Glued-on beads soften in per-chlorethylene (a common solvent used by normal cleaners) and lose their finish, some actually dissolve. Cleaners using Stoddard solvents often have a better chance in cleaning without any damage to beads or fancy embellishments. Before cleaning your gown you should have the beads tested by the cleaner. This is very simply done by placing a bead in solvent for five to ten minutes. The bead is then checked to see if any finish or any part of the enamel has dissolved. If you notice a cloudy finish to the bead then it is best to find a cleaner who uses another type of cleaning solvent.

Following cleaning, the gown should be available for inspection. The dress should then be wrapped in blue, acid-free tissue paper and stored in a cardboard box. Stuff the skirt and the sleeves with tissue paper so the dress is not packed into creases.

Trimmings, particularly of gold colour, should be covered with tissue paper. Ensure that the gold does not touch the white fabric.

Deter moths and silverfish

Scatter Epsom Salts on the bottom of the cardboard box to deter moths and silverfish; don't let the salts touch the fabric of the dress.

Make-up stains

Cover the mark with white talcum powder. Cover the powder with a white tissue.

Wash your hands in very hot water. Dry them. With a thick towel covering the hand under the stain, press the other hand onto the top of the tissue. Hold it there for a few minutes before brushing the powder off. Repeat the treatment a couple of times until the stain disappears.

Perspiration stains

Perspiration can oxidise and become rusty. Dampen the stained area with lots of cream of tartar. Leave for about two hours, and then brush off. Sponge with wool wash. Do not wash or try to whiten a very old, precious, hand-embroidered wedding dress. Simply pack it in blue, acid-free tissue paper and keep it away from moths or silverfish.

Veil

Do not fold the wedding veil, but roll it in blue, acid-free tissue paper and keep in a cardboard box. If the veil has a small moth hole dip a piece of veiling into thin raw starch. Place it over the tear. With a handkerchief over the tulle, press on the wrong side with a warm iron. It will attach.

Restoring an old wedding dress

Stains on an old satin dress should be entrusted only to a commercial cleaner who also redresses fabric. New satin fabric is usually made with synthetic fibre and is probably washable. Check the label. If the satin is washable, rust marks can be removed by covering them with a paste made with salt and lemon juice. Leave the paste on for about twelve hours before brushing off. Sponge with a cloth, dipped in a solution of one tablespoon baking soda in half a cup of warm water.

Wedding heirlooms

Write the story of the wedding heirloom and keep it with the article so that those coming after you will know its history and value to the family.

Colours

Create your colour scheme around the type of wedding that you will be having. If the wedding is to be in a park why not choose greens and green blue for your dresses. Use the colours of the stained glass in the church to create a colour scheme. If it is a beach wedding go for the colours of the sand and water.

The reception

The wedding table

Generally the wedding table consists of the bride and groom and the attendants. If the wedding party is small it may include the parents of the bride and the groom. However, this can be isolating and some prefer to do the table arrangements in different ways. One way to do it is to not have a head table and instead have a 'sweetheart' table, which would be just for the bride and the groom. While this is untraditional, it's fine.

Decorating a hall

If your wedding is taking place in a hall, cover those pictured-covered walls with hanging drapes of fabric from ceiling to floor. Use a colour that complements your wedding flowers and attendants' dresses. Later the fabric can be sewn into table clothes and given as gifts. For a more dramatic flare, up light the walls . . . 'wash' them in colour.

The usher

An usher is another term for groomsman, meaning that an usher is an official member of the wedding party. As such, ushers are expected to wear the suit picked out by the groom for all his attendants, stand beside him during the ceremony, and, of course, give a wedding gift.

Themed weddings

When creating a themed wedding take into account:

- **Food** – select a menu that suits your theme, but be sensitive to the needs of all of your guests.
- **Location** – be sure to decide if you want to have an indoor or outdoor wedding. Have an estimate of the number of guests you will be having before booking a venue.
- **Decoration** – hire a professional or get help from friends.

Music

Music is most important and should not be overlooked. Music sets the mood, creates ambience and accompanies us when we are happy or sad. We dance to it, work to it, sleep to it, eat to it and make love to it. 'If music be the food of love, play on' (Shakespeare, *Twelfth Night*).

Best months for weddings

January – is the luckiest month.
The couple are marrying in the summer and their lives will be happy and fruitful.
February – good for marriages that will last and last.
March – the bride and groom will travel the world together.
April – good fortune will shine upon the happy couple.
May – the couple that marry in May will have many hurdles to cross on their journey, but they will pull together and be stronger for it.
June – ancient Romans believed that June was the special month chosen by the gods and they named it after the goddess of fortune and plenty, Junos.
July – yours will be a fiery marriage where there will be many debates and disagreements and many passionate makings up.
August – your partner is true and loyal and will stick with you until death.
September – yours will be a harmonious marriage with never an unkind word.
October – the only thing that you will bicker about will be money.
If you can make enough of it so that it isn't an issue, you will have a blissful union.
November – you are the lucky couple.
Everything that you touch seems to turn to gold.
December – there will be much laughter and happiness in your home.

The wedding reception is a celebration of love with food and music. The theme wedding can centre on the music played during the church ceremony and wedding dinner.

Classical class

A touch of class can be provided by a string quartet or trio, playing chamber music. In a sea of chaos, they are calm and steadfast. Besides classical pieces, some quartets and trios can belt out decent pop tunes to the delight of your guests more accustomed to contemporary music. This is great to listen to, sets the scene and is not too loud so as to impinge upon conversation.

Other music

Consider a classical pianist or a harpist. A country band that will sing of love and love lost. A good band can lull your guests into having a great time and makes it more enjoyable for everyone. A young covers group will provide excellent dance music. Have a karaoke at your wedding and make the event less formal and more enjoyable for everyone.

Outfits

Inform your designer of the theme you are having and listen to his/her suggestions. Remember to wear only something you can move around comfortably in.

Guests

Choose a theme your guests will be comfortable with. If your theme involves guest participation, give them ample time to get involved. If not, surprise them!

The fairy tale

You can live your Prince Charming and Cinderella fantasy, complete with evil stepmother-in-law!

- Food – serve food that's fanciful and dreamy. Have each course served amid dry ice to conjure up the magical.
- Location – wave the magic wand and decorator-transform your function room into your palace.
- Décor – create the image of being in the enchanted kingdom. Think ice carvings.
- Outfits – a princess like ball-gown, with a magic wand instead of a bouquet. Groom has to wear a tuxedo.
- Guests – persuade your guests to arrive in costumes. Have the wedding party go to town on the costumes.

Elizabethan wedding

Elizabethan weddings were the first to feature many of the customs we use today.

- The exchanging of vows and rings.
- The creation and eating of wedding cakes.
- The passing of the garter.
- The idea of a bridal party procession.
- Brides wore wreaths of blossoms and carried bouquets trimmed with love knots.

Wedding dresses tended to fall into two categories:

- Heavy brocades ornamented with threads and lace in gilt and metallic colours.
- White, billowy dresses with long sleeves, antique lace and bows, and a number of tiny buttons.

The dress usually had a plunging neckline that revealed ample cleavage. Otherwise, the bride's body was fully covered with a number of petticoats and corsets and a ball-gown style skirt.

Hair
Women's hair was worn long, often to the waist, and loose. Women would create soft, flowing curls for special occasions. No proper bride would be seen without a crescent-shaped cap of herbs adorning her head.

Herbs
Elizabethans associated herbs with secret meanings and mythical qualities. The prominence of herbs is the most distinct element of the Elizabethan wedding. They were infatuated with both the fragrance and historical significance of these plants. Elizabethans of all social classes infused herbs into every possible part of a wedding, from the bride's headdress to the embellishment of candelabra at the dining tables. The most commonly used herbs were thyme, lavender, rosemary, parsley, 'Blue Ribbon' echinus, sage, chive, marjoram and the daisy-like feverfew.

Tussie-mussies
For weddings, bridesmaids carried small bunches of herbs called 'tussie-mussies'. These were little tied posies of sweet-smelling herbs. Often, each tussie-mussie was different from the others, giving each girl her own unique bouquet. The posies complemented each other in fragrance and colour.

Colours
Typical colour schemes for Elizabethan weddings included soft golds, dusty pinks, yellowy creams, and sage greens – much as one would picture in a tapestry from the era.

Bridal bouquet
The bride's bouquet took the form of a 'pomander', or flower-ball. Usually about twice the

size of the bridesmaids' tussie-mussies, the essential function of the pomander was to perfume the air around the bride. Herbs used in the pomander included marjoram, various shades of sage, thistle, and occasionally small flower blossoms in muted yellow or purple. Typically, a wide piece of colourful ribbon or gauze was used as a handle. After the wedding ceremony, they were used to decorate a house or reception room, often hanging from iron railings and knobs by the aforementioned piece of ribbon.

When re-creating an Elizabethan wedding, it's important to focus on the big picture. Elements such as:

- Full dresses in brocade, gilt, or even white, with a revealing décolletage.
- Long hair parted in the middle, preferably worn with loose curls.
- Plentiful use of herbs in rounded bouquets, as well as in headpieces, and centrepieces.
- A muted colour scheme.

Romantic candlelight wedding

Have your wedding day on the Feast of Michaelmas, on 29 September. Light up with many candles. Create an ambience of romance.

Medieval/Renaissance wedding

For the traditionally romantic, the age of the Renaissance is one of the most rich and beautiful in European history. A medieval/Renaissance wedding, complete with knights in shining armour, may be the perfect choice for you.

If you wish to have a church ceremony, try to find one that looks Gothic with stained-glass windows and arches.

If you are having your wedding in a modern building, you will need to improvise. Decorate the space with:

- Plenty of ivy, the traditional wedding plant of the era
- Use black iron candelabras
- Scrolls
- Banners of family crests
- Large baskets of flowers
- Flowered garlands on wooden and/or iron poles
- Big, chunky wooden candle holders

Reception

A good choice would be an old castle or castle-looking building that can be used as a party location. Most of these places are used to holding medieval weddings, and know how to put them on.

Say it with flowers wedding

Your love is in full bloom, and is reflected in your choice of buds.

Choose one flower such as an iris and have the usher give out a stem to each person as they enter the church. They then pass the stem onto the bride and groom as they enter the church.

Combine different flowers in a similar colour. Have hanging baskets of your favourite blooms everywhere around the venue. Flowers can be used to decorate the church, the reception area, the home and even the food display. The same flower(s) can be used in the bouquets and the car decoration.

Present your guests with a stalk of your favourite flower. Ask that guests take home the flower arrangements/hanging baskets from their table. Perhaps you can make a gift of a packet of seeds or a bulb of that flower as each gift, so that they may plant it and think of you.

Heart-to-heart

Decorate everything with hearts, whether in different colours or in a single colour. Big hearts, small hearts. Sew little hearts onto your wedding gown. A heart-shaped wedding cake. Sprinkle little hearts over the white tablecloths.

Medieval wedding

A medieval wedding is one of the most dramatic and possibly the most romantic.

- Stone castles
- Tudor fashions
- Gothic design
- Sweeping velvet gowns
- Stunning wildflowers
- Men in tights!

The dress

If you are going to have a medieval wedding, a white dress is not for you. Brides in the Middle Ages wore dark and regal velvet dresses in such colours as hunter green, burgundy wine or deep purple. Often these dresses were laced up the sides and/or back, had long, pleated skirts, and were floor-length and long-sleeved. They were usually relatively low-cut. A metallic (gold or silver) braided ribbon often ran throughout the design. The torso of the dress often was cut like a coat. Stick to such a dress for both the bride and the bridesmaids.

The hair

Hair is worn long and flowing, with loose curls, braids or roles. Instead of a veil, wear a wreath of ivy, herbs and flowers, possibly with ribbons attached and hanging loose over the back of the head. The dress for men is tights, breeches, tunics, pirate shirts, laced vests and boots. If his hair is long, it too can be worn loose. Anything in a tapestry pattern is perfect for either the bride or the groom, as well as anyone in the wedding party. Try hiring your costume from local costume shops or theatre groups.

The flowers

This era is characterised by the prominent use of herbs. Rosemary, thyme, basil and even garlic are often interspersed with the chosen flowers. This custom originated from what was then believed to be the mystical, even religious, significance of various herbs in both health and destiny. The flowers displayed should be rich, darker shades such as red, orange, purple, green, brown and bright yellow. All the flowers should appear as rustic and natural as possible. Wheat, considered symbolic of fertility, played a vital role in marriage ceremonies.

The invitations

The most appropriate invitation to a medieval/Renaissance wedding is one made of ivory or beige parchment paper, with the announcement written, or printed in black ink. The paper can then be either rolled like a poster and clasped with a napkin-like ring, or it can be sealed with hot wax.

Bursting with love

Use balloons as a theme when love is in the air.
You can use balloons anyway you please.
They come in all colours and sizes and shapes.
Flood the ceiling with helium-filled balloons.

Other ideas

- Shanghai wedding
- Ethnic theme

- Seashell wedding
- A beach wedding
- A garden wedding
- A wedding at the zoo
- I'm in Heaven

Favours

These are not necessary but if you do choose to have them, choose something in line with the wedding theme so guests have something to take home with them.

Wedding album

At some weddings the photographer decrees the order of happenings and controls the day. Decide whether you wish to spend up to four thousand dollars documenting your wedding, only to have your photographs and videos put away in a cupboard while you and your partner get on with your life. You really need only a half dozen good photographs. To do this you can:

- Place disposable cameras on each table and invite your guests to take photos during the reception. Have them processed and voila!
- Ask a friend to stand in as your photographer for the day. Remember, the difference between getting good photographs or not, is often simply in the number of shots you take. Give him/her lots of film.
- Ask your favourite aunt, the one who gets along well with people, to stand at the entrance to the ceremony and take a photograph of everyone as they come in. Just when they are looking their very best!

Other wedding tips

Best days to wed

Monday – your emotions and feelings are paramount. Your marriage will be blessed.
Tuesday – your marriage will be energetic and long-lived.
Wednesday – don't do it. It is best that you avoid this day, as it is unlucky.
Thursday – yours will be an unconventional marriage as this is not a common day to marry.
Friday – yours will be a prudent union where you live within your means in a modest but happy marriage.
Saturday – the most popular day of the week to marry. Yours will be a conventional marriage, where you strive for the good things in life and have 2.1 children.
Sunday – yours is a marriage that is loving and giving and you shall be blessed with a large and happy family.

Restoring a wedding album

Use a good-quality white leather shoe cleaner to restore a white leather wedding album that has yellowed. Wipe over with methylated spirits on a soft cloth to remove finger marks.

Wedding cake

To keep an un-iced wedding cake, wrap in two layers of brown paper. Store in a cardboard box in a cool dry place. Add some silica gel, making sure the silica gel does not touch the cake. To keep an iced cake, before icing, paint the cake all over with egg white, which has been lightly beaten with a fork. Let the egg white dry before icing the cake. This helps to keep the icing white. Wrap an iced cake in two or three layers of paper and continue in the same vein as for an un-iced cake.

Or put the cake into a freezer bag. Pump all the air out. Seal and store in the freezer.

Dress colours

White

White is the traditional colour for a wedding gown and signifies virginity and virtue. It is indicative of the exclusivity of the relationship between these two people, that they are each other's only lover and that the love that they have, has not been given to any other. It promises devotion and purity. It should only be used for first couplings.

Green

Green is the colour that signifies prosperity and money. The wearer of green, especially if it is in an outdoor ceremony, is cool and elegant. She likes good things and attracts riches. She is cool in her decision-making and she will require the best for her family.

Silver

Silver is the colour of the moon. The wearer of silver will be totally emotionally committed to her husband and family. She will be a gentle soul in a loving family.

Her home will be harmonious and the relationship romantic.

Blue

Blue is the colour of certainty and cool judgment. It says that I know that I have found the right man. We will do this together and we will have fun along the way.

I know that this is the man for me. I have no doubts. This is the man that I will laugh with, live with and love for the rest of my life.

Red

Red is the colour of passion. To wear red on your wedding day means that your marriage will be a passionate relationship with high highs and low lows. Each day will bring new adventure. The wearer of this colour will have a kitchen full of friends.

It will never be boring.

Gold

Gold is the colour of the sun. This is a happy union where the couple are proud of each other and their family. The wearer of a gold costume is a lucky person who will always fall on her feet. She will be loyal and true, warm and sweet.

Black

Black and grey are theatrical costumes, which should only be worn by a Goth who is out to make a social statement. This person is not afraid of anything. She does not care for public approval and will always march to her own tune. Her family will be strong and resilient.

Flowers

Fresh flowers symbolise new life and smell great.

You can spend a fortune at the florist and have your flowers professionally done.

Or you can make your own posies using some of the following flowers:

The meaning of flowers

Roses – Roses are the traditional symbol of luck and romance.

Daisies – Daisies are for simplicity and no fuss.

Orange blossom – Orange blossom is for old-fashioned values.

Sprigs of rosemary – Rosemary is for remembrance and to remind the bride and groom of the good things from the past.

Lilies and orchids – Lilies are for purity and clarity. Orchids are for luxury.
Posy – A posy of mixed flowers means that you will take life as it comes, for better and for worse.
Violets – Violets are for humility and sensual awareness.
Gerberas – Gerberas mean that the wedding party will be a blast.

Assemble your own bouquet

You can hand each guest a single stem – rose, gerbera, iris and lily – along with the order of service. Have them give the stem to either the bride or the groom as they enter the ceremony. This breaks the formality as the happy couple will take the flower, kiss or embrace the guest who hands it to him/her, exchange a word or two and everyone will feel part of the ceremony.

The bride and groom can give out little seed packets you can get at any hardware store. They pick some flowers (usually perennials) they like, and personalise it by attaching a sticker or tag that says 'Please plant these flowers in your yard. Each year when they grow, think of us and enjoy them'.

Ways to keep your bouquet

In order to extend the life of your flowers, keep them out of the sun. Place them in a shadow box or glass container to keep the dust off them.

Freeze-dry your bouquet

One popular method, and the most costly, is freeze-drying. After the moisture is removed in this way, the flowers keep their shape. A post-treatment solution is also applied to the flowers to keep the moisture in the air from going back into the petals.

Make your bouquet using roses that have already been freeze-dried and using other materials that have already been preserved. The look is beautiful, very much like fresh flowers and greens.

Go to the Net and type in freeze dry flowers to your search engine or www.ninemsn.com.au and you will find the people who provide this service in your area, where you can hire equipment to do it yourself and the method to use.

Air-dry your bouquet

Roses can be air dried (hung upside down) and silica dried (follow directions on a can of silica gel). Freesias can be silica dried, but they are extremely delicate. Carnations can be silica dried as well. Tulips and orchids are more difficult to silica dry because the waxy substance on the petals slows down the movement of moisture from the petals to the silica. After silica drying, protect the flowers by dipping individual flowers in hot paraffin. This gives them a nice protective coating and it keeps moisture in the air from getting back into the flowers.

Green plants preserve nicely with a glycerine solution. Some flora will draw up the solution through the stems. Others, like ivy, do best if you immerse the leaves with their stems completely in the solution.

Glycerine solution and method

Mix one part glycerine to two parts boiling water. Add green food colouring to prevent the leaves from turning brown. Leave the greenery in the solution until it does not drink any more solution or until two weeks have passed.

Bubbles instead of confetti

Hand each guest a bubble-blowing kit (they can be bought from party supplies) and ask them to blow bubbles instead of throwing confetti. It's great fun and it gets people talking to each other – and looks great in photos. Also, no cleaning up needs to be done.

The wedding cake

The wedding cake is traditional and signifies the hospitality of the bride and groom, as it is the first gift that they give as a couple. The wedding guest has in the past taken a piece home and slept with it under the pillow so that they could dream of good fortune. It was traditionally decorated with icing and symbols.

- Bells protect the couple from evil influences.
- Keys open the door to a new life.
- Figurines of the bride and groom increase good fortune.
- Fruits symbolise fertility.
- Flowers symbolise a good sexual relationship.
- Hearts unite the two hearts of the bride and groom.
- Ribbons and bows symbolise unity in the marriage.
- A horseshoe is for good luck along life's journey.

How the groom can make a good impression

Arrange to have floral arrangements delivered to your home and your bride's home on the day before the wedding. Add an 'I love you' note to your beautiful wife to be, and thank the parents for their love and support.

Have flowers in the honeymoon suite awaiting your arrival. Add a bottle of champagne, wine or non-alcoholic wine.

To keep that romance going, write down the names and colours of the flowers and file it. On your anniversaries, pull out that list and call your favourite florist. Avoid any floral fragrance that is going to compete with the aromas and flavours of the food.

A second wedding

With a second wedding there is a more difficult minefield to negotiate between several extra major players.

Children of divorce

Children of divorce may have very mixed feelings about a mother or father actually marrying someone new. They may feel disloyal to the other parent if they embrace the idea too readily and attend the wedding. They may feel devastated when they realise that their secret dream of mum and dad reunited will never come true. Reassure the children about the changes that may take place after the wedding.

Talk to them about how they can take an important part in the day. Include your children in your wedding day plans; provide them with happy memories of your wedding day. Those families who all go to the altar together and take part in the rituals have the happiest days of all.

If the news has gone down well when you told your children about your wedding, and they want to be involved, how can they be best included?

- Bridesmaid
- Pageboy
- Best man (or woman)
- Usher
- Flower girl
- Children are also often happy to perform the honour of 'giving the bride away'

Involve the children

Children can be a part of the preparations by helping to make things and to prepare the celebrations.

- Involve them in the planning.
- Your child may like to sing at the wedding.
- Some prefer jobs behind the scenes.
- They may like to suggest colours, flowers and perhaps the music.
- Your wedding day is a great excuse to buy an extra special outfit for the children.
- The children could help with handing out order-of-service sheets, helping to direct people to their places and giving out handfuls of confetti. Alternatives to confetti could be wildflower seeds, rose petals, rice or bubbles.
- Perhaps the children could make a prayer of the faithful, asking that their new family be blessed.
- Have the children stand with you as you make your vows. This will go a long way towards making them feel included on your wedding day.
- You could all join together in lighting a unity candle.
- Perhaps the celebrant could ask the children 'Do you promise to love and obey your new stepfather/mother?' To which they may answer, 'I do'. The new parent could be asked, 'Do you promise to love and support these children from this day forward?'

If there has been pain or grief in the past, nothing can be nicer than to see a new family bonding together to make this a joyous and happy occasion. All the evidence shows that if children are involved in the wedding of a parent they are more likely to accept the marriage.

Beware of a small boy carrying the rings on a pillow if they are not fixed on firmly!

Ex-partner

The ex-partner should be told about the forthcoming wedding well in advance. When the first partner is dead, this is often the time to put grief aside and for all the family to join in celebrating the new union. Consider inviting your ex-parents-in-law so that they can see their granddaughters as bridesmaids.

Wedding Anniversaries

1	Cotton, clocks
2	Paper, china
3	Leather, crystal
4	Fruit, flowers
5	Wood
6	Sugar
7	Copper
8	Bronze
9	Linens and lace
10	Tin
15	Crystal
20	China
25	Silver
30	Pearl
40	Ruby
50	Gold
60	Diamond
75	Diamonds, Gold

Travel
Before you go
Six months before you go
- Check that your passport is still valid.
- If not, begin the process to get a new one.
- Will you require a visa in the countries to which you are travelling?
- Finalise your itinerary.
- Learn what you can about your destination, its customs, its laws and climate.
- Check to see if the country that you are travelling to is safe for travel.
- Are there things that you should know for your own safety?
- Do you need to make a will?

Three months before you go
- Book your ticket.
- Get appropriate travel insurance.
- If you have special needs, check that they can be catered for at your destination.
- Check that your medicines are legal in the country of destination.
- Start thinking about your wardrobe and what you will pack.

Six weeks before you go
- Have a medical check-up at least six weeks before you travel.
- Are your vaccinations and medications up to date?
- Pack a simple medical kit.
- Have a dental check-up
- Have an eye check-up
- Pick up your tickets.
- See your bank about the currency you will require, travellers' cheques, credit cards, etc.
- Leave a copy of your itinerary with a responsible person, so that somebody is aware of your movements.
- Arrange for somebody to look after your house, pets, etc.
- Inform your neighbours of your impending trip and ask them to keep an eye on your house.

In the final two weeks
- Finalise security arrangements for your house.
- Check developments and the state of the politics in the country of destination.
- Cancel newspapers and all other deliveries.
- Arrange for somebody to take junk mail and ordinary mail from your mail box.
- Prepay any bills that may come while you are away.
- Pack and label your luggage.
- Leave a copy of your itinerary, passport photo page, travellers' cheques and your credit card with a friend or relative. Arrange to keep in regular contact.
- Photocopy your documents so you can keep them separately from your handbag.
- Always carry additional copies of your passport photo with you.

Leaving
- Put a container with a few drops of lavender oil in it in each room. This will discourage insects and prevent that musty smell.
- Turn off the power and the gas.
- Lock all the windows and doors.
- Have the car serviced and full of petrol.
- Check the fan belt and radiator hose to see that they are in good condition.

Plants

Look after your plants while you are away.

Ask a neighbour whom you can trust to water your garden for you.
If that is not possible do the best to ensure the health of your plants:

- Give the garden and your plants a good soak before you go.
- Water large, hard-to-move pots by filling a large bottle with water and inverting it into the soil near the stem of the plant.
- Dig outdoor plants into a hole in a shady part of the garden.
- Immerse bricks in water then stand the pot on top.
- Stand pot plant inside a plastic bag, draw the bag up and secure with an elastic band. Leave only the plant uncovered.
- Install an automatic timer on your watering system.

Check-ups

Have a dental check-up and if you wear glasses or contact lenses take a spare pair and your prescription. If you need to take medication, take the prescription or a letter from your doctor with you.

Cross-cultural calculator

Buy a gadget, which includes a digital clock, calendar and calculator, to work out those exchange rates. After all, how can you call yourself a serious haggler if you don't know the prices?

Driver's licence

If you plan to drive overseas, make sure your Australian driver's licence is current and obtain an international driving licence before you leave.

Equipment

Buy a small luggage bag. That way, you won't over-pack. Test cameras and lenses before you leave. Store your camera gear and films in a sealed bag.

First aid kit

Pack aspirin or paracetamol, antihistamine, antibiotics – take your prescription – Band-Aids (especially for blisters), insect repellent, sunscreen, chap stick and your antimalarial drugs. Take extras such as a sewing kit, a pocket knife and adaptor plugs.

Fitness

Do the hard work *before* you go. There's nothing worse than feeling out of breath and tired in the middle of the day when you're at a fantastic holiday spot.

Guidebooks

When buying a guidebook, make sure it is current. Check out the date it was published.

Health Insurance

Buy a travel insurance policy to cover theft, loss and medical treatment in an emergency. Invest in top medical cover if you're heading to the United States, where medical treatment will cost you an arm and a leg if you're not covered. If you plan to dabble in adventure sports, make sure they're covered in the insurance policy.

Passport

Check the date when your passport expires. Make sure your passport is valid for at least six months after the time you intend to travel overseas.

For information on passports and the safety of the area you plan to visit, contact the Australian Department of Foreign Affairs at www.dfat.gov.au/passports.

Phone card

If travelling overseas, buy a phone card instead of using your mobile phone. If you purchase an international sim card for your mobile phone, you must pay the extra call costs when someone rings you. Pricey.

Roll clothes

When packing, you will find that your clothes pack better and arrive less crinkled if you roll them up, rather than lay them flat.

Research

A good way to find out the feel of a place is to read a novel or see a film set in the area before you go.

Travel agents

Shop around for a knowledgeable travel agent. It can make all the difference as to whether your holiday is a hit or a nightmare.

Travel books

Buy a travel book about the place where you are going. Lonely Planet's *World Food* books on Morocco, Vietnam, Italy, Thailand and Spain are excellent. As well as featuring local delicacies, each book comes with a brief dictionary at the back, with phrases from 'please' and 'thank you' to 'I'm a vegetarian' and the essential 'where's the toilet?'.

Weather

Check out what the weather will be like in the countries you plan to visit before committing to an itinerary. Sightseeing in sweltering heat is no picnic. Likewise, remember that travelling in winter will mean shorter days and less daylight to see the sights.

Working holidays

A great way to see the world without having to be a millionaire. To line up a working holiday, read, 'Work Your Way Around the World: Vacation Work', published by Vacation Press.

International travel tips

Airport shuttle bus

Take an airport van or a bus to and from the airport. They are usually much cheaper than taxis and, if you ask nicely, they may drop you off at your hotel door.

Basic language

Make an effort to learn basic language greetings to use at bus stops, restaurants and bars. That way, you'll get to meet the locals.

Beware thieves

Flaunting camera gear, jewellery and designer shopping bags can encourage theft. Be discreet. Try not to look like a tourist. Also, read the map and get your bearings before you head out into the streets.

Beware of scams

While it's great to be open-minded, the reality is that you need to be on guard when strangers approach you and strike up conversation. One scam includes the hustler bumping into you, pushing an ice-cream on your shirt and in the following mayhem, nicking your wallet.

Camera

Know thy camera. Consider taking a photo class before you leave for mind-blowing shots on your travels. Don't forget to label each roll of used film as you go.

Check with embassy

If you're considering travelling to a politically troubled country, contact the relevant embassy in Australia before you go to identified troublespots.

Children

Travel With Children, by Maureen Wheeler, is essential reading for those travelling with little ones. It's published by Lonely Planet.

Clothing

Layer and go for clothes that don't need ironing. You'd be mad to pack a white 100% cotton shirt for a business trip. Light colours show dirt. Pack a tie or a top for an impromptu glamorous night out. Never ever pack shoes you haven't worn before. Blisters will happen.

Credit cards

When it comes to activating your credit card at automatic teller machines, look for the Maestro and Cirrus signs. These two brands can, theoretically, accept your credit card worldwide. Check with your bank before you leave home.

Crime

If the worst happens and you are the victim of theft, go straight to the police station and file a police report. This is necessary to obtain a new passport and to make an insurance claim.

Disabled travellers

Information for travellers with disabilities can be found at Independent Travellers, 167 Gilles St, Adelaide.

Drink responsibly

Don't get visibly drunk in a public place such as a bar and then walk back to your hotel alone late at night. You're asking for trouble.

Drive away program

In the United States, a perfect way to drive vast distances is through the drive away program. Basically, you drive a car across the country and deliver it to its owner. You pay the petrol costs. Look in the American Yellow Pages under 'Automobile Transporters'.

Email

To stay in touch with folks back home, set up a free email account at hotmail:
(www.hotmail.com).

Empty film containers

Empty film containers are ideal for keeping small items safe – especially when travelling.

Eurail passes

Eurail passes give you unlimited travel on Europe's rail network in seventeen western
countries of Europe. Eurail passes are available as consecutive day passes or flexipasses.
They must be bought in your home country.

Guided walks

If you're new to a city, the best way to get your bearings is to take a guided walking tour.
That way, you won't spend every waking moment with your nose in a guidebook, worried
about getting lost.

High altitudes

If trekking from sea level to high altitudes, take it easy. Give your body time to adjust to
the thinning air. Carry adequate drinking water.

Immunisations

Have the required injections at least six weeks before you leave. Ask your doctor whether
you need immunisation against hepatitis A, hepatitis B and typhoid.

If you're travelling to Africa, consider cholera immunisation. If you're travelling to Asia,
consider immunisation against Japanese B encephalitis. Immunisation against meningo-
coccal meningitis may be a good idea for travellers to certain parts of Asia, India, Africa and
South America. Immunisation against polio, rabies and tetanus is a good idea for every traveller. In some countries, proof of vaccination against yellow fever is required.

In every instance, consult your doctor.

Itinerary

Double-check your itinerary before you leave. Even after you've been through it with your
travel agent. Double-check that you have all entrance tickets and the relevant visas.

Jet lag

Jet lag isn't pretty. If you arrive in the day after a long flight feeling like a drowned rat, fight
the temptation to sink into the hotel bed and never rise. Go for a walk to stay awake.

A New Age approach to curing jet lag is to try essential oils such as eucalyptus, geranium, grapefruit, lavender, lemongrass or peppermint dabbed on your forehead or on the
balls of your feet.

Lunch

When travelling, it is better to make lunch the main meal of the day as many restaurants
charge more for dinner at night.

Markets

A perfect way to take in the scenery and the food in a foreign land is to have a picnic
lunch from market produce. Beats bland fast-food takeaway any day.

Money
To avoid being stuck with no money, divide your money into cash, traveller's cheques and credit cards and keep it on different parts of your body.

Nerves of steel
If buying a campervan, remember that it may be difficult to manoeuvre it down narrow country lanes in places such as England. Also, you need to be a good navigator and have nerves of steel to negotiate your way through the traffic snarls of Europe.

Plastic bags
Plastic bags are very handy when you are travelling. Use them for:

- Wet clothes
- Shoes
- Toiletries
- Dirty laundry
- Keeping tickets, passports, visas and other documents together

Postage bags
Padded postage bags are handy for nail-polish, cosmetics, etc.

Pyjamas
If you're arriving at your destination at night, pack your pyjamas on the top so you don't need to turn your luggage inside out to find it.

Road safety
When crossing the road, look in both directions and remember that traffic may be coming from the opposite direction. Stop at the curb. It sounds elementary, but so many people have near-death experiences when crossing roads overseas.

Safety
Don't walk down deserted streets or in parks late at night. If you do get mugged, don't be argumentative. Give the mugger what they want and don't make any sudden movements.

Stopovers
If you're travelling vast distances, include a stopover trip to reduce jet lag.

Take sunscreen
If you are snorkelling or swimming, make sure that your back and all other exposed areas are well covered by sunscreen.

Taxis
Before you take a taxi anywhere, work out the shortest route. This will avoid the problem of sitting in the back as the meter clicks away, being given the long 'scenic route' by a shrewd cabbie.

Theatre
To book tickets to shows and events overseas, visit www.latestevents.com.

Time difference

Note the international dialling code and the time differences of the places where you will be travelling. If in doubt, take two watches. That way, you won't get your friends back home out of bed at three in the morning for a chat.

Timing

When planning a holiday to southern USA or Mexico, keep in mind that hurricanes sometimes hit the Gulf of Mexico from June to November.

Tipping

If you're heading to the United States, tip 15%. So, for instance, for a $20 bill, tip $3. In Europe, tip 10%, that is $2 for a $20 service.

Travel sickness

To combat travel sickness, take ginger and vitamin B6 one hour before boarding. Aromatherapy oils said to reduce travel sickness symptoms include mandarin, peppermint, spearmint and lavender.

Destination tips

Egypt

Pack a torch and cold water in your day bag when you're visiting the pyramid tombs in Egypt.

Islamic countries

Females heading to non-Western countries, such as Islamic countries, should wear loose clothes. Dress in long skirts and pants and don't bare your shoulders. Shorts are out altogether.

Men will do best in long summer-weight pants and loose, long-sleeved shirts. Shorts and open-necked shirts are inappropriate.

Luxury accommodation

For the ultimate in dead gorgeous accommodation, dip into 'The Small Luxury Hotels of the World Directory'. Even if you can't afford a night in the properties mentioned, it's fun to see how the other half holiday. Fairytale French chateaus, Indian palaces, English manors and Austrian chalets are all mentioned. Key in www.slh.com.

New York

Serious shopaholics heading to New York should not miss the bargain-priced designer label clothes available from Century 21 at 12 Cortland Street and at Filene's basement at 620 6th Avenue.

Back home

Storing a suitcase

When storing a suitcase, place an unwrapped piece of soap inside. It will smell fresh when you next use it.

Eating abroad

Safe foods when travelling

Anything that is steaming hot or packaged

Unpeeled fruit
Ripened cheeses
Cooked vegetables

Unsafe foods when travelling
Raw fish
Cold salads
Cold sauces
Hamburgers
Peeled fruit
Cold desserts
Fresh soft cheeses
Strawberries

Safe drinks
Carbonated
Bottled water
Boiled water
Iodised water
Packaged ice
Fresh fruit juice
Irradiated milk

Unsafe drinks
Tap water
Chipped ice
Non-pasteurised milk

Overseas holidays
Africa
In Africa, you can grab adventure with both hands.

See wildebeest roaming across sun-drenched savannahs, and visit ancient tribes. Africa spans from the Mediterranean in the north, through the world's largest desert, the Sahara to majestic Mount Kilamanjaro in the east and to the south the Swaziland and then Cape Town at the southern tip.

It pays to play it safe in Africa. There's current political unrest in places such as Algeria, Angola, the Congo, Sierra Leone and on the border of Ethiopia and Eritrea. Check with the government website for warnings before you embark on your trip to anywhere in Africa.

Cape Town and South Africa
Cape Town is at the southern tip of Africa at the Cape of Good Hope. Table Mountain, a 100-metre plateau, overlooks the city. Take the cable car for awesome views from the top. Visit the ultra-trendy beaches at Clifton and see wildlife in the Cape of Good Hope nature reserve. Take a day trip to the wineries of the tollenbosch, which date back to the 1700s. Cape Dutch buildings from the era remain.

Kenya
Kenya, bordering the Indian Ocean, is safari land. From the capital Nairobi, organise a safari to the Masai Mara National Reserve on the Tanzanian border for the annual wildebeest migration.

Morocco

Marrakech, Morocco, is a buzzing, chaotic and colourful city – a ferry ride from the south of Spain. Hit the markets to haggle for rugs, silver teapots, ceramics, and brassware and sandalwood boxes. Sip sugary mint tea and eat a barbecued meal at the Market Square, Djemma el-Fna, where snake charmers and acrobats vie for your tip.

Lome

Lome is in West Africa near the Gulf of Guinea. The Marche des Feticheurs is voodoo culture at its best. Animal potions, organs and mysterious bottles promise a remedy to every medical problem. The market is eight kilometres from Lome.

Zimbabwe

If you visit Zimbabwe, chances are you'll have Victoria Falls on your itinerary. At the falls, the Zambezi River tumbles 107 metres into the river below, sending huge clouds of spray into the air and making a deafening rumble. For a different view, take a flight over the falls, or spend some time white-water rafting or canoeing further down the river.

Europe

Europe – where do you start? The area is loaded with fine art and architecture. Iceland, Great Britain, Spain, Italy, France, Greece and Turkey are just some of the highlights. Wherever you end up, you'll need to pace yourself to prevent sightseeing overload. Visiting a glut of medieval churches and countless galleries in a short period of time can put you off travel for life. Try not to overload yourself. Choose a couple of destinations and enjoy time to explore and to learn about the history and culture of the area. Take time out to live with, and watch, the locals going about their day.

Rome

It's easy to see why they say all roads lead to Rome. This city is oozing classical antiquity. Eat a wedge of authentic pizza at the Spanish Steps, and throw coins into the marble Trevi Fountain in the heart of the city. Take a step back in time to ancient Rome. The Forum ruins were the political epicentre of the modern world 2000 years ago, and the Colosseum, situated nearby, opened in AD 80.

Barcelona

Spain is the home turf of the great artists, Dali, Picasso and Gaudi. Envelop yourself in their art and learn to understand and love their work and lives. In Barcelona, see architect Antonio Gaudi's whimsical unfinished church, La Sagrada Familia, which hovers eccentrically over the city skyline. Wander through the Ramblas, a wide pedestrian thoroughfare lined with buskers and Art Nouveau street lamps. Stop for lunch at the Bouqueria Food Market nearby, and eat tapas in a loud lively bar late at night.

London

Stop at hip Neal's Yard in Covent Garden, see a West End production in Drury Lane and buy a ticket for the world's biggest Ferris wheel at the Millennium Dome.

Pop into the National Gallery at Trafalgar Square, once the site of the Royal Mews.

London has red double-decker buses, beautiful bridges, fine architecture, the Queen and all the pomp in the world. It's where it all happens.

Athens

Despite the ugly modern office blocks, the Parthenon and the Acropolis, shrines to the classical era, continue to stand out on the city skyline. Take a day trip to Delphi for more classical ruins and a museum depicting what life was like in Ancient Greece.

Greek Islands
White-washed villages perched on cliffs, the sound of bouzouki playing in tiny cafés and dozens of islands with that picture-postcard look. Visit the famous island of Santorini for ouzo drinking and Greek dancing. But also try some of the islands off the beaten track. After all, island hopping is the name of the game here.

Iceland
Can't find enough hours in your day? Well, head to Iceland, in the middle of the North Atlantic. See the midnight sun at Eyjafjordur at Lake Myvatu. From the capital Reykjavik take a few day trips into the remote countryside. There are fjords to the east, mountains to the north and glaciers, hot springs and waterfalls to the south. There are Eskimos.

Dublin
Have a chat with a local at a pub over a pint of Guinness. Enter Dublin Castle which dates back to the 13th century and is now the state apartments for the Irish president. Take a tour of Trinity College, founded by Elizabeth 1 in 1591. Up until 1966, only Protestant students were allowed at the university. Famous students included Oscar Wilde and Samuel Beckett. Go out into the Irish countryside and enjoy the accents and the pub culture.

North America
From Alaska and the Rockies, to California in the east, through the central Great Plains, across to New York in the west and down to the Deep South, contradictions abound. From honky-tonk towns to the power base of Washington. From Gospel and jazz to hip hop. From fast food and cable TV to refined architecture and acclaimed 20th-century art. It's these contradictions which make North America get under your skin.

Chicago
By the Great Lakes of America's mid-west lies Chicago, Illinois. It's renowned for its blues and jazz, and mind-boggling architecture, from city skyscrapers to the work of architect Frank Lloyd Wright. You can visit the Oak Park house where he lived and worked from 1898 to 1908. Make time for a trip to the Art Institute of Chicago and view the impressionist and post-impressionist works. Take a 'Gangster Tour' of old-time Chicago and visit the haunts of Al Capone.

New York
Manhattan is the place for fast-paced, in-your-face urban living. Take a gospel tour to Harlem, jump on the ferry to Staten Island. See a TV show taping. Eat a lox bagel at Dean & Deluca's deli in Soho. Get your art fix at the Met, the MOMA and the Guggenheim. Stop for a hot pretzel at Central Park. Shop at Barneys, Macy's and Sak's Fifth Avenue. And if you still have energy, walk across the Brooklyn Bridge.

Washington
See the free Smithsonian museums, including the NASA museum, the Holocaust Museum and the National Museum of American History. Catch a train to the Arlington National Cemetery dedicated to those killed in war. Tour the Capitol Buildings. Eat, drink and hit the clubs at funky Dupont Circle.

New Orleans

New Orleans in Louisiana borders the Mississippi. Jazz rules. Head to Bourbon Street in the French Quarter for blues, zydeco, cajun or Dixieland live music. Try some Cajun Creole cooking and try the chicory coffee and beignets at the renowned Café du Monde in the French Quarter. It's open twenty-four hours. Veteran jazz musos perform at Preservation Hall, near Bourbon Street. And if you're in New Orleans in early January, the Mardi Gras parade is compulsory viewing.

Hollywood

Dripping with nostalgia, Art Deco, palm trees and clipped lawns, this is a throwback to the old movie days when stars once had true glamour. See the famous sign, 'HOLLYWOOD', perched on Hollywood Hills which is on many a postcard.

Take a trail up the hill for a closer view. See the concrete prints of more than 150 film stars on Hollywood Boulevard outside Mann's Chinese Theatre. Drop in at the visitor's centre, Janes House, on Hollywood Boulevard to book a roadside tour of houses formerly owned by Holly-wood legends.

Central and South America

This area stretches from the Central American countries of Mexico and Cuba, through the Panama Canal and beyond to the southern continent, where you'll find the Amazon rainforest, the tango and the samba and the Andes. Jungles and ancient ruins and absolutely gorgeous beach resorts are thick on the ground. Check with the relevant embassy before embarking on a trip to countries in South America.

Rio de Janeiro

People come to this city on the Atlantic in Brazil for the crowded beaches, such as Copacabana and Ipanema. Body watching has been raised to an art form. Travellers also go to Rio for the sexy street dance party, Carnaval in February/March. For a higher form of culture, see an opera at the Teatro Municipal, built in 1905. The best view can be had 396 metres above the city in a cable car.

Santiago

From Santiago, Chile, you can see the 6000-metre snow-capped Andes some 100 kilometres away. Santiago is big on museums. Take a breather from the crowds, the smog and the traffic at Cerro Santa Lucia, a sprawling garden with fountains on the hill above the city.

Cancun

Cancun, Mexico, is a sand-spit resort on the Yucatan peninsula. It's the playground of choice for filthy-rich Americans in search of sun, cocktails, warm water and lavish resorts. Cancun even has its own international airport. This is the place to park yourself on a deckchair with a cocktail by the warm waters of the Caribbean and not budge an inch for the entire day.

Buenos Aires

Buenos Aires in Argentina is on the Rio de la Plata in western South America. Take a catamaran tour along the Delta to the nearby island, Isla Martin Garcia. It's a lush tropical park and a welcome escape from sardine-packed Buenos Aires. See a soccer game and soak up the atmosphere of the Feria de San.

Machu Picchu

At the top western edge of South America lies the stone archaeological site of Machu Picchu, in Peru. The city ruins hark back to the time of the Incas, but the date when they were built remain a mystery. The city has sundials, shrines and long winding staircases in abundance. Take a tour of the site at night when there's a full moon for an unforgettable experience, but don't try to camp there – guards check the site at sundown to make sure no one stays the night.

Asia

From hi-tech cutting-edge electronic outlets in Tokyo to the surreal sight of a geisha in full kimono gliding down a busy street. From Buddhist monks begging for alms outside temples to crowds of office workers at a noodle house at midday. No matter how many times you visit Asia, you'll always discover a town, a restaurant or an inn owner who offers an entirely new perspective on the place.

Thailand

When it comes to shopping bargains, Bangkok is the perfect place to give your credit card a workout. But it'll give your nerves a workout at the same time . . . Bangkok is brash and loud. That said, there's more to Bangkok than shopping. Visit the National Museum for a brush-up lesson in Thai art, history and culture. The museum has everything you've ever wanted to know about Thai culture and more. Visit some of the many Buddhist temples dotted throughout the city.

Hanoi

Hanoi is the capital of the Socialist Republic of Vietnam. There are lakes and temples galore. You can see the glass sarcophagus encasing former leader Ho Chi Minh at the Ho Chi Minh Mausoleum.

Tokyo

The Ginza district is the final word in shopping and dining out in Japan. A ten-minute walk away is the Imperial Palace, home to the Japanese emperor. Wander through the gardens and take a photo of Nijubashi Bridge. Art buffs should head to the National Museum of Modern Art for a review of Japanese art.

Myanmar

Formerly known as Burma, Myanmar is home to a multitude of Buddhist monks, highly visible in their bright orange robes. The floating markets, homes and gardens on the Inle Lake in the south-east are a must-see. Boats and canoes are the only form of transportation.

Singapore

Dine in luxury at the Raffles Hotel, which offers a window into the Singapore of old, before the rise and rise of modern shopping malls. Take a tour on the harbour in a Chinese junk to the rubber plantations nearby, and book yourself in for a walking tour of Chinatown.

The Pacific

For Australians, the Pacific is the ultimate place for island living minus the jet lag.

From family-run inns at traditional villages to islands sporting multimillion-dollar resorts, the accommodation choice is virtually limitless. What's more, the Pacific has rainforests and water sports sorted. This, as they say, is living.

Rotorua

On New Zealand's North Island, Rotorua is a tourism hub. Don't let that put you off, it's worth the visit to see the bubbling mud and hissing steams in the Taupo volcanic region. There's also black-water rafting at the nearby Waitomo caves. This involves floating through dark underwater channel . . . if you dare.

Noumea

Noumea, New Caledonia, blends French colonial architecture, with cafés, nightclubs, lagoons and tropical beaches. Oh, and it's a great place to practise your school-level French.

Langkawi

Langkawi is a Malaysian island of mountainous steamy jungles, which lead onto powdery white beaches. It has a handful of ritzy resorts, which resemble small towns in themselves – complete with golf courses, restaurants and tour guides. Head there between October and April to avoid the wet season, when the mozzies come out in force.

Bali

The low rupiah makes Bali a bargain basement package tour destination for Australians. But to get the most out of a holiday in Bali, you need to venture away from the brash back-packer zone at Kuta and head to the more refined Sanur and beyond. Also worth a visit is Nusa Dua. The gentle Balinese are suffering greatly since the terrorist attacks.

Middle East

At the moment the Middle East is a good place to stay away from. Let's pray that peace will descend upon the good people of that region soon. The Middle East has ancient cul-ture at every turn. Watch long robed men and women at village markets straight out of Biblical times, walk around an old walled city with winding dirt alleyways, and take in the vastness of the desert.

Cairo

Cairo is a mix of Middle East, African and European cultures. Archaeologically, Cairo's got the lot. The pyramids of Giza take family graves to a new level. Those towering mausoleums were for a grandfather, a father and a son – Cheops, Chephren and Mycerius. Watch a night-ly sound-and-light show at the Sphinx, which stands watch in front of the pyramids. Glide down the Nile, visit a camel market, and see a performance of Sufi dancing.

Istanbul

With Asia on one side and Europe on the other, Istanbul is a good stopping-off point dur-ing a trip to either continent. Istanbul is in the Bosphorus Strait on the Black Sea.

It is loaded with history from the Roman, Byzantine and Ottoman empires, and jam-packed with museums, markets, mosques and castles.

Israel

The Dead Sea is the beach health spa nirvana of Israel. Some people swear by the spa baths as cures for all sorts of ailments. The Dead Sea is a sixty-minute drive from Jerusalem and a two-hour drive from Tel Aviv. It is not a good place to visit at the moment and it won't ever be until they manage to sort out the Palestinian problem.

Driving holidays

Have the car serviced before you go to ensure that you will not be caught stranded on the side of a hot dusty road. Take with you:

- Insect repellent
- Water bottles
- Wet weather gear
- A good road map
- A compass
- Activities to keep the children amused, while travelling and when stopped

Motoring holidays with children

Holidays with children can be fun. It is a bonding time for the family when the daily stresses of life are absent. With proper planning and a positive mindset your family holidays will be remembered as the best times of your life. However, with a negative mindset and no planning they could be living hell.

Limit driving time

Try not to travel too far in the one go with children. Break your journey into two-hour segments. Stop so that the children can have a run or play in a park. Share the driving between you and your partner.

Eight hours travel a day

It is possible to travel eight hours each day without complaints from anybody:

- It is a good idea to start early, two hours before normal breakfast time.
- Travel for two hours before breakfast.
- Stop at a fast-food outlet where the children can play.
- Travel another two hours.
- Stop at a park near a bakery and have a cup of tea while the children play on a playground.
- Travel another two hours and stop for lunch and a play.
- Travel for two more hours.
- Stop for the day in time for a play and dinner before bed. Don't leave it too late so that you are thinking about stopping as the sun goes down.
- Get up the next day and start again.

Rotate seats

Rotate seats after every stop, so that family members are not sitting next to the same person all of the time. It gives everyone a chance to relate to a different person each time the seating is changed and relieves boredom and entrenched hostility. This means Mum and Dad too! It goes like this:

Dad starts out driving and at the first stop he moves into the rear driver-side seat, the whole family rotate so that back passenger side moves to the front, and Mum moves to the driver's seat. Next change, Dad goes back to the driver's seat, Mum sits in the back and back passenger side moves to the front, and so on. Whoever is in front with the driver, gets to play their choice of music.

Music

Have each person bring their own music that they can play when they are sitting in the front passenger seat. This encourages discussion and helps Mum and Dad become familiar with their children's culture. Give everyone a sixty-minute tape each – or blank CD if you have a burner – and tell them to put fifteen of their favourite tracks on it. Mum and Dad, too! That way everyone gets a chance to play what they want. Near the end of the trip you can have a vote to see who has the best compilation, in terms of content, artists, technical expertise, etc.

Fun pack

Have some games, stories, pencils and paper and a pack of cards so that if things get boring there is something to do.

Snow

Don't be caught tearing down the slopes without waterproof clothing, and layer your clothes. Wear a hat. Half of your body heat can be lost through your head.

Emergency supplies

Pack a first aid kit and a fire extinguisher.

Picnics

Children love finger foods. They enjoy mini sausage rolls, sandwiches, breads and dips, crackers, cold meats, cheese, carrot sticks, cherry tomatoes.

Picnic where there is a barbecue, it opens up all sorts of possibilities for eating.

Don't forget to take:

Plates
Plastic glasses
Cutlery
Corkscrew
Insect repellent
Sunscreen
Wet ones
Flask of tea/coffee
Iced water in bottles
Games to play – cricket bat, Frisbee, football

Local travel tips

Weather

In Australia, the monsoon season goes from November to March. It will rain every day and there may be cyclones.

If you're bound for the snow, make sure there is anti-freeze in the radiator.

Walking

When walking the golden rule is never to walk further than the capabilities of your youngest child.

Box jellyfish

In north Queensland, watch out for box jellyfish if you plan to swim. They are present in the water around Cairns from late October to June, and in Rockhampton from December to March. Box jellyfish thrive after local rain when the sea is calm.

Baby

When travelling with a baby, take a packet of bicarbonate of soda with you. If the baby vomits a sprinkle on the baby's clothes with the bicarbonate of soda will take away the odour when brushed off.

Rules for camping holidays

Never pitch a tent or park a caravan under large trees. Branches can fall on you and kill you.

Never camp in empty river beds. Flash floods can turn a dry river bed into a torrent.

Wash laundry while you travel

If you are travelling from place to place, keep your laundry under control. Half fill a plastic rubbish bin with water. Add detergent and your soiled clothes. Place the lid on firmly. Wedge bin in the corner of the van or car. The movement will wash the clothes. When you arrive at your destination, rinse clothes and hang out to dry.

All-purpose apron

A towelling apron with two large pockets is very useful in camp park laundries for holding pegs, soap, things left in pockets, etc.

Quick camp snacks

Fill a flask with boiling water. Add instant soup mix. It will be ready for you next time you are hungry.

Fill an open-necked flask with boiling water and frankfurts. Drain at mealtime and place into rolls.

Baked beans or canned spaghetti make delicious fillings for toasted sandwiches.

Tinned sausage stew tastes great in a toasted sandwich if you are hungry enough.

Bushwalking precautions

Before you set off, always tell someone where you are going, and what time you expect to be back. Plan where you are going by checking maps or charts, and asking locals for advice, rather than charging off down the trail. Do not aim for a return time that will be perilously close to nightfall. Leave plenty of time between your expected return and sundown.

Never walk alone. A group of four is the best and safest. Always keep each member in view at all times, especially children. Take with you enough water and energy foods to cover all contingencies. Wear clothing in layers. Take a box of matches, paper and a pen/pencil.

Continually check the map, matching up the features and surroundings. If something on the map does not become obvious, retrace your steps and try that section again. If you cannot find an anticipated trail, abandon the walk and return to base. Get all the best available forecast information on the likely weather for the day.

If the weather looks worse than anticipated, play it safe, go home, watch a video and come back another day.

If you do get lost . . .

If you get lost, dampen all feelings of panic, sit down and calmly work out where you believe you are. Keep everyone together and rationally discuss your situation.

Retrace your steps, but be very careful about this. If, after a few hundred metres at most, you are still not sure where you are, then stop, make a camp and wait for the search party. Slogging on aimlessly is not going to do you or anyone any good.

Make a camp with whatever equipment you have and light a fire with the box of matches we recommended you take with you. This will not only provide warmth and comfort but give searchers something to aim for.

Select a camping spot that will help keep you dry and warm – trees with big canopies, rocks, caves, hollow logs or trunks.

Lean long branches at a 45° angle onto a rock, and place branches and brush on top to construct a makeshift tent to keep out the cold and wind.

Keep the fire going at all times.

Camping next to water sounds a great idea in terms of sustenance and comfort, but it is wise not to stay too close because the sound of the running water might drown out the calls and noise of the search party.

It is not wise to move from your emergency camp, tempting as it is. You risk heading further into unknown territory, burning up energy, and frustrating attempts of the searchers, who will have estimated approximately where you are.

If you do move, identify the trail you take by leaving markings on trees or breaking sticks, and so on. And if you do move on, leave a message explaining which way you headed, what time, where you intend on heading, and what is the physical condition of everyone in the group. Always keep movement down to a minimum to conserve energy. Keep everyone's spirits up.

Reassure young members of the group that you have everything under control, you are in no danger, and you will be found by the search party. Make regular calls or distress signals. Not random shouting, but three consecutive noises – such as from a whistle, shouting or banging – at regular intervals.

House exchange

Exchanging your house with another person or family in a different state or country is a great way to enjoy a holiday, especially as it eliminates the cost of accommodation.

Do:
- Join a reputable house exchange organisation, for example:
  www.seniorshomeexchange.com
  www.sunswap.com
- Ask for email addresses of previous exchanges.
- Trust that the person you are exchanging with is just like you.
- Set out clearly in writing who pays for what.
- Check your bills when you get home.
- Leave good, reliable written instructions for the running of your home.
- Leave a list of local attractions and how to get there.

Don't:
- Exchange with a family if you don't have children yourself.
- Leave valuables in the house.
- Do it if you can't relax and trust that the other person has given you his house.

Garden

Dos and don'ts for your garden before you go on holiday:

- Do not fertilise your garden in the weeks before you go on holiday. Fertilisers encourage growth which in turn requires more water.
- Apply a wetting agent to your soil instead. This will ensure maximum penetration and better retention.

- Mulch the garden with soil containing moisture retentive organic materials from your compost heap.
- Wrap your terracotta pots in plastic before you give them a final watering to prevent the pots from drying out.
- Group your pots together in a shady spot out of the wind.
- Use the 'wick' watering system where a wick (such as pantyhose, rope, or some other porous material) is placed in a bucket of water and runs down to the pot. Capillary action will draw the water into the pot.
- Install an automatic watering system that will water your plants at the same time each day.
- Have a neighbour come and check and water your garden regularly.
- Consider paying somebody from a gardening/lawn mowing business to keep your garden going.
- Consider paying your neighbour's children to come and turn the hoses on twice a week.

Going off-road

If you have purchased a new or second-hand 4WD, there are a few things to remember when you go off-road. And by that we mean going really off-road into the Outback, mountains, or far away from your usual metropolitan haunts.

Partner

Travel with at least one other vehicle. Despite your best preparations, there is always the risk of getting stuck, having a breakdown, or being involved in an accident. When travelling with another car, or among a group, always keep within sight of at least one other car.

Communication

And don't think that because you have a mobile phone, if the rest of the party disappears out of view that you can get to them. Despite the increasing proliferation of phone towers around Australia, there are still lots of Outback areas where they simply do not work. CB radio was devised for this sort of journey and it is wise to have one on board.

Vehicle

There are 4WDs – and 4WDs. Many are the muscular bush-bashers that were built specifically for the tough going. But more and more boutique 4WDs are coming on the market, where the accent is on luxury and about-town driving rather than strength. Make sure you are aware of your vehicle's true capabilities. It can be tough out there.

Where to?

For your first journey, pick a relatively easy trail. Books such as *Explore Australia by Four Wheel Drive* have excellent trips for beginners. Wherever you are going, get the most detailed map you can, showing all bush tracks.

Time

Allow plenty of time. Your average speed on a bush track can be very slow, especially if there are deep holes, fallen trees, rivers, and mud to negotiate.

Prepare

Make sure your battery and tyres are in good shape, and that the 4WD is fully serviced.

Safety

- When you reach the dirt, improve traction by getting out and lowering the tyre-pressure until the sidewalls bulge slightly.
- Drive with your thumbs and fingers on the outside of the steering wheel. You can strain or break a finger when the wheel kicks back on you.
- Drive slow for safety.
- If an obstacle such as a rock, tree or river appears into view, get out and look if you are unsure as to what challenge it poses and work out your strategy.
- Do not stop when halfway through trying to get up a slope.
- Never turn around on a hill. If you come to a stop, reverse.
- Don't drink and drive.
- Even though you are away from the bitumen and going slowly, belt up.

Driving

- When climbing, keep the revs up and your foot off the clutch or it can burn out.
- If you have an automatic transmission, select a low gear and hold it.
- When descending, use a gear that acts as a brake as well.
- Avoid mud-holes.
- Take hills and downslopes straight-on in low range, low gear.
- Take logs, ditches and rocks at an angle, one wheel at a time.
- Do not straddle large rocks.
- Cross creeks slowly in low gear and keep the revs up.

Survival

Always have on board:
- Medical kit
- Water
- Tool kit
- Shovel
- Axe
- Fire extinguisher
- Torch
- Jumper leads
- Winch
- Snatch straps and buckles
- Tent
- Cooking equipment
- Fold-up chairs
- Food
- Drink
- Insect repellent
- Spare fuses, pipes, hoses
- Ropes
- Two spare wheels
- Silicone gasket fixer
- Radiator stop leak
- WD40 spray
- Tube of glue
- Extra fuel
- Pump
- Tape

Boating

Recreational boating is one of the most popular sports of all. Remember most states now are introducing a Boat Operator Licence. You must pass a test on boat safety and waterway regulations and rules.

Basic safety gear

- Life jacket for each person on board.
- Mobile telephone or radio.
- Five gallon water container filled with water.
- Flare.
- V-sheet, which is a large orange flag with a large black V printed on it to attract attention of rescuers.
- Light stick or emergency waterproof light, which will allow boaters to read flare instructions, attract attention, check the engine and act as a general all-round emergency light.
- Mirror to attract attention.
- Whistle to attract attention in poor visibility or if the boater is in the water.

Know your boat

Boats capsize for reasons as simple as the people on board moving around it inappropriately. Know your boat's capabilities. Pay attention to the pattern of the ocean.

Talk to the locals who will tell you about the sand bars, and the local conditions. If you are crossing a sand bar have your life jacket on. Always let somebody know when you are going and when you expect to get back.

Local destinations

Northern Territory

Given its location at the tip of Australia, the Northern Territory is often said to have two seasons instead of four – the wet and the dry. In summer, the monsoons come, making the deserts thrive with greenery – and torrents of water pour from the waterfalls. For the rest of the year, the climate is hot and dry. But nights can be cold. Roughly one quarter of the Northern Territory's population of 180,000 are Aboriginal, and the Northern Territory is one of the best places in Australia to learn about Aboriginal culture, the oldest surviving culture in the world. It is said to stretch back to 60,000 years ago. The long tradition of bush tucker, dancing and story-telling continues.

Uluru (Ayers Rock) is in Uluru – Kata Tjuta National Park.
Darwin, the capital of the Northern Territory, is in the Top End of the territory. Darwin is a laidback, relaxed capital. It has a casino and you can sail on Darwin Harbour.

South of Darwin, lies Alice Springs, in the heart of Australia. It is a desert community, with a population of 20,000. It was established in 1870 as a telegraph line site. The town of Tennant Creek is a flashback to the old mining days. It is where miners last panned for gold in the 1930s. If you have the time, make sure you get to see Katherine Gorge. Take a boat trip and a plunge into a cool deep waterhole.

Ooraminna Bush Camp

Ooraminna Bush Camp is a thirty-minute drive south of Alice Springs. It's on a family-owned cattle station, between the MacDonnell Ranges and the Simpson Desert. This has to rate as the true blue, warts-and-all taste of the Aussie Outback. You get to sleep under a canopy of stars in a swag, eat a stockman's dinner cooked on an open fire, take an escorted horse ride amid red sandhills and rocky outcrops, and even have a crack at cattle droving.

You can also do a four-wheel drive cattle station tour, and bushwalk. Best of all, despite the opportunity to 'rough it', the camp does provide creature comforts. You can stay in the 'pioneer hut' instead of camping out. The Camp is owned and operated by Bill and Jan Hayes who have a strong pioneer heritage. They go back six generations. William and Mary Hayes were one of Alice Spring's pioneer families, arriving in 1884 with horses and bullock teams loaded with steel telegraph poles to replace the original wooden poles. Nowadays, the Hayes operate Deepwell and Maryvale Stations, as well as managing Ooraminna Bush Camp.

Transfers are available from Alice Springs airport, bus terminal and railway station. Pack wisely. All shops are about thirty km from the camp. But the Ooraminna Homestead Store on site does sell basics like snacks, toiletries and film. While in the store, listen to 'School of the Air' on the radio. Tel: (08) 8953 0170, www.cbl.au/ooraminna.

Central Australia
Shimmering heat, gorges and waterfalls and Aboriginal Dreaming encapsulate the mood of Central Australia. The Northern Territory is best known for Uluru (Ayers Rock). But the Dreamtime heritage of dancing, bush tucker and story-telling can also be seen in other parts of the Centre. For breathtaking beauty, try Kings Canyon. It's a cool fern-clad escarpment away from the midday sun.

Natural attraction
Nourlangie Rock, Kakadu National Park, is one of the world's oldest open-air galleries. Some 50,000 years ago, Aborigines painted on this rock underhang in ochre. Their detailed works remain. Depicted are such characters as Namarrgon, 'Lightning Man', which illustrates the strong spiritual bond between the Aboriginal people and the land. The main rock art is adjacent to a paved track, but the Nourlangie Art Site Walk is a circular route of 1.5 km. Park rangers conduct guided tours of the site during the dry season. The site is open from 7am to 7.30pm.

South Australia
South Australia, with a population of 1.4 million, is known for very fine food and wine. Yet for decades, the capital, Adelaide has attempted to shrug off its wowserish tag as the puritan city of churches, referring to the inordinately large number of churches dotted throughout the city. While the churches are architectural highlights, there are plenty of groovier attractions to visit. There's a thriving pub and nightclub scene and great wines. It's a pretty city too, framed by the Mt Lofty Ranges and the Gulf St Vincent, and it has a temperate climate. The Adelaide Arts Festival is held in March in even-numbered years. In odd-numbered years, Womadelaide, Adelaide's outdoor festival of world music and dance, is on in February.

Sandwiched between Adelaide and Melbourne is the Flinders Ranges, an 800-km range. This is desert country, providing a taste of the Aussie Outback. (Visit in winter or spring to avoid meltdown.) If you get a kick out of natural landscapes, check out the natural basin known as Wilpena Pound which is framed by 1000-metre cliffs.

And of course, there's the wine. The fifty wineries in South Australia's Barossa Valley are a sixty-minute drive from Adelaide and the wines from this district are world-renowned. Most sell direct to the public. The wineries are wonderful places to spend a day, eating and drinking. Since the vines are pruned during winter, the most aesthetic time to visit the Barossa is from March to May, when the grapes are harvested. Once you've done the Barossa, try some of the other wine-growing regions of the state, like the Penola, Coonawarra and Padthaway in the south-east, Clare Valley in the north of the Barossa and McLaren Vale on the Fleurieu Peninsula.

German people who were escaping religious wars in Prussia and Silesia settled South Australia in 1842. The German tradition is evident at Hahndorf, the oldest German settlement in Australia. It is 29 km south-east of Adelaide. The coastal areas of Robe and Kangaroo Island are also well worth a visit.

Tourist attraction

The *Adelaide River Queen* ninety-minute Jumping Crocodile cruise shows you all the menace of a salt-water croc up close. It sounds morbid but at the same time, this is one hell of a fascinating trip. With amazing ferocity and speed, salt water crocodiles, their jaws slightly apart, carve a smooth path through the water and suddenly leap bullet-like into the air, clenching chunks of meat with their jaws before retreating into the muddy depths. And you thought *Jaws* was scary! Cue the cello music. Location: Adelaide River Bridge, Arnhem Highway, Adelaide River. Open daily from 9am to 3pm.

Tasmania

Traffic jams in Tasmania just don't happen. About 472,000 people live on the southern island of 68,331 square kilometres. The local economy thrives on tourism, farming and fishing, and the production of beers and cool-climate wines.

To the west of the island are rugged mountains and rainforest, in the centre is a hilly plateau dotted with lakes, and to the east, the land is flatter and the climate drier and warmer. About 35,000 years ago, when Tasmania was still connected to the mainland, Aborigines inhabited the area that became Tasmania. But the harmony of the island was disrupted when the British arrived in 1803. The British decimated the Aboriginal population and transformed Tasmania, which was known at the time as Van Diemen's Land, into a British convict outpost. It was not until 1852, after about 70,000 convicts had been sent to Van Diemen's Land, that the convict system was abolished and the name of the island was changed to Tasmania.

The city of Hobart, Tasmania's capital, is in the south-east. Launceston, the second largest city in Tasmania, is on the Tamar River up north.

One of the best tourism assets of Tasmania is its wilderness. The untouched beaches and coves of Freycinet National Park in Tasmania's east are a good example. Here, take the trek to Wineglass Bay. Also, the Overland Trek at Cradle Mountain is excellent if you enjoy bushwalking, but you'll need to be fit. It's a five-day walk through the mountain range in Lake St Clair National Park, a World Heritage Area. King Island, Port Arthur, the Franklin and Gordon Rivers are other key tourism attractions. If you want to work on your golf handicap, you've come to the right place – Tasmania has more than eighty golf courses.

Hobart

With a population of only 127,000, set in a harbour and framed by mountains, Hobart has a village feel. Known for its arts and crafts, Hobart's Salamanca Market on Saturdays always attracts a crowd. Hobart is also loaded with natural assets. It is located on the Derwent River overlooking a busy harbour, and mountains surround it. The streets are filled with Georgian buildings and sandstone warehouses. People from the mainland may knock Hobart for being provincial, but the laid-back pace is a big holiday asset. This is a place to switch off the mobile phone and take it easy. Shoppers will be kept happy wandering through the many arts and crafts shops in the city. If you have time, take a walking tour of the town to discover the city's convict past.

Natural attraction

To see Hobart from on high, hire a car or take a tour bus to Mt Wellington. (Wait for good weather or you may as well not bother.) The summit of the mountain is 22 km away from the heart of Hobart. Also visible from the summit is the Derwent Valley and the Southern Ocean. And on a very clear day, you can see Port Arthur, where 12,500 convicts were imprisoned between 1830 and 1877.

Tourist attraction

The Cadbury Chocolate Factory at Claremont – a 20-minute drive from Hobart – is seventh heaven for those with a sweet tooth. Many from the mainland make the pilgrimage to this place for the ultimate chocolate fix. The smell of cocoa as you walk into the building is divine. The factory was opened in 1921. The guided tour around the huge steel vats includes eating-trays of chocolate samples. After the tour, stock up on discounted chocolates at the factory shop. Tour bookings are essential.

The factory is closed from mid December to mid January. Opening hours: Monday to Friday (excluding public holidays).

New South Wales

This is the birthplace of European Australia. Captain General Arthur Phillip, along with ships of convicts and whalers, sailors, builders and traders, set anchor in Botany Bay in January 1788.

Head out of the Olympic city for peace and quiet. It takes two hours to drive north to the Hunter Valley wine region. Stop off along the way on the Central Coast to enjoy the natural bushland of Bouddi National Park, Brisbane Water National Park and the Hawkesbury River. Lord Howe Island is part of New South Wales. The island, 11 by 1.5 km, has rainforests, coral reefs and volcanic peaks and is accessible by air.

Head south and you'll pass pristine empty beaches and charming coastal towns such as Berry and Eden.

Head west from Sydney and you'll come to the Blue Mountains, so-named because of the bluish haze created by eucalyptus oil evaporating from gum trees covering the mountain ranges. Beyond the Blue Mountains are the beautiful country townships that developed during the gold boom and the agricultural boom. Spend a few days at a traditional farm homestead, perch your elbows on the bar of a local pub and chat with the locals. To the north on the coast is Byron Bay, famous for its New Age atmosphere and thriving café and restaurant culture. There's a dolphin sticker on every second kombi van. Byron is the perfect place to 'chill out' and to enjoy the excellent surf, the beaches and comfy accommodation. BYO surfboard and a laid-back attitude.

Sydney

People often whinge that Sydney is brash, fast-paced, and irreverent – but that's what makes it such a fine place to visit. It's a good idea to take advantage of the competitive airline prices. Challenge yourself by climbing the Harbour Bridge for awesome 360 degree views. From the top of the bridge, you can see Homebush, the home of the 2000 Olympic Games, in the distance and the sight of watercraft moving about the harbour underneath the bridge is picturesque.

The colony took hold at The Rocks, at the foot of Sydney Harbour. Take a ferry from Circular Quay to the seaside suburb of Manly, shop 'til you drop at Double Bay and ultra-trendy Paddington. Body surf at Bondi. Take a sailing lesson at the Spit Bridge in Mosman. The Festival of Sydney in January, the Sydney to Hobart yacht race from Boxing Day and the Gay & Lesbian Mardi Gras in February/March help make Sydney internationally famous.

Natural attraction

Palm Beach is a forty-five–minute drive from the heart of Sydney. Put on your walking shows after a swim at the beach and allow a few hours for a climb to the Barrenjoey Lighthouse, a sandstone structure built in 1881. To access the lighthouse, turn left at Governor Phillip Park and walk up Pittwater Beach until you see the entrance sign. The climb up a rocky path takes about forty minutes. It's worth it . . . There are green views of Broken Bay to the north, and Palm Beach and Pittwater to the south.

Tourist attraction

The Sydney Fish Market, Pyrmont, is home to the southern hemisphere's biggest seafood sale at 5.30am each weekday. In total, 65 tonnes of fresh catch with everything from live mud crabs to sashimi salmon, to king prawns and coral trout are auctioned daily and sent off to retailers and restaurants. The Sydney Seafood School at the Sydney Fish Market runs fantastic cooking classes, but you must book. Tel (02) 9552 2180.

Catch the light rail from Central Station, Haymarket or Darling Harbour to the Fish Market stop across the road from the market. The light rail operates every twelve minutes, twenty-four hours a day, seven days a week.

Victoria

Victoria, with a population of 4.7 million, is the second most-inhabited state after New South Wales. For a taste of the lifestyle outside Melbourne, the Great Ocean Road, carved from limestone cliffs, has stunning coastal views at every turn. It is a three-hour round trip to one of the road's highlights, the coastal town of Lorne. Alternatively, head down the Mornington Peninsula to the seaside towns of Sorrento and Portsea. For utter pampering, the mineral spring health spas at Daylesford are a hot spot.

And if a vintage Shiraz tickles your fancy, there's the Yarra Valley or the Mornington Peninsula. Meanwhile, Victoria's goldfield heritage can be found at Ballarat and Bendigo where gold was first discovered in Victoria in 1851. Nature lovers can bushwalk at the Grampians. Wander through the fern-clad Dandenong Ranges. Take a houseboat up the Murray or see the penguins waddle up the beach at Phillip Island as the sun sets. Sail on the beautiful Gippsland Lakes and visit the Buchan Caves. Melburnians are sports-mad. The Australian Open tennis championship kicks off in January, the Australian Grand Prix is in March; Aussie Rules football is played nationally from March to September and the Melbourne Cup, a horse race which stops the nation, is run on the first Tuesday in November.

Melbourne

Melbourne is an eclectic urban playground. You can watch rowers from the banks of the Yarra River, sip a decent latte at a sidewalk café (Melbourne does great coffee) and join the fashionistas at Chapel Street, South Yarra. Alternatively, join the fired-up crowd at an Aussie Rules football night game at Colonial Stadium. Watch a performance by the Australian Ballet, hear late night jazz and choose from a plethora of multicultural restaurants for your evening meal.

Melbourne was founded in the early 1800s when Queen Victoria was on the throne. This accounts for the abundance of Victorian architecture, parkland and wide tree-lined streets of the city. The free burgundy city tram circles the CBD, taking in many of the city sights from the Queen Victoria Market to Chinatown to the Old Melbourne Gaol.

Macedon in Victoria

The Macedon Ranges are about a sixty-minute drive north-west of Melbourne. To get there, head out to the Tullamarine Freeway and turn off to the Calder Freeway. Macedon is the first town in the Macedon Ranges. To get to Mount Macedon and Hanging Rock, take Mount Macedon Road to the north. If you want to explore further afield, the Calder Freeway runs northwest from Macedon through Woodend, Kyneton, Malmsbury, Taradale and Elphinstone. Perhaps you want to venture into Daylesford in Spa Country. If so, turn east onto the Pyrenees Highway from Elphinstone to Castlemaine. Follow the Midland Highway south to Hepburn Springs and Daylesford. Your mineral spa and massage awaits.

Natural attraction

Hanging Rock, at Mt. Macedon, is about 75 km north-west of Melbourne. Peter Weir's film *Picnic at Hanging Rock* (1975), based on the novel by Joan Lindsay (1967), has established the rock as part of local folklore. The story goes that on St Valentines Day 1900, three schoolgirls and a governess went for a walk at the rock during a picnic. One girl returned hysterical, another girl returned suffering from amnesia and the third schoolgirl and the governess were never seen again. The annual Hanging Rock Picnic in late February, and the New Year's Day Hanging Rock Horse Races are calendar highlights.

Tourist attraction

If you plan on enjoying the wineries of the Macedon region, having a designated driver is essential. Let someone else do the driving while you do the drinking. Day tours to the Macedon Ranges takes place with a minimum of two guests and a maximum of eight guests. The tour encompasses a mix of small, boutique wineries with a cellar door. Climbing Hanging Rock is an option of the tour. The tour includes a morning tea stop at one of Mount Macedon's picnic spots, plus lunch.

Queensland

Queensland has a population of 3.2 million. The state's capital, Brisbane, is in the south-east. The tourism jewel in Queensland's crown is the Great Barrier Reef – stretching for around three-quarters of the length of Queensland's east coast.

It's the world largest marine park and spans a whopping 345,000 square kilometres. There are hundreds of islands near the reef, and about twenty have resorts. Snorkelling and scuba diving allow visitors to get up close with the reef marine life.

Queensland is warmer than its southern counterparts. The average maximum temperature is 25.2°C and the average minimum temperature is 15.7°C. Head to Brisbane, the riverside capital, for cultural events and a well-established nightlife. It's Australia's third largest city after Sydney and Melbourne. Brisbane came of age when it hosted the 1982 Commonwealth Games and Expo '88. The Gold Coast and the Sunshine Coast are blessed with some of Australia's best beaches and warm water, powdery white sand and thundering surf. Up north in tropical Queensland, go white-water rafting on the Tully near Cairns, the far north's main city.

World Heritage primeval rainforests are to the north of Cairns, at the Daintree Rainforest and further north at Cape Tribulation. Even further up is Cape York. Head inland and you'll come to the Atherton Tablelands and then on to the grasslands of the Gulf Savannah.

Port Douglas

The sixty-minute drive north from Cairns airport is the stuff of island dreams. You'll pass palm trees and mango trees, and gaze out onto an expanse of turquoise sea.

It can be muggy from November to March. With a population of about 6000, Port Douglas is a sleepy tropical resort town. The main stretch, Macrossan Street, is lined with gift shops, clothing boutiques and upmarket restaurants that serve the freshest of seafood from barramundi to mud crab. Sidewalk tables are everywhere. Walk to the end of Macrossan Street and you'll come to Four Mile Beach, a safe beach with a shark net where the water is usually warm. That's not surprising, given the fact that Port Douglas is on the same latitude as Tahiti.

Port Douglas is a good launch pad to the World Heritage rainforest at the Daintree or Cape Tribulation. Take a guided tour or head off on a four-wheel drive safari. Trips to the Great Barrier Reef also operate from Port Douglas. You can go diving, snorkelling or hop aboard a yacht as you head out to places such as Low Isles or Agincourt Reef. Other options include taking a day trip to historical Cooktown and a champagne sunset cruise up the mangrove mudflats, or get your adrenalin fix by riding the rapids in a day of white-water rafting on the Tully River. The Port Douglas Visitors Bureau is at 5/12 Grant Street, Port Douglas.

Hamilton Island, the Whitsundays

Set in the Whitsundays, Hamilton Island is a one-stop shop resort. Granted, it's a formulaic holiday, but who cares? It's fun, and you can relax without feeling duty-bound to sightsee every day. Hamilton has a new hook – The Beach Club. Geared towards the romantic market, it's a brand new fifty-five–room boutique hotel on Catseye Beach where you can wallow in five-star luxury.

The best part about The Beach Club is that each guest is given the services of a butler.

Yes, a personalised host to cater to your holiday whims, from booking a massage to organising a seaplane to take you and your loved one to a secluded Whitsunday beach for a picnic. It's adults only.

There are three other hotels on the island geared towards the family market with childcare facilities. At Hamilton Island, there's no such thing as too much choice.

You can even get married on Hamilton Island, choosing from a beach, garden or chapel ceremonies. Every day, guests can select from eighty-five activities. These include Barrier Reef cruises, clay pigeon shooting, gymnasium activities, water-skiing, PADI diving accreditation, windsurfing catamaran and yacht sailing, tennis, game fishing, whale watching (from mid July to September), scenic flights and safari tours. It makes you breathless just thinking about it.

If you can't be bothered lifting a finger, take your book and your towel to one of the six resort pools and simply chill. What's more, there are sixteen restaurants and food outlets on the island. You can swim year-round in the Whitsundays. During winter, day temperatures rarely dip below 20°C. Qantas flies regularly to Hamilton Island. It's a one-hour flight from Brisbane, two hours from Sydney and three hours from Melbourne.

Western Australia

Western Australia is huge. It stretches across one-third of Australia for some 2.5 million square kilometres. Key industries in Western Australia are gold, iron ore, gas and minerals. Dutchman Dirk Hartog was the first recorded European arrival in Western Australia in 1616 when he dropped anchor at Shark Bay. It's best to pack for four seasons on a trip to WA because the weather varies, depending on where you are in the state. It can be baking hot in the Kimberley in the north, and freezing in Perth and further south.

If you're eating out in Perth, Northbridge and Fremantle are famous for southern European and Asian cuisines. Of the 1.8 million people who live in WA, 1.38 million of them live in the capital Perth, close to beaches and vineyards. Western Australia is full of natural wonders, and there are plenty of places to enjoy adventure sports in natural settings, from abseiling to white-water rafting. Head north to the Kimberley to view the 350-million-year-old Bungle Bungles – a towering range of odd-shaped red rock formations. View gorges and waterfalls in the Pilbara region up north. The Shark Bay World Heritage is in the Gascoyne region. To the south-west is the Margaret River coastal area, home to premium vineyards, which were established more than 170 years ago. The kauri forests of Stirling Range National Park also lie in the south-west of the state. To glimpse a whale or a dolphin, head to Monkey Mia and further north to the Ningaloo Reef, a beautiful sanctuary for fish and sea life.

Western Australia has sublime beaches, from Esperance in the south to beautiful Broome in the North.

Broome

Broome has a slightly raffish feel harking back to its early pearling days. It's a good place to chill out for a few days if you're planning on roughing it into the Kimberley.

At dusk, take a trip down to Cable Beach to view a gorgeous sunset . Sit yourself in a deckchair at Sun Pictures for an outdoor movie under the stars.

El Questro Wilderness Park

When you blend ecotourism in a remote location with an assortment of accommodation choices, you end up with a place like El Questro Wilderness Park.

This is final frontier territory. But it's not all dry and barren. Far from it. Expect to see craggy ranges, tidal flats, rainforest pockets, gorges and waterfalls. Animals, birds and fish congregate on the rivers and waterholes, freshwater springs and salt-water estuaries.

As for activities, try barramundi fishing with El Questro's rangers, or explore canyons and gorges by boat or on foot. Expect to see brumbies, wild donkeys, bustards, frilly lizards, goannas, sea eagles, brolgas, jabirus and parrots. Make sure you go boating in the Chamberlain Gorge, a waterhole stretching for three km. At one end are excellent examples of Wandjina rock art. Zebedee Springs is a short walk off the graded road through to a series of thermal pools. Sport fishermen love the area.

Barramundi season runs from March to December, although other fish including mangrove jack, bream, salmon and catfish bite all year. It doesn't get wilder than this. El Questro, on the eastern fringe of the Kimberley, extends eighty km into the centre. Most of the property has never been explored on foot.

Opened in 1991, El Questro offers four accommodation experiences. There's the bottom-of-the-rack riverside camping option, the air-conditioned family bungalow, and the Emma Gorge resort. And finally there's The Homestead, which serves up gourmet meals and comes with organised tours and an open bar.

By four-wheel drive, El Questro is 100 km west of Kununurra. That's fifty-eight km on sealed Great Northern Highway towards Wyndham, and the remainder is on graded-gravel Gibb River Road. El Questro is open from 1 April to mid November each year. Gibb River Road, via Kununurra, Western Australia. Telephone: 61 08 9161 4318, www.elquestro.com.au.

The Australian Capital Territory

Think Australian Capital Territory and no matter how hard you try, politicians in Canberra will instantly spring to mind. But there's more to the ACT than the trials and tribulations of politics. The national capital Canberra, with some 313,000 people, has many cultural attractions and a lively nightlife to service the large university population. Canberra was settled in the 1820s. Its name is derived form a local Aboriginal word 'Kamberra', meaning 'meeting place'. Canberra was established as the result of bickering between Sydney and Melbourne. After federation in 1901,the cities couldn't agree on which city should become the Federal capital. The dispute was settled in a roundabout way. In 1908,Canberra, which is located between both states, became the political epicentre of Australia. The inaugural parliament session took place in Canberra in 1927.

The grid town plan design is by American architect Walter Burley Griffin, who won a competition to design the city in 1912. The artificial lake in the heart of the city bears his name. There are two pedestrian bridges across the lake.

On Capital Hill, visitors are welcome at Parliament House. Topped with an 81-metre flag post, it's hard to miss. When parliament is sitting, visitors can take a seat in the public gallery. Other tourism attractions are Old Parliament House, the National Gallery of Australia, the High Court of Australia, the Australian War Memorial, and the Australian Institute of Sport.

Country and heritage towns surround Canberra. In this region, orchards, wineries, wool and cattle properties abound. Worth a look is the Canberra Deep Space Communication Complex, which is one of three NASA tracking stations. The others are in California and Spain. The Australian Botanic Gardens at the base of Black Mountain near the capital is *the* place to view an impressive assortment of native plants.

8
Finance

Money management
The most important thing to do to organise your finances and investing plan is to just do it. Ask yourself do you wish to work all your life for your money or do you wish your money to work for you. Review your personal finances. Make a budget. Free up some money by making simple and small changes.

Questions to ask your financial advisor before you employ him or her
- Who owns your company?
- Is it a bank or a funds management company or anybody else that may have a vested interest?
- How is the advisor renumerated?
- Does the advisor get incentives and commissions for selling some financial products?
- Is payment a fee for service or a commission-based fee?
- Is it upfront or ongoing?
- Is the advisor restricted in the number or types of products or platforms that they are able to recommend?
- Can he explain why he has recommended the products that he has and has he done a set of comparisons for you to see?

Getting the most from your tax return
Keep accurate records of tax deductible expenses. If you earn over $60,000 a year, every $100 of tax deductible expense is worth $48.50 in your pocket. If you earn between $30,000 and $59,000 per year, every $100 spent on tax deductible expenses is worth over $30 to you. Keep all receipts and documentation.

To claim these deductions
- Record the date on which the expense occurred.
- The name of the business that supplied the services.
- The amount.
- Details of the goods and services.

Checklist of eligible deductions
- Travel expenses
- Car repairs, maintenance and running costs
- Insurance
- Public transport and taxis
- Interests on loans and overdraft
- Use of home office
- Bank charges/financial institutions duty
- Bad debts
- Business losses
- Donations to charity
- Tools of trade
- Subscriptions to professional journals and associations
- Professional library

- Telephone
- Internet
- Stationery
- Postage
- Uniforms, including laundry costs
- Staff amenities

Reduce the taxman's split

You should try to offset any capital gains that you make in a tax year with a capital loss. Reduce the taxman's share of the household income by splitting your income with your spouse. Transfer investments to a non-earning spouse so that you are not paying tax at a higher rate.

Credit cards

It's plastic fantastic.
Buy now, pay later.
A cheap way to borrow.
It can also ruin you!

Consider two scenarios:

First scenario:
You're in a shop, you see a shirt you must have. You are not carrying any cash. You whip out the credit card and, presto, you have a new shirt. A month later you get the bill and pay off the amount in full. You had free use of the shirt while you waited for the bill.

Second scenario:
You're in a shop, you see a shirt you simply must have. You don't have a cent to spare. The last pay-cheque has gone and the next one's already spent. You whip out the card, buy the shirt. You take the card to the auto-teller and 'borrow' some cash.

When the bill comes in, you still don't have any money. So you let it go a while . . . Six weeks later you get a reminder from the credit card company, plus interest owing at 16% calculated daily. You still can't pay what you owe for the shirt, much less what you borrowed, and you get another reminder with more interest added. Eventually they cancel your card, and you go onto public record as a bad creditor, making it hard to ever get a bank loan or another card.

Remember:
- Most financial institutions will give anyone over eighteen a card as long as they can show they have some capacity to pay it off.
- Cards have either an interest-free period, or charge interest immediately a purchase is made but at a lower rate. Some charge annual fees.
- The interest rate is usually considerably higher than the official cash rate.

All this should only be of concern if you have trouble paying back what is essentially debt! Enjoy your shirt.

Credit card tips

If you use a credit card, be sure to pay off the entire amount owed every month. If you maintain a balance owing you will end up paying substantial amounts in interest. Don't surpass your credit limit or you'll be charged for that, too. Try to have only one or two credit cards, and choose those with low interest rates and/or low annual fees.

If you have to make a large purchase and will not be able to pay off the amount in a single month, pay as much as you can. Consider switching to a credit card that offers a lower interest rate.

Credit cards in business

- Properly used a credit card can be a real asset and can offer interest free money.
- Wrongly used it can be the cause of disaster and you may end up paying huge interest on a loan that you never seem to be able to reduce.
- Always pay your credit card by the due date. In this way you enjoy an interest free period and don't incur any interest charges.
- Don't buy things on your card that you can't afford to pay for at month's end.
- Use credit cards in preference to cheques as they are cheaper. However you must then be able to repay the money within the interest free period.

Credit card fraud

These common-sense tips will help ensure you are not a victim of credit card fraud.

Do . . .

Sign your new card as soon as you receive it. Most new cards take effect as soon as you use them for the first time.

Avoid carrying your credit cards in your wallet. Keep them in a separate folder or business card holder or in a zippered compartment of your purse.

Make a list of all your charge account numbers, their expiration dates, and the address and telephone number of the issuing company. Keep the list in a secure place.

Watch as the sales clerk swipes your card. Get your card back as quickly as possible after a purchase. Especially if the store is busy or if your card has been taken away to complete the transaction (such as in a restaurant), make sure the card returned to you is your own.

Draw a line through any blank spaces above the 'total' line when you sign the receipt, to ensure no charges can be added later.

Make sure the receipt is marked void if a mistake is made during a transaction.

Remember that most charge card receipts no longer include carbon paper. If you receive an older-style receipt, be wary and destroy the carbon paper once you've signed the receipt.

Keep all your receipts together, so that when the monthly statement arrives you can be sure the amounts match.

Reconcile the credit card account every month, just as you should do with a cheque account.

Report any mistakes, such as a charge you didn't make or that is otherwise questionable. Call the card company and back up your complaint with a letter.

Advise the credit card company if you change your address.

Call the credit card company immediately if you lose your card or believe it has been stolen.

Don't . . .

Let someone else use your credit card or account number.

Leave cards or receipts in places where others could read or take them.

Sign a receipt that has not been completely filled out with the amount and details of your purchase.

Publicise your account number, for example by writing it on the outside of the envelope when you write to the credit card company or submit payment.

Make credit card purchases over the telephone or online unless you know you are dealing with a reputable store or firm. If you haven't bought something from the company before, it is a good idea to call a consumer protection office or Better Business Bureau and ask about it before buying anything.

Insuring your future

Insurance is one of those things we all think we don't need. Until it is too late. While premiums can seem expensive, recovering financially from a loss, whether of income, property or valuables, can take years. It is a good insurance to be insured.

What to insure depends largely on where you are in life

- Life insurance is advisable if you have dependents relying on income you provide.
- Health insurance is a must if you want to choose your own doctor in hospital.
- Trauma insurance covers major illnesses such as heart attack, stroke or cancer, and is paid whether you are working or not.
- Income protection insurance, protecting a vital asset, is gaining popularity.
- Third party car insurance, covering injuries to passengers, other drivers and pedestrians, is compulsory and included in the registration fee. Cover to your own car and others is optional, and bought in much the same way as home and home contents insurance. It could prove invaluable.

Shop around

- It pays to look at different deals being offered by insurance companies, as premiums can vary widely depending on your age, whether you smoke, how long you have been driving, or, in the case of home contents, what area you live in.
- Some insurance companies offer discounts if you have all of your insurances with them.
- An insurance broker will take all your details and requirements and shop around for a deal they think best suits your needs. But they take a commission on the products they sell.
- Either way, always read the fine print on the contract for details of how long it takes to pay a claim and in what circumstances claims aren't accepted.

Superannuation

You can never beat the Grimmest of all Reapers, the Tax Man. But superannuation gets you close! A low tax rate of just 15% on investment earnings makes it very attractive, especially for people earning above, say, $30,000.

There is a reason

The government takes so little tax because it wants us to save for our retirement, rather than having to pay us a full pension. A compulsory scheme called Superannuation Guarantee has been operating for the past eight years. It requires employers to pay-in a designated amount, worked out on a percentage of employees' wages, to an employee superannuation fund. The figure will be the equivalent of 9% of each employee's wages. The money is only accessible when you reach Preservation Age – at least fifty-five and retired. Your benefits are paid out either as a lump sum or a pension paid over a number of years. The average wage earner on $40,000 a year will go on a retirement income of $18,000, half from an age pension and half from super.

How much you'll need in retirement depends on two factors:

- Whether you are male or female. Average figures show women retiring at sixty-five live a further twenty-two years, and men sixteen.
- What sort of lifestyle you want to lead. A modest existence? Or going out for dinner and travelling?

Salary sacrifice into your superannuation fund

Arrange with your employer to reduce your salary by an agreed amount and to pay that money into your superannuation. This allows you to increase your super savings in a most tax effective manner. It saves you on tax as your salary is in a lower tax bracket. Make a superannuation contribution for your spouse. If you are under sixty-five you will receive a rebate on contributions up to a certain amount. These contributions are treated as unde- ducted contributions and can be returned tax free upon retirement. Earnings within a super fund are taxed at a lower rate of 15%.

Borrowing money
Do your sums

Don't borrow more than you can afford to pay back. Shop around for the best possible interest rates. Borrow against the equity in your home. Home loan interest is the cheapest source of money so it makes sense to use the equity in your home to borrow to buy essen- tials like a new car. It doesn't make sense to borrow if you have money available in an 'emergency fund'. Save interest by using that and if a real emergency arises use a credit card.

Borrowing from a bank usually costs less than borrowing from a credit society. Use a mortgage broker to guide you. It is often worth far more than the fee you pay as they have an overall picture of the money market and will be able to point you in the direction of the loan that is most suitable for you. Life insurance companies often offer cheap money secured against the surrender value of the policy that you hold. If you are using borrowed money for an investment then the cost of that money may be used as a tax deduction.

Savings
Budget

The hardest part about doing a budget is being honest with yourself! How much do you really spend on going out? On clothes? On your rather strange hobby, the World's Biggest Bottle Top Collection? You shouldn't have to feel guilty about how much you spend on any of these. A budget will simply make sure you are spending less than you are earning. If you've tried budgeting before and given up, chances are you were being too unrealistic.

Start by listing all expenses
- Home (including mortgage repayments or rent, repayments on an investment proper- ty, rates, telephone, gas, furniture, maintenance)
- Family (school fees, child-care, pets, sports, memberships, papers, clothing, entertain- ment, holidays, gifts)
- Food (groceries, alcohol, cigarettes, takeaway, morning coffee, lunches, restaurants)
- Health (medical, dental, pharmacy, gym)
- Car (registration, petrol, maintenance)
- Insurance (house, contents, income protection, death cover, car)
- General (superannuation, personal loan, credit cards)

Then list income
- After-tax income
- Any rental from investment property
- Any income from savings accounts
- Any shares dividends

Your total income less your total expenses is your savings
Don't panic if it is less than you thought, or even negative! Listing where you spend your money will help you identify potential savings:

- Taking lunch to work twice a week saves $500 a year.
- One less takeaway a week could mean savings of $300 a year.
- One less packet of cigarettes a day saves $2500 a year.

And, for example, do you need two cars? Registration, insurance, petrol, etc., can add between $2000 and $5000 a year. The most important thing is to do something.

Use the savings to pay off your mortgage, buy something you're saving for, establish a separate bank account. Invest in more bottle tops…

Make a budget and stick to it
Include all things on your budget. Work out total costs for the year and divide by twelve.

These are your costs for the months. Anything over can be saved. Sometimes it may be helpful to make envelopes stating the budget area and putting the monthly money in this. Others may be able to do it without this concrete aid.

Sample budget
- Mortgage payment
- Food and groceries
- Drinks and alcoholic beverages
- School fees
- Electricity
- Gas
- Water
- Rates
- Car payments
- Petrol
- Registration
- Parking
- Tolls
- Entertainment
- Clothes
- Presents and gifts
- Medications/medical
- Dental
- Donations
- Transport
- Telephone
- Internet
- Pets
- Walking-about money
- Anything else

Before signing up for a savings plan
- What is the commission?
- What are the administrative costs?
- What are the penalties for withdrawal?

Loose change
Tired of loose change cluttering your house, purse and pockets? Turn an annoyance into a family project by establishing a special coin jar, where everyone in your household can deposit his or her spare change. In six months or a year, tally up your savings, then vote on a summer or holiday family treat funded by all that loose change.

Investments
Before making an investment decision, thoroughly research the market and gather all the information together. Gearing may increase gains, but it also increases losses. Make decisions on a long-term basis. Decide on an investment and then allow it time to mature.

Learn from past mistakes. Cutting your losses is just as important as taking profits. It is always worth waiting for the right investment at the right price. Independent thought is necessary to make the right decisions.

Investment companies
Finding the right business
A good investment business has:

- Predictable earnings
- High turnover
- High market share and limited competition
- Management must act as if they are the owners of the company
- Profits must be created in cash

Don't invest in a company that:
- 'Makes' money through accounting tricks rather than in cash.
- Management seeks to aggrandise their position and gain personal advantage.
- The company relies too heavily on one large contract.
- The company has a large debt.
- The company is reliant for profit on matters beyond their control.
- There are many government regulations governing the sector.

Managed funds
The title says it all. A managed fund is your money managed for you by someone else.

They are ideal for:

- People who don't have large amounts of money to invest in the stock market directly.
- People who do not have the time to investigate which companies to invest in.

For as little as $1000 you can gain access to a managed fund. Basically, your money is pooled with that of hundreds of other investors. This gives you added buying power and access to a broad range of investments, which are managed and monitored by professionals. There are hundreds of managed funds on offer from a range of financial institutions. Which one best suits you depends a lot on your own circumstances including your age and how much risk you can take. If you are close to retirement you might be a bit wary about putting your money into a managed fund, which invests only in technology stocks, as these may take longer to return healthy profits.

Diversified managed funds
A less risky fund would be a diversified fund, which spreads its money across the four main asset classes:

- Shares, domestic and international
- Property
- Fixed interest
- Cash

Money managers
Managers move money in and out of the funds they manage, depending on how they believe they are going to perform in the future. They also have access to the best information about financial markets and economic trends. Not every fund achieves the same results, so it is important to choose an organisation that has a track record and good credentials.

Licensed financial advisers are a good place to start your search. But remember that many financial advisers receive a commission every time they introduce a new investor.

You can find a local, licensed financial adviser through the Australian Securities & Investments Commission.

Investment in shares

Investing in shares is really a gamble. The good investor needs to beat the odds and have a clear understanding of the financial performance of a company and the company's management. This requires research and if you are not prepared to do the research, then you would be best to put your money into a managed fund where professional investors will do it for you.

Define your objectives

It is essential to define your objectives before you start investing.

- Set goals
- Develop a positive approach
- Be decisive

Take these things into account:
- Capital gains
- Income
- Safety
- Ease of management
- After tax return
- Liquidity

Best times to buy

Monday is a good day to buy. Companies like to release bad news on a Friday so as to give the market time to absorb it over the weekend. Therefore prices are often down on a Monday morning.

On days other than Mondays, prices tend to rise in the first hour of trading, stay stagnant all day and rise a little towards the end of trading.

Prices are usually higher than average on days preceding a holiday.

The January effect is one that has been noted. Prices tend to rise before Christmas and continue to rise until the New Year.

The end of the financial year generally brings a glut in sales as people sell to take losses and balance their tax debts.

October has long been a notorious month for sharemarket slumps. This is a good time to buy.

'October is a particularly dangerous month to speculate in stocks.

The others are July, January, February, March, April, May, June and December.' (Mark Twain)

Successful investors 'buy on rumour, sell on news'.

If everyone is selling, then this is probably a good time to buy (and vice versa).

Useful share market tips

It pays to read a prospectus as it tells you all about the company and you can make an informed decision as to whether you wish to become a shareholder.

Investors in many newly floated companies do not make money in the short term. They are long-term investments.

Only take up a rights issue if you are comfortable with the company's future growth prospects.

Don't invest in shares unless it is money that you are prepared to lose.

Don't borrow money to invest in shares.

Many stockbrokers have a minimum charge. This makes investing in small parcels expensive.

Brokerage is negotiable.

You can save money by using a discount stockbroker.

Be wary of the Internet. Be aware that Internet advice is not always reliable. Often suppliers of such advice have a vested interest in the share price that they are recommending.

If you are an investor in the stock exchange, make it your business to read the business news in your paper daily. Keep up with what is going on.

If you buy a share in the period between when a dividend has been declared and when it is paid, you may receive the dividend even though you have only held the shares a short time.

It is important that shares are liquid. Liquidity is the measure of how easily you can sell a share without losing money.

Government bonds are easy to buy and sell.

Think and act long term. Don't become emotionally involved in the short-term twists and turns of the market.

Single males are the greatest risk takers.

First-born children are the most conservative risk takers.

If a share or other investment is under-valued there probably is a reason for it.

Don't be greedy. Take your profit and leave enough for the next person.

Your shares are not the family pets, don't keep them too long.

When you are on a winner, sell half of your shares when they have doubled in price.

Cut your losses quickly. Admit your mistake and get out.

Diversify. Buy shares over a range of sectors and reduce your risk.

Review the balance of your portfolio regularly.

Be careful of investing too heavily in the industry in which you already work. You already have a major investment in that sector.

A franked dividend is one on which the tax has been paid.

Just because the shares are 'blue chip' does not mean that you cannot lose money on them.

Keep an eye on the Saturday papers and see which directors of which companies are buying and selling their shares. If they are selling, then you should sell, too. If they are buying then it may be a good time to buy.

If you are investing in Unit Trusts, don't make the mistake of investing small amounts in many trusts. This increases the costs.

When to sell a share

- The company misses paying a dividend.
- It has gone up in value 50% or more.
- It has been held for two years and hasn't appreciated in value.
- Earnings fall to a point where the P/E is 50% higher than when you bought it.

Advantages of shares over other investments
Liquidity

Shares are easily bought and sold. Funds become available within a few days.

Flexibility

Each person may hold his own portfolio of shares that reflect his or her individual investment choices and with the level of risk that he or she is prepared to endure.

Diversification

Shares, unlike property can be bought in bundles ranging in value from a few thousand dollars to millions.

Tax effectiveness

Shares that pay franked dividends provide tax rebates.

Income
Dividends provide a regular income stream.

Growth
Prospects for growth are provided if the shares increase in value.

Income versus growth
Concentrate on growth in income, rather than growth in share value. This will provide you with a tax efficient income stream, which will increase as the years go by.

In summary
- When buying stocks or shares you are buying an interest in a company.
- Long-term shares generate the highest return, compared with property, bonds and cash. Short-term, however, share returns fluctuate more.
- Shares are bought and sold via a stockbroker, who charges a fee depending on the level of advice given, and are traded on the Australian Stock Exchange (ASX).
- Trading online via the Internet is gaining popularity, but there is usually no buying/selling advice given.
- When picking stocks, it depends on your financial requirements and risk-tolerance levels.
- Some risk is reduced if shares are held in a number of different companies in different industries.
- Some advisers say to invest only in companies where you understand what they do.
- Some say to also look to income through the dividend payments.
- Returns will be volatile, the value of your shares rising and falling at various times. This is because of external factors including interest rates, the economy and performance of overseas markets; and internal factors including competition, productivity and consumer demand.

Glossary of sharemarket terms
Bear market – A falling market.
Bid – The price that someone is prepared to pay to buy a certain share.
Blue chip stocks – Shares in a company that has the reputation of being a solid company that turns profits in good times and in bad.
Bonus issues – An issue of shares that is funded by the company to existing shareholders in proportion to existing shareholdings.
Bull market – A rising market.
Convertible note – A loan made to a company at a fixed rate of interest, which can either be converted into ordinary shares or redeemed at a predetermined date.
Debenture – A loan made to a company at a fixed rate of interest and for a fixed period of time.
Dividend yield – Dividends per share calculated by dividing dividends per share-by-share price X 100/1.
DPS - Dividends per share over a twelve-month period.
EBIT – Earnings before interest expense, abnormals and tax attributable to each fully paid share over a twelve-month period.
EPS – Earnings per share measures the earnings that are attributable to each fully paid share over a twelve-month period.
Ex – Without. Ex-dividend, without the current dividend.
Float – The initial raising of capital by public subscription to shares in the company.
Franking rate – A dividend paid by the company to a shareholder, on whom the company has already paid tax is a franked dividend. The franking level represents the percentage of the dividend of which tax has been paid.
Industry classification – Can be one of twenty-four categories and indicates the industry sector into which the company has been classified.

Market capitalisation – The market value of the share capital of the company, and is calculated as follows: Fully paid ordinary shares x market close price.

Option – Rights given by the company to take up its shares by a predetermined future date at a certain price.

Preference share – A share that ranks above ordinary shares, but below creditors.

Rights issue – A new issue of shares, usually at a discount to the market, made to existing shareholder in proportion to their existing shareholding.

Share registry – Share registry name, address and contact details.

Things you need to know before you venture into the share market

- If you wish to become a millionaire while playing the stock market, simply start out with $2 billion.
- The safest way to double your money is to fold it and put it in your pocket.
- An income is what you can't live without or within.
- Gambling is a sure way to get nothing for something.
- Misers aren't much fun to know when they are alive, but they make wonderful ancestors.

Futures

Futures contracts used to be traded by waving, screaming men and women in brightly coloured jackets on the trading floor. This mayhem has now been replaced by computer screens.

A futures contract is an agreement to:
- Buy or sell a commodity (such as wool or wheat), or a financial instrument (such as bonds or shares).
- At a fixed time in the future.
- But at a price agreed on today.

The difference between futures and shares

What makes futures different from shares is that the delivery period, quantity and quality of a futures contract is standardised and specified, while the price is set at the time the contract is opened. Organisations use futures for risk management. Futures contracts enable risk to be transferred from those exposed to risk, to those who are happy to assume risk, in the hope of making profit. Unlike shares, there is no need to be in possession of the commodity or security at the time at which a futures contract is entered into. The contract simply represents a commitment to either deliver (sell) or accept delivery (buy) the commodity on the expiry date. Therefore, one can sell a futures contract just as easily as buying a futures contract. Participants thus have the ability to benefit from a fall in prices as well as a rise in prices.

Hedging

Investors can hedge or protect the value of their assets (shares, bonds, etc.) against the risk of price fluctuations in a commodity or financial instrument. An investor taking a position in the futures market, which is opposite to that held in the physical market, does this. The rationale is that the investor will benefit on the futures position should prices move adversely. The Share Price Index (SPI) closely follows a basket of shares on the stock market.

Property trusts

Effectively you are purchasing a share, or unit, in a company or trust that invests in property and is listed on the Australian Stock Exchange. Property trusts generally invest in a broader range of properties than you could buy as a single investor.

These include commercial, industrial and retail buildings, factories, hotels and shopping centres. These are usually in prime locations and are managed to attract long-term tenants.

As well, trust units are easy to buy and sell on the share market so, should the need arise, you have quick access to your funds.

Property

For most of us, property means our home – bricks and mortar. Buying additional real estate as an investment is one way to increase your wealth. First you have to find the property, then obtain or extend a loan to finance it. It doesn't have to be a home or a unit. You can also invest in commercial, retail or industrial properties to give some diversity.

The pitfalls of property

- In times of a poor economy it may be difficult to maintain tenants and/or increase rents to cover the repayments.
- Property prices can fall.
- The property requires maintenance; otherwise its value could be affected by normal wear and tear.
- Property can be hard to sell if you need the money in a hurry.

Advantages of property

There are three distinct tax advantages, not available to other investments:

- If it is your home, then you do not have to pay capital gains tax on the profit when you sell it.
- If it is an investment property, and you borrow money to buy it, the interest on the loan and all associated expenses, such as maintenance, agent's fees, bank fees, insurance and bank charges, are tax deductible.
- You can live in it.

Investment mortgages

Banks, building societies, insurance companies, credit unions and mortgage originators lend money to buy property.
They either:

- Use the property you are buying as security against the loan.
- Or ask you to take out mortgage guarantee insurance as protection in case you default on the loan.

Avoid telemarketing fraud

When you receive a telephone solicitation, suggest the caller mail you detailed written information about the item, service or opportunity they are promoting or the charity they are working for.

Get accurate details

Get the full name of the company or organisation and check it out before you give or send any money. Ask how the company and the industry it operates in is regulated. Or if you're speaking to someone representing a charity, find out its registration number and double-check with the appropriate government agency.

Never rush into anything

Even if you're tempted by the product being offered, don't let the caller bully or badger you into making a decision or purchase on the spot.

Beware of testimonials

They are promotional statements from so-called happy customers and you have no way of knowing whether these people exist or if their statements are fact or fiction.

Ask questions

Do not buy or invest in something if you don't understand all the details of the purchase or agreement you are being asked to make. Ask that the relevant information also be sent to your accountant, bank manager, lawyer, or someone else who can provide financial or legal advice.

- What happens if you aren't happy with the product or service?
- Will you get your money back in full?
- How much time do you have to evaluate your purchase?

Don't tell all

Avoid providing personal information, and especially financial details such as your credit card number, over the telephone. Give only the information absolutely needed for the transaction.

If the caller makes you uncomfortable or persists in his sales pitch after you have said 'no', just hang up.

Starting your own business
Credit

Unless you have money of your own you will need credit to start a business. Although many unforeseeable things come our way and strain our pocket books, unfortunately, creditors and others don't view these events as we do. Set some credit goals as quickly as possible. Speak with a friend or mentor who has a solid credit history.

Make an appointment with a financial expert. Ask them for strategies and advice for getting credit. Make a brand new start for yourself in the credit department.

Networking

Work on building credibility and image for your business. Network: let people know that you are here and tell them what you do. Join a professional organisation. Join community organisations. Go to professional network breakfasts or dinners. Let people know that you're in business and that you are good.

Business plan

Before jumping into the sea of entrepreneurship you have plenty of steps to climb. The first step, however, is your business plan. If you haven't started to develop one for your business, do that right away. Use another one from any business as a format.

Your business plan is your map or game plan. Determine your purpose, your objective, action items on how to reach that point, and what to do once you get there.

Go to your local Small Business Development Centre and get free assistance in the development of this plan. Your plan will tell you how much capital you truly need because it'll force you to break things down. You'll develop a capital equipment list whereby you can see what items are absolutely necessary for you to have to start your business, thereby leaving the other items for a later date when you're much more prepared financially. You'll also have an opportunity to seek an audience and find out whether or not the interest is truly there.

Paying yourself in your own business

Open a separate cheque account for your business. This is essential for you to know how well your business is doing. You want to know how much money your company earned before compensating yourself for your service and work within the business.

You also want to know how much you've received as personal compensation for your efforts in the business. You must be able to distinguish between business expenses and personal expenses. By accurately recording all your income and all your expenses, you see how much your company earned.

One bookkeeping tip is to be sure you accurately record any withdrawals of money removed from your business for personal purchases. Do this whether you remove a flat salary or some percentage of the earnings or some more complex withdrawal. If you're a sole proprietor, it's entirely up to you how much profit you remove from your business. You and your company are considered the same economic entity.

Partnership

If you're in a partnership, the situation is more complex, because one partner might not like seeing the other partner raid the partnership piggybank. Your tax situation was determined when you determined your business structure. You will pay taxes as a sole proprietor (or a partner) on your net profits.

Other considerations

Taxation isn't the only factor to consider when paying yourself money from your business. Before you go paying yourself, know your business books well. How much money is coming in? What expenses do you need to budget for? Because the earnings and cash flow of operating a company aren't exactly correlated, paying yourself as the money comes in is not a good idea.

Cash budgeting

Projecting cash needs in the future is often called 'cash budgeting'. How much money you must leave in your business is dependent upon how much money your business needs to cover your current and near-future expenses.

Set aside growth funds

You will want to retain capital to launch new products or marketing initiatives.

Don't forget about taxes!

As a business owner, you're responsible for paying taxes on your profits. So planning and cash budgeting is crucial. Once you have a handle on how much your company earns regularly and what your regular costs are, you'll invariably have a good idea of how much money should be retained within your company.

Why would you want your own business?

- Self-reliance
- Pride in a job that is all your own
- Allowing your own opinions and ideas to lead projects and staff members
- Reap the rewards from a job that is well done

Ten tips for when your enthusiasm for business wanes
1. Don't overwhelm yourself with too many to-dos

This is one of the easiest ways to suck the energy right out of your day. If your to-do list looks like a never-ending novel, then you will feel overwhelmed before you even begin! Instead, list eight goals – one for every hour. That gives you enough time to complete each assignment and if you finish early, you can revel in the satisfaction of a job well done.

2. Visualise yourself achieving your goals

You can mentally recharge by envisioning yourself achieving what you want more than anything.

3. Take a break and focus on yourself

You are the boss. Without you, your business will fail. Increase your mental and physical stamina by getting healthy! Get a good night's sleep every night.

4. Surround yourself with positive people
Optimism is contagious. Gather up a team of happy-go-lucky, energetic people who will feed into your self-esteem and create some infectious positive energy. They don't need to be employees, they can be supportive friends and family.

5. Boost morale
Do anything and everything to make the job fun!

6. Progress reports
Praise yourself and your employees with monthly progress reports. Do *not* focus on what you have *not* done, but talk about what you *have* done.

7. Inspiration
Find a successful mentor. His/her insights and experiences will inspire and encourage you and feed your goals.

8. Chronicle your journey in a portfolio
Take a day to look back on what has brought you to your current position. Gather up photos of you in various stages of your career, any newspaper clippings, letters of achievement, awards, recognitions, profit sheets, and employees. Put this all together in a photo album and sit it on a shelf in your office.

9. Get busy on a new project or tackle a big obstacle
Start something new and exciting. Create and build. What do you want to do? Where do you want to go next? Create a business plan for your next adventure and go for it!

10. Lower your expectations
Perfection is man's ultimate illusion. It simply doesn't exist in the universe. Perfectionism is self-defeating, it lowers your self-esteem and is hauntingly pessimistic. Lower your expectations to focus on progress only. So what if it isn't perfect? Gain experience with your imperfections.

Security
Precious and sentimental possessions can have more value than you imagine. In case of burglary, both for regaining possession of your valuables, or for claiming the insurance you should:

- Have them valued regularly.
- Have photographs, sketches or a video of everything of any value.

Never leave your home without checking that all windows and doors including garden sheds and garages are locked securely.

Thieves come in all shapes and sizes. Don't presume what a thief will look like: sly, scruffy, wearing a beanie and gloves and dressed in black. Many thieves dress in a suit as a businessman, or in overalls as a tradesman.

Easy targets
Homes which are easier to target, are those where there is a high fence or bush so the thief can't be seen.

A thief will look for signs like the mail not being taken in, or the lawn not being cut, or the bin left out in the street.

Thieves also tend to stay away from homes which have security systems.

Mobile telephones

- Keep your mobile phone with you.
- Never leave your mobile phone in your car unattended.
- Never put it down in a public place or leave it unattended.
- Switch it to 'vibrate' mode in circumstances where a ring tone might attract the attention of a thief.
- Make use of your mobile phone's security features.
- Notify your Network Carrier immediately in the event of loss or theft of your mobile phone.

Spare keys

Do not leave a spare key where a thief could find it!

Do not place spare keys under a doormat, a flower pots or in a meter box.

Key boards

This problem also extends to keys kept within the home where key hooks are commonly used and are openly displaying keys to anyone legally or illegally entering your home. Keep you keys out of sight in a drawer.

Last will and testament

What's going to happen to your favourite Pooh Bear when you die? If you care at all about your possessions after you conk out, then you must forward plan. Failing to prepare for death – not a particularly endearing thought, but, alas, it strikes us all at some point - may mean your assets are given to people you wouldn't normally want to go near. Imagine, Pooh Bear in the hands of some ill-mannered lout who pulls his ears off!

Estate planning

The transfer of assets on death is called estate planning. A properly drafted will is essential to any estate plan.

The will

A will is a legal document that comes into effect after a will-maker (a testator) dies.

It specifies how and to whom the estate is to be distributed. The estate consists of all the assets that the testator legally owns at the date of death. Dying without a will (intestacy) causes all sorts of problems. A person's next of kin (eg, spouse or parents) will usually be left to sort out the deceased's affairs which often means expensive legal and court costs. It's estimated almost 50% of people die without a valid will. Many who die with one, often have a will that's out of date or inappropriate

Probate

When a person dies, application must be made for probate. Probate is the process used to determine the authenticity of a deceased's will. It is therefore important that the will isn't damaged in any way. A will can be challenged, on the grounds of insanity of the person who made the will or undue influence or duress exerted on that person.

An aggrieved spouse or child could also seek changes to the way assets are distributed. It can be a very expensive time-consuming process. Meanwhile, leaving Pooh out in the cold…

Banking
Savings and cheque accounts

It is hard enough to get the cash together to stash it in an account, without the bank taking their cut via fees! When selecting a savings account, one of the biggest things to be aware of is the fees and charges that can erode your money. Competition means you can shop around to avoid the worst of these while looking for the best rate of interest.

Remember:
- Basic or everyday accounts are widely available and particularly attractive to low income earners.
- Bank fees are waived on these accounts, on the condition you stay within set withdrawal lines.
- You are allowed to make a set amount of deposits and withdrawals a month.
- However, do not expect these accounts to pay much interest or have a cheque facility.

While more and more payments can be done electronically, cheque facilities can still be incredibly handy to pay bills, repay loans, etc. Transaction accounts are usually the ones with a cheque facility.

- Competition means most of the banks offer a reasonable rate of interest, and waive account-keeping fees, as long as you keep a minimum balance in the account.
- You can make money by moving anything above the minimum to an account that pays greater interest, such as a cash management account.
- A fixed term deposit is another way of saving excess funds. Your money is locked away for between six months to five years, at competitive rates of interest.

One of the best ways to start saving is to work out how much excess money you have after your expenses. To do that you need to prepare, dare we say, a budget.

Bank fees
Compare banks, it may pay you to change
Ask for an up-to-date list of all cheque account and other fees charged by your bank. Some banks offer low fees for accounts with a low minimum balance requirement (or even none at all). Some banks do not charge fees if you have a certain minimum balance. Shop around. You can save a great deal of money in bank fees.

Some banks will waive or decrease your cheque account fees if pay cheques or social security cheques arrive via direct deposit. Another good reason for using direct deposit is that it ensures your money is secure.

Savings and investments
There is an ever-increasing range of savings and investment options available through banks and financial institutions. You should be aware that not all options are safe options. Before opening any account, ask whether your funds will be protected.

Investment options with a high annual percentage yield and very low risk include certificates of deposit and treasury bills or notes.

When you have narrowed down your list of possible savings or investment products, ask several financial institutions about their rates and fees for each type. Variables can make a big difference in the interest you will earn over time.

Mortgages
Your home is one of the most expensive items you will buy in your lifetime. It is also the best investment that you will ever make.

Reduce the interest and therefore the cost of your home mortgage
- Pay off your mortgage as quickly as you can and save tens of thousands of dollars over the term of the loan.
- Use an offset account where you have your salary paid into your offset account so that everything that you earn automatically reduces your mortgage.
- Make your payments fortnightly rather than monthly.

- Make a slightly higher payment than is required.
- If you have extra money at any time, make a lump sum payment.

Keeping bank fees to the minimum
- Many accounts charge high fees when the monthly balance falls below a certain level. Ensure that your account is always above this level.
- Have one account with a higher monthly balance rather than many small accounts.
- Only have one credit card.
- Plan your withdrawals as fees are charged if you go over a certain number each month.
- Take extra money out when you are shopping. Decide how much money you need for the week and take that in one go.
- Read all the fine print before you agree to any banking agreement.
- Internet banking fees are considerably less than those for using ATMs or over the counter services.
- It is better to be a bank shareholder than a bank depositor.
- Dividends often offer greater value for money than interest.
- Change to an account that pays interest on the daily total in your account.

Mortgage loans
Short-term mortgages can save you tens of thousands of dollars in interest over the long term. For example, if you borrow $100,000 at a fixed rate of 8% per year, a fifteen-year mortgage results in $90,000 less in interest payments than a thirty-year mortgage. You will have to pay a higher monthly payment than with a longer-term loan.

Even a small difference in interest rates can mean thousands of dollars, so it's a good idea to shop around for a mortgage loan with the lowest rate and fewest points available. Your local newspaper probably prints a list of mortgage rates available at various banks or financial institutions. Telephone several lenders and compare their rates, points and fees.

How will you calculate the best loan for you?
- Some banks will help you determine exactly how much each mortgage option will cost and its tax implications.
- You can also ask an accountant for an independent assessment.
- If you would like to do the analysis yourself, some common financial management computer programs will calculate mortgage loan costs for you.

Choosing your mortgage
Which financial institution you choose should be based not only the interest rate on offer, but also on:

- Loan establishment fees, which range from $0 to $700.
- Bank charges on your account.
- Whether you can vary the payments.
- Whether you can change from a fixed rate to variable rate and vice versa.
- Whether you can pay the loan out without penalty, say if you win Lotto.

Variable rate mortgages
Variable rate mortgages will, as the title suggests, rise and fall depending on the official interest rate as set by the Reserve Bank of Australia. If rates rise, so do your repayments.

Fixed rate mortgages
Fixed rate mortgages remain fixed for set periods of time and can be popular when interest rates are rising. Not only are you protected if rates rise, but you always know what your regular repayments are, and can budget accordingly. Most lenders will lend between

85% to 95% of the property's value, but the bigger the deposit the less interest you end up paying. Lenders also require that repayments, worked out over twenty-five years, do not exceed 30% of gross monthly income. Get a calculator, do your sums.

Adjustable rates

If you are thinking of having a mortgage loan with an adjustable rate, remember that the rate can fluctuate greatly over the lifespan of the mortgage. If your rate was to jump by several percentage points, your monthly payments could rise by hundreds of dollars.

Mortgage refinancing

If your current mortgage is at an interest rate at least 1% higher than what the financial institutions are offering now, consider refinancing. This advice is especially valid if your mortgage has several years to run. An accountant can help you figure out whether this move will be advantageous once you factor in up-front fees or penalties etc.

Home equity loans

Many finance companies are targeting seniors with advertising for home equity loans. Be cautious. Home equity loans decrease the equity you have built up in your home, in other words, the degree to which you own it. If you find yourself unable to meet the payments, you could be forced to sell your home. If you are considering taking out a home equity loan, compare the rates and options from at least four banks or financial institutions. Take into account the annual percentage rate, points, closing costs, other fees, and the impact of changes to any variable.

Acronyms

Depending on your success or otherwise in investment, at varying stages of your life, you will belong to at least one of these categories:

BOBO	Burnt Out But Opulent
DUMP	Destitute Unemployed Mature Professional
OINK	One Income, No Kids
YUPPIE	Young Upwardly Mobile Professional
PUPPIE	Poncy Upwardly Mobile Professional
YAPPIE	Young Affluent Parent
PIPPIE	Person Inheriting Parent's Wealth
SCUM	Self Centred Urban Male
SILKY	Single Income, Loads of Kids
SINBAD	Single Income, No Boyfriend, Absolutely Desperate
SITCOM	Single Income, Two Kids, Outrageous Mortgage
WOOPIE	Well Off Older Person
GOLDIE	Golden Oldie Lives Dangerously

Car loans

If you have some money in the bank that is not earning a high rate of interest, it can be more advantageous to use this money to make a large down payment on a car, rather than to finance the car purchase with a loan. Car dealers/manufacturers sometimes offer low financing rates to entice you to buy. Shop around.

You may be able to get a car loan at a low rate from your bank or credit union, as well. You can then choose the car you really want.

Buying a car

It is said the two most stressful situations that people face during their lives are the death of a loved one and purchasing a house. Buying a car must surely be up there with them! Whether it is:

- Sitting amid the potted plants of a new car salesroom.
- Trawling through the used vehicle yards.
- Or haggling with a private seller with one foot in the gutter.

Work out what you want

Whether it's a new or used vehicle, you can take much pain out of this process if you sit down and work out what sort of car you really want. There is not much point hocking yourself into financial oblivion on a two-door roadster when the family already has three children, and a fourth pregnancy has just been confirmed.

Know thine product

Read the test drives, read the ads, ask around. Be confident that you know the car inside out before you blurt out those irrevocable words: 'Excuse me, can you tell me about this model . . . '

Hang loose

It's easy to get carried away amid the sparkling chrome and the alluring 'new-car' smell of a showroom.

- Don't appear anxious to sign up, even if you are beside yourself with anticipation.
- Make it clear there are still plenty of options to be considered before you sign up.

Beware the improved trade-in

Be careful when the salesperson boosts the trade-in offer on your old banger.
What happens is that he or she is upping the new vehicle's price by the same margin. 'Let's work out a final changeover figure,' they say.

- Insist on keeping the two prices separate.
- Until the actual purchase price is made clear, don't bring the estimate of your trade-in into the discussion.

Price first, payments later

Avoid discussing finance until the final price is locked in. Talking about monthly payments too soon in the negotiations only does two things:

- It distracts everyone from the real issue at hand, that is, what the new car is worth.
- Secondly, having the price portrayed to you as 'only' so many dollars a month, suddenly makes it sound very attractive – whether it is in your budget or not.

Extras

Don't forget that after the price of the car, there are compulsory charges involved, including:

- Delivery charge
- Registration
- Government stamp duty and transfer fees
- And in some states, number plate fee

On top of that, you will have to pay your first year's insurance on the car.

Ordering
Often the car is not in the yard and you will sign an Order Form to have one brought in from the factory. Remember, an Order Form is legally binding. You can't sleep on the buy, ring up next day, say you have changed your mind.

Check everything
Before signing an Order Form, check that all details – model number, year, colour, etc. – are set out correctly.

Get-out clause
Do not sign the deal without an escape clause. Have it noted that the deal is subject to you satisfactorily finding finance from a chosen credit provider.

Sign nothing until...
Never, never, sign anything that you do not understand. If the words or phrases are meaningless or ambiguous, admit that you do not know what they mean, and seek clarification from the salesperson. If necessary, get an independent opinion.

The black hole
Often contracts have blank sections in them, which can be filled in later. Before you sign, either cross out, or get the salesperson to cross out, any blank or non-applicable sections. It is preferable for you and the dealer to date and initial any cross-outs.

Say what?
By the very nature of the car selling business, words flow freely, and sometimes aspects such as 'extras' are discussed and ordered. Or were they? Make sure any verbal agreements – for example, extras such as driving lights, air-conditioning, or specific exterior/interior finishing – are fully detailed in the contract.

Say when?
Make sure a specific date is written down for the Date of Delivery. The phrase ASAP could lead to an interminable wait, no matter how confident the salesperson is. Also ensure that the contract carries no clauses that allow for any factory/retail price increases that are announced while you are waiting for your car to be delivered, to be passed on to you.

Women buying cars
Skilled, confident women – capable of running a home, operating a business, or working in a pressure job – are still angered, amazed and astounded by the treatment they get from some car salesmen. Attitudes include:

- Not letting the woman test-drive the car, but instead putting her in the passenger seat and driving it himself.
- Actually allowing her to drive the car, but only after piloting it himself to a quite, low-traffic area where she 'won't do much damage' and allowing her to take over from there.
- Asking, when she enters the showroom by herself: 'Where's your husband?'
- If told it is a company car she is going to buy, asking: 'Isn't your boss with you?'
- Diverting women away from their first choice of car – 'You don't need something like that, that's a bloke's car!' – to a tiny hatchback or lipstick-coloured four-door.
- Comparing the car to her. 'It's like you – a nice bottom and a cute smile.'
- If she has brought a male companion along – even though the woman is going to drive the car and foot the bill – directing all the conversation to the man.

Some useful tips
- Be prepared. Read up about the car market in newspapers, magazines and the Net.

- Select the make and model you want, or a couple of alternatives. Fun though it may be, don't buy on impulse.
- Work out the price ranges, and set your own spending level.
- Research the model you've selected, especially about the options available.
- Talk to family and friends about where they got their car, and get their dealer recommendations.
- Try three or four dealers. See how much variation there is in the final price, and on your trade-in.
- Don't take any patronising treatment from a male dinosaur. Don't be afraid at any stage to get up and walk away.
- Remember, he needs the sale to keep his job. It won't hurt to tell his superiors, or write to the manufacturer, stating that his attitude is unacceptable.
- If you feel more comfortable, ask for a woman sales rep, if there are any on the staff.
- Do not let the salesperson 'test-drive' the car for you. You are buying it, you are going to drive it, you want to know what it feels like!
- Make it clear that this is your deal, your dough, your decision.
- Leave all male counterparts at home, even if they do know a lot about cars. You run the risk of the conversation being directed at them, and you being cut out of the negotiations.
- If you are a mum, it's better to leave the kids at home and concentrate on the task at hand, exciting though it may be for little ones. Bring them second-time around, when the deal is done, and they can enjoy the thrill of the new purchase.

Car finance

You've found the car, you love the car, you want to buy the car. Now, how are you going to pay for it? Here are the major considerations:

Hire purchase

This is the traditional form, and most common way for individuals or families to buy a car. These days it is also called a 'consumer loan'. It is based on:

- Monthly repayments.
- A term varying between one and usually five years.
- An interest rate calculated on the current market rate, the amount of loan, and the risk.

Basically, you pay the payments, and that's it, the car is yours. An add-on is the 'balloon payment option'. That is, deciding on a one-off amount that will be the final payment at the end of the contract. For example:

- The all-up cost of the car is $40,000.
- But you choose to select a balloon payment of $10,000.
- You now pay off $30,000 over the agreed period, say, five years.
- At the end of the term, you pay the $10,000.

This reduces your monthly payments across the term. The bigger the balloon payment you set, the less you are paying off in the short term, and therefore the less your monthly payments are, thus helping out your domestic budget. But, remember, at the end of the term, you either have to pay out the balloon amount in one hit, or refinance it, and continue paying it off in monthly instalments.

Guaranteed buyback finance

This procedure is similar to the balloon payment version of hire purchase. But the difference is that the balloon or guaranteed buyback figure determined at the start of the contract is based on the length of the loan term and also prevailing used car values. The buyback figure is generally called a residual. In effect, it is what the car will be worth after the loan term expires. Under Guaranteed Buyback Finance, the customer has four options to consider at the end of the term. Having paid monthly payments for the set term, he/she can then:

- Hand the car back and walk away with no further obligation.
- Pay out the buyback (residual) figure and keep the car.
- Refinance the buyback (residual) figure and keep the car.
- Trade-in the car on a new vehicle, and set up a new deal.

Leasing the car
Finance lease
In this situation, no deposit is put down, or trade-in made on the car. A monthly payment is worked out by the finance company, based on:

- The length of term of the lease.
- Interest on the finance.
- Residual value of the car at the end of the term.

You should be able to walk away at the end of the lease. However, if at the end of the term, the market indicates that the car is now not quite worth what was predicted when the lease began, then the responsibility lies with you to make up the dollar difference, so that the contract can be finalised. Under the rules and definition of a lease, you do not gain any equity in the car. Nevertheless, you can usually make an offer for the vehicle at the end of the term – paying out or refinancing the residual and thus taking ownership.

Novated lease
If you are in a relatively high tax bracket, then it may be worth it to take up a version of the Finance Lease called the Novated Lease. The idea is to make the car part of your salary package, and therefore reduce your taxable income. Novation is a Latin word meaning the substitution of a new debtor of contract for a former one. You will need your employer to take part in this.

- A finance lease is taken out on the car.
- Under the novation agreement, the monthly payments are paid by your employer.
- In turn, the lease payments, running costs and fringe benefits tax are then taken out of your pre-tax salary.

This reduces your taxable income, either dropping you into a lower tax-bracket, or preventing 'bracket creep' into the next higher level. The important point is that this agreement remains in place only as long as you remain with the company. If you leave, then responsibility for the car and all remaining monthly lease payments lies with you. As with the standard lease, when it comes to an end, you should be able to walk away. But the residual is also your problem, too. If the market indicates that the car is now not quite worth what was predicted when the lease began, then the responsibility lies with you to make up the dollar difference, so that the contract can be finalised. At the end of the lease you can also:

- Keep the car by turning it over into a new lease.
- Trade it on a new car on a new novated lease.
- Purchase the vehicle through a third party.

Operating lease
This is basically a long-term rental.

- At the end of the term you hand the car back and walk away.
- You do not gain any equity in the car.
- But the advantage is that any risk of the residual lies with the finance company. You do not have to make up any difference.
- Payments are fixed monthly.
- The lease can be tailored so that the car can be fully maintained. All upkeep costs, apart from fuel, are included in the one monthly payment.

This system is good for a company in that you are taking no risk on a depreciating asset, and is proving popular with cars at the top end of the market – BMW, Mercedes, Jaguar, Lexus, etc.

Where to go for money

For purchase finance:

- Banks
- Credit unions
- Finance companies

Finance companies specialise in this kind of loan. Many are either extensions of the banks (for example, Esanda is owned by the ANZ) or linked directly with the car manufacturers (for example, Holden and GMAC). Banks offer a lesser interest rate but will require more security than a finance company or a guarantor.

For leasing:
- Finance companies
- Specialist leasing firms
- Vendor finance

Vendor finance is simply the car-maker, such as BMW, Mercedes or Volvo, setting up the lease.

Second-hand cars
What model?

Do your research and confirm in your mind, the following:

- Make
- Model
- Age

Enter the car-yard jungle confident about what you wish to discuss. Remember, there are models within models – versions of the same model that have variations in engine-size, external décor, internal layout, comfort and safety. Read up on what version has which variations so the dealer won't confuse you.

Same again?

Select a particular type of car and then, if they are on the car-lot, drive two or three versions of the same one before making a decision. You will be surprised to see the difference between what appear to be identical cars. Much depends on how they have been driven and cared for by their previous owners.

Before you jump in – insurance!

Dealers should have insurance coverage on the car, and so there is usually no problem taking it for a drive. But in a private purchase, do not test drive a car until you have seen proof that it is insured. You may be only going around the block near the seller's home and think it is safe, but if something happens, the financial aftermath could be dreadful.

Test drive it for as long as you like

- Insist on a long drive.
- This is going to be your transport for at least the next couple of years and you want to know if it really does go OK.
- Select a route that mixes up familiar roads with tracks that will put the car to a test.

Which pedal? And how hard?

On the test drive:

- Push the brake pedal hard and monitor the response.
- If it's a manual, feel whether the clutch pedal feels firm and sound when you depress it to change gears, rather than heavy or only kicking in at the end of the movement.
- Hit the 'go' pedal hard a couple of times too, to see how the car accelerates.

Car check
Auto

An automatic transmission gearbox is an expensive item, and you don't want to be paying out on a new or reconditioned one straight-away. The major sign that there is something wrong is the 'crawl'. Put the selector in Neutral, as distinct from Park, and if the car creeps forward, then beware. Any delay in time between the selection of a gear and it going into action is also a danger sign.

Brakes

You could be lucky and the 'spongy' feeling when you depress the brake pedal could just mean the brake fluid reservoir needs a top up.

- If it requires too much pedal to pull the car up, then something more serious – such as worn discs and pads – could be involved.
- The steering wheel pulling to one side when you hit the brake pedal could mean the brakes need attention or that the wheels need alignment.

Exhaust

There is a vast difference between the hearty throb of a motor coming out of a healthy exhaust/muffler, and the ear-splitting roar exiting what appears to be a rusty drain-pipe. If it's loud and nasty there are probably holes in the muffler and/or exhaust, and that means expense.

Get an expert

- An independent check by a qualified mechanic could save you from disaster.
- A mechanic knows what problems, signs of wear and tear, and pointers to disaster to look for.
- It will cost between $100 to $150, but will be well worth it.
- A dealer will usually accept a mechanical check, but if a private owner refuses an inspection, then move on.

History

If this is a private buy, ask questions about the car's history, and what sort of driving it has done:

- Long journeys?
- Stop-start trips around town?
- Carrying heavy loads etc.?

Read the body language to see if the answer is truthful or not.

Is it hot?

It is vital you check the car is not stolen, or that it still has finance owing on it, or that it has been reconstituted out of another car(s).

- Use the phone service supplied by your state motor registration authority to check its status.
- You need at least the registration number, but preferably also the serial number on the plate fastened to the engine bay.

Kilometres

Turning the odometer back is illegal. Nevertheless, there are still unscrupulous people who try this old favourite.

- Check any maintenance/service stickers on the windows, doors or air filter.
- If any of those figures are more than the figure on the clock, move on.
- Same, too, if the odometer reads under 20,000 kilometres and it is obvious from

pedal-wear or scratches and marks, especially around the ignition, that the car has done more than that.
- Generally speaking, service documents should verify how many kilometres the car has been driven.

Manual

See whether the clutch pedal feels firm and sound when you depress it to change gears, rather than heavy or only kicking in at the end of the movement.

- If selecting any gear is met with a crunch or stubbornness, the gearbox could be wearing out.
- Sloppy gear levers and 'airy' changes are also indicators of gearbox grief.
- Crunching gears can also mean a worn-out clutch.

Any of these signs are a warning you are shortly going to be up for expensive repairs.

Oil

Look underneath the car and check for oil leaks. Pull out the dipstick and see if there is foaming white goo on it. That means that water and oil is mixing and the car is prone to overheating.

Panels

By observing the car from different angles and running your hands along the metal:

- Check to see that all panels are original.
- Make sure that the panels align properly.
- Make sure the doors shut flush.
  If not, the car may have been in a sizeable accident, affecting the body structure, and causing further problems.

Roadworthy

You buy a car without a Roadworthy Certificate at your own risk!

- A roadworthy examination includes the state of ordinary, everyday components such as the windscreen, tyres, exhaust and lights.
- While they may look all right to you, any of these can be later deemed un-roadworthy, and you will be up for expensive replacement/repair costs.
- Unless you are a mechanical genius intent on a rebuild and know what you are letting yourself in for, play it safe.

Insist on a Roadworthy Certificate.

Rust

Check to ensure that the magnificent, sturdy-looking beast standing before you is not a rust-bucket held together by a couple of coats of paint. Rust is a cancer that will eat your car and turn it into a deathtrap.

- Tap your fingers along the panels and listen for the muted, dead sound of filler.
- Check all areas that collect water, including the wheel arches, doors, light fittings, boot lid and bonnet, fuel-cap, and window-sills.
- Look under floor mats for rust spots.

S-s-s-smokin'!

The true test is when you start the motor up. Is that blue smoke pouring out the back?
Turn it off, jump out, and try elsewhere. It's using up too much oil and will shortly cost you heaps to fix.

Suspension

Suspension is one of those grey areas that many car-owners know little about.

But it is important, especially for your own safety.

- The bounce test is worth trying. Press down with both hands on the boot or bonnet. If the car bounces too easily, new struts, which maintain its stability, might be needed.
- Drive the car over a few bumps, and listen for 'clunking' sounds. These indicate worn suspension components.

The boot

A peek in the boot – not always necessarily done by buyers – can be a very revealing exercise.

- The condition of the carpet or rubber gives a good indication of the general condition of the remainder of the car.
- See if there is any rust.
- Check if the spare is in reasonable condition.
- Find out if the tool kit is still complete.

Wheel alignment

Check how straight the car steers to see whether there is a wheel alignment problem, which in turn can lead to, among other things, tyres being scrubbed out.

Be brave

Most sellers will anticipate a bit of haggling – some thrive on it.

- Dealers often advertise cars above the generally accepted price, so try for a 10% cut up front.
- It won't hurt and the seller can only say no.

Deposit

In the heat of the moment, it's too easy to get carried away and offer a huge deposit to be absolutely certain that the car is yours.

- A figure of $200 to $500 is enough as a holding deposit.
- Remember, a deposit is a display of faith on both sides, and if necessary, go to 5% of the price.
- 10% is too much.

Shopping
Shopping on the Internet

The Internet is being used more and more for convenience shopping. We are able to buy almost anything we want over the Internet and many of us do. However, as it is early days yet, there are still some concerns regarding security and bone fides of Internet businesses.

Some considerations about shopping on the Net

Know about the business that you are contacting. Check that it has an address, a telephone number and that it is legal. Make sure that it has a bricks and mortar presence.

Only enter sites that the browser recognises as secure sites and don't enter financial information that is not needed for the purchase.

Check the privacy provisions. Will your personal details be passed onto anybody else? Is that what you want? Do not enter information about you that is not needed for the sale.

Do your research before you jump on the Net. Know what you want and know your prices.

Pay securely. Keep a credit card with a low limit just for Internet purchases. That way you limit your losses if somebody does get hold of your details illegally.

Check your contract. Understand terms and conditions and check the delivery date and whether you need to be home for it. Understand the small print and the conditions of sale.

Double-check costs. Calculate extras such as currency conversion, taxes, customs duties, delivery fees, packaging and posting costs.

Keep records. Print your order before you send it and note any reference numbers. Confirm the order. You should be given a chance to either confirm or reject the order. Resolve any problems with the trader. If a satisfactory conclusion is not reached, contact the ombudsman.

Be wary of scams
- Confirm your order. You will be given a chance to confirm or reject your order before you pay for it.
- Keep a record of your order. Write down any reference number.
- Resolve problems promptly. Contact supplier if you have a problem, if not satisfied contact the relevant dispute resolution body for that industry.

If something looks too good to be true, then remember, it probably is!

Internet shopping for food
While the mail order/Internet industry enjoys a good safety record, ordering food over the Internet may cause concerns about food safety, shelf life and distribution. This is especially true for meat, poultry, fish and other perishable foods such as cheesecake, which must be carefully handled in a timely manner to prevent food-borne illness. The following food safety tips will help the purchaser and recipient determine if their perishable foods have been handled properly:

- Make sure the company sends perishable items, like meat or poultry, cold or frozen and packed with a cold source.
- It should be packed in foam or heavy corrugated cardboard.
- The food should be delivered as quickly as possible, ideally, overnight.
- Make sure perishable items and the outer package are labelled 'Keep Refrigerated' to alert the recipient.
- Tell the recipient if the company has promised a delivery date. Or alert the recipient that 'the gift is in the mail' so someone can be there to receive it.
- Don't have perishable items delivered to an office unless you know it will arrive on a work day and there is refrigerator space available for keeping it cold.

Buying a home
When you are looking to purchase a home, the following guidelines should help you through the process.

Take time to get to know the market
Do your research. Look through the open house listings to get a feel for home pricing by size and neighbourhood.

Make a list of priorities
What are the things that are essential and what are the things that you can compromise on. Be sure in your own mind what you want, but be open enough to know a good deal when you see one.

Select a real estate agent that you are comfortable working with
It can also make an offer more attractive to a seller if they know you already qualify for the loan.

Set a price
Let your real estate agent know what price range you are looking in and any amenities you desire to have included. Be firm in your own mind as to how much you can afford to spend. They can then prepare a list of home listings that fit these criteria.

Search

Make sure to preview as many houses as possible before making any offers. Know in your own mind what you want and what you are prepared to accept. When you are interested in making an offer, request a second showing of that house.

Advice

Make an appointment with your mortgage loan officer to get pre-approved finance. This will give you an idea of the price range of homes to look at. When requesting information from a lender, be sure to ask for any related costs in addition to the interest rate.

Love at first sight

Go on your gut feeling. Houses have their own feel and this is a purchase that is one of the biggest that you will make. Ask yourself, 'Can I see myself living here?' If you can't, this is not the house for you.

Fund raising

We all find ourselves on fund raising committees at some time during our lives. It begins at play group and continues through kindergarten, schools, sports clubs, service clubs, charity organisations and charity institutions. It is a community building thing to do and can be lots of fun. Here are a few tips to make it a rewarding experience for you.

Know what is expected

What is the total operating budget of the organisation?
How much do you expect to raise?
How much was raised in previous years?
How was it raised?

Set your goals

Write traditional/compulsory commitments in on the calendar. Decide whether you need a couple of big events or a number of smaller ones. Aim a little higher than you think is necessary to allow for contingencies.
This will depend upon:

- The size of the group.
- How much money needs to be raised.
- The number of supporters.
- The prevailing mentality of the group.
- Geographical locations of group members.

Make the most of your resources

Know your members, what they do for a living, their areas of influence and interests.

Laws governing fundraising

It is incumbent upon the fundraiser to ensure that all activities which are conducted on behalf of his/her organisation comply with the laws of the state in which the activities are to occur, and to adhere to them.

Asking for donations

Determine which people are most likely to help you and why they would want to help. Consider:

- Past students
- Family members
- Local neighbourhood

- Charity trusts
- Big business
- Local business

What can you offer?
- Recognition
- Advertising
- Tax deduction
- Goodwill
- Custom

How are you going to ask for help?

What are you going to tell the organisation from whom you are seeking funds, about your organisation?

- What is the best way to get the message across?
- Why, on this occasion, are you asking for help?

Ensure that the quality of your request and the way it is presented stands up to scrutiny.

Fundraising ideas
Raffles

There are raffles of many kinds. Depending on your organisation, you may wish to raffle something as simple as an Easter egg basket made up of donated eggs, for a school, to a boat on a trailer for a Fishing Club. Do your sums well, comply with government regulations and make sure you get the tickets out there and sold. Raffles are a relatively simple and lucrative money raiser.

Advertising space

Sell advertising space in your newsletter.

A casino night

Arrange games of chance. Instead of cash as prizes arrange for tokens that may be converted to prizes from a pool of prizes which have been donated by local people.

Auctions

Goods are donated by local business. A local estate agent donates his services for the night. It is usually preferable to have the auction following a dinner as people will be more relaxed and likely to spend more.

Ball

In some organisations these are regular events, either annual or biannual. Choose a theme and a band that is good to dance to. This is a big night out and is a dressed-up affair.

Art show

Participants pay an entry fee to hang their art work. A commission is charged for any art work sold. Coffee and cakes or wine and cheese can be sold.

Bike gymkhana

A great family event. Hire an oval and set up events such as:

- Long distance races
- Short sprints
- Precision riding
- Laps against the clock
- BMX course
- Balancing on one wheel the longest time
- Riding on one wheel

Day on the river/lake
A picnic and BBQ on the day. Hire the boats at discount from the hire boat operator. Sell rides to members.

Blanket coin throw
Obtain permission to take the blanket around the inside perimeter of the local sporting oval at an athletics meet, football match etc.

Book sale
New books can be bought from wholesalers. Second-hand books can be donated by well wishers. Good profits can be made.

Selling of sweets
You can buy attractive and tasty sweets at wholesale prices and on-sell them to club members, their neighbours and families.

Break-open cards
The cards can be bought in batches and may have money prizes inside. They are often sold in pubs over the bar and provide a steady source of income. A football club might consider selling envelopes with winning scores inside and a cash prize going to the person who has the exact winning margin for that week's club game.

Calcutta sweep
A variation of the sweep is the Calcutta sweep. This makes much more profit than an ordinary sweep, as many more tickets can be sold. The horses 'names are put in one hat. The ticket-holders are put in another. A horse's name is drawn out, and then the name of the ticket-holder (either an individual or a syndicate) who gets that horse is drawn. Let's call person who got the first horse Punter A. Then an auction follows whereby the horses are put up for auction and sold to the assembled punters. When the horse is sold, Punter A gets a percentage, usually 50%, of the price that his horse fetches at auction. 30% goes to prize money and 20% to the fundraiser. Punter B, the person who is the successful bidder, gets to keep the horse in the coming race. The punter whose horse wins the race is rewarded handsomely, as is the fundraiser.

Car boot sale
People pack their car boot with unwanted items and take them to the venue. They pay a fee to the club for a site. The club adds value by having a sausage sizzle and a drinks stall.

Car rally
Arrange for a Sunday and require contestants to follow a map, find information and arrive at a predetermined venue for a group picnic/meal.

Car wash
Many people are more than happy to have their car hand washed by a local charity at a reasonable price. It costs very little to do and the rewards are good.

Delivery of junk mail
Contact your local pamphlet distributor and ask for an area to deliver to. Roster members to do the job.

Delivery of the telephone book
Contracts are available for local organisations to deliver the phone book.

Easter eggs
These can be bought cheaply in quantity and resold at a profit at Easter. Calendars, greeting cards, gift wrap, and so on, may be either bought cheaply from the wholesalers and on-sold. You could have club/charity cards printed especially for sale. Beautiful and individu-

ally made cards and wrapping paper can be made by members at a working bee and then offered for sale.

Fetes and fairs

Fetes are fun. They are community building and relationship enriching. A group of people coming together with a common aim can form friendships that will last a lifetime as they tackle the task of putting a great fair together. Kids love them and are excited by them.

Stalls you might have:

Cake stall

Cakes are made and donated by the group's members and supporters. They can also be sold at the local shopping centre or other locale.

Fairy floss

You can hire a fairy floss machine. The hire company will instruct you on the use of the machine.

Gourmet food stall

Use the talents of all the good cooks in the club. Buy in some food at wholesale prices.

Wine tasting

Buy wine in bulk. On the day of the fair have a wine tasting and take orders. Arrange a day for bottling. Deliver the orders.

Devonshire teas

You will need scones made. Jam and cream can be brought in. Teas and coffee made and served. Dress the tables up so they look inviting.

Second-hand clothes

This is an excellent stall for a school fete, as most will have clothes that are still quite good but that children have grown out of. Second-hand school uniforms can also be sold.

Hot popcorn

Machines can be hired. Staff will be trained.

Amusements

Can be hired with attendants. There is a wide variety and decisions will need to be made about which ones are chosen.

Basketball throw/skipping/running laps

Ask children to obtain sponsorship for an amount per hoop/skip/lap. On the day of the fete children complete their contract and collect their sponsorships.

Trash and treasure

One man's trash is another man's treasure. People love to seek through donated goods to find a bargain.

Craft

Enlist the talents of the arty crafty people who will enjoy making things to sell at your store.

Sausage sizzle

A great one for the dads. Dress them up in aprons and a chef's hat. Give them a pair of tongs and a long fork. Make sure that you have onions cooking as they tempt the tastebuds.

Hamburgers

Another easy to cook taste tempter that can be cooked on a BBQ.

Plant stall

Get members propagating plants well before the event as plants take time to take root.

A local nursery will very likely be happy to supply plants at a discount.

Other suggestions
- Face painting
- Hair braiding
- Manicures
- Dunk the coach/teacher/president
- Ghost train
- Pony rides
- Mobile farm
- Secret auction
- Raffles

Fun runs/walks
Determine the venue. Send letters requesting participants and a separate letter asking for sponsors. On the day record the distances walked. Collect the promised amounts.

Games tournament
Can be cards, scrabble, chess, checkers. Let members pit their skills against each other. Should be arranged over a couple of days.

Golf day
A social day. Obtain a discount from the golf course. Charge members a higher fee.

Golf driving competition
A golf driving range will most likely give you a good price for the hire of their facilities. Charge per given number of balls.

Group travel
Group travel experiences are fun and can range from a day at the country races to a full on overseas excursion. More profit can be made from the short day or weekend trips, as pricing becomes very rigid the further you travel.

Horse-riding trial
Can be arranged through a horse-riding farm. Suitable for clubs with younger membership.

Joint projects with local businesses
These may be in the form of sponsorships where a club will advertise that business in return for monetary patronage. Which goods or services does your group use regularly? Who are most likely to benefit by gaining your group's custom? Think about what you can offer the business in return for their support. How are you going to conduct a mutually successful relationship?

Joy flights
If you live near a small airport this is a good activity for clubs whose members have not flown very much.

Juke box and hamburger night
Juke boxes can be hired. Booths set up 50s style. Sell hamburgers and drinks.

Link with other local clubs
The local RSL may offer its venue to the school music group to play on a given night.

In return the RSL will do more business from the parents who come to support their children. Two sports clubs may combine to fundraise for improved facilities which they both will share. An athletic club may shake the tin at half time at the local football game. The possibilities are endless.

Lamingtons and snowballs

There are specialist suppliers of lamingtons and most families don't mind buying a couple of packets as they can be frozen and used for lunches.

Lucky envelopes

Envelopes contain sealed numbers from one to 100, which are sold for a set amount.

Prizes are set for certain numbers and the envelopes are sold.

A mammoth garage sale

Ask all members and supporters to empty their homes of unwanted goods and to bring them to the club rooms on a certain day. Advertise the number of households who will be joining together for the sale. Advertise some of the items.

Meat/chook raffle

Sheets of cards are sold at a given amount per sheet. A number of draws for meat prizes take place over a given time of about one hour.

On the day raffles

These are conducted at each meeting. Prizes are arranged for that day by the members. It could be a prize is given as a result of something that happens that day.

For example, the number of the first player for the football team to get a goal gets a prize.

Pies and sausages

Can be ordered through smallgoods wholesalers. Orders are taken before delivery so there is no wastage.

Club merchandising

You can organise merchandise in club colours which will build morale and make money for you. This could include T-shirts, jackets, track-suits, bags, plaques, mugs, tea-towels, towels, key rings, pens and so on. These are very popular. There are always new things on the market for clubs and organisations to sell as fundraisers. Keep your eyes and ears open. Observe what other clubs are doing.

Pub sports

Dart, hooky, pool, dominoes. Book a local pub. The bar benefits from sale of drinks and food. Charge admission to games.

Restaurant nights

Negotiate a price with the chosen restaurant. Charge a bit more. Great for encouraging and cementing relationships.

Rock and roll night

Have good music. Provide supper. Can include a dress-up element with prizes for best period costumes.

Hole in one competition

Arrange a hole whereby participants can aim to hole in one. Insure against the eventuality. Sell balls to entrants.

Sausage sizzle

Can be dressed up by offering an array of international sausages and shashliks.

Spit roasts

Hire the gear from the butcher who will also arrange the right quantity of meat. Members provide salads.

Shop until you drop
Hire a bus for a shopping expedition to the factory outlets in your area. Members pay a certain amount for the hire of the bus and lunch. What is left over is profit.

Slave and supper night
Encourage local business people to offer their services to be auctioned. It can be anything from a handyman, babysitter to a lawyer. Over a basket supper and wine auction the 'slave'. The person who bids the highest price gets the service at that price.

Spinning wheel
Tickets are sold. The wheel is spun. The winning number gets to pick a prize.

Sweeps
Usually associated with a big horse race in the town or city. Punters buy a ticket for the draw. Horses and punters names are called and married up. The person who owns the winning horse wins the sweep.

Tennis night
Hire the entire indoor courts for the night. Provide supper for a price. Conduct a round robin competition.

Theatre nights
Buy a block of tickets cheaply. Sell to members at normal prices. Some cinemas will arrange for champagne and chicken to be served either before or after the show.

Triathlon
Running
Swimming
Bicycle riding

Great for sporting clubs. Needs a lot of organising. Once you have produced a couple of good triathlons, then athletes will pencil it into their calendar as an annual event.

Trivia night
Devise a series of trivia questions and games that will challenge the memory and amuse the crowd. Don't allow it to go too long. Allow time for people to socialise with each other by making for breaks between questions.

Wine tasting
Select a local wine merchant and arrange to feature good wines and tasty cheeses. Consider a blind tasting game. Send individual invitations with a RSVP and payment upon return.

9
Words of Wisdom . . .

Sayings to live by

Here are some wonderful philosophic sayings and other reflections to help guide you through life:

- When you sail you must follow the curve of the river.

Don't look for the flaws as you go through life,
And even if you find them,
It is wise and kind to be somewhat blind,
And to look for the virtues behind them.

- It is a great thing to be thankful for your lot, even if it is not a lot.

If your lips you'd keep from slips,
Five things observe with care
Of whom you speak, to whom you speak,
And how, and when, and where.

- It's nice to be important, but more important to be nice.
- There is nothing wrong with men possessing riches. The evil comes when riches possess them.
- Opportunities are often disguised as hard work, so most people don't recognise them.
- The person who has everything usually sits next to you in the doctor's surgery.
- Memories are the key, not to the past, but to the future.
- Our virtues are learnt at our mother's knee. Our vices are learnt in some other low joint.
- By the time I had acquired my nest egg, inflation had turned it into chicken feed.

The seven deadly sins

1. Pride
2. Greed
3. Lust
4. Envy
5. Gluttony
6. Anger
7. Sloth

The four cardinal virtues

1. Prudence
2. Justice
3. Temperance
4. Fortitude

An old Irish curse

May those who love us, love us,
And those that don't love us,

May God turn their hearts.
And if he doesn't turn their hearts,
May he turn their ankles
So we'll know them by their limping.

More thoughts
* Better to be quarrelling than lonesome.
* Time, like a snowflake, disappears while we're trying to decide what to do with it.
* When the fish are biting there is no problem that is big enough to be remembered.
* Poverty is no disgrace, but it is an inconvenience.

'Man is interested in what is real even though it may not be desirable.
A child is interested in what is desirable, even though it may not be real.'

* The fellow who says that he is going to call a spade a spade is probably getting ready to dig dirt.
* Success has one hundred fathers, failure is an orphan.

An Irish blessing
May the road rise to meet you.
May the wind be always at your back, may the sun shine warm upon your face, the rains fall soft upon your fields and, until we meet again, may God hold you in the palm of his hand.

Things to know when you go sailing
* To see a dolphin while you are at sea is very lucky.
* Killing a dolphin or a seagull will bring disaster.
* Bananas are considered unlucky for sailors. True seamen never take a banana on board.
* Always put your right foot on board first. If you step with your left then disaster is sure to follow.
* No good will ever come of changing the name of your boat.
* Always put a coin under the mast before setting sail.
* Redheads and umbrellas are bad news.
* Never take anything green on a boat.
* It is bad luck to take the ship builder on the maiden voyage with you.
* Whistling on board is bad luck as one may 'whistle up the wind'.
* Black travel bags bring bad luck for sailors.
* Women and clergy are bad news on board a boat.
* Saturday is a good day to start a voyage, but Friday is considered unlucky.
* Never say the D word while on board. You can only say 'drowned' on shore.

Children's days
Monday's child is fair of face,
Tuesday's child is full of grace,
Wednesday's child is full of woe,
Thursday's child has far to go.
Friday's child is loving and giving,
Saturday's child works hard for a living,
And the child that is born on the Sabbath day is bonny, blithe, good and gay.

May you have . . .
Enough happiness to keep you sweet,
Enough trials to keep you strong,
Enough sorrow to keep you human,
Enough hope to keep you happy,
Enough failure to keep you humble,
Enough success to keep you eager,
Enough friends to give you comfort,
Enough wealth to meet your needs,
Enough enthusiasm to look forward,
Enough faith to banish depression,
Enough determination to make each day better than yesterday

Index